Corporate Strategy for Irish Companies

Text and Cases

Corporate Strategy for Irish Companies

Text and Cases

2nd Edition

Gerry Gallagher

Chartered Accountants Ireland

Published by
Chartered Accountants Ireland
Chartered Accountants House
47–49 Pearse Street
Dublin 2
www.charteredaccountants.ie

This publication is designed to provide accurate and authoritative information in regard to the subject matter covered. It is provided on the understanding that the Institute of Chartered Accountants in Ireland is not engaged in rendering professional services. The Institute of Chartered Accountants in Ireland disclaims all liability for any reliance placed on the information contained within this publication and recommends that if professional advice or other expert assistance is required, the services of a competent professional should be sought.

ISBN: 978-1-907214-65-3

Typeset by Compuscript
Printed and bound by the MPG Books Group

To
Fiona, Cormac and Ciara

Education is not the filling of a pail, but the lighting of a fire.

William Butler Yeats.

Summary Table of Contents

Chapter

1. Understanding Strategy 1

Part One: The Foundation

Introduction to the Foundation 29

2. Leadership and Organisational Culture 31

3. Vision, Mission, Goals and Objectives 74

4. Corporate Governance, Business Ethics, and Corporate Social Responsibility 106

Part Two: Strategic Analysis

Introduction to Strategic Analysis 149

5. Examining the Business Environment 151

6. Evaluating an Organisation's Strategic Capability 195

Part Three: Developing Strategy

Introduction to Developing Strategy 231

7. Corporate-level Strategy 233

8. Business-level Strategy 263

9. Developing Strategy Options 274

10. Diversification 311

11. Alternative Methods of Developing Strategy Options 334

12. Decision-making 363

Part Four: Implementation

Introduction to Strategy Implementation 393

13. Strategy Implementation 395

14. Leading Organisational Change 433

Case Studies 459

Bibliography 533

Glossary 547

Index 555

Detailed Table of Contents

Chapter

1. **Understanding Strategy**...1
   - Introduction 1
   - Definition of Strategy 2
     - The Nature of Corporate Strategy 2
     - Challenges in Corporate Strategy 5
   - Strategy Applies to all Organisations 7
   - Levels of Strategy within the Organisation 8
     - Corporate-level Strategy 9
     - Business-level Strategy..9
     - Operational Strategies 9
     - Functional Strategies 10
   - Core Areas of Strategy...10
     - The Foundation 12
     - Strategic Analysis of the Business Environment and Organisational Capability 12
     - Developing Strategy 13
     - Strategy Implementation 14
   - Development Processes 14
     - Intended Strategy Development...15
     - Emergent Strategy Development..19
   - Conclusion 23
   - Summary 24

Part One: The Foundation

Introduction to the Foundation 29

2. **Leadership and Organisational Culture**..31
   - Introduction 31
   - Leadership 32
     - Leaders and Managers...34
     - Managers 34
     - Leaders..34
   - Leadership Theories 35
     - Trait Theories of Leadership..35
     - Behavioural Theories of Leadership...38
     - Situational Theories of Leadership 40

Chapter

Charismatic Leadership 41
'Level 5' Leadership 42
Functions of Leadership 44
Creating a Vision 45
Building Teams 45
Motivation 47
Development 47
High Performance Organisation 48
Succession Planning 49
Bringing about Change 49
Decision-making 50
Failures in Leadership 51
Organisational Culture 53
Understanding Culture in Organisations 53
Classification of Organisational Culture 56
Handy's Four Types 56
Miles and Snow Typology 57
Peters and Waterman Excellence Model 58
Thompson *et al.* Cultural Strength 58
Management Philosophy 60
Subcultures 60
The Nature of Culture 61
The Importance of Organisational Culture 61
Establishing and Maintaining Organisational Culture 62
Identifying an Organisation's Culture 64
Organisational Culture and Performance 64
Intercultural Differences 65
Conclusions 66
Summary 66

3. Vision, Mission, Goals and Objectives 74

Introduction 74
Vision 75
Benefits of a Vision 77
Components of an Organisation's Vision 78
Leadership 78
Values 79
Purpose 83
From Vision to Strategic Intent 84
Sharing the Vision 87
Mission 88

Chapter

Goals and Objectives...89

Setting Organisational Goals and Objectives – Getting the Balance Right 91

    The Balanced Scorecard 91

    Strategy Map...94

    Strategy Map: Five-star Hotel..95

    Translating Strategy into Great Performance 97

    Setting Goals and Objectives – Individual Level...98

    Motivational Aspect of Goal Setting..99

    Rewards 100

Conclusion 101

Summary 101

**4. Corporate Governance, Business Ethics, and Corporate
Social Responsibility**..**106**

Introduction 106

Corporate Governance 107

    Company Structures..107

    Chain of Governance 108

    Company Directors..108

    Differing Board Structures 114

    Investment Information 114

Business Ethics...115

    Introduction 115

    Historical Background 116

    Teleological Ethical Systems 117

    Deontological Ethical Systems 117

    Ethical Relativism 118

    Integrative Social Contracts Theory 118

    Code of Ethics 119

    Evidence of Unethical Behaviour...120

    Relating Ethics to Business...122

Whistle-blowing...122

    Whistle-Blowers' Charter 124

    Punishing Whistle-Blowers 126

Organisational Approaches to Ethical Behaviour..126

Corporate Social Responsibility..127

    Introduction 127

    Criticisms of Corporate Social Responsibility 127

    Stakeholders...128

    Stakeholder Mapping..131

    Areas of Concern in Corporate Social Responsibility......................................134

Chapter

Reasons for Corporate Social Responsibility...136
Good Business 138
Conclusion 141
Summary 142

Part Two: Strategic Analysis

Introduction to Strategic Analysis..149

5. **Examining the Business Environment** 151
Introduction 151
The Macro Environment 153
The Global Environment...153
The European Union 153
Other Trading Blocks..157
Organisation for Petroleum Exporting Countries (OPEC) 158
The World Trade Organisation 159
Porter's Diamond 159
PESTEL Analysis 164
Implications for Organisations 171
Scenarios...172
The Micro Environment..173
Understanding the Industry's Economic Structure 173
Competitive Forces 175
Industry Life Cycle..180
Driving Forces 181
Identifying the Industry Driving Forces 182
The Impact of Driving Forces 183
Segmentation, Targeting and Positioning 183
Strategic Group Mapping...184
Key Success Factors..186
Opportunities and Threats...189
Conclusion 191
Summary 191

6. **Evaluating an Organisation's Strategic Capability** 195
Introduction 195
Resources 196
Competences 198
Capabilities...199
Human Resource Management 199
Finance 200
Marketing 201

Chapter

Operations 203
Research and Development 204
Information Systems 204
Knowledge Management 205
Cost Competitiveness 206
Value Chain Analysis 207
The Value System 211
Supply Chain Transparency 212
Strategy Maps 213
Benchmarking an Organisation 214
Performance Metrics 215
Removing Cost Disadvantages 216
Yield Management 217
Competitive Analysis 219
SWOT Analysis 222
Strengths 222
Weaknesses 222
Opportunities 223
Threats 223
Conclusion 224
Summary 224

Part Three: Developing Strategy

Introduction to Developing Strategy 231
Developing Strategy 231
7. Corporate-level Strategy 233
Introduction 233
Corporate Headquarters – Defining the Business 234
Scope 234
Corporate Governance 235
Information Systems 235
Leadership 237
Employees 237
Motivation 238
Culture 239
Creativity 239
Structure and Strategy 240
Organisational Structure 240
No Formal Structure 241
Functional Structure 241

Chapter

Multi-divisional Structure 242
Matrix Structure 244
Flexible Structures 246
Control Styles 247
Allocating Resources 249
Financial Decisions 250
Capital Structure 250
Dividend Policy 251
Management Incentive Schemes 251
Managing Risk 252
Uncertainty 256
Conclusion 257
Summary 258

8. Business-level Strategy **263**
Introduction 263
Generic Strategies 264
Low-cost Provider Strategy 265
Broad Differentiation Strategy 267
Best-cost Provider Strategy 269
Focused Low-cost Strategy 270
Focused Differentiation Strategy 270
Managerial Skills 271
Linking with Corporate Level 271
Summary 272

9. Developing Strategy Options **274**
Introduction 274
Corporate Strategy Directions 275
Capability and Innovation 276
Capability 276
Innovation 276
Market Penetration 278
Market Penetration 278
Consolidation 279
Withdrawal 279
Product Development 280
Definition of Products 281
Product Line and Product Mix 282
Research and Development 283

Chapter

Product Life Cycle 287

First Mover Advantage 288

Brand Management 289

Market Development 290

New Segments 290

New Uses 291

International Markets... 292

International Drivers.. 293

Competitive Advantage 294

Selecting Markets 294

Risks 296

Strategies for Entering Foreign Markets...................................... 296

Exporting.. 297

Licensing and Franchising... 299

Strategic Alliances and Joint Ventures... 299

Foreign Direct Investment 300

Strategies for Operating Internationally...................................... 300

Global Strategy 300

Transnational Strategy... 301

Multi-domestic Strategy.. 302

Globalisation or Localisation... 303

Conclusion 305

Summary 306

10. Diversification 311

Introduction 311

Choosing a Diversification Strategy... 312

Reasons for Diversifying.. 312

Types of Diversification... 313

Related Diversification 314

Unrelated Diversification 315

Performance... 316

Adding Value – Diversification.. 317

Competences 320

Strategies for Achieving Diversification 321

Internal Start-up 321

Joint Venture 322

Acquisition.. 322

Managing the Portfolio 322

Boston Consulting Group Matrix 323

Chapter

Directional Policy Matrix 326
Corporate Parenting 328
Conclusion 331
Summary 331

11. **Alternative Methods of Developing Strategy Options** **334**
Introduction 334
Internal Development 335
Strategic Alliances 337
Types of Alliances 338
Consortia 338
Joint Ventures 339
Licensing 341
Franchising 341
Outsourcing 344
Networking 345
Managing Alliances 345
Mergers and Acquisitions 346
Benefits of Mergers and Acquisitions 348
Variety of Mergers and Acquisitions 349
Process 350
Review of Acquisition 353
M&A Approval 354
Alliance or Acquisition 355
Industry Conditions: Tailoring Appropriate Strategies 356
Emerging Industries 357
Growth 357
Maturity 357
Decline 358
Conclusion 359
Summary 359

12. **Decision-making** **363**
Introduction 363
Decision-making Process 364
The Rational Model 365
Diagnosing the Problem 365
Identifying Different Solutions 365
Evaluating the Alternatives 365
Making a Decision 366
Implementing the Decision 366

Chapter

Evaluating the Outcome 367
Limitations of the Rational Model 367
Time Requirement in Decision-making 368
Escalation of Commitment 369
Group Decisions 370
Groupthink 371
Decision-making Styles 373
Decision Support Systems 375
Strategy Evaluation 376
Consistency 376
Suitability 377
Feasibility 378
Business Risk 379
Return 380
Mutually Exclusive Projects 384
Cost–Benefit Analysis 385
Stakeholder Reaction 385
Strategic Plan 386
Conclusion 387
Summary 387

Part Four: Implementation

Introduction to Strategy Implementation 393

13. Strategy Implementation 395
Introduction 395
Strategic Capability 396
People 397
Leadership 398
Management Team 398
Employees 400
The Human Resources Function 402
Other Resources 403
Finance 403
Marketing 404
Information Technology Systems 405
Operations 408
Building Competitive Capabilities 409
Procedures for Good Strategy Execution 410
Business Process Re-Engineering 410
Total Quality Management 411
Six Sigma Quality Control 411

Chapter

Project Management 415

Project Life Cycle 417

Processes 417

Project Integration Management 418

Project Scope Management 418

Project Time Management 419

Project Cost Management 420

Project Quality Management 420

Project Human Resource Management 421

Project Communications Management 421

Project Risk Management 421

Project Procurement Management 421

Successful Implementation 422

Incentives and Strategy Execution 422

Structural Designs 423

Control Processes 424

Direct Controls 424

Indirect Controls 426

Conclusion 428

Summary 428

14. Leading Organisational Change 433

Introduction 433

Forces of Change 435

Technology 435

Market Changes 436

Demographics and Sociological Changes 437

Types of Change 437

Balogun and Hope Hailey 437

Generic Typology of Change 439

Theory 'E' and Theory 'O' 439

Challenges for Understanding Change 439

Leadership 440

Context 442

Culture 442

Resistance to Change 443

Why People are Resistant to Change 443

Forcefield Analysis 444

Manifestations of Resistance 445

Models of Planned Organisational Change 446

Lewin's Change Model 446

Strategic Change Model: an Integrated Approach 447
    Phase One – Identifying the Need for Change 448
    Phase Two – Choosing the Appropriate Strategy 448
    Phase Three – Implementing the Change Programme....................... 449
    Managerial Imperatives 454
    Phase Four – Monitoring Results 454
Conclusion 455
Summary 455

Case Studies **459**
Introduction: Case Study Analysis.. 459
Case Study – Subject Matrix 462
BP and Deepwater Horizon 463
HSBC – Changes at the Top 473
Four Seasons Hotels and Resorts 480
Eason & Son Ltd – A New Chapter 493
Bonuses at the Bank 499
Ryanair.. 506
ESBI – Internationalisation in Action... 514
Ernest Shackleton – Leading Change 521

Bibliography **533**
Glossary **547**
Index **555**

Lists of Illustrations, Figures and Tables

Illustrations

Illustration 1.1	The PPARS System in the Health Service Executive	6
Illustration 1.2	Strategy Formulation – Dublin Docklands Development Authority	17
Illustration 1.3	PulseLearning and Emergent Strategy	20
Illustration 2.1	Personalised Power	33
Illustration 2.2	Behavioural Theories – Antarctic Expeditions	39
Illustration 2.3	Charismatic Military Leaders	42
Illustration 2.4	Dress Code and Corporate Culture	55
Illustration 3.1	Differentiating Vision, Mission, Goals and Objectives	75
Illustration 3.2	PulseLearning	76
Illustration 3.3	Diageo and its Stated Values	80
Illustration 3.4	The Johnson & Johnson 'Tylenol' Crisis	81
Illustration 3.5	Long-term Goals – The Apollo Programme	86
Illustration 3.6	Examples of Mission Statements	89
Illustration 4.1	The Watergate Scandal	122
Illustration 4.2	Corrib Gas Project	132
Illustration 4.3	Dove and the 'Campaign for Real Beauty'	139
Illustration 4.4	Croke Park – An Environmentally-friendly Stadium	140
Illustration 5.1	Tayto Crisps in China	158
Illustration 5.2	Ireland's Corporate Tax Rate	166
Illustration 5.3	Technology Changing the Business Model – Dream Ireland	170
Illustration 5.4	The Commission for Energy Regulation	174
Illustration 5.5	Bord na Móna and its Changing Environment	190
Illustration 7.1	Organisational Structure – Kerry Group Plc	243
Illustration 7.2	Risk Management – Bank of Scotland Ireland	255
Illustration 8.1	Low-cost Provider Strategy at Dell	266
Illustration 8.2	Differentiation Strategy – Four Seasons Hotels and Resorts	268
Illustration 9.1	Investment in Broadband	284
Illustration 10.1	Diversification Strategy – The Quinn Group	318
Illustration 11.1	Insomnia Coffee Company	336
Illustration 12.1	Groupthink – Our Lady of Lourdes Hospital, Drogheda	371
Illustration 13.1	Data Mining at Tesco	406
Illustration 13.2	Shannon Aerospace – Lean Transformation	414
Illustration 14.1	Ernest Shackleton – Leading Change	434

List of Figures

Figure 1.1 The Levels of Strategy 8
Figure 1.2 The Strategic Planning Model 11, 29, 150, 232, 393
Figure 1.3 Strategy Development Processes 15
Figure 2.1 Level 5 Leadership 43
Figure 2.2 Model of Organisational Culture (Schein) 54
Figure 3.1 Illustrates the three elements of a vision, and the relationship
          between an organisation's vision, its mission and its goals and objectives. 78
Figure 3.2 The Balanced Scorecard: A Five-star Hotel 93
Figure 3.3 Strategy Map for a Five-star Hotel 95
Figure 3.4 Customer Relationship Management 96
Figure 4.1 Diagram of Ethical Framework for Decision-making 119
Figure 4.2 Organisational Stakeholders 128
Figure 4.3 Stakeholder Mapping – Royal Dutch Shell and the Corrib Gas Project 131
Figure 5.1 Porter's Diamond 160
Figure 5.2 PESTEL Analysis 165
Figure 5.3 Five Forces Analysis 176
Figure 5.4 Industry Life Cycle 181
Figure 5.5 A Strategic Group Map of Some of the Main Hotels in Dublin 185
Figure 5.6 A Strategy Canvas for Five-star Hotels 188
Figure 5.7 Crisis: Danger and Opportunity 190
Figure 6.1 Strategic Capability 196
Figure 6.2 Product Customer Relationship 202
Figure 6.3 The Value Chain 207
Figure 6.4 The Value System 211
Figure 6.5 Activity Map – Ryanair 213
Figure 6.6 Weighted Competitive Strength Assessment 221
Figure 7.1 A Functional Structure 241
Figure 7.2 Multi-divisional Structure 242
Figure 7.3 Matrix Structure 245
Figure 8.1 Five Generic Strategies 264
Figure 9.1 Ansoff's Matrix 275
Figure 9.2 Product Life Cycle 287
Figure 10.1 The Boston Consulting Group (BCG) Matrix 323
Figure 10.2 Industry Attractiveness – Competitive Strength Matrix 327
Figure 10.3 The GE/McKinsey Portfolio Planning Matrix 328
Figure 10.4 Parenting Matrix: (the Ashridge Portfolio Display) A Diversified
          Buildings Material Group 329
Figure 12.1 Average Decision-making Styles for Highest Compensated 20%
          of Managers 374

Figure 13.1   Project Management Framework 416
Figure 13.2   Project Life Cycle.. 417
Figure 13.3   Precedence Diagramming Method (PDM) Network Diagram 419
Figure 14.1   Types of Change 438
Figure 14.2   Customer Relationship Management.. 441
Figure 14.3   Forcefield Analysis 445
Figure 14.4   Styles of Leadership Change 451

List of Tables

Table 2.1   Miles and Snow Typology... 57
Table 3.1   Objectives.. 90
Table 5.1   European Union Members and Eurozone Countries.................... 156
Table 6.1   Financial Ratios 215
Table 6.2   Weighted Competitive Strength Assessment: Henry Morris
               Manufacturing Ltd 220
Table 10.1   Market Attractiveness 326
Table 10.2   Relative Strength of the Company 327
Table 11.1   A Selection of Franchise Businesses Operating in Ireland 342
Table 12.1   Determining the Suitability of Strategic Options 377
Table 12.2   Payback Period... 381
Table 12.3   Net Present Value Method 384
Table 12.3   Strategic Plan 386

Introduction

"It was the best of times, it was the worst of times, it was the age of wisdom, it was the age of foolishness, it was the epoch of belief, it was the epoch of incredulity, it was the season of light, it was the season of darkness…". So begins *A Tale of Two Cities* by Charles Dickens. In many ways, those words could easily describe the last number of years in Ireland.

Since the 1st edition of this text was published, the Irish economy has suffered the worst recession in many decades. The enormous prosperity that was enjoyed by so many Irish people in the late 1990s and the early part of this century, has vanished like early morning mist being burned off by the summer sun. It was the result of so many factors, from greed to hubris. It was, above all, a failure of leadership.

It is, however, very easy to focus on the negative news and information that flows on an almost daily basis from the media. While the current recession is having a devastating impact on so many Irish companies, it is important to recognise that there are also good-news stories for both existing companies and start-ups. Despite the current difficulties, many Irish companies are succeeding. In any discussion about the economy or the recession, it must be remembered that there is no such entity as "Ireland Inc." There is the Irish State, of which the economy plays a central part, along with the institutions of State, and most importantly, its people. As a nation, we have no choice but to galvanise all our resources into rebuilding the country. We must also learn from experience to ensure such a debacle never happens again.

Revision

This 2nd edition of *Corporate Strategy for Irish Companies* covers the entire spectrum of managing organisations at a strategic level. The 1st edition has been updated to reflect recent developments in Ireland, and around the world, and the entire text has also been extensively revised. In particular, the chapter on leadership and corporate culture has been considerably expanded. The 2nd edition also contains a selection of detailed case studies (more case studies are also available online). The beginning of each case briefly summarises the main topics covered. These cases will help the reader develop their understanding of the various elements of strategy outlined and will also develop critical thinking skills.

Part 1 of this text lays the foundation for strategy within the organisation. Given all that has happened in Ireland over the past few years, this part must be seen as a vital part of the process of developing strategy in organisations. When things go wrong, the implications for all stakeholders are far too great. The social cost to this country as a result of the recession has been enormous.

Parts 2, 3 and 4 then explain the strategic process that is required in formulating and implementing strategy: analysing the business environment and the internal capability of the organisation; examining different strategic options; picking the optimum course of action; and finally, implementing the chosen strategy and dealing with changing circumstances.

Though the book is divided into four distinct parts, it must be remembered that these parts are not separate entities: they are all interlinked. The 2nd edition contains an introduction to each of the four parts in order to assist the reader put the chapters in that part into perspective. The text is aimed primarily at students preparing for exams. It will also be useful for those working in business who wish to develop a more strategic approach to running their company.

An Irish Text

While there are numerous texts on strategy available, this book presents the concepts of corporate strategy in an Irish Context. There are many examples included to illustrate the theory being discussed. Some of these examples are developed in greater detail and presented in separate illustration boxes. The examples cover large multinational companies that operate on a global basis, and also focus attention on the Irish economy and Irish companies. In some cases, such as with Kerry Group Plc, the 'local' example is also a 'global' one. Such examples are important as they reflect what is happening in the business world in Ireland and demonstrate that strategic management is not an abstract science but is directly relevant to every manager. By reflecting on these examples, it is hoped that the reader will appreciate the importance of corporate strategy in successfully guiding an organisation within a competitive environment. The case studies provided at the end of the book, and also as extra online resource, will provide a greater opportunity for the student to understand the theoretical concepts explored in the text.

While there are obvious differences in meaning between terms such as 'organisation', 'company', 'corporation' and 'firm', for the purpose of this book, the terms are used interchangeably.

Research

The material contained in this 2nd edition comes from an extensive literature review of what the leading international experts say about different aspects of corporate strategy. This review has been extensively updated. Some of the studies referred to have taken teams of researchers years to gather and interpret the relevant data. Such research provides valuable insights into corporate strategy. There are perhaps thousands of books and journal articles covering strategy in general, as well as more specific areas of research. The research referred to in this book is designed to give the reader the breadth and depth required to equip them with good, rounded knowledge of the subject matter. It is brought together in a comprehensive way and applied in a critical analysis to the business environment in Ireland.

Referencing

In discussing the academic literature in this area, the original source of material is given, and is reference using the Harvard System. This gives the author's name, the date of publication and where a specific page is referenced, this is also included after the date. The full reference to the book or journal article can then be found at the end of the relevant chapter. This will allow readers to develop their knowledge in greater detail if desired or required. In many cases, additional recommended reading on the subject matter is provided. A bibliography is also provided for all the books, journal articles, newspapers and other sources consulted in writing the text.

There are numerous quotes throughout the book that are drawn from English literature and many other different disciplines. These are intended to demystify corporate strategy and help the reader to realise that underpinning the subject is a lot of common sense, and that we can draw inspiration from all around us. William Shakespeare, in particular, demonstrated remarkable insight into human behaviour, especially in his commentary on different types of leadership. It will be seen throughout the text that people play a central role in the success of organisations. While many aspects of leadership and management have evolved over time, there are many other aspects that are immutable and are the same today as they were 400 years ago when Shakespeare was writing his plays.

Principles of Strategic Management

Regrettably, some of the Irish companies mentioned in the 1st edition have now ceased trading – casualties of the very difficult times in which we live. There remain enormous challenges ahead, and, unfortunately, there will be many more companies that go out of business over the next few years. Consequently, some of the examples used in this book may date more quickly than would normally be the case.

Gandhi once said: "It's not that Christianity has failed; it's just that it has never been tried." While the examples themselves may lose their significance, the principles and theories outlined in this text remain valid despite the turmoil and, indeed, will assume even greater importance. It is relatively easy to make profits in business during a boom period. In a recession, it is a lot more difficult. The challenge for those managing companies will be to step back from the day-to-day issues in their organisations and think strategically. In many situations, it is a case of getting back to the basics.

Each chapter begins by setting learning objectives, which are intended to assist the reader focus on the material contained therein. For example, the learning objectives for Chapter 2 are as follows:

LEARNING OBJECTIVES
On completion of this chapter, you will be able to:
- Distinguish between the different types of leadership
- Evaluate the effectiveness of different leadership styles
- Assess the relationship between leadership and corporate culture
- Critically examine the role of leadership in the formulation and implementation of strategy

While the material is grouped into parts and chapters as much as possible, it should be remembered that there is a strong link between all the various elements running through the entire text. At the end of each chapter, there is a summary of the main points. Discussion questions are also provided, which are designed so that the reader can reflect on the material contained in that chapter.

Definitions

There are a number of definitions and terms that are used throughout this book. These are standard terms used in the world of strategic management. They are defined and explained the first time they appear in the text and are highlighted for the reader as in the following example:

Corporate Strategy is charting the future direction of a company by developing long-term goals that reflect stakeholders' interests and achieve sustainable competitive advantage.

A glossary of these terms is also included at the end of the text to facilitate understanding.

Acknowledgements

Once again, I am deeply indebted to a great number of people who have helped in the writing of the second edition of this text.

To Pat Costello and all the staff at Chartered Accountants Ireland. To Ronan O'Loughlin, Diarmuid Breathnach and all the FAE team for their on-going help and support. To the Publishing team: Michael Diviney, Agnieska Pobedynska and Jennifer Thompson for all their patience and assistance throughout the project, and for making the first edition a success.

To the Band of Brothers – a big note of thanks to all my former Army colleagues who have helped both directly and indirectly, and most of all for the tremendous friendship over the last thirty-plus years.

To my colleagues in the Institute of Technology, Tralee, and in particular to Mary Rose and the business team. A special word of thanks is due to all the library staff, who assisted in the search for books and journal articles.

To the numerous people in the various organisations who provided information and advice. In particular, I would like to thank the following for their time in contributing case studies for this text: Felicity Kelliher and Chris O'Riordan, Mary Rose Stafford, Breda O'Dwyer, Ann Sayers, Catherine Moylan, Sheila O'Mahony, Fearghal McHugh, Aine Culloty, Charlotte Curtin, Niall Horan, Sarah Scanlon, Aaron Spring, Bernard Harmon, Michelle Buckley. Thank you also to Paul O'Connor for all the technical back-up.

Finally, I would like to thank Fiona for all her support throughout the process. Writing a text such as this demands endless hours of work, and it would not have been possible without such support.

Tralee, August 2011.

Understanding Strategy

LEARNING OBJECTIVES

On completion of this chapter, you will be able to:

- ■ Evaluate corporate strategy and its various elements
- ■ Distinguish between the different levels of corporate strategy
- ■ Critically examine the four core areas of corporate strategy
- ■ Analyse the various ways in which strategy is developed

INTRODUCTION

'Strategy' is a term used to describe the actions of a company. In essence, it is about the long-term direction of an organisation. It takes into account its vision and mission, its interaction with the world around it, looking at the company's current situation, deciding where it needs to go from its present position, and how it is going to get there. Ultimately, the chosen strategy should result in better company performance and a sustainable competitive advantage.

Chapter 1 gives an overview of how strategy is developed in organisations. It begins with defining strategy and examines the nature of corporate strategy. It then examines some of the challenges involved in developing a strategy for an organisation and how strategy applies to all types and sizes of organisations. There are various levels of strategy within organisations and these are discussed.

It then examines in detail the various elements of the process of formulating and implementing strategy. The chapter begins by looking at the definition of strategy and examines some of the challenges involved in developing strategy and how it applies to different levels of an organisation.

There are four core areas of strategy:
- • the foundation
- • strategic analysis
- • strategy development
- • strategy implementation

These are introduced to the reader in this chapter and will be developed in greater detail throughout the book. The final part of this chapter examines the variety of different ways in which strategy is actually developed within organisations.

DEFINITION OF STRATEGY

There are many terms used for strategy and strategic management. These include 'corporate strategy', 'business policy' and 'competitive strategy'. While each has its own nuance, they are essentially synonyms; so, for consistency, the term used here is corporate strategy.

 Corporate Strategy is charting the future direction of a company by developing long-term goals that reflect stakeholders' interests and achieve sustainable competitive advantage.

The Nature of Corporate Strategy

Adopting a strategic focus is of vital concern for all organisations. In the present turmoil in world markets, some managers may focus on the immediate issues that are pressing on the organisation. Without doubt, these matters must be attended to, but so too must the long-term strategic issues. They are not mutually exclusive. What is important is that the day-to-day issues are examined in the context of the overall strategic direction of the company and are supporting the attainment of its strategic goals. Adopting a strategic focus, therefore, requires senior managers to step back from the organisation and look upon it in a holistic manner with an eye to long-term sustainability. The challenges facing organisations today make it far more difficult to adopt such a strategic focus, yet it is vital that managers meet that challenge. In good times, a company will find it relatively easy to succeed. When times get tough, sound strategic decisions will make the difference between survival and oblivion.

According to McCarthy *et al.* (2010), a lack of business skills is one of the main reasons behind Ireland's loss of competitiveness. The report by the Irish Management Institute (IMI) *Closing the Gap* draws on research from the London School of Economics and McKinsey and found that underperformance in management skills leaves the country uncompetitive in relation to other European states and could be costing Ireland in the region of €2 billion a year (McKinsey & Co, 2009). In particular, small to medium-sized enterprises (SMEs) are lacking the necessary management skills to compete internationally. The Government has directed its efforts to improving skills among employees, which is of course a necessary step in improving competitiveness. However, the report also highlights the necessity to concentrate on improving skills among managers, as there is a direct correlation between management skills and company performance. One of its recommendations is that managers in all companies, particularly SMEs, focus specifically on long-term strategy. This text will help underpin the academic knowledge required to develop those strategy skills.

Definitions can be useful to help focus attention on a particular subject. There are many characteristics of strategic decisions that are implicit in the definition of corporate strategy given above. These characteristics can be summed up as:

Complex In general, strategic decisions are complex in nature: they demand rigorous analysis, and, in looking to the future, there will inevitably be significant uncertainty as to the best course of action. There are a number of analytical tools available to assist executives in deciphering the information available to them in order to make decisions that are appropriate to their company.

Tailor-made strategies In developing options for the future, it is essential that those options are tailored for each individual organisation. What is right for one company may not be right for another. Therefore, while much can be learned from observing other companies in operation, care must be exercised in applying those lessons to each individual company. There are many examples and company illustrations to explain the concepts in this text. The strategy of a company can be identified in a number of ways, such as observing its action in the market place, noting what the company says about itself in its annual reports, marketing material, press releases, etc. (Such analysis forms an integral part of environmental analysis in Chapter 5, which discusses how companies analyse the competitive environments in which they operate.) While it may be difficult to acquire some relevant information on competing companies, a considerable amount of it is readily accessible and just requires constant environmental scanning (the process of collecting information about the forces at play in the organisation's environment) and analysis.

Subjectivity In using analytical tools, one may get the impression that strategy is an exact science. While it is important to analyse the data, particularly financial data, there is still a large element of subjective judgement required by the executive. This is particularly true for all industries at present, as companies grapple with the uncertainty of collapsing markets and financial turmoil. By being well-informed and having a good grasp of the use of strategic tools, executives can, however, be more objective in their deliberations.

Holistic view In thinking strategically, senior executives require a holistic view of the organisation rather than focusing on just one specific area. It must be remembered that there are strong links between all parts of the organisation, and decisions made in one area will impact on other parts.

Resources Usually, large resources will be needed to implement these decisions, and such resources will have to be identified and allocated. These resources are often tied up for a considerable period of time, so there is often an opportunity cost involved, i.e. by using resources to support one particular strategy they are then not available for others. Strategic decisions, therefore, require careful consideration before committing to them. In the current climate, this is more important than ever. These resources should be seen as an investment rather than a cost; Huff *et al.* (2009) observe that strategy should generate more resources than it uses in terms of revenue, reputation and commitment.

Change Factors such as Ireland's membership of the European Union, and increasing globalisation in many markets, mean that the environment within which the organisation is operating is constantly changing. Change is not always obvious, and so the organisation must recognise any changes that are taking place and be able to spot opportunities when they arise. In response to the changing environment, organisations themselves must change (see Chapter 14).

Competitive environment All organisations, even not-for-profit ones, operate in a competitive environment, so whatever business the organisation is in, it is about doing it better than its rivals and at lower costs. Strategic decisions, therefore, require a thorough understanding of the capability (the resources and competences) of the organisation, as well as using that capability in the most effective manner possible to achieve its goals. Competition must be increasingly seen in global terms, particularly in such an open economy as Ireland. The internet has radically altered the nature of competition not just in terms of the source of competition, but also the speed at which the competitive environment can change.

Sustainability Whatever course of action an organisation is following, it must be sustainable over the long-term and not focused merely on immediate gain at the expense of its continuing viability. A company must obviously respond to the competitive threats that it faces. However, in the search for opportunities, it has to strike a balance between managing for today, while simultaneously positioning itself strongly for the future. The implosion in the banking industry in Ireland highlights this need very clearly. Outside of the banking industry, private sector companies do not fall under the mantle of 'systemic importance' and do not qualify for state assistance. All strategy decisions must, therefore, be made with the long-term sustainability of the company in mind.

Defining the organisation and industry Strategic decisions, through the goals that are generated, will generally define the organisation under consideration. Defining the organisation refers to whether it is a single business operation or a conglomerate (a collection of different businesses within a group); which products and markets the company is involved with; and, just as importantly, those products and markets that they are *not* involved in. It also defines the boundaries of the industry. Some industries are clearly defined in terms of what they do and fall within set parameters, e.g. the cement manufacturing industry. Others are more difficult to define, such as the tourism industry. Tourism crosses over many other industries, such as the airline industry and the restaurant business. However, each of these elements of the tourism industry also provides a service to people who are local to the area and clearly could not be described as tourists.

Long-term Strategic decisions are generally long-term in nature, rather than about day-to-day operational issues, though such operational decisions will ultimately derive from strategic decisions that have been taken in the organisation. The time-frame involved in developing and implementing strategy will differ from one industry to another. For example, in the software industry a year will see many changes. In the oil exploration industry, 20-year planning periods are not unusual. Given the turmoil in international markets at present, such time-frames are getting shorter, though on average the time-frame for strategic decisions can be taken to mean a three-to-five-year period. However, for all organisations, flexibility is required as time-frames can change quite considerably depending on the level of turmoil in the environment within which it is operating. It should also be noted that different strategies will necessarily have different time-frames, depending on the nature of the course of action being undertaken. Therefore, some strategies will be effected within a one-year period, while other strategies might be rolled out over a three- to five-year time-frame. (This point will be developed further in Chapter 3 in discussing Balanced Scorecards.) One very important aspect of the timing of different strategies is that the nature of the strategy must be clearly communicated to employees at all levels in the organisation. In most instances, strategies will have different elements and employees must understand what element the organisation is currently focused on and what part they play in that process.

Inclusive approach An important aspect of the above definition of corporate strategy is the inclusion of 'stakeholders'.

Stakeholders are people, both groups and individuals, who have a direct or indirect interest in the organisation and its goals, including shareholders, directors, managers, employees, trade unions, government, and the wider community.

Many companies focus on their obligations to shareholders, often to the exclusion of the other stakeholders. The interests of an organisation's stakeholders will differ, and these should be balanced in driving the organisation forward. The values of an organisation should also inform its strategy, and these values need to reflect those of its stakeholders. (This point will be developed further in Chapter 4 when discussing corporate governance.)

Challenges in Corporate Strategy

Corporate strategy has become more complex in recent years due to various forces impacting on organisations, including globalisation and technological change. Individually and collectively, these forces have radically changed the manner in which many businesses operate. Globalisation is having a major impact on competition, not just in terms of more competitors, but in the dynamic pace at which competition can change in just a short period of time. There is now much greater mobility of people internationally (particularly within the European Union) and it was estimated by the Central Statistics Office (CSO) in 2007 that there were 420,000 foreign nationals in Ireland, representing some 10% of the total population and 14% of the working population. These people have brought much-needed skills and experience, but this also presents challenges in terms of cultural integration. Since 2009, many foreign nationals, particularly eastern Europeans, have left Ireland and returned to their native country the working population in Ireland can still. However, be regarded as multicultural.

Technology is rapidly changing the cost structure of business and how products and services are delivered to the customer, and technology will become even more important in the future. Yet technology *per se* is not the panacea for every problem. Ultimately, technology is an aid to decision-making and efficiency. It should not be regarded as an end in itself. According to Collins (2001), technology is "an accelerator of momentum, not a creator of it". In addition, care must be taken regarding the choices about the type of technology systems that are used. There are many examples of enormous sums of money being spent on IT systems that simply do not deliver on their promise. The Health Service Executive (HSE), for example, abandoned the roll-out of the PPARS computer system having spent approximately €150 million (see **Illustration 1.1**).

In making strategic decisions, it is becoming more difficult to keep up-to-date with changes in the complex environment of contemporary business, and to understand the implications at individual company level. This often leads to what Johnson *et al.* (2011: 33) call **strategic drift**, where "the

Illustration 1.1: The PPARS System in the Health Service Executive

PPARS, the Personnel, Payroll and Related Systems project was originally designed in 1995 by the Department of Health to computerise the Payroll and HR systems of the 130,000 health service staff and assist the health boards in the efficient management of all the various functions dealing with employees. The initial cost of the project was estimated at just less than €10 million. The project itself began two years later and covered five health board areas (the health boards were later amalgamated into the Health Service Executive) and St James's Hospital in Dublin.

It was estimated that the project would take three years to complete employing commonly-used SAP software. However, from the beginning, the project was very poorly managed and the scope of the system did not take into account the needs of those who would be using the system. PPARS had a project manager who reported to a National Project Board made up of members from the various health boards. As often happens with different vested interests involved in a project, getting agreement among members who represented the separate and autonomous health boards often proved extremely difficult, and the Board often did not have the authority to implement decisions.

Despite problems arising with PPARS, the decision was made to stick with the project. Throughout its development, there were numerous changes made to the scope of the programme. This 'scope creep' added significantly to both cost and time. There were many criticisms of the decision-making process and the communication channels used. In general, there was much acrimony among the participating groups and an overall lack of ownership of the project by those involved.

By 2007, when the project was eventually suspended, the cost had multiplied to €150 million (estimates vary as to the complete cost) while the project itself covered only a small part of its original intended scope.

Source: Dept of Health and Children; C & AG Report; *Prime Time*, 6 October 2005

strategy of the organisation gradually drifts away from the realities of its environment and towards an internally determined view of the world. This can lead to significant performance downturn, and potentially the demise of the organisation."

This text is designed to provide you with strategic tools to assist in the formulation and implementation of strategy. Kaplan and Norton (2008) believe that most companies' underperformance is due to a breakdown between strategy and operations. They stress the importance of understanding the management cycle that links strategy and operations, and knowing what tools to apply at each stage of the cycle.

Every company will face its own challenges in implementing strategy. In their book, *The Strategy Focused Organisation*, Kaplan and Norton (2001) articulate five principles that are common to each organisation when meeting that challenge:

- Translate the strategy into operational terms to which people in the company can relate and understand.
- Align the organisation to the strategy – individual strategies must be linked and integrated and the organisation must support the implementation of these strategies.
- Make strategy part of everyone's everyday job. It needs to be moved from the boardroom to the backroom. All employees must understand the company's overall strategy and conduct their day-to-day business in a manner that supports it.
- Make strategy a continual process. It should be an on-going process with constant reviews that involves everyone in the organisation. It should also be an opportunity for learning.
- Mobilise change through executive leadership. The single most important condition for success is the active involvement and sense of ownership of the executive team. Strategy involves change in the organisation and this change must be led from the top. Leading change is also a central theme of Kotter (1996, 2002).

STRATEGY APPLIES TO ALL ORGANISATIONS

When one thinks of strategy, large multinational companies come to mind. However, strategy is relevant to *all* organisations. The examples in this text are drawn from a wide variety of industries and different-sized companies. It must be remembered that such companies would not have grown to be multinationals unless they made the right decisions along the way.

The Tralee-based company Kerry Group is now one of the largest and most successful food ingredients companies in the world. The company was founded in Listowel, County Kerry in 1972, and grew steadily throughout the 1970s. In 1986 it became a public limited company, listing on the Dublin and London stock exchanges. Since then it has continued to grow by internal development and acquisitions. With its headquarters in Tralee, the Group now employs 22,000 people throughout its manufacturing, sales and technical centres around the world, and is regarded as a leader in its chosen markets. This success did not happen by accident. It needed sound strategic decisions from its beginnings as a small company, and right through each stage of development.

Equally, strategy is just as relevant in service organisations as it is in manufacturing. It is axiomatic that, as economies develop, a greater percentage of GDP will be derived from service industries. It is estimated that €58 billion in Irish exports in 2007 represent service exports, accounting for 40% of total exports. Increasingly, there is much greater focus on public sector bodies to ensure that they are delivering value-for-money to the taxpayer. Such bodies also need a clear understanding of strategy. The same can be said for aid agencies and other not-for-profit bodies. There are some 24,000 not-for-profit organisations in the Republic of Ireland and 7,500 charities. The sector employs 63,000 people and accounts for 8% of GDP (McKay, 2009). The purpose of these organisations differs from commercial bodies, yet they too operate in a competitive environment, competing for resources, and this requires effective strategies. While the circumstances of all of these organisations may differ, the basic principles of strategic management are common to all.

LEVELS OF STRATEGY WITHIN THE ORGANISATION

Strategy exists at three main levels in the organisation: corporate-level, business-level and operational strategies forming the following hierarchy:

- Corporate-level strategy
- Business-level strategy
- Operational strategy

These three levels are set against a background of functional strategies. These levels of strategy are shown graphically in **Figure 1.1**.

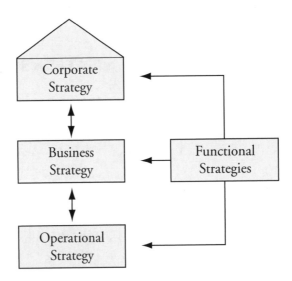

Figure 1.1 *The Levels of Strategy*

Corporate-level Strategy

Corporate-level strategy refers to the decisions that are taken at the corporate headquarters and these decisions will impact on the entire organisation. They are concerned with deciding whether a company will operate as a single-business entity, in which case corporate-level and business-level strategy are the same, or in a number of different industries, in which case strategy governs the relationship between the headquarters and the various strategic business units (SBUs) of the organisation. A **Strategic Business Unit** is a unit within the organisation that has its own distinct market for its goods or services, and is distinct from other SBUs. While a large company may have many SBUs operating in different markets, the actions of these SBUs will have to be co-ordinated at this level. The corporate headquarters does not, in general, deal directly with customers, and thus does not generate revenue directly. It must, therefore, concern itself with adding value to the different elements of the organisation.

Corporate governance is an important element of strategy at this level and has come in for considerable attention in recent times in Ireland. The board of directors of the company will give its imprimatur to the strategies that are proposed by senior management. Decisions taken at this level will also have to accommodate the expectations of the different stakeholders, and these expectations should be reflected in the strategy. (This point will be developed further in Chapter 4.)

Business-level Strategy

In the case of a single business operation, or a Strategic Business Unit, business-level strategy involves competing successfully in different markets. It concerns decisions about the markets in which the company operates and what goods and services to offer in those markets. Competitive strategy is a core element, as this will distinguish market leaders from followers. For commercial organisations, profitability will also be important, though there may be some circumstances where a particular SBU might be subsidised by other SBUs within the organisation for other strategic reasons (see Chapter 10). Such cross-subsidy would need the approval of senior management. Strategies at business-level should be consistent with corporate-level strategies, as ultimately this is how the overall organisation will achieve its desired results.

Operational Strategies

Strategy is meaningless until it is reflected in the everyday operations of the company. Lynch (2008) considers strategy as existing only at corporate-level and business-level, and does not include operational-level strategy. Other writers such as Johnson *et al.* (2011: 7) and Thompson *et al.* (2008: 40) include operational strategies directly in the overall hierarchy of strategy. Operational strategies are concerned with how the front line managers in different parts of an organisation translate the corporate and business-level strategies into delivering goals and objectives. Operational strategies require the effective use of people and resources, as well as control and other processes. While on the one hand, operational strategies do not fit neatly into the definition of corporate strategy, which is essentially long-term in nature, they are still part of the process of how organisations achieve their goals. In that regard, they can be considered part of the overall hierarchy of strategy.

Functional Strategies

Some writers such as Thompson and Martin (2005), Hill and Jones (2009), and Huff *et al.* (2009) refer to functional strategies as either being another layer in the hierarchy or else as an alternative name for operational strategies. In reality, functional strategies form an integral part of all levels of strategy that have been discussed:

- Corporate-level strategy
- Business-level strategy
- Operational strategies

Consequently, functional strategy forms a backdrop that runs from corporate-level strategy down through the hierarchy (see **Figure 1.1**). Take the accounting function in a large company, for example. The group financial controller will set financial policy for the entire group in terms of the financial structure of the company – master budgets, consolidation of accounts and accounting policy to which the entire organisation will adhere. Each SBU will develop its own financial policy in line with the overall directives of the organisation. It will formulate budgets for the SBU and adapt its accounting procedures to comply with the laws of the jurisdiction within which it is operating. In turn, each part of the SBU will develop its own budgets and accounting procedures relevant to its section. While conforming to the agreed policies for the SBU, the budget and other accounting functions needed in the production department will obviously differ from those for the marketing department.

It should be noted that all three levels of strategy: corporate, business and operational, should be aligned both horizontally (across the organisation) and vertically (from corporate to operational) and, if such alignment is not achieved, then problems will occur in the organisation's strategy.

CORE AREAS OF STRATEGY

In broad terms, strategy can be divided into four core areas:

1. The Foundation
2. Strategic Analysis
3. Developing Strategy
4. Strategy Implementation

These four core areas of strategy are not separate, sequential stages but are very much integrated and concurrent processes. An organisation might be in the process of implementing a particular strategy when changes in the environment cause it to modify or even abandon that strategy. These four core areas, forming the strategic planning model, are represented graphically in **Figure 1.2** below.

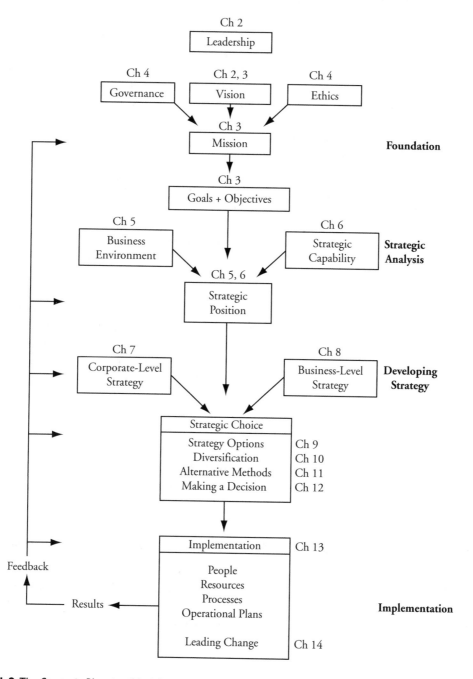

Figure 1.2 *The Strategic Planning Model*

The Foundation

An essential part of the process of developing and implementing strategy for any organisation is the laying down of a proper foundation. The foundation for developing strategy consists of understanding the processes involved within that particular organisation and establishing a vision and mission. Leadership is an essential element of the process that drives and underpins all aspects of strategy. It also involves establishing proper corporate governance procedures and ethical structures that will guide decision-making. With these foundation stones in place, the organisation can then develop a competitive enterprise that will stand the test of time and also moral scrutiny.

Before examining the business environment in which it operates, the organisation should be clear about its purpose and mission as these will influence the interpretation of all further analysis, both internal and external. The organisation then needs to decide what it wants to achieve and to set clear goals and objectives. These goals and objectives should be both legal and ethical, and reflect to varying degrees the various expectations of all its stakeholders.

Warren Buffett, one of the richest men in the world, once famously said: "It is only when the tide goes out that you see who was swimming in the nude". It is now abundantly clear that many Irish companies have been caught by the tide going out. So many companies, not least of all the banks and property developers, went in naked pursuit of the maximisation of profit but had failed to establish a proper foundation that would create, or in some cases continue, a sustainable business model. There are currently several official enquiries into the conduct of some key players, and it remains to be seen if any laws were broken. What is clear at this juncture, however, is that their business models provided incredible short-term gain but at the expense of their companies and their employees. It was, for many, a Faustian pact.

In addition, whatever about the legality of the way business was conducted, in some cases the behaviour of those involved was highly unethical at best. Given the enormous impact on the Irish economy and its international reputation, as well as the impact on Irish citizens, there can be no doubt that there will be much greater scrutiny in the future with regard to the decisions that executives make. There will be tougher regulations, and higher standards will be demanded of companies and those charged with running them.

Strategic Analysis of the Business Environment and Organisational Capability

The next step in the strategic management process is an analysis of the business environment within which the organisation operates and of the company's own strategic capabilities. Such analysis should be an on-going process, as change in the business environment is continuous. Indeed, such small changes can, over a period of time, constitute major change and can have a serious impact on performance.

Organisations are open systems that interact with their environment: strategic analysis consists of the development of a detailed understanding of that environment. While there are a number of strategic tools available, it is a difficult process that involves making assumptions about the future, something that inevitably entails uncertainty. The organisation needs to anticipate any changes but, at the very least, it must be able to react when such changes occur.

Environmental analysis examines the **macro environment**: all the wider political, economic, socio-cultural and technological factors that impact on the organisation's industry or industries. It also looks at the **micro environment**: the level of competition within the organisation's particular market or industry, and how the organisation is positioned within this competitive environment. It also examines the changes taking place – the driving forces and the key success factors required for operating in the industry. The purpose of carrying out environmental analysis is to develop a fuller understanding of the opportunities and threats that exist. (Environmental analysis is discussed in detail in Chapter 5.)

Internal analysis of the organisation follows on from the examination of the external environment. (This is examined in Chapter 6.) Its purpose is to understand the strategic capability of the organisation. Such analysis highlights the organisation's strengths and weaknesses and, combined with the opportunities and threats identified earlier, will enable it to complete a detailed Strengths, Weaknesses, Opportunities and Threats (SWOT) analysis. SWOT analysis can provide the basis for strategic options that the organisation could develop further.

Developing Strategy

The third major stage of strategic management is the development of strategies for both corporate and business unit levels. As described above, companies must first decide on their corporate-level strategy, as this will impact on business-level strategy. Issues such as what businesses it will include in its portfolio, what range of products it will manufacture and what markets, both at home and internationally, it will operate in must be decided. Such decisions will depend on the level of resources at its disposal, along with the skill and competences that are needed to support such decisions.

Business-level strategies are formulated in line with corporate-level strategies and are translated into specific strategies for each individual SBU. Porter (1985) defined three generic business-level strategies: cost leadership, differentiation and focus. These generic business strategies have been further developed by other writers and are discussed in detail in Chapter 8.

Once business-level strategies have been chosen, the company can then set about generating possible strategic options. It is important that managers generate as many options as possible before making a decision on the future direction of a company. Often there is a tendency to pick the most obvious choice, but this may not necessarily be the best option. Possible options here include:

- **Market penetration** – building up market share
- **Product development** – developing new products for existing markets
- **Market development** – developing new markets with existing products
- **Diversification** – moving away from existing businesses into new parts of the industry or, indeed, new and different industries

All of these options must be underpinned by the necessary capability to pursue a specific course of action. This will vary considerably from one organisation to another (see Chapter 6). As competition becomes more intense and diverse, it will also need to be underpinned by a culture of innovation.

For each of these possible directions, there are different methods by which such strategies can be pursued. For most organisations, growth by **internal development** will form an important part of their future plans. **Mergers and acquisitions** provide a quick method for expansion, or alternatively, they may consider various forms of **strategic alliances** with other organisations. (Chapters 9, 10, 11 and 12 examine these factors along with methods of analysing the various options.)

Strategy Implementation

The fourth stage of strategy is its implementation. Without successful implementation, the chosen strategy remains merely a plan or aspiration. Implementation requires putting an appropriate strategic architecture in place, along with ensuring that all the necessary resources (human, financial, physical and technological) are made available when needed. In most instances, implementing the chosen strategy will involve change for the organisation, and this process has to be carefully led.

While implementing the strategy, it is also necessary to monitor its suitability as well as monitoring the process of implementation itself. In that regard, the entire process of developing and implementing strategy is an iterative process whereby executives should be constantly referring back to all stages of the process to ensure that the strategy being implemented remains the best course of action. A number of questions should be asked to test the suitability of the strategy that has been chosen:

1. Is the strategy consistent with the vision and mission of the organisation?
2. How well does the strategy fit the company's situation? (The company must have the resources and competences to deliver on the strategy.)
3. Is the strategy different from what competitors are doing, and will it help the company develop a competitive advantage that is sustainable in the long-term?
4. As the strategy is being implemented, is it achieving the intended results? (This should include a balance between financial and strategic goals.)
5. What corrective measures need to be taken?

DEVELOPMENT PROCESSES

The division of strategy into the four core areas that have been discussed above (the foundation, strategic analysis, developing strategy options, and strategy implementation) implies that strategy is developed in an organised and sequential manner. The reality for most organisations is different and, in most instances, the strategy that an organisation is actually pursuing is constructed in a combination of different ways. It is useful to examine these various processes, as it is important for executives to understand all of the various influences that impact on the strategy-making process.

It will be seen that it is not a case of senior executives deciding on a course of action, and then giving directions to ensure its implementation. The planning of such a course of action by those at the top of the company is, of course, a very important part of the overall process, but it does not paint the full picture. According to Mintzberg (1985), the strategy development process can be divided into two broad categories:

- intended strategy development; and
- emergent strategy development.

This is depicted in **Figure 1.3** below. It is only by understanding all of the processes involved, and the mixture of those constituent parts, that executives can play a truly effective role in formulating and implementing strategy in their organisation.

Intended Strategy Development

Organisational Leadership For any organisation, leadership plays a central role in its success. In the context of strategy formulation, leadership fulfils two important functions. First, leaders provide a clear vision for the future of the company. Secondly, they create an environment within the organisation in which all members can develop to their full potential and work together towards achieving the strategic goals that have been agreed. In this regard, leadership also provides the environment in which all the other processes of both intended strategy development and emergent strategy development take place. (The role that leadership plays in formulating strategy will be further developed in Chapter 2.)

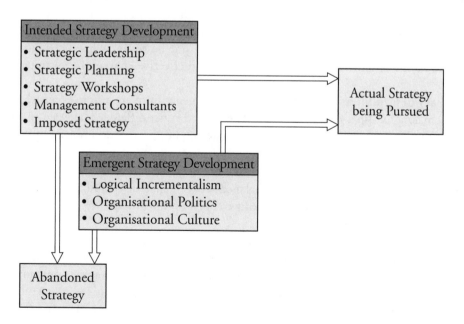

Figure 1.3 *Strategy Development Processes*

Strategic Planning The development of a strategic plan is an essential element of the overall process of strategy development. Strategic planning provides a structured means for the organisation to take a longer term view of strategy and to evaluate both its environment and its capabilities. The plan can be used to formulate goals and objectives and move the organisation in the desired direction. The plan, and its resulting budgets, also help co-ordinate the various divisions within the organisation and help them work in unison.

In the 1960s and 1970s, most multinational corporations had large planning departments staffed with specialists whose job it was to produce a series of plans for the approval of senior management. It was very much a top-down process based on the intentions of senior management and backed up by the appropriate resources. This process would have had its antecedents in the military, in that armies would have been the precursors of large corporations in the organisational sense.

During the 1990s, the planning process in corporations became much less formal. Apart from the costs of having such large planning departments, formal planning can create problems in that those who are involved in developing the plans have no responsibility for their implementation, and this can result in a lack of ownership of the plan by those whose job it is to deliver on the objectives.

Mintzberg (1994) highlighted many problems associated with such formal planning systems:

- **The fallacy of prediction** – the world is supposed to stay still while the plan is being developed and implemented. This clearly does not happen in reality.
- **The fallacy of detachment** – the system does the thinking and the strategists are detached from operations. There is often a relentless search for the 'one best way', while flexibility is usually required. Business unit managers must take full and effective charge of the strategy-making process.
- **The fallacy of formulisation** – implies a rational sequence from analysis to eventual action, but strategy making is also a *learning* process. There is a distinct difference between planning and strategic thinking. Planning cannot generate strategies, but it can help implement them.

Planners do, however, have a very important role in the process in terms of general analysis and acting as catalysts. There also needs to be a balance between analytical thinking, bringing order to the organisation, and creative, intuitive thinking to open up the process.

Strategy Workshops Most organisations now involve managers at all levels in the development of strategy, giving people a meaningful input into the process. This is often done using strategic workshops where people meet (often off-site) and discuss the issues facing the company and how they might be addressed. It still feeds into a formal strategic plan, but it is as much a bottom-up process as a top-down approach, and it enables those responsible for the execution of the plan to participate meaningfully.

Having started off with a very autocratic style, Jack Welch, former CEO of General Electric, gradually switched to a much more inclusive one, getting his managers involved in strategy 'workout sessions'. These were sessions where managers at many levels would debate the issues facing the company and how best to tackle them, debates which would be facilitated by outside people, such as university professors who had 'no axe to grind'. Managers were taught how to identify the root cause of any problem and quickly find a solution so that the company could move forward (Welch, 2001).

Illustration 1.2: Strategy Formulation – Dublin Docklands Development Authority

The **Dublin Docklands Development Authority (DDDA)** is one Irish organisation that has used workshops involving multiple stakeholders to help formulate strategy. While the Authority has been in the news in recent years for among other things its involvement in the consortium that purchased the Irish Glass Bottle site in Ringsend, Dublin for €413 million, the DDDA nevertheless has achieved many successes through its involvement with its stakeholders in developing its strategic plans. The DDDA was established in 1997 with a remit covering the social and economic redevelopment of the docklands area in Dublin. To enable them to achieve this, the Authority developed a five-year strategic 'master plan'. This was subsequently updated in 2003, and their new master plan is currently being developed. These plans cover all aspects of the development of the docklands area. The establishment of the International Financial Services Centre (IFSC) in Dublin was the initial part of the physical regeneration of the area. This progress has continued year after year and there are now many stunning contemporary buildings north and south of the River Liffey, including the National Conference Centre, which was opened in 2010.

These magnificent buildings are only one element of the regeneration. An integral part of the overall development is the social regeneration of the area, which was home to long-established communities that had worked for generations in the labour-intensive docks. As shipping companies moved to containerisation in the second half of the last century, unemployment became endemic in the area. An extra challenge for the Authority is how to integrate the new residents, that have come to work and live in the area with the established residents, to develop a vibrant community in the docklands.

To be successful, any developments have to be community-led rather than adopting a top-down approach. The DDDA has been very successful in working hand-in-hand with all of the community stakeholders: young people, senior citizens, community groups, educational establishments, sports clubs, Gardaí, business groups, and many more, to discuss issues of mutual concern. For many years, the DDDA hosted a Social Regeneration Conference and invited over 200 delegates, representing a complete cross-section of the community. The conferences were addressed by international speakers, and these talks were followed by workshops for the delegates where the main issues facing the community were discussed and action points developed.

At the beginning of each annual conference, there was an update on all of the action points from the previous year. In so doing, the Authority demonstrated its commitment, as the vast majority of objectives that were adopted the previous year were completed, with an update given on the progress of the others. In addition to these conferences, the DDDA holds regular meetings throughout the year with different groups of stakeholders. The purpose of these consultations is to feed into the master plan and develop goals and objectives that will have real meaning in the development of communities and not just in the physical infrastructure.

A new DDDA Master Plan has been developed for the period 2008–2018. As a result of these plans, there has been an enormous improvement in the quality of life of those living in the docklands.

Source: Docklands Master Plan and interview with former CEO Mr Paul Maloney

The concept of strategic workshops does not just involve managers, but a much wider group of stakeholders working on the premise that good ideas can come from anywhere, not just from those at the top. By including various stakeholders, a workshop is likely to create much greater acceptance of the outcome.

Management Consultants On occasions, outside consultants may be brought in to assist in the process of strategy development, to provide expertise and experience not available in-house. This may apply to every size of organisation, from the small family-owned business to international corporations seeking advice on major strategic initiatives, such as mergers and acquisitions or perhaps a flotation on the stock market.

There are a number of advantages in bringing in outside consultants. It can give the management a perspective that they did not have before, as they may be too close to the problems at hand. In other cases, the management may lack the specific skills needed at crucial times such as the development of an integrated information technology system. Yet, on other occasions, consultants may be brought in to justify cost-cutting measures and redundancies. What is important from the management's point of view, regardless of the advice obtained, is that they take ownership of the strategy that is being proposed.

Imposed Strategy There are occasions where organisations may have strategic plans imposed upon them. This has happened with semi-state companies where the Government had a political imperative that took precedence over the commercial imperative. An example is the postal service (An Post), which continues to operate small rural post offices that are not commercially viable, but which provide a very valuable social service in isolated communities.

Another example of imposed strategy in the public sector in Ireland is the provision of electricity. In 1927 the Electricity Supply Board (ESB) was established as a semi-state company for the purpose of supplying the country with the electricity it needs for commercial and domestic use. For most of its life, the ESB was in a monopolistic position. The market is now opened up to competitors and the ESB has been split into two organisations, one generating electricity and the other company,

ESB Networks, responsible for operating the national grid network. The grid operator must accept electricity from all suppliers in the country. Ireland does not have nuclear power and the ESB has traditionally used coal, peat and gas burning stations as well as hydroelectric power. Apart from water and wind, the other sources of electricity generation are contributing to greenhouse gases and they are finite in terms of supply. As part of the government's 'green' strategy, it has directed that by 2020 the ESB must be generating one-third of its electricity from renewable sources. It will generate 1,400 MW of electricity from wind generation and will also exploit the potential of wave, tidal and biomass resources. As a semi-state company, managers are obliged to accept this imposed strategy, and the board has approved a strategic framework with a €22 billion investment programme to 2020. It aims to halve the carbon emissions by the ESB by 2020 and have zero emission by 2035 (ESB, 2011).

Imposed strategy also happens in commercial organisations where the corporate headquarters may impose a strategy on a SBU or subsidiary company when a certain balance is required in its corporate portfolio. (This is discussed in detail in Chapter 10.)

In addition, for companies quoted on the stock exchange, the capital markets are in a powerful position to impose a particular strategic direction on a company. Senior managers in such companies regularly meet their large institutional shareholders to brief them on their company's plans. If such large shareholders were to express strong views about a strategy, it would, in many cases, be adjusted to take account of those views. The net result is that strategies are often imposed on the company by these large shareholders and bond holders as the threat of withdrawal of funds is enough to steer the company in a direction that reflects their views. (In Chapter 4, **Illustration 4.2**: the Corrib Gas Project illustrates how powerful stakeholders can impose strategy on an organisation.)

Emergent Strategy Development

Logical Incrementalism Von Moltke, the famous Prussian general, once remarked that "no plan survives contact with the enemy". In commerce as well as in combat, circumstances can often change rapidly, rendering the original plan useless. Companies often develop strategies that result in success, not as a result of a detailed strategic plan, but as a result of choices made between alternatives, and decisions taken that have evolved the strategy in one particular direction over a period of time. Robert Frost in his poem "The Road Not Taken" describes travelling on a road, coming to a junction and having to make a choice about which direction to proceed, knowing that whichever road he chooses would take on a momentum of its own, to the exclusion of other options:

> "Two roads diverged in a yellow wood,
> And sorry I could not travel both…
>
> Oh, I kept the first for another day!
> Yet knowing how way leads on to way,
> I doubted if I should ever come back. …"

Definition Quinn (1980: 58) describes this process as: "**logical incrementalism**" — the development of strategy by experimentation and learning from partial commitment rather than through global formulations of total strategies.

There are a number of underlying reasons for the logical incrementalism approach, including the lack of a long-term understanding of where the organisation is heading, uncertainty of the environment in which they are operating, keeping objectives broad, and the need to retain complete flexibility to be able to take advantage of opportunities when they arise. Social processes play a major part in the development of such strategy.

Pascale (1984) describes the entry of Honda to the US motorcycle market in the 1960s and how they had to adjust rapidly to circumstances different to those which they had expected. An Irish example of a company that has had to react quickly to rapidly changing circumstances is the e-learning company, PulseLearning – see **Illustration 1.3**.

Illustration 1.3: PulseLearning and Emergent Strategy

Founded in November 1999 by Jim Breen, PulseLearning survived the dot-com bubble. Operating in the technology sector, it is in a hyper-dynamic environment. Specific plans, therefore, would have a short life-span. The strategies and the business model that the company has pursued have evolved significantly in response to a changing environment in the years since its establishment.

As CEO Jim Breen explains: "the strategies that made the company successful over the first three years would not deliver success in the following three years. In turn, those strategies also had to change". Because of the dynamic nature of the markets in which the company operates, its approach is to 'engage and see' – enter the market and be prepared to change the plan as the need arises. The company has grown substantially and now employs 85 people in Ireland, the US, Canada and Australia. An important element in this success has been its flexibility and willingness to adapt as circumstances changed.

Source: interview with CEO Mr Jim Breen

A vital element in the concept of logical incrementalism is the people working in the organisation. The success of a strategy, particularly one that requires a great deal of flexibility, requires having the right people on board. Jim Collins in his book *Good to Great* cites the example of the American bank Wells Fargo:

"Wells Fargo began its 15-year stint of spectacular performance in 1983, but the foundation for the shift dates back to the early 1970s, when then-CEO Dick Cooley began building one of the most talented management teams in the industry. Cooley foresaw that the banking industry would eventually undergo wrenching change, but he did not pretend to know what form that change would take. So instead of mapping out a strategy for change, he and chairman Ernie Arbuckle focused on 'injecting an endless stream of talent' directly into the veins of the company. They hired outstanding people whenever and wherever they found them, often without a specific job in mind. 'That's how you build the future', he said. 'If I'm not smart enough to see the changes that are coming, they will. And they will be flexible enough to deal with them'."

Collins (2001: 42)

The allocation of resources can also play a major role in emergent strategy. The organisation will have made strategic decisions in the past that will have directed it along a certain route. Resources will have been allocated to support that strategy and, inevitably, this will create further momentum. Bower and Gilbert (2007) believe that the cumulative impact of the allocation of resources by an organisation's managers at all levels ultimately has a significant impact on strategy development.

Spotting an opportunity when it arises and knowing when to move on a 'window of opportunity' is an essential element of leadership. Timing is of the essence. Shakespeare summed it up thus:

"There is a tide in the affairs of men, which taken at the flood leads on to fortune. Omitted, all the voyage of their life is bound in shallows and in miseries. On such a sea we are now afloat and we must take the current where it serves or lose our ventures."

Julius Caesar. Act IV, Sc. 3

Organisational Politics Aristotle believed that man was by nature a political animal. Business organisations are social constructs. They are designed by people to work together towards achieving certain goals. It is inevitable that, in many instances, different stakeholders will have different views about what those goals should be, and how best to achieve them. Shareholders will want a good return on their investment, and workers will want the best working conditions. While this dichotomy is not necessarily mutually exclusive, it does point to differences in personal aims. If these aims are deemed to be mutually exclusive, who wins? In all companies a certain amount of negotiation and bargaining will take place, and this brings much greater subjectivity into the more objective planning process. Such battles can also take place in family-run businesses. Collins (2007) describes many sibling battles that made their way into the public domain in Irish family-run companies such as Dunnes Stores.

With different people having perhaps very different views of what direction a company should take, this can have a big impact on the strategy that is eventually chosen. According to Johnson *et al.* (2011: 141), **stakeholder mapping** can be used to ascertain people's support or opposition to a particular strategy, depending on their level of interest in a particular course of action being taken and the level of power they possess to either implement or block a certain strategy. Those with a high level of interest and power are in a key position to influence strategy one way or another (see Chapter 4).

Baggage handlers in Ryanair went on strike in 1998 seeking union recognition, but had to abandon their strike after a couple of weeks when the airline made alternative arrangements (Creaton,

2004). Ryanair still does not recognise unions. On the other hand, the unions in Aer Lingus have traditionally wielded a lot of power, although this power has gradually been eroded over the last number of years. In January 2011, there was a standoff between management and unions in Aer Lingus in regard to rosters for cabin crew. The company wanted to reduce costs substantially by imposing new roster arrangements for staff which amounted to considerable changes to their terms and conditions. Many of the cabin crew refused to work the new schedules and were dismissed by the airline (Cooke, 2011).

When embarking on a particular course of strategic action, it may be the case that not everyone in the organisation will agree with the direction being taken. However, it is vital that the CEO has the support of senior managers for the chosen course of action. Without their support, the proposed strategy would surely flounder. Before deciding to invade France, Henry V sent for the Archbishop of Canterbury to ascertain his legal right to claim France, and then discussed the expedition with his nobles. He knew he had their support when Westmoreland replied:

> "Never King of England had nobles richer and more loyal subjects, whose hearts have left their bodies here in England and lie pavilion'd in the fields of France."
>
> *Henry V.* Act 1, Sc.2

The flow of information plays a major part in organisational politics. There are ethical issues to be considered here. By filtering certain information and feeding it into the decision-making process, or alternatively, by withholding vital information, decisions may be swung one way or the other. Even the choice of words used in an argument can have an emotive impact and this can channel thinking in a particular direction.

The bargaining involved in organisational politics can, in some instances, have a positive effect. It can challenge staid thinking and result in innovative approaches by the company. A CEO should be confident about a chosen course of action and be able to defend it to managers within the organisation. If, on the other hand, it cannot be justified, then it is time to go back to the drawing board.

Organisational Culture The culture of an organisation will also have an impact on its strategy. Culture is often described simply as 'the way things are done around here'. Just as an individual person has their own personality, an organisation has its own culture:

 Culture can be defined as: "a set of beliefs, values and learned ways of managing – and this is reflected in its structures, systems, and approach to the development of corporate strategy. Its culture derives from its past, its present, its current people, technology and physical resources and from the aims, objectives and values of those who work in the organisation" (Lynch 2008: 608).

The culture of an organisation can be a very powerful force in either blocking or supporting a strategy. The problem for managers is that, in addition to being powerful, culture is also a difficult phenomenon to observe and understand. Johnson *et al.* (2011:174) refer to the paradigm in an organisation as: "the set of basic assumptions held in common and taken for granted in an organisation".

The paradigm guides how people in the organisation view that organisation and its environment. Faced with uncertainty, managers try to define the environment in ways that are familiar and in light of past experience. Such cultural influence can be a strong force supporting a particular strategy, but it can also have a major negative impact when change is required. Trying to understand the underlying assumptions of an organisation can be difficult and Johnson *et al.* recommend use of a 'Cultural Web' to analyse the different elements of an organisation's paradigm. This consists of the organisational structures; control systems; rituals and routines; stories; symbols; and power structures. Through an awareness of these elements, an understanding can be gained of the organisation's culture and how it will impact on strategy.

Abandoned Strategy Organisations may have spent a considerable time developing a particular strategy, whether it be a deliberate strategy or one that has gradually emerged over a period of time, and then find that the circumstances in which they are operating have changed dramatically, thus calling that strategy into question. It might be that the strategy no longer makes sense, and a decision may have to be made to abandon that course of action. This can be a very difficult decision to make as a large amount of money might have already been spent in the process, and this investment would have to be regarded as a sunk cost (where resources have already been committed and these costs cannot be recouped if the project is abandoned).

In October 2007, the US biotechnology group Amgen announced that it had "postponed indefinitely" its €800 million plant at Carrigtwohill in County Cork. The plant had already 79 people employed and had a planned workforce of 1,000 by 2010. The decision followed an adverse ruling by the US regulator, the Food and Drug Administration (FDA), about two anaemia drugs that account for close to half of Amgen's revenues. The company had already announced the loss of 2,600 jobs worldwide in August and the closure of two US plants (Roche and Coyle, 2007).

It is not only companies that abandon strategy. As a result of the deep economic recession currently enveloping Ireland, the Government will have to cut current and capital spending by some €15 billion over the next few years. As a result, many of the major infrastructural projects that were planned for the country have now had to be abandoned.

CONCLUSION

Strategy is developed using a variety of the methods described above. Organisations will differ in how they mix these elements together. In all cases, some elements of each will be detected, despite the predominance of any one particular type. There are certain occasions when detailed planning is vitally important. Even when the environment is changing rapidly, mergers and acquisitions still require meticulous planning. However, on its own, strategic planning will never be the only process used in the formulation and implementation of strategy. In general, company statements and reports give the indication that all moves by the organisation are carefully orchestrated by senior managers as part of a carefully thought-out plan. However, close observation of the actual strategies being pursued by various companies will reveal a lot more about the strategy-forming processes involved than that articulated by the management in official communiqués.

SUMMARY

Chapter 1 has introduced you to strategic management. Strategy applies to every type of organisation: big and small, commercial and non-profit. Understanding how strategy is developed will assist when examining more specific areas of developing and implementing strategy.

There are three broad levels of strategy in an organisation:

- At the top, there is **corporate-level strategy** dealing with the type of decisions taken at the corporate headquarters concerning the portfolio of businesses and markets in which the company operates.
- The next layer is **business-level strategy** dealing with how a single business operates in a competitive environment.
- Both the corporate-level and the business-level strategies have to be **operationalised** in the day-to-day routines of the company.
- **Functional strategies** covering areas such as finance and marketing form a backdrop to all three levels.

The crafting and implementation of strategy can be divided into four distinct elements. The first part is laying **the foundation** for the organisation and the type of strategy it will pursue. This involves establishing a vision for the organisation and proper corporate governance structures based on sound ethical principles and leadership. **Strategic analysis** is concerned with making sense of the environment within which an organisation is operating, along with understanding its own capabilities. **Strategy development** examines all of the possible options open to the company as a means of achieving its objectives. Choices will have to be made as resources are limited, and so it includes a decision-making framework. Once that decision has been made, it must be **implemented** by the organisation. This involves putting the correct structures and processes in place and supporting the strategy with the necessary resources. It also requires the organisation to deal with changing circumstances.

The final section of this chapter examined the different process by which strategy is developed. There are two broad divisions. First, **intended strategy development** includes the formal strategic planning process underpinning much of this text. It also includes strategic workshops, which is a more inclusive process involving managers at different levels of the organisation. The section on intended strategy also examined how outside management consultants may be brought in to advise the company on the way forward. On other occasions, strategy may be imposed on an organisation, either by the government, as in the case of public sector bodies or on a strategic business unit by its corporate parent. Finally, there are occasions where strategy has to be abandoned because changed circumstances would make it non-viable.

The second broad division includes **emergent strategies.** This covers logical incrementalism, where strategy is developed by experimentation and learning from partial commitment, rather than through global formulations of total strategies. It requires strategic flexibility, and an essential element is having the right people involved. Emergent strategies also look at the impact of organisational politics and culture. It has to be remembered that organisations consist of many different stakeholders, each with their own view of how strategy might suit their needs.

DISCUSSION QUESTIONS

1. Ireland is currently experiencing a very difficult trading environment. This will present many challenges for managers. Taking an organisation of your choice, critically analyse the major strategic challenges facing that organisation.
2. In reference to question 1 above, what opportunities present themselves to Irish companies?
3. Distinguish between the different levels of strategy in an organisation.
4. With regard to the four cores areas of strategy, discuss the importance of laying a solid foundation for strategic decisions.
5. Choose an Irish public limited company and evaluate the strategy-making processes that you can identify that form part of their chosen strategy.
6. Analyse each of the strategy development processes described, and state the different circumstances in which one method might be more suitable than others.

REFERENCES

Ambrose, S., 2003, *Eisenhower: Soldier and President*, London, Pocket Books

Bower, J. and Gilbert, C., 2007, "How everyday decisions create or destroy your company's strategy", *Harvard Business Review*, February 2007, Vol. 85, Issue 2, pp.72–79

Breen, J., 2009, *Interview with the Author*, 20 April 2009

Collins, J., 2001, *Good to Great*, London, Random House

Collins, L., 2007, *Irish Family Feuds*, Dublin, Mentor Books

Cooke, N., 2011, "Plane Talker", *The Sunday Business Post*, 30 January 2011, p.17

Creaton, S., 2004, *Ryanair*, London, Aurum

ESB, 2011, http://www.esb.ie/main/sustainability/strategy-to-2020.jsp, Accessed 26 January 2011

Hill, C. and Jones, G., 2009, *Theory of Strategic Management with Cases*, New York, South-Western Cengage Learning

Huff, A. *et al.*, 2009, *Strategic Management: Logic and Action*, Hoboken, NJ, Wiley

Irish Management Institute, 2010, "Closing the Gap", Dublin, IMI

Johnson, G. *et al.*, 2011, *Exploring Strategy, Text and Cases*, 9th Ed., Harlow, Essex, Prentice Hall Financial Times

Kaplan, R. and Norton, D., 2008, "Mastering the Management System", *Harvard Business Review*, January 2008, Vol. 86, Issue 1, pp.62–77

Kaplan, R. and Norton, D., 2001, *The Strategy-Focused Organisation*, Boston, Harvard Business School Press

Kiberd, D., 2007, "There's no stopping the service sector", *Sunday Times*, 28 October 2007, Business, p.4

Kotter J. and Cohen D., 2002, *The Heart of Change*, Boston, Harvard Business School Press

Kotter, J., 1996, *Leading Change*, Boston, Harvard Business School Press

Lynch, R., 2008, *Strategic Management*, 5thEd., Harlow, Essex, Prentice Hall Financial Times

Lynch, S., 2010, "Irish management skills weak", *Irish Times*, 21 December 2010, p.17

McKay, S., 2009, "The Kindness of Strangers", *Irish Times*, Magazine, 14 March 2009, p.17

McKinsey & Co., 2009, "Management Matters in Northern Ireland and Republic of Ireland", Dublin, Forfás

Mintzberg, H., 1994, 'The Rise and Fall of Strategic Planning', *Harvard Business Review*, January/February 1994, Vol. 72, Issue 1, pp.101–114

Mintzberg, H. and Waters, J., 1985, "Of Strategies: Deliberate and Emergent", *Strategic Management Journal*, Vol. 6, Issue 3, pp. 257–272

O'Brien, J. and Marakas, G., 2008, *Management Information Systems*, 8th Ed., New York, McGraw-Hill

Pascale, R., 1984, "Perspectives on strategy: the real story behind Honda's success", *California Management Review*, Spring 1984, Vol. 26, Issue 3, pp.47–72

Porter, M., 1980, *Competitive Strategy: Techniques of Analysing Industries and Competitors*, New York, The Free Press

Quinn, J., 1980, *Strategies for Change*, Homewood, Ill, Irwin

Roche, B. and Coyle D., 2007, "IDA Confident Despite Loss of Amgen Plant", *Irish Times*, 4 October 2007, p.1

Thompson, A. *et al.*, 2008, *Crafting and Executing Strategy: The Quest for Competitive Advantage*, New York, McGraw-Hill

Thompson, J. and Martin, F., 2005, *Strategic Management: Awareness and Change*, 5th Ed., London, Thomson Learning

Wall, M. 2006, "Inefficiency and High Labour Costs Blamed for Expensive Electricity", *Irish Times,* 2 October 2006, p.5

Welch, J., 2001, *Jack: What I've Learned Leading a Great Company and Great People*, London, Headline Publishing

PART ONE

The Foundation

Introduction to the Foundation

Part One of this text deals with the philosophical foundation of strategy. It comprises three chapters on: leadership and organisational culture; vision, mission, goals and objectives; and corporate governance, business ethics and corporate social responsibility. The business environment in Ireland is currently experiencing one of the worst recessions since the foundation of the State. Many companies are

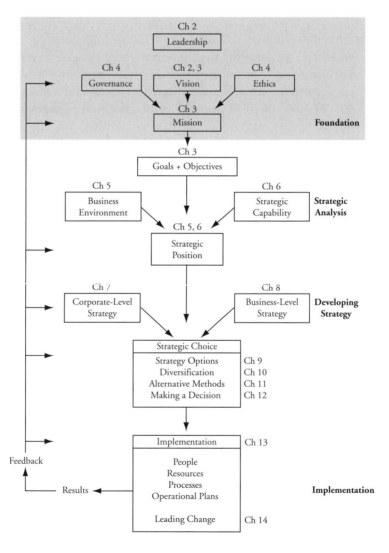

Figure 1.2 *The Strategic Planning Model*

struggling to survive, while many more have gone into liquidation. The majority of banks in the country are in state ownership, and if they were not of systemic importance to the economy, they too would be gone. The elements outlined in the Foundation (**Figure 1.2**) play an essential role in the long-term sustainability of organisations.

Part One begins with a chapter on leadership and organisational culture (Chapter 2). One of the biggest failures across Irish corporate life in recent years was one of leadership. The economy was awash with money and many companies were making substantial profits despite having no clear leadership or vision. Many companies, like the economy itself, were on autopilot. When the downturn came, the lack of proper leadership meant that many of these companies could not survive.

It is vital, therefore, that those running companies have a clear understanding of what their core business is and to whom they are targeting their products and services. The goals and objectives that they set need to be aligned with the organisation's vision and mission. Chapter 3 examines the nature of an organisation's vision – the leadership that drives it, the values that support it and the purpose that justifies it. The mission stems from the vision, and in turn guides the setting of goals and objectives.

There are many legal, fiduciary and other obligations placed on limited companies, and so Chapter 4 deals with governance – how senior executives are held to account to various stakeholders. Too much legislation would stifle the day-to-day operations of companies, and so business ethics guide decision-makers when the law does not prescribe an answer. The final part of Chapter 4 deals with corporate social responsibility (CSR) – the responsibility that organisations have to the wider community in which they operate.

If a building does not have sufficient foundations, sooner or later it will come crashing down. Likewise, companies will not survive if they do not have a solid foundation underpinning their strategy. Good leadership and a results-oriented corporate culture, supported by good governance structures, will guide the company successfully through turbulent times, as well as the boom times. Good governance ensures not just legal compliance; it also provides the organisation with a moral framework that will withstand any scrutiny.

Leadership and Organisational Culture

LEARNING OBJECTIVES

On completion of this chapter, you will be able to:

- Distinguish between the different types of leadership
- Evaluate the effectiveness of different leadership styles
- Assess the relationship between leadership and corporate culture
- Critically examine the role of leadership in the formulation and implementation of strategy

"The great leader is he who the people say 'we did it ourselves'."

Lao Tsu

INTRODUCTION

Leading an organisation to achieve its goals is central to its success. Leadership exists at many levels: the directors on the board, the chief executive and other senior executives and those heading up the different divisions and sections throughout the organisation, right down to supervisor level. It should underpin the values and expectations of the company and is the catalyst behind the energy and commitment of its employees. As such, it is an essential element in laying the foundation of strategy, as well as the other phases of strategy formulation and implementation.

This chapter looks at leadership from a number of different perspectives. Having defined leadership, it then draws a distinction between management and leadership. While many theorists suggest that leadership is a function of management, there is an important distinction between the two. These theories include examining traits, behaviour, situations and charismatic leadership.

The functions that leaders perform in organisations are also explored:

- Creating a vision
- Building teams
- Motivation

- Development – individual and organisational
- Creating a high-performance organisation
- Succession planning
- Leading change
- Decision-maker

The chapter refers to a wide range of authors and theories on leadership. William Shakespeare, in particular, showed a tremendous understanding of human nature and how it applies to leadership. Four hundred years later, his insight holds true.

The final section of the chapter deals with organisational culture, how it is established and maintained and the different types of culture in an organisation. Leaders play an important role in developing and maintaining organisational culture. In turn, culture plays an important role in supporting those leaders in the organisation in achieving results.

LEADERSHIP

Leadership can be defined thus:

Leadership is the ability to inspire and motivate others to work willingly towards achieving organisational goals.

Inspiration Strategic goals are achieved by senior management working with the employees of the organisation. This implies being able to motivate and inspire people, so that the collective effort can enable the organisation to achieve goals that individuals on their own could never achieve. There are many ways in which people can be influenced. There has been much research over the years on influence tactics. Yukl *et al.* (1993) propose generic influence tactics ranging from rational persuasion (using logic and reason) to legitimating tactics (using one's authority and organisational rules). Ultimately, rational persuasion and inspirational appeals, building on employees' values and ideals, are much more effective than having to exert authority.

Power Leadership also implies power. There are two dimensions of power in organisations. The first is *socialised power*, which is aimed at helping people to achieve their goals. The second is *personalised power*, which is directed at helping oneself. When discussing organisational leadership, it is socialised power that enables people and organisations to achieve their goals.

History shows many examples of people who amassed personal power. In some cases, personalised power was used in an autocratic manner but for what the leader presumed was the good of the people. When the Duke of Wellington became Prime Minister of Britain in 1828, he obviously had some trouble making the transition from the army to political life (he was a strong opponent of parliamentary reform). In describing his first cabinet meeting, he is quoted as saying: "An extraordinary affair. I gave them their orders and they wanted to stay and discuss them!"

In other cases, power has been greatly misused, with devastating consequences. In modern business, many of the major ethical scandals were due to people amassing personal power and wealth (for example, Kenneth Lay in Enron). In the context of business, it is important that power is used for the benefit of the organisation rather than the individual. In that respect, it is important that leaders and managers reflect on the source of their power and realise that it is organisational and positional, rather than personal.

Illustration 2.1: Personalised Power

In their book *Wasters*, Ross and Webb (2010: 52–56) describe many examples in the Irish semi-state sector of individuals mistaking organisational power for individual personalised power. What epitomises this was perhaps the resignation of the former Director General of FÁS, Rody Molloy, over enormous expenses that were run up on numerous trips abroad. In an interview with Pat Kenny on RTÉ Radio One, Mr Molloy explained how he brought his wife on one of the trips "at no additional expense to FÁS because I traded down my travel entitlement to allow her to travel so that it comes in at less expense to the organisation". He went on to explain that he was "entitled" to travel first class. Between 2002 and 2008, FÁS spent €4.7 million on foreign travel which included 4,400 flights, of which 1,000 were long-haul flights. The investigation by the Comptroller and Auditor General (C&AG) found that 27% of the long haul flights were either business class or first class. They also established that there was no entitlement to first-class travel, and, therefore, any down-grading of a ticket should have resulted in a saving to the State. Mr Molloy's retirement package caused similar controversy. The C&AG report estimated the package to be almost €900,000 in excess of what it ought to have been.

Ross and Webb (2010) also detail many abuses by politicians in regard to expenses. While many of the examples they cite relate to one particular political party, it needs to be stated that there are examples right across the political spectrum. These expenses were deemed 'legitimate' in the sense that the politicians interpreted these trips to be a normal part of their job. To the ordinary observer, a different interpretation might easily be taken. In addition to expenses, there have also been many examples of politicians evading tax, taking corrupt payments and not co-operating with tribunals of inquiry. The net effect of all this has been to greatly undermine the integrity of politics in general and political leadership in particular.

In addition to the dimensions of power, there are different **bases for power**. The most widely used classification is that devised by French and Raven (1959), who argued that there are five bases for power:

- Reward power – obtaining compliance by granting rewards
- Coercive power – threat of punishment or actual punishment
- Legitimate power – derived from one's position in the organisation
- Expert power – having expert knowledge or information
- Referent power – using one's personality or charisma to influence people

CEOs of an organisation will, by virtue of their position, have legitimate power. To be effective, they should be able to rely on expert power and, to a lesser extent, on some referent power. Power underpins so many of our interactions. It must be carefully used, not abused.

Leaders and Managers

The above section reminds us that simply holding a management position at the top of an organisation does not make one a leader. There is an important distinction between leadership and management. While 'management' and 'leadership' overlap as activities, they each have their own distinct characteristics. The word 'management' derives from the Latin word '*manus*', meaning a 'hand'. Management literally means 'handling' the organisation, whereas leadership involves showing the way. A succinct summary of the difference between leadership and management was that provided by Bennis and Nanus (1985):

"Managers do things right. Leaders do the right thing."

Managers

Mintzberg (1973) studied a variety of organisations and observed that managers performed 10 different roles (of which leadership was one). The managerial functions identified by Mintzberg are integral to the running of any organisation. Many earlier writers looked on leadership as a function of management, but more recent writers, such as John Adair and John Kotter, regard leadership, while still being linked with management, as being an essential role in its own right.

Leaders

The above section reminds us that holding management positions at the top of an organisation does not make one a leader. Leadership is a much broader concept than just a function of management. Leadership is concerned primarily with inspiring and motivating others in the organisation. Leaders develop a vision of the future and how the organisation will get there. In Chapter 3 we will see that that vision encompasses a moral element, which underpins the notion that 'leaders do the right thing'. There is a strong inter-personal element to the role of leaders and how they relate to people both inside and outside the organisation.

Not every manager will be a leader, even those who make it to the top of their respective companies. When corporate strategy is being developed and implemented, the emphasis is much more on leadership than on management. In discussing leadership here, the main focus will be on those running the organisation. However, it must be stressed that leadership takes place at many different levels in an organisation. Each divisional or functional head should also lead those within their own unit. This should happen at every level, right down to front-line management. Also, leadership is not exclusive to positions of authority and there are often situations where leadership is demonstrated by individuals who 'rise to the occasion'. (A study of the Antarctic exploration by Scott and Shackleton shows that Tom Crean from County Kerry displayed great leadership qualities, despite the fact he was not in a position of formal authority (Smith, 2000; Nugent, 2003) — see **Illustration 2.2** below).

At the time of writing, there are many inquiries on going into the conduct of business 'leaders' by authorities including the Gardaí and the Director of Corporate Enforcement. Whether criminal prosecutions arise from these investigations remains to be seen. What is clear, however, is that there has been widespread abuse of power in organisations that demanded respect. This raises serious questions on how organisations develop leadership qualities in their people (as opposed to developing management skills). Part of their leadership training should be teaching them how to handle power properly and behave in an ethical manner.

These problems have developed over a long period of time, and are partly caused by a societal deference in Ireland to people at the top of their organisations, whether they are church, state, professional or commercial. What is required, therefore, is a more open approach internally and externally to leadership and governance. The Report into the Catholic Archdiocese of Dublin, known as the 'Murphy' report (Murphy *et al.*, 2009:23) states:

> "Institutions and individuals, no matter how august, should never be considered to be immune from criticism or from external oversight of their actions. In particular, no institution or individual should be allowed such pre-eminent status that the State, in effect, is stymied in taking action against it or them should there be breaches of the State's laws."

Across the board in Irish business and society, there have been failures in leadership, and there has been enormous collateral damage – the implications go far beyond the organisation itself. In future, there will have to be far greater openness and accountability by business leaders for their stewardship of the company with which they have been entrusted. It will require a more inclusive approach recognising that the actions of executives have far-reaching consequences on a wide group of stakeholders.

LEADERSHIP THEORIES

Different theories have evolved over time to understand the nature of leadership, and these can be classified as follows:

- Trait Theories
- Behavioural Theories
- Situational Theories
- Theories of Charismatic Leadership
- The 'Level 5' Theory of Leadership

Trait Theories of Leadership

Historically, it was believed that leaders were born, not made. This belief underpinned the concept of hereditary monarchs and, with the advent of the Industrial Revolution, expanded to include 'captains of industry'. It was assumed that such people possessed certain innate traits or personal characteristics that set them apart as leaders.

Studies on leadership early in the last century focused on innate traits, which included qualities such as intelligence, vision, self-confidence, initiative, lateral thinking, the need for power and achievement, being goal-driven, etc. This view of leadership continued until the 1950s. For example, Stogdill (1948) identified five common traits that differentiate leaders from their followers: intelligence, dominance, self-confidence, level of energy, and task-relevant knowledge. However, Stogdill's study, and a later one by Richard Mann in 1959, showed that, while leaders possess many of these traits, the concept of leadership was much more complex than just identifying certain individual traits.

Perhaps the greatest limitation to the traits theory is its inability as a predictor of leadership – by identifying these traits in an individual, can one identify a leader? It is also difficult to measure these traits in an individual, and leadership is also dependent on an employee's perception of what constitutes effective leadership. According to Buelens *et al.* (2008: 47) a '**leadership prototype**' is a mental representation of the traits and behaviours that a person believes is displayed by a leader. Thus, a person is regarded as a leader if their behaviour is consistent with people's leadership prototype. The task of predicting leaders is made more difficult by the fact that this concept of leadership prototype is culturally bound with differences between English-speaking and non-English speaking countries and between different clusters of countries in Europe. In other words, it is "influenced by national cultural values".

While the presence of leadership traits in a person is not necessarily a predictor of leadership qualities *per se*, such traits are usually present in leaders. Research is once again looking at traits. Kouzes and Posner (1995) sought to examine the qualities that people admire in their bosses. Results from around the world indicate that leaders should be "honest, forward-looking, inspiring and competent". Jack Welch, the former CEO of General Electric, refers to the four Es: "energy; ability to energise others; the edge to make tough decisions; and execution…" (Stewart, 1999)

Perhaps an important distinction to make is between the redundant concept that people are born with these traits, and recognition that nurturing plays an important role in developing the necessary traits required to lead an organisation. Writers such as Kotter (1996) and Goleman (2002) firmly believe that leadership can be taught. Armies around the world, for example, place a strong emphasis on developing leaders, and such development takes place throughout the person's career using a mixture of theoretical concepts and command experience. Many commercial organisations now recognise the importance of leadership development, either in their own in-house training centres (such as GE's Crotonville Management Development Centre), or externally as part of MBA programmes.

Emotional Intelligence Goleman (1995 and 2002) linked the concept of emotional intelligence to leadership. Emotional intelligence (EQ) is the extent to which people can understand their emotions. He argues that such traits are not innate but can be learned. Goleman believes that emotional intelligence increases with age, but it does require a sincere desire and concerted effort on behalf of the individual. Quoting Ralph Waldo Emerson: "Nothing great was ever achieved without enthusiasm."

According to Goleman (1995), there are five components of emotional intelligence at work:

- **Self-awareness** – how we can recognise and understand our moods, emotions and what drives us, as well as recognise their effect on others. The hallmarks of self-awareness include self-confidence, and a self-deprecating sense of humour. It gives leaders a strong sense of who they are and helps them align their personal values with work values.
- **Self-regulation** – how we control our impulses and moods and the ability to think before acting. Our emotions are driven by biological impulses, but these impulses can be controlled. Self-regulation is characterised by trustworthiness and integrity, openness to change and being comfortable with ambiguity, all of which are very necessary attributes for a leader. Self-regulation is important for a number of reasons. First, it creates an environment of trust and fairness. Secondly, it enables people to cope with change. Finally, it helps build lasting relationships with stakeholders.
- **Motivation** – intrinsic motivation goes well beyond financial rewards or status, along with the energy and persistence to pursue goals. It manifests itself in a strong desire to achieve, optimism even in difficult circumstances and a commitment to the organisation. Motivation creates a passion for work and an eagerness to explore new ways of doing things. People who are motivated are forever raising the performance bar.
- **Empathy** – the ability to understand and respond to the emotional makeup of other people. It requires cross-cultural sensitivity, service to both clients and customers, and an expertise in building and retaining talent. It is important to recognise that empathy does not mean adopting other people's emotions or trying to please everybody. It does, however, mean considering employees' feelings, in conjunction with other factors, when making decisions.
- **Social skill** – a proficiency in managing relationships and building networks and an ability to build a rapport with people. These attributes are important in working with and through people and team-building, and social skill is a particularly important attribute in leading change. Organisations are social constructs — designed by people to enable people to work together towards the attainment of agreed goals. Social skill entails finding common ground with employees and motivating them towards those end goals. In essence, it is the combination of the other four dimensions of emotional intelligence.

As leadership is primarily about relating to people, emotional intelligence plays an integral part in successful leadership. While emotional intelligence is undoubtedly an important attribute in leaders, there is debate in the literature about its validity. This is based primarily on the difficulty of measuring it and its predictive ability. Yet, it is difficult to dismiss it. Shakespeare's plays on leadership show a deep understanding of human emotions. Before the battle of Agincourt, King Henry recognised the fear in his men, being totally outnumbered by the French, yet he was able to appeal to their emotions:

"If we are marked to die, we are enough to do our country loss; and if to live, the fewer men, the greater share of honour…
We few, we happy few, we band of brothers.
For he today that sheds his blood with me shall be my brother…".

Henry V. Act 4, Sc. 2

On the other hand, Shakespeare's Coriolanus, while a brilliant general, lacked any emotional connection with his troops.

Cultural Intelligence According to Early and Mosakowski (2004), cultural intelligence is similar to emotional intelligence, but picks up where emotional intelligence leaves off. Those with emotional intelligence are able to distinguish between what makes us human and, at the same time, individual. Cultural intelligence enables us to identify features that are common to all groups of people: those peculiar to a particular person, and those that are common to specific ethnic groups.

In leading a multicultural group, cultural intelligence is particularly important in understanding the behaviour of people in that group. It allows the leader to suspend judgement – to think before acting. By understanding cultural patterns, one can read body language and anticipate how people will react in a certain situation. Early and Mosakowski believe that, while some cultural intelligence is innate, much of it can be learned. They believe that there are three components to cultural intelligence: cognitive; physical; and emotional/motivational.

The cognitive element concerns learning about different cultures such as that provided by corporate training programmes. However, while one can learn much about the beliefs and customs of foreign cultures, one cannot be prepared for every situation. The physical element concerns itself with how well a person adopts the habits and mannerisms of a culture, e.g. the amount of personal space that should be allowed when in conversation with another person. Finally, the emotional element relates to how willing a person is to relate to, and embrace other cultures.

At a basic level, having such cultural intelligence can prevent leaders from insulting employees or customers through cultural ignorance. When it is cultivated, it can enable leaders to understand people from different cultures and so relate to them more effectively. In the past 15 years, the demographics of the workforce in Ireland have changed dramatically, with many companies having employees from a wide variety of countries. In addition, Irish companies are now dealing in markets all over the world. As a result, cultural intelligence is a vital trait for leaders to have.

Behavioural Theories of Leadership

The limitations of the trait theories prompted a wider study of leadership (particularly in the United States) during the Second World War, when there was a strong imperative to develop effective leaders for the army. The emphasis shifted from the possible traits that leaders might possess, to their behaviour. Two major, and somewhat overlapping studies on leadership behaviour emerged – the Ohio State University study and the University of Michigan studies.

The **Ohio** research was extremely extensive, but was eventually narrowed down to just two independent variables, based on a manager's focus on the needs of his employees, known as **considerate style**, and the manager's focus on getting the job done, referred to as **initiating structure**. The combination of these two factors resulted in four types of leadership behaviour, with a high initiating structure/high consideration style being considered the best (Stogdill and Coons, 1957).

The **Michigan** studies investigated the behavioural relationship between effective and ineffective leaders. Like the Ohio study, they came up with two similar variables centred on employees (employee-orientated), and on achieving results (production-oriented). Results indicated that effective leaders balance a supportive, employee-centred approach with a focus on setting and achieving high performance goals (Likert, 1961). Blake and Mouton (1962) developed the 'managerial grid' to determine the one best style of leadership. Again, they use two dimensions (each divided into nine units): concern for people and concern for production.

Behavioural research was an important development in the study of leadership, as it explored different leadership styles. It was also seen that the effectiveness of leadership style depended on the particular context, a realisation which gave rise to the development of situational theories of leadership.

Illustration 2.2: Behavioural Theories – Antarctic Expeditions

Accounts of the early Antarctic expeditions by the Norwegian explorer Roald Amundsen, the British explorer Robert Falcon Scott, and Irishman Ernest Shackleton provide a fascinating study of contrasting leadership styles and their effectiveness.

Scott, a strong disciplinarian in the Royal Naval tradition, sought to be the first man to reach the South Pole. However, he lacked focus in his vision. Scott had included a large team of scientists to explore conditions on the continent. While such exploration had perfect validity in its own right; in terms of the race to be the first to reach the South Pole, it detracted from his primary mission. Scott also had inadequate resources, and had failed to master the use of one vital resource – teams of dogs to pull the heavy provisions. He regarded the use of dogs as "not the right thing to do". But by man-handling sledges (in four-man teams) weighing approximately 360kgs, they were operating at a much slower rate, and it was exhausting work in what are the most severe conditions on the planet (temperatures as low as minus 40° centigrade and 80 km/h winds).

Behind his strong authoritarian approach, Scott had poor leadership skills. In particular, he was indecisive. During the expedition, he waited until the last minute to decide on picking the team that would make the final push to the South Pole. This had major implications for the men concerned. The team picked to reach the South Pole should have been relieved of heavy pulling work at an early stage in the trek in order to conserve their energy for the final push. Instead, they were physically exhausted by the time they got to the Pole. This undoubtedly contributed to their death on the return leg.

He also made a poor decision in leaving Tom Crean behind (the strongest and probably the most capable member in the entire group), and did not have the courage to be direct with him in telling him he was not included. On hearing the Irishman cough, Scott used that as an excuse not to include Crean in the final team. He said: "You have a bad cold there Crean". The ever-loyal Crean understood he was not being included but was not about to let such a poor excuse pass by. He retorted: "I understand a half-sung song, Sir!"

In addition, Scott picked a *five*-man team including himself, Bowers, Wilson, Oates and Taff Evans, while all along, the training and division of supplies had been based on a four-man team. They reached the South Pole on 17 January 1912, only to find that they had been beaten by the Norwegian team led by Roald Amundsen. On the way back to the main group, Scott and his colleagues perished (Alexandre, 1998; Smith, 2000).

Roald Amundsen by contrast, was completely focused on his mission to be the first to reach the South Pole, which he achieved on 14 December 1911, a month before Scott. A team leader to the end, he insisted that all five members simultaneously plant the Norwegian flag at the South Pole. This was his vision, and for years he had prepared for it, acclimatising himself to the severe cold, mastering the use of skis and the use of dog-teams for pulling sledges, as well as learning all of the survival skills needed to operate in such harsh conditions from native Norwegians living in the far north of the country. Amundsen and his team made far greater progress than Scott, averaging 36km a day compared to Scott's 24km a day. By the time Scott had reached the South Pole, Amundsen was already safely back at his Franheim base having covered the round trip of over 3,000 km in just 99 days (Smith, 2000).

Ernest Shackleton's 1914 expedition to cross the Antarctic went terribly wrong when his ship *The Endurance* was crushed by ice in the Weddell Sea, and turned into one of the greatest survival epics ever known. It is an incredible story of leadership and change management. (Shackleton's leadership ability is explored in a case study later in the text.)

Situational Theories of Leadership

The study of leadership traits and behaviours showed that leadership is a great deal more complex than previously thought and that there was still a general lack of understanding about the effectiveness of leadership styles. It was seen that context was also an important element. Different situations require different leadership styles, and as the situation changes, so too must the style. This effectively contradicted the notion that there is one best leadership style. This section will examine two situational theories: Fielder's Contingency Model and House's Path–Goal Theory.

Fielder's Contingency Model examines leadership in different work situations. There are two interconnected elements: leadership style and the situation context. The leadership styles examined by Fielder were similar to previous studies in that he isolated two styles:

- **Relationship-motivated style** which focused on developing relations between the leader and followers.
- **Task-motivated style** where the focus is on accomplishing the particular task.

Fielder then developed a measurement instrument called the **'Least-preferred co-worker'** to ascertain a person's leadership style, whether it is relationship-motivated or task-motivated. He believed that leaders had a particular style of leadership (a dominant style) and they were reluctant to change or modify that style.

House's Path–Goal Theory has strong links with Vroom's 'expectancy theory' of motivation (1964) where the effort put into work is linked to performance and, in turn, impacts on the outcome. People are motivated by the value that they receive from the outcome. According to House (1971), leaders should focus their attention on identifying goals and helping employees achieve them. The attainment of those goals is linked to rewards. The leader should clarify the path to achieving the goals and help remove any obstacles along the way (hence the name path–goal). House identified four different leadership styles:

- Directive leadership – a prescriptive approach to how employees should carry out the task
- Supportive leadership – being friendly, approachable and supportive
- Participative leadership – taking on board the ideas of employees when making decisions
- Achievement-oriented leadership – enabling employees to perform at their best in achieving goals

In contrast to Fielder, House believed that leaders can exhibit more than one style, and their ability to help employees achieve their goals is dependent on how well they can adapt the style to the situation. In turn, this is linked to two situational variables: employee characteristics (locus of control, task ability experience, need for achievement and need for clarity) and environmental factors including the employee's task, the work system in place and the work team to which they belong.

In reality, most individual CEOs are probably slow to change their leadership style. Organisational needs will vary from time to time, and so the appropriate leadership style is dependent on the strategic issues facing the organisation at that particular time. As a result, it may well be that the existing leader does not have the appropriate style to bring the organisation through its current difficulty. In such situations, the organisation may require a different leader with a different set of skills, an example being a company in a crisis situation where strong, directive leadership may be more appropriate than a more inclusive style. On the other hand, this directive style would be inappropriate for organisational learning.

Charismatic Leadership

The types of leadership discussed above (trait, behavioural and situational) are generally referred to as **transactional** leadership, where leaders use a mixture of rewards and sanctions to achieve organisational goals.

Charismatic leadership, by contrast, is **transformational**. It has a profound effect on employees and is responsible for appealing to their values and beliefs, and gives them a sense of direction. As a result of its ability to get to the heart of employees, it plays a significant role in bringing about organisational change (see Chapter 14).

One of the primary functions of charismatic leadership is providing a vision for the organisation and creating a belief that such a vision can be achieved. According to Bass (1990) transformational leaders are charismatic role models for their organisation; they inspire and motivate, provide intellectual stimulation and coach and advise staff.

Illustration 2.3: Charismatic Military Leaders

Admiral Nelson was a charismatic leader who had a profound effect on the morale of his officers and men. As he arrived at the Royal Navy fleet anchored at Cadiz just before the battle of Trafalgar in 1805, "the mood of the fleet changed as its seventeen thousand men realised that Nelson was amongst them" (Pocock, 1987: 318). Despite the British fleet being outnumbered by the combined French and Spanish fleets, the 'Nelson Touch' is believed to have had a major impact on the outcome of the battle.

Napoleon too had a similar effect on the French nation and its army. His great nemesis, Wellington, recognised the impact that Napoleon had on the Grande Armée when he said:

> "I used to say of him that his presence on the field made the difference of forty thousand men."

Unfortunately for Napoleon, when it came to the Battle of Waterloo, the Prussian general Marshal Blücher made up the numbers before the day was done.

While there is evidence to support the concept of charismatic leadership, and good examples in politicians like Nelson Mandela and John F. Kennedy, and business people like Anita Roddick (founder of the Body Shop) and Richard Branson (Virgin Group), charismatic leadership seems to be somewhat elusive in reality. Manfred Kets de Vries, who lectures at INSEAD in France, is particularly critical of the concept of charismatic leaders. He believes that there is a negative or 'shadow side' of leadership that can have a detrimental impact on the whole organisation. This is mainly because these people surround themselves with subordinates who will not challenge, nor will they seek advice, believing that they know best (Kets de Vries, 2001). This criticism of charismatic leadership is also shared by Collins (2001) who argues that the most successful type of leadership is 'Level 5' leadership.

'Level 5' Leadership

In sharp contrast to the concept of charismatic leadership is what is termed 'Level 5' leadership. In his book *Good to Great*, Jim Collins (2001) examined the factors that underpin companies that constantly achieve greatness. His research team contributed 15,000 hours of work to the project and initially examined 1,435 'Fortune 500' companies, involving both qualitative and quantitative research. They picked a 15-year period for the study in order to show sustained long-term results, rather than companies that achieve good short-term, but unsustained results. They picked companies with results that were three times the market average. Next, they chose comparison companies and sought to ascertain what the good-to-great companies shared in common, defining what distinguished them from these comparison companies. The comparison companies were divided into two groups: similar companies in the same industry and other companies that showed short-term good results, but failed to maintain them.

The results covered a range of topics from strategy to the use of technology. One result that surprised the team was the style of leadership in the highly-successful companies:

"We were surprised, shocked really, to discover the type of leadership required for turning a good company into a great one. Compared to high-profile leaders with big personalities who make the headlines and become celebrities, the good-to-great leaders seem to have come from Mars. Self-effacing, quiet, even shy – these leaders are a paradoxical blend of personal humility and professional will."

He refers to these leaders as 'Level 5' leaders – the highest level in a hierarchy of executive capabilities. They are ambitious people, but their ambition is directed for the benefit of the company, not for themselves. The five levels are:

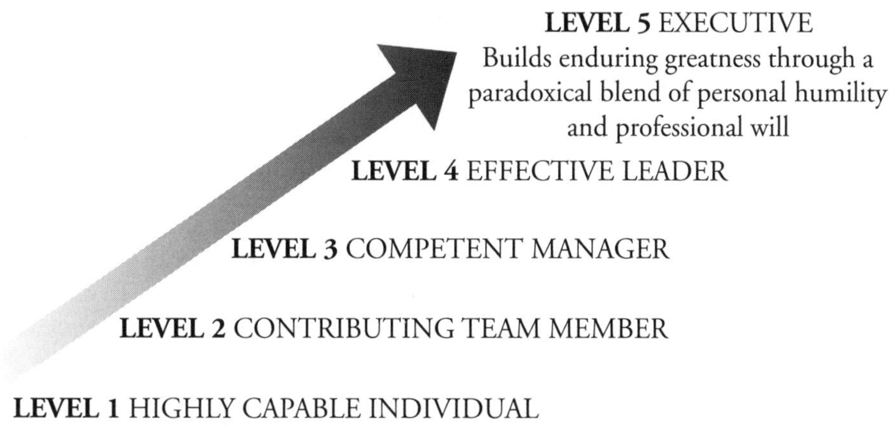

LEVEL 5 EXECUTIVE
Builds enduring greatness through a
paradoxical blend of personal humility
and professional will

LEVEL 4 EFFECTIVE LEADER

LEVEL 3 COMPETENT MANAGER

LEVEL 2 CONTRIBUTING TEAM MEMBER

LEVEL 1 HIGHLY CAPABLE INDIVIDUAL

Adapted from Collins, J., 2001, *Good to Great*, London, Random House Business Books

Figure 2.1 *Level 5 Leadership*

Interestingly, the team did not set out to investigate the role of leadership; rather, Collins had initially told the team to downplay the role of top executives. As the study continued:

"The research team kept pushing back, 'No! There is something consistently unusual about them. We can't ignore them'. When they examined the evidence, they found that all of the good-to-great companies had Level 5 leadership at the time of transition."

(Collins, 2001: 22)

A number of interesting and important observations about these leaders emerged from the research. 'Celebrity' CEOs who come in from the outside were negatively correlated with going from good to great. In practically all cases the good-to-great CEOs came from inside the organisation, whereas comparison companies chose outside CEOs six times more often. There are, however, some exceptions. There has been much criticism of Irish banks in promoting insiders. When the chief executives of Bank of Ireland and Allied Irish Bank were forced to resign as a result of the financial crisis, they were replaced by insiders. Many people considered that the banks should have recruited from outside, as it was believed that appointing senior executives who were also board members at the time of the crisis would not inject the fresh thinking that was required to lead the banks out of the mess and, in particular, change banking culture. Despite these exceptions, the evidence still suggests that promoting from within produces better results for the organisation (see case study on the Four Seasons Hotel).

According to Collins, the style of work of Level 5 leaders was more reflective of a "plough horse rather than a show horse". They were fanatically driven towards achieving sustainable results and would make whatever decisions were necessary. They displayed a compelling modesty, were self-effacing and understated, whereas the comparison companies usually had leaders with enormous egos who contributed to the continued mediocrity or the demise of the company. When things did go wrong for Level 5 leaders, they took the responsibility. On the other hand, when things went right, they attributed the success to factors other than themselves. It was the opposite with the CEOs of the comparison companies.

FUNCTIONS OF LEADERSHIP

The previous section examined the various schools of thought on the nature of leadership. It is also necessary to consider the various functions that leaders fulfil in organisations. To do this, we should look at leadership in its widest function, as in many cases those at the top of the organisation may not be directly involved themselves in these areas, but what is important is that they *create the environment* within which these activities can take place. By creating the environment, the people within the organisation become empowered and can achieve their full potential. When employees fulfil their potential, then the organisation will achieve competitive advantage. Lao Tsu, the Chinese philosopher (b.604 BC) who inspired Confucius, identified the type of leader who would enable an organisation to achieve that competitive advantage:

"The great leader is he who the people say 'we did it ourselves'."

These leadership functions are many and varied, and are important in making everything happen within an organisation. There are a number of functions that leaders perform:

- Creating a vision
- Building teams
- Motivation: individual and organisational
- Development
- Creating a high-performance organisation
- Succession planning
- Bringing about change
- Decision-making

Creating a Vision

A vision plays a vital part in giving direction to an organisation and, as will be seen in Chapter 3, goals and objectives are then chosen to reach the desired end state for that organisation. Leaders play a vital role in creating that vision and this, in turn, helps motivate people to work toward achieving success. It will also be seen in Chapter 3 that organisational values are an integral part of creating a vision.

People are often attracted to organisations that display values similar to their own (see Chapter 4). For senior executives, the values of the organisation and their own values are likely to be strongly linked. They are the people who make the strategic decisions, and inevitably, their own values will be reflected in the type of decisions that are made. Likewise with ethics: those at the top of an organisation must be able to stand over their decisions from an ethical standpoint.

Chapter 4 offers a cogent case for strong organisational values. Prahalad (2010) argues that managers are the custodians of society's most powerful institutions and must hold themselves accountable to a higher standard. In short, leaders must achieve success with responsibility. He reminds us that, over a long career, leaders will experience high points and low points and "humility in success and courage in failure are hallmarks of a good leader". Achievement must be balanced with compassion for others, and learning with understanding. It must be remembered that leaders should lead by example. If they do not display strong values in their own actions, it cannot be expected of others. An essential element in all of this is how leaders communicate their vision. Hamm (2006) believes that, all too often, people leading organisations fail to communicate what they are thinking, and talk in a manner that is unclear and vague to employees. It is imperative that all members of the organisation know exactly what is required of them in terms of their contribution to achieving organisational goals.

Building Teams

Many influential writers, such as Peter Drucker and Manfred Kets de Vries, believe that teams are playing an ever-increasing role in business organisations. Being able to pick the right team is a valuable competence required to implement a chosen strategy. Different people have different skills, and being able to recognise those skills and then motivate people to use them to the best of their ability is an essential element in achieving organisational success.

> "All the world's a stage, and all the men and women mere players: they have their exits and their entrances, and one man in his time plays many parts, his act being seven ages."
>
> *As You Like It.* Act 2, Sc. 7

According to Adair (1983) leadership is about teamwork and the creation of teams. Teams tend to have leaders and leaders tend to create teams. Teams do not happen by accident. First it requires finding the right people and then getting the mix right. Nowhere is this more evident than in Irish Rugby. The panel that is chosen to represent Ireland consists of many very talented individuals. One of the greatest challenges for Declan Kidney and his fellow coaches is picking the optimum team based on individual skill, performance, motivation and, most importantly, an ability to work together towards a common goal. The same principles also apply to every company.

One must distinguish between groups and teams. Teams have been defined as "a small number of people with complementary skills who are committed to a common purpose, performance goals and approach for which they hold themselves mutually accountable" (Katzenback and Smith, 1993: 45). The concept of the team is also central to Adair's **Action-Centred Leadership** model, which was developed while he was lecturing at the Royal Military Academy, Sandhurst. There are three overlapping elements to the model for which the leader is responsible:

- **Task** – creating a vision and purpose for the group, developing a plan to achieve the task, providing resources and monitoring progress.
- **Team** – establishing and agreeing standards of behaviour, culture, ethics, building up team spirit and resolving conflict, developing roles within the group, changing team members as necessary, establishing open communication and giving feedback to the group and gradually developing greater autonomy for the group.
- **Individuals** – understanding each individual's needs, skills, hopes and aspirations, training and developing the individuals to undertake the necessary tasks both individually and as members of a team, assigning responsibility and giving recognition to people for work well done.

Each of these elements is mutually dependent on the other two and failure in one can affect the others. Leadership is common to them all.

According to Buelens *et al.* (2006: 375) for work teams to be effective, they must achieve a level of performance that meets users' expectations. They must also be viable, meaning that members must be satisfied and willing to continue contributing. Work teams must be supported by the organisation if they are to be successful. Factors here include strategy, organisational structure, technology, culture, the reward system and administrative support and training. They also list five important factors of the internal processes of work teams, including member composition, interpersonal dynamics, purpose, resources, and co-ordination with other work groups. Leaders play an important role in creating the environment in which teams can operate effectively. When work teams fail, it is often the result of a hostile environment where there is poor staffing of the teams, poor communication and a lack of trust. Team members themselves can also be responsible for failure in taking on too much and having poor interpersonal skills.

In every team there will be those who are effective and those who are not. Performance evaluation is another important function of leaders in aligning the efforts of individuals to the goals of the organisation. There are many reasons why people may not achieve goals that were assigned to them, from the goals being too difficult in the first instance, to a lack of necessary training, or simply a case of the person underperforming due to a lack of effort. Performance evaluation, when carried out objectively, should discover the underlying reason so that it can be rectified. In many cases, various incentives such as bonus payments are linked to performance. To be motivational, it is imperative that employees view the system as being fair and impartial. At times, leaders will have to make tough decisions, not just on whether incentives should be paid, but also on who should be promoted, and whether an individual actually belongs in the team.

Motivation

People working in an organisation will only 'go the extra mile' when they are motivated. This applies equally to people at every level of the organisation, not just those at the top. In turn, leaders at each level must energise those working in their section, which has a cascading effect as managers motivate those with whom they work directly. Motivation is a complex process and it is necessary that leaders have a proper understanding of what works for different individuals.

There is a variety of different theories of motivation. In broad terms, theories of motivation can be divided into two broad groups. First, content theories which identify people's needs and the goals they want to achieve to attain those needs, e.g. Maslow's Hierarchy of Needs. Secondly, process theories explain the actual process of motivation and acknowledge people's personal decisions, e.g. Adam's Equity theory and Vroom's Expectancy model.

The main objective of motivation from an organisational perspective is to improve work performance. Clear communication is an essential element of motivation. People must understand clearly what is expected from them. There is also an onus on leaders to ensure that staff members have the ability to do the job that is being asked of them and that they also have the opportunity to perform the job in terms of organisational support and time. It must also be remembered that people model the behaviour of managers who, in turn, must constantly demonstrate good behaviour and reinforce it. Buelens *et al.* (2006:174) suggest that the link between motivation and improved productivity is also dependent on three factors: direction, intensity and persistence. Direction is whether people prefer intrinsic rewards (personal growth) or extrinsic rewards (bonuses). Intensity refers to the intensity of the response once the person makes the choice. Finally, persistence refers to how long a person will channel their energy and effort to attain a goal.

As Ireland moves more and more towards a high-knowledge economy, organisations will require people that have achieved a much higher level of educational attainment. In turn this will place a greater onus on executives to provide leadership and motivate team members. In most situations, a prescriptive form of management will not suffice.

Development

Individual Development Coaching and mentoring are important elements of leadership. There are different aspects to coaching. In order to develop individuals to their full potential, their strengths and weaknesses need to be identified. It is only then that the weaknesses can be lessened or eliminated and the strengths built upon. It is a good deal easier for another person to identify these points in us than we can do ourselves. It is the exact same with organisations. Leaders need to be developed and encouraged in order to achieve their potential. Stewart and Rigg (2011) identify such development as being an essential element in a high-performance culture.

The development process is continuous. To quote Darwin Smith, former CEO of Kimberly-Clark (one of the good-to-great companies identified above): "I never stop trying to become qualified for the job," Collins (2001:20). Development also involves reflective practice – getting the individual to reflect on how he or she handled a particular situation. This is not to be confused with performance evaluation (which is also necessary), but rather facilitating the person in a non-confrontational way to learn from the process that they have been through. Mentoring involves taking an individual and helping to develop their career by being there to guide them when required. It is ensuring that the person gets the right work experience in terms of different markets and skills, and once that has been attained, moving on to the next appointment. In Shakespeare's *King Henry IV, Parts 1 and 2*, the young Prince Hal enjoyed a wild lifestyle, but all the time he was getting to know and understand his future subjects. He does so in preparation for the time that he will accept the crown from his dying father:

> "My gracious liege, you won it, wore it, kept it, gave it me; then plain and right must my possession be; which I with more than common pain 'Gainst all the world will rightfully maintain."
>
> *Henry IV Part 2.* Act 4, Sc. 5

Martin and Schmidt (2010) highlight a number of potential pitfalls when identifying talented individuals that are potential future leaders. It should not be assumed that just because employees are talented, that they are engaged. Talented employees need to be given stimulating assignments and need to be recognised in a variety of ways, not just pay. It should also be remembered that those who are performing well in current roles do not always have the potential to progress to higher levels – employees being considered for promotion need to be tested for three critical attributes: ability, engagement and aspiration. These employees must be placed in assignments where new capabilities can be acquired and they must be involved in the development of future strategies. The development of future leaders should be managed primarily at corporate level – line managers may try to hoard high-performing individuals for the benefit of their strategic business unit, rather than do what is best for the overall company – or the individual.

Organisational Development Organisational development occurs at both individual and organisational levels and the two are interwoven. At present, the Irish economy is becoming knowledge-based. This implies a greater move by organisations to what Garratt (1987) referred to as "the learning organisation", a concept later made popular by Senge (1990). A learning organisation is one that has a culture that supports challenging assumptions around a common vision and one that is capable of regeneration through continuous learning by its members. Inherent in organisational development is a focus on innovation. There is a growing need for organisations to be constantly innovating. In dealing with intelligent and highly trained staff, a different type of leadership is required. A number of writers have discussed the importance of organisational learning, and leadership is an essential element in promoting such organisational development.

High Performance Organisation

Perhaps one of the biggest challenges for any leader is creating a high-performance organisation. There are a number of different aspects to this. It begins with laying the foundation for strategy development in terms of the values and governance of the organisation. The type of values that the organisation has will impact on many of the decisions that it takes, and the organisation and all its members will take its cue from the values displayed by those at the top.

Strategic analysis, in the form of analysing the business environment and, more importantly, understanding and building the strategic capability of the organisation, is also an integral part of the development process. The paradigm that is created will influence the type of strategy that the organisation develops. However, there is no 'acid test' to prove that any one strategy is the best one. Yet, the chosen strategy will have a profound impact on the organisation and its performance in the market place. Implementing the chosen strategy is the final element in creating a high-performance organisation. Up to this point, the strategy is merely a blueprint and the implementation process must be led properly for it to be successful. It involves putting constant, constructive pressure on the organisation to achieve results, and adapting the strategic plan to meet changing circumstances.

A high-performance organisation is underpinned by that organisation having a high-performance culture. It will be seen in the section on culture below that there is a strong link between leadership and culture.

Succession Planning

Good leadership plays a very important role in the success of any organisation. Leaders come and go but there must be continuity in the leadership process. A very important role of leadership is planning the succession of leaders at every level, from the top down. This involves identifying people that display leadership potential and developing their skills and experience. Vacancies in critical areas may come about unexpectedly due to a person leaving, illness or death. For that reason, it is important to prepare and groom future leaders at every level. Without proper planning, a vacuum will occur and the wrong person could be appointed to the position.

When approaching retirement, Jack Welch conducted an exhaustive search within General Electric for the person who would succeed him (Welch, 2001). King Lear planned his succession on a more spurious basis. Addressing his three daughters, he asked:

> "Since now we will divest us both of rule, interest of territory, cares of state — Which of you shall we say doth love us most? That we our largest bounty may extend where nature doth with merit challenge."

King Lear: Act 1, Sc. 1

Kerry Group is an example of a public company that has made a very successful transition from Denis Brosnan, its first CEO, to Hugh Friel and now to Stan McCarthy. Throughout that time, the company has maintained and built on its vision and developed steady and sustainable growth.

Bringing about Change

Every organisation undergoes change in their environment (see Chapter 5). As Charles Darwin discovered in terms of evolution, it is only those species that can adapt to a changing environment that can survive. The subject of change will be discussed in detail in Chapter 14 but, in the context of leadership, it is important to stress the role that the leader plays in bringing the organisation through the change process. One of the most notable experts on change, John Kotter, stresses that change must be led rather than managed (Kotter, 1996). Similarly, Brown (1994) argues that effective leaders are those that understand the nature of the change affecting their organisation and can transform their organisation to create competitive advantage.

Coping with change is something most employees find very difficult, and so being able to motivate them is an integral part of the change process. Motivation also plays a much wider role in the attainment of organisational goals. Change involves taking tough decisions and being able to stand over them. This is particularly so when the organisation has to downsize and people are made redundant. While decision-making is an integral part of management, leaders will often take decisions that require great courage and can have a profound impact on the organisation. One major difficulty in leading change is balancing the necessity to create stability in the organisation, while anticipating and implementing the change that must take place to secure its future. Leaders also play an essential role in how they interpret and deal with uncertainty.

In the current climate, the nature of the challenges that change will bring about will also place many pressures on the leader of the organisation. Perhaps one of the biggest challenges on a human level is how to counter adversity with resilience. Resilience is the capacity to respond quickly and constructively to crises. According to Margolis and Stoltz (2010), dealing with a crisis needs a shift from cause-oriented thinking to response-oriented thinking. It requires leaders to: turn their attention to what they can control; focus on identifying positive effects that action may bring about; assume the crisis is specific and can be contained; and, finally, take action on addressing the problem immediately.

Prahalad (2010) reminds us that "leadership is about self-awareness". The importance of coaching in developing the potential of leaders was discussed above. While this is important in all aspects of the leader's job, it is particularly so in helping the leader to cope with change. If on a personal basis, the leader is having difficulty in coming to terms with a new reality, there is little hope of leading the organisation through the crisis. To facilitate this process, O'Donovan (2009) provides a framework known as CRAIC (Control, Responsibility, Awareness, Impetus and Confidence), which demonstrates how coaching can unlock the potential in individuals and help them maximise their performance. The leader must first focus on Control, which refers to the feeling of control over one's environment and is important in terms of self-esteem, motivation and self-efficacy. He or she must then take Responsibility for change and exercise control and self-discipline in terms of committing to action. Successful action is dependent on our level of Awareness of our thinking patterns – a vital element in creativity and developing workable solutions. In turn, this requires the Impetus to begin, and sustain effort towards achieving goals. Finally, it requires the Confidence to take the necessary action. Napoleon once described leaders as "dealers in hope". To be able to inspire hope in others, leaders must first be masters of themselves.

Decision-making

Underpinning all of the above functions is the ability of the leader to make decisions. According to Brousseau *et al.* (2006), a manager's decision-making style should change as the manager advances within the organisation. This is due to changes in the nature of the work being done and the demands on the individual. Lower down the organisational chain, action is at a premium and managers are required to be more directive and focused on specific tasks. At senior executive level, managers are required to make decisions that involve multiple courses of action that may evolve as circumstances change. In general, for senior executives the emphasis should be on a more participative style of leadership and decision-making. (Decision-making is discussed in detail in Chapter 12.)

Failures in Leadership

The last few years have laid bare many unedifying examples of poor leadership across the globe. Ireland has been no exception, and the consequences have been extremely serious for all concerned. It is essential to acknowledge and examine such failures and, most importantly, learn from the mistakes that were made. To paraphrase Karl Marx: history has happened, first as tragedy; it must not be allowed repeat itself as farce.

Many international factors have contributed to the deep recession in Ireland. However, despite the initial widespread denial by many politicians and those at the top of many organisations (banks in particular), there can be no doubt that Ireland is responsible for a large portion of the problems that caused the crisis. In particular, a failure of leadership played a major part in creating that problem. As a leader article in the *Economist* put it: "hubris was followed by nemesis" (*Economist*, 2011). Inevitably, the collapse of the banking industry in Ireland had a major consequential effect on the rest of the economy and, as Regling and Watson (2010: 5) state: "Ireland's banking crisis bears the clear imprint of global influences, yet it was in crucial ways 'home-made'." The report into the Irish banking crisis by the Governor of the Central Bank (Honohan, 2010: 6-10) was even more unequivocal about the causes of the financial crisis in Ireland blaming a number of factors: domestic macroeconomic imbalances (Government pro-cyclical policies), a systemic failure in regulation both in terms of having reliable information and a lack of "intrusiveness and assertiveness on the part of regulators in challenging the banks". He also laid the blame firmly with "the directors and senior managements of the banks that got into trouble".

In any country, there is a strong overlap between politics and business. In Ireland, this overlap is clearly illustrated by a number of writers including: Cooper (2009), Leahy (2009), O'Toole (2009), Ross (2009), Ross and Webb (2010), O'Toole (2010), Lyons and Carey (2011). For those who have been observers of political and business affairs over the last 10 years or more, these writers provide a useful summary of events that have unravelled so many of the enormous gains made by the Irish economy since the early 1990s. Criticism of these blunders is not restricted to what some termed the "four angry men" (four journalists/authors who wrote polemics on the corruption in Irish business and politics: Matt Cooper, Pat Leahy, Fintan O'Toole and Shane Ross). A trawl of the international press, from the *Financial Times* to the *Washington Post*, over the last number of years does not present the country in a very flattering way. As far back as April 2005, Brian Lavery and Timothy O'Brien of *The New York Times* controversially branded Ireland as "The wild west of European Finance" (Lavery and O'Brien, 2005). While many in Ireland took offence at this comment, our "light touch" regulation has clearly failed.

International commentary by respected journals and rating agencies is important, as it will inevitably impact on the decision by foreign companies to invest in Ireland (as well as the rate of interest charged on Irish sovereign bonds). It also has impacted negatively on other sectors such as tourism. The number of overseas visitors to Ireland declined from 7.7million in 2006 to 6.9millon in 2009 (CSO 2010). While there are many reasons for this decline, including lack of competitiveness, the perception by potential visitors of the economic problems in Ireland is also playing a part. The country had to receive an €85 billion bailout loan from the EU/IMF in November 2010. Many of the banks are in state ownership. The unemployment rate is expected to be 13.5% in 2011, and it is estimated that up to 100,000 Irish people will emigrate in 2011 and 2012. To put this in perspective, the highest rate of net outflow in the 1980s was when 44,000 people emigrated in 1989 (ESRI, 2010:1).

The failure of leadership has been across the spectrum of organisations in Ireland. The "Murphy Report" by Yvonne Murphy into the Archdiocese of Dublin (Murphy, 2009:4) is a dreadful indictment of those at the top who were preoccupied with "the maintenance of secrecy, the avoidance of scandal, the protection of the reputation of the Church, and the preservation of its assets. All other considerations… were subordinated to these priorities." While all churches usually operate at a remove from the business world, they can also be involved in running key services such as many of the country's hospitals. On a broader level, they have traditionally played an important part in framing societal values which, in turn, inform how people in business conduct their affairs. Investigations such as the Murphy Report and also the Ryan Report (2009) clearly undermine the central message that should underpin such values.

The above examples do not reflect well on many of those who were entrusted with leadership positions in this country and hubris has played a large part in causing such a depth of problems. In moving on, we first of all need to learn from the mistakes and to recognise the importance of true leadership in successfully guiding organisations of every type.

Fr Harry Bohan is founder of the Céifin Centre in Ennis and chair of an annual conference that attracts leading commentators from the world of broadcasting, business, religious groups, the health sector, academia, etc., to examine the changes taking place in our society. Fr Bohan believes that leadership is one of the critical challenges facing Irish society in the 21st Century. He calls for a redefinition of leadership at every level and in every sphere:

> "The 20th Century was very much the era of the institution. Our lives were shaped by institutions – whether financial (banks), spiritual (church), corporate (big business) or political (parties). Problems arose when those institutions that were central to our lives became ends in themselves and lost the notion of service upon which they had been founded. Trust has been broken in many instances and broken trust is not easily mended. Many institutions have to return to first principles and ask themselves some basic questions. What are banks for? What is the church for? Is politics about parties or people? How can business and community connect?" (Bohan, 2009)

Bohan goes on to criticise top-down leadership – command and control model – and what he terms the disconnect between those at the top of the organisation and those at the bottom. Instead, he calls for a new kind of leadership – "a leadership of service" (Bohan, 2009).

ORGANISATIONAL CULTURE

Every type of society has its own culture or set of cultures. Societal culture is a product of many different factors such as ethnic background, politics, economic conditions, religion and language. In larger countries, there may be differences between regions in terms of culture, e.g. the northern part of Germany has quite a different culture compared to the south. Our culture impacts on our assumptions about how we perceive things, how we think, act and feel. It is an integral part of who we are and, hence, it is inevitable that we bring our societal culture to work with us in the form of our values, customs and language. Societal culture impacts directly on our personal values and assumptions, and societal culture also impacts on organisational culture. When we join an organisation, its culture will also impact on our values. The combined effect of societal culture and organisational culture on the individual will ultimately direct people's behaviour in organisations (Buelens *et al.* (2006: 591). In the context of strategy, it is, therefore, important that we understand organisational culture and how it impacts on the decisions that are made by individual organisations.

Understanding Culture in Organisations

Just as each society has a culture of its own, an organisation likewise has a particular culture that defines its own separate identity. Charles Handy (1999:180) sums it up thus:

> "Anyone who has spent time with any variety of organisations, or worked in more than two or three, will have been struck by the differing atmospheres, the differing ways of doing things, the differing levels of energy, of individual freedom, of kinds of personality. For organisations are as different and varied as the nations and societies of the world."

Organisational culture is extremely difficult to observe and understand. It has so many levels, it has been described by Trompenaars and Hampden-Turner (1998) as being like the layers of an onion. A number of writers have proposed various frameworks that can be used for the purpose of understanding culture. Though there are no truly common themes running through these frameworks, it is worth reviewing a selection of theories for a better understanding of organisational culture.

One of the most cited researchers in the area of organisational culture is Edgar Schein, Sloan Fellows Professor of Management Emeritus at the Sloan School of Management at MIT, who defines organisational culture as:

> "A pattern of shared basic assumptions learned by a group as it solved its problems of external adaptation and internal integration, which has worked well enough to be considered valid and, therefore, to be taught to new members as the correct way to perceive, think, and feel in relation to those problems."

Schein (2010:18)

53

According to Schein, organisational culture can be observed at three different levels which can best be described by drawing an analogy to an iceberg. The **artefacts** are above the waterline and are easy to see, but difficult to decipher. The **espoused beliefs and shared values** are below the waterline and are not as easily seen. The **basic assumptions** are deep down and are barely discernible.

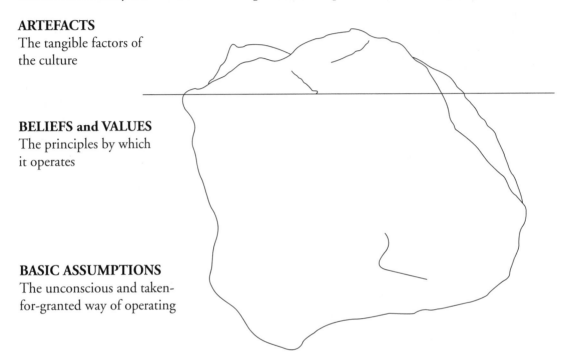

ARTEFACTS
The tangible factors of
the culture

BELIEFS and VALUES
The principles by which
it operates

BASIC ASSUMPTIONS
The unconscious and taken-
for-granted way of operating

Figure 2.2 *Model of Organisational Culture (Schein)*

Artefacts Artefacts are the visible, tangible phenomena that represent an organisation's culture. They include: the stories and legends that are told about the organisation by its staff and outsiders; the rituals and ceremonies that define organisational life; the language used by its staff; the physical manifestations such as buildings and office layout, logos and branding style; and organisational dress code (see **Illustration 2.3**). Schein believes that it is dangerous to try to infer deeper assumptions from artefacts alone as a person's interpretation of those artefacts is a projection of that person's own feelings and reaction.

Espoused Beliefs and Values In solving problems, a group will develop a shared understanding of what will work for that particular group and will thus be validated by them. The shared values of an organisation (see Chapter 3) are the principles by which people in it operate. They define what the organisation considers important and guide decision-making. They provide meaning and comfort for group members. These beliefs remain conscious and are explicitly articulated as they guide the group in tackling situations and they train new members in how to behave. In some cases, these beliefs and values may not be congruent with employee behaviour and other artefacts. Espoused beliefs and values often do not present a full understanding of an organisation's behaviour and so, to get a fuller understanding, one must examine the basic assumptions of that organisation.

Basic assumptions When basic beliefs and values are applied in an organisation over time, and they are seen to constantly work, they gradually evolve into shared assumptions. These are the unconscious, taken-for-granted beliefs held by people in the organisation. They are deep beneath the surface and cannot be readily observed by those looking in. It is how the group perceives reality, and it means that there is little variation within the social group in terms of its actions. Basic assumptions tend to be non-debatable and because they are shared, they are mutually reinforced and, hence, difficult to change. They are implicit (rather than explicit) assumptions and they are very powerful, as they guide people as to the correct way to perceive, think and feel. When events do not conform to people's assumptions, group members often resort to defensiveness and denial.

Illustration 2.4: Dress Code and Corporate Culture

The style of clothes worn by employees says a lot about the corporate culture of an organisation. While companies in the software industry usually have no fixed rules about employees' dress code, things are a little different in the Swiss bank UBS. According to a report in *The Wall Street Journal*, the dress code consists of a 40-page illustrated book, which gives very prescriptive rules for staff on what is considered appropriate dress for work. The book is designed to inform new employees about the culture in the bank and it is being piloted in a number of branches. It has been designed to differentiate UBS in the minds of its customers and, if successful, may be adopted as a code for all staff.

The book contains some general sections, and in terms of the colour of clothes, it says that suits should be dark grey, navy-blue or black, since these colours "symbolise competence, formalism and sobriety". Suits should also be stored on large, rounded hangers to preserve their shape. Furthermore, the code includes pointers about eating and smoking. Staff members are encouraged not to smoke and should not spend time in smoke-filled rooms. Garlic and onion-based dishes are also to be avoided.

There are also separate sections for male and female staff. Men are not allowed to wear short-sleeved shirts and stubble or excessive facial hair is to be avoided. They should have their hair cut every four weeks. Socks should be black and high enough to prevent skin from showing when legs are crossed. They must use tie-knots that match the bone structure in their face. Shoes must be black and highly polished. Men should not dye their hair, and their finger nails should not be any longer than 1.5 millimetres. Men are not allowed to wear jewellery but are encouraged to wear a wrist watch as it suggests "reliability and great care for punctuality".

For women, the guide recommends wearing pearls and illustrates details on stitching. Trendy glasses should not be worn. Hair should be well-cared for and cut by a stylist. Women must wear flesh-coloured underwear and must ensure that they do not get foundation on their collars. Makeup should consist of foundation, mascara and discreet lipstick which will "enhance your personality". The hemline of skirts should hit the middle of the knee. Scarves, if they are worn, must be tied in a certain manner. Fragrances should be applied as soon as one gets out of the shower (Berton, 2010).

All in all, there does not appear to be a lot of room for individualism. Rock 'n' Rollers need not apply.

CLASSIFICATION OF ORGANISATIONAL CULTURE

A trawl of the literature will reveal that there is no universally accepted way of classifying organisational culture, and many writers approach such typologies in very different ways. This is probably due, in no small way, to the nature of organisational culture and how difficult it is to observe, let alone understand, the culture of a particular company. To gain a fuller appreciation of organisational culture, it is perhaps useful to examine a number of the different typologies that are applied, including:

- Handy's Four Types
- Miles and Snow Typology
- Peters and Waterman Excellence Model
- Thompson *et al.* Cultural Strength
- Management Philosophy

Handy's Four Types

Charles Handy (1999:183-191) built on earlier work by Harrison (1972) and draws together the structure of organisations (see Chapter 7) and the type of culture associated with them. He describes four manifestations of culture:

1. **Power culture** This is normally found in family-run or small organisations where one person is the sole authority and everything revolves around their vision. The boss will personally select staff members, and will recruit employees that will fit into the culture. The centralised nature of this form of organisational culture can have the advantage of quick decision-making, particularly in a highly competitive market. However, while the individual may have the necessary energy to drive the organisation forward, they may lack the broad managerial skills required to achieve success. Handy used a web to represent the power culture organisation, with all power resting with the "spider" in the centre of the web.

2. **Role culture** Role culture applies to large organisations. Here Handy uses a Greek temple to depict this type of organisational culture where power is retained at the top of the organisation. The pediment at the top is where decisions are made. It is supported by pillars which represent the various functions and departments of the organisation with information flowing up and directions flowing down. It is bureaucratic and highly structured in nature and lends itself to organisations like government departments, banks and oil companies. This form of organisational

culture is not particularly suited to a dynamic environment. Decision-making is centralised at the top of the organisation, and there is a clear career structure in place for members.

3. **Task culture** This type of organisational culture is focused on getting the job done by bringing together in the organisation all the necessary people and expertise. It is represented by a net or matrix structure and is best suited to volatile markets and project management where a team has to be formed that can respond quickly and effectively to differing circumstances. Examples include management consultancies and advertising agencies.

4. **Person culture** With this form of organisational culture, each individual in the organisation may be the focus at any one time, depending on their specialisation. As such, there is a high level of individual freedom in approaching work assignments. It is represented by a galaxy of stars and is most suited to professional practices or consultancies, where a number of people are required to work together to meet the needs of a particular client. There is no formal authority as such, and people cooperate together as required.

Miles and Snow Typology

Miles and Snow (1978) developed a typology linking different types of organisational culture and strategy. Based on different sets of values, each organisation will develop strategic goals in line with its values. The first three strategy types – Defenders, Prospectors and Analysers – are all viable options. The fourth type – Reactors – will ultimately fail unless they adopt one of the other strategies.

Table 2.1: *Miles and Snow Typology*

Type	Characteristics	Emphasis	Example
Defender	A conservative company that sets low-risk strategies that will secure its current markets and customers. Slow steady growth.	Long-term planning. Efficiency.	Marks & Spencer Dunnes Stores
Prospector	Concerned with innovation and growth. Always searching for new opportunities. Willing to take risks and can handle uncertainty.	Visionary company. Change.	3M Kerry Group
Analyser	Maintains its current markets while searching for new markets. A mid-way point between Defenders and Prospectors.	Planning. Moderate innovation.	IBM Ryanair
Reactor	No clear strategy. Reacting slowly to changes in the environment.	Delayed reaction.	Waterford Wedgewood Some professional organisations.

Peters and Waterman Excellence Model

In their book *In Search of Excellence* Peters and Waterman (1982) attempted to identify one best form of organisational culture for American organisations. Their research was conducted using data from client companies of McKinsey, a large American consulting company. They concluded that the best run companies operated on the basis of eight cultural tenets that underpinned their success:

1. ***A bias for action*** – a quick reaction, make things happen approach
2. ***Stay close to the customer*** – listening to your customers and understanding their needs
3. ***Autonomy and entrepreneurship*** – empower employees and encourage innovation
4. ***Productivity through people*** – employees are the most important resource, and it is through employees that productivity is delivered
5. ***Hands on, value driven*** – the organisation must have clear values and managers must demonstrate their commitment to work and organisational values
6. ***Stick to the knitting*** – reducing risk by sticking to what the organisation does best, and not be distracted by diversifying into areas where the company lacks expertise
7. ***Simple form, lean staff*** – creating a flat organisation that is flexible in its response
8. ***Simultaneous loose-tight control*** – striking a balance between the controls and values that are necessary but giving staff autonomy to take action

There has been much criticism of the work by Peters and Waterman, particularly around their methodology, and the fact that many of the companies identified subsequently failed (Martin, 2005:496; Tiernan*et al.*, 2006:38). However, the eight cultural tenets they identified still provide a useful insight into organisational culture and performance. It must be remembered that, in many cases, companies lose sight of the fundamentals of their business and no longer practise the basic principles that helped them achieve success in the first instance. Irish banks are a perfect example of this.

Thompson *et al.* Cultural Strength

Thompson *et al.* (2010: 390-96) classify organisational culture according to its strength and influence and divide it into five categories:

- Strong
- Weak
- Unhealthy
- High performance
- Adaptive

Strong culture companies A strong organisational culture has deeply-rooted values that strictly regulate the conduct of a company. These values are articulated and practised by managers who insist that others in the company do likewise. By constantly reiterating the importance of these values, through words and deeds, a strong message is communicated to staff members about what the company considers important. There is significant peer pressure on staff members to conform, and those who dislike the company's values tend to leave. Strong leaders tend to play a pivotal role in establishing strong organisational cultures which become enduring qualities of the company.

Where there is a strong culture-strategy fit, it can play a major part in the success of that strategy. It can also provide continuity in an organisation, particularly during a time of changeover from one chief executive to another. However, problems can sometimes arise when the environment changes and strategies evolve, but the culture of the organisation remains the same. This is a problem that successive chief executives in Aer Lingus have faced over the last 10 years. A strong culture can also lead to 'group think' which is a form of pervasive thinking that people engage in when making decisions that clouds clear judgement (see Chapter 12).

Weak culture companies Companies with weak organisational culture lack values and principles that are widely shared. This often happens where there is a succession of CEOs, each with a different set of values and views about what the organisation should be doing. As a result, there is no dominant organisational culture that drives staff in one direction, and they are left with little emotional attachment to the organisation. A weak culture provides little assistance in pursuing a particular strategy, as there are no common bonds that managers can use to assist the process of strategy formulation and implementation.

Unhealthy cultures Unhealthy organisational cultures are those that impact in a negative way on company performance. There are different reasons for such unhealthy cultures. Internal political factors can impact on strategy formulation and internal rivalries can result in personal empire building and political manoeuvring, all of which diverts attention away from what the organisation should be doing to develop and execute strategies. Cultures that are resistant to change will impede progress in the organisation. Change affects people and impacts to a greater or lesser degree on every company. The organisation that cannot adapt will soon lose market share, and will eventually go out of business. The predominant culture in such companies is to maintain the status quo, and people do not take risks in case they make mistakes. This obviously constrains attempts to develop new products and processes and make the necessary changes that reflect a different environment.

Similar to change-resistant culture is an insular culture, where people in an organisation believe that they know best, leading to an arrogance that causes the company to ignore what customers are telling them and not see the changes taking place in the marketplace. These companies are resistant to any deployments that were not initiated internally, and this leads to a diminution of the strategic capability of the organisation.

Unethical companies are the final, and perhaps the worst, manifestation of unhealthy organisational culture in that they can potentially do far greater harm to a wider group of stakeholders (see Chapter 4 for a fuller discussion of issues on ethics and corporate governance). Prior to the collapse of the banking industry in Ireland, many attributes of an unhealthy culture could be clearly identified in the strategies that were pursued.

High-performance culture An organisation with a high-performance culture is one that has a can-do spirit and is results-orientated. It requires its staff to be accountable, with an expectation that they will learn from their mistakes. There is a strong sense of personal involvement by staff members, and the organisation is very clear on what it expects people at every level to achieve, with a strong emphasis on creativity and initiative. High-performance culture inspires loyalty and dedication by staff and, for those who achieve results, the rewards follow. This form of culture is an integral part of achieving organisational excellence and the implementation of strategies that will perpetuate that excellence.

Adaptive culture An adaptive culture is one that reacts quickly to a changing environment and all the challenges that it brings. Employees are quick to innovate and take risks, and the organisation is supportive of staff who identify issues, evaluate the implications for the company and develop an appropriate workable solution to the problem. For their part, employees will embrace change when they see that it does not compromise the core values of the organisation and when it meets the legitimate needs of all stakeholders. While change is something that impacts on all organisations, an adaptive culture is particularly important in a fast-changing business environment, such as the software industry and technology companies.

Management Philosophy

The final approach to classifying an organisation's culture is the management philosophy that underpins it. Press (1990) argues that the culture of an organisation is related to one or more philosophies based on its relationship with the company's stakeholders. There are two intersecting axes: outcome-oriented measures/resource-based measures on one axis and external perspective/internal perspective on the other axis. This results in four different philosophies:

- **Market focus** – importance of satisfying customer needs
- **People focus** – building on the expertise of its people and meeting their expectations
- **Shareholder focus** – based on maximising shareholder return
- **Resource focus** – minimising costs and achieving efficiencies

Companies obviously need to take all these philosophies into consideration, but each company will differ in terms of where it places its priorities.

Each of the five methods of classifying culture that were examined above present a very different approach and a different insight into culture. When examining the culture of a particular organisation, there will be traces of each classification identified in that organisation and the strategies that they are pursuing.

Subcultures

The discussion on culture in this chapter is primarily centred on the dominant culture of an organisation – the culture that is widely shared throughout the organisation. It is also quite common to have different subcultures within organisations, particularly if an organisation is large and/or diversified. The values and beliefs in these subcultures can vary quite considerably depending on factors such as the type of business unit, geographical location or functional division involved. These differences can manifest themselves in various ways. According to McShane and Von Glinow (2009), some subcultures can support the dominant culture with parallel values and assumptions, while other subcultures act as countercultures in that they work against the dominant values of the organisation.

Countercultures can create many problems for the company by creating unnecessary conflict and can be disruptive in terms of developing and implementing strategy. They often have their own objectives which run counter to organisational objectives. Elton Mayo identified this in the early 1930s in the Hawthorn experiments in the Western Electric Company. In the last of the experiments, known as the 'Bank Wiring Observation Room experiments', Mayo and his team observed the existence of informal groups that created their own rules of behaviour separate to the 'official' culture of the company (Tiernan *et al.*, 2006:22). In cases where subcultures clash within an organisation, managers must act to resolve the problem. This is particularly so when a company merges with another, or more commonly, when it makes an acquisition. In general, a high percentage of mergers and acquisitions fail, and irreconcilable cultural differences play a substantial part in such failures, where, according to Buelens *et al.* (2006:603) it "multiplies the chance of failure".

On the other hand, McShane and Von Glinow believe that countercultures can also serve a number of useful functions by challenging a dominant culture and generating useful ideas. In turn, this can help an organisation to align with the needs of the market in which they are operating. Finally, countercultures can also be of benefit in not tolerating illegal or unethical behaviour (Chapter 4 will deal with the issue of whistleblowing).

When the culture of a society changes over a period of time, problems can arise if the internal culture of particular organisations does not change in tandem with it. This can manifest itself in different ways. Johnson *et al.* (2011:158) refer to **strategic drift** where there "is the tendency for strategies to develop incrementally on the basis of historical and cultural influences, but fail to keep pace with a changing environment". Martin (2005:500) refers to it as "cultural fragmentation" which can create particular challenges for public services. Irish society has changed enormously in the last number of years with large ethnic groups living and working in the country. Organisations such as the Health Service Executive and the Gardaí face cultural diversity in the workplace in a way that would have been considered unimaginable even 15 years ago. Policing foreign groups, for example, requires more than the ability to speak a particular foreign language. In essence, it requires police men and women from those ethnic groups who will fully understand all of the cultural issues at play and, in turn, this creates a challenge for police organisations to ensure full cultural integration of their members.

THE NATURE OF CULTURE

The Importance of Organisational Culture

Culture serves a number of valuable functions in an organisation, according to Smircich (1983). First, it gives people working in the organisation a sense of identity and belonging and a sense of pride in what they do. Armies throughout the world, for example, have long recognised the importance of the sense of identity which soldiers have for their own particular unit. *Esprit de Corps*, or morale, is an essential attribute in the fighting soldier. The same positive effect can be experienced by commercial organisations in galvanising their workforce behind a chosen strategy. Just as staff members identify with the organisation, it must be remembered that organisations are also social constructs, and so providing a stable social system for employees is important. This point was illustrated by Elton Mayo in the 1920s during the Hawthorne Experiments which first identified the impact of the social structure of employees in an organisation on their productivity (Tiernan *et al.,* 2006).

Organisational culture can help employees make sense of their environment and what the organisation stands for. With aid agencies, for example, the culture of the organisation and the values of the individual volunteers working for it are usually aligned in a powerful synergy. Communication is an important element here in terms of induction for new employees and feedback on performance to ensure the organisation's culture is maintained.

Establishing and Maintaining Organisational Culture

The initial culture of a company is normally established by its founders, who impose their philosophies and beliefs on the organisation. This will happen to a greater or lesser extent depending on the individuals concerned. Some will give it a great deal of consideration and set very clear standards for others to follow. Whole Foods Market, for example, is the world's largest retail chain of natural and organic foods and was founded in Austin, Texas in 1980. It is an example of an organisation that has established a corporate culture based on very clear principles which reflect the values of its founder, John Mackey. Whole Foods Market now has 300 stores across the United States and the UK, and the company employs 54,000 people. The values that underpin its culture are practised daily in every aspect of the company's dealings with its customers and its employees. The organisation describes its values as being constant – not changing from time to time or from person to person. Each employee is part of the company culture. They believe the organisation's values transcend their own and they are the soul of the company. Whole Foods Market's values centre around the quality of natural ingredients and organic foods; delighting their customers with their produce and highly-trained staff; supporting their staff in their personal development; caring about the community and environment; and educating customers on healthy eating (Whole Foods Market, 2011).

How leaders embed culture is important for an organisation's success. Schein (2010:236) proposes a number of primary and secondary measures to help establish and embed culture. The primary embedding mechanisms include:

- The issues that leaders pay attention to, measure and control
- How leaders react to critical incidents
- How resources are allocated within the organisation
- Criteria for allocating rewards
- Recruitment and selection, as well as retention
- Role modelling and coaching

According to Schein, the secondary articulation and reinforcement mechanisms include:

- Organisational structure
- Building design and layout

- Systems and procedures
- Organisational rituals and ceremonies
- Formal statements by the organisation concerning its philosophy
- Stories about important people and events that have happened within the organisation

Just as the actions of the founders of an organisation are important in establishing organisational culture, the behaviour of senior managers also plays a vital role in maintaining the culture. Employees will reflect the values they see practised by those running the organisation, rather than whatever values are being espoused. The culture of the company, and what it stands for, will have to be communicated clearly to all new staff members. This is achieved through a socialisation process, and it plays a major role in maintaining the culture over time. It will require staff to learn and to adjust to their new surroundings. A three-phase model of socialisation was proposed by Feldman (1981):

1. **Pre-employment socialisation** – where people research the company in terms of the type of employment conditions they can expect and the compatibility of their values with those of the organisation. The organisation should be open about itself and paint a realistic picture of what it is like to work there. Recruitment and selection processes are time-consuming and expensive, and it does not serve anyone's purpose to create unrealistic expectations about the organisation. By clearly defining its culture, the company can more effectively select potential new employees that will be compatible with that culture and the values embedded in it. As a consequence, the employees that it selects are more likely to stay longer, thus reducing recruitment costs.

2. **Encounter** – the person has now signed the contract and started in the organisation. They have to start making the necessary adjustments to fit in with the work demands placed upon them. They will have to reconcile differences with regard to what they previously expected and the reality they now face. Many will encounter what is known as reality shock – stress associated with reconciling preconceived notions about the company and the realisation of the day-to-day routine they are now experiencing. Some people may decide to leave at this point.

3. **Adaptation** – once they have gotten over the initial stages, the process of adaptation to the company will have to continue, and new employees must learn to fit into the work practices that exist within the organisation. They learn to internalise the values and the norms of the organisation and, over time, become "insiders". In addition, they will have to understand the social hierarchy of their new colleagues and resolve workplace conflicts.

Clear communication is essential to help employees clarify what is expected of them. This will include formal briefings about the company, its vision and the values that underpin its culture. Some organisations will provide mentors to help new employees make the transition into their new role and to ensure they understand the company's philosophy. Explanation about the rewards' system operating in the company will also be important. While a company's official induction programme is very important, it must be remembered that an informal process will also take place, especially in the absence of a proper company programme. Managers must, therefore, take the initiative and ensure the induction process is comprehensive.

Identifying an Organisation's Culture

A number of different ways of classifying culture were discussed above. Similarly, there are different ways of identifying which type of culture is dominant within an organisation. Identifying the culture of an organisation is by no means an exact science, however, given the rather nebulous nature of culture. Despite the difficulties involved, it is important for managers to develop an understanding of their organisation's culture, as this culture will either help or impede the development of certain strategies, and it is probably one of the most difficult aspects of leading change in an organisation (see Chapter 14).

Perhaps the most comprehensive framework for understanding the culture of an organisation is that by Johnson *et al.* (2011:176) who suggest using a **Cultural Web** to "show the behavioural, physical and symbolic manifestations of a culture". They place the organisational "paradigm" or basic assumptions at the centre of a web which includes the following overlapping elements, all of which impact on the central paradigm:

- **Routines and rituals** – the daily routines that show how things are done in the organisation, as well as the rituals that are emphasised
- **Symbols** – "the objects, events, acts or people that convey, maintain or create meaning over and above their functional purpose"
- **Power** – how people in the organisation use their influence over others to achieve certain outcomes
- **Organisational structures** – the structure of the organisation and its reporting lines
- **Control systems** – not just the formal control systems but also the informal systems that support people

Johnson *et al.* believe that understanding the central paradigm or basic assumptions is central to understanding the organisation's approach to strategy. The central paradigm is the managers' judgement on what they consider to be important. However, the difficulty lies in developing an awareness of the paradigm, particularly as an outsider. By observing the different elements above, a greater understanding of an organisation's culture can be developed. In isolation, no one element will present a full picture, but examined together, a cultural web will convey a reasonably comprehensive understanding of the culture that exists in that organisation. In reality, it takes a lot of time and questioning before that understanding emerges clearly. For example, statements made in a company's annual reports about its values may not truly reflect the way it operates away from the glare of the media.

Organisational Culture and Performance

Of critical importance to leaders is the relationship between organisational culture and an organisation's performance. Peters and Waterman's study (above) has been criticised, and while many of their recommendations remain valid, no direct correlation can be drawn between the culture they advocated and organisational success. McShane and Von Glinow (2009:280) looked at the relationship between strong organisational culture and performance. They suggest "that only a modestly positive relationship exists between culture strength and success". There are a few reasons for this. First, once the external environment shifts, strong organisational cultures can impede success, in that the company may no longer be responding to the needs of its customers. Secondly, very strong cultures can restrict decision-makers when searching for solutions to problems or for new opportunities. Finally, strong cultures can suppress dissenting voices within an organisation and also suppress diversity.

Barney (1986) concluded that superior financial performance is dependent on sustained competitive advantage. In turn, organisational culture plays an important part in building competitive advantage providing that: the culture is valuable and facilitates high performance; it is rare; and it is not easily copied by competitors. Ryanair is perhaps a good example. It is a highly-profitable airline, and its approach to low costs is deeply embedded in its culture and facilitates high performance. It is rare, in the sense that Ryanair has perfected this culture, and, thus, it is very difficult for any rival airline to copy it.

Intercultural Differences

At the beginning of this chapter, the influence of national culture was examined in relation to organisational culture. For many Irish companies understanding national culture is a relatively straightforward affair, as they are subject to similar national cultural forces. For multinational companies, be they foreign or Irish, different national cultures will impact on internal organisational culture in a number of different ways, including: language, both verbal and non-verbal; religion; values; customs and manners; and social institutions such as clubs and societies. These are all factors that need to be considered when expanding abroad, whether by foreign direct investment or by acquisition. According to Hofstede (1985), some of the main considerations include:

- **Individualism v collectivism** Societies differ in terms of whether their focus is on the individual (US and Britain), where people pursue their own self-interest and expect to be rewarded accordingly, or on the extended family and wider community (France, Germany and most Eastern countries, such as China, etc.).

- **Power distance** refers to how much inequality people expect to find in their dealings with organisational and governmental bodies. The higher the power distance score (Philippines, Mexico and India) the greater the distance between those at the top and the bottom. A low score implies closer links (Sweden and Denmark).

- **Uncertainty avoidance** refers to how people deal with uncertainty. People in societies with high uncertainty avoidance require strong institutional procedures and control to help them cope (Greece, Portugal and Japan). Societies with low uncertainty avoidance are better at coping with risk and will accept a variety of different views (US, Sweden and the UK).

- **Masculinity v Femininity** Masculine societies place emphasis on achievement and making money, and jobs tend to be gender based (Japan and Australia). Feminine societies place greater emphasis on people and quality of life (Sweden, Denmark and Finland).

What Hofstede's study and similar investigations show is that there is no one correct way to lead people from across different cultures. The earlier discussion in this chapter on cultural intelligence highlights the importance of leaders having a strong sense of cultural awareness and sensitivity. Cultural differences can have very practical implications for an organisation in terms of people's perception of time (punctuality), personal space, communication, socialising and, in general, how people adapt to foreign assignments, as well as the level of company support that might be needed to help the employee adjust. Recognising the existence of intercultural differences is a useful starting point.

CONCLUSIONS

Leadership plays a vital role within organisations in giving them direction and in establishing strong values that will form the bedrock of organisational culture. Leadership is about inspiring and motivating others to work towards achieving organisational goals. It is quite separate from management. It is about doing the right thing. Unfortunately, in Ireland, as indeed across the globe, those that are entrusted with leadership do not always live up to the mark. Jim Collins's "Level 5 Leader" provides a useful framework for aspiring leaders. Central to all the functions of the leader is the ability to get the best from people. Trust is a vital element in achieving that. While there are many different types of organisational culture, the leader of an organisation must understand the nature of the dominant culture that exists in their company, and they must also ensure that the prevailing culture supports the company in achieving its goals.

SUMMARY

Leadership plays a vital role in the success of organisations. It is the catalyst for the entire strategy process from development through to implementation. Various theorists view leadership differently, some regarding it as a function of management, others as a separate function in its own right. Whatever way it is viewed, leadership requires very different skills compared to normal day-to-day management skills. While every leader displays a number of different traits, effective leadership is dependent on a number of different variables.

Leadership involves giving direction to organisations. There is an important distinction between **leadership** and **management**: managers do things right; leaders do the right thing. Leadership is concerned primarily with inspiring and motivating others at every level in the organisation.

Early studies on leadership focused on traits, which generally included qualities such as intelligence, vision, self-confidence, initiative, lateral thinking, the need for power and achievement, and being goal-directed. Behavioural theories looked at the way leaders act. The Ohio State University study and the University of Michigan studies examined leadership styles that were based on either getting the task completed or a focus on the employees. Another theory by Blake and Mouton (1962) developed the 'Managerial Grid' to determine the one best style of leadership. Again, using two dimensions, it sought to measure leadership style.

Later studies saw that **context** was also an important element in leadership – different situations require different styles. Fielder's model looked at the leadership style and the situation context to come up with the most effective style. House's theory examined the role that goals play in **motivation**, and how leaders can help employees achieve organisational goals.

Charismatic leadership has a profound effect on employees, is responsible for appealing to their values and beliefs, and gives them a sense of direction. In reality, examples are rare and there is conflicting evidence as to the effectiveness of this style. In contrast, Level 5 leaders are self-effacing and shy, with a paradoxical blend of personal humility and professional will.

There are a number of **functions** that leaders can perform in organisations. Effective leaders are those that understand the nature of the change affecting their organisation and can transform it in such a way as to create competitive advantage.

Those leading the organisation should do so ethically and instil sound values that guide people in the decisions that they make.

Being able to pick the right **team** is a valuable competence required to implement a chosen strategy. Teams have to be built up and maintained, and different people will each have their own contribution to make to the team. **Development** occurs at both individual and organisational levels, and the two are interwoven.

A **learning organisation** is one that has a culture that supports challenging assumptions around a common vision and one that is capable of regeneration through continuous learning by its members.

Leadership is also a catalyst for establishing and maintaining the **culture** of the organisation. Good strategy must be supported by an appropriate culture as it underpins all aspects of the process and guides people in the decisions that are made.

Every organisation will have its own individual culture. **Organisational culture** is defined by Schein as "a pattern of shared basic assumptions learned by a group as it solved its problems of external adaptation and internal integration, which has worked well enough to be considered valid, and therefore to be taught to new members as the correct way to perceive, think and feel in relation to those problems".

It can be observed in organisations at three different levels:

- **Artefacts** – aspects of the culture that are visible to outsiders;
- **Espoused beliefs** – the values that members hold and use to guide their decisions; and
- **Basic assumptions** – the unconscious, taken-for-granted beliefs held by people in the organisation.

There is no universally accepted way of classifying organisational culture. Different approaches examined in the chapter include:

1. **Handy's Four Types** which draws together structure and culture
2. **Miles and Snow typology** examines the link between culture and the strategy being pursued
3. **Peters and Waterman's Excellence Model** – the link between organisational culture and the success of the organisation
4. **Thompson *et al.*** classify culture according to its strength and influence
5. **Management philosophy** regards the culture of an organisation as a function of the underlying philosophy of management

While most studies on culture focus on the organisation as a whole, it is also quite common to have **subcultures** within the organisation that represent different groups and geographical divisions. Sometimes these subcultures support the dominant culture but, on other occasions, they can work to undermine it. Mergers and acquisitions provide a major challenge for organisations when it comes to reconciling different cultures.

Culture serves a number of important **functions** in organisations. It gives people a sense of identity and belonging. It also provides a stable social structure for people to work together, and it can help them make sense of the environment within which they are working.

The culture of an organisation is established initially by its founder, and there are a number of primary and secondary embedding mechanisms that can be used to perpetuate the culture. The example given by managers is of vital importance. So too is the **socialisation** process by which the culture of an organisation is passed on to new members. There are three phases: pre-employment socialisation, the encounter, and adaption. Clear communication plays a pivotal role in this process.

Identifying an organisation's culture can be a very difficult process, but Johnson *et al.* suggest using a **cultural web** to show the "behavioural, physical and symbolic manifestations of a culture". It involves examining the routines and rituals; the symbols; power; organisational structures; and the control systems.

Intercultural differences can pose many difficulties for managers in dealing with staff members from different national and ethnic groups. It requires a much greater awareness of such differences and an ability to bring people together to achieve common goals.

For those who wish to read more on different topics discussed in this chapter, the following is a list of suggested readings.

For a contemporary exploration of the wide-ranging debates surrounding the relationships between business and society in 21ˢᵗ Century Ireland read:

Hogan, J. et al.	2010	*Irish Business and Society: Governing, participating and transforming in the 21st Century*	Dublin	Gill & Macmillan

For enduring insights on leadership from the Drucker Foundation:

Hesselbein, F. and Cohen, P	1999	*Leader to Leader*	New York	Jossey-Bass

For a practical and accessible guide for talent development in organisations:

Stewart, J. and Rigg, C.	2011	*Learning and Talent Development*	London	CIPD

For a comprehensive view of organisational culture and leadership:

Schein, E.	2010	*Organisational Culture and Leadership* 4th ed.	San Francisco	Jossey-Bass

There is a wide selection of books that will provide the reader with an understanding of the business and political events that have led both directly and indirectly to the current state of the country:

Carswell, S.	2006	*Something Rotten: Irish Banking Scandals.*	Dublin	Gill & Macmillan
Cooper, M.	2009	*Who really runs Ireland: The story of the elite who led Ireland from bust to boom… and back again*	Dublin	Penguin Ireland
Creaton, S. and O'Cleary, C.	2002	*Panic at the Bank: How John Rusnak lost AIB $691,000,000*	Dublin	Gill & Macmillan
Leahy, P.	2009	*Showtime: The inside story of Fianna Fáil in power*	Dublin	Penguin Ireland
Lyons, T. and Carey, B.	2011	*The Fitzpatrick Tapes: The rise and fall of one man, one bank and one country.*	Dublin	Penguin Ireland
Murphy, D. and Devlin, M.	2009	*Banksters: How a powerful elite squandered Ireland's wealth*	Dublin	Hatchette Books
O'Toole, F.	2009	*Ship of Fools: How stupidity and corruption sank the Celtic Tiger*	London	Faber & Faber Ltd
O'Toole, F.	2010	*Enough is enough: How to build a new Republic*	London	Faber & Faber Ltd
Ross, S.	2009	*The Bankers: How the banks brought Ireland to its knees*	Dublin	Penguin Ireland
Ross, S. and Webb, N.	2010	*Wasters: The people who squander your taxes on white-elephant projects, international junkets and favours for their mates – and how they get away with it*	Dublin	Penguin Ireland

Suggested further reading on the expeditions to the South Pole

Alexandre, C.	1998	*The Endurance: Shackleton's Legendary Antarctic Exhibition*	New York	Alfred A. Knopf
Heacox, K.	1999	*Shackleton: The Antarctic Challenge*	Washington	National Geographic
Hurley, F.	2001	*South With Endurance: Shackleton's Antarctic Expedition 1914–1917. The Photographs of Frank Hurley*	London	Bloomsbury
Lansing, A.	1959	*Endurance: Shackleton's Incredible Voyage*	New York	Carroll & Graf
Nugent, F.	2003	*Seek the Frozen Lands: Irish Explorers 1740–1922*	Cork	The Collins Press
Smith, M.	2000	*An Unsung Hero: Tom Crean – Antarctic Survivor*	Cork	The Collins Press

DISCUSSION QUESTIONS

1. Discuss the role that power plays in leadership.
2. Distinguish between leadership and management.
3. Critically analyse the relevance of emotional intelligence as a necessary trait in leaders.
4. Discuss the nature of leadership in organisations and state whether you think leadership exists only at the top of the organisation or if it is reflected at all levels.
5. Explore the role that leaders play in supporting organisational culture.

REFERENCES

Adair, J., 1983, *Effective Leadership*, Aldershot, Gower

Alexandre, C., 1998, *The Endurance: Shackleton's Legendary Antarctic Voyage*, New York, Alfred A. Knopf

Argyris, C. and Schon, D., 1978, *Organisational Learning: A Theory of Action Perspective*, Wokingham, Addison-Wesley

Barney, J.B., 1986, "Organisational Culture: Can it be a source of sustained competitive advantage?", *Academy of Management Review*, Vol. 11, Issue 3, pp.656–665

Bass, B., 1990, "From Transactional to Transformational Leadership: Learning to Share the Vision", *Organizational Dynamics*, Winter, 1990, p.22

Benis, W. and Nanus, B., 1985, *Leaders: The Strategies for Taking Charge*, New York, Harper and Row

Berton, E., 2010, "Dress to impress, UBS tells staff", *The Wall Street Journal*, 14 December 2010, http://online.wsj.com/article/SB10001424052748704694004576019783931381042.html?mod=djemTMB_t, Accessed 21 February 2011

Bohan, H., 2009, "A new kind of leadership now required", *The Irish Times*, 06 October 2009, p.14

Brousseau, K. *et al.*, 2006, "The seasoned executive's decision-making style", *Harvard Business Review*, February 2006, Vol.84, Issue 2, pp.110–121

Brown, A., 1994, "Transformational Leadership in Tackling Technical Change", *Journal of General Management*, Vol. 19, Issue 4, pp.1–10

Buelens, M. *et al.*, 2006, *Organisational Behaviour*, 3rd Ed., Maidenhead, McGraw-Hill

Collins, J., 2001, *Good to Great,* London, Random House Business Books

Cooper, M., 2009, *Who really runs Ireland?*, Dublin, Penguin Ireland

CSO (Central Statistics Office, Ireland), 2010, http://www.cso.ie/Quicktables/GetQuickTables. aspx?FileName=TRDA1.asp&TableName=Overseas Visits to and from Ireland&StatisticalProduct=DB_TM, Accessed 30 January 2011

Early, P.C. and Mosakowski, E., 2004, "Cultural Intelligence", *Harvard Business Review*, October 2004, Vol.82, Issue 10, pp.139–146

ESRI, 2010, *Quarterly Economic Commentary,* Winter 2010, Dublin, ESRI

Feldman, D., 1981, "The Multiple Socialisation of Organisation Members", *Academy of Management Review*, April 1981, pp.309–18

French, J. and Raven, B., 1959, "The Basis of Social Power", in *Studies in Social Power*, Ed. Cartwright, D., Michigan, University of Michigan Press

Goleman, D., 1995, *Emotional Intelligence*, London, Bloomsbury

Goleman, D. *et al.*, 2002, *The New Leaders*, London, Little, Brown

Hamm, J., 2006, "The Five Messages Leaders Must Manage", *Harvard Business Review*, May 2006, Vol. 84, Issue 5, pp.115–123

Handy, C., 1999, *Understanding Organisations*, London, Penguin

Harrison, R., 1972, "Understanding your organisation's character", *Harvard Business Review*, May-June 1972, Vol. 50, Issue 3, pp.119–128

Honohan, P., 2010, *The Irish Banking Crisis, Regulatory and Financial Stability Policy 2003-2008*, Dublin, Central Bank of Ireland

House, R., 1971, "A Path-goal Theory of Leader Effectiveness", *Administrative Science Quarterly*,16 September 1971, pp.321–338

Johnson, G. et al., 2011, *Exploring Corporate Strategy,* 9th Ed., Harlow, Pearson Education Ltd

Kanter, R.M., 1989, *When Giants Learn to Dance*, London, Simon & Schuster

Katzenbach, J. and Smith, D., 1993, *The Wisdom of Teams: Creating the High-PerformanceOrganisation*, New York, HarperBusiness

Ket de Vries, M., 2001, *The Leadership Mystique*, London, Financial Times. Prentice Hall

Kouzes, J. and Posner, B., 1995, *The Leadership Challenge*, San Francisco, Jossey-Bass

Lavery, B. and O'Brien, T., 2005, "Insurers' trails lead to Dublin", *The New York Times*, http://query.nytimes.com/gst/fullpage.html?res=9805EED9103FF932A35757C0A9639C8B63, Accessed 30 January 2011

Leahy, P., 2009, *Showtime: The Inside Story of Fianna Fáil in Power*, Dublin, Penguin Ireland

Likert, R., 1961, *New Patterns of Management*, New York, McGraw-Hill

Lyons, T. and Carey, B., 2011, *The Fitzpatrick Tapes: The Rise and Fall of One Man, One Bank and One Country*, Dublin, Penguin Ireland

Margolis, J. and Stoltz, P., 2010, "How to Bounce Back from Adversity", *Harvard Business Review*, January/February 2010, Vol. 88, Issue 1, pp.86–92

Martin, J., 2005, *Organizational Behaviour,* 3rd Ed., London, Thomson

Martin, J. and Schmidt, C., 2010, "How to keep your Top Talent", *Harvard Business Review*, May 2010, Vol. 88, Issue 5, pp.51–61

McShane, S. and Von Glinow, M. A., 2009, *Organisational Behaviour*, 2nd Ed., New York, McGraw-Hill

Miles, R. and Snow, C., 1978, *Organisational Strategy, Structure and Process*, New York, McGraw-Hill

Murphy, Y. *et al.*, 2009, *Report into the Catholic Archdiocese of Dublin*, Dublin, The Stationery Office

Nugent, F., 2003, *Seek the Frozen Land*, Cork, Collins Press

O'Brien, J. and Marakas, G., 2008, *Management Information Systems*, 8th Ed., New York, McGraw-Hill

O'Donovan, H., 2009, "CRAIC - A model suitable for Irish coaching psychology", *The Coaching Psychologist*, December 2009, Vol. 5, Issue 2

O'Toole, F., 2009, *Ship of Fools: How Stupidity and Corruption Sank the Celtic Tiger*, London, Faber and Faber Ltd

Peters, TJ. and Waterman, R.H., 1982, *In Search of Excellence: Lessons from America's Best-run Companies*, New York, Harper & Row

Pocock, T., 1987, *Horatio Nelson*, London, Brockhampton Press

Prahalad, C.K., 2010, "The Responsible Manager", *Harvard Business Review*, January/February 2010, Vol. 88, Issue 1, p.36

Press, G., 1990, "Assessing competitors' business philosophies", *Long Range Planning*, October 1990, Vol. 23, Issue 5

Regling, K. and Watson, M., 2010, "A preliminary report on the sources of Ireland's banking crisis", Dublin, Government Publications Office

Ross, S., 2009, *The Bankers: How the banks brought Ireland to its knees*, Dublin, Penguin Ireland

Ross, S. and Webb, N., 2010, *Wasters*, Dublin, Penguin Ireland

Ryan, S.*et al.*, 2009, *The Commission to Inquire into Child Abuse*, Dublin, Government Publications Office

Schein, E., 2011, *Organisational Culture and Leadership*, 4th Ed., San Francisco, Jossey-Bass

Senge, P., 1990, *The Fifth Discipline: The Art and Practice of the Learning Organisation*, London, Doubleday

Smircich, L., 1983, "Concepts of Culture and Organisational Analysis", *Administrative Science Quarterly*, September 1983, Vol.28, Issue 3, pp.339–58

Smith, M., 2000, *An Unsung Hero*, Cork, Collins Press

Stewart, J. and Rigg, C., 2011, *Learning and Talent Development*, London, CIPD

Stewart, T.A., 1999, "The Conquest for Welch's Throne Begins: Who Will Run GE?", *Fortune*, 11 January 1999, p.27

Stogdill, R. and Coons, A., 1957, *Leader Behaviour: Its Description and Measurement*, Columbus, Ohio, Ohio State University Press, Bureau of Business Research

Stogdill, R.M., 1948, "Personal Factors Associated With Leadership: A Survey of the Literature", *Journal of Psychology*, 1948, pp.35–71

The Economist, 2011, "Irish Mist", *The Economist*, 19 February 2011, p.14

Tiernan, S. *et al.*, 2006, *Modern Management: Theory and Practice for Irish students*, 3rd Ed., Dublin, Gill & Macmillan

Trompenaars, F. and Hampton-Turner, C., 1998, *Riding the Waves of Culture: Understanding Cultural Diversity in Global Business*, 2nd Ed., New York, McGraw-Hill

Vroom, V., 1964, *Work and Motivation*, New York, John Wiley & Sons

Welch, J., 2001, *Jack: What I've Learned Leading a Great Company and Great People*, London, Headline

Whole Foods Market, 2011, www.wholefoodsmarket.com/values/, (accessed 11 February 2011)

Vision, Mission, Goals and Objectives

LEARNING OBJECTIVES

On completion of this chapter, you will be able to:

- Analyse the different elements of a company's vision
- Differentiate between a company's vision and its mission
- Assess the importance of goals and objectives for an organisation and be able to distinguish between them
- Using the Balanced Scorecard, identify suitable goals and objectives for an organisation

"Nurture your mind with great thoughts, for you will never go any higher than what you think."

Benjamin Disraeli

INTRODUCTION

Leadership plays a vital role in organisations. It is the leader who sets the scene within which all those in the organisation work together to achieve their purpose. But what is that purpose and how is it shared throughout the organisation?

In *Alice's Adventures in Wonderland*, when Alice asks the Cheshire Cat in which direction she should go, the Cat advises her:

"That depends a great deal on where you want to get to."

Every organisation needs direction and if you don't know where you are going, any road will take you there. This chapter distinguishes between the vision and mission of an organisation and how goals and objectives are set. This is a vital part of strategy formulation. If the organisation is not clear about these essential elements of its foundation, it will not succeed for very long in a competitive environment. Yet, it would appear that there is a lack of clarity among many organisations about the concepts that are examined in this chapter.

A company's vision concerns its long-term future direction. What company would it like to be, in say 10 years' time? This vision will guide the company through difficult times and keep it focused. The vision consists of the values and purpose of the organisation, and it is driven by leadership at the top. They are all interlinked.

The mission works hand-in-hand with the vision. The essential difference is that the mission is more concerned with the here and now. What type of company is it currently and what does it do? Every organisation will have resources to support its strategies. These resources are scarce and expensive, and they must be used to maximum effect. Goals and objectives are not set in isolation, but are formulated to help the process of using those resources to fulfil the mission in the most efficient manner possible. Goals are broad, general statements of intent, in line with the mission, and are usually qualitative in nature. Objectives are also statements of intent but are much more specific in terms of the desired outcomes.

Illustration 3.1: Differentiating Vision, Mission, Goals and Objectives

Vision
A Vision is the desired end-state of an organisation, which consists of its values and purpose, underpinned by leadership and expressed in motivating terms to inspire its members. Achieving the vision is a long-term process that will stretch the capabilities of the organisation.

Mission
A Mission guides the members of an organisation in making decisions that will achieve strategic goals and objectives.

Goals
Goals are a broad general statement of intent in line with the mission, focused on achieving a certain outcome, and they are usually *qualitative* in nature. A goal may have a number of objectives emanating from it.

Objectives
Objectives are also statements of intent but are much more specific in terms of the desired outcomes to be achieved. They are, generally speaking, *quantitative* in nature.

VISION

Jonathan Swift described vision as:

"The art of seeing what is invisible to others."

Companies should differentiate between the need for a constant focus on what the company is trying to achieve, while retaining flexibility to respond as circumstances change. Chapter 1 examined the concept of emergent strategies and the difficulty in strategic planning because of rapidly changing circumstances. What links that long-term focus and the challenges that currently exist is vision. According to Kotter (1996), developing a vision plays a major part in leading change (see also Chapter 14).

Collins and Porras (1996) found that companies that have taken the time to craft a proper vision have outperformed the general stock market by a factor of 12 since 1925: "Companies that enjoy enduring success have core values and a core purpose that remain fixed, while their business strategies and practices endlessly adapt to a changing world."

Collins and Porras regard a well-conceived vision as consisting of two major components:

- A **Core Ideology** consisting of core values and core purpose – what the company stands for and why it exists; and
- **Envisioned Future** – what the company aspires to become; where long-term objectives are set (what they refer to as "Bhags" – "Big Hairy Audacious Goals") and how these objectives are communicated to all concerned. This is, in effect, a vision statement.

Thompson *et al.* (2008: 22) outline the characteristics of an effectively worded strategic vision. It should be:

- Graphic – paint a picture of the kind of company management want it to be.
- Directional – forward-looking; charting the strategic course.
- Focused – specific enough to guide actions without being prescriptive.
- Feasible – the company should be able to achieve it, within the time frame.
- Desirable – in the interest of stakeholders.
- Easy to communicate – preferably summed up in a simple statement.

The environment for many industries is changing at an ever-increasing rate, making long-term planning, in particular, extremely difficult. As a result, companies have to be flexible and adaptable when opportunities arise. Without vision, companies could take the wrong direction. Vision enables organisations to spot opportunities as they arise and provides the end goal for effort. There are many ways of achieving that end goal, and those methods will change as circumstances unfold. Essentially,

Illustration 3.2: PulseLearning

An example of a successful technology company, PulseLearning was one of the Ernst & Young 'Entrepreneur of the Year' finalists in 2006. It was also voted Deloitte Fastest Growing Technology Company in 2007. Jim Breen, CEO of PulseLearning, is very clear about the importance of having a vision. "The vision of PulseLearning is to be the number one e-learning technology company in the world in its chosen markets." For a company in the Southwest of Ireland, operating in a global market, this may seem an unrealistic aspiration. Yet, when one examines the meteoric rise of companies like Microsoft and Dell, people could have said the same about them. As the winner of numerous awards in its sector, PulseLearning is well on the way to achieving its vision. As G.B. Shaw said:

"You see things and ask why: I dream of things that never were and ask why not."

PulseLearning believes their vision should be shared by all the employees of the company throughout the world, and it is through this shared vision that the company will achieve the level of growth required to become the number one e-learning company in its chosen market.

Source: Interview with CEO Jim Breen

however, vision is about creating an environment in which managers at every level can work in harmony towards agreed objectives, rather than about the nuts and bolts of every decision.

One of the most famous quotations (indeed it is usually mis-quoted) regarding vision statements was made in 1993 by Louis Gerstner, the then newly-appointed CEO of the computing giant IBM:

"There's been a lot of speculation as to when I'm going to deliver a vision for IBM, and what I'd like to say to all of you is that the last thing IBM needs right now is a vision."

Gerstner's statement made great copy in the business press. However, he claims he was quoted out of context. In his autobiography he states:

"A lot of reporters dropped the words 'right now' from my vision statement when they reported my stories. And so they had me saying that 'the last thing IBM needs is a vision'. That was inaccurate ... I said we didn't need a vision right now because I discovered in my first ninety days on the job that IBM had file drawers full of vision statements."

While Gerstner had a drawer full of vision statements when he took over the company in 1993, there were many critical operational challenges facing IBM that had to be dealt with as a matter of urgency. By March 1996, having turned his attention to the most pressing issues, he was then in a position to look to where the company was heading in the future. The emphasis could now shift from urgent, pressing issues to a more long-term focus. As with all companies, IBM's long-term effort needed clear direction: "What IBM needs most right now is a vision" (Gerstner, 2002).

Benefits of a Vision

Vision plays a very important role in business. First and foremost, having a vision for a company provides its senior executives with a clear and shared understanding of where the organisation is going over the long term. This will inevitably impact on the decisions that are made, which correspond with achieving that vision. Vision also serves as a guiding light for the entire organisation, both in terms of lower-level managers setting departmental objectives, and in terms of employees buying into the process. Finally, vision will guide the organisation through inevitable periods of change and uncertainty.

Components of an Organisation's Vision

Collins and Porras (1996) spoke of the core ideology consisting of values and purpose. One essential element of a vision that they did not discuss is the driving force behind it – the leadership required to give the process energy and direction. Therefore, building on the framework provided by Collins and Porras, it can be argued that there are three essential components of an organisation's vision:

- Leadership
- Values
- Purpose

Leadership

Leadership, values and purpose together constitute the organisation's vision. Chapter 2 examined leadership in detail. In particular, it examined the role of leadership in creating and promoting values. It can be seen from **Figure 3.1** below that leadership, values and purpose are all integral components of vision. Leadership is discussed in this context in regard to how it drives and supports the other two elements of a company's vision – values and purpose. Values and purpose do not exist in isolation. Leadership plays a very important part in the process of building and sustaining the values and purpose of the organisation. **Illustration 3.4** (see below) examines the Johnson & Johnson 'Credo' – the stated values of the Johnson & Johnson company. It will be seen that the Credo was developed by Robert Johnson, the then-CEO of the company, who was setting

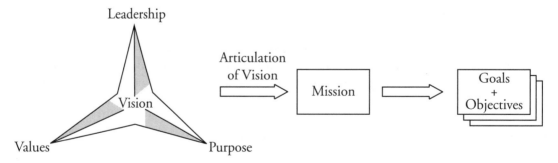

Figure 3.1 *Illustrates the three elements of a vision, and the relationship between an organisation's vision, its mission and its goals and objectives.*

out his stall as chief executive with regard to the type of corporate values that he thought were important for the company to practise in its dealings with all its stakeholders. Other functions of leadership that were discussed in Chapter 2 are also relevant here, namely, building teams of people that are culturally compatible with the values and purpose of the organisation, as well as developing individuals as future leaders who will ensure the continuity of the values and purpose of the organisation.

Building and sustaining a vision, by its nature, is a long-term process. Therefore, an important function of leadership is to maintain the level of motivation and commitment within the organisation, while simultaneously achieving the mission and objectives. In 1942, Winston Churchill was quick to recognise the importance of the victory at the battle of El Alamein, while at the same time keeping in sight the long struggle that the Allies still faced: "Now this is not the end. It is not even the beginning of the end. But it is, perhaps, the end of the beginning."

Perhaps the most important function that binds leadership and vision is the necessity to bring that vision to fruition. All of the other elements – values and purpose – can be present, but without leadership, the vision will not be realised:

"Leadership is the capacity to translate vision into reality."

Warren Bennis

Values

 Dose (1997) defined **values** as: "standards or criteria for choosing goals or guiding actions, and they are relatively enduring and stable over time".

While societal values are relatively enduring and stable, it is natural that they will evolve over time. The fact that values can evolve is important. Rokeach (1973) argues that social change would not take place if values were absolutely stable. On the other hand, if there were a lack of stability with regard to values then there would be no continuity in society. Each set of values ultimately reflects the society in which it exists.

Buelens *et al.* (2006: 91) distinguish between 'content' and 'intensity' when considering values. The content aspect relates to what people find important, while the intensity aspect deals with how those values are ranked according to their intensity — a value system that can be described as "an enduring organisation of beliefs concerning preferable modes of conduct or end-states of existence along a continuum of relative importance". It is generally accepted that people are not born with an internal set of values, but that they are acquired through a process of socialisation during their lifetime from a variety of sources including family, peers, school, work and national culture. Initially, values are learnt in isolation from each other in an absolute, all or nothing sense. As people mature, they learn to integrate these isolated values into a hierarchy of importance. Schwartz and Sagie (2000) consider that there are a number of value types that are common to most societies. This has obvious implications for global companies in terms of creating common values throughout their organisations.

Business organisations are social constructs. They are designed by people to enable them to work together to achieve collective goals. When the strategy of an organisation is being discussed, it must be remembered that it is the people in that organisation who develop its strategy. Consequently, when looking at values, it is important to recognise that there is a link between organisational values and individual values.

Ross *et al.* (1999) state that work values are expressions of basic values in the work setting and are ordered by their importance as guiding principles for evaluating work outcomes and settings, and for choosing among different work alternatives. Thus, corporate values ultimately reflect the personal values of those running the company. Ireland has become a multicultural country, and this can present challenges for organisations. Various cultures may differ in their values, but there will still be shared core values to which they can all aspire.

In turn, the values of an organisation will ultimately attract people whose personal values reflect those of the organisation. Examples of organisational values attracting like-minded people are aid agencies such as Goal or Concern. Each year, such organisations attract a wide variety of volunteer doctors, nurses, engineers and others, who often give up the opportunity to earn good salaries at home, operating in hostile physical conditions to alleviate the plight of their fellow human beings in the developing world. **Illustration 8.2** (see Chapter 8 below) gives the example of Isadore Sharp, CEO of Four Seasons Hotels and Resorts using a promotional video on the recruitment section of the company's Website. In the clip, he describes the culture and values of the organisation. For any potential new employee it sends out a clear message about the personal values that they are required to have: "It's not something they train for. This is the way they are brought up."

Values guide an organisation in its dealings with all its stakeholders. While values might be explicitly stated, they are ultimately of intrinsic value to the organisation and do not require any justification to outsiders. Each company will generate their own values. There is no right answer *per se*; what is important is that they have core values. Collins and Porras (1996) recommend having only a few – perhaps three or four – as only a few values can be truly core and define what is central to company beliefs.

Illustration 3.3: Diageo and its Stated Values

Diageo, the parent company of Guinness, defines its values thus:

"Diageo has placed these five values at the heart of our business. They are a critical element of our corporate strategy – influencing the way we work, every day and everywhere:

- **We are passionate about consumers** – our curiosity and consumer insights drive our growth. We cherish our brands; we are creative and courageous in pursuing their full potential. We are innovative, constantly searching for new ideas.

- **We value each other** – we seek and benefit from diverse people and perspectives. We strive to create mutually fulfilling relationships and partnerships.
- We are **proud of what we do** and how we do it – we behave responsibly with the highest standards of integrity.
- We give ourselves the **freedom to succeed** – we trust each other, we are open and seek challenge, and we respond quickly to the opportunities this creates.
- We strive to **be the best** – we are always learning, always improving. We set high standards, we stretch to exceed them and we celebrate success."

www.diageo.com

As guiding principles, values should be largely independent of the environment in which they operate. The acid test of a core value is if it would still be applied even if this meant that the company would be put at a competitive disadvantage. Perhaps one of the most famous examples of stated values being used to guide an organisation's actions is the Johnson & Johnson credo.

Illustration 3.4: The Johnson & Johnson 'Tylenol' Crisis

Established in 1884, Johnson & Johnson is a multinational manufacturer of pharmaceuticals, diagnostic, therapeutic and personal hygiene products, and a household name for many products such as talcum powder and sticking plasters.

They also make the pain reliever Tylenol®. It was with this product that the company showed the importance of the values embodied in their 'Credo' in guiding daily action. In 1982, the product was indirectly responsible for the death of seven people when some bottles containing the tablets were interfered with in a Chicago drugstore, and poison was inserted. At a cost of over $100 million, the company withdrew the product from the shelves until they were sure of the cause of the problem. In the process, they also developed the first tamper-proof containers for medicines. The action by Johnson & Johnson is still used as a case study on how a company should respond to a crisis. Over time, public confidence was restored, and the company more than made up for lost revenues.

First written in 1943 by Robert Wood Johnson, the Johnson & Johnson 'Credo' has been updated slightly from time to time. The company has used this Credo for over 60 years to guide their daily decision-making. They describe the Credo as:

"A set of values that we live by, we work by. It is the North Star, the guiding light, the foundation of Johnson & Johnson and everything we stand for and everything we are."

The Credo identifies four types of stakeholders:

- The company's first responsibility is to "the doctors, nurses and patients, to mothers and fathers and all others who use our products or services…
- "We are responsible to our employees, the men and women who work with us throughout the world. Everyone must be considered an individual. We must respect their dignity and recognise their merit…
- "We are responsible to the communities in which we live and work and to the world community as well. We must be good citizens…
- Robert Wood Johnson and his successors in managing the business have believed that, if the Credo's first three responsibilities are met, shareholders will be well served.

www.Johnson&Johnson.com

Rosabeth Moss Kanter believes that values are truly a primary consideration which help companies find business opportunities and motivate employees and partners. They require "the serious nurturing of hearts and minds." Once people are in agreement as to what their collective values are, they can then make decisions independently. Kanter believes that there are many benefits for companies with embedded values:

- It helps integration, which in turn permits collaboration among diverse people
- It enables the transfer of knowledge and technical innovation
- It assists in post-merger integration
- Values allow people to make consistent decisions, even under pressure

Values can be a strong motivational tool that provide people with a basis of engagement with their work, a sense of membership in their organisation and stability during change.

Sam Palmisano, the CEO of IBM, considers values to be of absolute importance to an organisation: "Management is temporary; returns are cyclical. But if we use these values as connective tissue, that has longevity. If people can get emotionally connected and have pride in the entity's success, they will do what is important to IBM." (Kantor, 2008)

Many organisations will have espoused values. Stating values is one thing, but practising them is another. Enron had espoused corporate values including respect, integrity, communication and excellence, yet displayed very different values in its actions. (Enacted values reflect the actual values that employees demonstrate in the workplace.) In the case of Enron, greed took over and a number of senior executives were involved in 'creative accounting', which gave investors and staff alike the impression that the company was doing extremely well. However, huge debts were allowed to mount up, and the company was eventually put under Federal investigation and declared bankrupt in Autumn 2001. Many of the senior executives were found guilty of fraud and were given jail sentences. The chairman and former CEO Kenneth Lay was found guilty, but died of a heart attack in prison while awaiting sentencing. He had taken over $300 million from Enron. The accounting firm Arthur Andersen was the firm's auditors and were found to be complicit in the cover-up of Enron's accounting procedures. Tons of paper documents were shredded by Andersen to hide their role in the affair from investigators. The firm collapsed in 2002.

In conclusion, the values of a company should underpin the actions of all members of the organisation and be exemplified by its leaders.

Purpose

The third element of a vision is purpose. The Irish playwright, George Bernard Shaw wrote in *Man and Superman*:

> "This is the true joy in life: being used for a purpose recognised by yourself as a mighty one; being a true force of Nature instead of a feverish little clod of ailments and grievances complaining that the world will not devote itself to making you happy. I am of the opinion that my life belongs to the whole community, and as long as I live, it is my privilege to do for it whatever I can. I want to be thoroughly used up when I die. For the harder I work, the more I live. I rejoice in life for its own sake. Life is no brief candle to me; it's a sort of splendid torch which I've got to hold up for the moment and I want to make it burn as brightly as possible before handing it on to future generations."

It might seem a little incongruous quoting Shaw in a text about corporate strategy. However, organisations as well as individuals need a sense of purpose. Purpose is the organisation's *raison d'être*. While business objectives will change, Collins and Porras (1996) suggest that you cannot fulfil the organisation's purpose; it is like a guiding light on the horizon, forever pursued but never reached. While the purpose itself does not change, it inspires change.

Many companies describe their mission statement as their purpose. However, the purpose *precedes* the mission. The mission statement may embody the purpose (as we shall see later), but there is a fundamental difference between discovering the organisation's purpose and its public manifestation in a mission statement. The importance of purpose in an organisation is illustrated in Collins and Porras's (1996) quote from David Packard in a speech to the employees in HP in 1960:

> "I want to discuss why a company exists in the first place. In other words, why are we here? I think many people assume, wrongly that a company exists to make money. While this is an important result of a company's existence, we have to go deeper and find the real reasons for our being. As we investigate this, we inevitably come to the conclusion that a group of people get together and exist as an institution that we call a company so that they are able to accomplish something collectively that they could not accomplish separately – they make a contribution to society..."

This is as relevant today as it was 50 years ago. According to Mourkogiannis (2006), purpose both drives a company forward and helps build sustainable advantage. Purpose becomes "the engine of the company". Collins and Porras (1996) believe that a purpose should not be descriptive in terms of its current product lines. For the Sony Corporation it is not about televisions or PlayStations, it is: "to experience the joy of advancing and applying technology for the benefits of the public". For the American company 3M it is: "to solve unsolved problems innovatively". The best way of developing purpose is the '**five whys**'. Start with the descriptive statement: we make X products or we deliver X services, and then ask, why is that important? Then repeat the process five times. After a few whys, you will get down to the fundamental purpose of the organisation. Core purpose is not about the maximisation of shareholder wealth. As Peter Drucker pointed out in his 1954 book *The Practice of Management*: "The purpose of a business is to create and keep a customer". If the focus is only on the creation of wealth, the customer will not be looked after, and business will decline, taking wealth along with it. The collapse of the Irish banking industry is raw proof of this. In the absolute pursuit of profit maximisation, Irish banks lost focus of their purpose and their customers, and were ultimately the architects of their own downfall. A primary function of core purpose is to inspire, and not many people in the organisation will be inspired by a purpose based on maximisation of shareholder wealth. Many people in business are wealthy beyond their dreams and still remain passionate about their work. For others, wealth does not come into it. As Peter Drucker pointed out, the best and most dedicated people are ultimately volunteers, for they have the opportunity to do something else with their lives.

From Vision to Strategic Intent

The vision of the company consists of its values and purpose and is driven by those leading the organisation. In order to achieve this envisioned future, the company must translate the vision into a more tangible form. Collins and Porras (1996) refer to the second component of the vision framework as being the **envisioned future** consisting of a 10- to 30-year audacious goal and a **vivid description** of what it would be like to achieve that goal. In many ways, however, these are just the articulation of the organisation's vision rather than being an integral part of it. There is a saying that every journey of a thousand miles begins with the first step. In reaching for this envisioned future, there will be many steps to be taken along the way. It is the function of those leading the company to decide on what the priorities should be and to galvanise the entire organisation behind the process. The process of striving towards the envisioned future is often referred to as 'Strategic Intent'.

Definition According to Hamel and Prahalad (2005): "**Strategic Intent** envisions a desired leadership position and establishes the criterion the organisation will use to chart its progress".

They first coined the phrase in 1989 when they compared how Western and Japanese companies attained their long-term goals. Japanese companies, they argued, developed among their employees the desire to succeed and maintained it by spreading the vision of global leadership. Rather than setting goals to fit their resources, Japanese companies developed 'stretch targets' that forced them to innovate, and so succeed on world markets. They cite a number of Japanese examples, such as Komatsu taking on Caterpillar, and Canon taking on Xerox, and succeeding to become world players. One of the big differences was that Western companies tailored their ambitions to fit their resources while Japanese companies had leveraged their resources to achieve seemingly impossible goals. They invested heavily in core competences (see Chapter 6) as well as in product-market units.

With these Japanese companies, their strategic intent is stable over time and so, in terms of formulating strategy, it lengthens the organisation's attention span rather than just focusing on the here and now. It also sets a target that deserves personal effort and commitment, not in direct terms of contribution to shareholder wealth, but indirectly towards global leadership. The latter has a much greater motivational impact on employees. In essence, strategic intent is more like a marathon than a 200-metre sprint. To be effective, management and staff must understand it and see the implications for their own jobs. Hamel and Prahalad (2005: 153) suggest that there are a number of challenges that face management:

- Creating a sense of urgency throughout the organisation
- Developing a competitor focus at every level of the company through widespread use of competitive intelligence (hard information about what approach other companies are taking in the market place)
- Providing employees with the skills they need to work effectively. This should be an on-going process
- Giving the organisation time to digest one challenge before launching another
- Establishing clear milestones and review mechanisms (discussed later in this chapter)

The process of developing strategic intent involves a different approach with an emphasis on engaging employees emotionally and intellectually in the development of new skills and in reciprocal responsibility for competitiveness. They believe that cost reductions are achieved not through lower wages but from better working methods developed by employees. A winning strategy is achieved by creating tomorrow's competitive advantages quicker than competitors can copy the ones your company possesses today. This requires a constant focus on innovation, building layers of competitive advantage over time, exploiting areas that competitors are not immediately concerned with; changing the terms of engagement (here Hamel and Prahalad cite how Kodak and IBM tried to take on Xerox, but it was Canon who changed the rules of engagement by standardising machines and components to reduce costs and selling through office product dealers rather than trying to match Xerox's huge sales force); and finally, through licensing, outsourcing agreements and joint ventures (see also Chapter 11).

Thompson *et al.* (2008: 33) describe strategic intent thus:

> "A company exhibits strategic intent when it relentlessly pursues an ambitious strategic objective, concentrating the full force of its resources and competitive actions on achieving that objective."

Ambitious companies that establish exceptionally bold strategic objectives, and have an unshakable commitment to achieving them, almost invariably begin with strategic intents that are out of proportion to their current capabilities. Starbucks' strategic intent is to make the Starbucks brand the world's most recognised and respected brand. In 1987, the company had nine stores in Seattle; it has grown each year since, and currently has over 15,000 stores worldwide.

John Lonergan (2006) the Governor of Mountjoy Prison in Dublin stated at a Social Care conference in Tralee that: "Vision without action is a daydream. Action without vision is a nightmare." An integral part of the process of developing a vision for every type of organisation is developing long-term goals that will translate the vision into reality. This process of creating 'audacious goals' (goals that will stretch the organisation) is about giving practical reality to strategic intent.

These long-term goals can be a narrative description of the general long-term direction – articulating the vision of the company. There is also a need for management to spell out precisely the short-, medium- and long-term strategies to achieve the vision, so that employees can play a meaningful part in helping the organisation achieve its goals. This cannot be achieved if people do not understand the strategy. The Balanced Scorecard (see below) helps achieve this by explaining precisely what is required.

Illustration 3.5: Long-term Goals – The Apollo Programme

One example of an audacious goal was the American Apollo space programme. President Kennedy, in his address to Congress on 25 May 1961, stated that the US would land a man on the Moon before the decade was out. This caught everyone (including NASA!) by surprise. However, it has to be seen in the context of the time. The Russians had beaten the US in the space race by launching the first spacecraft to orbit the earth when the cosmonaut Yuri Gagarin circled the earth on 21 April 1961. This was happening at the height of the Cold War, and the defence of the West was predicated on technological superiority, and missile technology in particular. The US had to increase spending dramatically (estimated at the time to be $40 billion (Daller, 2003)). It resulted in an intense focus on the space programme, and one that caught the popular imagination. There is an anecdotal story told of President Kennedy visiting NASA some time later. During his tour of the space centre, he asked one elderly gentleman (whose job it was to keep the toilets clean) what his role was in the centre. Straightening his back, he said proudly: "Mr President, I am helping put a man on the Moon". A number of years later on 21 July 1969, Apollo 11 landed on the Moon and Neil Armstrong uttered the famous words: "One small step for man, one giant leap for mankind".

When Jack Welch became CEO of General Electric he set the objective for the company to "become number one or number two in every market we serve and revolutionise this company to have the strengths of a big company combined with the leanness and agility of a small company" (Welch, 2001). In 1984, Michael Dell started Dell computers with $1,000, and the company rapidly grew. By 1990, he set a long-range objective for the company to become one of the top three PC companies in the world. By 1998, he had achieved his target and, by 2005, Dell Computers was the number one seller of PCs worldwide.

Sharing the Vision

A vital part of the process of achieving a vision is getting others to buy into the process – getting them to picture what the organisation will look like when vision has been achieved. Covey (1994: 97) suggests that we "begin with the end in mind" – and work backwards to where we are currently at". This involves describing that vision and then deciding what needs to be done to achieve it. That vision has to be shared with everyone in the organisation and their support for the process galvanised. President Kennedy's inauguration speech in January 1961 – "…The torch has been passed to a new generation of Americans… tempered by war, disciplined by a hard and bitter peace" – was an exhortation that appealed to their sense of patriotism and duty: "And so my fellow Americans: ask not what your country can do for you – ask what you can do for your country."

Two years later, the civil rights leader Martin Luther King Jr (1963) delivered perhaps one of the most famous vision statements of all time in his "I have a dream" speech. Repetition is a powerful oratorical tool, and in his speech, King used the word 'dream' 10 times. His speech is a very powerful vision of society without racial prejudice and conflict. It is a speech with vision which he relates back to the dream of freedom in the Declaration of Independence: "They were signing a promissory note to which every American was to fall heir. This note was a promise that all men, yes black men as well as white men, would be guaranteed the unalienable rights of life, liberty and the pursuit of happiness…".

It is a speech with values, with encouragement, with urgency. It is a speech that recognises the problem of racial inequality, and the enormity of the struggle. It is a vision laced with hope for a better future: "I have a dream that one day this nation will rise up and live out the true meaning of its creed: we hold these truths to be self-evident that all men are created equal. I have a dream…"

America has come a long way, and while further progress needs to be made, who would have thought that a black senator from Illinois would be inaugurated President of the United States in January 2009?

Other vision statements are much shorter, such as Henry Ford's vision of a car for every family. The Model T Ford was the first mass-produced car in the US that was affordable to wage-earning people. A century later, Ryanair is achieving a similar vision in making air travel available to the ordinary person. For Nike it is: "To bring innovation and inspiration to every athlete in the world."

MISSION

There is a clear distinction between a strategic vision and a mission statement. In essence, a vision concerns the company's future business – where it is heading in the long term. A mission, on the other hand, defines the company's current business: "who we are, what we do and why we are here". In essence, the vision guides the mission, and the values and purpose described in the vision will often be reflected in the mission statement. It is important that the company gives a great deal of consideration to defining the mission because, in turn, the mission guides the selection of goals and objectives. The mission, therefore, gives all employees a shared sense of direction that points them towards opportunities. A mission can be defined in the following terms:

Definition	**A mission** guides the members of an organisation in making decisions that will achieve strategic goals and objectives.

Kotler (1999: 88) describes a mission as an "invisible hand" within the organisation. The company's mission is derived from the vision and describes the current position of the company in terms of what it does. According to Dibb *et al.* (2006: 42), creating a mission statement is very difficult because there are a number of complex variables involved. However, the process is an important one because the mission statement can benefit the organisation in five ways:

1. It gives the organisation clear direction, keeping it on track.
2. It helps differentiate the organisation and sets it apart from competitors.
3. It keeps the organisation focused on customer needs.
4. It guides managers in making decisions about what opportunities to pursue.
5. It acts like a glue in holding the organisation together, particularly in the case of large multinationals operating across the globe.

Ideally, mission statements should be brief, allowing them to be remembered easily by employees and customers. Mission statements take a long-term view, but they do evolve over time. Therefore, they should also be phrased in a manner that allows flexibility. Product lines and technologies come and go, but the mission statement should be reasonably broad and flexible enough to cater for such changes without the need for redrafting, and so should last over time. While vision statements are by their nature more aspirational, mission statements should be realistic regarding what the company is capable of doing, given its current capabilities. Most of all, mission statements should motivate employees, and appeal to outsiders. It must be remembered that statements like "maximising shareholder wealth" is not a great motivator for staff unless they all have large share options. In reality, mission statements vary considerably in length as well as content.

As stated in Chapter 1, strategic management applies to all types of organisations, from big to small, in the public sector and private sector, and from entrepreneurial start-ups to long established corporations. The following is a selection of mission statements that reflect such a variety of organisations. (Some organisations embrace the principles of constructing mission statements better than others.)

Illustration 3.6: Examples of Mission Statements

The Health Service Executive (HSE):
"To enable people to live healthier and more fulfilled lives."

Enterprise Ireland:
"Our core mission is to accelerate the development of world-class Irish companies to achieve strong positions in global markets resulting in increasing national and regional prosperity."

Oxfam:
"To work with others to overcome poverty and suffering through the most effective and appropriate means."

Castleknock College, Dublin (a secondary school run by the Vincentian Order):
"Our mission is to have a college which is concerned with the development of the whole person in a Christian atmosphere which encourages involvement in a balance of religious, intellectual, cultural and sporting activities which promotes the growth of self-worth and respect for others in the spirit of St Vincent de Paul."

J.J. Kavanagh & Sons (Ireland's largest privately-owned coach company):
"Our mission is to provide our customers with the highest levels of service, quality, comfort and safety."

FBD Insurance:
"In our target markets, to be the leading customer-focused insurance group, delivering long-term sustainable value."

Intel:
"Delight our customers, employees and shareholders by relentlessly delivering the platform and technology advancements that become essential to the way we work and live."

Source: company/organisational websites

GOALS AND OBJECTIVES

In order to achieve the mission, the company must translate it into more immediate goals and objectives (which will ultimately help the organisation achieve its audacious goals). In texts about management and strategy, the terms 'goals' and 'objectives' are often used interchangeably. There is a large overlap between the two terms, but there is a distinction, nonetheless, and both are necessary in linking the mission with achieving results.

Goals are a broad general statement of intent in line with the mission, focused on achieving a certain outcome, and they are usually *qualitative* in nature. A goal may have a number of objectives emanating from it.

Objectives are also statements of intent but are much more specific in terms of the desired outcomes to be achieved. They are, generally speaking, *quantitative* in nature.

The distinction between goals and objectives can be illustrated by the following example. To be successful in business, it is vital that customers have a high level of satisfaction with a company's products or services. Following a review of internal capability, it might be decided that improvements need to be made in the area of customer satisfaction. Improving customer satisfaction then becomes a necessary goal. Bill Hewlett of Hewlett Packard once said: "what gets measured gets done".

However, measuring customer satisfaction can be somewhat difficult as it is a broad concept that can mean different things to different people. As a goal, customer satisfaction can be further broken down into specific objectives, along with the appropriate metrics as follows:

Goal: Improve customer satisfaction in ACDB Limited within a three-month period.

Objectives: The following objectives relate to the goal of increasing customer satisfaction (see **Table 3.1**):

Table 3.1: *Objectives*

Objective	Description	Metric	Timeframe for results
1	Introduce staff training in customer care	All staff to complete three days' training in customer care	31 January
2	Reduce waiting time for answering phone calls	All phone calls to be answered within 10 seconds	20 January
3	Reduce customer complaints about staff interactions	No more than one complaint per 500 staff/customer interactions	28 February
4	After-sales follow-up	All customers to be contacted within two weeks of purchasing items	31 January

SETTING ORGANISATIONAL GOALS AND OBJECTIVES – GETTING THE BALANCE RIGHT

In setting goals and objectives for an organisation, it is essential that they reflect all aspects of the organisation. The use of the Balanced Scorecard will assist in this process.

The Balanced Scorecard

Most organisations set goals and objectives based on financial performance. Depending solely on financial measures of performance does not give a balanced view of how well the organisation is performing overall. One of the big problems associated with financial performance is that the measures used are lagging indicators – the focus is largely on what has happened in the past, and these are not necessarily a good indicator of future performance. Moreover, financial reports may indicate areas that need improvement, but without necessarily indicating how these improvements might be made. Leading indicators of the company's future strategic position show whether the company will be in a stronger or weaker position in the market place.

For example, by setting ambitious targets for the coming year, and achieving those targets, in all likelihood the end of year financial results will be strong. On the other hand, if after a good year, the company rests on its laurels, it is unlikely that the results will be anything more than mediocre. The targets that are set for the organisation must reflect a balance between financial and strategic goals. This is achieved by use of a Balanced Scorecard, which combines both qualitative and quantitative measures that reflect different aspects (and stakeholders) of the company. The Balanced Scorecard also ensures a link between the organisation's vision, its mission and the resulting goals and objectives.

Robert Kaplan of the Harvard Business School and his colleague David Norton first developed the **Balanced Scorecard** in 1992 arguing that organisations should monitor both financial and operational metrics simultaneously, and that the perspective should be forward-looking. They draw an analogy to a pilot flying a jet. The pilot does not rely on just one instrument but is simultaneously monitoring various gauges such as airspeed, bearing, altitude, fuel and other indicators, all of which build up an integrated and comprehensive picture of overall performance. In isolation no one instrument would provide all that information. Likewise, executives need an overview of the entire organisation when goals and objectives are being formulated. The Balanced Scorecard is primarily a planning device, but it also serves as a control device in the implementation of strategy. It also plays a very important role in the process of change and helps the organisation keep market-focused.

According to Kaplan and Norton (2005), there are four elements to the Balanced Scorecard:

- The customer perspective
- The internal perspective

- The innovation and learning perspective
- The financial perspective.

Customer perspective – how do our customers see us and do our products/services meet or exceed their expectations? A company must be customer-focused if it is to remain in business. It must be able to supply a range of products that will satisfy customer demand. In particular, when examining customer service, it is essential to look at it from the perspective of the customer and then develop specific measures that the customer considers important.

Internal perspective – knowing what our customers want, we then need a clear understanding of what we have to do internally in order to deliver on those expectations. The organisation must examine all its internal systems and procedures to ensure that it can meet and exceed customers' expectations. The most important factors here are those that have the greatest impact on customer satisfaction. In a service industry, the calibre of people delivering the service is of the utmost importance. Placing a priority on choosing good quality staff and on training will ensure that they meet customers' needs regarding time, service and quality. Appropriate cost control systems and management supervision will reduce any unnecessary cost in running the business.

Innovation and learning perspective – expectations will change over time. What measures are we taking now in order to be able to deliver good results in the future? Can we improve on what we are doing? In a competitive environment, standards keep rising, so it is essential that the company is able to anticipate and satisfy future customer demand. The ability to innovate and develop new products and processes that will meet future customer needs is, therefore, essential. To do that, the organisation must be constantly striving to improve its performance and to learn. It must be able to innovate and launch new products, penetrate new markets and increase revenue and profits. Building a relationship with customers is essential for receiving accurate feedback in current performance and on what customers would like to see improved. Spending quality time with key clients will, therefore, also be essential. Many of the measures here will overlap with others, such as improvement in staff training and performance.

Financial perspective – how is the organisation doing financially, and is it delivering good returns to its investors? Financial control is an essential part of any organisation and is, therefore, an integral part of the Scorecard. The financial measures will examine how the organisation is doing in the various departments and how they are contributing to the bottom line. It must be remembered that it does not always follow that improvements in the other areas of the Balanced Scorecard will automatically result in financial improvements. For example, improving the number of front-line staff will improve service levels and the level of customer satisfaction but, beyond a certain ratio, it will have a negative effect on the bottom line.

All four elements of the Balanced Scorecard are linked together, and what impacts on one will impact on the others. For example, the innovation and learning perspective is dependent on the provisions of adequate finance to support innovation and, in turn, will affect the internal

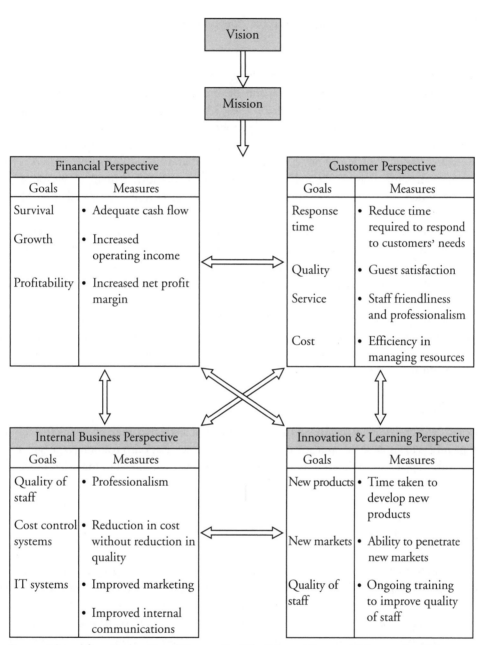

Source: Adapted from Kaplan, R. and Norton, D., "The Balanced Scorecard: Measures that Drive Performance", *Harvard Business Review*, July/August 2005, Vol. 83, Issue 7/8, p.174.

Figure 3.2 *The Balanced Scorecard: A Five-star Hotel*

perspective on customer satisfaction. It thus provides a forward-looking and holistic perspective on the performance of the organisation.

A number of goals are listed for each element along with appropriate metrics to gauge performance. By limiting the number of measures used, the Balanced Scorecard helps minimise information overload – it forces managers to concentrate on those measures that are of critical importance to the organisation. It brings all the critical information together from different elements in to one report and helps prevent sub-optimisation by showing managers the inter-relationship between those parts. Improvements in one area should not be at the expense of another. While some trade-offs between different measures may have to be made, those trade-offs should not involve key success factors – those areas where the organisation must excel if it is to be successful (see also Chapter 5).

The Scorecard for each individual business will be different because of variances in market situations, strategies and competitive environments. Each business unit will, therefore, have to customise the Scorecard to fit in with its own particular circumstances. It will have to be updated regularly as circumstances change, while at all times remaining consistent with the company's long-term strategy.

Since the Balance Scorecard was first developed, Kaplan and Norton have worked with many major international corporations using it as a strategic tool. As a result of the feedback they have received, they have consistently developed the concept of the Scorecard and how it might be applied. One major innovation was the use of strategy maps.

Strategy Map

Kaplan and Norton (2008) recommend the development of a **strategy map** as a powerful tool to help all staff members to visualise the strategy, and its cause and effect relationship among strategic objectives. It begins with the long-term financial objectives, and these are then linked to the other processes:

- The customer perspective
- The process perspective
- The learning and growth perspective

Larger organisations will have an overall strategic map for the entire company and then connect it to strategic maps for each operational unit. These are then linked to corresponding measures and targets. The process of developing a strategy map can be simplified somewhat by using just three to five strategic themes. A **strategic theme** is a vertical slice within the map that consists of a set of related strategic issues. These themes have a number of advantages: they all manage to customise the various themes to suit their particular circumstances while, at the same time, help integrate the different objectives with the overall strategy. The themes can also be developed to deliver results over different time periods. This will help executives to manage short-, medium- and long-term value-creating processes simultaneously.

The strategy map is then linked to **performance metrics** for each objective. Such metrics are a vital part of the process in terms of managing and improving the organisation. Another essential element is authorising and allocating the resources necessary for attaining the desired results, along with the strategic initiatives required. Kaplan and Norton believe that achieving results requires an integrated and cumulative impact of the different themes across the organisation. Finally, they recommend that a senior manager is assigned responsibility for each theme, as this allows for much greater co-ordination between different parts of the organisation and provides for greater chances of success. Each of the metrics can be assigned a colour-coded, traffic-light indicator (green, orange and red) that will focus management attention on the most pressing issues that require their attention. This will form a central part in the implementation of strategy which will be discussed in Chapter 13.

Strategy Map: Five-star hotel

The example below (**Figure 3.3**) is applied to a five-star hotel, and takes three themes: operational excellence, customer service and customer relationship management. These themes can then be superimposed on the four perspectives of the Balanced Scorecard.

Strategy Map for a Five-star Hotel			
Themes *Perspectives*	**Operational Excellence**	**Customer Service**	**Customer Relationship Management**
Financial	Increase margins ↑	Create higher margins ↑	Increase revenue and ROCE ↑
Customer	Increase contribution from customer ↑	Customer-focused service Create a compelling place to visit ↑	Add and retain high value customers ↑
Internal Process	Develop efficient internal processes, to include environmental processes and CSR ↑	Create seamless and co-ordinated service between departments Minimise absence New product and service development ↑	Create a comprehensive customer database to include detailed information about likes and dislikes ↑
Learning and Growth	Develop a capable and efficient Workforce Develop a customer-focused competence in staff		

Figure 3.3 *Strategy Map for a Five-star Hotel*

In turn, each of these themes is supported by the appropriate metrics, strategies and budgets that will manage performance. **Figure 3.4** below will elaborate on the third theme (above) from the strategy map: Customer Relationship Management.

(Theme 3): Customer Relationship Management					
	Strategy Map (Figure 3.3)	**Measure**	**Target**	**Initiative**	**Budget**
Financial perspective	Increase revenue and ROCE ↑	Revenue mix Revenue growth	New: + 10% Existing: + 25%		
Customer perspective	Add and retain high value customers ↑	New customers Increase in repeat visits Longer stay	15% increase in new customers 10% increase in repeat visits (calendar year) 1 night extra per guest per visit	Marketing campaign Discount for extra night	€ __
Internal Processes Perspective	Create a comprehensive customer database to include detailed information about likes and dislikes ↑	Targeted marketing. Improve process for customer feedback. Develop integrated database	Complete database of all customers c/w personal preferences, interests etc.	Data mining Social media Email/write to targeted customers	€ __ € __
Innovation & Learning Perspective	Develop a capable and efficient Workforce Develop customer-focused competences	Staff training Staff development	Certification awards Top rating for Customer feedback Staff Incentive scheme	Internal training External Training Secondment/ Posting to other hotels and resorts Profit sharing	€ __ € __ € — € __

Figure 3.4 *Customer Relationship Management*

The Balanced Scorecard framework thus provides a clear link between the vision that has been crafted for the organisation, the mission, and the subsequent goals and objectives. The scorecard illustrates the precise targets and the initiatives that are required to deliver the desired results and gives managers a clear understanding of where they need to be focusing their attention. Different time-frames can be applied to the different themes, and so they can tie in with short-, medium- and long-term objectives.

In itself, the Balanced Scorecard does not guarantee a winning strategy. What it can do is assist managers to operationalise strategy throughout the organisation in a co-ordinated and market-oriented manner, while helping the organisation to make all the necessary changes as the environment around it evolves. It helps managers to examine the link between operations and finance and, more importantly, it represents a fundamental change in the assumptions about performance measurement in the organisation.

Translating Strategy into Great Performance

Translating strategy into great performance can be a difficult process at the best of times. Setting clear goals and objectives that reflect all aspects of the organisation is obviously very important. When corporate goals are not achieved, where does the fault lie? Is it because the goals were unrealistic in the first instance or is the problem in the execution of those goals?

According to Mankins and Steele (2005: 67) companies realise only 63% of their potential because of defects in planning and in the executing phases of strategy. If senior executives do not fully understand the cause of the failure, then the wrong corrective action will be taken. Moreover, when goals are not realised on a regular basis, it will foster a culture of under-performance in the company. They argue that the gap between planning and performance can be closed by focusing on better planning *and* better execution simultaneously. They list seven rules that are applicable to organisations wishing to achieve high performance:

Rule 1 – Keep it simple, make it concrete Often, the organisation's strategy is quite abstract and does not lend itself to translation into plans that can be executed. It should be expressed in clear language to enable people to understand what the strategy includes and does not include. Everyone needs to be going in the same direction.

Rule 2 – Debate assumptions, not forecasts Planning in an organisation is often a political process. Forecasts usually understate short-term performance and overstate long-term performance. Financial forecasting is often done in isolation from the marketing or strategy functions. Forecasts should drive the work the company does. Therefore, the assumptions underlying their long-term plans should reflect the actual market realities. Cross-functional teams will help achieve detailed information on the profitability of different markets as well as costs. There should be discussions about the assumptions that would drive each unit's long-term financial performance, not on the actual performance itself.

Rule 3 – Use a rigorous framework, speak a common language It is vital that there is open dialogue between the corporate headquarters and SBUs in terms of the potential profit available in each market in terms of size and growth. Then the centre can create the financial projections that will drive the SBU. It is critical that the framework establishes a common language between the centre and the SBU that can be used by all functions.

Rule 4 – Discuss resource deployments early An important part of the process is making an early decision about critical resource requirements. Once agreements are reached, they are then factored into the plan and put in place to support the execution of the strategy.

Rule 5 – Clearly identify priorities Not all tactics are equally important — some steps must be taken at the right time. The priorities that will have the *greatest impact* on performance must be identified and acted upon with clear timetables, budgets and key performance indicators.

Rule 6 – Continually monitor performance Seasoned executives will know instinctively the correct amount of resources to allocate for a project. They also need real-time performance tracking to help the process. They must constantly monitor the use of resources against the plan. These reviews should indicate 'red light' events that require instant action by management.

Rule 7 – Reward and develop execution capabilities Management is key to success and companies must motivate and develop staff. There are huge hidden costs in hiring bad employees. Incentives must be built into the delivery of good results.

Mankins and Steele (2005: 72) consider that "the prize for closing the strategy-to-performance gap is huge". Improvement in performance often achieves a cultural multiplier effect as people become more confident about what they can achieve, and they become willing to make stretch goals that both inspire and transform their companies. The Balanced Scorecard can go a long way towards closing the strategy to performance gap.

Setting Goals and Objectives – Individual Level

Once the organisation is clear about what it wants to achieve, these corporate goals and objectives must be understood by all concerned within the organisation. The role of the manager then at every level is to translate these organisational goals and objectives into goals and objectives for each department. In turn, departmental/unit goals and objectives are further broken down until each individual in the organisation is assigned personal goals and objectives. There must be a straight alignment between corporate goals at the top of the organisation right down to those of the individual. Each person must have a clear understanding of how their personal goals will fit into and contribute to the attainment of their departmental goals. As objectives are specific elements of goals, the principles involved in setting goals and objectives overlap. For that reason, the following framework suggested by Buelens *et al.* (2006: 222) can be applied to both goals and objectives:

1. Set Goals Goals and objectives can be set in a number of ways: managers looking at the past performance of employees and then setting targets; the manager and employee participating in the process; or through benchmarking whereby best practice can be the target. There is no best way, as it depends very much on circumstances and the personalities of the employees. Some are happy to have the goals set for them, others, particularly those with what McClelland (1961) referred to as a high 'Need for Achievement' will want to have an active involvement in the process. The acronym SMART is often applied to setting objectives. SMART stands for:

- **S**pecific – should be expressed in precise rather than vague terms and be quantifiable when possible.
- **M**easurable – some form of measurement is needed to confirm when the goal or objective has been achieved.
- **A**ttainable – challenging, but not impossible.
- **R**esults-oriented – corporate goals should focus on the results that are needed by the organisation. In turn, the goals set for each individual should be supporting the objectives of the particular division and the organisation as a whole.
- **T**ime-bound – there should be a date set for the completion of objectives.

2. Promoting goal achievement When employees consider that goals are fair and reasonable, they are much more likely to commit to achieving those goals. Such goal commitment should not be taken for granted, and there are many ways in which managers can develop it. The rationale for the goal should be explained clearly, along with demonstrating how the individual's goals form part of the organisation's goals. It is important that the goals are challenging and, where employees demonstrate a willingness to be part of the goal-setting process, those employees should be included.

3. Provide support and feedback It is important that employees are encouraged to achieve their results and that they are given whatever support is required. Training, for example, may be needed to enable them to accomplish the task, or other resources and supports not currently available. Feedback is also vital. It plays a dual role: instructional and motivational. To be effective, feedback should be timely and specific. In addition, it should be credible, accurate and fair.

Motivational Aspect of Goal Setting

Setting goals and objectives is an integral part of the strategic management of any organisation. Frederick Taylor's concept of 'scientific management' was based on setting goals for each worker. This was developed in much greater detail by Peter Drucker (1954) in his book *The Practice of Management*, in which he coined the term: 'Management by Objectives' (MBO). Management by Objectives is a process where managers and employees participate in decision-making, goal setting and feedback. According to Buelens *et al.* (2006: 218), research has shown a substantial gain in productivity in organisations that used Management by Objectives, provided top management commitment to the process is high. Setting performance goals increases individual, group and organisational performance.

Csikszentmihalyi (1990) believes that clear goals play a central role in creating flow in the workplace. In that regard, goal setting also plays an important role in motivating individuals. According to

Locke and Latham (1990: 126), there are four motivational components in goal setting that are reasonably common across cultures:

- Goals focus one's attention on what is relevant and important.
- The level of effort involved in completing a goal is related to the difficulty of the goal, and consequently motivates people. In general, there is a strong relationship between goal difficulty and performance – the greater the level of difficulty, the greater the performance. However, if the individual perceives the goal to be beyond their reach, then performance drops considerably as many people will adopt the attitude it is not worth the effort trying to achieve their goals.
- Goals develop persistence and, over a period of time, people tend to see obstacles as challenges to be overcome, rather than something that would cause them to give up. People are generally committed to achieving goals when they are committed to the goals themselves. Consequently, it is important for managers to get those involved to 'buy into' the process.
- Goals encourage people to develop action plans in order to achieve their goals.

Rewards

Achieving goals and objectives is often linked to monetary rewards, particularly at senior executive level. In some organisations, it is considered to be an important part of attracting and motivating senior executives, and it can represent a significant payment for some. Such payments need to be looked at in a more holistic way, however, as research by Bloom (1999) examined the effects of pay dispersion (the pay gap between high-level and low-level employees) and found that the smaller the gap, the better the individual and organisational performance. In motivating those at the top, the motivation of management at levels below, as well as employees, should also be taken into account.

Many large organisations use appraisal systems to rate the performance of their employees. These appraisals would normally be conducted on an annual basis, and they are used to guide departmental managers in awarding bonus payments to staff. For those whose performance was considered exemplary, the rewards can often be significant. These rewards must be shared throughout the organisation by those that contributed to achieving the organisation's goals. At the other end of the scale, for those who are constantly under-performing, decisions will have to be made concerning the future of that employee. There has been much criticism in recent years, however, of enormous bonuses being paid to top executives, particularly in the banking sector, despite dismal performance.

There are a number of such examples in Ireland. Michael Fingleton, Chief Executive of the Irish Nationwide Building Society, received a €1 million bonus in 2008. The payment was made after the society was rescued by the Goverment's bank guarantee scheme. His total package for 2008 was €2.34 million, which made him the highest-paid boss of the guaranteed banks in 2008. This was in addition to the €27.6 million pension that he had built up in the society. The bonus caused outrage and in March 2009, Mr Fingleton agreed, under considerable pressure, to hand back the €1 million bonus. However, to date, he has failed to do so despite Irish Nationwide being bailed out by the state to the tune of €5.6 billion (Ross, 2009).

Another example refers to employees of the Capital Markets division of AIB (Lynch, 2010). As a result of a High Court ruling in November 2010, AIB had to pay backdated bonuses to approximately 90 employees. The ruling affected employees in the Capital Markets division of AIB (the division comprises Global Treasury, Investment Banking and Corporate Banking Division) and relates to their performance in 2008. The case was taken by one trader who sued the bank for non-payment of a €161,000 bonus who claimed in court that the non-payment would cause "unjustified hardship" to himself and his family. The bank said it would honour contractual payments for 2008 but that it has no plans to pay any bonuses for 2009 (Lynch, 2010:18). The Minister for Finance subsequently intervened and prevented further payment of bonuses to AIB members.

As well as enraging shareholders who have lost a considerable amount of their wealth, the payment of bonuses to top executives who have underperformed also exacerbates the de-motivating impact on lower-level employees of the pay dispersion referred to above.

CONCLUSION

The recession is going to place even greater pressure on organisations than ever before, and managers will have to get greater efficiencies from the resources they are using. During the boom years, many businesses were poorly run but still made a profit. That will no longer be the case and every week we see more and more companies going into liquidation. It is, therefore, imperative that senior managers have a clear vision for their company and understanding of what they want to achieve. The mission statement will derive from the organisation's vision and, in turn, it will guide the setting of strategic goals and objectives. One of the biggest lessons that can be learned from recent business failures is the absence of a sustainable plan for the organisations in question. By developing a balanced approach, that puts responsibility on each individual in the organisation, the chances of succeeding are greatly enhanced.

SUMMARY

This chapter has dealt with setting a vision, mission, goals and objectives for an organisation. Such a process is vital in order to ensure the effective and efficient use of resources so that the organisation can survive in a competitive environment.

Research by Collins and Porras (1996) and Mourkogiannis (2006) has indicated a strong link between visionary companies and success. There is a necessity for leaders to stand back from the day-to-day issues that confront their organisations and develop a clear understanding of what it is they are trying to achieve. Such a vision needs to be holistic and take into account a balanced stakeholder perspective. There must be a direct connection between the vision, the mission and the objectives that the organisation is trying to achieve, as it is only through those objectives that the original vision can be realised.

Vision plays a very important role in organisations in that it gives senior executives a clear and shared understanding of where the organisation is heading over the long term. It also serves as a guiding light for the entire organisation, both in terms of lower-level managers in setting departmental objectives, and in terms of staff members buying into the process. Finally, it will guide the organisation through a change process. A vision statement should be graphic, directional, focused, feasible, desirable and easy to communicate.

There are three broad elements to vision:

• Leadership
• Values
• Purpose

Leadership is vital to the process of developing a vision in that it sets the scene which allows the entire process of creating a vision and developing the mission, as well as the goals and objectives, to take place. Creating the **Vision** is a long-term process, and so another function of leadership is to maintain the level of motivation and commitment in the organisation while this process is taking place.

Values were described by Dose (1997) as: "standards or criteria for choosing goals or guiding actions, and they are relatively enduring and stable over time", but they can, and do, change. Regarding people's values, there is a distinction between 'content' (what people find important) and 'intensity' (how those values are ranked). People are not born with a set of values; they are acquired in a process of socialisation during their lifetime from a whole variety of sources, including family, peers, school, work and national culture. There is a link between organisational values and individual values, and this link is important in recruitment. Where there is congruence of values between the organisation and the individual, the result for the organisation can be quite powerful. Values guide a company in its dealings with all its stakeholders. They are principles that focus the attention of senior managers on what the organisation truly considers important. As guiding principles, values should be largely independent of the environment in which they operate and of current fashions.

The organisation's **Purpose** is its reason for being. While business objectives will change, you cannot fulfil a purpose; it is like a guiding light on the horizon – forever pursued but never reached. While the mission statement should embody the purpose, the purpose precedes the mission. A successful purpose both drives a company forward and helps build sustainable advantage and becomes "the engine of the company". The purpose should not be descriptive in terms of its current product lines. A primary function of the purpose is to inspire and, therefore, the purpose should not be based on maximisation of shareholder wealth.

The vision of the organisation, in terms of leadership, values and purpose, has to be translated into a '**Strategic Intent**' or long-term goals, and must be communicated clearly to the entire organisation. This can have a powerful motivating effect.

There is a clear distinction between a strategic vision and a mission statement. A mission describes the company's current business – 'who we are, what we do and why we are here'. In essence, the vision guides the mission. In turn, the mission statement, and subsequent goals and objectives, all provide guidance for the planning process. Mission statements ideally should be brief and should be flexible. They should be realistic with regard to what the company is capable of doing, given its current competences and capabilities. Most of all, mission statements should motivate the employees, as well as appeal to outsiders.

A company must translate its mission into goals and objectives. **Goals** are a broad, general statement of intent in line with the mission, dealing with a certain topic and are usually qualitative in nature. A goal may have a number of objectives emanating from it. **Objectives** are also statements of intent but are much more specific in terms of the desired outcomes to be achieved. They are, generally speaking, quantitative in nature. **Balanced Scorecards** can assist in the process of setting goals and objectives that are focused on the future and represent a broader perspective on how the organisation should develop, rather than using financial metrics only. There are three steps involved in setting goals and objectives: set the goal; promote its achievement; and provide support and feedback. Goal setting plays an important role in motivating individuals, and it is often linked to rewards.

DISCUSSION QUESTIONS

1. Distinguish between an organisation's vision and its mission.
2. Taking a selection of organisations, examine whether a clear vision for their future direction can be identified.
3. In light of so many recent corporate scandals in Ireland, discuss the need for values underpinning corporate strategy.
4. Construct a Balanced Scorecard for an organisation with which you are familiar.
5. Examine the process for developing individual goals and objectives in your organisation. What changes or improvements to the process would you suggest?

REFERENCES

Bloom, M., 1999, "The Performance Effects of Pay Dispersion on Individuals and Organisations", *Academy of Management Journal*, Feb 1999, pp.25–40
Breen, J., 2008, Interview with the Author, September 2008
Carroll, L., 1989, *Alice's Adventures in Wonderland*, London, Hutchinson
Churchill, W.S., 2004, *Never Give In! The Best of Winston Churchill's Speeches*, London, Pimlico
Collins, J. and Porras, J., 1996, "Building Your Company's Vision", *Harvard Business Review*, Sept/Oct 1996, Vol. 74, Issue 5, pp.66–77
Covey, S., 1994, *The Seven Habits of Highly Effective People*, London, Simon & Schuster

Csikzentmihalyi, M., 1990, *The Psychology of Optimal Experience*, New York, Harper Colllins

Dallek, R., 2003, *John F. Kennedy: An Unfinished Life 1917–1963*, London, Penguin

Dibb, S. *et al.*, 2006, *Marketing Concepts and Strategies*, Boston, Houghton Mifflin

Dose, J.J., 1997, "Work Values: An Integrative Framework and Illustrative Application to Organisational Socialisation", *Journal of Occupational and Organisational Psychology*, September 1997, pp.219–40

Drucker, P., 1954, *The Practice of Management*, New York, Harper Row

Early, P. C. and Mosakowski, E., 2004, "Cultural Intelligence", *Harvard Business Review*, Oct 2004, Vol. 82, Issue 10, pp. 139–146

Gerstner, L., 2002, *Who Says Elephants Can't Dance?*, London, HarperCollins

Hamel, G. and Prahalad, C., 2005, "Strategic Intent", *Harvard Business Review*, July/August 2005, Vol. 83, Issue 7/8, pp.148–161

Kanter, R.M., 2008, "Transforming Giants", *Harvard Business Review*, Jan 2008, Vol. 86, Issue 1, pp.43–52

Kaplan, R. and Norton, D., 2001, *The Strategy Focused Organisation*, Boston, Harvard Business Press

Kaplan, R. and Norton, D., 2005, "The Balance Scorecard: Measures that Drive Performance", *Harvard Business Review*, July/August 2005, Vol. 83, Issue 7/8, pp.172–180

Kaplan, R. and Norton, D., 2006, "How to implement a strategy without disrupting your organisation", *Harvard Business Review*, March 2005, Vol. 84, Issue 3, pp.100–109

Kaplan, R. and Norton, D., 2008, "Mastering the management system", *Harvard Business Review*, Jan 2008, Vol. 86, Issue 1, pp.62–77

Kotler, P. *et al.*, 1999, *Principles of Marketing*, New Jersey, Prentice Hall

Kotter, J., 1996, *Leading Change*, Boston, Harvard Business School Press

Locke, E. and Latham, G., 1990, *A Theory of Goal Setting and Task Performance*, Upper Saddle River, N.J., Prentice Hall

Lonergan, J., 2006, Address to Social Care Conference, Institute of Technology, Tralee

Lynch, S., 2010, "AIB to pay up to €10m in backdated employee bonuses", *Irish Times*, 10 November, 2010, p.18

McClelland, D., 1961, *The Achieving Society*, New York, Free Press

Mankins, M. and Steele, R., 2005, "Turning Great Strategy into Great Performance", *Harvard Business Review*, July/Aug 2005, Vol. 83, Issue 7/8, pp.64–72

Mourkogiannis, N., 2006, *Purpose – The Starting Point of Great Companies*, New York, Palgrave Macmillan

O'Brien, J. and Marakas, G., 2008, *Management Information Systems*, 8th Ed., New York, McGraw-Hill

OECD, 2009, Corporate Governance and the Financial Crisis: Key Findings and Messages, OECD, http://docs.google.com/viewer?a=v&q=cache:ZaMONnyAq7EJ:www.oecd.org/dataoecd/3/10/43056196.pdf+oecd+corporate+governance+and+the+financial+crisis&hl=en&gl=ie&pid=bl&srcid=ADGEESgGKyXtMlC1TWuVFGm1I6IvAzmGpo0xtzE50tf-3wtURuUuB8r7uUQT7bno816D_r6yIjOXvfzSEqUEottHhAPr054o7D1V5LBoI2R8WDMjDXSsl9yJb7D-APpANpMNfNMpMiSs&sig=AHIEtbQOp4BQvgUaxAya5bbhFWdmZP9i7g, Accessed 14 November 2010

Rokeach, M., 1973, *The Nature of Human Values*, New York, The Free Press

Rokeach, M., 1979, *Understanding Human Values*, New York, The Free Press

Ross, M. *et al.*, 1999, "Basic Individual Values, Work Values and the Meaning of Work", *Applied Psychology: An International Review*, Jan 1999, pp.49–71

Ross, S., 2009, *The Bankers: How the banks brought Ireland to its knees*, Dublin, Penguin

Schwartz, S. and Sagie, G., 2000, "Value Consensus and Importance: A Cross-National Study", *Journal of Cross-Cultural Psychology*, July 2000, p.468

Thompson, A. *et al.*, 2008, *Crafting and Executing Strategy*, 16th Ed., New York, McGraw-Hill

Welch, J., 2001, *Jack: What I've Learned Leading a Great Company and Great People*, London, Headline

Corporate Governance, Business Ethics, and Corporate Social Responsibility

---

LEARNING OBJECTIVES

On completion of this chapter, you will be able to:

■ Critically examine the corporate governance structures of an organisation
■ Differentiate between various ethical approaches
■ Evaluate actions from an ethical perspective
■ Assess the actions of an organisation from a corporate social responsibility perspective

"It is necessary only for the good man to do nothing for evil to triumph."

Edmund Burke

INTRODUCTION

Corporate Governance, Business Ethics and Corporate Social Responsibility are the subjects of the final chapter in Part 1 of this book, which deals with three related and important elements concerning the foundation of corporate strategy. This is an important chapter because it lays down an ethical foundation for the entire text. It is an approach that should underpin all of the decisions that managers take in the development and implementation of strategy.

The first section of the chapter discusses corporate governance, which is concerned with how the various structures are put in place to ensure that proper control is exercised on the direction an organisation is pursuing and that it is compliant with the law.

The middle section of the chapter examines business ethics. Corporate law governs much of what an organisation does, laying down specific and prescriptive rules about how it conducts its affairs. Making VAT returns and submitting company accounts are some of the many legal obligations that an organisation must fulfil. There are also a number of other decisions that managers must make that are not so clear-cut. What is the right thing to do and what is wrong when the law does not prescribe an answer? Ethics guide the manager as to what the correct course of action should be. Included in this section is a discussion on whistleblowers. When one sees something wrong being done by a company, does loyalty to the organisation override the obligation to have the practice stopped? It is often the case that the practice will cease when it is brought into the public domain.

The final section of this chapter, on corporate social responsibility, recognises that the organisation has obligations to groups other than shareholders. The obligation to provide financial returns to shareholders must be balanced with its obligations to all its stakeholders. Companies are slowly beginning to recognise that, by fulfilling those obligations, it is not really costing anything, and in many cases, it is actually providing a sound financial return -- in addition to doing the right thing.

It will be seen throughout this text that strategic decisions are rarely cut and dried in regard to the correct course of action. It is often only after the event that one can see whether the correct course of action was chosen in terms of the financial benefits. With strategic decisions, there is also the added complication as to whether the actions stand up to moral scrutiny. Often, companies make good returns without the actions supporting those returns coming under investigation. On other occasions, it emerges that the company was operating in a manner that was either illegal or unethical or both. Reputations or companies come crashing down.

CORPORATE GOVERNANCE

Corporate governance is an important factor in how strategic decisions are made. It will vary considerably depending on the type of company and from one country to another.

 Corporate Governance is the control mechanism by which board members and senior executives are accountable to stakeholders for the strategic direction of an organisation and for legal and ethical compliance.

There are a number of factors that need to be considered when examining corporate governance including:

- Company structures
- Chain of governance
- Company directors
- Differing board structures
- Investment information

Company Structures

Strategy applies to all types of companies, both big and small. In terms of corporate governance, therefore, there is a large variation between the different types of ownership. Many people in business are self-employed and answer only to themselves in terms of their decisions. The owner and the manager are one and the same person. Once a limited company is formed, there are more legal and accounting formalities to be observed. The majority of companies in Ireland are small companies, employing perhaps just a few staff, some of whom may be family members. The law prescribes rules in regard to the appointment of directors and their duties. If the company is a private limited company, most aspects of corporate governance will be straightforward. Once the company goes public and is listed on the stock exchange, the corporate governance structures change significantly, and the number of people involved in the process grows considerably.

Chain of Governance

A large, listed company could have tens of thousands of shareholders – the people who own the company. In such situations, there is separation of ownership between those who own the company and those who run it on a day-to-day basis. The managers are employees of the organisation. In a public company, the managers are accountable, through the board of directors, to the shareholders for the decisions that are made. This is known as the chain of governance. It describes the different roles that various people have to play in the running of the company and who is answerable to whom. While publically quoted companies will have many individuals as small shareholders, perhaps owning a couple of thousand shares each, a large proportion of the shares will be held by pension funds and investment managers. When money is paid into pension funds by individuals, it is invested on behalf of the trustees of the fund by professional fund managers. These fund managers will place the money in various public companies according to the level of confidence they have in the management of the company to deliver growth in the value of the shares through dividends and capital growth. The board of directors is the main group in charge of authorising strategy within the organisation, but these fund managers are in a very powerful position, albeit vicariously. While they do not have any formal authority to approve strategy, by moving funds in or out of the company, they show their confidence in the management to achieve results, and thereby influence strategy. Fund managers and investment analysts are in a powerful position in how they deal with companies, and this imposes strong moral and ethical obligations on how they perform their work.

Company Directors

Directors are elected by the shareholders at an annual general meeting. In exercising their functions as directors, they owe a fiduciary duty to act in good faith on behalf of the company as a whole and for the purpose of the powers invested in the directors. They are free to exercise unfettered discretion in how they vote, which should be in the best interests of the company. They owe a duty not to be in a position where there is a conflict of interest, and there is a liability to account to the company in regard to benefits obtained by their position of directors. In addition to fiduciary duty, directors also owe a duty of skill, care and diligence in how they exercise their duties as directors. If a director does not exercise such duties, he or she may be held legally liable. The onus is, therefore, on the director to be acquainted with company law and to ensure that the company is being run in a proper manner.

An important issue here is defining those to whom a duty of care is owed. Is it simply the shareholders or do they have a wider duty of care to balance the interest of all stakeholders (see Chapter 1)? This text takes the view that companies are answerable to all stakeholders, albeit in different ways. This includes a duty of care to employees, and the people who purchase products and services from the company.

Former CEO of General Electric, Jack Welch, was traditionally one of the strongest proponents of the shareholder value movement. Over the years he had a change of heart on this subject. In an interview in the *Financial Times* (Guerrera, 2009), he is quoted as saying:

> "On the face of it, shareholder value is the dumbest idea in the world. Shareholder value is a result, not a strategy…[Y]our main constituencies are your employees, your customers and your products."

This responsibility will be examined in greater detail later in the chapter under 'Corporate Social Responsibility'.

Public companies will have a mixture of executive and non-executive directors on their board. The executive directors are full-time managers in the company with specific responsibilities for the day-to-day running of the company. Non-executive directors are appointed from outside the company, and their purpose is to provide a balanced and an independent perspective to the board. There should be a majority of independent directors to ensure that managers are operating the company according to the rules and in the interest of all interested parties. Being independent means not being in a business relationship with the company, or receiving consultancy payments or share options. In 2003, the Chancellor of the Exchequer in the UK commissioned a report on the role and effectiveness of non-executive directors. Building on the earlier work on corporate governace by Sir Adrian Cadbury, Derek Higgs compiled a very extensive review of these responsibilities. One of its more important recommendations (para. 5.7) states that a chief executive should not become a chairman of the same company (Higgs, 2003). Interestingly, in two cases where public limited companies were in the spotlight in recent years, their chief executives were subsequently appointed chairmen: DCC and Anglo Irish Bank. In both cases, the chairmen subsequently had to resign.

One issue that needs to be addressed regarding the composition of boardroom members is gender balance. The percentage of women members on boards of directors across the globe is low, and in Ireland it is particularly low. Research carried out by Clancy *et al.* (2010:2) on Irish PLCs and semi-state companies found that women are significantly under-represented on boards of these leading companies: overall, just 11% of the 572 directors of the top Irish companies were women; the position was worse in the private sector, where only 7% were women. In the public sector, women's representation on boards was somewhat higher, where 18% of the directors were women. Some countries such as Norway have introduced a quota system for women on boards of directors, whereby women must comprise 40% of all boards. Spain will implement a similar quota by 2015 and France by 2016 (*The Economist*, 2010). Such prescriptive approaches are, however, controversial.

In addition to the gender imbalance, Clancy *et al.* (2010: 2-14) also state that "all the available evidence shows a lack of diversity across other characteristics, such as social background, occupation and age". Their research has shown that a small number of executives (39 individuals) in Ireland held a disproportionately high number of directorships between them. One group of nine directors simultaneously sat on the boards of up to five of the top 40 Irish publically quoted or semi-state companies. Each one of that group was also a member of the boards of up to 17 other companies. These directorships also included a number of cross-directorships (where an individual on the board of company A is offered a seat on the board of company B, and vice versa).

Multiple directorships, and in particular, cross-directorships, have the potential to undermine good corporate governance in a number of areas. First is the independence of board members (in particular where there is a crossover of membership of remuneration committees). Second, is the lack of diversity of those members. Third, it raises serious questions about the amount of time that those individuals can devote to the complexity of board matters. The Walker Report in the UK was commissioned by the then Prime Minister Gordon Brown in 2009 to review corporate governance in UK banks and other financial entities. It recommends that the overall time commitment of non-executive directors in financial institutions should be greatly increased and should in future be a minimum of 30 to 36 days a year (Walker, 2009:14). In Ireland, the Financial Regulator is bringing in legislation that will limit the number of directorships in financial institutions that can be held by any one individual.

The main purpose of the board is to scrutinise the actions of the managers and to ask hard and probing questions about their work. They must make independent judgements about the strategy proposals being made by managers, and satisfy themselves that the proposals are in the best interests of the company and have been properly analysed. This should take the form of asking incisive questions about the rationale and methodology behind the proposals and about how management will implement company strategy if given approval. This will include examination of the element of risk involved in the proposals. Assessing risk is one very important role of directors, especially non-executive directors. Jim O'Leary wrote an opinion piece in the *Irish Times* (O'Leary, J. 2010) in which he admits that he should have been "more pushy in opposing risk-taking" at AIB. Mr O'Leary was a non-executive director at AIB from 2002 until 2008 at a time when the bank grew exponentially through funding development loans and mortgages. He says, that in retrospect, the amount of lending now seems reckless, but at the time, the board was predominantly of the view that there would be a "soft landing", and this formed the central case in designing strategies. There are a few points that he raised which need examination. First, he spoke about the "asymmetry of information" where bank executives have all the information they need, but non-executive directors are totally dependent on those executives to supply them with relevant and accurate information. He does qualify this by saying that: "... this is not a formula for exonerating boards. Boards of directors are ultimately responsible for running the business." He also speaks of the importance of trust: "I would say that directors placed too much trust in management." He stated that it is a matter of personal judgement as to who one should trust and to what extent.

However, in both cases it must be remembered that it remains the responsibility of each director to analyse the information presented to them and to form an independent judgement on the quality and accuracy of that information and its implications for the company. He said he was sceptical of the "soft landing" view taken by the board and declared: "it is a matter of profound personal regret to me that I wasn't more forceful in setting out the contrarian view and didn't work harder at analysing its implications." The evaluation of risk will also be examined in Chapter 7.

Proper oversight of the accounting procedures of the company is a very important element of the board's work. They must ensure that all of the proper accounting standards and regulations are being complied with. There will usually be a special audit committee consisting of non-executive directors to scrutinise the financial affairs of the company and to ensure that proper procedures are in place to prevent fraud (see example in Chapter 13).

There is an obvious distinction between economic success and moral probity, and there are many examples in recent years where boards and individuals failed in this regard. Another very important role of the company's board is to test the moral dimension of the strategies being proposed. This is something that is not clear-cut, such as seeing whether the accounts have been properly compiled. It requires much more subjective judgement. That does not lessen its importance in any way and, indeed, with strategy in general, there is a great deal of judgement required. Given the company's obligation to a wide group of stakeholders, ensuring high ethical standards in the actions of the company is an essential part of the remit of the board.

There should be no doubt about this responsibility when one examines the social fallout from the meltdown of global financial and other markets. Much of the responsibility lies with the strategic decisions taken in boardrooms across the world. To dismiss it as a by-product of the free market for which no one is responsible, or to view it as 'just one of those things', is not just simplistic; it is a total abrogation of moral responsibility. For a market to operate, it needs society and people who have the means to purchase goods and services. The strategic decisions of companies must reflect the needs and well-being of society. The board of directors must show ethical leadership in their own actions and send out a strong message to the company as to the high level of standards that are expected by all employees from the chief executive down.

Compliance has not always measured up to the mark, however. The Financial Regulator, Matthew Elderfield, stated: "The old rules were too generous in their nature and encouraged box ticking as a means of compliance. Most disturbingly, all of the evidence points to some boards that were seriously out of touch with what was happening on the ground in their organisations." (Handcock, 2010: 18). Perhaps the most incisive comments about corporate governance, and specifically about the role of directors in banks, was made by Niall Fitzgerald. Mr Fitzgerald is a former CEO of a multinational company, Uniliver, and he is perhaps one of the most successful Irish-born businessmen of his generation. In an interview in *The Irish Times* in March 2010, he spoke about being a bank director in Ireland in the 1990s. He said that he had recently posed an awkward question at a dinner party to some friends of his (all of whom acted as bank directors):

"I want to confront you as a friend with a very difficult question. Because unless we all together and individually learn from this, I'm not sure it has been of any great value. The question you have to ask yourselves is: did you know what the institution was doing and the full consequences of what it was doing? Because if you did, you were complicit with the recklessness. Or if the answer is you didn't know, then you cannot have been discharging your responsibility as a director of that company properly."

He also spoke about the importance of the values that he learnt at home, particularly from his mother. Her basic rule was you should never depart from treating people as you would wish to be treated yourself. Her litmus test was the mirror – if you are unsure if it is the right thing to do, look in the mirror and if you find you are averting your eyes, then you have a problem. There are many business leaders that could learn from that simple piece of advice.

O'Toole, F. (2010)

A number of significant high-profile cases around the world have prompted many governments to bring in regulations governing how companies operate. After the collapse of major companies such as Robert Maxwell's Communications Corp in the early 1990s (owing £440 million to the company's pension fund), and the Bank of Credit and Commerce International (BCCI), the British Government commissioned Sir Adrian Cadbury in 1992 to chair a committee to investigate the British corporate governance system and to make recommendations. Many of these recommendations have already been discussed. In the US, the Sarbanes-Oxley Act came into being in 2002, and its aim is to combat fraud, improve the reliability of financial reporting and restore investor confidence. Similarly, this was brought in after the collapse of a number of companies such as WorldCom and Enron. The act itself is short. Perhaps the two most important elements are Sections 302 and 404:

- **Section 302** – Corporate responsibility for financial reports. The CEO and the CFO must personally certify the accuracy of financial statements and disclosures and that those statements fairly present in all material aspects the results of operations and financial condition of the company. Section 906 deals with white-collar crime penalties, and states that wilful failure by the Chief Executive Officers (CEOs) and Chief Financial Officers (CFOs) in regard to complying with the regulations can result in fines of up to $5 million and imprisonment for up to 20 years.
- **Section 404** – requires companies to have annual evaluations of internal controls and procedures for financial reporting, and to include this internal report in their annual reports.

www.sarbanes-oxley.com

Among other requirements, it obliges publicly-traded companies to have a code of ethics (see section on Business Ethics below). Rather than considering the Sarbanes-Oxley Act a financial burden, Wagner and Dittmar (2006) believe that it can be turned to a company's advantage, bringing operations under control while driving down compliance costs.

Reaction in Ireland to the many lapses in corporate governance prompted the Companies (Auditing and Accounting) Act 2003, which is similar to the Sarbanes-Oxley Act. In addition, the Company Law Enforcement Act was passed in 2001 and it established the Office of the Director of Corporate Enforcement (ODCE), which has responsibility for, *inter alia,* ensuring compliance with the Companies Acts 1963 to 2003, which are the relevant pieces of legislation covering companies in Ireland. In May 2010, the Financial Reporting Council in the UK introduced the UK Corporate Governance Code (this was formally known as the Combined Code on Corporate Governance or just the "Combined Code"). The Corporate Governance code, like its predecessor, operates on a "comply or explain" basis, whereby companies must either comply with the regulations, or where they deviate from those regulations, the reason must be explained in their annual report. The Irish Stock Exchange (ISE) has adopted these provisions for Irish listed companies. Other provisions relating to Irish companies are contained in the ISE Listing Rules (ISE, 2010).

For those who consider that the 'business of business is business', it is important to remember that the cost of non-compliance with ethical standards can be extremely high. Thomas *et al.* (2004) list three levels of cost of ethical failures:

- **Level 1 Costs** – These include government fines where laws have been broken, e.g., BP in the Gulf of Mexico, which caused a large environmental disaster. Level 1 costs also include penalties arising from any civil law cases. Generally speaking, these will also result in falling share prices.
- **Level 2 Costs** – include all the costs incurred by the company in investigating possible breaches of regulations and also the costs involved in rectifying the situation, e.g., the costs incurred by the banks involved in the DIRT Inquiry (see section on Business Ethics).
- **Level 3 Costs** – these costs are much more intangible, but real nonetheless. They include the loss of customers as a result of the company's actions, the damage to the company's brand (e.g., the damage caused to Shell by the Brent Spar incident — this is discussed under the heading Corporate Social Responsibility), and the impact it has on staff morale, which often results in high staff turnover.

If things go wrong, the process of repairing the company's shattered reputation is both costly and time-consuming. The third part of this chapter deals with corporate social responsibility, which advocates a proactive approach to how companies interact with all of their stakeholders. It will be seen that, in addition to being the 'right thing to do', it also confers significant advantages on the organisation.

Implicit in all of the discussion above is that the board must satisfy themselves as to the calibre of the executives and their ability to do the job. This is particularly so in relation to the chief executive and the leadership he or she exercises. Very often, a significant part of the remuneration package of senior executives is given in the form of a bonus payment, and this is decided by the board (or a subcommittee thereof). Another one of the more important recommendations of the Higgs Report relates to the separation of the role of chairman of the board from that of chief executive (Paragraph 5.3). This is to ensure the independence of the chairman from the day-to-day management responsibility of the company (Higgs, 2003). This separation of roles is considered best practice and is adopted by most Irish public companies. In many situations there may be dissent in the board over certain proposals and the chairman must act in a decisive and independent manner to encourage debate, but also to bring the discussion to a conclusive end.

The role of directors has become a great deal more onerous in recent years. The Institute of Directors in Ireland was established in 1980 as an independent, non-political body whose aim is to support and develop the role of directors in Irish business. While most of the discussion in this book will centre on the role of executives in formulating and implementing strategy, the board of directors plays a very important role in the oversight of the company.

Differing Board Structures

There is no standard international structure for boards of directors. In Ireland, there is a single board whose function is to supervise the management of the company. This is often referred to as the Anglo-Saxon model or the shareholder model and is common to most English-speaking countries, such as the UK, the US, Australia and Canada (Johnson *et al.* 2011: 129). Within this structure, there tends to be widespread ownership of shares and these shares trade regularly. The relationship of banks to these companies is largely limited to contractual arrangements with regard to overdrafts and loans. In many European states, a more inclusive corporate governance structure exists. The norm is for two-tier structure boards, which comprise a fixed level of worker representation which enjoys powers of co-determination and veto. As such, it goes much further than consultation, and amounts to joint decision-making (O'Leary, K. 2010: 280). In the two-tier structure, the first tier consists of managers who are responsible for the day-to-day supervision of the company. The upper tier is a supervisory board whose role is to oversee the management board. Banks tend to be more involved in what the company is doing and in Japan, for example, the banks tend to have a long-term relationship with the companies by taking out equity investment. This was one of the reasons why it took Japan so long to emerge from the recession in the 1990s. It took the banks a long time to recover because of their direct involvement in failing businesses and, in turn, the banks were unable to lend money to support recovery in the business sector.

Investment Information

The detail and level of information available to members of the governance chain will vary considerably depending on their position. One of the major strategic benefits of IT is that it can provide managers with accurate and detailed information in a timely manner (and on occasions, in real-time). Such detailed information is necessary for managers to make the correct decisions. However, much of this information will be highly confidential and will need to have restricted access within the company. Shareholders will also want information about the performance of the company as they will base their investment decisions largely on this information. However, the information given to shareholders will be largely confined to that issued in the annual accounts. Public companies must publish their results every six months in Ireland, while in the US it is every three months. One of the big drawbacks to such short reporting periods is that it can put undue pressure on executives to come up with short-term gains at the expense of the long-term interests of the company, which is central to corporate strategy.

Stockbrokers and investment managers, while they will not have access to internal management reports, will compile detailed information about industries and companies in those industries, and this will form the basis of their investment decisions. It is common, however, for corporate executives to meet with investment managers to discuss the strategy being pursued and to explain the rationale behind it. When Ryanair bought its 29% shareholding in Aer Lingus in 2006, it caught the investment community by surprise, and Ryanair CEO Michael O'Leary had to meet with the large institutional investors to satisfy them that the move was part of a coherent plan. Without such assurances, fund managers could quickly remove large amounts of money from investment in the company, causing the share price to fall dramatically.

BUSINESS ETHICS

Introduction

In recent years, there has been a much greater focus on how businesses and individuals conduct their affairs. There have been many high profile cases of serious lapses in ethical standards not just around the world, but also here in Ireland. Ethics, of course, covers all aspects of how we live our lives and each of the various professional bodies has their own code of ethics. Medical ethics is obviously different to ethics in the accountancy profession, but each serves to guide people as to what is right and what is wrong. There are rarely clear-cut answers when it comes to ethics:

> "The business of philosophy is not to give rules, but to analyse the private judgements of common reason."
>
> Immanuel Kant

The Walker Report in the UK made the following observation in relation to regulatory changes:

> "The behavioural changes that may be needed are unlikely to be fostered by regulatory fiat, which in any event risks provoking unintended consequences. Behavioural improvement is more likely to be achieved through clearer identification of best practice and more effective but, in most areas, non-statutory routes to implementation so that boards and their major owners feel 'ownership' of good corporate governance."
>
> (Walker, 2009: 9)

By recognising that not every aspect of governance can, or indeed should, be governed by regulation, we see that ethics clearly plays an important role in how companies operate.

The focus of this section relates to how individuals in business make decisions from an ethical perspective.

 Business ethics can be defined as the ethical conduct of people within organisations and the impact it has on decisions they make at corporate and individual level.

This section will deal with business ethics under a number of headings:

- Historical background
- Ethical theories: teleological ethical systems, deontological ethical systems and ethical relativism
- Code of ethics
- Evidence of unethical behaviour

- Relating ethics to business
- Whistle-blowing
- Organisational approaches to ethical behaviour

Historical Background

While most management theory is relatively new, the study of ethics goes back to the beginnings of philosophy. To understand modern business ethics, it is perhaps useful to understand the development of philosophy over the millennia. The study of ethics is an entire body of knowledge in its own right, and just part of a chapter cannot possibly do it justice. The purpose of this section is merely to highlight its influence rather than catalogue its development over time.

Early philosophy began by trying to understand the world through the use of reason. The three great Greek philosophers, Socrates, Plato and Aristotle, brought it to a new level. Socrates, born in 470 BC, and unlike earlier Greek philosophers, was not concerned with the natural world, but believed what mattered most is how we ought to live our lives. Regarded by many as the founder of moral philosophy, much of his work centred on finding the answer to questions such as: 'What is justice?' 'What is right?' 'What is good?' Having the answers to these questions would have a profound effect on our lives. His style was to pose questions: he did not necessarily know the answers himself, but sought to create discussion and debate in order to increase the level of understanding of philosophical questions. He was the first to teach about the importance of personal integrity in its own right rather than in response to the law or deities (Magee, 1998).

Plato, the greatest pupil of Socrates, and who recorded in writing much of Socrates' teaching, concerned himself with a much broader range of topics and regarded mathematics as key to understanding the natural world. Plato's most famous work, *The Republic,* applies the principles of philosophy to political affairs and covers a whole range of social and moral issues.

In turn, Aristotle was a pupil of Plato's Academy for 20 years. His teachings were very broad, but in the context of this discussion, his development of our understanding of virtue ethics is important. He believed that people want to be virtuous, and that self-indulgence will only bring us into conflict with others. According to Aristotle, 'the golden mean' was a virtue, the midway point between two extremes (vices). Thus, courage was the midway point between rashness (excess) and cowardice (deficiency). Other virtues included temperance, magnificence, magnanimity, proper ambition, patience, truthfulness, righteous indignation, modesty and friendliness (Aristotle, Ed.1976: 104). His discussions also cover topics such as moral goodness, moral responsibility, justice and the intellectual virtues.

The teachings of Socrates, Plato and Aristotle laid the foundation for generations of philosophers that have influenced ethics over the years. Many regard virtue ethics as being a classification in its own right. Certainly, there are necessary prerequisites for ethical leadership in managers and board members. These virtues are not innate but are developed in the individual over time. The fact that virtues are developed over time is in keeping with the concept of the learning organisation (Senge, 1990), and consequently managers must pay due cognisance to developing a culture of ethical compliance in their organisation.

There are a number of classifications used for ethical theories. The classifications used here are:

- Teleological ethical systems – dealing with consequences
- Deontological ethical systems – dealing with universal principles
- Ethical relativism – allowing for regional variation in standards

Teleological Ethical Systems

Teleological ethics is based on the concept that the morality of a decision is measured by examining its probable outcome and consequences. It is closely linked with the theory of utilitarianism, which was developed by Jeremy Bentham and John Stewart Mill in the 19th Century. Utilitarianism is very similar to the managerial concept of cost-benefit analysis. It involves examining a decision from the point of view of its costs and its benefits, and that the decision should yield the greatest possible benefit. (In many ways, it underpins the decision-making process described in Chapter 12.) It appears a simple concept at first, and easy to apply in theory, but on closer examination, it is not so clear-cut.

In order to make morally correct decisions, it requires discussion on the issue and full knowledge of the problem and likely consequences. Inaction must also be considered as well as action (acts of omission and acts of commission). In reality, it is often very difficult to foresee all consequences. The question of measurement is another problem. Financial cost and benefits can be measured, but how can happiness be calculated, for example, or goodness? Another version of teleological ethics is **distributive justice**. Developed by Harvard professor John Rawls, the theory is based on a concept of fairness. Distributive justice believes that ethical acts are those that lead to an equitable distribution of goods and services (Hartman, 2002).

Deontological Ethical Systems

Deontological ethical systems are based on universal principles or concepts of what is right and wrong. They are termed universal in that they transcend cultures and societies. The person most credited with developing the theory was the German philosopher Immanuel Kant (1724–1804). Actions are considered right or wrong regardless of the consequences of the action or its impact on others. The concept of goodwill is central to Kant's philosophy. A person's moral worth is based on their decision to discharge their duty. In deciding what is right, a person is guided by the categorical imperative — what a rational person would believe to be universal laws that apply to all mankind (Hartman, 2002).

Deontological ethical systems underpin general principles such as the UN Declaration of Human Rights, which sets out the universal rights of people around the world. It also underpins legislation such as the Equality Act 1998 which prevents discrimination on nine grounds. It is a prescriptive law: a manager cannot discriminate on age grounds because he or she does not agree with the legislation. Deontological ethics also prescribes that people should perform acts because those actions are the right thing to do, rather than from fear of the consequences, such as being fined or going to jail.

In some respects **virtue ethics** are linked with deontological ethical systems, in that virtues like honesty, truthfulness, and many more are held in esteem by most societies and, in that regard, are universal. Such virtues guide human behaviour in making ethical decisions. There is also a strong overlap between deontological ethics with most of the world's religions. Christianity, Judaism, Islam and Buddhism all share prescriptive rules as to how one should lead one's life – such as the Ten Commandments. Virtue ethics and religion were brought together by St Thomas Aquinas, who divided virtue into two categories. Theological virtues included faith, hope and charity, and intellectual virtues included wisdom, justice, temperance and fortitude. Aquinas considered that virtue was not innate but something that was learned or acquired (Hartman, 2002).

Ethical Relativism

Universal principles cover many aspects of what is right and wrong. According to Thompson *et al.* (2008: 319), ethical relativism believes that different societies and cultures have divergent values and that there are also various political systems. Consequently, there can be no absolute rules guiding business activities. When there are regional differences about what is considered proper behaviour, it is appropriate to allow local standards to prevail and take precedence over ethical standards applicable at home. Common dilemmas faced by multinational corporations are whether or not to pay bribes or use underage labour. Deontological or universal ethics would dictate that the use of child labour is always totally wrong. Ethical relativism would have us examine the issue in a different way. Is it wrong to employ the child if the child's family is dependent on that wage for subsistence living? What are the consequences of not employing the child? What are the alternatives for the individual: starvation, prostitution? It is evident that these decisions are more complex than they first appear. Ethical relativism believes that there are few absolute rules, and one size does not fit all. Therefore, companies must tailor their decisions according to local customs. For a local company operating in just one location, it is an ethical dilemma. For a multinational company operating in over 100 countries worldwide, it would be an administrative nightmare, in addition to being a moral dilemma. Thompson *et al.* (2008: 321) argue that such a position is "tantamount to rudderless ethical standards" and "is morally unacceptable".

Integrative Social Contracts Theory

Donaldson and Dunfee (1994) propose a compromise between universalism and relativism. The integrative social contracts theory suggests that a company should, as much as possible, adhere to universal ethical principles that control company action while also taking into account local customs that further define ethically acceptable behaviour. Where there is a conflict between the two, then universal principles take precedence. The universal rules about right and wrong, to which groups around the world subscribe, form a binding social contract between the company and society. It is essentially a universal system, with some flexibility built in. Ethical relativism might be 'morally unacceptable', but the variations in ethical standards from one country to another make universalism very difficult to operate in a competitive environment. The integrative social contracts theory goes a long way to reconciling the two.

While universal laws are very prescriptive, in reality they often require some interpretation. Measurement of human rights in a country, for example, cannot be calculated in the same precise manner as, for example, measuring temperature. It requires managerial judgement. From that point of view, the integrative social contract theory seems to safeguard universally accepted principles while allowing for managerial judgement. However, when one re-examines the universal system above, it must be recognised that Kant allowed for interpretation: "The business of philosophy is not to give rules, but to analyse the private judgements of common reason."

Code of Ethics

Many organisations have drawn up a code of ethics to guide managers in making difficult judgements. A code of ethics is a written statement of what the organisation considers to be important values and standards of behaviour. It is important that time and effort goes into making this a meaningful document. Enron had a values statement, but it was meaningless. According to Lencioni (2002: 113), "empty value statements create cynical and dispirited employees, alienate customers, and undermine managerial credibility". Lencioni provides a framework for drafting meaningful company values:

- Managers must understand the different types of values and what actually constitutes the company's core values.
- The values statement must be aggressively authentic; something that the company considers integral to the success of the company rather than a slogan more fitting to a greeting card.
- It must be owned by the company and be reflected in how it operates.
- The values must be woven into every aspect of the company.

In addition to guiding ethical decisions, values are also important for the company's vision. It will be remembered from the previous chapter that Collins and Porras (1996) regard values as an integral part of the company's vision.

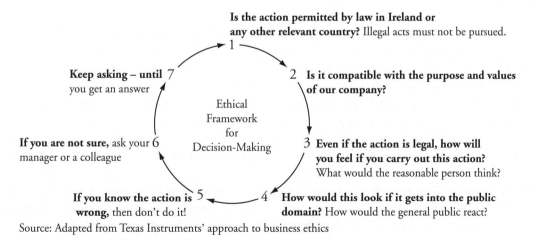

Source: Adapted from Texas Instruments' approach to business ethics

Figure 4.1 *Diagram of Ethical Framework for Decision-Making*

The framework above will help guide managers and employees in making day-to-day decisions concerning their work. The aspiration for all employees should be to behave in an ethically sound fashion, dedicated to maintaining the highest standards. Managers should exercise ethical leadership. This entails not only complying with the law on all matters, but ensuring that all aspects of their work reflect high moral standards. That includes ensuring that there are no unintentional acts or ethical breaches as well as deliberate ones.

Evidence of Unethical Behaviour

There are many examples of unethical and illegal behaviour around the world. There are various reasons for such behaviour. If it were to be summed up in two words, they would be: human nature. Despite the ideals expressed by the great philosophers, there have always been those who will act in their own self-interest and believe, to borrow the line from the original 1988 movie *Wall Street*, that "greed is good". It is unfortunate for the majority of people who work in an honest and ethical fashion, that they should be affected by such behaviour. With the recent collapse of the banks in Ireland, it was not only thousands of small investors who lost their money in the destruction of the share price; tens of thousands also saw the value of their pension funds destroyed. In both cases, this will have a severe long-term impact on their net wealth. In addition, many staff members employed at the banks will lose their jobs over the next few years. Because of cases like this, the wider stakeholder approach to corporate governance is advocated.

Companies must ensure that there are procedures in place, supported by an ethical culture, to prevent unethical conduct by employees. While a company cannot directly account for an individual's excessive pursuit of personal wealth, there are ways in which it can ensure proper corporate behaviour. In particular, it must ensure that the pressure on staff members to reach financial targets is fair and reasonable. Once the company prioritises the bottom line over ethical behaviour, it starts on a slippery slope. As discussed above, the company's values statement must be woven into every aspect of its work.

Examples of unethical behaviour are not just confined to large multinational companies. There are a whole range of Irish examples that do not reflect well on our collective attitude to ethics. The various tribunals of inquiry do not show the country in a good light. While much of the focus is on politicians, it must be remembered that the allegations of misconduct also involve business people. Over the years, there have been many cases of abuse of various forms of EU funding. In recent years, there has been evidence of price fixing in a number of industries. Many of the ethical scandals involved Irish banks. In the 1970s and 1980s, businessman Des Traynor ran a complex banking system that facilitated many Irish businesses and professional people to deposit large sums of money in a bank in the Cayman Islands in order to evade tax. The money was routed through the Guinness & Mahon bank in Dublin. The Ansbacher affair as it became known was finally exposed in 1997. By 2006, €56 million was collected by the Revenue Commissioners, including interest and penalties, from 108 Ansbacher depositors, which included some of the most respected business people in the country. In 2004, AIB made a statement saying that five former senior executives had broken Irish tax laws by investing money in the British Virgin Islands using an offshore investment company called Faldor. This company had been managed by AIB Investment Managers (AIBIM).

There have also been numerous instances of inappropriate selling of financial products and overcharging of bank customers, whereby various charges were loaded onto people's accounts without their knowledge. In addition, Irish banks facilitated large-scale tax evasion by enabling people to avoid paying deposit interest retention tax (DIRT) on savings purportedly belonging to individuals living abroad. It must, however, be remembered that in order for people to avail of this benefit, they had to *knowingly* sign a declaration that they were living abroad, when that was untrue. At a time when exchequer finances were in very poor condition, millions of pounds were withheld in tax payments to the State. The DIRT inquiry was set up in 1999 to investigate the extent of bogus non-resident accounts. By 2006, the Revenue Commissioners had collected €838 million in relation to these bogus accounts from non-compliant taxpayers and financial institutions (Carswell, 2006). The most high-profile tax settlement came about following the Flood Report in 2002 when the Bailey brothers, Mick and Tom, paid €22.17 million to the Revenue Commissioners (Ross, 2009). While many would claim that these incidents are in the past, the 2008 report by the Comptroller and Auditor General said "there is still a culture of non-compliance and non-payment of tax in Ireland".

In commenting on the Comptroller and Auditor General's report, de Bréadún (2008) noted: "During 2007, while 12 people were imprisoned as a result of welfare fraud, none of the nine people convicted for serious tax evasion during 2007 are likely to spend any time behind bars." It would appear that as a society, we still have a problem viewing the payment of tax as an ethical and legal imperative.

In 2007, the Supreme Court found that DCC Plc and its then CEO Jim Flavin had engaged in insider trading. At the time of writing, there are ongoing inquiries into the activities of the CEO and later chairman of Anglo Irish Bank, Sean Fitzpatrick, over the movement of tens of millions of Euro in directors' loans out of the accounts of the bank. Throughout the banking sector at present, there are almost daily revelations of what can, at best, be called questionable practices by those charged with running many of these organisations.

Dr Diarmuid Martin, Archbishop of Dublin, speaking at the World Economic Forum meeting in Davos, Switzerland in January 2009, talked about the responsibility that bankers have in "creating a climate of responsibility from within". He believes that bankers have responsibility not just to themselves, their boardrooms and investors, but also to economic and social sustainability. Commenting on the excessive amount of "irresponsible lending and irresponsible management of lending" that had taken place in recent years, the Archbishop said that this will have enormous social consequences for Irish people. Martin believes that "morals and ethics cannot be injected from the outside", and that the business and financial community were part of the problem in the first instance, but they would also have to be part of the solution (Carswell, 2009).

The repercussions of these revelations go far beyond the reputation of the institutions involved. The reputation of the country as a place to do business has been severely damaged as a result. One thing is certain at this point: the approach to corporate governance and regulation will have to undergo major reconstructive surgery. The comment by Marcellus in Hamlet could easily be applied here in Ireland:

"Something is rotten in the state of Denmark."

Hamlet. Act 1, Sc. 4

Relating Ethics to Business

The above relates to serious ethical failures in business. Ethics also concerns everyday decisions that managers have to make. Organisations are open systems, meaning they are dealing with a wide variety of stakeholders, and ethics shapes all of these relationships. Chapter 6 will deal with the value chain and the value system: how organisations deal with their suppliers and distributors. Each person and organisation that the company deals with is entitled to be treated fairly, and to share in the overall profit. The organisation also deals with the wider community, with the government, and other groups. Ethics also concerns internal issues: how it treats its employees in terms of pay and conditions, does it treat them in a respectful manner, does it provide them with stimulating jobs? How the organisation deals with these stakeholders will be examined in detail in the next section on corporate social responsibility. Another topical ethical issue that requires examination is whistle-blowing.

WHISTLE-BLOWING

Whistle-blowing occurs when a member (or ex-member) of an organisation discloses any action by others in that organisation that is either illegal or unethical. It covers issues such as when a company is causing harm, directly or indirectly, to members of the public, violating human rights, or doing things that are illegal either under statute law or common law. It may also be an action of a serious nature that is contrary to the purpose of the company. All of these situations can be as a result of managerial action or, in other cases, a lack of such action.

Illustration 4.1: The Watergate Scandal

Long before Julian Assange became famous for releasing sensitive, classified information on his controversial Wikileaks website, Mark Felt was one of the first and most famous whistle-blowers. Felt, who went by the alias "Deep Throat", was number 2 to Interim Director L. Patrick Gray of the FBI at the time of the break-in at the Democratic National Committee's Headquarters in the Watergate office complex in Washington in June 1972. It later emerged that it was members of President Richard Nixon's campaign team that broke into the offices to spy on the Democratic Presidential campaign. Mark Felt was the source that helped reporters Bob Woodward and

Carl Bernstein of the *Washington Post* break the Watergate scandal. He insisted on remaining anonymous and it was Woodward and Bernstein's editor that came up with the alias. He fed the reporters information on the break-in bit by bit and the reporters eventually cracked the story that ultimately brought down President Nixon. The Nixon Administration did everything in its power at the time to subvert the FBI's investigation into the break-in and the subsequent cover-up of the crime.

The year prior to the scandal, Mark Felt had been passed over for promotion as Director of the FBI after J. Edgar Hoover retired. Was being passed over for promotion his motivation or was it disgust at the abuse of political power? Felt died in 2008 at the age of 95 and, while his identity was only made public three years before, his motivation was never made clear.

> "Soft you; a word or two before you go. I have done the state some service, and they know't; No more of that."
>
> *Othello*. Act 5, Sc. 2

Regardless of his motivation, Felt's actions changed US history and strengthened democracy.

Whistle-blowing raises a number of ethical issues. First, one must examine the motivation of the person making the disclosure. It could be for perfectly laudable reasons or it may be because the employee has a personal grudge against the company, such as not being considered for bonus payments or not being promoted. For the purpose of the discussion here, it will be assumed that there are genuine reasons for any disclosure and that it is of substantial interest to the wider public.

Employees must distinguish between loyalty owed to the organisation on one hand, and the wider public on the other. This can pose a dilemma for the employee in question. Loyalty to an organisation is something that is generally fostered and is seen to be a good thing. Working closely with colleagues further develops this sense of corporate identity and commitment. In the course of their work, employees will come across information that is commercially sensitive and confidential. For that reason, every employee owes loyalty to that organisation. It is qualified, however, in the sense that each and every individual has to take responsibility for his or her actions, and if those actions by the company are illegal, it is immaterial if the employee was acting under the direction of a manager or not.

Any work being carried out in commercial life has to be within the bounds of what is legal. Where any activity is illegal or morally wrong, the employee has a clear duty to report it. However, this can often have grave consequences for the individual involved. If the organisation is involved in illegal activity, it will not take kindly to those actions being made public. The whistle-blower concerned may not be promoted in the future, may find themselves out of a job, and could face difficulties in finding another job, as the company may destroy their reputation in the industry. If a person is the breadwinner in a family, such a prospect is quite daunting. On the other hand, doing nothing is not a moral option. In the words attributed to Edmund Burke: "For evil to flourish, all that is necessary is for good men to do nothing."

The consequences of whistle-blowing can be very serious for all concerned. There is an onus on the individual to ensure that, in making a public disclosure, they have accurate information. If it is inaccurate, not only will it damage the reputation of the company, but it will also besmirch the reputation of fellow workers – without justification. In many cases, the facts may not be all that clear-cut and there will be a question of judgement involved as to whether it should be reported or not. In many aspects of law, the acid test is what would the reasonable person think? The person concerned will have to take into account the seriousness of the situation, as well as the immediacy of the problem. Where possible, the whistle-blower should endeavour to obtain documentary evidence. In making or not making a disclosure, the person involved must take responsibility for their own actions.

In the first instance, the person should seek to have the problem redressed within the company. There are many occasions in which illegal activity is carried out without the knowledge or approval of those at the top, as in the case of rogue traders such as Nick Leeson (Barings Bank). As a result, one's duty to the organisation takes precedence over making such knowledge public. Indeed, it may jeopardise any legal action that the company may wish to take against the individual concerned. Again, this can pose a dilemma. Is the activity being carried out at a lower level or at the very top of the organisation? Unless one has genuine grounds to believe that the activity concerned is being undertaken with the approval of top management, there is an obligation to exhaust all internal channels before bringing it to the attention of those outside the organisation. Going outside the organisation should be the last resort.

From the perspective of good corporate governance, the organisation should be run in such a way that makes whistle-blowing something that should never have to happen in the first instance. The organisation has a clear moral duty to its employees to ensure that they are not being asked to do anything illegal or compromising. By having clear corporate goals based on ethical principles, and by ensuring that the organisation is run in a clear and transparent manner, employees should then feel free to notify management of any wrong-doing without fear of any repercussions. This again highlights the need for sound corporate leadership. Just as the organisation should not cause the situation in the first instance, it also has a moral duty to protect employees who highlight illegal practices by the corporation.

Whistle-Blowers' Charter

Many organisations are now developing a 'whistle-blowers' charter', which is designed to enshrine the rights of employees in disclosing any untoward practices. To ensure that such a charter is based on substance rather than rhetoric, some companies will subject themselves to an independent audit to validate the charter. In order to give employees confidence that the company's attitude to whistle-blowing is serious, it may set up a separate division that will allow employees to bypass the normal chain of command and report directly to a company-nominated or an outside investigator, perhaps anonymously. The investigator can than examine the claim and take whatever action is appropriate. Central to the policy of whistleblowing must be the clear expectation by the employee that they will be protected by the organisation and not be victimised in any way. On the other hand, employees must be aware that making false or malicious allegations will be considered a serious disciplinary matter.

While many private organisations have brought in their own charter, there is no statutory provision in Ireland to protect whistle-blowers. This is despite the fact that there have been numerous examples in recent years where many organisations stood over wrongdoing, and where numerous people in those organisations were aware of what was going on and yet did nothing. This became quite evident in the Morris Tribunal findings in relation to Garda members in Donegal. There are many reasons, no doubt, why people who are aware of illegal or unethical behaviour do nothing about it, but without proper protection in place, fear must play a part.

In the Lourdes Hospital Inquiry in 2006, Ms Justice Maureen Harding Clark noted that there was little turnover in staff and there was significant job insecurity that "may have influenced a climate of silence" (Harding Clark, 2006: 38). In that case, it was a whistle-blower that brought to light the appalling wrong carried out by Dr Michael Neary in the Lourdes Maternity Hospital, Drogheda over a 25-year period. Judge Harding Clark also noted that during the inquiry: "We heard comments to the effect that whistle-blowers would never get a job in Ireland…". (The Lourdes Hospital Inquiry will be developed further in terms of 'groupthink' in Chapter 12.)

In the UK, the Public Interest Disclosure Act 1998 came about as a result of a number of disasters that could have been avoided if employees had been able to voice their concerns without fear of retribution. In their 2008–2009 annual report, the UK's Committee on Standards in Public Life highlighted the importance of such channels: "Whistle-blowing, following agreed procedures can be an instrument of good governance and an important safeguard against fraud, malpractice or maladministration" (Committee on Standards in Public Life, 2010:41). In Ireland, however, there are many who disagree. In 2007, all but two of the Company Law Reform Group, chaired by Dr Thomas Courtney of Arthur Cox Solicitors, rejected the notion of a law on whistle-blowers' protection. The group comprised representatives from the Irish Banking Federation, the Irish Stock Exchange, the Institute of Directors, IBEC, the Law Society, the Bar Council, leading individual law firms, government departments, the Financial Regulator, the director of corporate enforcement and SIPTU. Despite many examples of failure of corporate governance over the decades, the report stated that it found no evidence of endemic failure in corporate governance or in its enforcement that would require enhanced whistle-blowing provisions. However, in May 2010, James Hamilton, the Director of Public Prosecutions, called for such protection in order to secure prosecutions arising from the behaviour of some bankers, saying that in many cases, without a whistle-blower, there would be no case (Barrington, 2010).

In the 2009 Code of Practice for the Governance of State Bodies, section 2.11 deals with confidential disclosures: "The Board should put in place procedures whereby employees of the State Body may, in confidence, raise concern about possible irregularities in financial reporting or other matters and for ensuring meaningful follow-up of matters raised in this way." This requirement goes a small way towards providing protection to whistle-blowers but it falls far short of what is required.

Punishing Whistle-Blowers

The need for legislation to protect whistle-blowers is self-evident. There are many examples of people who did speak out and were victimised or punished for whistle-blowing. Eugene McErlean was former Group Auditor for AIB. He was wrongly blamed for not preventing the operations of rogue trader John Rusnak, who lost $691 million at AIB's US subsidiary, Allfirst. Mr McErlean was effectively forced to leave the bank when AIB issued a press release which likened his departure to the Rusnak affair (Ross, 2009). Mr McErlean had previously uncovered systematic overcharging of customers at AIB as well as the use of off-shore companies to trade in AIB shares by AIB's stockbroking subsidiary, Goodbody. He reported the matter to his superiors in AIB and to the Financial Regulator. However, nothing came of it at the time, and it was only after RTÉ ran an investigative programme a few years later that the matter was properly dealt with. Nobody in AIB was disciplined over the affair, although Mr McErlean hasn't worked since leaving AIB in 2002. It took until May 2009 before the then CEO of AIB, Eugene Sheehy, finally apologised publicly to Mr McErlean for the way in which he had been treated by the bank.

ORGANISATIONAL APPROACHES TO ETHICAL BEHAVIOUR

Different companies will adopt different ethical stances on how they conduct their affairs. This will largely be a reflection of the culture of the organisation and of the individual managers and their ethical standards. There are various frameworks, usually based on a continuum. Thompson *et al.* (2008: 333) list four organisational approaches to ethics:

- **The unconcerned approach** – where executives believe that the notion of right and wrong is dictated by government in its laws and regulations. Once it keeps within the law, the company is entitled to do what it likes, and management's time should not be wasted by concerning itself beyond what it is legally required to do.
- **The damage control approach** – managers are wary of scandal and adverse public comment. They will adopt a code of ethics for the purpose of window dressing, but company personnel are not required to adhere to its contents. It will turn a blind eye to shady practices as long as there is no danger of public exposure.
- **The compliance approach** – where executives will comply with a high ethical standard in their dealings with staff and customers, and it is strictly enforced. However, much of the motivation for this approach is a desire to avoid damage to the company's reputation.
- **The ethical culture approach** – top executives believe in a high ethical approach that becomes ingrained in the corporate culture and governs everything the organisation does.

Every organisation will fit somewhere along the continuum. It is towards the latter end of the continuum that companies will engage in corporate social responsibility, which is discussed in the third section of this chapter.

CORPORATE SOCIAL RESPONSIBILITY

Introduction

Corporate Social Responsibility (CSR) is an aspect of business that has gained great importance over the last few years. In 2004 and again in 2007, the Economist Intelligence Unit carried out a survey on the degree of priority given to CSR by global executives. There was a sharp increase in just a three-year period and this trend is expected to continue over the coming years (Franklin, 2008: 4). Companies recognise that it is no longer an optional extra but a concept that must be embraced. The only question remaining is in what way should companies adopt CSR? The European Commission defines CSR as: "A concept whereby companies integrate social and environmental concerns in their business operations and in their interaction with their stakeholders on a voluntary basis."

Criticisms of Corporate Social Responsibility

While increasing profits is clearly a strong imperative for commercial organisations, the belief that it is the only view, as we shall see, is both outdated and incomplete.

However, before dealing with the importance of CSR, it is important to recognise that it is a concept which does not have universal approval. The Nobel Prize-winning economist Milton Friedman was of the opinion that: "The social responsibility of business is to increase profits." He was not a fan of the concept of CSR! This is a view shared by some contemporary writers such as Robert Reich who served as President Clinton's Labour Secretary. Reich (2008) believes that by companies getting involved in CSR, democracy has become less responsive to its citizens. He argues that business and politics should be kept distinct.

Many business executives would agree with the above commentators that it is the role of governments to look after the needs of society and that companies should concentrate on doing what they do best – making profits for their shareholders. That is making an assumption that governments everywhere operate in the best interests of society. Not all governments are democratically elected and, clearly, there are many who do not act for the benefit of their citizens, and some who engage in human rights abuses. In the spring of 2008, the government in Burma actively impeded international aid efforts to save stricken refugees left homeless after a devastating typhoon. As globalisation impacts on so many industries and companies, such companies have to face a variety of different types of governments and standards in their day-to-day operations. There is, consequently, a moral imperative on organisations to take a more active role.

Other critics consider that for executives of companies to engage in CSR is dealing in shareholders' funds – to which they have no right. Such funds belong to those who have invested in the company. Are such criticisms valid? Professor Kellie A. McElhaney, Faculty Director at the Haas School of Business in the University of California, Berkeley, defines CSR as:

> "A corporate strategy that is integrated with (1) core business objectives and (2) core competencies to create financial and social/environmental returns and is embedded in corporate culture and day-to-day business operations."

(McElhaney, 2008)

When we examine the definition above, we see that it creates *financial* as well as social/environmental returns. This is often referred to as the 'triple bottom line effect' of economic, social and environmental performance and helps ensure the sustainability of the programme. The World Business Council for Sustainable Development uses the definition of sustainability developed by Gro Harlem Brundtland (the former Norwegian Prime Minister): "Meeting the needs and aspirations of the present without compromising the ability of future generations to meet their own needs" (Brundtland, 1987).

For those companies who engage in CSR, there is the potential (but it must be managed strategically) to create even greater shareholder wealth than they otherwise would. CSR is not about how you spend the money you make; it is about how you make the money you spend. When one examines corporate scandals such as Enron, one can see how greed – both at corporate and individual level – can destroy not just the company itself, but also have a devastating impact on all of its stakeholders.

Stakeholders

Inherent in the concept of CSR is the view that organisations are open systems dealing with multiple stakeholders (see Chapter 1). These relationships are ever-present and dynamic and they are also inter-related. It involves discussing with stakeholders the issues that are of common interest and

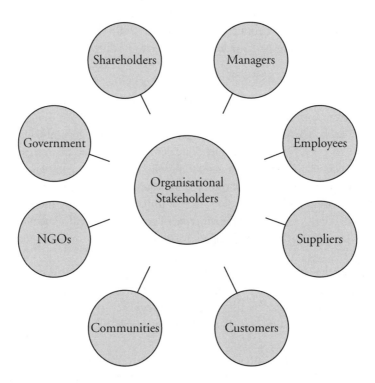

Figure 4.2 *Organisational Stakeholders*

then incorporating them when developing strategy. While the concept of stakeholders has been discussed previously, it is necessary to revisit it in the context of CSR.

Shareholders There has to be an acceptance by the major shareholders that they want the organisation to be involved in CSR. Without this support, it would be difficult for managers to fully engage in the process. According to Franklin (2008: 4), one out of every nine dollars under professional management in the US now involves an element of 'socially responsible investment'. Many of the big banks such as Goldman Sachs have started to integrate environmental, social and governance issues into some of their equity research.

Managers CSR takes many different forms. Many companies pay a proportion of their profits to chosen beneficiaries. Others allow staff members to become involved in projects and pay for their time doing this work. While these have to be sanctioned by management, and can be very important for the beneficiaries, the main emphasis should be on *strategic* CSR. That will not succeed if those at the top of the organisation are not fully committed, and they must lead by example. They are ultimately the engine driving CSR in the organisation. Marks & Spencer has come up with a CSR programme called 'Plan A' (so called because they believe that there is no Plan B). It is a €200 million, business-wide plan and each store has a dedicated 'Plan A' champion. This is a very comprehensive programme that includes 100 action points to be achieved by 2012, which include becoming carbon neutral, increasing the amount of organic food and fair-trade cotton, eliminating waste going to landfill and many others (http://plana.marksandspenser.com.2008).

Employees Employees and management need to work together as a team to ensure that the company policy of CSR is implemented at an operational level. Many companies are coming under pressure from their employees to engage and be part of the process. Perhaps one of the first Irish examples of this was in the 1980s when the workers in Dunnes Stores in Dublin refused on principle to handle South African goods in protest against the apartheid regime. This resulted in a long strike, and much financial hardship for the workers, but it succeeded in bringing attention to the issue of apartheid. Throughout the world, workers are recognising the importance of working for a company that has a policy of CSR, and it is also an important tool for organisations in the recruitment of people who will fit in with such values and culture.

Suppliers Companies cannot engage in CSR in isolation. The clothing apparel company Nike came in for much criticism in the early 1990s because of their practice of using poorly-paid labour in developing countries. Companies and their suppliers have to work together in the supply chain to ensure the process is meaningful and transparent. With globalisation and outsourcing, this can often be difficult to achieve in practice, but it can be done. (This will be further examined later in this chapter.) There are conflicting demands here. Porter's Five Forces analysis – bargaining power of buyers, in particular, suggests that a company should pay the lowest possible price for its supplies (Porter, 1980). However, suppliers too are entitled to reasonable remuneration for their goods (it does not always follow that cheaper inputs result in lower prices for the consumer – often it is just greater profits for the manufacturer/retailer). Fair trade coffee, for example, ensures that the coffee growers receive a reasonable price for their produce.

Customers The demand for CSR often originates from the company's customers and, consequently, organisations must be in tune with these demands. A survey of 25,000 people carried out by Marks & Spencer showed that 75% of consumers in Britain are interested in green shopping (Franklin 2008: 16). Customer power is not to be underestimated, and it ranges from positive action in purchasing, on one hand, to boycotting companies on the other. Ultimately, no company can afford to alienate potential customers.

Communities When corporations are negligent or are prepared to exploit resources for their own profits, it is often local communities that suffer, and sometimes the consequences can be devastating. In December 1984, an explosion at the Union Carbide pesticide factory in Bhopal, India, caused 27 tons of deadly methyl isocyanate to leak, quickly spreading to the nearby city of Bhopal where half a million people lived. It is estimated that some 20,000 people have died to date as a result. The plant was loss-making from the start and managers allowed the equipment to fall into disrepair, and it was inevitable that such an incident would happen. The surrounding area is still contaminated and over 120,000 people are still suffering the effects of the disaster (www.bhopal.org. 2008). Here in Ireland, the Hanrahan family ran a mammoth legal battle during the 1980s with the chemical company Merck, Sharp and Dohme in County Tipperary. The family ran a 256-acre farm adjoining the factory. Their cattle were dying mysteriously, and the family believed emissions from the factory were causing their deaths. They lost their case in the High Court, but the Supreme Court found in their favour on 5 July 1988 in a landmark ruling (Coogan, 2003).

However, there are also examples of positive interaction. The Dublin Docklands Development Authority works very closely with the local community to ensure that they are an integral part of the development of the Docklands area. This is done in both its direct contact with the community groups and also acting on behalf of those community groups in their dealings with the many corporations being established in the area. In general, communities benefit from a company's policy of CSR, and both the organisation and the community need to work together to ensure that maximum benefit is obtained from the available resources. Collaboration is a vital part of the process. In some instances it is local communities who benefit, but in recent years there has been a move towards the globalisation of CSR. Now, it is often distant communities who reap the benefits, such as with fair trade coffee.

NGOs The term NGOs (non-governmental organisations) covers a wide spectrum of organisations that campaign or operate on a variety of issues that include charities, the environment and human rights. Initially, it was often NGOs who highlighted unethical, and, indeed, illegal practices by companies. Such intervention led to antagonistic relationships between both groups. Now, as we shall see, both sides have much to gain by co-operating and working towards the same goals. Such co-operation can pre-empt difficulties from arising in the first instance and lead to a win-win situation for all concerned.

Governments To ensure maximum the benefit of CSR programmes, it is also necessary to work closely with governments, particularly in developing countries. In Ireland and, indeed, throughout the EU, the government is bringing in much tighter regulations covering the entire spectrum from climate change to health and safety. While responsible firms may complain about the 'nanny state', it ensures that the damage caused by irresponsible companies is kept to a minimum and when breaches occur people will be held accountable.

Stakeholder Mapping

The ability of management in a company to pursue a particular strategy will depend on a number of influences, not least of all the reaction of the various stakeholders involved. If a strategy is likely to be controversial in any way, a useful exercise for managers is to develop a stakeholder map (see **Figure 4.3** below) which plots the level of interest and the level of power that each stakeholder may have in regard to that strategy.

Interest: The proximity of a stakeholder to the company indicates their level of interest in a particular strategy. The closer the stakeholder is to the company, the higher their level of interest. The level of interest on its own, however, is not sufficient to either block or promote a particular strategy.

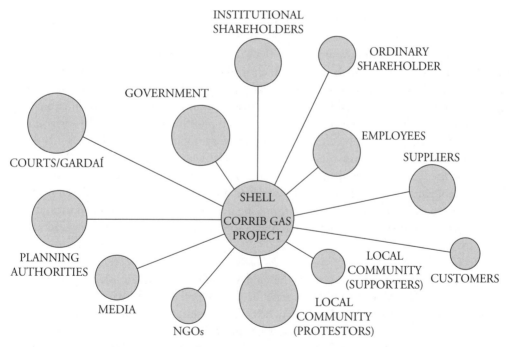

Key: The proximity of the stakeholder to the Company indicates Level of Interest.
The size of the circle of each of the stakeholders represents their level of power to influence the strategy.

Figure 4.3 *Stakeholder Mapping – Royal Dutch Shell and the Corrib Gas Project (see also **Illustration 4.2** Corrib Gas Project)*

Power: the size of the circle representing each of the stakeholders indicates their level of power to influence the company in regard to the strategy. The bigger the circle, the greater their level of power.

The process of developing a stakeholder map will focus the mind of managers on the likely reaction of the different groups of stakeholders to a particular strategy. Consequently it can assist management in successfully implementing the strategy by taking appropriate and timely measures to gain support for the strategy and by lessening any possible objections. By anticipating the reaction and taking appropriate measures, it is likely that most of the opposition can be negated, and thus unnecessary confrontation can be avoided.

Illustration 4.2 is an example of how Royal Dutch Shell interacts with its various stakeholders in relation to the development of the Corrib Gas Field off the coast of Co. Mayo. **Figure 4.3** above represents this relationship on a stakeholder map.

Illustration 4.2: Corrib Gas Project

In 1996 natural gas was discovered in the Slyne Trough basin (block 18/20) off the coast of Co. Mayo. Known as the Corrib gas field, the project involves the development of the Corrib gas field itself, the construction of a natural gas pipeline and a gas processing plant where the pipeline comes ashore. It is estimated that the field contains some 1,000 billion cubic feet of natural gas, over half of which is recoverable. The gas is 3,000m below the earth's surface, which in turn is in waters 350m deep. The field is of particular importance to Ireland as it is the first find of natural gas off the Irish coast since the Kinsale field was discovered in 1973, and it is hoped that the Corrib field will supply some 60% of the natural gas needs of the country for the foreseeable future. Since 2002, when Enterprise Oil – one of the original developers – was acquired by Royal Dutch Shell, the operator of the field is Shell E&P Ireland. In turn, it is part of a consortium consisting of Royal Dutch Shell (45%), Statoil (36.5%) and Vermilion Energy Trust (18.5%).

Royal Dutch Shell proposed to develop the field as a sub-sea production facility and to bring the gas ashore to Co. Mayo by an 83km pipeline, before processing it (dry the gas and remove any impurities) some 9km inland at Bellanaboy. The processed gas would then be fed into the Bord Gáis grid. Development of the project began in 2004, but was delayed in 2005 due to protests from locals in the Bellanaboy area in Co. Mayo, who had concerns over the safety of the pipeline and its proximity to houses in the area. There were also concerns about the discharge from the processing plant into Broadhaven Bay, an area which contains EU Special Areas of Conservation and Special Areas of Protection.

Shell contended that all of the facilities involved were in line with best international practice. The project, however, received unwelcome publicity on many occasions due to protests by the "Shell to Sea" campaign. Some of the protestors, known as the "Rossport Five", spent time in jail as a result of these protests, but much of the media coverage of these events was sympathetic to the locals involved. The protestors have, on occasions, damaged property belonging to Shell, and Gardaí have had to intervene to protect Shell workers. In 2005, Mr Peter Cassells was appointed as an independent mediator in the dispute.

In addition to the disruption caused by local protests, the project has not had a smooth run with the various planning authorities, and in 2009 An Bord Pleanála (the statutory authority that deals with planning appeals) directed that Shell redesign its pipeline to direct it away from residential areas as it constituted an unacceptable risk.

Despite the negative publicity that the project has received, there are many supporters. From the Government's perspective, it will bring much-needed employment to a rural part of Co. Mayo, both in the construction phase (up to 1,000 jobs) and in on-going operations (130 permanent jobs), and this is naturally supported by many of the local population (Pro Gas Mayo). Shell E&P Ireland is now involved in funding many community projects in Mayo. The company states that they are committed to employing local people wherever possible. The Department of Communications, Marine and Natural resources has commissioned independent safety reports on the project.

In addition to the benefits brought by employment in the area, the Government estimates that the well could be worth up to €1.7 billion in tax over the life of the gas field. In 2007, taxation rates of 25% were imposed, although in some cases, this can increase to 40% for very large finds. In addition to having a strong interest in the project, the government is also in a very powerful position in terms of granting licences. However, there are many critics of Government policy in regard to the taxation of oil and gas revenues, claiming that exploration companies can write off 100% of costs before declaring a profit and that the terms for the exploration companies are among the most favourable in the world.

The project is already a number of years behind schedule and millions of euro over budget, and the dispute has not yet been resolved. Shell Ireland has admitted that the project was initially handled badly by the company and that it should have taken greater interest in the concerns being expressed by various stakeholders from the beginning. In 2008, Mr Andy Pyle, the previous managing director of Shell E&P Ireland Ltd (SEPIL), retired and was replaced by Carlowman, Mr Terry Nolan. Prior to his new appointment, Mr Nolan spent two years living in Mayo building links with the local community. How smoothly the project will run from now on remains to be seen.

Source: this illustration was obtained from a variety of sources including: www.shell.ie/; www.shelltosea.com; www.colmrapple.com; newspapers and television reports.

The stakeholder map (**Figure 4.3**, above) is a snapshot in time. It will be seen that the Local Community (protestors) have a deep interest in the project (note the closeness of their circle to the company), and they also have a high level of power (the size of the circle representing their group). The Shell project is now many years behind schedule and many millions of euro over budget as a result of various protests and court actions taken by the protestors. Government is also very interested, and also very powerful in terms of granting licences etc. The level of interest of customers is currently low, as is their power. However, this was not always the case, as in the past many customers boycotted Shell filling stations around the country in protest over Shell's handling of the affair. The planning authorities have a low level of interest (once proper procedures are followed), but have a high level of power as they can ultimately prevent progress on grounds of planning or safety.

As a result of a particular event happening, the level of interest in a strategy may increase or decrease and also the level of power may change, e.g. protestors could get a court injunction preventing work from continuing, thus placing them in a very powerful position. Many of the different stakeholders will have links with other groups of stakeholders. The media for example will have contact with the company itself, local supporters, protestors, Gardaí and the Government. In turn, the media will inform the opinion of other groups such as customers. The links between other stakeholders (apart from the media) can also sway opinion in a positive or negative direction.

There are many influences on the response of the various groups of stakeholders with regard to a particular strategy. These influences encompass economics, social policy, sociology, law, government, ethics and values. How these factors are communicated and represented are of vital concern. The company must be open and honest in its communication and not misrepresent its position. If that happens, trust is lost and it can be difficult to regain. In turn, this can have significant implications for the success of the strategy. Inevitably, it will strengthen a company's position when it is acting not just legally, but in an ethical manner. It is also imperative that the company recognises that different stakeholders have legitimate interest and concern in various strategies, and these must be taken on board by the management when examining the various options open to them.

Areas of Concern in Corporate Social Responsibility

There are many different areas in which companies can become involved in CSR. A pressing issue for many companies is climate change and the environment. In the past, a number of large companies engaged in practices that were extremely harmful to the environment.

British Nuclear Fuels at Sellafield has been involved in a number of scandals concerning discharges of radioactive material into the Irish Sea, and attempted to cover up its actions. In 1995, Shell tried to sink an obsolete oil rig, the Brent Spar, in the North Sea in order to minimise the cost involved in its disposal. This, however, would have had major consequences for the environment. Greenpeace has played a large part in highlighting issues such as these. Other situations were accidental, but nonetheless caused major environmental damage, such as the Exxon Valdez oil spill in Alaska. That incident ultimately cost the shipping company billions of dollars in the clean-up operation and in fines. There is now much greater awareness by the majority of companies of the potential damage to their brands, and their responsibilities to the environment, and much more is being demanded by both employees and consumers.

Throughout the world, countries are beginning to realise the damage that is being done to the environment. In a report in *The Economist* (2008) by McKinsey Consultants, the environment ranked number one or number two in issues that will be most important over the next five years for both developed and developing nations. For a variety of reasons, there is now a much greater awareness among companies of the potential damage their operations can cause and, as a result, they are taking action to minimise such damage. Other companies are taking a much more proactive role in protecting the environment. Toyota, for example, has been a pioneering company in developing green motoring. Given the finite reserves of petroleum products, such work may well also play a vital role in the future success of the company.

Many organisations are becoming acutely aware of their carbon footprint and are taking active measures to reduce this, while at the same time expanding their operations. For some companies, it is an imperative because in the future customers will want to see supply chains shortened, particularly in regard to food items that might be transported thousands of miles to be sold in supermarkets. In addition, regulators will apply new and more restrictive rules. Measurement of CO_2 emissions, while not a simple task, is key to the process, as companies need to know their base line before any statements of reduction can be meaningful. Once again, top management commitment is essential to the success of such operations, and it needs to be embedded in the corporate culture.

Water conservation is also very much allied to the protection of the environment and its preservation for future generations. Access to water sources is of strategic importance to countries, such as the Golan Heights, which is part of Syria, but has been occupied by Israel since the Six Day War in 1967. The Golan supplies much of northern Israel with fresh water and for that reason alone it is unlikely that it will be returned to Syria in the near future. Jean Ryan of KCB Asset Management, who was key speaker at the Irish Association of Pension Fund Managers conference in Dublin in 2008, described water as the "blue gold", as demand increases worldwide. In an interview with Samantha McCaughran (2008) of the *Sunday Business Post*, Ryan said: "Environmental issues are here to stay, the whole issue of climate change has moved to the centre stage and it has become a major issue for investors". She pointed out that, while the search is going on for alternative energy sources, such as wind generated electricity, water has no substitute and its supply is finite. If it is not found where it is needed, it is extremely expensive to transport. Not only is water critical for human life, it can also be critical from a commercial perspective, e.g. for beverage companies such as Ballygowan.

The health of the world's population is another important theme for CSR. There is obviously a strong link between availability of clean drinking water and the health of people, particularly in developing countries, but that is only one aspect of health. In addition, many such people are suffering from diseases that are either curable or at the very least containable. In poorer countries, people often cannot afford the necessary drugs. The reputations of many large pharmaceutical companies were damaged by their refusal to make cheaper generic drugs available to combat AIDS in Africa. That is changing and many pharmaceutical companies are now making HIV drugs available at cost price.

Education is an essential component in raising the living standards of a nation. In Ireland, we benefited over a long number of years from the largesse of the Irish-American billionaire Chuck Feeney and his company Atlantic Philanthropies. Millions of dollars were donated to help develop Irish universities under strict conditions of anonymity. It was only years later that Feeney's involvement became public. Feeney made his fortune in the duty-free business and is committed to the principle of giving while living. He has now broadened the scope from education to building hospitals and other projects. It is his objective to spend the entire fortune of some $4 billion by 2015 on suitable development projects around the world. One essential criterion in terms of the selection of projects by Atlantic Philanthropies is that they must be self-sustainable in terms of generating future benefit (O'Cleary, 2006).

In addition, other Irish millionaire business people have contributed to the building of various business schools on university campuses in return for naming rights. Such contributions have played an important role in the development of educational facilities, particularly in the light of chronic under-funding by successive governments. However, it also raises other ethical issues. Many of these business people are tax exiles. The laws relating to foreign domicile are quite generous (one has to be out of the country for in excess of 183 days in the year). This poses the question: are they Irish people living and working abroad with the odd trip home, or are they substantially living and working in Ireland, and not contributing to the exchequer here? Nobody particularly likes paying taxes. However, for 99.9% of the population, they have no choice but to pay taxes in Ireland, and then decide to give to other causes. However, it is those taxes that provide the services from which all of society benefits. Taxes are not, as the New York hotel millionaire Leona Helmsley once famously said, "only for the little people".

Reasons for Corporate Social Responsibility

There are many reasons why organisations engage in CSR. First, many companies would have given a small percentage of their profits to what they considered to be deserving causes. It would have been viewed as important to give something back to the community – it was the right thing to do. This moral imperative on its own is often no longer sufficient for many reasons. Most importantly, it does not address the question of how the money was made in the first instance. Cigarette companies donating money to projects may not sit easily with the recipients, knowing that the product that generated those profits caused people to die of cancer. As stated earlier, CSR is not about how you spend the money you make, it is about how you make the money you spend. One difficult challenge for executives is trying to decide which compelling cause the organisation should support. There can be many pressing choices, each providing ample justification for inclusion. It involves balancing values and making a choice that few organisations are adequately equipped to do from a moral perspective.

It can also be difficult to measure the effectiveness of the spending, particularly in balancing social and financial costs. However, while various mechanisms are being developed to maximise the potential of CSR, this moral imperative has to remain a very important foundation that underpins the actions of the company. There are times when 'doing the right thing' is justification enough.

Secondly, many companies have begun to pursue CSR either to minimise damage to their brands or to develop and enhance those brands. There are many examples of companies that suffered damage to their brands because of their actions. In an age of instant communication, organisations cannot realistically hope to get away with wrongdoing for very long before being exposed. Such companies can be punished severely by governments and by consumers for their actions, and this can have long-lasting and severe consequences for their image. Sometimes it may be about avoiding tighter regulations being brought in. For those companies, it is all about minimising risk, and many are now co-operating with governments, NGOs and communities in order to be more responsible corporate citizens. Sometimes companies may be unwittingly caught up in controversy through their value chain. In 2007, Mattel the toy manufacturer had to recall millions of toys made in China because of concerns over safety. The threat of legal action can be a major factor in directing the action of companies. In the US, the Alien Tort Claims Act allows American companies to be sued in American courts for human rights violations committed abroad.

Other companies may not have been involved in scandals but see CSR as an opportunity to make their brand more appealing. Brand equity is the marketing and financial value associated with a brand's strength in a market. It can represent a sizable investment. In 2010, the top five brands in the world were Coca-Cola ($70.5 billion), IBM ($64.7 billion), Microsoft ($60.8 billion), Google ($43.5 billion), and General Electric ($42.8). The only non-US company to make it into the top 10 rankings was Nokia with a brand valuation of $29.5 billion (Interbrand, 2010). With so much money at stake, companies will do all they can to protect that investment. The danger here is that it is largely a defensive stance and the process is mainly cosmetic with limited positive impact for communities and for the company itself.

The third and most compelling reason is the opportunity to create value and become part of the company's competitive advantage. This is where sound business objectives overlap with corporate social responsibility. It is this category that separates the leaders in the field from the laggards and shapes the kind of company it will be. It has been termed 'enlightened self-interest', and contradicts the notion that CSR is not part of a profit-making business. By developing a competitive advantage through CSR, it is in fact creating even greater shareholder value, and at the same time benefiting all of the other stakeholders as well – in a sustainable manner. It requires a strategic framework to be developed that encompasses CSR as an integrated component of its business model. The pet food manufacturer Pedigree has a campaign entitled 'We're for Dogs'. Part of this includes an 'adoption drive' which involves making a donation to help find abandoned dogs a new home. In finding homes for these dogs, there will be an increased demand for dog food (including Pedigree), and so increase their profitability, while at the same time providing a valuable service to the community (Pedigree, 2011).

Good Business

If CSR is to benefit the organisation and the community, then it must be approached in a strategic manner. In this regard, it is very much linked to the vision and values of the company as well as to corporate governance. Again, this shows the need for the organisation to embrace a stakeholder approach. CSR is not about management, it is about leadership. According to McElhaney (2008), CSR strategy must fit two things:

- **Core business objectives:** increase sales, penetrate new markets, engage employees, reduce operating expenses, improve reputation, protect the brand and beat competitors.
- **Core competences:** the processes and activities that give a competitive advantage that others cannot easily match.

Adopting a strategic approach, CSR can add huge value to the organisation by attracting and inspiring employees, enhancing and redefining the brand and increasing brand loyalty. It also creates a distinctiveness about the company and its products.

Porter and Kramer (2006) provide a framework to ensure that it meets the needs of society, while anchoring it in the strategies and activities of the organisation. The first thing that needs to be done is to identify the points of intersection between a company and society. They suggest a two-stage framework involving:

- **Inside-out linkages** – using the value chain (see Chapter 6) to identify the different aspects of the business and to examine the positive and negative impacts of those activities. For example, in relation to the value chain's primary activities such as 'Operations', covering how the company treats worker safety, energy usage, etc. Secondary activities such as 'Technology Development' include aspects such as ethical research and product safety.
- **Outside-in linkages** – external social conditions that influence the organisation. Here they suggest using the diamond framework (see Chapter 5). The four points of the diamond are: Context for the company's strategy and rivalry (such as fair and open competition); Factor conditions (like availability of appropriately trained human resources – vital for the pharmaceutical industry in Ireland); Local demand conditions (such as demanding regulatory standards); Related and supporting industries (such as availability of local suppliers). All four aspects impact on the organisation as it operates externally and interacts with its stakeholders.

The next stage of the process, according to Porter and Kramer, is choosing the social issues with which to be involved. As stated above, there are many possibilities, but the organisation must choose those that intersect with and are of value to its own particular business. There are three categories, namely: generic social issues; value chain social impacts; and social dimensions of competitive context.

1. **Generic social issues** – those issues that may be important to society but are not significantly affected by what the company does and will not impact on its long-term competitiveness. Ford

supported research on cancer and, while such research is of major concern to society in general, it does not relate to the company's core competences.

2. **Value chain social impacts** – those issues that are significantly affected by the organisation as it carries out its operations. Fighting disease in developing countries would be a value chain impact for pharmaceutical companies.

3. **Social dimensions of competitive context** – those issues in the external environment that fundamentally underpin its competitiveness. Reducing carbon emissions is both a value chain impact and a competitive issue for car manufacturers such as Toyota.

All of these factors will vary considerably from one organisation to another. What could be just a generic social issue for one company could be central to the competitiveness of another. In some cases, there may be opportunities to collaborate with industry colleagues in areas of mutual

---

Illustration 4.3: Dove and the 'Campaign for Real Beauty'

Dove, the soap manufactured by the multinational company Unilever, recognised that the cosmetic industry in general raised serious ethical issues in how it portrayed women. Generally, advertisements seem to only include women that were both young and beautiful, and research carried out by the company found that this was having a very detrimental effect on the self-esteem of many women worldwide. To counteract this, Dove has repositioned itself as a brand. It started the 'Campaign for Real Beauty' which aims to boost the self-esteem of the majority of women who do not fall into the idealised notion of beauty that many have come to accept. This repositioning is bringing the parent company into line with its values: "As a multi-local multinational we aim to play our part in addressing global environmental and social concerns through local actions and in partnership with local governments and organisations". Its corporate purpose states that: "To succeed requires the highest standards of corporate behaviour towards our employees, consumers and the societies and world in which we live".

The 'Campaign for Real Beauty' involves using ordinary people (including older women) for their advertisements (and not having the images digitally re-mastered), as well as trying to encourage mothers to educate their daughters about what constitutes real beauty. Girls are exposed to this idealised notion of beauty every time they open a magazine, watch television or pass advertising hoardings, thus creating unrealistic expectations that will ultimately damage their self confidence (… 'talk to your daughter before the beauty industry does'). The Dove Self-Esteem fund aims to educate and develop young girls and their image of themselves, and create discussion about beauty stereotypes. In addition to contributing money to various organisations, such as the Girl Scouts of America self-esteem fund, Unilever employees are also allowed time off work to mentor girls as part of the programme. Feedback from consumers to the campaign has been very positive and it has had a major impact on sales of their products – increasing by 6% in the first year as well as increased brand awareness (www.Dove.com 2008).

concern. The company has to go beyond the categorising of social issues and 'create an explicit and affirmative corporate social agenda'. This is more than just being a good corporate citizen (which should go without saying) and goes beyond minimising any harmful effects of its operations. Both of these constitute responsive CSR. What is required is a strategic approach that goes beyond best practice and chooses a unique position, involving both the 'inside-out' and the 'outside-in' approach simultaneously. By looking at value chain activities, the company can identify aspects of that value chain that can benefit the company and society.

According to Porter and Kramer (2006) pioneering value chain innovations and addressing social constraints to competitiveness are both individually important, but the effect is even more powerful if they operate together and reinforce one another. It then becomes an integrated part of the

---

Illustration 4.4: Croke Park – An Environmentally-Friendly Stadium

Many organisations are developing a much greater awareness of corporate social responsibility and the impact that their activities are having on the environment. One such organisation is the Gaelic Athletic Association (GAA). Having built a magnificent stadium in Croke Park, the GAA wanted to put in place a programme covering its electricity, water and waste management systems. Cúl Green was launched in 2008 and is a joint initiative between the GAA and the Electricity Supply Board (ESB) designed to minimise the stadium's impact on the environment, and eventually make it carbon-neutral.

Achievements to date include:

- 11.7% less electricity used in 2009 compared with the previous year
- 52% of waste being recycled
- A reduction of 312,000 litres of water per day
- ISO 14,001 certification
- The first stadium in the world to receive a BS8901 certification

The ESB is providing expertise in environmental management and both it and the GAA are working closely to implement internationally-recognised best practice systems. The GAA has involved fans in the project, and over 18,000 people have made a carbon saving pledge. It is hoped that the initiative will have greater implications than just making Croke Park carbon-neural, and will generate far greater environmental awareness in the wider community. It is also being held up as the model that other stadiums worldwide should be working towards.

As part of its certification, the stadium is audited under three main categories: environmental, social and economic. The environmental category includes recycling, a reduction of the stadium's carbon footprint and a reduction in energy usage and water. The social category includes health and safety, community relations, and the involvement of its workforce and volunteers. The third category, economic, covers best practice models in financial and legal compliance, supply chain management and working with contractors.

Cúl Green is a strategic environmental initiative, driven from the top of the organisation. Stadium director, Peter McKenna, sums it up:

> "We decided from the beginning of the process that there could be no half measures when it came to sustainable development. It was going to be the way we managed all of our processes at Croke Park. From our organisational principles right through all our operational activities and those of our contractors, sustainability is now the key pillar in the way we manage our business."

> (Cúl Green, 2011)

business. In order to increase the supply of milk, coffee and cocoa, Nestlé has worked very closely with farmers in India and has invested large sums of money in providing equipment, technology, healthcare and education to the local communities. It has resulted in a major increase in production of high quality supplies for the company, while at the same time increasing the economic well-being of the farmers.

For CSR to be truly strategic, it must have a unique value proposition where the company meets the needs of its customers in a way that competitors cannot. It is an approach to business that requires leadership, as well as configuring the organisation to support the strategy. Many attempts at CSR are abandoned because the focus is on the wrong areas instead of measuring social impact. It requires a different paradigm. It is also selective.

According to McElhaney (2008), companies must carefully select a limited number of compatible partners that fit in with its mission. They must then work together to select clear objectives that can be measured. Ideally, it should be a long-term partnership that involves all the stakeholders, recognising that each one will bring its own strengths to the relationship. All alliances require active management. Trust and open communication also play a vital part in this relationship. No one company can address all the social issues that it identifies. Instead, it must select those opportunities that provide it with a competitive advantage as well as having a positive impact on society. In short, it is about creating shared value.

CONCLUSION

The collapse of the banking industry in Ireland has highlighted many corporate governance failures. Regardless of whether there are prosecutions in the courts, it is certain that there will be many changes to the regulations governing how business is operated. This will greatly increase the cost of compliance for Irish companies and will place a greater burden of responsibility on company directors. In turn, this will increase the necessity for appropriate professional training for people who sit on company boards. While regulations will be tightened, there will be also be a greater onus on executives to behave in an ethical manner, and there will have to be greater public accountability than has been the case heretofore. This accountability will extend not just to individual behaviour, but to how companies fulfil their corporate social responsibility. The impact of the collapse of the banking industry on society has been too great for anyone to argue that the responsibility of organisations is solely to their shareholders. A more pluralistic, stakeholder approach is required.

The three elements of this chapter – corporate governance, business ethics and corporate social responsibility – are all interlinked and form an integral part of the foundation of a company's strategy.

SUMMARY

Corporate governance is an important factor in how strategic decisions are made. It is concerned with the structures and systems of control by which management are held accountable to those who have a legitimate stake in an organisation.

There are a number of factors that need to be considered when examining corporate governance, including:

- Company structures – it will vary with the size and type of company.
- Chain of governance – this is concerned with how the decision-making process is dealt with. The board of directors has ultimate responsibility for the actions of the company.
- Company directors – their role has increased greatly in recent years. They are responsible for the oversight of the company, and they must be familiar with how the company is operating and that it is complying with all legal requirements. Failure to do so can cause directors to be held liable, and it can severely damage the reputation of the company.
- Differing board structures – the structure of the board of directors will differ from one country to another. In Ireland, the board consists of a single tier, to whom management report.
- Investment information – different stakeholders will require, and will be entitled to, different amounts of information about the company. Senior executives will obviously require detailed information about the performance of the company.

In recent years there has been a much greater focus on how businesses and individuals conduct their affairs. There have been many high profile cases of serious lapses in ethical standards, not just around the world, but also here in Ireland. There are rarely clear-cut answers when it comes to ethics: "The business of philosophy is not to give rules, but to analyse the private judgements of common reason."

Business ethics concerns the application of general ethical principles and standards to the actions and decisions of companies and the conduct of company personnel. While the majority of management theory is relatively new, the study of ethics goes back to antiquity. The three great Greek philosophers, Socrates, Plato and Aristotle, brought it to a new level. Socrates is regarded by many as the founder of moral philosophy. Much of his work centred on finding the answers to questions such as: What is justice? What is right? What is good? Plato concerned himself with a much broader range of topics including a whole range of social and moral issues. Aristotle believed that people want to be virtuous, and self-indulgence will only bring us into conflict with others. According to Aristotle, 'the golden mean' was a virtue, the midway point between two extremes (vices).

There are different classifications used for ethical theories. The classifications used here are:

- **Teleological ethical systems** – based on the concept that the morality of a decision is measured by examining the probable outcome and its consequences. It is closely linked with the theory of utilitarianism and is very similar to the managerial concept of cost-benefit analysis.
- **Deontological Ethical Systems** – based on universal principles or concepts of what is right and wrong. They are termed universal in that they transcend cultures and societies. The person most credited with developing the theory was the German philosopher Immanuel Kant. Actions are considered right or wrong regardless of the consequences of the action or its impact on others.
- **Ethical relativism** – argues that different societies and cultures have divergent values and different political systems. Consequently, there can be no absolute rules guiding business activities.

Donaldson and Dunfee (1994) propose a compromise between universalism and relativism. The integrative social contracts theory suggests that a company should, as much as possible, adhere to universal ethical principles that control company action while also taking into account local customs that further define ethically acceptable behaviour. A code of ethics is a written statement of what the organisation considers to be important values and high ethical standards.

Whistle-blowing is when a member (or ex-member) of an organisation discloses any action by others in that organisation that is either illegal or unethical. It covers issues such as when a company is causing harm directly or indirectly to members of the public, violating human rights or doing things that are illegal either under statute law or common law.

Different companies adopt different ethical stances in how they conduct their affairs. This is largely a reflection of the culture of the organisation and of the individual managers and their ethical standards. There are various frameworks, usually based on a continuum. It is towards the latter end of the continuum that companies will engage in corporate social responsibility (CSR).

CSR is defined as: a concept whereby companies integrate social and environmental concerns into their business operations and into their interaction with their stakeholders on a voluntary basis. For those companies who engage in CSR, there is the potential to create even greater shareholder wealth than they otherwise would. CSR is not about how you spend the money you make, it is about how you make the money you spend.

Inherent in the concept of CSR is the view that organisations are open systems dealing with multiple stakeholders. These relationships are ever-present, dynamic and inter-related. It involves discussing with stakeholders the issues that are of common interest and then incorporating them when strategy is being developed. There are many different areas in which companies may become involved in CSR.

For example, a pressing issue for many companies is climate change and the environment. In the past, a number of large companies engaged in practices that were extremely harmful to the environment. The health of the world's population is another important theme for CSR, as is education.

There are many reasons why organisations engage in CSR or in giving something back to the community. One difficult challenge for leaders is trying to decide which compelling cause the organisation should support. There can be a number of pressing choices. Many companies have begun to pursue CSR either to minimise damage to their brands or to develop and enhance those brands. Other companies see CSR as an opportunity to make their brand more appealing. The third and most compelling reason is the opportunity to create value, which becomes part of the company's competitive advantage. This is where sound business objectives overlap with corporate social responsibility. It is this category that separates the leaders from the rest.

If CSR is to benefit an organisation and the community, it must be approached in a strategic manner. It must have a unique value proposition where a company meets the needs of its customers in a way that competitors cannot. It is an approach to business that requires leadership, as well as configuring the organisation to support the strategy. It is about creating shared values.

DISCUSSION QUESTIONS

1. Corporate governance in Ireland has been the subject of much criticism in recent years. Discuss whether such criticism is valid or not.
2. "Ethics cannot be taught." Discuss the role that ethics plays in the education of business students.
3. As chief executive of a large Irish corporation, you wish to put in place a charter for whistle-blowers. What are the main elements that should be included in the charter?
4. "The business of business is business." Critically analyse this statement in light of recent corporate scandals in Ireland.
5. Taking a company of your choice, critically analyse the opportunities for creating value through corporate social responsibility.

REFERENCES

Aristotle, Translated by Thomson, J., 1976, *Ethics*, Harmondsworth, Penguin

Barrington, K., 2010, "Truth-seekers are left to whistle down the wind for real protection", *The Sunday Business Post*, 23 May 2010, p.5

BBC, 1998, http://news.bbc.co.uk/2/hi/europe/221508.stm, Accessed 23 July 2010

Beasley, A., 2010, "McCreevy quits over 'privileged' position", *The Irish Times*, Saturday, 9 October 2010, p.17

Bruntland, G. H., 1987, http://www.thegoalfocusedway.com/?p=112, Accessed 12 March 2011

Carswell, S., 2006, *Something Rotten: Irish Banking Scandals*, Dublin, Gill & Macmillan

Carswell, S. "Bankers must create 'Climate of responsibility' says Archbishop", *Irish Times*, 29 January 2009, p.21

Clancy, P. *et al.*, 2010, *Mapping the Golden Circle*, Dublin, TASC

Clancy, P. and Murphy, G., 2006, *Outsourcing Government: Public Bodies and Accountability*, Dublin, TASC

Collins, J. and Porras, J., 1996, Building your company's vision, *Harvard Business Review*, Sept/Oct 1996, Vol. 74, Issue 5, pp.65–77

Committee on Standards in Public Life, 2010, *Review and Annual Report 2008–2009*, London, Committee on Standards in Public Life

Coogan, T.P., 2003, *Ireland in the Twentieth Century*, London, Hutchinson

Cooper, M., 2009, *Who really runs Ireland?*, Dublin, Penguin Ireland

Cúl Green, 2011, *A cleaner, greener Croke Park*, http://www.culgreen.ie/en/About_en.aspx, Accessed 12 March 2011

de Bréadún, D., 2008, "Still a culture of Non-compliance and Non-payment of Tax", *Irish Times*, 23 September 2008, p.9

Dibb, S. *et al.*, 2006, *Marketing Concepts and Strategies*, Boston, Houghton Mifflin

Donaldson, T. and Dunfee, T., 1994, "Towards a Unified Conception of Business Ethics: Integrative Social Contracts Theory", *Academy of Management Review* 19, No.2 April 1994, pp.252–284

Dublin Docklands Development Authority, 2008, 6th Annual Social Regeneration Conference, Dublin, DDDA

Early, P.C. and Mosakowski, E., 2004, "Cultural Intelligence", *Harvard Business Review*, October 2004, Vol. 82, Issue 10, pp.139–146

Economist, The 2010, "Skirting the Issue", *The Economist*, 11 March 2010

Fáilte Ireland, 2007, Tourism and the Environment, *Fáilte Ireland's Action Plan 2007–2009*, Dublin, Fáilte Ireland

Flemming, L., 2010, "Whistleblowing and White Collar Crime: Why Ireland needs Legislative Change", *Accountancy Ireland*, December 2010, Vol.42, Issue 6

Franklin, D. *et al.*, 2008, "Just Good Business" Special Report, London, *The Economist*, 19 January 2008

Freeman, R.E., 1985, *Strategic Management: a Stakeholder Approach*, Boston, Ballinger

Grant Thornton, 2010, Corporate Governance Review, 2010, Dublin, Grant Thornton

Greenpeace, 2007, http://www.greenpeace.org/international/en/about/history/the-brent-spar/, Accessed 23 July 2010

Griffin, R., 2005, *Management*, Boston, Houghton Mifflin

Guerrera, F., 2009, "Welcsh condemns share price focus", *Financial Times*, 12 March 2009

Handcock, C., 2010, "Elderfield says level of mortgage arrears likely to get worse but should not destabilise banks", *Irish Times*, 9 November 2010, p.18

Harding Clark, S.C., Judge Maureen, 2006, *The Lourdes Hospital Inquiry: An Inquiry into Peripartum S. C., Judge Maureen Hysterectomy at Our Lady of Lourdes Hospital, Drogheda*, Dublin, Stationery Office

Hartman, L., 2002, *Perspective in Business Ethics*, New York, McGraw Hill

Higgs, D., 2003, *Review of the role and effectiveness of non-executive directors*, London, The Stationery Office

Honohan, P., 2010, *The Irish Banking Crisis: Regulatory and Financial Stability Policy 2003–2008*, Dublin, Government Publications Office

Humphries J., 2004, "Women hold 5 per cent of seats on Irish Boards", *Irish Times*, 23 January 2004

Interbrand, 2010, *Best Global Brands 2010*, http://www.interbrand.com/en/best-global-brands/best-global-brands-2008/best-global-brands-2010.aspx, (accessed 12 March 2010)

ISE, 2010, *Irish Stock Exchange Adopts New Rules in Relation to Corporate Governance*, Dublin, Irish Stock Exchange

Johnson, G. *et al.*, 2011, *Exploring Corporate Strategy*, 9th Ed., Harlow, Pearson Education Company

Lencioni, P., 2002, "Make Your Values Mean Something", *Harvard Business Review*, July 2002, Vol. 80, Issue 7, pp.113–117

Magee, B., 1998, *The Story of Philosophy*, London, Dorling Kindersley

McCaughran, S., 2008, "Investors looking for blue gold", *Sunday Business Post*, 20 July 2008

McElhaney, K., 2008, *Just Good Business*, Williston Berrett-Koehler

Morley, M. and Heraty, N. (Eds), 2000, *Strategic Management in Ireland*, Dublin, Gill & Macmillan

O'Cleary, C., 2007, *The Billionaire Who Wasn't*, New York, Public Affairs

Murphy, D. and Devlin, M., 2009, *Banksters: How a Powerful Elite Squandered Ireland's Wealth*, Dublin, Hachette Books Ireland

New, S., 2010, "The transparent supply chain", *Harvard Business Review*, October 2010, Vol. 88, Issue 10, pp.76–82

O'Brien, J. and Marakas, G., 2008, *Management Information Systems*, 8th Ed., New York, McGraw-Hill

O'Leary, J., 2010, "I should have been more pushy in opposing risk-taking at bank", *The Irish Times*, Saturday, 24 July 2010, p.11

O'Leary, K., 2010, "Partnership in Enterprise Level in Ireland", in J. Hogan et al. (eds), *Irish Business and Society*, Dublin, Gill & Macmillan

O'Toole, F., 2010, "Balancing profit and loss, ups and downs, right and wrong", *Irish Times*, Saturday, 6 March 2010, Weekend Review, p.7

Pedigree, 2011, Adopt a dog, http://www.ie.pedigree.com/adopt-a-dog, (Accessed 12 March 2011)

Plato, Translated by Lee, D., 1974, *The Republic*, Harmondsworth, Penguin

Porter, M., 1980, *Competitive Strategy: Techniques for Analysing Industries and Competition*, New York, Free Press

Porter, M. and Kramer, M., 2006, "Strategy and Society", Boston, *Harvard Business Review*, December 2006, Vol. 84, Issue 12, pp.79–92

Regling, C. and Watson, M., 2010, *A Preliminary Report on the Sources of Ireland's Banking Crisis*, Dublin, Government Publications Office

Reich, R., 2008, *Supercapitalism: The Battle for Democracy in an Age of Big Business*, Cambridge, Icon

Ross, S., 2009, *The Bankers: How the banks brought Ireland to its knees*, Dublin, Penguin Ireland

Ross, S. and Webb, N., 2010, *Wasters*, Dublin, Penguin Ireland

Senge, P., 1990, *The Fifth Discipline: The Art and Practice of the Learning Organisation*, London, Doubleday

Thomas, T. *et al.*, 2004, "Strategic Leadership in Ethical Behaviour", *Academy of Management Review*, 18, No.2, May 2004, p.58

Tiernan, S. *et al.*, 2006, *Modern Management Theory and Practice for Irish Students*, Dublin, Gill & Macmillan

Wagner, S. and Dittmar, L., 2006, "The Unexpected Benefits of Sarbanes-Oxley", *Harvard Business Review*, April 2006, Vol. 84, Issue 4, pp.133–140

Walker, D., 2009, *A Review of Corporate Governance in UK Banks and Other Financial Industry Entities*, London, The Walker review secretariat

PART TWO

Strategic Analysis

Introduction to Strategic Analysis

There is often a debate as to whether organisations should set goals and objectives *after* they have analysed the organisations's external and internal environment. Certainly, short-term goals and objectives will have to take this analysis into account and adjustments may be made to accommodate the reality facing the organisation. However, there are very strong arguments in favour of developing a vision, along with goals and objectives, as the starting point for the strategic process. First, given the considerable resources that are needed by a company to compete in the market, it is necessary to have a very clear understanding of what the company is trying to achieve so that all activity can be directed towards the achievement of its vision. The strategies that will be chosen are the means of achieving those strategic goals, and there are many possibilities. Second, while realism must prevail, companies must also be positive in their outlook. Many companies thrive in a recession, simply because they did not let the constraints of the recession hold back their thinking and their action. While some see crises, others see opportunities and they go after them.

In many ways, the process of internal and external analysis is not so much sequential to setting strategic goals and objectives, but rather, it should be an on-going process, effectively without a start or finish. Events change in the external environment. These changes can range from very gradual, and almost imperceptible adjustments, to situations where the response by the organisation has to be rapid and determined.

Chapter 5 looks at the external environment. Analysing the external environment is outward looking in its focus – factors often outside the direct influence of the company. It examines the international and national environment that will ultimately impact on every organisation in some shape or form. It also examines the particular industry within which the company is operating. Such analysis includes examining the competitive situation as well as examining how the market is segmented. Finally, it identifies what the critical success factors are for operating in that industry.

Evaluating the organisation's strategic capability is the subject of Chapter 6. Analysing strategic capability is inward looking in that it examines the capability of the organisation to pursue a course of action. While resources may be a constraining factor in the short-term, that does not mean that those necessary resources cannot be obtained or developed. In all cases, a critical factor is the quality of leadership and the quality of the people in the organisation. If Ireland is to operate in the smart economy, it is critical that there is a substantial investment in people – both at national level and in every organisation.

When the external and internal analysis is complete, the company can then construct a detailed SWOT analysis (strengths, weaknesses, opportunities and threats). Ultimately, the company will endeavour to capitalise on its strengths to pursue whatever opportunities that are available. The variety of different strategic options open to the company will be considered in Part Three of this book. The strategic options that are chosen will be predicated largely on the results of the SWOT analysis. While such analysis is somewhat subjective, it nevertheless forms a vital layer in the strategy-development process.

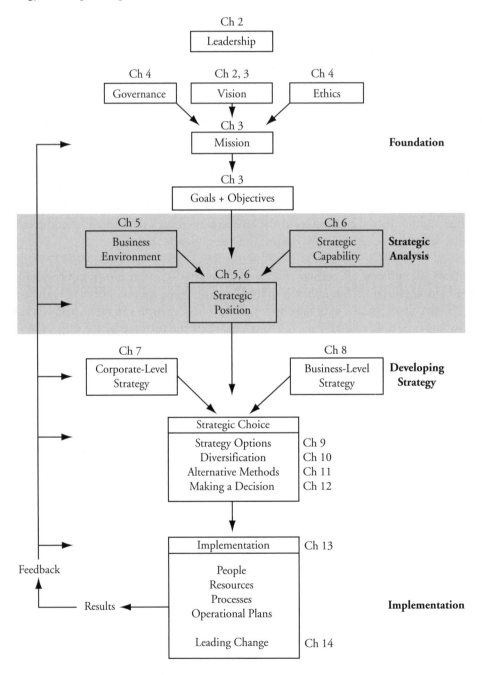

Figure 1.2 *The Strategic Planning Model*

Examining the Business Environment

LEARNING OBJECTIVES

On completion of this chapter, you will be able to:

- Differentiate between the macro and micro environments
- Evaluate the different factors impacting on an organisation
- Assess the competitive forces operating in an industry
- Conduct an analysis of the opportunities and threats facing an organisation

"We must not cease from exploration. And the end of all our exploring will be to arrive where we started and know the place for the first time."

T.S. Eliot

INTRODUCTION

The poet John Donne wrote: "No man is an island". Just as no man can live in isolation, neither can an organisation. Each one is part of a much greater business environment that impacts directly and indirectly on every aspect of its operations. The environment is ever-changing, and analysing it is a complex affair. While some of the issues will be obvious, others will be much more subtle and may well impact on an organisation before that organisation is even aware of it. For that reason, environmental analysis is not something that is done once every couple of years; it should be an on-going appraisal. Environmental analysis involves scanning the business environment to get a better understanding of what is happening in the economy and how it will impact on the company.

Definition	**Environmental scanning** is the process of collecting information about the forces in the environment.

Environmental scanning involves monitoring newspapers, journals, magazines, radio and television programmes, the Web, government publications and other relevant publications, as well as meeting people working in whatever industry one is operating in. For many executives, the volume of information coming at them can be overwhelming, and they must focus on and analyse those issues that are of real relevance to their company. There are a number of different analytical tools which will be examined in this chapter to assist in such analysis. However, there are no set guidelines for the interpretation of whatever information is available and, consequently, experience plays an important part. Analysing and interpreting the environment can be difficult:

"Reports that say that something hasn't happened are always interesting to me, because as we know, there are known knowns; there are things we know we know. We also know there are known unknowns; that is to say we know there are some things we do not know. But there are also unknown unknowns – the ones we don't know we don't know."

Donald Rumsfeld, US Secretary of Defence (2001–2006)

The ultimate aim of environmental scanning and analysis is to be able to spot the opportunities and threats that are facing the organisation. As the Duke of Wellington put it:

"All the business of war, and indeed all the business of life, is to endeavour to find out what you don't know by what you do; that's what I called 'guessing what was at the other side of the hill'."

Environmental analysis consists of two main divisions:

The Macro Environment This consists of all of the factors that will impact internationally on all countries and the factors that are more specific to the country that we are operating in. A multinational company will obviously have to take into account how these issues differ in each of the countries in which it operates.

In this chapter, examination of the macro environment will include:

1. The Global Environment
2. Porter's Diamond
3. PESTEL Analysis
4. The use of scenarios

The Micro Environment The micro environment looks at what is happening in the particular industry in which we are operating. These factors will have a more direct and possibly much greater impact than any of the macro factors. They include:

1. Understanding the industry's economic structure
2. Five forces analysis
3. Industry life cycle
4. Industry driving forces
5. Strategic groups
6. Market segmentation
7. Critical success factors
8. Opportunities and threats

THE MACRO ENVIRONMENT

The first aspect of the macro environment that needs to be considered is what is happening generally in the global environment, as this will ultimately impact on an organisation, however indirect that relationship may be. There is a very large overlap between what is happening in the global environment and in the more immediate macro environment in each country. In some cases, such as multinational companies, the relationship is reasonably seamless. For smaller companies operating in the domestic market here in Ireland, the difference is more pronounced. However, even for these companies, knowledge of what is happening in the global marketplace will help give an understanding of the changes that are taking place at home.

The Global Environment

In examining the global environment, it becomes apparent that there are different types of economies operating around the world. However, many of these can be grouped into different trading blocks. The nearest, and from Ireland's perspective the most important, is the European Union.

The European Union

The European Union has a major influence on every aspect of Irish life, but most especially on our business environment. It is a unique economic and political partnership between 27 democratic countries with the aim of providing peace, prosperity and freedom for its 490 million citizens. There are various bodies to enable the Union to function. These include:

- The European Parliament (representing the people of Europe). Its members are directly elected every five years.
- The Council of the European Union (representing the national governments).
- The European Commission (representing the common EU interest).

Background The European Union had its antecedents in the signing on 9 May 1950 of the Schuman Declaration (named after the French Foreign Minister at the time) which established a European Coal and Steel Community. This came into effect a year later with the Treaty of Paris. This put in place a common market in coal and steel between the six founding members: Belgium, the Federal Republic of Germany, France, Italy, Luxembourg and the Netherlands. On 25 March 1957, these six countries signed the Treaty of Rome, which established the European Economic Community. This was a much broader agreement covering a wide range of goods and services. Customs were abolished later and common policies on trade and agriculture were put in place. In 1973, Denmark, Ireland and the United Kingdom joined, and at the same time new social and environmental policies were put in place. The European Regional Development Fund, from which

153

Ireland benefited greatly, was established in 1975. Four years later, in 1979, the first elections to the European Parliament took place.

In 1987, the Single European Act came into force which enshrined the concept of a single market, which was to be achieved by 1993. The Berlin Wall fell in 1989, and this led to the reunification of Germany in October 1990. In December 1991, the Maastricht Treaty was signed (coming into force on 1 November 1993) adding areas of intergovernmental co-operation to existing integrated Community structures, thus creating the European Union (Europa, 2011).

The Single Market The creation of the single market has had important implications for the way in which business is conducted within the European Union, and Ireland in particular, as we shall see below. There are four main areas in which barriers have been removed.

1. **Physical Barriers**: All border controls on goods and services have been removed, together with customs control on people. Police controls still remain in place for security reasons. The Schengen Agreement signed in 1985 governs police co-operation and common asylum and immigration policy (Ireland and the UK are not party to this agreement). The enormous growth that took place in the Irish economy up to 2007 would not have been possible without the number of eastern Europeans coming to work here in every area, from construction to the tourism industry. According to the CSO, some 204,018 PPS numbers were assigned to foreign nationals in 2006. There is, however, a large drop-off each year in the number of these workers who stay in Ireland (www.cso.ie). The current economic downturn in Ireland has meant that many more have left over the last few years.

2. **Technical Barriers**: Throughout the European Union any product legally manufactured and sold in one member state must be allowed to be placed on the market in all others. This has had major positive implications for Ireland in attracting foreign direct investment into this country. For example, the pharmaceutical company Pfizer, with its manufacturing bases here in Ireland, is able to sell its products right throughout the European Union without any restrictions. One area in which Irish people have benefited enormously is in the deregulation of the airline industry which allowed companies like Ryanair to be established, resulting in airfares now being a fraction of what they were in the early 1980s. While obstacles remain in the services sector, this too has been freed up considerably.

3. **Tax Barriers**: These have been reduced through the partial alignment of national VAT rates. Each member state still has control over the rates of taxation. Ireland's corporation tax rate of 12.5% has come under much criticism by other member states as they see it as giving Ireland an unfair advantage in attracting foreign direct investment. There is also an integrated market for financial services which cuts the cost of borrowing for businesses and consumers and will offer savers a wider range of products from which to choose.

4. **Public Contracts**: All public contracts awarded by national, regional or local authorities must be open to bidders throughout the EU.

There is much work in progress at EU level that will also impact on how business operates, such as the recognition of professional qualifications, protection to prevent piracy and counterfeiting of EU goods, further liberalisation in the area of transport, particularly land transport, and liberalisation of services (the Services Directive) which will introduce competition in the area of services throughout the EU. This will have huge economic implications for Ireland.

Monetary Co-operation In 1971, the United States abolished the link between the dollar and the official price of gold, thus putting an end to the system of fixed exchange rates. European countries responded by preventing exchange fluctuations of more than 2.25% between member countries. This led to the development of the European Monetary System in March 1979. Ten years later in 1989 at an EU Council meeting in Madrid, the EU leaders adopted a three-stage process to achieve economic and monetary union. This later became part of the Maastricht Treaty in December 1991.

The first stage of the process to achieve economic and monetary union allowed for the free movement of capital within the EU, and further developed the structural funds to remove inequality between regions and accelerate economic convergence. The second stage in 1994 established the European Monetary Institute (EMI) in Frankfurt. This was made up of the governors of the central banks of the EU countries. It also allowed for the independence of national central banks and rules to apply to curb national budget deficits. The third stage saw the introduction of the Euro on 1 January 1999 which was adopted by 11 countries, including Ireland. The European Central Bank took over from the EMI and became responsible for monetary policy. Euro notes and coins followed on 1 January 2002 and are the only form of legal tender for cash and bank transactions in the Eurozone.

Under monetary co-operation there are five convergence criteria that member countries must meet in order to qualify for euro membership, including:

- Price stability in relation to the three member states with the lowest rate of inflation
- Inflation – long-term rate of inflation not greater than 2%
- Budget deficits below 3% of GDP
- Public debt less than 60% of GDP
- Exchange rate stability

The Stability and Growth Pact was signed in 1997 which provided for a permanent commitment to budgetary stability and allowed for penalties to be imposed on member countries whose budget deficit exceeded 3%. This pact was subsequently reformed in 2005. New member states are due to adopt the Euro when they meet the criteria.

Member Countries Expansion of the European Union continued in the intervening years, right up to January 2007. There are now 27 Member States in the European Union,

17 of which are members of the Eurozone. They are as follows (Eurozone members in Brackets):

Table 5.1 *European Union Members and Eurozone Countries*

Austria (Euro)	Latvia
Belgium (Euro)	Lithuania
Bulgaria	Luxembourg (Euro)
Cyprus (Greek part) (Euro)	Malta (Euro)
Czech Republic	Netherlands (Euro)
Denmark	Poland
Estonia (Euro)	Portugal (Euro)
Finland (Euro)	Romania
France (Euro)	Slovakia (Euro)
Germany (Euro)	Slovenia (Euro)
Greece (Euro)	Spain (Euro)
Hungary	Sweden
Ireland (Euro)	United Kingdom
Italy (Euro)	

The financial turmoil with the Euro began with the bailout of Greece in April 2010, followed by Ireland later that year. It highlighted many structural weaknesses in the common currency. The Maastricht Treaty was meant to keep all member countries in line by keeping budget deficits less than 3% of GDP. Including the bank bailout, Ireland's budget deficit was 32% of GDP in 2010, and nearly all the other EU member states were above the 3% level. According to Donovan (2011), one inevitable consequence of this will mean that, in future, there will be considerable interference in individual country's fiscal policies.

Ireland's budget deficit represents the difference between what the country is spending on the services it provides and the amount of revenue generated through various forms of taxation. The figure is 10 times the limit of the 3% allowable for Eurozone members and is the highest ever recorded by a developed economy in peacetime (the US had a deficit of 30% in 1943 due to the massive expansion in the production of war matériel). The figure of 32% includes the cost of the banking crisis, and if that cost were factored out, it would still be 11.6% – a similar figure to Sweden in 1993 and Argentina in 2002. Indeed, in Japan in the 1990s (which has been termed their "lost decade" due to their banking crisis), their deficit peaked at 8.7% in 1999. Even in comparison to the dark days of the 1980s in Ireland, the worst deficit was in 1985 when it reached 8% of GNP (the deficit was previously measured by the CSO as a percentage of GNP (Gross National Product) which is considered a more accurate figure as it excludes profits repatriated by multinational companies). The period from 1995 to 2007 saw a continuous budget surplus (where revenue exceeded the cost of running the country). This figure peaked in 2000 where the surplus reached 7.8%, falling to 4.3% in 2007. In 2008, the figures went into the red with a deficit of 2%, followed by a deficit of 14.6% in 2009 (*Irish Times*, 2010).

The EU refused to allow the Irish government to keep the cost of the wider banking crisis off Ireland's balance sheet in 2010. The money going into Anglo Irish Bank and Irish Nationwide is not regarded as an investment that will ever produce a return for the exchequer. This money is a one-off event, so the deficit will drop significantly in 2011. The target for 2011, as agreed with the European Commission, is to reduce borrowing to 10% of GDP or around €17 billion. The target is getting harder to reach because growth is slow, the level of GDP will be lower, and limiting our borrowing to 10% of this reduced figure will be more challenging. There will be lower tax revenue due to lower consumer spending, and there will be higher welfare payments because more people are unemployed and claiming benefits. The tax take in Ireland is around 30% of GDP compared to an OECD average of 35–36% and an EU average of 39–40%. If tax is measured against GNP, which is probably a more accurate measurement given the distortion caused by the repatriation of profits by multinational corporations, this brings our tax level up to around 35%. Almost half of earners are not in the tax net due to generous allowances. Public sector pay accounts for around 35% of total day-to-day spending. While the EU has insisted that the money committed to Anglo and Irish Nationwide be accounted for in 2010 as part of our borrowing requirement, it will be drip-fed to the banks over a period of years. The deficit is expected to gradually fall to 3% by 2015 (Taylor, 2010).

Other Trading Blocks

The North American Free Trade Agreement (NAFTA) which consists of the United States of America, Canada and Mexico, operates as a free trade zone where tariffs and quotas have been eliminated. As a trading block, it is somewhat similar to the EU, but one important distinction is that it does not cover the free movement of labour. There are similar arrangements between many of the Caribbean (CARICOM) and South American countries.

The Far East has also become a very important trading bloc with powerful economies such as Japan, Singapore, Hong Kong, South Korea, and Taiwan. There are other economies emerging in the area including the Philippines, Vietnam, Thailand, and Malaysia. China, with a population of 1.3 billion, is re-emerging as a huge economic powerhouse, not just regionally, but globally. Two centuries ago, China was also a dominant power accounting for 30% of world GDP. It then began to decline because of outdated political, economic and social systems due to domination by feudal overlords and foreign powers. The People's Republic of China was established by Mao Zedong in 1949. After Mao's death in 1976, Deng Xiaoping initiated changes, introducing Western-style market systems and opening up the country to foreign trade. China became a member of the World Trade Organisation (WTO) in November 2001. China's economy has been growing at almost 10% each year for the last decade, and now has a major trade surplus with the United States. The rise of China as a world power has major implications for the West both in terms of competition with European and American companies, and also in terms of increasing demand for Western goods and services.

In recent years, there has been an enormous increase in foreign direct investment in China, which offers preferential tax treatment to steer investment to desired locations, preferred industries and also to encourage specific investment modes, such as forming strategic alliances. China strongly prefers the formation of strategic alliances between foreign companies and indigenous companies as it provides a means for home industry to gain access to vital Western technology. Traditionally, most investment in the country occurred along the coastal region which had the best infrastructure. However, this was leading to a widening economic gap between the various provinces and, since 2005, China has encouraged foreign investment in its interior (Tian, 2007).

Doing business in China is very different from Western countries, not just because of language difficulties, but in terms of the entire business culture. Nowhere is this more pronounced than in the importance of relationships. The Chinese term is *guanxi,* which would best be described as close-knit connections. It also implies obligations for continued exchange of favours. When *guanxi* is present, it can open up many doors. The difficulties in operating in China can be overcome, and many Irish companies are succeeding in this vast country (see **Illustration 5.1** Tayto Crisps in China). The Chinese economy recently overtook that of Japan in terms of size and it is expected to become the world's biggest economy in another 15 years.

Illustration 5.1: Tayto Crisps in China

While potato crisps are manufactured in many different countries, Tayto crisps are something of an iconic Irish brand. The company was founded by Joe Murphy in Moore Street, Dublin in 1954 with a total investment of £500, and quickly developed a market in Ireland. It was Tayto that invented the famous "cheese and onion" flavour. Tayto is now owned by Largo Foods and is based in Ashbourne, Co. Meath, and also in Co. Donegal. Largo is a leading manufacturer of premium snack foods and sells to shops in Ireland, the UK and continental Europe. It has an annual turnover in excess of €90 million (Largo Foods, 2010).

Selling Tayto crisps in China probably would not have been on the radar of Largo Foods. However, in 2010, Qian Wei, an Irish-Chinese entrepreneur, approached Largo Foods with the idea of selling Tayto in China. Mr Qian now operates the office of Largo Foods in Shanghai and is selling Tayto through a number of retail chains. Known as *tudoushenshi shuping*, which translates as "Potato Gentleman Crisps", its flavours are very different to the flavours that dominate the Irish market. The flavours that appeal to the Chinese palate include Thai sweet chilli, hot and sour soup, and French chicken. The crisps retail at 50 yuan (€5) for a 50 gram packet, and so far, the reaction by consumers has been very positive. If sales continue to improve, it is planned to open a factory in Shanghai which will focus initially on Shanghai city and neighbouring Zhejiang province (Coonan, 2010). Shanghai has a population of 20 million, so getting a foothold there could prove very lucrative for Tayto. It could also illustrate the opportunities that are there for other Irish companies willing to consider markets outside Europe or the US.

Organisation for Petroleum Exporting Countries (OPEC)

The Organisation for Petroleum Exporting Countries (OPEC) covers many, but not all, of the oil producers and sets the price of oil for world markets. The price of oil has emerged as a major factor in the cost of doing business for companies around the globe. At the beginning of this decade, oil was approximately $25 a barrel. By July 2008, oil had reached $147 a barrel, but then fell back considerably. Nevertheless, the price of oil remains volatile on world markets. Unrest in Arab countries, including Egypt and Libya, in 2011 saw oil prices hit a new high. Some industries are hit directly by rising oil prices, such as the airline industry, the haulage industry, the fishing industry and many more. However, in the long run, all industries are hit as input costs soar. While the search for alternative energies continues, it will be a long time before oil can be effectively replaced, and until then the pace of economic development may well be severely curtailed (www.opec.org).

The World Trade Organisation

The General Agreement on Tariffs and Trade (GATT) was established in the wake of the Second World War in an effort to promote world trade in a balanced way that would not see the rich countries develop at the expense of poorer ones. On 1 January 1995 the World Trade Organisation (WTO) came into being to replace GATT. The WTO is headquartered in Geneva, Switzerland and consists of 150 member countries and accounts for 97% of world trade. Its principal objective is to help trade flow freely, fairly and in a predictable manner. Its main functions include:

- Administering WTO trade agreements
- Providing a forum for trade agreements
- Handling trade disputes between nations
- Monitoring national trade policies
- Providing technical assistance and training for developing countries
- Co-operation with other international organisations

Negotiations under the WTO are referred to as 'Rounds'. These agreements are made by the entire membership and are then ratified in members' parliaments. The WTO's top level decision-making body is the Ministerial Conference and below this is the General Council (ambassadors and heads of delegation). It has a number of sub-groups including the Goods Council, Services Council and Intellectual Property Council, as well as various specialised committees and working groups. The WTO secretariat in Geneva has a staff of 673 and is headed by a director-general. (The previous chairman of BP, Irishman Peter Sutherland, is a former director-general.)

The Uruguay Round began in 1987, lasted until 1994 and ultimately resulted in a wide range of trade liberalisations, in areas such as telecommunications services, information technology products and financial services worldwide. The present round began in Doha, Qatar in November 2001 and has a wide agenda including agriculture, services, WTO rules on dumping and subsidies, investment, competition, as well as a range of issues faced by developing countries in implementing present WTO agreements (www.wto.org).

Porter's Diamond

Later in this chapter we will examine competition within industries. However, it is also important to look at competition at a macro level. In his book, *The Competitive Advantage of Nations*, the

Harvard Business professor Michael Porter argues that some countries are more competitive than others, and why some industries within those countries are also more competitive.

According to Porter (1990 and 1998), countries can create their own prosperity by taking a number of steps which are not dependent on their supply of natural resources. (These steps will be discussed below.) As a result, there are major variations in competitiveness between countries, and no one country will be competitive in all industries. Porter considers that traditional economic theory on competitiveness is no longer relevant. Companies will become competitive through acts of (incremental) innovation in technology and in new ways of doing things and anticipating foreign and domestic needs, e.g. Volvo's reputation for safety. Innovation is the result of sustained effort and must be constantly upgraded and sustained as any advantage can be imitated – Korean companies have successfully copied Japanese electronics companies. Porter suggests there are two prerequisites to achieving competitiveness. First, adopt a global approach, selling the product worldwide under its own name and channels. Secondly, make existing advantages obsolete, even while it is still an advantage. He believes that innovation and change are inextricably linked.

So why then are some nations more competitive than others? The answer, according to Porter, lies in four broad attributes of a nation. These attributes, individually and together as a system, constitute the diamond of national advantage. They are:
- Factor conditions
- Demand conditions
- Related and supporting industries
- Firm strategy structure, and rivalry

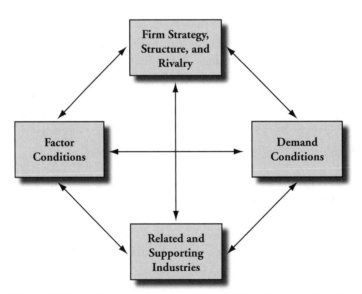

Source: Michael E. Porter, *The Competitive Advantage of Nations*, London, Macmillan, 1998

Figure 5.1 *Porter's Diamond*

Factor Conditions Traditionally, basic factors of production such as land, labour, natural resources and capital dictated the wealth of a nation, e.g. Britain during the Industrial Revolution. Previously, Ireland was considered to be deficient in natural resources, and capital was in short supply and, for many decades after independence, traditional economic thinking such as this restricted Ireland's development. Porter argues that, in the modern world, countries must instead create skilled human resources or a scientific base which must be upgraded and deployed to meet the *specific* needs of different industries. Countries and industries need to create specialised factors and then work continuously to improve them.

Countries that have a disadvantage in the more basic factors of production can encourage a company to constantly innovate and upgrade, e.g. labour shortages in Switzerland after the Second World War led to huge improvements in productivity. Similarly, high labour costs in Ireland will make productivity increases imperative if we are to regain competitiveness in global markets. This is particularly important at present where wage costs have increased substantially compared to our European neighbours. Transforming disadvantages to advantages, however, requires favourable circumstances elsewhere in the diamond: access to people with the appropriate skills, strong home demand conditions, robust domestic rivals and strong company goals that lead to a sustained commitment to the industry.

In recent years in Ireland, there has been a large increase in those attending third-level education, and the government has targeted science as being particularly important for the future development of the economy. Nevertheless, Ireland's ability to turn out sufficient numbers of suitably-qualified graduates is not as secure as some may think. In December 2008, Google abandoned plans to locate up to 100 jobs in Ireland for software engineers because they could not find enough suitably-qualified graduates. Instead, the jobs went to other locations in Europe. According to the head of Google's European Division, Dublin-based John Herlihy, there has been a "dumbing down" of educational standards in Ireland (Paul, 2008).

The development of the nation's physical infrastructure is also of vital importance for our future economic wellbeing. 'Transport 21' is an integral part of this and €34 billion was due to be spent between now and 2015 to develop a world-class transport system, which would see the development of Metro/Luas lines, heavy rail, roads, buses and regional airports. Communication systems, including broadband, will also need to be further developed. However, the current recession has had a major impact on the roll-out of 'Transport 21'.

The Hunt report on higher education advocated that research should "focus additional priority resources on a smaller number of challenges in strategically important domains that we can address effectively and in which we can make a difference. Priority should be given to research areas with the greatest potential for national economic and social returns and which will be characterised by partnership across disciplines, across the sciences and humanities, across institutions, and with industry and other relevant agencies nationally and internationally." (Hunt, 2010:55)

Ireland's gross expenditure on R&D as a percentage of GNP has risen from 1.41% in 1998 to an estimated 1.68% in 2008 and is now approaching the EU average. Under the Lisbon agenda, however, Ireland is committed to investing 2.5% of GNP in R&D by 2013, while the Programme for Government has increased this commitment to 3% of GDP (Forfás, 2009:11). The Hunt report suggests that, notwithstanding the current pressures on public finances, it is essential that the government delivers on this commitment as it is vital for the future well-being of the country (Hunt, 2010: 56).

One final point with regard to factor conditions is that it is not just their presence, but the efficiency with which those factor conditions are deployed, that is important.

Demand Conditions Porter believes that, despite living in a globalised economy, the home market is very important as it can have "a disproportionate effect on how companies perceive, interpret, and respond to buyer needs". As a result, this information puts pressure on firms to innovate. If the home demand conditions are very high in terms of the standards expected, then any company that can survive in that home market can be confident that they can withstand any competitive pressure from elsewhere in the world. In this regard, Ireland has changed very significantly in recent years. While Ireland is still a small country, the size of the home demand is less significant than the character of its demand. The market puts pressure on companies to meet high standards, to improve and to innovate constantly, e.g. small Japanese apartments created a demand for miniature electronics that was not met by American or European manufacturers. If the home market becomes saturated at an early stage it will encourage firms to export. Many Irish companies are now competing very successfully in global markets, e.g. PulseLearning (see Chapter 1).

Related and Supporting Industries Suppliers that are located in the home base that are also internationally competitive can achieve a number of advantages in the value system. They can deliver supplies and components in an efficient and cost-effective way. They also provide close working relationships that cause innovation and upgrading, especially when located near each other, e.g. the Italian footwear cluster (shoe producers, leather manufacturers and fashion houses are mutually advantageous and self-reinforcing). The internationally successful horse breeding business in Ireland has also led to the development of internationally successful horse feed companies such as Connolly's 'Redmills' in Kilkenny.

Being located in close proximity to suppliers also means shorter lines of communication, facilitating the sharing of information on customers' needs and also facilitating innovation. Companies achieve most if suppliers are global competitors. It does not benefit companies to create captive suppliers who are dependent on the home producers, as this is likely to impede innovation at supplier level. It is not necessary that all supplies can be sourced at home. Other necessary components can be sourced abroad. Innovation in one industry often transfers into related and supporting industries. A home-based related industry helps create new skills and entrants, e.g. the Japanese became world leaders in electronic keyboards from acoustic instruments and consumer electronics.

Firm Strategy, Structure and Rivalry Countries differ in many ways such as culture, demographics and infrastructure. A number of different national circumstances influence how companies are managed. Porter cites Italy as an example where many companies are privately owned and operated like extended families. This lends itself to creative industries such as the fashion industry. In Germany companies tend to be more hierarchical in organisation and management practice – suitable for production-type industries such as car manufacturing or chemicals. Despite these differences, no one system is universally appropriate, e.g. Ireland has become famous for its wealth of literary and musical talent, as well as software development. These require an individualistic, artistic approach, and a hierarchical structure would be totally inappropriate in fostering such creativity.

Competitiveness in a specific industry results from a convergence of the management practices and organisational modes favoured in the country. The goals that companies and individuals seek to achieve are also important. In Germany and Switzerland, where shares are held for a long time (often by banks), companies do well in mature industries. In the US, there is a considerable amount of risk capital available, thus supporting new industries like software. Competitive advantage is dependent on individual attitudes to work, and improving competences is also important. Local rivals play an important role as they create pressure on companies to innovate and improve, lowering costs and improving service. Geographic concentration magnifies competitive advantage, such as in Silicon Valley in California. Companies are less likely to be hooked on government aid and they look abroad for markets. Up to the 1970s, many indigenous Irish companies were protected by barriers and tariffs and did not survive open competition when we joined the EEC in 1973. Now Irish companies have learnt to compete successfully in global markets.

The Diamond as a System Porter suggests that each point on the diamond is self-reinforcing and 'together constitutes a system'. Domestic rivalry is particularly important: it promotes improvement, stimulates development of specialised factors, upgrades domestic demand and promotes related and supporting industries. Working as a system, the Diamond also tends to create 'clusters of competitive industries' linked through supply chain relationships, e.g. Japanese laptops/portable products/LCD display watches. They are often linked geographically as well as in clusters. The obvious example is Silicon Valley in California. In Ireland, there is a large cluster of (competing) pharmaceutical companies operating in Cork.

Governments play an important part in developing national competitiveness, but not in the traditional way by protecting industries through tariffs or barriers. The role of government should not be to prop up industries that are not sustainable, nor should governments preside over an unregulated market on the other. The failure of the 'light touch' approach to financial regulation in Ireland proves the necessity for an appropriate level of regulation.

According to Porter, a government's function is to act as a catalyst and challenger: it should focus on specialised factor creation that is advanced, specialised and applied to industry. It was mentioned above that the government here in Ireland is putting resources into developing a greater

163

interest in science. This will be essential in ensuring a future supply of science graduates (including PhD students) for the pharmaceutical industry. However, there has been recent criticism of the government in this regard. The general manager of Hewlett-Packard (HP) Ireland stated that the government is not doing enough to promote foreign direct investment and said "Ireland needed to get back into the game". He also said that "more needed to be done to fund technology at primary and post-primary levels. The other challenge is to increase the number of high-end researchers we get into Ireland." The Managing Director of Microsoft Ireland made similar comments in the context of the 2009 budget (O'Brien, 2008).

Porter suggests that governments should avoid intervening in currency markets in terms of devaluing currency, as it works against upgrading industry. Ireland no longer has the ability to devalue our currency as we did in the early 1990s as we are now part of the Eurozone. Instead, the focus should be on ensuring strict product safety and environmental standards, as this promotes domestic demand. We have witnessed this in recent years with stringent safety measures brought in by Irish law. Governments can also play a big role in fostering a climate of R&D in a country. Some of this can be done collaboratively, but it is best done by individual companies. Governments give certain tax incentives to encourage this. Competition must be deregulated as a lack of competition stifles rivalry and innovation. A good example here is the airline industry before and after it was deregulated.

In addition to the government, individual companies must play their part in developing a competitive advantage. It requires leadership that 'harnesses and amplifies the forces to promote upgrading'. The CEO should create a pressure of innovation within the company that responds to sophisticated buyers' needs and channels, e.g. the 3M Corporation. Companies should welcome competition rather than trying to be protected from it, as competition will improve performance and deliver a competitive advantage. By working closely with suppliers and distributors, they can upgrade the entire value chain, thus creating a more competitive product that will satisfy the end consumer, regardless of what part of the globe that consumer is found. Porter's Diamond can be used by both governments and individual companies to understand the nature of the global factors that are affecting competition in different industries and build a sustainable competitive advantage.

PESTEL Analysis

Continuing with analysis of the macro environment, it is necessary to look at other factors in the environment that will impact on the organisation, both directly and indirectly. Johnson *et al.* (2011: 50) suggest the PESTEL framework to examine the list of possible influences. PESTEL stands for:

- Political
- Economic
- Sociological
- Technological
- Environmental
- Legal

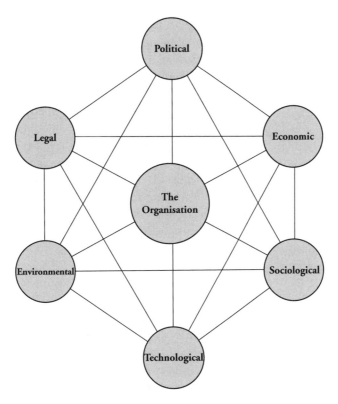

Figure 5.2 *PESTEL Analysis*

Inevitably there is a big overlap between many of these factors, and what is important when examining them is not which category any one item falls into, but the likely impact they are going to have on the organisation. For example, the government's annual budget overlaps a number of categories: Political – it is the government's budget for running the country; Economic – it impacts on the economy; Sociological – it also impacts on our standard of living; and Legal – when passed in the Finance Act, it becomes law and will be enforced by the courts.

When we looked at the definition of strategy in Chapter 1, we saw that strategy deals with the long-term direction of a company. It is, therefore, important that, when we are looking at the different factors, we assess their impact not just in the present time, but try and understand how they will change over the next few years. While there will be many possible factors facing the organisation, it is important to focus on those that will have a major impact. It is sometimes argued that the macro environment is outside the control of an organisation. However, regardless of whether it is or is not outside their control, it is imperative that managers are aware of these developments and plan accordingly. It should also be noted that, while it may be outside the remit of any one firm, most industries have representative associations that lobby government and the EU on issues facing the industry. One just has to look at the various farmer groups in Ireland, such as the Irish Farmers Association (IFA), to see the impact of such lobbying. Finally, the PESTEL framework is not just relevant when developing strategy here in Ireland, but any Irish company wishing to expand abroad would also need to use it to analyse the target country.

Political Political factors include the EU, government stability, and whether there is a favourable climate for business in the country. Obviously, the EU has, and will continue to have, a major influence on how business operates. Calls for tax harmonisation, if they were to be adopted, would significantly change the attractiveness of Ireland with regard to foreign direct investment. At present in Ireland, the rate of corporation tax is 12.5%, which is extremely low by international standards and has been very important in attracting foreign direct investment into the country. It is government policies such as these that have a major impact on the economy. Government policy directly affects the standard of living and quality of life of its citizens through investment in infrastructure and services such as health and education, which in turn influences people's decision to live and work in Ireland.

Government stability refers more to the type of government rather than any particular political party in power. A socialist government would have a different view of business than a centre-right party. A stable political system allows companies to plan for the future with a degree of certainty. It must also be remembered that governments are also major buyers of products and services in their own right, and this can have a strong impact on the economy. 'Transport 21', the current infrastructural plan for Ireland, will play a vital part in the future development of not just Irish society, but also the economy. Through its laws and regulatory bodies, the government also plays a very important part in creating the environment in which business operates. In the section on 'Porter's Diamond' above, we examined the essential nature of competition. There must be a level playing field for all companies to operate and prosper, underpinned by appropriate company law.

Illustration 5.2: Ireland's Corporate Tax Rate

A low rate of corporation tax has been the bedrock of industrial policy in Ireland since the mid-1950s. It began as an exemption on export sales profits in order to encourage foreign direct investment in Ireland. The incentive has continued in some form or another since then. The rate is currently 12.5% for all companies. Over the last number of years, the European Commission has been discussing the idea of a common consolidated corporation tax base (CCCTB) for member states. This measure would include regulations on what may or may not be written off by companies for tax reasons. It would also include rules for multinationals as to how profits made in different countries would be apportioned between member states for tax purposes. It is argued that the CCCTB would make it much cheaper and easier for businesses, as they would effectively need to engage with just one tax system. However, others argue that it is the first step towards tax harmonisation, and it is believed that the amount raised by the Irish Exchequer through corporation tax would fall significantly if harmonisation were introduced.

The low rate of corporation tax in Ireland has come under increasing pressure in recent times, particularly from the French and German governments. As Ireland was forced to accept EU money as part of its bailout plan, it will become increasingly difficult to continue to ignore such pressure. However, what will strengthen Ireland's case is a detailed comparison drawn up in a report by the World Bank and PricewaterhouseCoopers. According to Keena (2011), the report compares different countries and found that most countries apply two rates of corporation tax: a nominal or headline rate and the actual rate paid by companies after all tax write-offs have been included. The nominal rate in many European countries such as the UK, France and Germany is around 30%. However, one of the biggest critics of Ireland's 12.5% rate is President Nicolas Sarkozy of France. Yet French companies pay an actual rate of only 8.2% – a considerable reduction from their nominal rate. In Germany, the actual rate is 22.9% and in the UK it is 23.2%. While the German and UK rates are above Ireland's rate, they are still considerably less than their respective headline rates. In Ireland, the effective tax paid by corporations is 11.9%, almost identical to the nominal rate.

Controversially, the PWC report does not recommend cutting the rate of corporation tax paid in Northern Ireland. There had been many calls to bring it in line with the Republic. The report says that matching the Republic's rate would cost Northern Ireland around £280 million, with no guarantee of an equivalent benefit. In 2009, Northern Ireland, which represents only 3% of the UK's population, secured 10.3% of all new foreign direct investment jobs that came into the UK. The report says that, while the low rate of corporation tax was an important factor in the development of the Irish economy, it was only one of many factors that contributed to the success of the Irish economy during the "Celtic Tiger" years (BBC, 2011).

While the EU bailout might weaken Ireland's case for holding on to the 12.5% rate, on the other hand, maintaining a low rate is probably more important now than ever as the country struggles to get its budget deficit down to 3% by 2015. Having foreign multinational companies operating in Ireland will be vital for Ireland's recovery – and being able to pay our sovereign debt.

Economic Economic factors consist of interest rates, GNP/GDP, inflation, unemployment, disposable income, money supply etc. The economic conditions in a country are of vital importance to the success of any company. Interest rates are set by the European Central Bank (ECB). There have been advantages and disadvantages to this but, in general, it has given Ireland great financial stability. However, there have been times when the rate set by the ECB for Europe as a whole had not suited Ireland's economic conditions at that time. For many years, Ireland had phenomenal growth in GNP, but the next few years will see little or no growth. The higher the level of growth, the greater will be the demand for products and services. Inflation in Ireland has long been higher than the rest of Europe, leading to a loss of competitiveness (inflation rose from 2.5% in 2004 to 4.9% in 2007, but has since dropped significantly (www.cso.ie)). Some of the reasons for inflation are domestic, but other factors are outside our control such as interest rates (set by the ECB) and the price of oil.

Unemployment and emigration were for many years seen as a fact of life in Ireland by successive governments. The various partnership programmes agreed between the government, employers, trade unions and other bodies, are largely credited with finally tackling this social and economic evil. While unemployment was coming down, the Irish labour force also grew from 1.49 million people in 1998 to 2.09 million in 2008. It has since fallen back to 1.8 million workers. The expansion of the workforce not only provided wonderful opportunities for individuals, but also enabled companies to expand. Indeed, such was the level of expansion that some industries found it very difficult to recruit the amount of staff that they needed, and this in turn led to considerable wage inflation as companies sought to recruit staff with more attractive salaries. The depth of the recession has sadly brought emigration to the fore once again. It is expected that 100,000 Irish people will emigrate in 2010 and 2011.

The nature of the Irish economy has also changed a great deal in the last 20 years, with a shift in emphasis from manufacturing to the services sector. The International Financial Services Centre (IFSC) is an example of the importance of services to the economy. After many years of a booming economy, the economic climate in Ireland is deteriorating rapidly. The country is now deep in a recession that may last for several years.

Sociological The factors that are relevant here are population, levels of education, income distribution and general socio-cultural changes that are taking place. The population of Ireland has changed enormously in percentage terms over the last 20 years for various reasons – not least being the reversal of what was an accepted policy of emigration. The boom in the economy during the 1990s and the early part of this century has seen the 2006 population grow to 4.24 million. (By comparison, in 1961 the population was only 2.8 million, growing to 3.5 million by 1991.)

The structure and nature of the population has also changed significantly. Family size is much smaller, there are more one-parent families, and people are moving away from their home town searching for jobs, all resulting in a much higher demand for housing relative to the overall population size. In turn this impacts on the demand for a wide variety of services and products. The population of Ireland has a much higher proportion of young people than the majority of European countries, particularly Germany and Italy. This has important implications with regard to the type of products bought and the services required. For example, an ageing population will have a much higher demand for health-related products and services. The ethnic mix of the population has also changed dramatically in the last 15 years. These people entering Ireland have brought with them much needed skills and experience, but it has also brought challenges in terms of integration and the management skills required to manage a diversified workforce.

As stated above, the overall population growth has been a very necessary ingredient in the growth of the economy. However, one of the problems associated with this is the very large concentration in the greater Dublin area, and this has an impact on income distribution. Ireland now has a very high level of participation in third level education in the school-leaving age cohort. This is also a very necessary ingredient of economic growth. There have also been many social changes in this time. Part of the rise in the workforce can be accounted for by the fact that there has been a large increase in the number of women working outside the home. With people being cash-rich but time-poor, there has been a big increase in demand for services such as childcare and convenience foods.

The nature of employment is changing, with more and more people working part-time or on contract, rather than in permanent jobs. As a result of EU membership, there have been important changes in legislation dealing with employees, including protection of part-time staff, maternity leave, minimum wages and many more. All of these factors impact on costs and how companies are managed, as well as having important social implications. Finally, the culture of a country needs to be considered in as much as it overlaps with business. Business ethics and corporate social responsibility have already been discussed in Chapter 4 and these are important considerations for society.

Technological This includes technological development and the rate of diffusion, the rate of obsolescence, spending on research and development, and development of e-commerce, etc. Technology impacts on every type of organisation. Production methods are constantly changing and this has a knock-on effect on production costs, production times and the ability to customise products. Product life cycles are getting much shorter and products are becoming obsolete much earlier than before.

Many products are also becoming smaller, as their capability increases. The Sony Walkman® represented a big breakthrough in consumer electronics 30 years ago. It was limited in that it played one cassette tape and additional tapes were bulky to carry. Now, MP3 players can contain hundreds of albums and are only a fraction of the size. Developments such as these can often lead to whole new industries. Such is the speed of diffusion, that many new developments quickly become industry standard, putting pressure on other companies to follow suit. The importance of new product development will be dealt with in greater detail in Chapter 9.

There is a need for much greater emphasis on research and development (R&D) in order to keep up with worldwide competition. Irish companies tend to lag behind in this regard. According to a Forfás annual report (2009: 16), spending on R&D in Ireland was 1.68% of GNP in 2008. This compares with an OECD average of 2.24%. If we were to take out the spending by foreign-owned multinationals on R&D, such as in the pharmaceutical industry, it would show that the spending by Irish companies is very low. The section above on 'Porter's Diamond' emphasises the importance of innovation and its link to R&D. The government has been trying to encourage greater spending on R&D and has greatly increased funding in third-level colleges in this regard, particularly in science-related areas.

The roll-out and speed of broadband here is still very slow and this has obvious limitations on the ability of businesses to engage in e-commerce. This development is revolutionising how many businesses operate, including the airline and banking industries. It involves companies establishing websites that show the range of products and services they have available, and how the customer can purchase them. It also includes much information about a particular company. While many companies operate on a brick and click method (maintaining a traditional building where customers can come in and shop, as well as a Website for Internet purchases), other companies, such as Kenny's bookshop in Galway, have moved exclusively to Internet sales.

A distinction can be drawn between business to consumer (B2C) websites, such as www.aerlingus.com, and business to business (B2B) sites. The latter forms a very important part of how businesses operate within the supply chain. This will be discussed further in Chapter 6. Technology also plays a big part in determining where people work. Mobile communications and broadband allow people to work from home and on the move, reducing the requirement for office space.

Illustration 5.3: Technology Changing the Business model – Dream Ireland

Dream Ireland Holiday Homes based in Kenmare, County Kerry offer holiday home rentals in Ireland with add-on companies offering holiday rentals in Europe. The supply of holiday homes to the Irish market grew at a phenomenal rate from 2000 due to generous tax allowances. The source of rental business for holiday homes in Ireland was a mix of 82% domestic market and 18% international visitors. The majority of the international business was booked through tour operators or travel agents based in other countries. Initially, all business was booked by telephone or post.

As the importance of the Internet grew, Dream Ireland lobbied hard to get broadband to Kenmare, Co. Kerry. Once broadband was available, the company focused on two main areas, namely an on-line booking service and greater efficiency on administration internally. The on-line reservations needed to be driven by search engine optimisation coupled with exposure in normal print media and incentives for booking on-line. The international market was very quick to make bookings on the website. This opened up a new direct overseas booking market that had previously been very difficult to access and was handled mainly through third parties, thereby reducing the revenue received after commissions had been paid out. Airlines were now offering easy on-line booking systems with cheap airfares, so the tourist quickly became their own travel agent. The domestic market was slightly slower to react for reasons varying from insufficient broadband coverage nationally to a reticence towards booking on-line. As familiarity with and popularity of booking and buying on-line grew in Ireland so did Dream Ireland's Irish bookings. Internet bookings now account for 30% of all reservations, and the figure is increasing. Dream Ireland is currently working on a new version of their website which will allow the company to integrate seamlessly with large booking engines, such as www.bookings.com who book 165,000 rooms per day. Dream Ireland has also employed a direct marketing associate who will handle the social media side of the business, such as Facebook, Twitter, blogs, etc. Social media is seen as an important part of the company's growth strategy, as it will allow Dream Ireland to target their market with precision.

Source: Interview with CEO Dream Ireland, Mr Tony Daly

Environmental This includes issues such as energy costs and consumption, environmental protection, disposal of waste material, etc.

The environment has taken on a new importance over the last couple of years for a variety of reasons. It is partly pro-active and partly reactive. Chapter 4 has dealt with Corporate Social Responsibility (CSR) and examines how companies are beginning to take a much broader perspective on how they relate with stakeholders other than shareholders. This includes taking responsibility for the environment in which we live, over and above what is required by law (CSR can even become a competitive advantage for such organisations). For those who do not regard such obligations as part of their remit, much tougher laws protecting the environment have come into play in recent years, and this trend will continue. When one considers the amount of illegal dumps that have been discovered in Ireland, many containing toxic materials, our record in this regard has not been exemplary.

What is of major concern to businesses and consumers alike is the rise in the cost of energy. Many economists are predicting that oil will soon reach $200 a barrel. In the first couple of years of the 21st Century, it was approximately $25 a barrel. This is obviously having a huge impact on the cost of doing business and, more than concern for the environment, will concentrate minds on how this cost can be reduced. It will certainly affect airline companies.

Legal Health and safety, employment law, consumer law, company law and competition law all come under this heading. Laws are put forward by the Oireachtas (the Irish Parliament) and signed by the President of Ireland. It is then up to the courts and the regulatory bodies to ensure that they are complied with. As a result of the numerous laws that have been passed in recent years, the HR function in companies has become quite a specialised area. Other areas of law and regulation, such as company law and competition law, often require more specialised outside advice. As with many of the other factors mentioned above, these all have important implications for how companies are run, and the responsibility rests with management to be informed about developments in relevant laws and regulations, and ensure compliance.

Implications for Organisations

As we have seen, there are myriad factors impacting on organisations that have to be taken into account when formulating strategy. They will all vary in terms of importance: some have little or no relevance; while others will be central to an organisation's competitiveness. Obviously, it is the latter that will require management's attention. The question needs to be asked: what impact will a factor have on the organisation? It must also be stressed that they are not static, and in some cases will be quite dynamic, particularly the economic factors. For that reason, management must be constantly aware of these issues and factor them into their decision-making. It is particularly important to try to understand how they will be in a couple of years' time, as strategic decisions are, by their nature, long-term. The point has already been made that there is a huge overlap in each of the sections. Thus, it is not so much individual factors that have to be taken into account, but their combined effect. Finally, it must be remembered that consideration must be given not just to the combined factors as they exist now, but how they are likely to change in the coming years.

Scenarios

Change is a factor that affects every organisation, some to a small extent, while others are affected to a much greater degree. For every organisation, trying to predict the future can be difficult and, where there is a great amount of uncertainty, it can prove almost impossible to do this. In such situations, the development of different scenarios can be particularly useful in helping organisations understand the nature of change.

Definition **Scenarios** provide an outline of alternative future developments and their impact on an organisation.

Scenarios can be used to examine developments at the macro-environmental level and, perhaps, to a lesser extent at industry level, e.g. examining the effect on a business if a major competitor were to pursue a certain strategy. However, events at industry level are in most cases more predictable, and for that reason, the use of scenarios is more suited to examining major changes at global and national level.

Using scenarios is not about trying to predict the future. Scenarios take into account different perspectives on what might happen in the future, and examine the implications to the organisation if such an outcome were to happen. It is advisable to use an even number of scenarios, either two or four, as there can be a tendency to opt for the middle one, which may defeat the purpose of properly examining all possible future situations.

Scenarios should be constructed around events that potentially would have serious implications for the future of the company. An example of this would be the cost of oil for the airline industry. Oil costs are entirely outside the control of the industry (even governments), but yet have major implications for the industry. It is expected that many airlines will make a loss in 2009 because of the rise in the price of oil (while the price of oil on world markets has dropped again, many airlines would have hedged the price of oil at a much higher level). Against such a background, retrenchment rather than expansion would probably be a more appropriate strategy.

In Chapter 1, when examining how strategy is formulated, the use of strategy workshops to debate the issues facing organisations was discussed. Such workshops can be particularly useful in developing and debating scenarios and play an important part in organisational learning. The ultimate aim is to develop contingency plans for each of the scenarios. One should avoid assigning probabilities to these scenarios, as it can confer a false sense of certainty to what is essentially an unpredictable future. As the circumstances become clearer with time and with more information, managers can then make a decision as to the most appropriate response to the unfolding circumstances. With the contingency planning completed, they are then in a position to react quickly, and develop a strategy that is suited to the particular scenario that is unfolding.

One obvious failure to properly utilise scenario planning was the collapse of the financial sector in Ireland. According to O'Leary (2010), speaking about the time he was a non-executive director at AIB, he stated that directors did examine more malign scenarios but "they trusted the systems

Single Electricity Market (SEM) — was activated by the CER and the Northern Ireland Regulator. Such co-operation is seen as a vital element in ensuring a sustainable and reliable supply of electricity across the island.

A central part of the CER's remit is to promote competition in the electricity and gas sectors for consumers, as the various companies are forced to compete on price and service. This is not just left to the open market. As part of their licence agreement, companies must conform to minimum standards of service and codes of practice and, in particular, safety. The CER is headed up by three Commissioners (one of which is chairman) and there are four divisional directors:

- Director of Operations and Electricity Markets
- Director of Gas, Legal and Renewables
- Director of Electricity Networks and Retail
- Director of Safety and Consumer Affairs

The CER has a five-year strategic plan (2010-2014) which provides for the delivery of the Commission's mission and statutory objectives. In a fast-changing energy environment, it is monitoring international developments and formulating strategies that will meet the needs of energy consumers over the coming years.

Source: CER (2011)

Competitive Forces

Porter (1980: 3) has developed a generic framework for examining competition in an industry. Competition puts a ceiling on profits, and the greater the level of competition, the lower the profits will be. It is relatively easy to look upon competition as the other companies operating in the industry. While this is totally valid, there are also other forms that must be taken into account. Porter describes five such competitive forces operating in any given industry. One important point about the Five Forces Analysis is that it should be used at strategic unit level rather than for the company as a whole, as competition will differ for each strategic group. One should not look at the forces in isolation, as there is a connection between them all. Similarly, there is often a connection between elements in the macro environment and the five forces that needs to be considered.

The **five forces** are:

1. The threat of new entrants
2. Rivalry among existing firms
3. The threat of substitute products
4. The bargaining power of buyers
5. The bargaining power of suppliers

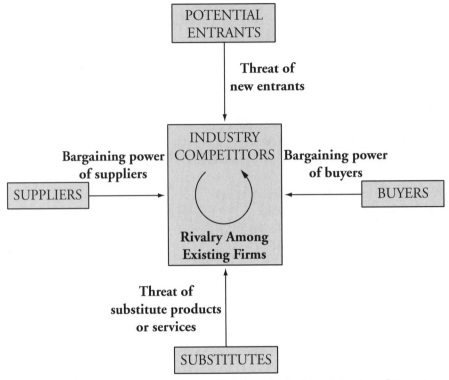

Source: Michael E Porter, *Competitive Strategy: Techniques for Analysing Industries and Competitors*, New York, The Free Press, 1980

Figure 5.3 *Five Forces Analysis*

1. The threat of new entrants The competitive market in any industry can often change as new companies enter, bringing with them extra capacity. When we examine many industries in Ireland, we see that a large amount of new capacity was added in the last 10 years. As a result, competition in these industries has intensified enormously. The likelihood of new entrants depends on the existence of barriers to entry – whether there are obstacles that they must overcome. Such barriers should not be seen as permanent but factors that will at best delay entry. According to Porter, there are six main barriers to entry:

- **Economies of scale** – some industries require economies of scale in order to be profitable. Economies of scale exist when unit costs come down, as production goes up. It normally happens where there are high fixed costs. Pharmaceutical production requires large economies of scale in order to cover the very substantial investment required in R&D.
- **Product differentiation** – where a product is differentiated in the minds of the consumer, thus creating brand loyalty and allowing the company to charge a premium. Such brand loyalty would be difficult for a new company to overcome.

- **Capital requirements** – if there is a requirement to invest large sums of money in plant and machinery, it poses an obvious problem for a new company that would not have such resources. Oil exploration, for example, requires huge investment in rigs and drilling equipment.
- **Switching costs** – switching costs are costs that may be incurred if a customer moves from using one company to another. Changing production or computer equipment to that supplied by another company may require considerable retraining for example.
- **Access to distribution channels** – companies require distribution outlets for their products. Access to supermarket shelves can be very difficult to achieve for newcomers, as the supermarkets will often prefer to stick with well-known brands that are guaranteed to be purchased by the consumer.
- **Cost disadvantages independent of scale** – established firms can often have an advantage due to factors such as a favourable location (a restaurant), favourable access to raw materials or employees, or because of the existence of an experience curve, where costs decline as companies become more knowledgeable and efficient, such as a law firm.

2. Rivalry among existing firms In developed countries, monopolies are essentially a thing of the past and, therefore, organisations of every type, including not-for-profit organisations such as aid agencies, face competition. There will be strong rivalry to gain market share and companies will use a variety of means to strengthen their position and increase profits. Ultimately, all of the other forces at play will impact on competitive rivalry. For example, if there are low barriers to entry, then new players are likely to enter the industry, thus increasing competition. Some forms of competition such as price competition often leave the industry worse off as companies try to match each other on price, and profits fall. On the other hand, advertising battles can potentially raise the level of demand generally. There are a number of factors that influence the level of competitive rivalry:

- **Balanced competitors** – the more balanced competitors are in terms of market share, the more each one is likely to try and increase its market share. If one company is in a dominant position, it is likely to impose a discipline on the market generally.
- **Slow industry growth** – because of little growth in the industry, when one firm tries to expand, it is at the expense of others. Consequently, they will retaliate to hold their share.
- **High fixed costs** – there is pressure on firms to fill capacity in order to cover high fixed costs such as capital investment. To generate profit, they will try to increase volume sales, often prompting a sales war.
- **Lack of differentiation** – if the product is perceived as a commodity by consumers, purchasing decisions are based primarily on price.
- **Capacity added in large increments** – where economies of scale dictate that extra capacity is added in large increments, it can cause temporary over-supply in the industry, thus causing a lowering of prices to fill that extra capacity.
- **High exit barriers** – these exist where assets are specialised and hard to dispose of, or companies are facing high redundancy costs. In such cases, companies stay on in the industry fighting for market share despite poor profitability.

While many companies will naturally focus their competitive attention on existing rivalry, it must be remembered that the nature of competition is changing rapidly with the emergence of new developing markets. This combined with changes in technology, particularly with regard to the Internet, makes understanding the true nature of existing rivalry much more difficult. On the other hand, the use of technology can also present opportunities.

3. The threat of substitute products The existence of substitutes for products will ultimately put a ceiling on the price that can be charged for that product, particularly if consumers see the substitute as a close second. A substitute refers to a product that provides a similar function to other products. There are different types of substitution. First there is product-for-product substitution. Regional flights in Ireland save a good deal of time for busy executives. In most cases there is probably only one operator flying between the regions and Dublin. For example, Ryanair currently has the contract to operate flights between Kerry and Dublin and, on the face of it, it would appear that there is no competition. However, in recent years, intercity rail has improved greatly, and while the actual journey does take longer, it is often less expensive and without lengthy security and check-in procedures, and so represents a viable alternative.

There is also substitution of need where new developments may render other products obsolete, even though they are quite different. For example, some people do not wear watches, but instead use their mobile phone to tell the time. Obviously, they are very different products *per se,* but both tell the time. Finally, it must be remembered that in a competitive world where people have only a certain amount of disposable income, choices have to be made with regard to spending. Thus, a garage selling cars is not only competing with other car dealers, but is perhaps competing with, say, the travel industry, as limited funds may require that a choice has to be made between taking a holiday or changing the car.

4. The bargaining power of buyers Organisations require customers to purchase their products and services. If those customers/buyers are in a position to exert pressure on the company to sell at a lower price, that represents a form of competition and places a ceiling on the price that can be obtained. The ability of buyers to obtain more favourable prices from their perspective depends on their bargaining power. A distinction needs to be drawn between the buyer and the ultimate consumer. A person dining in a restaurant and purchasing a bottle of wine is the ultimate consumer. The price paid is that marked on the wine list, and there is no negotiation. The restaurant, on the other hand, is the buyer and, particularly if it is part of a chain of restaurants, will buy the wine in considerable quantities perhaps directly from the vineyard, and will have strong bargaining power. The buyer will have high bargaining power when the following are present:

- **Concentration of buyers** In some cases, certain buyers account for a very large proportion of a company's sales, which puts these buyers in a powerful position when negotiating price. For example, a cheese producer who may be in a situation where a supermarket chain is willing to buy their entire output, in which case the supermarket, as the buyer, will drive a hard bargain. The choice for the producer is do they go with one buyer that will purchase all of their output at a lower price, or sell to perhaps hundreds of smaller retailers, at a higher price? In the latter case, distribution and other selling costs will also have to be factored in, as well as the time involved in trying to secure sales.

- **Standard products** If the products are standard or un-differentiated, there will usually be alternative suppliers from which the buyer can obtain the necessary inputs.
- **Lower switching costs** Switching costs were discussed above in looking at the threat of new entrants. If a buyer can switch easily from its current supplier to another, it puts the buyer in a strong position.
- **Full information** If the buyer has full information about the market and prices, the buyer is in a stronger position to negotiate favourable prices for the products. The growth of the Internet is an important factor here as buyers can check out prices in other countries and, if cheaper, deal directly with that company.
- **Backward integration** If there is a possibility that the buyer can move back along the value chain and take over supply of the materials themselves, it puts them in a stronger position.

5. The bargaining power of suppliers In many ways, the bargaining power of suppliers is a mirror image of the bargaining power of buyers. The next chapter will deal with the value network in detail, showing the relationship between an organisation and its suppliers. In this context, there are occasions where the supplier can exert considerable bargaining power in supplying the necessary raw materials or components to a company. Bargaining power is said to be high when:

- **There is a concentration of suppliers**. If there are only a few suppliers of necessary inputs, then a company that needs those inputs is not in a position to 'shop around', thus allowing the supplier considerable leverage in negotiating price. It is said that diamonds are 'a girl's best friend', and they are associated with wealth. As a commodity, there are considerable reserves of diamonds, but the flow of diamonds onto the world market is strictly controlled by a handful of suppliers and, along with high demand, maintains a huge premium.
- **A supplier's product is an important input into the buyer's business**. In this case, it places greater pressure on the buyer to ensure that the quality and quantity is correct, thus putting the supplier in a stronger position.
- **There is a threat of forward integration**. If the supplier can move up the value chain to take over the distribution of their product and, in so doing, cut out the intermediary, it increases their bargaining power.
- **There are high switching costs**. A production company may have installed a system of equipment that is compatible only with other machinery supplied by that supplier. In changing one part of the system, the company may well be tied in to the original supplier as it would mean having to change the entire system and not just one machine, if they were to move to another supplier.

Analysis of each of the five competitive forces will present different answers. The threat of new entrants might be high, existing rivalry might be moderate to low, etc. For that reason, it is necessary to form an overall judgement with regard to the level of competition, and thus the overall level of attractiveness of that industry. If competitive forces are weak, it will present a good opportunity to invest in that industry. It must also be remembered that competitive forces are dynamic – they can and do evolve. Companies must be constantly monitoring competitive developments and take appropriate offensive or defensive action to counter the threat. An example of an offensive move to counter competition is acquiring a rival company, thus reducing the level of competition being faced. On the other hand, increasing the level of advertising or investment in R&D would be regarded as defensive moves.

Five Forces analysis does have limitations. The bargaining power of suppliers, for example, suggests an adversarial approach between a company and its supplier. Driving too hard a bargain with suppliers undermines the relationship and works against the level of co-operation that is needed to make just-in-time management succeed. With regard to the threat of new entrants and rivalry among existing firms, the nature of rivalry suggested by Porter is probably more reflective of rivalry as it existed pre-globalisation and, in particular, pre-Internet, as many of the barriers to entry can be easily overcome as a result of the development of e-commerce.

Industry Life Cycle

Competition will also depend on the stage the industry is at in its life cycle. This variation is due to the number of competitor firms and the difference in buyer habits by consumers. There are four main stages:

- Introduction Stage
- Growth Stage
- Maturity Stage
- Decline Stage

See below, **Figure 5.4**.

In the **introduction** stage, there may well be only one manufacturer in the market (particularly if the new product is patent-protected). Even if there are a few, the competitors will be more concerned with building up the overall market as there tends to be just a small number of consumers due to a lack of familiarity with the product and high purchase costs. When flat screen TVs first came on to the market, for example, prices were in the region of €15,000, but now they can be bought for a couple of hundred Euro.

In the **growth** stage, sales begin to rise rapidly and more companies begin to enter the industry. The emphasis will still be on trying to grow the market overall, but competitors will also start trying to vie for market share. The initial players in the industry will now begin to recoup their development costs. In response to more competition, prices begin to drop significantly, making it possible for a larger group of people to purchase the product.

In the **maturity** stage, the sales curve peaks and begins to decline. There are no new customers and the industry is dependent on repeat custom. Competition now becomes severe, and many of the weaker players will be forced out of the industry. The hotel industry in Ireland has undergone enormous growth since the mid-1990s, much of it driven by tax growth. Ireland now has 35 Five-star hotels for a population of 4.2 million people. The Netherlands has 17 Five-star hotels for a

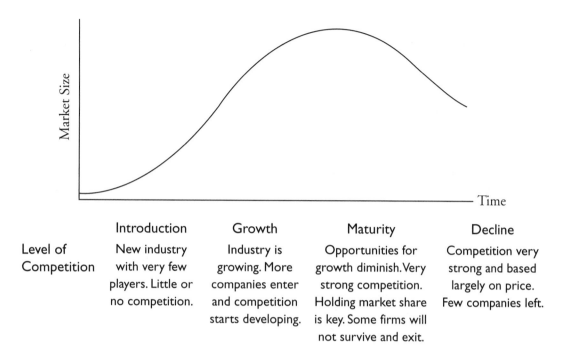

	Introduction	Growth	Maturity	Decline
Level of Competition	New industry with very few players. Little or no competition.	Industry is growing. More companies enter and competition starts developing.	Opportunities for growth diminish. Very strong competition. Holding market share is key. Some firms will not survive and exit.	Competition very strong and based largely on price. Few companies left.

Figure 5.4 *Industry Life Cycle*

population four times as large. Against a background of low economic growth in the home market and our main tourist markets, it is highly likely that there will be a number of hotels closing down in the Irish market in the coming years.

The final stage of an industry's life cycle is the **decline**. There is a large drop off in usage, and companies are concerned with minimising costs by cutting all advertising and minimising product offerings. There are likely to be only a few competitors left in the market at this point.

Driving Forces

Both at international level and at industry level, there will be many changes taking place that will sometimes alter the business environment in a fundamental way. This can happen in a relatively short period of time, but generally it will be part of longer term trends. If there are changes happening that are going to radically change the nature of the industry, it is vital that senior managers understand such changes and the impact that they are likely to have on the industry. These changes are often termed the industry driving forces.

 Industry Driving Forces are those changes taking place that are altering the fundamental nature and competition of that industry.

As such, they will have a significant impact on the future success of the company. For that reason, senior management must first be able to recognise the forces driving change in whatever industry they are operating. As factors in the global environment will also influence driving forces, these factors must also be taken into consideration. Secondly, they must assess the impact that those driving forces are likely to have. Lastly, once they have gained an understanding of these forces, action must be taken to position the firm accordingly.

Identifying the Industry Driving Forces

As stated, there will be many driving forces, and these will vary from one industry to the next. There are, however, many common issues facing most industries, and perhaps the two most important ones are technology and globalisation.

Technology Technology is constantly changing, not just in terms of product offering, but also in terms of how products are made and services are offered. This will impact on companies in different ways. As technology changes, it puts pressure on companies to innovate constantly. This point was discussed above in the context of Porter's Diamond. There is consequently a greater pressure on firms to innovate and upgrade their products to meet the demand of consumers. Failure to do so will see firms left behind.

Technology also provides opportunities. Electronics consumer companies such as Sony have now become firmly established in the digital camera industry, whereas before, it was dominated by Eastman Kodak and other 'traditional' camera companies. Firms must also be mindful of their costs, and process innovation is also an important factor that should be considered. The steel industry has seen enormous changes in the recent past in the way the product is manufactured. It was once an industry that required huge capital investment, but the development of mini-mill technology has now made it possible for small steel producers to compete successfully with larger operators.

Perhaps the greatest driving force brought about by technology is the Internet. This has changed radically the way business is carried out in so many industries, along with the nature of competition. While broadband rollout has been slow in this country, the number of people that have access to broadband is growing constantly. It has changed the way in which companies interact with their customers. In many cases it has resulted in cutting out middlemen from the channel of distribution. It is, therefore, of vital importance that companies develop attractive websites that are easy for customers to navigate.

One industry that has undergone much change as a result of driving forces is the travel industry. Up to 20 years ago, flights were booked solely through travel agents. In most instances nowadays, people book them directly with the airline. However, travel agents still have an important function, not just with straightforward package holidays, but in creating value-added itineraries and providing expert advice for travellers.

Globalisation In the context of driving forces, globalisation has radically altered the nature of competition and demand. For many products, there is a homogenisation of demand around the world, brought about to no small effect by, for instance, films and satellite television, as well as the removal of trade barriers and tariffs as a result of the EU and World Trade Organisation agreements. In turn, this puts pressure on companies to compete on a global basis in order to respond to the changing nature of competition, particularly with regard to economies of scale. From cars to computers, economies of scale are constantly rising in terms of the amount required by production runs and marketing. One way this manifests itself is through the outsourcing of production to countries with cheaper labour costs such as China or the Philippines. Tax laws can also result in a form of globalisation, and Ireland has seen many foreign multinationals establish here to avail of the low rate of corporation tax.

The Impact of Driving Forces

Driving forces will impact on organisations in very significant ways, and this impact will increase over time. Ideally, organisations should be able to spot these trends in the early stages and take action that places them ahead of their rivals. It is a difficult call to make, as a distinction needs to be made between passing fads and underlying drivers of change. In the case of the latter, managers need to be able not just to identify the basic trends, but to understand the impact they will have on the industry and their company in particular.

It must also be remembered that, while some forces will be pushing the industry in one direction, other forces may be pushing it in another. Thus, the overall impact of the various driving forces is what matters. Again, this highlights the importance of undertaking environmental analysis, as it is essential that managers fully understand the nature and impact of these driving forces in order to take effective action in response. The strategies that need to be considered by the organisation in light of these driving forces will be explored below.

Segmentation, Targeting and Positioning

Throughout this text, the importance of the customer is highlighted. In any market, whether it is a consumer market or a business market, different customers will inevitably have different needs. This concept is clearly illustrated by the vast range of items on sale in supermarkets, where there could be a large variety of any one item on sale, e.g. biscuits. Customers' needs must be understood by all companies operating in the market. While each individual will have their own specific requirements, these requirements can usually be grouped by companies into different segments. Therefore, when looking at the level of competition in an industry, it is necessary to examine the various segments that exist. The process by which companies identify different segments and decide which segments to pursue is known as Segmentation, Targeting and Positioning.

Definition **Segmentation** is the process by which diverse customers in a large market are divided into smaller groups that have similar needs.

Essentially it is a group that has similar products or buying needs. There are many segmentation variables that can be used such as age, gender, occupation, ethnic grouping, family size, life-cycle stage and many more. Segmentation may be done by single variable segmentation, for example a specific age group, or multivariable segmentation where more than one characteristic is used. The more variables that are used, the more homogenous will be the chosen group in terms of identifying their needs.

Once the market has been divided into segments, the next stage is identifying which of those segments the company wants to target with its product offering.

Definition The decision about which market segment(s) a company will focus on is known as **targeting.**

Again, the company can make a decision based on a concentration strategy, directing its marketing efforts towards a single market segment or a differentiated strategy aimed at two or more market segments. Positioning is the final stage of the process.

Definition **Positioning** involves creating an image of the product or service in the minds of the customer that will form a central part of its promotional strategy.

When the company has decided which segments to target, it must then meet the needs of those targeted customers with an appropriate marketing mix – a tangible mix of its products/services, place (where it is distributed), an attractive price, and promote it in a manner that will appeal to potential buyers. People will inevitably play a vital role in this process.

The Four Seasons Hotel in Dublin, for example, has a target market that is primarily aimed at wealthy visitors to the capital. It is marketed as a luxurious, relaxing venue that provides individual customer service that is unparalleled in the industry.

Strategic Group Mapping

There is a close connection between segmentation, targeting and positioning on one hand and strategic group mapping on the other. Segmentation, targeting and positioning is a response to customers' needs. Companies will make decisions on which segments to go after based on a number of factors, including their own strategic capability (see Chapter 6).

In examining the environment, it will become obvious that not all companies are alike in terms of size, market share, the range and quality of products, distribution channels, etc. This has implications in terms of assessing competition. Some companies will be direct competitors of a particular firm, while others will have little impact on it. Thus, when examining competition, the 'industry' is very often too large a concept to have any meaningful value. Therefore, the industry needs to be divided up by grouping together the players that possess similar characteristics and competitive approaches. They can then be analysed by way of strategic group mapping.

Definition A **Strategic Group Map** is a graphical depiction of the positioning of various companies competing within an industry.

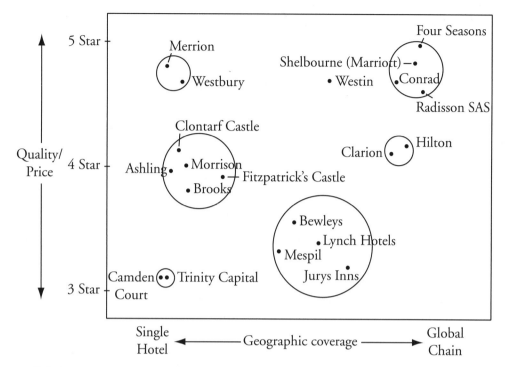

Figure 5.5 *A Strategic Group Map of Some of the Main Hotels in Dublin*

In positioning the rival firms, they can either be grouped together in a cluster or viewed separately, depending on the numbers involved.

There are many criteria available for comparing companies, and by choosing different variables, an alternative competitive picture emerges. For that reason, the exercise is often repeated using various characteristics, resulting in a more comprehensive analysis. The analysis should be based on how the firms compete with one another, for example on price, product range, etc. Having chosen the most appropriate variables for comparison, the various strategic groups can be analysed on a two-dimensional chart. Price/quality will often be chosen as one axis, while the other axis might represent, for example, product range or geographic coverage. The next stage is to examine all the companies operating in the industry and plot them on the chart according to the characteristics chosen. A circle is drawn around each one (or a group of rival companies when they display similar characteristics). The size of the circle should represent the size of market share that they possess in the industry. This will allow a quick, visual representation of the breakdown of the industry.

When selecting the variables for analysis, it is important to pick ones that are contrasting, otherwise the variables will be highly correlated along a diagonal axis on the map, and it will be of little value in analysing the industry. For example, price and quality are highly correlated, so with price on the x axis and quality on the y axis, it would result in a straight line from bottom left to top right of the map, with all the competitors grouped around the line.

Strategic group mapping is an important exercise in analysing where the real competition exists for any particular company. Those companies that are located close together on the map represent an immediate threat, while those located elsewhere, will be of lesser significance. Just as important, strategic group mapping will show that some parts of the industry are more attractive than others, reflecting the level of competition in any one cluster. This will consequently impact on profitability. For a new entrant into the market, it may well show up opportunities to gain a strong foothold where competition may be weak or non-existent. It must also be remembered that a strategic group map represents the industry at any one point in time, but the situation can change significantly over time. As mentioned above, the hotel industry in Ireland has changed dramatically in the last 10 years in all segments of the market.

An important part of the analysis, therefore, is to try and anticipate what changes are likely to be made by competitors. This information is not easy to come by, but a certain amount of it will be in the public domain by way of annual reports, company press releases, radio interviews with senior executives and many other sources. Anticipating such moves will give a company time to take offensive or defensive action to protect their position. Another part of the analysis should include an appraisal of the different strategies of the various companies: which strategies are working well and which are not? A company that has been a strong player in the past will not necessarily be so in the future.

This will all be necessary in trying to understand the opportunities that potentially exist for a company. Such opportunities must also be looked at against a background of consumer needs, and ultimately the product or service being offered must meet the needs of the target group. These needs will also change over time. In any business, staying close to the customer and being aware of their needs is vital. Meeting these needs will also form the basis of the strategy being pursued by the company. For example, for the price-conscious customer, keeping costs down is a vital part of the company's strategy.

Key Success Factors

The importance of understanding customer needs was made above. These needs will differ between different segments. The relative importance that customers place on certain product and service features will also vary. Some will be considered essential, while other features will be of lesser significance. Thus, from a company's perspective, there must be a clear understanding of these features and their relative value among the target group.

Definition   **Key Success Factors** (also known as critical success factors) are the resources and competences required by an organisation to be successful in a competitive industry.

Key Success Factors (KSF) are what separate the industry leaders from the minnows. KSFs will vary from one industry to another, such as in the clothing industry, where design and cost are of major significance, while in food items, branding and a strong distributive network are vital. When management have an understanding of the KSFs of the industry in which they are operating, they can then gauge how well they are performing against the criteria which customers (and not the company) consider important. This analysis requires an understanding of the company's strategic capability and this will be developed in the next chapter. Some of the most common types of KSFs include:

- Well-known brand name
- Range of products
- Customer service
- Supply chain management capabilities
- Quality control
- Skilled labour
- High utilisation of fixed assets
- Location (retail stores)
- Marketing skills
- Innovation in product design

Generally, there are probably about three KSFs, and certainly no more than five, operating within a particular industry. It is, therefore, an essential part of strategic analysis that senior management identify the KSFs operating in their industry. It is obviously easier for companies to understand KSFs when dealing directly with their customers, rather than operating through intermediaries. It is the view of the ultimate consumer that is important. Companies must be conscious that their decisions are based on hard evidence, rather than assuming that they know best. Those decisions must also be based on what the customer is looking for rather than what is convenient for the company to provide. It should also be noted that KSFs will vary over time and managers need to be aware of these trends, and not stick rigidly to out-of-date assumptions.

The strategy being developed by the company should incorporate these KSFs in such a way that they form an integral part of their competitive approach. In comparing how one company is doing against its main rivals, Kim and Mauborgne (2002) advocate the use of what they term a 'strategy canvas'. This is a visual representation of how different companies compare against the KSFs of that industry. They argue that, rather than preparing large documents filled with detailed numbers and jargon, companies should instead build the process around a graphical representation of the key issues. Such a picture will yield better results. See **Figure 5.6**.

According to Kim and Mauborgne (2002), a strategy canvas assists in visualising a strategic plan and helps understand the company's strategic positioning. It displays the following:

- Factors affecting competition among key industry players.
- Strategic profile of current competitors showing which factors they invest in.
- It draws the company's strategic profile or value curve showing how it invests in the factors of competition and how it might do so in the future.

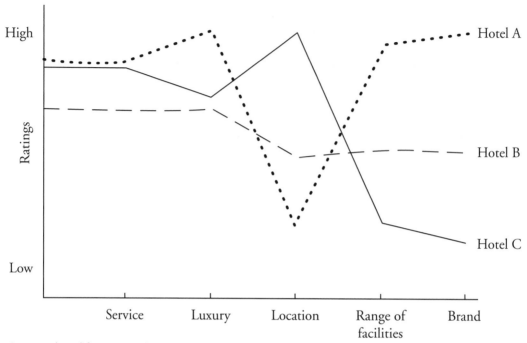

Source: Adapted from Kim and Mauborgne (2002): "Charting your Company's Future": *Harvard Business Review*, Vol. 80, Issue 6, p.76–83

Figure 5.6 *A Strategy Canvas for Five-star Hotels*

A strategy canvas assists the company to develop a clear focus on the areas in which it should concentrate on when developing strategy. In particular, it shows where a company should distinguish itself from competition, rather than following others. In this way, it can develop uniqueness and stand apart and may even create new ways of competing (e.g. Southwest Airlines began operating point-to-point travel between mid-size cities in the US rather than the traditional hub and spoke system).

A good strategy should also allow itself to be communicated clearly to customers. With Southwest Airlines, it is: "The speed of the plane at the price of a car." Southwest are a low-cost airline offering a basic, but inexpensive service.

The strategy canvas is a useful tool in visualising the type of strategy that an organisation might follow. Whether or not the organisation has the capability to pursue that strategy will be examined in Chapter 6. Care must, therefore, be taken when plotting a company's profile on a strategy canvas that it completed after a thorough analysis of the company's strategic capability.

In Chapter 6, we will examine a competitive strength assessment. In many ways, it is a similar exercise. However, in understanding an organisation's strategic position, it is necessary to identify the key success factors (KSFs) operating in that industry and how each company compares against those KSFs. It is also necessary to have a full understanding of our own company's strategic capability and to compare this capability against competitors.

Opportunities and Threats

Throughout this chapter, it was stated that the environment is constantly changing. Environment analysis must also be ongoing, both on a formal, and informal basis. The purpose of such analysis is to identify the opportunities and the threats that exist. A key element in this analysis is not a listing of different factors, but understanding the implications that they have for a company.

Opportunities exist in many forms. The industry may be in its infancy with large growth potential, and regulatory factors may have opened up what was previously a closed shop. A company may have a well-known brand which places it in a strong position, or it could have a good deal of retained earnings that would enable it to make acquisitions, etc.

Chapter 1 referred to the concept of the paradigm. Sometimes opportunities may not be obvious, but still exist. In the aftermath of 9/11, the airline industry around the world regarded the situation as dire. Michael O'Leary, the CEO of Ryanair, believed that, if prices were low enough, people would overcome their fear of flying. Ryanair cut their prices dramatically, and demand rose so much that the airline had to purchase additional aircraft to meet this demand (Creaton, 2004).

A company must also be mindful of threats. The competitive situation may have changed and become unfavourable – perhaps a large international player has come into the market, changing the dynamics. A downturn in the economy may make the entire industry vulnerable, particularly if the demand is elastic, such as in the tourism industry (a small increase in the cost of living can result in a big drop-off in demand for holidays as people struggle to buy the essential things).

The threats can come from a whole range of sources. It is vital that management recognises the threats that exist – ignoring them will not make them go away. For single business companies, it will be a case of trying to ride out the storm. For conglomerates, it may well mean deciding to exit a particular industry and concentrate on the other sectors in which it operates.

However, the existence of threats does not necessarily mean doom and gloom. What is important is how the company deals with them. The objective is to minimise the threats while capitalising on the opportunities. The next chapter will examine the competitive position of the organisation: the strengths and weaknesses and, together with the opportunities and threats, this completes the SWOT analysis. This analysis will subsequently dictate the choices that a company makes.

Illustration 5.5: Bord na Móna and its Changing Environment

One Irish company which has recognised that the environment is changing and accordingly needs to reposition itself is Bord na Móna. The company, which was founded in 1946, plans to move away from its traditional business of harvesting peat (the bogs used by the company will be depleted by 2025), and invest €1.4 billion over the next five years in expanding its business into wind farms, waste management and recovery, as well as horticulture. The company has been operating a wind farm in Oweninny in County Mayo which produces six megawatts (MW) of electricity every hour. They intend investing €500m in this project to bring its output up to 350MW which will supply power to 350,000 homes. Responding to environmental concerns about the use of peat moss in garden products, the company developed a system of converting organic waste into fertiliser. This has the positive effect of diverting waste material that would otherwise go to landfill.

Chief executive Gay D'Arcy realises that there are many changes coming down the line that will impact on the company. However, Bord na Móna has a 'strong bundle of unique capabilities' and these will be used to develop and reposition the company (O'Halloran, 2008).

The five illustrations in this chapter are typical of many companies in Ireland in terms of the challenges posed by a changing environment. It is, therefore, imperative that all organisations constantly monitor their environment, both from a macro and micro perspective, as the opportunities and threats that are identified are constantly evolving.

Many Irish companies saw the downturn coming, but very few would have anticipated the rapidity and depth of the current downturn. In Chinese, the symbol for crisis consists of two parts: danger and opportunity.

Figure 5.7 *Crisis: Danger and Opportunity*

Whether we determine something to be a crisis or an opportunity depends to a large extent on how we view things:

"For there is nothing either good or bad but thinking makes it so."

Hamlet. Act 2, Sc. 2

CONCLUSION

Even in times of recession, there are opportunities for companies to exploit. However, each company must be in a position to identify those opportunities, ideally before rival companies can spot them. Environmental scanning is, therefore, a vital part of the strategic management process. Circumstances are constantly changing, sometimes slowly, and sometimes major events can happen very quickly. Either way, managers must be constantly observing both the external environment within which they operate and interpreting how events will impact on their company. With many of these factors, managers will have very little direct control over them. On the other hand, they have control over how they act and, by taking appropriate action, they can minimise threats and position their company to take advantage of any opportunities. Monitoring the environment is a subjective process and managerial experience plays an important part in how events are interpreted. This judgement is built up over time. Thus, an important part of the process is creating a culture within the organisation where all these factors can be openly discussed, and lessons can be learned from past experience.

SUMMARY

The **Macro environment** examines what is happening generally in the global and national environment. There are many different **trading blocks** operating around the world, with the **European Union** of greatest concern to this country in terms of regulations, as well as providing a market of over 500 million people. The EU has been of huge benefit to Ireland in many ways. **Porter's Diamond** looks at how different countries develop a competitive advantage. It examines competitiveness under four headings: factor conditions; demand conditions; related and supporting industries; and firm strategy, structure and rivalry.

The **PESTEL framework** examines the Political, Economic, Social, Technological, Environmental and Legal factors that will impact on an industry. They are all inter-related and will vary in terms of importance. Some have little or no relevance; others will be central to the organisation's competitiveness. It must also be stressed that they are not static and in some cases will be quite dynamic, particularly the economic ones. Trying to predict the future can be difficult where there is a great amount of uncertainty. Scenarios offer plausible alternative views of how the business environment might develop in the future.

The **Micro environment** considers all of the factors that affect a specific industry and is of immediate concern to any particular company. There are a number of issues that need to be examined, including:

- Examining the **industry's economic structure** – an overall view of the attractiveness of the industry.
- **Five Forces Analysis** – Porter's model examines five competitive forces at play in an industry. They include the threat of new entrants, rivalry among existing firms, the threat of substitute products, the bargaining power of buyers and suppliers. These all put a limit on the amount of profit a company can make. Competition also depends on the stage at which the industry is at in its life cycle.
- **Industry driving forces** are described as those changes taking place that are altering the fundamental nature and competition of that industry. As such, they will have a significant impact on the future success of a company. These factors, such as globalisation, will have to be identified.
- Not all companies are alike in terms of size, market share, the range and quality of products, distribution channels, etc. This has implications in terms of assessing competition. **Strategic group mapping** is a technique for displaying market or competitive positions that rival firms occupy in the industry.
- **Market segmentation** is the process by which diverse customers in a large market are divided into smaller groups that have similar needs. There are many segmentation variables that can be used such as age, sex, occupation, ethnic grouping, family size and life-cycle stage, etc.
- **Key success factors** are the resources and competences required by an organisation to be successful in a competitive industry. Generally there are about three or four and include factors such as brand names, supply chain capabilities, skilled labour and many more.

Opportunities and threats Environmental analysis which must be ongoing, both on a formal and informal basis. The purpose of such analysis is to identify the opportunities and the threats that exist. A key element in this analysis is not a listing of different factors, but understanding the implications that they have for a company.

DISCUSSION QUESTIONS

1. Explore the relevance of understanding the macro environment in formulating strategy.
2. Discuss the use of scenarios in strategic planning.
3. Critically analyse the role of Porter's Five Forces Analysis in understanding the competitive environment of an organisation.
4. Taking an industry of your choice, explore the nature of the driving forces that are impacting upon it.
5. Evaluate the use of strategic group mapping as a tool for analysing competition.
6. The identification of Key Success Factors is a vital part of environmental analysis. Discuss how an organisation can use this knowledge to gain competitive advantage.

REFERENCES

BBC, 2011, "Cut in corporation tax 'could cost NI £280m', PwC says", www.bbc.co.uk/news/uk-northern-ireland-12128999, (Accessed 23 February 2011)

CER, 2011, http://www.cer.ie/en/about-us-overview.aspx, (Accessed 22 March 2011)

Coonan, C., 2010, "Chinese developing a taste for Irish Tayto", *Irish Times*, 28 December 2010

Dess, G. *et al.*, 2004, *Strategic Management*, Boston, McGraw-Hill

Dibb, S. *et al.*, 2006, Marketing Concepts and Strategies, Boston, Houghton Mifflin

Donovan, D., 2011, "Loss of fiscal sovereignty inevitable if euro is to survive", *Irish Times*, 13 January 2011, p.16

Early, P.C. and Mosakowski, E., 2004, "Cultural Intelligence", *Harvard Business Review*, October 2004, Vol. 82, Issue 10, pp.139–146

Europa, 2011, http://europa.eu/index_en.htm, (Accessed 22 March 2011)

Finlay, P., 2000, *Strategic Management*, Harlow, Essex, Prentice Hall. Financial Times

Fitzroy, P. and Hulbert, J., 2005, *Strategic Management: Creating Value in Turbulent Times*, London, Wiley

Forfás, 2009, *Annual Report*, http://www.forfas.ie/media/forfas100602-Annual_Report_2009_English.pdf, Accessed 21 March 2011

Hunt, C., 2010, *National Strategy for Higher Education*, Dublin, Strategy Group for Higher Education

Irish Times, 2010, "Budget deficit", *The Irish Times*, 8 October 2010, p.13

Johnson, G. *et al.*, 2011, *Exploring Corporate Strategy: Text and Cases*, 9th Ed. Harlow, Pearson Education Limited

Keena, C., 2011, "Corporation tax: unravelling the myths", *Irish Times*, 11 February 2011, Finance, p.5

Kim, C. and Maubourgne, R., 2002, "Charting Your Company's Future", *Harvard Business Review*, [June 2002], Vol. 80, Issue 6, pp.76–83

Kotler, P. *et al.*, 2007, *Principles of Marketing*, 4th European Ed., Upper Saddle River, NJ, Prentice Hall Europe

Largo Foods, 2010, http://www.largofoods.ie/about_us/corporate_history.asp, (Accessed 21 March 2010)

Levitt, T., 1983, "The Globalisation of Markets", *Harvard Business Review*, May/June 1983, Vol. 61, Issue 3, pp.92–102

Lynch, R., 2008, *Strategic Management*, 5th Ed., Harlow, Prentice Hall. Financial Times

Macaro, A. and Baggini, J., 2010, "The shrink and the sage", *Financial Times Magazine*, 27 November 2010, p.51

O'Brien, J. and Marakas, G., 2008, *Management Information Systems*, 8th Ed., New York, McGraw-Hill

O'Leary, J., 2010, "I should have been more pushy in opposing risk-taking at bank", *Irish Times*, 24 July 2010, p.11

O'Halloran, B., 2008, "Bord na Móna to invest €1.4bn over five years", *Irish Times*, 22 July 2008

Paul, M., 2008, "Ireland misses out on new Google jobs", *Sunday Times*, 21 December 2008, Business and Money, p.1

Porter, M., 1998, *The Competitive Advantage of Nations*, London, Macmillan

Porter, M., 1980, *Competitive Strategy: Techniques for Analysing Industries and Competitors*, New York, *The Free Press*

Porter, M., 1985, *Competitive Advantage*, New York, The Free Press

Taylor, C., 2010, "The Four Year Challenge", *The Sunday Business Post*, 10 October 2010, p.10

Thompson, A. *et al.*, 2008, *Crafting and Executing Strategy: the Quest for Competitive Advantage*, Boston, McGraw-Hill

Tian, X., 2007, *Managing International Business in China*, Cambridge, Cambridge University Press

Tiernan, S. *et al.*, 2006, *Modern Management. Theory and Practice for Irish Students*, Dublin, Gill and Macmillan

Welch, J., 2001, *Jack: What I've Learned Leading a Great Company and Great People*, London, Headline

www.cso.ie/releasepublications/documents/labour_markets/currentppsn.pdf, Accessed 18 June 2008

Evaluating an Organisation's Strategic Capability

"Make your life an affirmation, defined by your ideals, not the negation of others. Dare to the level of your capability then go beyond to a higher level."

General Alexander Haig, US Secretary of State 1981–1982

INTRODUCTION

The previous chapter looked at the external factors affecting an organisation. The primary purpose of such analysis was to identify the opportunities and threats in the business environment. In order to avail of any such opportunities, the organisation must have the necessary strategic capability. Except in the case of start-up companies, there will be an existing strategy in place, and it is important to review that strategy to see if it is achieving the strategic goals set in its existing strategic plan. While some aspects of the existing plan will change, inevitably much of it can remain. This chapter is concerned with analysing the capability of a firm to achieve its strategic goals, and provide management with an understanding of how best to get there.

First, it is necessary to examine the resources available to a firm. These include human resources, physical resources, financial resources and intangible resources. While such resources are essential, on their own they are of little benefit – it is how they are co-ordinated and utilised by an organisation that is important. The next stage in the process, therefore, is to examine the competences with which a company uses those resources. It is the mixture of an organisation's resources and competences that define its capability and what separates a superior company from a mediocre one.

In a competitive environment, all organisations must be concerned with their costs. Analysing costs is an integral part of understanding strategic capability. The value chain, and the wider value network, will assist in this process. In the final analysis, the strategic capability of any company is relative, and so we must compare performance with rival companies. This can be done with the use of a competitor strength analysis. Having carried out this analysis, management are in a position to fully understand the organisation's strengths and weaknesses. Together with the identification of the opportunities and threats from the last chapter, this completes the SWOT analysis and allows management to position the company strategically.

Carrying out a critical evaluation of an organisation's internal capability is an essential element of formulating strategy. It is also very difficult, as it requires the organisation to view itself in an objective manner. There will inevitably be vested interests involved that will lead to a more subjective rather than objective appraisal. The use of the strategic tools described in this chapter should ensure that such bias is kept to a minimum. Such analysis should focus the attention of management on the areas of most need. The strategic goals and objectives for an organisation have been set, and management must now ensure that they utilise all their resources in an efficient and effective manner so that those goals and objectives can be achieved. The strategic capability of an organisation is ultimately dependent on its resources and competences.

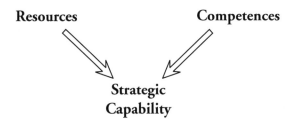

Figure 6.1 *Strategic Capability*

RESOURCES

The first stage of an internal analysis is a **resource audit**, examining all of the resources, both tangible and intangible, within an organisation. While it is necessary to examine all of the resources, the process is much more than just a listing of them. Ultimately, what is important is the value that they add to an organisation. The resources can be broken down into five main headings:

- **Human resources** – it is so often said by companies that their employees are their most important asset. For many firms, it is little more than rhetoric, and yet the reality is that staff are vital to the success of any organisation. As Ireland moves further into what Drucker referred to as the "knowledge economy" and companies move higher up the value chain, people will become even more important. One significant difference with human resources compared to other resources is that the company does not own the people who work for it. Irrespective of employment contracts, it is relatively easy for employees to leave and join rival companies. As a result, careful consideration must be given to HR policies to make the organisation an attractive place to work for employees at every level of the organisation, and this needs to be supported by the culture of the organisation.

- **Physical resources** – including buildings, plant, machinery and transport fleet, etc. There are a number of factors that need to be considered when examining such assets – their age, overall condition, location (buildings, for example, are specific to one particular location, which may or may not be an advantage). Their lifespan also needs to be taken into account. Perhaps the most important thing when considering physical resources is to examine their production capability, not just for present requirements, but also their future potential.
- **Information technology** – information technology systems are an essential part of the resources that can confer strategic advantage on an organisation in how it utilises all its other resources.
- **Financial resources** – such resources include the company's capital structure, retained earnings and other cash, debtors and creditors, as well as its relationship with its shareholders and bankers. Most options will involve substantial financial investment, and so financial resources are particularly important. Once finance is available, many of the other resources can be obtained, such as hiring talented personnel with a strong track record.
- **Intangible resources** – including goodwill, well-known brands, patents (particularly important in some industries such as pharmaceuticals), relationships with customers and customer databases, as well as business systems. Intangible resources such as brands also require considerable financial investment.

It must be remembered that it is not necessary to actually own the resources. Before the collapse of the banking industry, AIB and Bank of Ireland sold off many of their branches including their head office buildings and leased them back, thus releasing cash for developing the business. Lynch (2008: 126) believes:

> "It is useful to explore the reasons for an organisation to possess and use any resources beyond the minimum amount to stay in existence. Arguably, in an efficient market, there will be outside, more specialised suppliers that will be able to sell some activities more cheaply to the organisation than it can make them for themselves."

Outsourcing some of the value chain activities is becoming more common. Benetton, an Italian clothing company, outsources much of its production to a network of small local producers.

As a company grows in size, the amount of resources it has will also grow. Having resources somewhere in the firm is not enough. They have to be deployed where they are most needed and, consequently, flexibility is a very important aspect that needs to be considered, particularly with regard to the workforce. Given the huge level of investment in resources, it is imperative that an organisation gains maximum efficiency in their use. It must also be remembered that many resources can be easily imitated by competitors and so, on their own, resources will not give a company a sustainable competitive advantage. The next stage, therefore, is to examine the competences of the organisation.

COMPETENCES

Prahalad and Hamel (1990) first coined the term core competence in their *Harvard Business Review* article: "The Core Competence of the Corporation". They believed that "competitiveness derives from an ability to build, at lower cost and more speedily than competitors, the core competences that spawn unanticipated products". They regard core competences as the 'collective learning' in the organisation – the co-ordination of diverse production skills and integration of multiple streams of technology. It is about the organisation of work (particularly working across boundaries involving people at all levels and functions) and the delivery of value. In that sense they transcend business boundaries, such as SBUs, and allow a company to operate in what appear to be diverse areas. Canon, for example, has core competences in optics, imaging and microprocessor controls that has enabled it to succeed in diverse areas such as copiers, laser printers, cameras and image scanners.

The physical assets of any organisation deteriorate over time. However, core competences develop as they are applied and shared throughout an organisation, provided that those competences are nurtured by an organisation. They are built up over a long period of time, perhaps a decade or so, and this involves a process of continuous improvement: what the Japanese refer to as *Kaizen*.

According to Hamel and Prahalad, there are three tests to identify core competences. First, they provide potential access to a variety of markets. Second, in terms of the end user, it should make a significant impact in terms of perceived benefit. Third, it should be difficult for competitors to copy the core competence. The above example of Canon fits all three criteria: they operate in a variety of different markets; their products are of very high quality and represent good value for the consumer; and it will be difficult for competitors to replicate their processes.

Similarly, Honda has built a whole range of products, from cars and motorcycles to lawn mowers and chainsaws, from its competence in engine technology.

The building of core competences requires a strategic decision about where to build competence leadership within the organisation. This can often be built up through strategic alliances, as many Japanese companies have clearly done. Tesco has developed a core competence in managing customer information and using that information to guide the company in making decisions about what products to sell in their stores (see **Illustration 13.1** in Chapter 13).

Every organisation will naturally have to have a basic competence in all of the activities that it performs across its value chain.

 A **basic competence** should be seen as the minimum level of competence required to satisfy customers' requirements.

In a competitive environment, these basic competences are clearly not sufficient to support a leadership position in its chosen markets. Therefore, the company will have to develop core competences in one or more areas of their activities. As the company develops experience in different aspects of its business, it will build on the competences it has and develop them into a core competence.

Definition A **core competence** is an activity that the company has developed into a specialised activity that gives it a competitive advantage in that field.

Core competences will play a central part in the company's strategy and future development.

Over time, core competences can, of course, be copied by rival companies, thus eroding any competitive advantage. For many years, Volvo had a core competence for safety that gave them a strong competitive advantage. Now, many other car manufacturers such as Toyota, Renault, BMW, Mercedes, etc., have cars that are just as safe as Volvo's. Johnson *et al.* (2011: 92) believe there are four main barriers to copying core competences:

- Complexity due to internal and external linkages that deliver customer value. Innovation requires such linkages.
- The culture and history of the organisation where the core competences are embedded in its culture. 3M, makers of Post-it notes®, has a culture of innovation that is supported by inter-disciplinary groups working closely together to develop new products. Such co-operation is simply taken for granted.
- Causal ambiguity – where competitors find it difficult to understand the causes and effects underpinning an organisation's advantage.
- Change – the ability to innovate and keep ahead of competition.

CAPABILITIES

The combination of resources and competences that give an organisation its strategic capability. It is with this capability that a company can take advantage of the opportunities that have been identified. Just as key success factors will change over time, it is important to realise that the capabilities required for market leadership will also evolve as the business environment changes. When examining the capabilities of an organisation, it is important that they are viewed from the perspective of the customer. If there is no customer willing to buy a company's products or services, then such capabilities are of little use. These capabilities can be found throughout an organisation, and so a functional analysis can be of benefit to identify areas where the organisation is performing particularly well.

Human Resource Management

Organisations do not create strategies – it is the people within those organisations that do. Having talented managers and employees is of vital importance to every organisation. However, their presence alone is not enough – what is important is how they work together to achieve organisational objectives. In terms of capability, it begins with leadership, both in terms of setting the vision and achieving objectives. Being able to pick the right people for the job is in itself a key competence, which involves not just having the right skills and experience but also being able to blend new employees into the existing team. Leadership also involves creating and supporting the culture within which people will work together in a productive manner. Leadership at every level is important, from the CEO down to frontline supervisors.

In examining the capability of people in an organisation to support strategy, it is important to conduct such an analysis against the background of the culture that exists within that organisation. It can be difficult to fully understand the culture of an organisation, particularly for a manager joining the company from outside. Yet, it is essential to gain such an understanding in order to appraise the ability of the staff to support strategy. Johnson *et al.* (2008: 197) refer to the **'Cultural Web'** as a means of understanding the culture that exists within an organisation. The cultural web involves examining the paradigm of the organisation – how it sees itself and the world around it. It also involves examining the organisational structures; power structures; control systems; rituals and routines; stories and the symbols. By analysing all of these elements, not just individually but collectively, a picture can be built up of the company's culture and whether it is likely to help or hinder a particular strategy.

In terms of capability, it is also important to understand the power structures at play, as this will ultimately dictate what can be achieved. The adaptability of the people in the organisation is a crucial element in its ability to meet the changing needs of markets. It forms a central part of the ability to lead and manage change (this will be discussed later in Chapter 14). The growth in the diversity of the Irish workforce has brought with it challenges as well as opportunities. Most organisations are constantly looking at means of reducing staff costs by introducing automation. HR remains perhaps the most important function in relation to organisational capability, as with the right staff on board, everything becomes possible in terms of achieving strategic intent.

Finance

There are a number of issues that have to be looked at in terms of financial capability. In most cases, strategic decisions are likely to require significant funding, and decisions have to be made with regard to the source of capital. Most organisations use a mixture of debt, equity and retained earnings to fund major strategic projects. There are advantages and disadvantages to each. For example, the interest on debt is tax deductible, but it also increases financial risk. The debt has to be repaid irrespective of the fortunes of the company. Sometimes such finance may be difficult to raise, and there will be a certain level beyond which the risk increases substantially.

Since 2009, the 'Credit Crunch' has made it very difficult for firms to borrow even relatively small amounts of money from banks. On the other hand, the issue of shares (whether to new investors or through a rights issue) does not carry financial risk to the company but is more expensive. Retained earnings (profits accumulated over past years), if such exist, are an alternative way of financing projects. The overall cost of capital must be considered when evaluating the options using weighted average cost of capital.

There is an opportunity cost involved in financing projects, in that once the funds have been committed to a project, those funds are not then available for other opportunities that might arise. Consequently, an important capability is being able to appraise the various options available and pick the optimum one for the company. Return on capital employed, payback period and discounted cash flow analysis are all techniques which are used to evaluate strategic options, and these will be discussed below in Chapter 12. Managing cash flow is a vital financial skill, and problems with cash flow are all too often the reason why companies go into liquidation. Product lines and customers must also be screened to see where the company is making money and where the costs exceed the value.

Debtors must be constantly examined to ensure that they are paying on time. In recessionary times, many debtors will try to extend credit for as long as possible. Worse, there is a danger that some debtors' companies may go out of business, leaving large amounts of money outstanding and unsecured. The collapse in October 2010 of Pierse Contracting, one of Ireland's biggest building firms, left unsecured creditors of €51.5 million. Most of those companies who extended credit to Pierse were small building contractors who could not afford to absorb such losses. Even where a company is eventually getting paid by its debtors, it is important to remember that, while the company may be profitable overall, any delay in debtors' payment could result in short-term insolvency and an inability to meet day-to-day liabilities such as staff wages and electricity bills.

Costs cannot be controlled unless they can be identified. It is, therefore, essential that every company fully understands where all its costs are generated. Management information systems play a vital part in providing such information. The use of the value chain (see below) can be used as a framework to examine where costs are being generated in a company.

Marketing

 According to Dibb *et al.* (2006: 17): the **Marketing Concept** is "a philosophy that an organisation should try to provide products that satisfy customers' needs through a co-ordinated set of activities that also allows the organisation to achieve its goals".

It has been said that marketing is too important to be left to *just* the marketers. It is a way of thinking that covers all aspects of the organisation, and everything the organisation does must be market-focused. Without customers, there is no future for the business. There are many skills involved. First, a company needs to understand the market and customers' requirements. Sometimes this involves developing products for which customers have not yet identified a need. It also requires an ability to successfully segment the market, target and position the company. Developing the 'Five Ps' – product, price, place (distribution), promotion and people – is central to satisfying customers. In a competitive environment, building up and supporting brands is an essential element in separating companies and is directly tied in with the reputation of the company. Brands are capable of creating huge value for the company.

At the heart of any marketing function should be the customer. Over half a century ago, Peter Drucker (1954) identified the importance of the customer in *The Practice of Management* in which he stated that "a company's primary responsibility is to serve its customers... Profit is not the primary goal, but rather an essential condition for the company's continued existence". This approach is echoed by Martin (2010) who believes that the concept of maximising value for shareholders is inherently flawed and that shareholders actually do better when firms put the customers first. He believes that a better approach is to make customer value the top priority, and this in turn generates greater shareholder returns. He cites Johnson & Johnson and Procter & Gamble as examples of companies that have succeeded by putting customer value as their main focus. Staying close to the customer is an important part of customer value as it ensures that the company's products and services meet the needs of their customers.

Some companies deal directly with customers, without the use of intermediaries such as retail shops. One big advantage (apart from cost reduction) is that such a company can get direct feedback about what their customers *actually* want. For example, when people buy a Dell computer online, they can customise the specifications for that computer, adding in or leaving out components as required. This gives Dell a very accurate picture of what customers truly value in terms of their products and the items that those customers are willing to pay for. This information also plays an important part in Dell's research and development.

Rust *et al.* (2010) suggest that the focus on the customer requires a strategic shift within the organisation with the customer rather than the product placed in the centre.

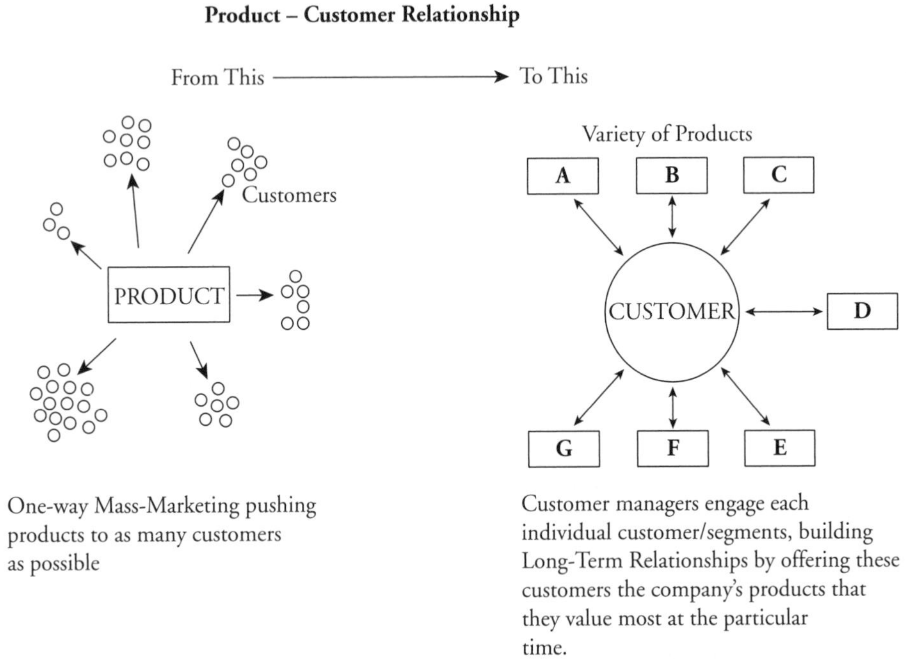

Product – Customer Relationship

One-way Mass-Marketing pushing products to as many customers as possible

Customer managers engage each individual customer/segments, building Long-Term Relationships by offering these customers the company's products that they value most at the particular time.

Source: Adapted from: Rust *et al.* (2010) "Rethinking Marketing", *Harvard Business Review*, Vol 88, Issue 1, p. 96

Figure 6.2 *Product Customer Relationship*

What is needed, they argue, is for the creation of a new position of Chief Customer Officer, reporting directly to the CEO, but senior to all product/brand managers. The primary purpose of the chief customer officer is to engage individual customers or narrow customer segments in two-way communications, building long-term relationships by promoting whichever of the company's products the customer would value most at any given time.

They propose new metrics for measuring the effectiveness of a customer-driven strategy. First there is a need to move the focus from product profitability to customer profitability. Second, pay greater attention not to current sales but to the customer lifetime value (the potential future profits that will come from a satisfied customer). Third, the focus should move from brand equity (the value of a brand) to customer equity (the sum of the lifetime value of their customers). Customer equity is also a good proxy for the value of the firm. Fourth, the company should pay less attention to market share and more attention to customer equity share (the value of the company's customer base divided by the total value of the customers in the market).

The information required by the organisation needs to be tracked at a number of levels, from the individual to the aggregate market level which, in turn, will require very close integration of the IT group within the organisation. Such transformation clearly needs to be driven from the top down.

Operations

The operations of a company are the means by which inputs are converted into outputs, and are at the heart of every organisation, whether in manufacturing or services. Such operations have to be carried out efficiently (achieving objectives using the least amount of resources necessary) and effectively (ensuring that the organisation is pursuing the correct objectives). The use of technology plays a very important part, and decisions have to be made about the level of technology and its cost vis-à-vis the cost of labour. This is complicated by the rate of change in technology development. Companies such as Toyota have made enormous savings by the development of what is termed 'lean production' techniques.

There are a number of major decisions that have to be made. The first is whether to make or buy. Some activities should be done in-house, while other activities can be safely outsourced. Nike has outsourced their production and is effectively a very successful marketing company that has created a lifestyle image which people buy into.

Other decisions include how to manufacture and where. Relationships with suppliers are very important, particularly for companies such as Dell, who rely heavily on just-in-time management to minimise inventory costs. Product design and the design of the production process itself are also central to the issue of costs. While there are differences between services and manufacturing, many of the principles overlap.

These days, outsourcing is an integral part of many companies' operations and it has many advantages. However, it is important that the relationship between the company and its contractors is managed very carefully to ensure quality. It also has important ethical considerations in terms of the possible exploitation of labour by contracted companies (with regard to corporate social responsibility and outsourcing, see below under **Supply Train Transparency**).

Research and Development

With product life cycles getting ever shorter, it is imperative that companies invest in research and development (R&D). It has been stated already that not enough money is being spent on R&D in this country in order to be competitive in a global market. The first decision, therefore, is the commitment to spending on R&D. Thereafter, it requires making decisions on what areas to invest in. There will be many areas that can show potential, but not enough finance to support them all. Decisions will then be required as to which areas to champion. Innovation is the life blood of any organisation and it requires a different way of thinking and a culture that supports it. As Albert Einstein put it:

> "The significant problems we face cannot be solved at the same level of thinking we were at when we created the problem."

James Dyson (of Dyson vacuum cleaners) spoke in Dublin in 2008 about the importance of developing a stronger manufacturing base in Ireland, and not just concentrating on the service industry, as bodies such as the IDA, Enterprise Ireland, IBEC and others seem to be doing. While we will be unable to compete on cost with large manufacturing countries such as China, Dyson argued that it is more important that we have the engineers that can come up with the ideas and patents that give us the intellectual advantage (Weckler, 2008).

The above section has examined the various functional areas where capability might be located. There are two main capabilities that bring together, and underpin, all of those parts, and these need to be considered in developing an understanding of capability in the organisation: knowledge management and cost competitiveness.

Information Systems

Throughout this text, the importance of Information Systems (IS) is a constant theme. Information Systems must be thought of not as an optional extra, but as an integral component of the strategic framework that supports competitive advantage in any organisation. It follows then that any discussion on strategic capability has to examine the information systems of the company to see how it creates value for both the company and the customer. This can be achieved in a variety of different ways from the use of data mining as a means of increasing sales, to control systems to minimise costs in the system. Yield management, which will be discussed later in this chapter, relies heavily on the use of information systems. Information Systems are also a vital element in the quality of decisions made by managers. Various types of Decision Support Systems are examined in Chapter 12.

Ireland has produced world-class companies that develop Information Systems, and given the peripheral nature of this island, e-business applications play an essential role in connecting Irish companies with their customers both at home and all around the world. This can be a major contributor to operational efficiency, productivity and customer service.

KNOWLEDGE MANAGEMENT

The concept of the 'Knowledge Economy' was mentioned above. As Ireland moves further into the knowledge economy, how companies manage knowledge will be of great importance in developing a competitive advantage. Indeed, some organisations such as accounting firms rely almost exclusively on the development of organisational knowledge.

Definition | **Organisational Knowledge** is the knowledge, values, understanding and experience that has been built up throughout an organisation over a period of time.

There are certain challenges in how organisational knowledge is managed, particularly as the organisation grows and develops into more and more divisions. Information technology has made the sharing and use of knowledge much easier, but is still dependent on the goals that management has set with regard to knowledge sharing. In General Electric, it is a central goal for each manager to share knowledge gained through the operation of their Strategic Business Unit with other parts of the organisation (Welch, 2001).

Knowledge can be shared in different ways. According to Nonaka and Takeuchi (1995), there is a difference between explicit and tacit knowledge. **Explicit knowledge** is expressed knowledge that is contained, for example, in standard operating procedure (SOP) manuals. Franchise operations such as McDonald's depend on a replication of such standardised procedures in all outlets, and this is achieved through strict reference to such manuals. The development of SOPs can be time-consuming and costly, but they ensure that all parts of the organisation are in tune. The danger is that rival firms can obtain these manuals and gain an understanding of how the company is operated, or just replicate the same procedures. While there are ethical issues involved, it would be naive to believe that such practice does not happen.

Implicit knowledge, on the other hand, is knowledge that people possess, but is not expressed in any formal way. In the course of their work, professional people, for example, will build up an enormous volume of knowledge that will inform their judgement and decision-making. A barrister doing a cross-examination in court will base her questions on a mixture of the knowledge of the law that she has built up over the years, along with her experience of previous cases, and what the witness has already said. It would be extremely difficult to codify such knowledge.

The organisation needs to put in place mechanisms for the sharing of as much information as possible so that as many people as possible benefit from it. With explicit knowledge, it is relatively easy in that this can be written down in books, manuals and policy procedures. For implicit knowledge, it is more difficult and relies on a social process within the organisation. This takes many forms. In the above example of a lawyer, a newly-qualified barrister is obliged to spend a year devilling (acting as an understudy) with an experienced colleague.

In a similar way, trainee doctors will shadow consultants doing their rounds in hospital wards. In both cases, it presents an opportunity to observe and ask questions and develop knowledge that would be very difficult to gain solely from books. Training seminars and in-house development programmes also provide an opportunity for people to mix together and share information. Ultimately, the value of the firm in terms of knowledge is the cumulative value of the knowledge of its entire workforce.

Information technology plays a pivotal role in how knowledge is managed within the organisation, and many companies are developing knowledge management systems (KMS) to assist them in managing organisational learning. According to O'Brien and Marakas (2008: 63), knowledge management systems facilitate organisational learning and knowledge creation. In many cases, organisations have more than sufficient information to enable them to make decisions. The problem for most, however, is providing that information in a form that is both useful and timely. Systems include the Internet and intranet websites, data mining, knowledge bases and online discussion groups.

COST COMPETITIVENESS

Central to the concept of capability is cost competitiveness, which covers every single aspect of an organisation. The human resource – the employees – must be able to generate revenue that justifies their salaries. Production costs must be kept in line. In selling products or services, it must be done at a price that customers are willing to pay and still allows the firm to make a profit. Managers have to be able to control costs and to do it on a continuous basis to achieve a competitive advantage. Johnson *et al.* (2008: 99) state that attention must be paid to **cost drivers** in order to manage costs effectively:

- **Economies of scale** In situations where there are high capital costs, these need to be recovered over a high volume of output. Some industries traditionally require economies of scale to be profitable, including chemical and car manufacturing.
- **Supply costs** Just-in-time manufacturing reduces overall costs by minimising the costs involved in supplying the necessary components. Scale is an important factor as well, in that companies buying in large quantities can negotiate more favourable prices. Location is also an important factor. Some manufacturing requires being located close to the raw materials because of the cost of transportation. Sheffield in England became synonymous with stainless steel as it was located next to plentiful supplies of coal and iron ore, both of which were required in the manufacturing process.
- **Product and process design** Streamlining product and process design can generate substantial savings. Yield management is central to the profitability of hotels and airlines. Software can direct pricing, depending on the demand, to maximise the revenue from a particular flight, explaining how two people sitting next to one another could have paid very different amounts for their tickets depending on when they booked them. Similarly with hotels: midweek specials are designed to level out the demand to ensure the hotel has full

occupancy all week and not just at weekends. (Yield management will be discussed in greater detail later in the chapter.)

- **Experience** The 'Experience Curve' describes how an organisation can reduce costs as it gains experience in whatever field it operates. As it gains this experience, it can operate in a more efficient manner and shorter timeframe.

VALUE CHAIN ANALYSIS

This chapter has already examined the capability of the organisation under each of the functional headings, such as HRM, Finance, etc., but understanding this capability requires a holistic view of all of these functional areas *working together* to see where value can be created. Managers also need to understand *how* such value is created. Porter (1985) developed the concept of the value chain to describe the activities of an organisation that are linked together to create value. It was originally designed to understand costs from an accounting perspective, but Porter suggested that it had wider application as a strategic tool. It enables managers to look at each part of the organisation to see where value is being created, and more importantly to understand the linkages between the different parts. It is a generic tool in that it can be applied to any business, whether manufacturing or service, and adjusted to meet the needs of a specific company, with some parts being more relevant than others.

As shown in **Figure 6.3**, the value chain can be divided into two main parts: primary activities and support activities.

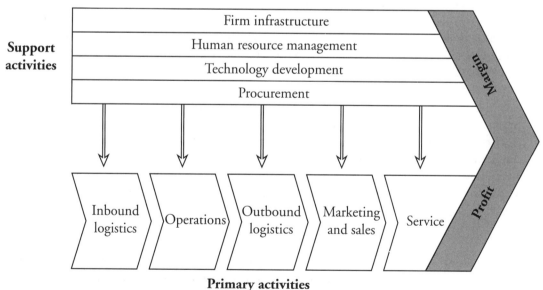

Source: Adapted from Michael E. Porter, *Competitive Advantage: Creating and Sustaining Superior Performance,* New York, The Free Press, 1985

Figure 6.3 *The Value Chain*

The **primary activities** consist of:

- **Inbound logistics** This is concerned with how the organisation interacts with, and receives goods from its suppliers, and the inspection of those goods to ensure appropriate quality. It also covers all internal handling and inventory management as the goods are stored and distributed to the operations division when they are needed. Companies such as Toyota have a very close relationship with their suppliers, ensuring just-in-time delivery of all necessary stock. The company knows exactly what parts are needed and, through electronic data interchange, so does the relevant supplier. The components are then dispatched immediately, replacing those that have been drawn from the company's internal stores. Only the bare minimum amount of stock is in the system at any one time, thus ensuring that costs are kept as low as possible for both the supplier and for Toyota.
- **Operations** This is the heart of the organisation – the operations where inputs are turned into outputs. It includes assembly, production, testing, packaging and getting the product or service ready for the customer. By carefully organising the operations, the firm can manage cost without impacting on the value obtained by the end user. For Dell, it means the assembly of the computer according to the specification requested by the customer. Nike outsources its production to manufacturing companies in the Far East. For Nike, 'operations' is more concerned with controlling the relationship with its subcontractors, rather than being directly involved in the manufacturing process itself.
- **Outbound logistics** Once the product has been manufactured it needs to be distributed to the customer. This section includes the storage of the finished product and the physical transportation through the distribution channel. Distribution channels will vary from one industry to another, but in the retail industry they would include wholesalers and retailers. Dell has recently decided to distribute its computers through select retailers, but the company still distributes most of its products directly to the customer using couriers.
- **Marketing and Sales** Whatever goods or services are produced by the organisation there have to be customers to purchase them. Marketing the company and its products is, therefore, an essential element of the process. Nike, for example, has a core competence in marketing its products and creating a lifestyle image that consumers want to buy into.
- **Service** This covers all of the activities associated with maintaining the relationship with the customer, both before and after the product has been sold. It also includes any training that might be required by the customer and the provision of spare parts and backup assistance. For many organisations, this is becoming a very important part of the overall offering to customers, and is very often the main factor that differentiates one company from another.

By examining each of the primary activities, the organisation can see where value is created. Each of the primary activities is, in turn, assisted by the four **support activities**, which are:

- **Procurement** Many organisations will have a dedicated department for procuring all of the resources needed by all of the primary activities. It will source these resources at the best price from suitable suppliers and it covers everything from spare parts for production machines to paper for office printers.

- **Technology development** New products are the lifeline of every organisation as it adapts to changing circumstances. Research and development and product design are integral to all parts of the value chain. (New product development will be discussed in detail in Chapter 9.)
- **Human resource management** This chapter has already covered the importance of human resources to the organisation. Every part of the company will need suitable employees from those involved in procurement to after-sales service. These must be recruited, selected, trained and integrated into the organisation. Given the high costs associated with staff turnover, suitable staff must also be retained and rewards systems must be put in place to support their retention.
- **Firm's infrastructure** This section includes everything from the structure and control mechanisms in the organisation to finance, administration, and the information technology systems required to support all aspects of a company.

On the right-hand side of **Figure. 6.3** is the margin or profit that the company makes. The outer line is the end price to the customer and the inner line represents the totality of the costs to the organisation. The difference is obviously the profit margin. To increase this margin, the outer line could be moved further to the right, to increase the selling price. In a competitive environment, this is very often not a feasible option. The alternative is to move the inner line further to the left, i.e. reduce costs.

By using the value chain, organisations can look at the various activities, both primary and secondary, to see where value is being created. It focuses management's attention on not just the different parts of the organisation, but, just as importantly, on the **linkages** between those parts. The importance of linkages within the organisation cannot be overstated. It is imperative that the organisation is acting in a unified manner, with the customer at the centre of its focus. Kanter (2008: 44) highlights the importance of being able to respond quickly and creatively to opportunities. This requires the co-ordination of all elements and business processes of the organisation, using various systems from common core values to IT platforms. Obviously, the focus on costs is very important, and by examining each component, it allows managers to isolate the costs for each activity and supports the process of activity-based costing. These costs can then be compared to industry averages. The value chain for each company will differ due to the way each one is configured and how they perform each activity. These differences will further evolve over time. Later in this chapter, we will examine how parts of the value chain might be reconfigured to improve value and cut costs.

It is also important that managers should examine value from the perspective of the customer. In a hotel, for example, 'service' is a *sine qua non* in terms of the customer, but a strict focus on costs may well trim back elements of the service that are considered so important by the customer. In particular, in some aspects of the value chain, such as the quality of the workforce, or management, it may be very difficult to place a precise cost on such activities.

Michael Porter's value chain (see **Figure 6.3**) brought the focus on value creation to a strategic level in the minds of executives and created an important focus on the customer in the value chain. While Porter's contribution has been very significant, there are also some important limitations that need to be considered. The model represents a traditional focus on the organisation, placing marketing and service at the end, with the primary focus on the profit that is made when the product or service is sold on to the customer.

Hines (1993) examined supply chains in Japanese companies and, adapting Porter's work, proposed an Integrated Materials Management system. He believes that a number of factors should be taken into consideration when examining the concept of value in terms of providing products or services. First, he believes that customer satisfaction and not company profit should be the main focus of the organisation. Second, while he acknowledges that Porter stresses integration between the different elements of the organisation, Hines believes the original model still shows a divided network not just between the divisions within the company but also between the various companies in the value network. Third, he considers the wrong functions are highlighted in the value chain.

Instead, Hines proposes that the value chain should be pointing in the opposite direction, placing the customer at the beginning of the process. The reason he suggests this is that it is the final customer that defines what value is, not any of the groups within the value chain. Thus the Integrated Materials Value System moves away from the traditional 'push' system as emphasised by Porter, to a consumer 'pull' system. The entire system needs to be a fully integrated system with one common purpose: customer satisfaction. Thus, the relationship between the different companies in the wider value chain is one of collaboration, rather than an adversarial one.

In addition, Hines believes that the primary activities should reflect a collaborative approach to defining value, starting with the customer and working back through the entire system to the supplier organisations. Hines lists marketing, materials, engineering, quality, R&D and design as the primary activities. These jointly define value at each stage. The secondary activities are activity-based costing, human resource management (HRM), total quality managemant (TQM), electronic data interchange (EDI) and profit. Perhaps one of the major differences between Porter's Value Chain and Hines's model, is that Hines believes profit is a facilitator and places it under the category of a secondary activity. He considers that a reasonable level of profit throughout the network is necessary to serve the consumer most effectively, stating that this is the approach most commonly taken by Japanese companies, reflecting a much more collaborative effort between all the different players in the system. Such collaboration is supported by a constant focus on innovation and the search to find better ways of delivering value to the customer. In so doing, it also combats many of the effects of the competitive forces at play within the industry.

One final observation that needs to be made about the value chain concerns IT. The capability of IT systems has transformed beyond recognition from the time Porter first proposed the value chain. IT must now be considered an integral part of any organisation from a strategic perspective. For example, the use of Data Mining (see Chapter 13) can greatly enhance the effectiveness of the "Marketing and Sales" part of the value chain. Those who have bought books through Amazon will have experienced how the company trawls though past purchases to pick new books that will suit the individual customer's choice. While there is a certain 'push' element to Amazon's strategy, it still ties in with the discussion above on the importance of working with customers to select products that match their requirements (Rust *et al.*, 2010).

The Value System

The above section dealt with the value chain of a single company. It would be quite unusual for one company to perform all of the value chain activities by itself.

The primary activities of inbound logistics and outbound logistics imply a relationship between the organisation and its suppliers and distributors. The price paid for a product by the customer also includes the cost of all parts of the entire chain from the supplier of raw materials/components to the retail outlet. This wider network is known as the Value System and must be included in the analysis by management in order to understand the totality of costs and value.

According to Kanter (2008: 49), in selecting external partners to work with, organisations require an open definition of purpose to "encourage exploration of partnership possibilities", which in turn requires managers to "think about the end-to-end possibilities to the whole ecosystem, from suppliers' suppliers to customers' customers and beyond – to society itself". It also provides opportunities to develop new products. Pepsi Cola uses its 'Power of One' strategy to work closely with its major retail partners in developing new products, identifying inefficiencies and creating joint promotions.

One of the major decisions that an organisation needs to consider is which parts of the value chain it will undertake itself, and which parts (if any) it will outsource. Only bigger companies can afford to have dedicated departments covering all aspects of the company's marketing activities. Smaller companies may employ a marketing manager, but all other aspects of the marketing function, such as advertising, are usually outsourced to an advertising agency. For most organisations, it makes sense to outsource advertising and PR to specialist companies who have the expertise and the necessary industry contacts. The main function of a marketing manager in this instance would be to liaise with the advertising/PR agency with regard to the specific needs of the company. The main advantages

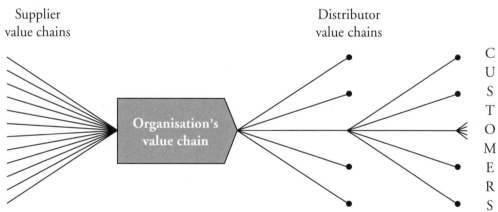

Source: Adapted from Michael E. Porter, *Competitive Advantage: Creating and Sustaining Superior Performance*, New York, The Free Press, 1985

Figure 6.4 *The Value System*

for the company in outsourcing is that they are getting expert assistance when required, without the overheads of maintaining staff that would not be fully utilised at other times. Thus, any discussion about managing linkages refers not only to internal linkages, but also to external linkages.

A detailed knowledge of costs is an obvious requirement of making decisions on outsourcing. Generally, an organisation should not outsource an activity if it is a core competence, as this will be a vital part of the organisation's capability. Another major decision to be made is which companies might be suitable to form alliances with. Any breakdown in the relationship between the partners will have serious consequences, and so it is vitally important that such alliances are carefully chosen. Like all relationships, they need to be nurtured on an ongoing basis. Porter pointed out that many aspects of a value chain can be copied by competitors. However, the quality of relationships could make it very difficult for competitors to copy, and so give the company a competitive advantage.

While production is often outsourced to developing countries where labour is cheaper, companies are coming under increasing pressure to shorten supply chains. This is primarily due to environmental concerns and the carbon footprint involved in moving goods half-way around the world. Increasingly, however, energy costs are also a major factor. According to Ghemawat (2010: 58), nearly one-quarter of all North American and European countries have taken steps to shorten their supply chain in recent years.

Supply Chain Transparency

It must be remembered that, from the perspective of corporate social responsibility (CSR), the company manufacturing products retains responsibility for its entire value system. Many companies have suffered significant reputational damage due to the actions of their immediate suppliers, or indeed companies supplying their suppliers, In Chapter 4, we saw that Mattel had to recall toys made in China because of concern over safety, raising questions about how much control it exerted over its supply chain. Thomas (2008) highlighted many unsavoury practices including *inter alia* the use of child labour in El Salvador in harvesting sugar cane that was used to supply Coca-Cola. Harvesting is hazardous and is classified as one of the worst forms of child labour by the UN. In its 2004 report on El Salvador, Human Rights Watch (2004: 60), identified that while Coca-Cola did not directly use suppliers that employed child labour, the company did indirectly benefit from such labour in their value network.

According to New (2010), companies are beginning to take much greater care to minimise adverse environmental effects all along the supply chain. Previously, customers had a limited view of supply chains, but now they pay considerable attention to the provenance of the goods they are buying. This applies not just to suppliers but to all parts of the distribution network. As a result, companies must take an active part in thoroughly investigating not just the companies that they are dealing directly with, but also other companies that their suppliers are dealing with.

Changes in technology in recent times have made this all the more important. While many of the technologies are not new, they are evolving in such a way that creates both opportunities and threats for companies. These technologies include microscopic labelling devices, a new generation of barcodes that can be read with mobile phones, as well as radio-frequency identification (RFID) tags which are becoming smaller and smaller. Technology can be used to store data directly and can be updated as it moves through the value chain. It can also be used to connect to a vast amount of web-based supporting data. This tracking of goods is already standard practice in many safety-critical industries where companies must be able to certify the quality of product components, such as in the aerospace industry, with pharmaceuticals and medical devices. As customers take greater interest in the origin and the authenticity of the goods they purchase, providing them with the means to track the supply chain can help increase brand value. Companies that fail to reveal this information may well have it exposed by activists who oppose certain supply chain practices, and in so doing, may cause enormous damage to corporate reputations (Human Rights Watch, 2004).

Strategy Maps

The importance of linkages in the value chain was discussed above. Porter (2006) considers the creation of customer value in organisations as a series of inter-connected activities. The challenge then for managers is to develop a strategic positioning by choosing which activities to engage in that will differentiate the company from its rivals. Some of these activities may be inconsistent with each other and a trade-off between those activities will be required, e.g. in order for Ryanair to reduce airfares, it is necessary to minimise passenger service. Thus, senior managers must decide on the priorities, and also make decisions about what not to do. These priorities must then be communicated to all staff members.

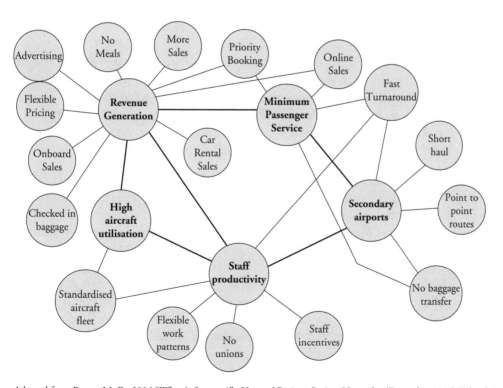

Adapted from Porter, M. E., 2006 "What is Strategy?", *Harvard Business Review*, November/December 2006, Vol. 74, Issue 6, p.73

Figure 6.5 *Activity Map – Ryanair*

These activities can be plotted on an Activity Map which shows both the main activities and related activities. Note that an Activity Map is a different concept to the strategy map that was discussed in the context of the Balanced Scorecard in Chapter 3. **Figure 6.5** is an Activity Map that could be applied to Ryanair. One major advantage of such a visual representation is that it shows the connection between all of the activities and how changing one activity can impact on others. It reinforces the importance of the fact that a company's capability lies not in any one particular function. It is a whole system of activities, rather than a collection of individual parts. This inter-connection plays a vital role in preventing competitors from imitating a particular company. There is no element of Ryanair's strategy that is difficult to interpret and copy. Its strength lies in how the company combines all these activities in a unified offering to customers, thus creating sustainability. The content of strategy maps can easily be created in draft form using Post-it® notes. The content can then be debated internally with regard to the importance of each element and the connections between them.

BENCHMARKING AN ORGANISATION

The value chain and value network examine the notion of cost and value in an organisation and its relationship in the wider value network. The capability of an organisation is relative, and must be compared with other organisations. Benchmarking is a process by which an organisation can compare its internal activities to best practice. It involves looking at how a company performs the different activities in terms of cost and efficiency. There are a number of ways in which a company can benchmark its activities.

The first process is historical analysis, which compares performance in the current year with performance in the previous year. Activities such as sales, administrative costs and many others can be examined to see if there has been an improvement or deterioration in performance. Airlines could compare passengers carried on a particular route with last year's figures. While such analysis is useful, it does not present a complete picture. A particular company may have improved its performance by perhaps 5%. However, if the industry expanded at a rate of 10%, then the company has lost relative market share.

A better form of benchmarking is a comparison to industry standards, to see if an organisation is performing well relative to other organisations in that industry. Most industries will have performance indicators that individual companies would be aware of and against which they can then compare their own results. The information can be obtained from a number of sources such as industry analysts, annual reports, other published reports, suppliers and customers. It can be obtained by the company itself, or there are companies who specialise in gathering data for benchmarking purposes and provide comparative data without identifying any of the participating companies. The analysis should focus management's attention on those areas that need to be improved. Discrepancies between company and industry averages could be due to poor implementation of internal procedures or outdated processes. The previous chapter looked at industry analysis and how the nature of the industry changes. It looked at how the photographic industry and the electronics industry converged and brought in new players such as Sony and Canon. Such changes in the boundaries of an industry have to be borne in mind when making an industry comparison.

One other drawback with industry comparisons is that the entire industry may not be performing to its potential. Prior to the deregulation of European airways, many national airlines such as Aer Lingus were very inefficient, but still profitable because of their protected position. Post-deregulation, huge structural changes were required to put these airlines on a sound commercial footing. In many industries, there can be a resistance to change because the industry standards are regarded by participants as tried and trusted. Yet, improvements in productivity can always be made. Therefore, benchmarking needs to go one step further and look at best practice, wherever that is found. The concept of Just-In-Time Management was first implemented by Toyota after some of its executives had observed how supermarket shelves were quickly restocked as customers bought the products. Having observed the process, they saw that it could be applied to car manufacturers in their dealings with suppliers. As a result, just-in-time manufacturing is now an integral part of the car manufacturing industry.

Performance Metrics

There are different ways in which performance can be measured. One important measurement technique is to apply financial ratios to evaluate a company's financial performance and strength. Different ratios will measure different aspects of the business, and ratios will also differ according to the type of industry. These ratios can be used for internal historical analysis and for industry comparison. Some of the more common ratios are:

Table 6.1: *Financial Ratios*

Ratio	Calculation	What it measures
Gross profit percentage	$\dfrac{\text{Gross profit} \times 100}{\text{Sales}}$	Indicates the efficiency of the producing department as well as the pricing policy of the business. It is a fundamental measure of the effectiveness of an organisation. The higher the rate the better.
Net profit percentage	$\dfrac{\text{Net profit} \times 100}{\text{Sales}}$	After tax profit as a percentage of sales. It indicates the relative efficiency of an organisation after deducting all expenses, but probably before interest and tax. The higher the better.
Expenses as a percentage of sales	$\dfrac{\text{Expenses} \times 100}{\text{Sales}}$	Measures the expenses involved in making sales. This should be kept as low as possible.
Return on capital employed	$\dfrac{\text{Net profit (before tax)} \times 100}{\text{Capital employed}}$	Shows the return the company is making on the total investment.
Return on shareholders' funds	$\dfrac{\text{Net profit (before tax)} \times 100}{\text{Shareholders' funds}}$	Shows the return the shareholders are getting as a percentage of their investment in the company.

Ratio	Calculation	What it measures
Earnings per share	$\dfrac{\text{Profits after taxes}}{\text{Number of ordinary shares}}$	Shows the profit attributable to each ordinary shareholder.
Price/earnings ratio	$\dfrac{\text{Current mkt price per share}}{\text{Earnings per share}}$	Shows the number of times' earnings a shareholder is willing to pay in order to purchase the share. The higher the rate, the greater the investor confidence.
Current ratio	$\dfrac{\text{Current assets}}{\text{Current liabilities}}$	Indicates the extent to which the amounts owed to short-term creditors can be met by assets which are expected to be converted into cash within the same time period.
Liquid or quick ratio	$\dfrac{\text{Current assets less stock}}{\text{Current liabilities}}$	The ability of the firm to pay current liabilities without having to sell stock.
Gearing	$\dfrac{\text{Total debt}}{\text{Total shareholders funds}}$	This is a term used to describe the extent to which the company's total capital is provided by fixed interest finance. High ratios show excessive debt.
Stock turnover	$\dfrac{\text{Cost of goods sold}}{\text{Average stock}}$	Measures the number of times that stock is sold in the year.
Average collection period of debtors	$\dfrac{\text{Total debtors} \times 365}{\text{Credit sales}}$	Indicates the average length of time it takes to convert debtors into cash.

Removing Cost Disadvantages

If an organisation is able to produce goods or services at a cost lower than its rivals, this will afford it a competitive advantage. On the other hand, if it is seen that the organisation is operating at a higher cost base than companies offering a similar product, remedial action needs to be taken quickly and decisively. Such cost disadvantages can occur anywhere in the company's value chain, or in the wider value system.

If the problem is internal, then managers have direct control over solving the problem. Using benchmarking, managers can identify best practice for the particular cost driver and make the appropriate changes. There can be numerous reasons for high costs: the company is carrying too much stock, administrative costs are too high, operations are badly designed, or manufacturing costs are too high. In recent years, many Irish companies have relocated to Eastern Europe or the Far East to avail of cheaper labour costs. In June 2008, Hibernian Insurance announced that it was outsourcing 560 jobs to India. According to the Group CEO of Hibernian, Stuart Purdy: "the issues relating to insurance in Ireland are 'relatively stark' and that profit levels in its life and pensions business are the lowest in the 27 countries in which its parent company Aviva operates" (McGreevy, 2008).

Costs disadvantages may also be found in the area of component supplies, and these also have to be rectified. The problem may be solved by finding a different supplier who can guarantee the same quality and service but at a cheaper price. As with the above example, it may be that savings are achieved from sourcing materials directly from abroad rather than from local suppliers. The answer may also be found by working more closely with the supplier and operating a just-in-time delivery system that reduces costs for both parties. If the supplier is in a strong bargaining position, this puts the onus back on the organisation itself to see if its operations can be redesigned in order to reduce costs.

Costs may also be found in the forward distribution channel, as distributors or retailers may be adding on too much of a markup. The company should work with the channel members to see if there are ways in which costs can be reduced and so preserve existing margins. In some cases, it may be necessary to bypass distributors and deal directly with the customer. Dell has traditionally operated in this manner. Likewise, Ryanair began using telesales in the late 1980s where passengers could phone and book their tickets, thus cutting out the 12.5% margin being made by travel agents. As the Internet gained widespread usage in the 1990s, passengers switched to booking online and now 99.5% of Ryanair tickets are purchased in this way. By reconfiguring their value chain like this, Ryanair made substantial savings in their cost base, which allowed them to pass those savings on to customers. In this manner, they turned a cost into a first-mover competitive advantage.

YIELD MANAGEMENT

The containment of costs is an essential capability of any organisation. By lowering costs, profits can be increased. The maximisation of revenue is also an important part of the equation of increasing profits. Most organisations are usually limited by competitive forces from increasing prices significantly. Therefore, in order to maximise revenue, the company must create a greater demand and sell more products at the standard, fixed price. If the demand is greater at certain times of the year, e.g. the Christmas toy market, then the products can be stockpiled in warehouses until they are needed. There are some industries that cannot stockpile goods for sale at a later date and, consequently, this could restrict their ability to maximise revenue. However, by using yield management techniques, greater profits can still be made by these organisations.

Definition | **Yield management** is the application of information systems and pricing strategies to maximise revenue from resources of a relatively fixed, but perishable, capacity, by anticipating and directing consumer behaviour.

Yield management was developed by the US company American Airlines in 1985 to enable it to compete with low-cost carriers following the deregulation of the airline industry. Throughout the late 1980s and early 1990s, yield management quickly spread to other airlines and transportation companies. Yield management is particularly relevant for sectors such as hotels, airlines, theatres, etc., that have relatively fixed capacity (over the short term). It is regarded as 'relatively' fixed as a 100-seater aircraft, for example, flying on a particular route is restricted to carrying 100 passengers on any one flight. Theoretically, the aircraft could be replaced by a larger aircraft if there was greater demand, but in the short term it is relatively fixed. Any seats that have not been sold on the flight are regarded as 'perishable' and cannot be resold on a later flight that might have a greater demand.

The same principle holds for many service industries where production and consumption is simultaneous, e.g. if U2 are playing in Croke Park, ticket holders must be present (consuming) as the concert is playing (production). If any fan was unable to make the concert on that night, the opportunity for that particular concert is missed forever.

With airline flights, demand is restricted by both capacity (the number of seats available) and time when the product is available, e.g. there are currently seven flights per day available on the Dublin–Stansted route. Inevitably demand will be higher or lower depending on the time the product is available. For example, airline flights on Friday evenings will usually have a greater demand as business people return home, and holiday makers wish to depart. Some customers will be willing to pay more to travel at a specific time, while others are more price-sensitive and are happy to travel at other times at a cheaper rate. Demand can also be altered by imposing minimum stay requirements. In addition to situations of fixed capacity, yield management is also relevant when there are high fixed costs and fairly low variable costs. With airlines, for example, there are high fixed costs (capital costs) associated with providing the aircraft, while the variable costs involved are very low. Therefore, any additional passenger, even at a low ticket price, represents a contribution to fixed costs. Once break-even point is reached, the contribution that each additional passenger makes can represent a significant rise in profit for that particular flight.

According to Kimes (2003), yield management using demand-based pricing helps ensure an even distribution of demand for the product by shifting it away from peak-demand periods to times when demand is lower. In order to ensure that each flight is full, differential pricing is used, which means that customers using the same service at the same time can pay different amounts, depending on when they booked the service. The object in both cases is to maximise revenue by using an appropriate pricing structure, information on the demand patterns of different market segments, information about historical demand and booking patterns, all of which are supported by an information system capable of handling such data. The computer system must be fully integrated into the overall IT structure of the company, underlining the strategic importance of information technology to the organisation.

Yield management requires a detailed knowledge of the market, which includes knowledge of segmentation – dividing the total market in different sub-groups that have similar needs or characteristics. It also requires the ability to forecast the requirements for the service using historical information to estimate future demand. Computer systems then analyse the demand on a real-time basis and adjust prices up or down accordingly.

While computers can assist in the process, yield management also requires subjective decisions by management and staff as some business will be last minute, e.g. direct enquiries by customers. In that regard, it requires well-trained staff to make appropriate decisions, as pricing too low will not maximise revenue, and pricing too high may turn away the business. Good sales staff will know when to make the right call, and direct contact with the customer can also provide an opportunity for selling other products, e.g. car rental, and so further increase revenue. In essence, yield management allows for a more structured approach to pricing decisions, taking into account marketing, customer and operational decisions.

COMPETITIVE ANALYSIS

Benchmarking will show the company whether they are stronger or weaker than their main rivals and in which areas. Such comparison is important, but the emphasis tends to be quantitative. There are also other qualitative factors on which companies compete and these must also be measured to ascertain whether the company has a competitive advantage or not. Thompson *et al.* (2008: 122) recommend carrying out a competitive strength assessment to compare a company with its rivals on a range of topics. These should include the key success factors for the industry (see previous chapter), and can also include other criteria that measure competitive strength.

The competitive strength analysis can be un-weighted or weighted. A weighted assessment is recommended as some of the factors will inevitably be more important than others and this should be reflected in the weighting allotted. The selection of the criteria, the weightings used and the scores allocated to each criterion, will inevitably be subjective. This might seem to undermine the purpose of the exercise. The process involved is, nevertheless, an important exercise in encouraging management to focus their attention on the important competitive issues facing their company. It should then direct action toward the areas that need strengthening.

There are a number of stages involved in constructing a competitive strength analysis:

1. List the industry's key success factors and most important measures of competitive strength/ weakness. Up to 10 factors should be chosen.
2. Apply a weighting to each factor reflecting its overall importance. The sum of all the weightings should equal 1.0.
3. List each company that the company is in competition with. (Strategic group mapping will assist this process.)
4. Each company is then given an allocated score for each of the criteria chosen on the left-hand column. This is then multiplied by the appropriate rating to give a weighted score for that criterion.
5. The process is repeated for all the criteria to be compared.
6. The scores for each company are totalled for all the criteria. The company with the highest score is the most competitive, ranging down to the least competitive.

It will be seen in the example in **Table 6.2** that there is a difference in the scoring between the un-weighted and the weighted scores. The weighting takes into account the importance

This is illustrated in **Table 6.2** (below):

Table 6.2: *Weighted Competitive Strength Assessment: Henry Morris Manufacturing Ltd*

(Scoring: 1 = very poor 10 = excellent)

Competitive Factor	Allocated weighting	Henry Morris Ltd		Rico Ltd		Galmul Ltd		Lowper Ltd	
		Allocated score	Weighted score	Allocated score	Weighted score	Allocated score	Weighted score	Allocated score	Weighted score
Brand reputation	0.20	8	1.60 (8 × 0.20)	7	1.4 (7 × 0.20)	9	1.80 (9 × 0.20)	4	0.80 (4 × 0.20)
Product Quality	0.15	7	1.05	7	1.05	8	1.20	4	0.60
Customer service	0.15	4	0.60	3	0.45	6	0.90	3	0.45
Distribution network	0.05	4	0.20	4	0.20	6	0.30	4	0.20
Overall Cost position	0.30	5	1.50	6	1.80	5	1.50	4	1.20
Financial strength	0.05	6	0.30	6	0.30	4	0.20	2	0.10
Production capability	0.05	4	0.20	5	0.25	7	0.35	5	0.25
Range of products	0.05	8	0.40	5	0.25	7	0.35	6	0.30
Sum of weights	1.0								
Un-weighted strength		46		43		52		32	
Overall competitive score (weighted)			5.85		5.70		6.60		3.90

Adapted from Thompson et al. (2008: 123)

of the various criteria in the mind of the customer and gives a more accurate reading. In the example above, Galmul Limited is the strongest in the market with a score of 6.60; followed by Henry Morris Limited at 5.85; then Rico Limited at 5.70; and finally Lowper Limited with a score of 3.90. The most important factor in the example is the cost position of the companies, which is given a weighting of 0.30.

An examination of the competitive strength assessment matrix will show the overall relative position of each company. It will also reveal the breakdown of where that strength lies and its importance from a customer perspective. Unlike the strategy canvas (see Chapter 5) it gives an overall assessment that includes a weighting in favour of the more important factors. This will give the company much more accurate feedback as to its true strengths and weaknesses, and consequently where it needs to take action. It will also guide management in making decisions about what type of action, either offensive or defensive, that needs to be taken. The information in **Table 6.2** can now be presented graphically in **Figure 6.6**.

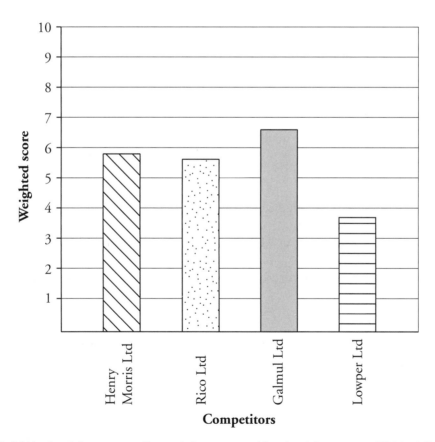

Figure 6.6 *Weighted Competitive Strength Assessment (Graphical Depiction of Table 6.2)*

SWOT ANALYSIS

A SWOT analysis lists the **s**trengths, **w**eaknesses, **o**pportunities and **t**hreats facing an organisation. In the previous chapter, we examined how opportunities and threats are identified from examining the environment. That chapter also looked at the organisation internally to examine its strategic capability. A number of strategic tools were used to analyse the resources and competences. The organisation is now in a position to draw all of these factors together in a SWOT analysis and this will form the basis of future strategic decisions. A SWOT analysis can be a useful strategic tool when it is properly utilised. It is **<u>NOT</u>** a mere listing of factors but a detailed analysis of the main issues facing the organisation.

Strengths

The review of resources, competences, functional analysis, value chain and value network analysis, and benchmarking will show a number of possible strengths. Such strengths could possibly include:

- Prime location
- State-of-the-art production facilities
- Strong economies of scale
- High quality/differentiated products
- Valuable patents
- Proprietary technology
- Highly-skilled staff
- Strong management team/clear strategic direction
- Strong balance sheet
- Well-known brand
- High relative market share
- Large customer database and loyal customers
- Strong e-commerce capability
- Core competences in areas such as R&D, marketing, supply chain management, etc.
- Strong cost competitiveness
- Strong internal/external linkages and strong strategic alliances

Weaknesses

Some weaknesses will be a major handicap to the organisation, while others will be insignificant. It is important that the difference between these is understood. In many respects, weaknesses will be a mirror-image of the strengths listed above:

- Out-dated production facilities
- High cost production relative to competitors
- Inflexible workforce

- Poor management team/lack of strategic direction
- High level of financial borrowing (highly geared)
- Falling profitability
- Poor/declining market share
- Poor brand image
- Lack of e-commerce capability
- Poor quality products/too narrow a product line
- Lack of core competences
- Poor competitive position

Opportunities

The opportunities and threats will have been observed from the external analysis. These will vary with industry conditions. It must also be remembered that opportunities can often be there around us – it is a matter of being able to spot them. In Chapter 2, it was shown how important it is to be able to seize the 'window of opportunity' when it arises. What may be an opportunity for one company may not be for another. Opportunities are also dependent on having the necessary resources to be able to exploit them. Opportunities may include:

- Expanding home market
- New market segments
- Growth in the economy
- Weak competitors/potential to expand relative market share
- Foreign markets
- Developing online sales
- Mergers and acquisitions
- Deregulation in the market
- Reduction in trade barriers
- New technologies
- Forward or backward integration

Threats

The organisation will want to take advantage of any opportunities in the market, but it also needs to be aware of any potential threats. Some of the threats will be to the industry in general, others will be more specific. The threats will also vary in terms of their possible impact on an organisation. Threats that are potentially significant in nature will have to be faced as a matter of urgency. Possible threats include:

- Declining economic growth
- Deregulation
- New technologies
- Declining home market/falling demographics
- Competitors gaining market share/increased competition

- Shift in consumer tastes
- Globalisation

SWOT analysis should not be just a listing of the various factors. Its use lies in the analysis and interpretation of those factors and the conclusions drawn. It is also about the action taken on foot of such analysis. The organisation will be trying to use its strengths to capitalise on the opportunities most appropriate to its situation, as that will give it the best chance of success. In particular, the company will need a strong match between its capabilities and the industry's key success factors.

When discussing PESTEL analysis in the previous chapter, it was stated that the organisation must examine the factors that are relevant now, and those that will impact on the organisation in the years to come. The same situation arises with a SWOT analysis. Strategy is about the long-term direction of an organisation. While some options may be able to be seized straight away, it may take many months or indeed years to put in place an appropriate strategy. Management will have to focus on those issues that are most pressing.

"Things that matter most must never be at the mercy of things which matter least."

Goethe

CONCLUSION

In the introduction to Part Two of this text, there was discussion regarding which should come first: the process of setting strategic goals, or analysis of the external and internal environments. This text argues that to achieve long-term strategic success, it is important that the vision drives the strategy-making process. Geometry tells us that the shortest distance between two points is a straight line. For a company, however, it is not always possible to move in a straight line in terms of achieving its vision. Cognizance must be paid to the environment within which the company is operating. For that reason, having conducted a SWOT analysis, the organisation may well wish to revisit the (short-term) goals and objectives that have been set, particularly in light of the resources available. While the short-term goals may be modified following this analysis, the resources available should not restrict the vision. Thus, the first part of the company's strategic plan (see Chapter 12) should now be complete. The strategies for achieving those goals will be the subject of Part Three of this text. It is at that point that the strategic plan will be finalised.

SUMMARY

The previous chapter examined the external environment to identify opportunities and threats. This chapter looked internally to examine the strengths and weaknesses of the company. Together they comprise a SWOT analysis. While the majority of people will be familiar with the term 'SWOT analysis', it will be seen that a considerable amount of analysis needs to be carried out before any meaningful conclusions can be drawn.

Every organisation needs resources and, in a competitive environment, they need to be the best available. These resources include tangible entities such as buildings, machinery, transport, etc. It also includes valuable, but intangible, resources such as brand names. Resources, on their own, are not sufficient. They must be utilised to maximum effect. The competences of an organisation describe its ability to use these resources, and together they make up its strategic capability. In pursuing a strategy, an organisation must have the strategic capability to support it; or if it currently does not have that capability, it must be developed.

The first stage of an internal analysis is a resource audit, examining all of the resources, both tangible and intangible, in the organisation. The process is much more than just a listing of them. Ultimately, what is important is the value that they add to an organisation. Resources can be broken down into five main headings:

1. **Human resources** – Employees are a company's most important asset and are vital to its success.
2. **Physical resources** – Buildings, plant, machinery and transport fleet. Their age and condition must be taken into consideration.
3. **Information technology resources** – IT systems that can confer a competitive advantage.
4. **Financial resources** Financial resources include the company's capital structure, retained earnings and other cash, debtors, creditors, as well as its relationship with its shareholders and its bankers. Implementing strategy will involve substantial financial investment.
5. **Intangible resources** – Includes goodwill, well-known brands, patents, relationship with customers, and customer databases, as well as business systems. Intangible resources such as brands also require considerable financial investment.

It is not necessary to actually own the resources. As a company grows in size, the amount of resources it has will also grow. Having resources somewhere in the firm is not enough. They have to be deployed where they are most needed and, consequently, flexibility is very important, particularly with regard to the workforce. Given the huge level of investment in resources, it is imperative that the organisation gains maximum efficiency in their use.

A basic competence should be seen as the minimum level of competence required to satisfy customers' requirements. In a competitive environment, these basic competences are clearly not sufficient to support a leadership position in a company's chosen markets. Therefore, the company will have to develop core competences in one or more areas of their activities.

A core competence is an activity that the company has developed into a specialised activity that gives it a competitive advantage in that field. Core competences will play a central part in the company's strategy and future development. Competences are built up slowly over time, and often in collaboration.

Strategic capability is the combination of resources and competences. It is with this capability that a company can take advantage of the opportunities that have been identified. Such capabilities can be found throughout an organisation, and so a functional analysis can be of benefit to identify areas where the organisation is performing particularly well. This involves carrying out an analysis of the company's human resources, finance, marketing, operations, research and development, and any other relevant functions. Knowledge management is an essential part of any organisation competing in what is often referred to as the 'knowledge economy'. **Organisational knowledge** is 'the collective experience accumulated through systems, routines and activities of sharing across an organisation'.

Central to the concept of capability is **cost competitiveness**. It covers every single aspect of an organisation. Managers have to be able to control costs and do it on a continuous basis to achieve a competitive advantage. Attention must be paid to **cost drivers** in order to manage costs effectively. These include economies of scale, supply costs, product and process design, and experience. Understanding the capability of the organisation requires a holistic view of all the different functional areas to see where value can be created.

The value chain describes the activities of an organisation that are linked together to create value. It enables managers to look at each part of the organisation to see where value is being created and, more importantly, to understand the linkages between the different parts. It is a generic tool in that it can be applied to any business, whether manufacturing or service, and adjusted to meet the needs of that specific company; for example, some parts will be more relevant than others. The value chain can be divided into two main parts: primary activities, including inbound logistics, operations, outbound logistics, sales and marketing and service; and support activities, including procurement, technology development, human resource management and the firm's infrastructure.

The price paid for a product by the customer also includes the cost of all parts of the entire chain from the supplier of raw materials/components to the retail outlet. This wider network is known as the **Value System** and must be included in the analysis by management in order to understand the totality of costs and value. One of the major decisions that an organisation needs to consider is which parts of the value chain it will undertake itself, and which parts (if any) it will outsource.

A competitive strength assessment compares a company with its rivals on a range of topics. These should include the key success factors for the industry and can also include other criteria that measure competitive strength. It can be un-weighted or weighted. The weighting takes into account the importance of the various criteria in the mind of the customer and gives a more accurate reading.

A **SWOT analysis** lists the strengths, weaknesses, opportunities and threats facing an organisation. The opportunities and threats were identified from examining the environment (see Chapter 5). This chapter looked at the organisation internally to examine its strategic capability. A number of strategic tools were used to analyse the resources and competences. The organisation is now in a position to draw all of these factors together in a SWOT analysis and this will form the basis of future strategic decisions.

DISCUSSION QUESTIONS

1. Differentiate between an organisation's resources and competences.
2. Taking an organisation of your choice, explore the various elements of that organisation and discuss where its capabilities lie.
3. Critically analyse the use of the value chain as a method of understanding an organisation's capability.
4. Discuss the role of benchmarking in evaluating organisational performance.
5. Evaluate the use of competitive analysis as a qualitative tool in inter-company comparisons.
6. Discuss how a SWOT analysis assists organisations in drawing up strategic plans.

REFERENCES

Coffey, A., 2010, "Managing Cash Flow", *The Sunday Times*, 7 October 2010, Business Section, p.5

Curran, R., 2011, "How BoSi paid a heavy price for its Irish property gambles", *The Sunday Business Post*, 20 February 2011, p. N8

Dibb, S. *et al.*, 2006, *Marketing Concepts and Strategies*, 5th European Edition, Boston, Houghton Mifflin

Early, P.C., and Mosakowski, E., 2004, "Cultural Intelligence", *Harvard Business Review*, October 2004, Vol. 82, Issue 10, pp.139–146

Ghemawat, P., 2010, "Finding your strategy in the new landscape", *Harvard Business Review*, March 2010, Vol. 88, Issue 2, pp.54–60

Hines, P., 1993, "Integrated Material Management: The Value Chain Redefined", *The International Journal of Logistics Management*, Vol.4, Issue1, pp.13–21

Human Rights Watch, 2004, http://www.hrw.org/reports/2004/elsalvador0604/elsalvador0604simple. pdf, (accessed 6 December 2010)

Johnson, G. *et al.*, 2008, *Exploring Corporate Strategy*, Harlow, Essex, Prentice Hall. Financial Times

Kanter, R. M., 2008, "Transforming Giants", *Harvard Business Review*, January 2008, Vol. 86, Issue 1, pp.43–52

Kimes, S., 2003, "A Strategic Approach to Yield Management", in Ingold, A. *et al.* (Eds), *Yield Management: Strategies for the Service Industry*, London, Continuum

Kotler, P. *et al.*, 2007, *Principles of Marketing*, 4th European Edition, Upper Saddle River, NJ, Prentice Hall Europe

Lynch, R., 2008, *Strategic Management*, 5th Edition, Harlow, Essex, Prentice Hall. Financial Times

Martin, R., 2010, "The age of customer capitalism", *Harvard Business Review*, January 2010, Vol. 88, Issue 1, pp.58–65

McGreevy, R., 2008, "Hibernian Insurance to Outsource Jobs", *Irish Times*, 3 July 2008

New, S., 2010, "The transparent supply chain", *Harvard Business Review*, October 2010, Vol. 88, Issue 10, pp.76–82

Nonaka, I. and Takeuchi, H., 1995, *The Knowledge-Creating Company*, Oxford, Oxford University Press

O'Brien, J. and Marakas, G., 2008, *Management Information Systems*, 8th Ed., New York, McGraw-Hill

Porter, M. E., 2006, "What is Strategy?", *Harvard Business Review*, Nov/Dec 2006, Vol. 74, Issue 6, pp.61–78

Prahalad, C.K. and Hamel, G., 1990, "The Core Competence of the Organisation", *Harvard Business Review*, May/June 1990, Vol. 68, No. 3 pp.79–91

Rust, T. *et al.*, 2010, "Rethinking Marketing", *Harvard Business Review*, Jan/Feb 2010, Vol. 88, Issue 1, pp.94–101

Thompson, A. *et al.*, 2008, *Crafting and Executing Strategy: The Quest for Competitive Advantage*, New York, McGraw-Hill

Thomas, M., 2008, *Belching out the Devil: Global Adventures with Coca Cola*, London, Ebury Press

Welch, J., 2001, *Jack: What I've Learned Leading a Great Company and Great People*, London, Headline

Woodall, P., 2003, "House of Cards", *The Economist*, 31 May 2003, pp.3–16

Wreaker (2008) "The Evolution of Invention", *Sunday Business Post*, 20 July 2008

PART THREE

Developing Strategy

Introduction to Developing Strategy

In every organisation, there will be a whole variety of options available with regard to the development of strategy. All these options will have to be carefully analysed to ensure their implications are fully understood. More and more, companies are delegating power for decision-making to those parts of the organisation that deal directly with their customers. This provides a faster response time and helps ensure that the company is meeting the needs of its customers. Major decisions will still have to be taken in the company's headquarters to ensure uniform policy in important functions throughout the entire organisation. For that reason, Part Three of this book begins by looking at corporate-level strategy. The factors considered in Chapter 7 will be relevant for all types of organisations. If the company is large, there will be a clear distinction between the headquarters and each of its strategic business units. Chapter 8 will then discuss business-level strategy which is designed to deal with the competitive factors in a specific market. If the company is small, that distinction between corporate-level and business-level strategy will be blurred, and there will be a large overlap between the two.

Developing Strategy

In order to be able to build up market share, a company must develop a range of products and services that will satisfy potential customers. This concept is central to the company's existence and is examined in Chapter 9. The company must also build up the actual markets in which to sell those products and services. To compete in the market place, the company must approach these challenges in an innovative way that will enable the company to stand out from its competitors. The company must also be constantly trying to improve its capability to deliver products and services at a price that people are willing to pay and that will also deliver profit to the company. Now that the Celtic Tiger years are well and truly over, there is an even greater onus on companies to be constantly trying to find new ways to satisfy customers who are looking for value. Chapter 10 will then examine how some companies move away from their main product ranges and diversify into different products and markets. Such diversification has advantages, but also poses many challenges in terms of how it is managed.

Most companies will want to grow their market share, and there are a number of ways in which this can be achieved: internal growth, strategic alliances and mergers and acquisitions. These are examined in Chapter 11. With all these choices open to managers, it is important that these strategies are all properly evaluated and a decision is made that is in the best long-term interest of the company. There have been many examples in recent times of decisions being made that were not sustainable. Chapter 12 will finish up this section by examining how decisions are made in a variety of settings.

It is important to remember that Part Three must not be examined in isolation. The options under consideration must be aligned to the company's vision, mission and its strategic objectives. The internal and external analysis will also dictate what the priorities are and what the organisation

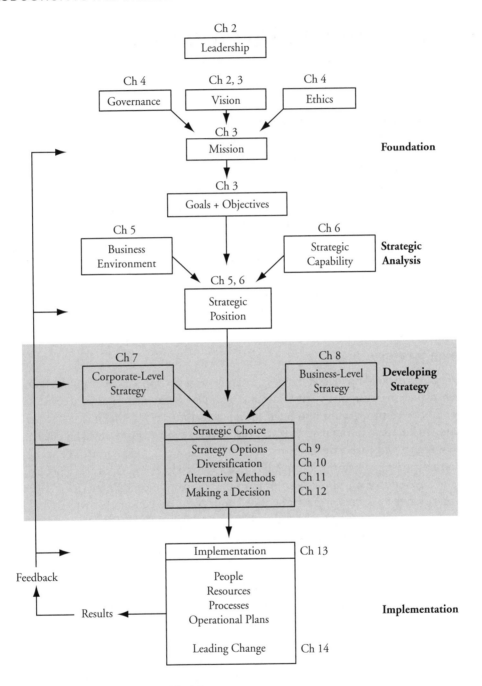

Figure 1.2 *The Strategic Planning Model*

is capable of doing in the immediate future. In one sense, examining and choosing these strategic options is a sequential process, but it is also an iterative one. Events in the last couple of years remind us just how quickly the business environment can change and the severe consequences of that change for every company. Flexibility and quick response times by managers are, therefore, essential.

Corporate-level Strategy

LEARNING OBJECTIVES

On completion of this chapter, you will be able to:

- Distinguish between different types of organisational structure
- Evaluate different parenting styles
- Distinguish between the various financial decisions that are made at corporate level
- Evaluate the level of risk that an organisation faces when considering a strategy

"It is not enough to have a good mind; the main thing is to use it well."

René Descartes

INTRODUCTION

There are many decisions that have to be made by a company in relation to its strategic direction. Managing a large corporation with many divisions brings with it very different challenges in comparison to running a small, single-business operation. It is inevitably a much more complex operation. This chapter is concerned with how the corporate headquarters makes decisions about the overall direction of the business. This begins with defining the scope of the business – where does the business begin and end? This process is directed by the vision that was outlined for the company and the objectives that were set. Strategy is all about the means towards fulfilling those objectives.

This chapter will also take an initial look at the structure of the organisation. The structure should support the strategy, and from that perspective, it is normally discussed in the context of strategy implementation. However, it is being included here because it is important to understand the existing structure and the relationship between the various parts of the organisation and how these relate to the development of strategy. This chapter will also discuss the nature of financial decisions, the capital structure, dividend policy and management incentives, as these decisions affect the entire company. The culture of the organisation will also be set at this level.

When examining strategic options at corporate level, there are many strategies available to the company based on product development, market development and diversification. These matters will be discussed in detail in Chapters 9 and 10. How the headquarters or corporate centre interacts with the different parts of the organisation and where the decisions are made, either centrally or by each of the Strategic Business Units, will also be discussed in this chapter. One way or another, the corporate centre should provide guidance and expertise to each of its divisions, and ultimately should add value to each of them.

CORPORATE HEADQUARTERS – DEFINING THE BUSINESS

Corporate headquarters can vary quite considerably from one organisation to another. Some can be very small units that set financial goals for the different divisions; other companies can have a very large headquarters that micro-manage the entire organisation. Irrespective of its size or approach, the corporate centre shapes the business in a number of inter-related ways which need to be examined under a number of different headings:

- Scope
- Corporate Governance
- Information Systems
- Leadership
- Employees
- Motivation
- Culture
- Creativity

The last five of these headings, from leadership to creativity, share the common theme of people and how they can contribute to the success of the organisation.

Scope

The centre defines the personality of the organisation in terms of its culture and how it relates to the world around it through its policy on corporate social responsibility. Developing strategy for an organisation is a means of achieving the goals and the objectives that have been set. Those goals and objectives are, in turn, a means of realising the vision. These are the factors that will help define the business in terms of the markets it is serving and the products and services it is delivering. Some companies will maintain a relatively narrow scope in terms of products and markets, while others will broaden out and diversify into entirely different lines. The level of diversification is a policy decision that is taken at corporate level as it ultimately brings many challenges in how such diversification is managed. Many companies, even large ones chose not to diversify (this topic will be discussed separately in Chapter 10). Either way, senior managers need to be clear about the type of growth they wish the organisation to achieve, and be single-minded in achieving it. All of the work and resources of the organisation should be supporting that effort. One of the primary functions of a corporate headquarters is to provide a clear sense of direction for the entire organisation, and often this has to be achieved against a background of conflicting stakeholder expectations. This means establishing a vision for its future direction, and goals and objectives that will stretch the organisation in terms of what it can achieve.

As an organisation grows more diverse, providing clear direction becomes a greater challenge. Yet diversified companies like Richard Branson's Virgin Group and General Electric manage to achieve such direction. This text examines a wide variety of different strategies, each designed to achieve different objectives. The strategies will need to be tailored for each organisation, as not only will their visions differ, but so too will the resources available to help deliver the strategies.

Ultimately, the corporate headquarters should add value to the company as a whole, which is greater than the sum of the divisions of that company if they were operating separately. Value can be added by being able to provide finance for worthwhile projects in situations where finance might not otherwise be available. The centre can also supply expertise to guide the division, particularly in turbulent markets. On the other hand, the corporate headquarters does not produce revenue directly, and represents a cost. All of the salaries and other overheads of the centre must be paid for by the divisions that generate revenue. There is a danger that the headquarters continues to grow in size and expense without adding extra value. The centre adds value through the decisions it makes in terms of providing overall direction, developing a strong corporate culture and management team, through mergers and acquisitions (M&As), and by directing or influencing the decisions of the various divisions.

Corporate Governance

Corporate governance is the control mechanism by which senior executives are held accountable to stakeholders for the strategic direction of an organisation and for legal and ethical compliance. Corporate governance plays a very important role in every company and there is an onus on the corporate headquarters to ensure the proper procedures are put in place to both direct and protect the organisation. Another important aspect of governance is the need to build trust with all the company's stakeholders and protect its reputation. Given such high-profile failures in this regard in recent years, it is an area that now requires close scrutiny in future years as the need for compliance is greater than ever.

Information Systems

Information Systems (IS) are a key and integral part of modern companies. O'Brien and Marakas (2008:4) define an information system as:

> "Any organised combination of people, hardware, software, communications networks, data resources, and policies and procedures that stores, retrieves, transforms, and disseminates information in an organisation."

Information technology (IT), on the other hand, refers to the hardware and software necessary for the system to operate. The nature of Information Systems is complex and constantly evolving. Consequently, while such systems provides many opportunities, there can be enormous costs associated with them (see **Illustration 1.1** in Chapter 1) and so management needs to be clear what purpose Information Systems are required to serve. IS must not be seen as an end in itself, but an integral part of the business process that will help deliver strategic goals. No matter how sophisticated Management Information Systems might be, it still requires the executive to make the decision.

The benefits of IS can have a positive impact on every part of a business. For that reason, rather than treat IS as a separate topic, it is discussed in the context of each part of the strategy process throughout this text. There are some elements of IS that need to be discussed at corporate level in terms of an overall policy framework.

One important issue that must be decided at corporate level is the nature and extent of the Information Systems that will be used in the organisation. If the company is divided into different strategic business units, it is imperative that there is an integrated system that is used throughout, and is capable of being expanded to meet future needs. When organisations merge one of the big difficulties in post-merger integration is linking up two Information Systems that were never designed to work together.

While dedicated systems can be very expensive, in general, overall costs are coming down as IT systems/applications have moved towards web-based IT applications which are delivered as part of 'cloud computing' platforms and software as service (SaaS) models. Cloud computing is the term applied to IT applications and data storage that are delivered across the internet, often on a pay-per-use basis. This has the added advantage of no major implementation issues that can often prove quite challenging for IT managers.

The importance of good communication throughout organisations cannot be overstated. Though good communication is primarily dependent on the communication skills of the people involved, and no amount of technology can make up for a lack of these skills, IT networks can play a vital part in the communication process by linking all parts of the organisation, regardless of how remote those parts may be. IT can provide accurate information for decision-making instantaneously. Policy decisions need to be made by the corporate headquarters in terms of the type of resources needed, including the physical resources (hardware), the information processing systems (software), the communication channels (networks) and data storage (data resources). Financial resources will then have to be provided to fund the purchase or development of the systems that will deliver business opportunities. This process must be managed in a cost-efficient and ethical way.

In essence, there are three fundamental roles for IS in any organisation:
- Support the business processes and operations of the company
- Support the decision-making processes
- Support strategies in achieving a competitive advantage.

These roles are integrated and mutually-supporting. Enterprise resource planning (ERP) systems provide a common interface that integrates all aspects of the company including planning, financial management, HR, inventory control, manufacturing, sales and customer service. IS should ultimately enable internet-based **e-business** (collaboration within a company and with customers and suppliers), and **e-commerce** systems (the buying, selling, marketing of goods and services over a variety of computer networks).

There are important ethical considerations in the use of information technology in organisations, and clear guidelines must be provided for all employees on what is considered acceptable behaviour. The security of the system is also vital, and security measures must be taken to prevent fraud, etc.

Finally, it must be remembered that IT is moving beyond internal corporate processes into the wider external social sphere. Businesses are now integrating their IT applications with social networking platforms. As a result, the internal/external divide is starting to be broken down.

Leadership

The importance of leadership is emphasised throughout this text. Leadership was defined in Chapter 2 as "the ability to inspire and motivate others to work willingly towards achieving organisational goals". Those at the corporate headquarters must provide clear direction and leadership for the organisation. They need to foresee developments in the industry and understand the implications for the organisation. This will require being able to deal with ambiguity and uncertainty and making sense of it all. Those at the top must also build a business model that is sustainable.

Leadership must be nurtured and the development of leaders must be seen as an essential investment in the future of the organisation. This begins effectively at the recruitment and selection stages. If the right talent is not selected initially, it will be difficult to develop those people in a manner that will meet the needs of a high-performance organisation. Kerry Group plc (see **Illustration 7.1**) runs its own graduate recruitment programme. Kerry's mission is to be an absolute leader in its markets through technological creativity, product quality, superior customer service and the wholehearted commitment of its employees. Therefore, the company places great emphasis on recruiting the best people with the requisite skills to manage the business.

Many large multinational organisations also have their own leadership programmes such as Johnson & Johnson's LeAD Programme which is a nine-month training programme designed to coach, develop and test employees who have been identified as having the potential to lead business units within the next three years. Martin and Schmidt (2010) remind us of the importance of such training being driven and co-ordinated at corporate level. There are many reasons for this. Such development will involve giving individuals a broad experience that will involve the entire organisation, rather than just one single unit. There is also a danger that managers at SBU level will, for purely selfish reasons, try to hold on to talented individuals and block their progress, even if only in the short term.

Employees

While leadership plays a central role in driving the strategy process, people throughout the organisation also play an essential part in helping it achieve success. Collins (2001) wrote about having the 'right people on the bus', and in the right seats. Corporate headquarters must develop the human resources of the company in a strategic manner. Huselid (1995) argues that human resources management (HRM) practices direct performance in three key ways:

- increase the knowledge, skills and abilities (KSAs) of employees;
- motivate employees to use their KSA to benefit the organisation; and
- empower the employees to take action.

HRM planning ties these three elements together. This implies designing the HR function so that it supports the objectives of the company. Liu *et al.* (2007) investigated numerous HRM practices based on data from 19,000 organisations, and concluded that human resource management adds significant value to organisations, in particular where human resource decisions are tied to strategy. Consequently, HR must be involved in the strategy formation process to ensure the organisation will meet its future needs in terms of suitable personnel in terms of numbers and skill. It is vital therefore that the organisation plans well in advance to determine its HR needs. The future needs must be compared with present resources, taking into account the supply of labour and the demand for labour. The organisation can then draft a HR plan that will satisfy its needs from internal and external sources (Gunnigle *et al.* 2006).

As well as a vertical alignment in terms of strategy, there should also be horizontal alignment where all elements of the HR system support one another. It is critical that HR professionals understand how one element of their policy impacts on others, e.g. recruiting people with a certain level of skill will affect the level (and cost) of training needed. In particular, policies must not contradict one another. An example of this is encouraging teamwork while only rewarding employees on the basis of individual performance.

Each organisation will have its own unique people-requirements. For larger organisations, each division will also have its own separate needs. The corporate headquarters set overall policy with regard to its employees, no matter where in the organisation they work. This will include guidelines on all aspects of HR policy from recruitment criteria, continuous professional development (CPD), promotion, gender balance, grievance procedures and employee compensation. While each division may subsequently adapt the HR policies as needs arises, there must be an overall consistency that promotes fairness, equality and develops talent.

Motivation

Motivation is a key aspect of leadership. Long-term productivity gains will only be achieved by motivating those employed in the organisation. Motivation is a complex subject, and each individual will respond to different stimuli. Money clearly plays an important part in the overall mix, and in times of recession, the ability of managers to increase pay is clearly constrained. It is therefore important for managers to examine the components of motivation that are within their control. There is often a discrepancy between the factors that managers *think* motivates their employees, and what *actually* motivates them.

Multi-year research carried out by Amabile and Kramer (2010) listed the factors that managers considered to be significant in motivating knowledge workers: recognition, incentives, interpersonal support, support for making progress and clear goals. The number one factor listed by managers was recognition (both public and private recognition). The research also examined what the workers themselves considered to be the important factors in motivating them. Their view was different. The number one factor for employees was, ironically, the factor that was ranked last by managers: progress. The research showed that knowledge employees are driven most when they feel they are making progress in their job or when they receive help in overcoming obstacles.

Perhaps the most significant thing about these findings is that progress is a factor that is largely within the control of managers. Managers have significant influence over the events within the organisation that will either facilitate or hamper progress. By having clear objectives, providing necessary resources and encouraging team members, managers can play an important role in facilitating progress. The research shows that negative events have a greater impact on motivation than positive events. Therefore, managers must be decisive in their actions; they should not change goals without consultation; or hold up resources that are needed. From an organisational perspective, the corporate headquarters should be mindful of the need for motivation as this will set the tone for the entire organisation. This is one clear way in which the centre can add value.

Culture

The nature of organisational culture was discussed in detail in Chapter 2. One important role for the corporate centre is establishing and maintaining a culture that is supportive of the strategy that is being pursued. Values are central to organisational culture and senior executives need to give careful consideration to the type of values they want to see practised within the company. While values will vary in their nature, there must be a strong ethical theme that runs through them. Executives need to be mindful of how they model that behaviour and also the importance of clear communication so that all employees fully understand what the company expects of them in their day-to-day operations.

It will be recalled that the main ways in which leaders embed culture is through the issues they pay attention to; how they react to critical issues; how resources are allocated; rewards; recruitment and selection (and retention): and role modelling and coaching. Secondary factors include structure, systems, building layout and others (Schein, 2010). While sub-cultures may exist in larger organisations, those at the top must take effective action to develop a high-performance culture that drives success. That high-performance culture should include a focus on creativity and innovation.

Creativity

In a global and competitive environment, there is a distinct need in every organisation for creativity, and it should exist right across all departments. Creativity is about the search for new ways of doing things and trying new approaches. A critical element in "Blue Ocean" thinking, creativity is more than just thinking in a certain manner. According to Amabile (1998), there are three broad elements to creativity:

- expertise – technical, procedural and intellectual knowledge;
- creative-thinking skills – these skills determine how people approach problems in a flexible and imaginative manner; and
- motivation – in particular intrinsic motivation that will develop a passion to solve problems.

There are many roles for the corporate headquarters in developing creativity. Hiring creative people is an important first step. Unfortunately, many organisation kill creativity through rigid policies and procedures. The challenge for managers is how to manage and cultivate creativity in a way that will help their company compete. Amabile (1998) argues that there are a number of measures that can be taken to foster creativity, beginning with matching people to the right assignments that play into their expertise and skills in creative thinking. While the senior managers will decide on the direction to be taken, staff must be given autonomy as to how to solve operational problems.

Resources in the form of time and money will be needed. Time deadlines can often help the process, provided such deadlines are based on real competitive pressures, while artificial deadlines can kill creativity. Careful attention must be paid to the design of work teams to provide sufficient diversity and mutual support. Motivation plays a central role in sustaining the interest of the group – their work must be recognised. Recognition should also include unsuccessful attempts where a lot of effort has been invested. In addition to motivation, wider organisational support should also be available – systems and procedures that emphasise the importance of creativity. Finally, organisational politics must not be allowed to hinder the process.

It must, therefore, be recognised that, while the importance of creativity may well be accepted by senior executives, creating such a culture within the organisation requires careful and deliberate nurturing. While creativity is important, Levitt (2002) reminds us that creativity on its own, is not sufficient. Businesses must also take into account the practical matter of implementation. (This will be discussed further in Chapter 9 when discussing innovation.)

Structure and Strategy

The decisions taken at corporate headquarters will impact on the entire organisation. Depending on the type of organisation, they will have a direct or indirect effect on each division. Therefore, it is necessary here to have an initial examination of the organisational structure. It needs to be emphasised that the structure of the organisation must support the strategy that is being followed. According to Chandler (1962), "structure follows strategy". For that reason, the structure will have to be revisited when examining the implementation of strategy. In the meantime, it will benefit the reader to have an understanding of the organisational structure of a large corporation as this will help illustrate how decisions are made at headquarters that direct each part of the company. There is no prescriptive structural form for a company. Each company will have its own variation on some of the structures that will be examined here. What matters is not the shape of the structure *per se*, but whether it supports the organisation in achieving its goals.

ORGANISATIONAL STRUCTURE

The structure of a company, as depicted graphically by an organisational chart, is effectively the skeleton that provides shape and form to that organisation. It depicts the various departments, the layers of management and the lines of responsibility in the company. For somebody joining the company, they can get an overview of its shape. Other factors, such as culture and control types, are separate elements (these will be examined later in Chapter 13) and are not immediately obvious when examining the organisational chart. Some of the basic generic structures are:

- No formal structure
- Functional
- Multi-divisional
- Matrix

No Formal Structure

Some types of companies may have no formal organisational structure at all. In the initial stages of establishing a company, there may be only a few individuals involved, and there is no formal structure. For example, Michael Dell began his company assembling computer components in his college dormitory. Similarly, the founders of Google, Sergy Brin and Larry Page, started their search engine company operating out of Stanford University before moving to offices of their own at Palo Alto. Despite the prominence of the many large multinational corporations in this country, Ireland relies very heavily on small businesses. This reliance will grow in years to come and the Government, through various agencies, provides a lot of support for start-up enterprises. Many of these small companies may have only a few people working in them, certainly in the initial phase.

Such informality regarding structure works well in the early days, as maximum flexibility is required. Those involved in establishing a business will be punching in long days and will tackle each job as it arises. Sooner or later, the newly-fledged company will need specialised personnel to deal with the different tasks that require specific skills such as finance, marketing, etc. In the case of Google, Larry Page and Sergy Brin realised that, while they had the technical expertise to build the company, they also needed business expertise, and their first appointment was Eric Schmidt as CEO. In turn, Schmidt built up the structures of the company.

Some start-ups will remain forever small, but others will begin to grow. For those that do begin to grow, within a relatively short period of time a more formal structure will be put in place, and the most common form is the functional structure.

Functional Structure

The functional structure is based upon a division of responsibility according to various functional departments such as finance, marketing, human resources, operations, R&D and IT. The company is likely to develop such a structure early in its life as it will require the expertise of people with those

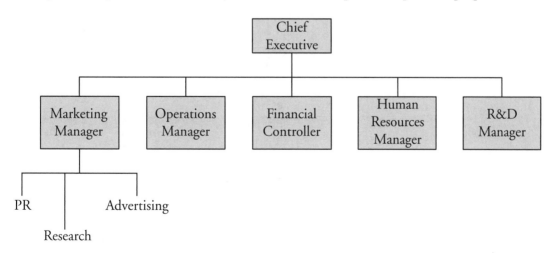

Figure 7.1 *A Functional Structure*

specialised skills. While the company may grow into a larger organisation, this functional structure will stay, as that expertise will always be required. The head of each department would be responsible for running that department and would report to, and provide expert advice to, the CEO.

Each of these functional divisions may be further subdivided, depending on the size and requirements of the organisation. For example, the marketing department may have sections dealing with sales, advertising, public relations and market research. The CEO is ultimately responsible for the success of the company overall and must ensure co-ordination between each of the divisions. One danger with this type of structure is that the divisions become autonomous units existing in their own right, rather than supporting the firm with functional expertise. This is often referred to as creating 'functional silos'. There are also potential problems with this structure as the organisation grows into a divisional structure.

Multi-divisional Structure

As organisations grow in size, their structures must adapt. The most common form of structure is the multi-divisional one, which allows the company to deal with a diversity of products and/or geographical spread. This was first developed by General Motors (Chandler, 1962) and is now used in some form by most large organisations. It can be seen from the diagram in **Figure 7.2** that there is still a functional structure in place, not just at corporate headquarters, but also in each of the divisions. This might seem like an unnecessary and expensive duplication, but it is necessary, as each division will have its own specialised requirements. For a company like GE, which manufactures a vast selection of products, the marketing of jet engines to aircraft manufacturers will be very different to the marketing of financial products to individual consumers.

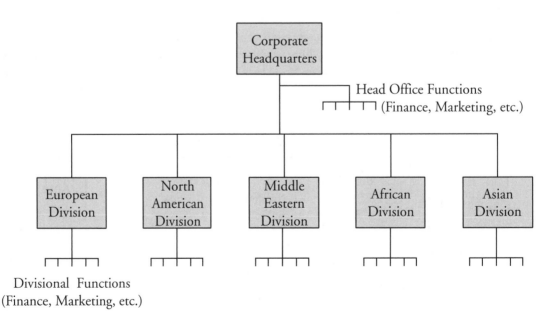

Figure 7.2 *Multi-divisional Structure*

One danger with the functional centre being in corporate headquarters is that HQ would try to impose policy decisions, where local decisions need to be made. An example would be in advertising, where not only does advertising have to be done in the local language, but it must also take into account local cultural sensitivities.

The multi-divisional structure gives the organisation flexibility in that divisions can be added or deleted as the need arises. In turn, each division may be subdivided into smaller divisions. Whether the divisions are based on product lines or geographical regions, it allows that division to develop particular expertise so that it can better meet the needs of its target market. Depending on the parenting style of the organisation, these divisions can operate as part of the greater organisation or as independent units. (This point will be developed later when examining portfolio management.) Either way, a structure such as this facilitates control and responsibility in each unit. In situations where companies own other companies, and allow them to operate autonomously, such parent companies are referred to as 'holding companies'.

In larger companies, this type of structure is important in giving potential senior managers the experience required by working in a variety of different divisions. Indeed, in most multinational companies such experience would be considered a prerequisite for promotion.

Illustration 7.1: Organisational Structure – Kerry Group Plc

From its beginnings in Listowel in North Kerry in 1972, Kerry Group Plc is now one of the world's leading agribusiness companies with annual sales of over €5 billion. It is headquartered in Tralee, employs over 20,000 people and has operations in 23 countries in five continents. The company is quoted on the Dublin and London stock exchanges and has a market capitalisation of over €4 billion. In recent years, Kerry Group has been restructured and is now organised into three divisions, as shown below:

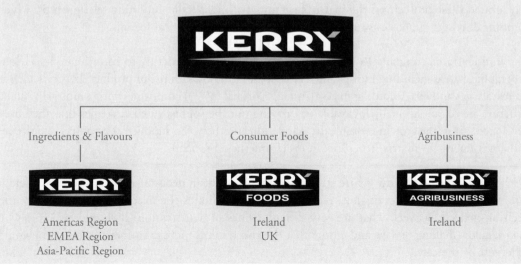

Kerry Ingredients and Flavours is the largest division of Kerry Group with 112 manufacturing bases across the Americas, EMEA and Asia-Pacific regions, producing over 15,000 ingredients, flavours and integrated solutions. It is a leading supplier of ingredients to the major food and beverage companies around the world. The division employs over 500 food scientists who work in partnership with the Group's customers to develop new products. The division has grown substantially over the years using a mixture of organic growth and acquisitions.

Kerry Foods has 20 manufacturing facilities located throughout Ireland and the UK. It is a leading supplier of value-added branded and customer-branded food products to the major supermarket chains, convenience stores and independent retailers. The division is subdivided into eight business units that market its various food products and services. These include: Brands Ireland; Brands GB; customer brands; direct to store/Kerry Connect; meat and savoury provisions; meat solutions; food service and dairy products. Kerry Foods has some high-profile brands in its portfolio, which include Denny, Dawn, Ballyfree, Golden Vale, and EasiSingles. The range of products is constantly evolving as it responds to meet changing consumer demand.

Kerry Agribusiness is based in Charleville, Co. Cork. Some 4,000 milk suppliers in the Southwest of Ireland provide it with high-quality milk in line with EU dairy regulations. It works closely with its suppliers to reduce production costs while maximising the quality of the milk.

Source: Kerry Group Plc

Matrix Structure

One of the potential problems with the multi-divisional structure is that there can be conflicts between different geographical areas and product divisions as to the level of standardisation/localisation required. Another problem can relate to the transfer of knowledge within the organisation. One way around these problems is the matrix structure, with its parallel reporting relationships, which combine different dimensions such as product lines and geographical regions.

The multinational company Royal Dutch Shell uses a matrix structure to co-ordinate its various geographical areas including Europe, the Far East and the US, with major product divisions such as chemicals, gas and oil. According to Bartlett and Ghoshal (1990) companies with a multi-divisional structure are organisationally incapable of carrying out the sophisticated strategies that they have developed, given the growing complexity of relationships between suppliers, customers, employees and governments. A matrix structure can overcome these problems.

With a matrix structure, the centre still has an involvement in decision-making and has different functional groups such as finance, etc. The process facilitates the necessary co-ordination and decision-making between what are very different lines of demarcation. It should also speed up that decision-making process and ensure that the end result is more customer-focused than would otherwise be the case.

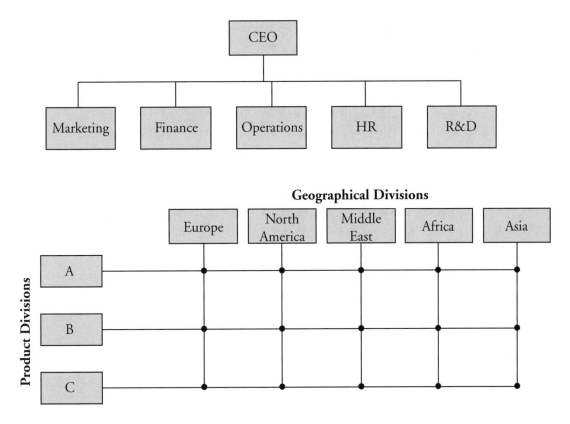

Figure 7.3 *Matrix Structure*

On the other hand, conflict can arise in matrix structures, such as personality clashes between key managers, and this can have the opposite effect. It can be further complicated by barriers of time, distance and culture. It will be necessary to have clear guidelines on who has responsibility for the final decision. As in all such situations, it is the responsibility of the CEO to ensure that the entire organisation is working towards common goals. As organisations grow in size, this can become increasingly difficult.

Bartlett and Ghoshal (1990) suggest that companies need to focus on the challenge of building up an appropriate set of employee attitudes and skills, and linking them together with carefully developed processes and relationships. They regard matrix management not as a structure, but as a frame of mind. The challenge for senior management is to provide clarity on the corporate vision, continuity in terms, sticking with strategic objectives and consistency in ensuring that everyone in the company shares the same values and objectives. The selection of the right people, along with their training and development (including managing complexity), is a vital part of the process. So too is charting out a career path for them. IBM is one major multinational company that uses a matrix structure and the company regards itself as a 'globally-integrated organisation'.

Many companies regard developing contacts and relationships between managers to be very important and this is done through common training processes and socialisation. Many of the large multinationals also ensure that managers get a broad experience across different functions, businesses and geographical areas in order to develop flexibility and a breadth of experience that will enable them to manage complexity and develop a corporate-wide understanding of the issues facing the company. It is then that managers can operate successfully in a matrix structure as they can make judgement calls and negotiate the trade-offs that will drive the organisation forward and achieve corporate objectives.

Flexible Structures

As stated, every company will develop some variation of the many structural types to suit their own particular circumstances. There is no set formula for designing an organisation's structure. Goold and Campbell (2002) suggest nine 'tests' to facilitate the selection of an appropriate structure for an organisation. These include:

- Market advantage – will the structure serve the needs of the market?
- Parenting advantage – can the centre add value to each element?
- People test – does it facilitate all the people working in the organisation?
- Feasibility test – does it meet the needs of all stakeholders?
- Culture test – does it support the culture of the organisation?
- Difficult links test – will it facilitate linking parts of the organisation?
- Redundant hierarchy test – is the company's structure sufficiently flat?
- Accountability test – are there clear lines of accountability and control?

Over a period of years, it is natural that the structure of organisations will evolve. On the other hand, it is important to have some continuity so that organisational members will understand the structure of the company and, in particular, the lines of responsibility. The challenges facing the organisation will vary and every situation will be different. A greater degree of flexibility is therefore required than such structures provide. To facilitate such flexibility, most organisations will leave the basic structures in place, but create special multi discipline teams to cater for specific eventualities. Team members operate together to deal with tasks such as new product development, where a wide variety of knowledge and experience is required.

In many organisations such teams are standing teams, where the team meets on a regular basis and the members are constant (allowing of course for normal transition due to people moving appointments or retiring). In other situations, special teams are put together for a specific project and are known as project teams or task forces. Government departments use a variety of teams and task forces to co-ordinate cross-departmental functions where a number of different departments may have a role. For example, the Department of Health and Children would have to work with other departments such as Education and Science, Justice and Law Reform, and Community and Family Affairs, in order to develop a holistic approach to child welfare.

Information technology plays an integral part in linking the various parts of an organisation. According to O'Brien and Marakas (2008:60), forming a 'virtual company' can be "one of the most important strategic uses of information technology". A virtual company uses information technology to create links between people inside and outside the organisation using the Internet, intranets and extranets.

Kaplan and Norton (2006) believe that the search for new organisational structures is driven by changes in competition and in the economy. Companies now derive their advantage not so much from managing physical and financial assets but more from how they align intangible assets such as knowledge management, R&D, and IT to the demands of their customers. In addition, the opportunities and challenges that globalisation brings are making many companies revisit many long-held assumptions about the management and control of both physical and intangible assets. They suggest that restructuring a company can be both expensive and distracting, and believe that it is far more effective to choose a design that works reasonably well, and then develop a strategic system to tune the structure to the strategy. To that end, they argue that the Balanced Scorecard framework (see Chapter 3) is the best way to align strategy and structure.

One way or another, the structure of the organisation is an important element in the implementation of strategy and must be designed to support it (see Chapter 13). Hamm (2006) believes that organisational charts represent much more than just the shape of the organisation. They also represent individual power and influence. Therefore, when change in the structure is needed, the CEO needs to take quick and decisive action or otherwise the organisation will grind to a halt while employees await decisions on who will be reporting to whom, and managers jostle for position. It then becomes a source of anxiety for all, rather than a supporting mechanism for strategy. Ultimately, it is about optimising the use of resources within the organisation.

In Chapter 6, the importance of linkages in the value chain was highlighted. Regardless of the type of structure chosen, such linkages must be created and strengthened. In response to pressure to adapt products and services to meet the specific requirements of different markets, many multinational companies are driving decision-making down the line to country managers. This allows for more responsive decision-making to meet the needs of each particular market, though it will place extra strain in terms of managing those important linkages. One essential task for senior management is to ensure that proper communication channels are developed, a process that can be difficult when different national cultures and languages are involved. It again highlights the importance of leaders having cultural intelligence (see Chapter 2). In addition to structure, the internal control systems used and how the company relates to other organisations is also important.

CONTROL STYLES

It was stated above that the corporate parent does not add value directly in its own right, but does so through interacting with the various divisions. Now that we have examined the different types of structure that organisations might adopt, it is important to explore the type of relationship between the corporate headquarters and each division. Central to this relationship are the concepts of centralisation and devolution.

With centralised decision-making, the corporate headquarters makes strategic and operational decisions that provide direction for the entire organisation. It is highly prescriptive and works on the basis that executives in the headquarters have greater knowledge and experience and thus can make more informed decisions. It is authoritarian and relies on a traditional command and control structure. It exerts tight managerial control over the organisation. It is bureaucratic, and slow in making decisions, and it is a somewhat obsolete structure for modern organisations.

At the other end of the spectrum is decentralised decision-making. Here the authority to make decisions is pushed down to the lowest level in the organisation that is capable of making such decisions. It means that unit managers are then responsible for what happens in that division, but takes into account that each market is different and these managers are best equipped to make decisions by considering all relevant factors. Because decisions do not have to be referred up the line, decision-making is much quicker.

Individual companies will differ in how they relate to their units. Goold and Campbell (1987) suggest different styles that describe the relationship between the centre and the different divisions:

- **Strategic Planning** This is a highly-centralised approach where all the major decisions are taken by the corporate headquarters and then prescribed to each of the divisions. It relies on the formal, traditional approach to planning, and the centre provides the necessary services by way of structure, operating procedures, finance and other resources. It can be appropriate where the executives in the centre have an in-depth knowledge of the business units and where all elements of the company are homogenous, e.g. a multinational hotel chain such as the Hilton. It can destroy value where the business units are quite different in terms of industries and markets, as headquarters staff could not possibly know more than unit managers and the cost of a bureaucratic headquarters would not be justified. It would also be very demoralising for divisional managers. In reality, most commercial organisations are moving away from this parental style.
- **Strategic Control** This is a mid-point between strategic planning and financial control and probably reflects a majority of major organisations. Here the centre will set the overall direction for the company, but work in tandem with the various business units in developing an agreed strategic plan. Part of the plan will include specific goals and objectives for each part of the organisation. The goals of each unit should support the overall goals of the corporation. In terms of resources and support, there will be a certain balancing act between the SBUs in proving those resources and the markets in which each is involved. The centre will endeavour to create linkages between all of the different elements of the company and facilitate organisational learning.
- **Financial Control** This is the parenting style normally associated with holding companies or highly diversified conglomerates. In such cases, the constituent companies will differ greatly in the nature of the industries that they are involved in, and the corporate centre could not possibly hope to add value by being directly involved. Instead, it sets financial objectives for each, and places responsibility on the management of those companies to deliver the results. The individual managers would have complete autonomy on how they achieve the results. One of the big drawbacks with this type of parental style is that there tends to be a short-term focus on results, often to the exclusion of longer-term development.

Culture can play a very important role in organisational control by ensuring work is done in a certain way and to a certain standard. This can be even more powerful than traditional methods of control that would be exercised through organisational structure, and does not require constant supervision. The 'Kerry Way' is a 200km walk through Ireland's most scenic county. It also refers to the culture in Kerry Group PLC and how things are done in one of Ireland's most successful companies.

ALLOCATING RESOURCES

It will be seen from the above section that an important role for the corporate headquarters is in allocating the necessary resources to, and developing the potential of, each SBU. There are a number of factors to be considered in this regard. First, there is finance. Strategic objectives will generally require substantial funds, and individual SBUs or companies within the overall organisation may not have sufficient finance to achieve their objectives. The headquarters will have to take an overview, looking at where the greatest profit potential lies and then investing in those SBUs. This point will be further developed later in Chapter 10 when looking at portfolio analysis.

The next point to consider, related to profit potential, will be a decision on the markets within which the company will compete. If the company intends to operate outside its home market, choices will have to be made on which market to enter. Some markets grow faster than others.

Thirdly, decisions will be required on the product range on offer. Should the current product range be broader or narrower than it currently is, and what new products should be developed (again requiring considerable finance)? Sometimes, organisations reach **strategic inflection points** that point them in a totally different direction. Nokia, now famous for mobile phones, was originally in the paper business. Finally, human resources play a very important role in the development of the organisation. This involves two dimensions: first, ensuring that each part of the organisation has the right people mix and skill range required at any one time and, secondly, it is also about developing future leaders by ensuring that they have the right experience in terms of different product areas and geographical regions.

All of these factors have to be balanced out by the corporate headquarters. Sometimes hard choices may have to be made that will not be popular with particular SBUs but are in the best interests of the corporation. Many factors will influence the decision, but much of it will be based on financial appraisal methods such as internal rate of return (IRR) and net present value (NPV). There will be more detailed discussion about methods for selecting particular strategies (Chapter 12) as well as product and market decisions later (see Chapter 9).

However, as a general principle, it can be taken that with a severe downturn in so many markets and the smaller margins that result, companies will have to be far more selective about investment decisions. This will have implications for portfolio management (see Chapter 10).

FINANCIAL DECISIONS

According to Fitzroy and Hulbert (2005), there are other decisions required at corporate headquarters level relating to the financing of the organisation, including:

- Capital structure
- Policy on dividends
- Incentive schemes for managers
- Managing risk

These will impact on all other corporate decisions.

Capital Structure

The gearing ratio of the firm refers to the relationship between debt and equity. The appropriate gearing ratio will differ according to the industry that it is operating in and the ability of the company to generate cash. Lenders will also take the company's credit history into account. The greater the level of debt, the greater will be the business risk. Ultimately, companies can decide not to issue dividends, but any loans must be repaid. If the company is experiencing difficult trading conditions, it often results in cut-backs in areas such as R&D, training or advertising. This will help the short-term position with regard to cash, but impact on its long-term growth. Even a temporary inability to pay debt would have very serious consequences for a company, and its ability to raise further debt in the future.

Every company will have a certain level of debt on its balance sheet and there are benefits to having some debt. The interest on debt can be put into the profit and loss account and so reduce the tax payable. The tax benefit will obviously depend on the tax rate applicable – the greater the rate of corporation tax, the greater the saving for the firm. With such a low rate of corporation tax in Ireland, it does not confer the same benefit as other jurisdictions. Debt is considered to be a cheaper form of finance than equity. There is also an argument that suggests that taking on debt will concentrate the minds of executives to ensure that they are getting a higher rate of return than the cost of debt. One of the biggest challenges at present, particularly for smaller businesses, is getting access to borrowing. Banks have not been lending in a way that meets the needs of these companies.

Gearing ratios are also influenced by the nature of the investment required. Heavy investment in capital equipment will normally require a greater use of equity than debt. The amount of debt that lenders are willing to give will also depend on the nature of the assets. If they are tangible assets, banks can place a mortgage on them, and the more liquid those assets are the better. However, intangible assets such as brands or goodwill do not have the same attraction to lenders. Finally, there will be international differences in the amounts that banks will lend. In Ireland, Britain and the US, the relationship with banks tends to be purely contractual. While companies may have a long-term relationship with a particular bank, each loan is essentially a separate contract between the company and the bank. In Germany and Japan, there tends to be a greater involvement by banks in the shareholding of companies that they do business with and, consequently, they have a much greater interest in the long-term development of those companies.

Dividend Policy

Another major decision to be made by companies relates to their dividend policy. Each individual company must decide if they will pay a dividend and, if so, how much? Some companies on the Irish stock exchange such as Ryanair do not pay a dividend. Investors must rely on the capital growth in the value of the share to get a return on their investment. Not paying a dividend, or paying just a small dividend, allows the firm to reinvest profits back into building up the company. In practically all cases, strategic decisions will require the investment of retained earnings in addition to loan capital to fund the project. Large dividends will be attractive to investors, but will lessen the amount that can be reinvested for the future growth of the company.

There are occasions where there may not be any suitable investment opportunities to hand, in which case there is a strong argument for returning the money to shareholders by either dividend payment or a share buyback. Traditionally, Ryanair is one of those companies that does not pay a dividend. In 2010, it broke with its own tradition and paid a dividend to its shareholders, a decision taken after negotiations with Boeing to purchase new aircraft failed to secure a deal and the company decided to return some of its cash to its shareholders. Share buyback has the advantage (in most cases) of increasing the capital value of the share and being more advantageous where the marginal rate of personal tax is greater than capital gains tax. Senior executives also need to be aware that dividend policy sends out important signals with regard to the future growth prospects of the firm. If the dividends are too high, it can be perceived that the company has no better use for the money, and needs to return it to the shareholders. If the dividends are too low, the markets may interpret that the future may not be as bright and the company needs to hold on to the cash. Finding the right balance can be difficult.

Management Incentive Schemes

Another corporate financial decision concerns incentive schemes for managers. Many large organisations will include share options as part of the remuneration package of senior executives. A share option is where the executive has the option of buying a specified number of shares in the company at a future date at a fixed amount (called the exercise price). The exercise price is set above the current share price. When the share price rises in value above the exercise price, the executive can take up the option to buy the shares at the exercise price and so make an immediate profit. The purpose is to provide an incentive to managers to make decisions that will increase the value of the company and such options effectively align shareholders' objectives with their own objectives. There are certain restrictions that must be adhered to and options also raise the issue as to how they should be treated in the company accounts.

One problem with regard to the efficiency of share options as a management incentive scheme is that they can reward mediocre performance. For example, the share price might go above the exercise price, thus rewarding the executive. However, the performance of that particular company could be lagging behind that of the industry in general. It is important in setting the exercise price that it is set at a level that will stretch the executives' skills in attaining the share price.

The TASC report *Mapping the Golden Circle* (Clancy *et al.* 2010:25) poses the question as to whether there is a ceiling beyond which no further level of motivation will occur and also draws attention to the traditionally high level of remuneration that occurs among board members of Irish companies, particularly in the financial sector. The payment of high salaries and bonuses to bank employees in Ireland has generated significant controversy in recent times, with the Minister for Finance directing that no further bonuses be paid by banks receiving State aid. The 2010 Grant Thornton Corporate Governance Review is critical of compliance regarding the composition and independence of remuneration committee board members in PLCs (Grant Thornton, 2010:29).

It must also be remembered in relation to the banking crisis, there is a strong link between the level of bonuses paid and the level of risk facing the company. Bonus payments were linked to the amount of lending by managers – the more money that was lent to customers, the greater the bonus that would be paid. Such short-term incentives overrode sound judgement and proper risk assessment.

While many organisations will retain incentive schemes for managers, a more prudent approach would be to create a much longer time-frame between the action that triggers the incentive, and its actual payment. A gap of a number of years would determine whether that action increased long-term shareholder value or not.

MANAGING RISK

Strategic decisions are long-term decisions. The company may be analysing the environment now and trying to extrapolate what the future is likely to hold in terms of return on investment. By using the appropriate strategic tools, the company may hope to gain a reasonably accurate insight into the future. But inevitably there is a level of uncertainty in such prediction and sometimes events happen that could not have been foreseen. Around the same time as the 9/11 terrorist attack in 2001, there was an outbreak of foot and mouth disease in Ireland that had a devastating impact on many different industries, from farming to tourism. Accordingly risk is an inherent part of every strategic decision, which can result in consequences different from those intended. Such risk can come about from changes in the environment, through selecting inappropriate options or through the poor implementation of the chosen strategy.

In general terms, there is a strong correlation between risk and return – the higher the potential return, the greater the level of risk. Drawing on a horse racing analogy, the horse that the bookies have put at 100/1 will potentially give a very healthy return to the punter, but the chances of that horse winning are fairly slim. Managers then need to balance the risk and return relationship.

Some decisions will encounter very little risk. Pension fund managers, for example, will transfer a person's pension into bonds and cash as he or she nears retirement in order to minimise the risk involved. In order to grow the pension in the earlier years, a portion of it will be put into speculative stock as the potential return will be far greater than normal run-of-the-mill investments. It is the same with all strategic decisions – the level of risk will vary depending on the nature of the decision. The level of risk will have to be balanced against the circumstances, and the implications involved.

The risk profile of every company will differ. Some will be risk-averse, some risk neutral and others will be risk-takers. There is no right answer in terms of what is an appropriate level of risk, as there are so many factors that need to be taken into account. In some cases, the future of the organisation may ride on a particular decision. For example, in aircraft manufacture, because of the enormous costs involved in the development of a new commercial aircraft, a wrong decision with regard to the type of aircraft to be manufactured (e.g. decisions on whether to develop wide-bodied, large capacity aircraft, or aircraft that can achieve greater speeds) could spell the end of the company.

In other cases, the level of risk may not threaten the continued existence of the company, but it can still have a devastating effect. Towards the end of 2008, fuel costs came down considerably having reached a new record of $147 a barrel in July of that year. However, many airlines would have hedged the price of fuel at a much higher rate before the price began to drop on world markets. As a consequence, their fuel (and total costs) was far higher in 2009 than would otherwise be the case. As a result, many airlines made a financial loss. In 2011, unrest in Arab countries such as Egypt and Libya caused oil prices to peak once again, increasing risk and causing further uncertainty.

There are different forms of risk other than examining whether a company will get an expected return on investment. In examining corporate social responsibility, we saw that companies are liable to suffer risk to their reputation, and companies can lessen this risk by acting in a manner that embraces all stakeholders. The nature of modern communications means that a company's reputation could be severely battered in a very short space of time as a result of environmental damage.

The strategic capability of an organisation could well rest on having very talented and experienced personnel working in the company. In such a case, it will need to ensure that its HR policies provide sufficient incentives to hold on to those personnel. Related risk would include health and safety issues. The cost of inputs can pose a big risk to companies. As mentioned above, it is common in the aviation sector to hedge on the price of fuel because it is such a large percentage of their total costs. With electricity costs soaring, many companies will be under pressure on costs over which they have little or no control. Fraud is an increasing risk for many companies. In 2002, AIB lost $691 million when John Rusnak accumulated losses on his foreign currency trading in AIB's US subsidiary Allfirst (Creaton and O'Cleary, 2002).

There is also a risk involved in doing nothing. There will be occasions when executives have reviewed a situation and come to the conclusion that 'steady as she goes' is the best course of action. Perhaps one of the biggest dangers is that, when direction is required in a company, managers do not take the appropriate course out of fear of making the 'wrong' decision. They keep putting off the decision, looking for more and more information before taking action – what is known as 'paralysis by analysis'. We should learn from Hamlet's soliloquy:

> ". . . Thus conscience does make cowards of us all; and thus the native hue of resolution is sicklied o'er with the pale cast of thought, and enterprises of great pith and moment with this regard, their currents turn awry and lose the name of action."
>
> *Hamlet.* Act 3, Sc. 1

In all cases, senior executives must examine all of the relevant information and assess the level of risk involved, including the likelihood of that event occurring and the consequences if it does happen. On a personal basis, we insure our homes against a variety of risks. Most people would hope never to have to claim on their policy, but the insurance is still taken out. A fire, for example, would have a devastating impact on the home owner if there were no insurance in place. Likewise, a company must assess the different types of risk that it faces, such as business or financial risk. Once a proper risk assessment has been carried out, appropriate steps can then be taken to control or mitigate such risk.

The assessment of risk by many Irish companies in the last few years leaves a lot to be desired, particularly in the financial sector. The recession has left many of these companies dangerously over-exposed. In the case of the banks, the exposure to risk left them totally dependent on state aid to continue in existence. In turn, this has had a devastating impact on the entire economy.

Speaking at the McGill Summer School in 2010, Jim O'Leary, who had been a non-executive director at AIB, spoke about how the bank directors "trusted the systems for monitoring and controlling risk". He referred to risk assessment at the bank:

> "But, mindful of the risk that something worse might occur, they carried out stress tests that purported to quantify the effects on profitability and on balance sheets of things going badly wrong. Almost without exception, these stress tests provided assurance that the banks would continue to make profits (albeit greatly diminished) and remain adequately capitalised and liquid. We now know these stress tests were seriously flawed." (O'Leary, 2010)

Ultimately, when evaluating any strategy for a company, it is the responsibility of the board of directors and senior managers to satisfy themselves as to an appropriate level of risk. Clancy *et al.* (2010:2) state:

> "The Irish Business environment, exemplified by a culture of excessive risk-taking in key sectors, together with a system of so-called 'light-touch' regulation, helped foster a weak and inadequate system of corporate governance. Some of the resulting failures have contributed to the economic crisis in Ireland."

They further state that "a high-pay culture also appears to have affected companies at the centre of the recent banking crisis by promoting a culture of short-termism." Clearly, all companies will have to review their procedures for evaluating risk. Unfortunately for many, the horse has already bolted and the stable door is wide open.

The situation is similar around the world. An international consulting group, Accenture, conducted interviews with 250 risk executives from 21 countries concerning their company's approach to risk-taking. Eighty-five per cent of them said they would be realigning their business risk strategies. One of the big issues for many of them is the lack of an integrated and scalable Risk IT infrastructure in place. Many of those interviewed said their risk management capabilities are not what they should be and that their culture encouraged irresponsible behaviour (Accenture, 2010).

Illustration 7. 2: Risk Management – Bank of Scotland Ireland

Halifax was the retail arm of Bank of Scotland (Ireland) – BoSi, which was a subsidiary of Halifax Bank of Scotland (and was subsequently taken over by Lloyds Banking Group in January 2009). The arrival of (BoSi) into the Irish market in 2000 caused a bit of a stir in banking circles. It dramatically changed the nature of competition in the banking industry in Ireland. Throughout the decade, BoSi's chief executive, Mark Duffy, lured customers away from the likes of Bank of Ireland and AIB through a mixture of lower interest rates on borrowing, higher savings rates and better opening hours. In so doing, they built up significant market share, particularly in retail banking. BoSi began giving 100% mortgages, requiring no deposit from the borrower. Also in 2000, BoSi bought a state-owned bank, ICC, for €340 million. For decades, ICC was a cornerstone of commercial life, lending to Irish businesses. This now provided a conduit into the property market as well as the consumer and residential markets. In addition to Anglo Irish Bank, BoSi began lending very aggressively in the property market. As a result of this industry realignment, the main Irish-owned banks became so consumed by trying to gain market share that they seemed to abandon any form of proper risk assessment. In the meantime, the price of commercial and residential property just kept rising. In turn, the loans got bigger and bigger. So too did the profits. By 2005, BoSi was firmly established in the commercial lending market. In 2007, profits peaked for BoSi at €272 million. That was when things began to turn.

According to Curran (2011), by the end of 2008, the five biggest customers of Bank of Scotland (Ireland) (BoSi) had borrowed €2 billion, and the top 20 customers had borrowed a staggering €4 billion between them. This was just before the bank began to make massive losses. The vast majority of the money borrowed was to property developers. In fact, of the top 20 borrowers, only three of them had a core business that was not based on property development. To put this borrowing in perspective, the money lent to the bank's top 10 customers represented 58% of its own capital. While the bank remained within the regulatory requirements that were then in place, this still constituted enormous exposure – and risk. By February 2009, its chief executive Mark Duffy had resigned.

While BoSi has shut its retail and commercial divisions in Ireland, it remains very heavily exposed here. Its new parent company, Lloyds, has had to inject €8 billion into Certus, a new company that has taken over the loan book of BoSi and is now managing its commercial portfolio. The bank had some of the big names in property development in Ireland, including: Liam Carroll who had a gross exposure of €750 million; Bernard McNamara, €610 million; financier Derek Quinlan's exposure, €330; David Kennedy (Formation Group) €280 million; and Jim Mansfield's HSS Group, €180 million. In some cases, the bank entered into a joint venture with developers. This would create potentially bigger profits for the bank if its projections were reached. It also increased the risk involved.

As far back as 2003, an article in *The Economist* identified a number of countries as being in danger of a property crash. Ireland was chief amongst them (Woodall, 2003). Ironically, while

BoSi initially proved very beneficial to consumers, it was reckless lending that ultimately caused so much damage, particularly for first-time buyers. Those who bought property between 2005 and 2008 are likely to be in negative equity for a long time. Once the property crash came, the bank's exposure to the market inevitably meant huge losses. Some of the larger borrowers have paid down part or all of their loans, but many others still owe enormous sums. To complicate matters, the companies owned by many of their big borrowers are now in liquidation. In many of these cases, the bank will have to write off huge amounts. For example, Bernard McNamara was the developer who bought the Burlington Hotel in Dublin with loans of €285 million. The hotel would now be worth a fraction of that amount.

As well as the big property developers, BoSi also lent to the buy-to-let market. With a huge over-supply of houses and apartments around the country, many small investors are left with vacant properties that were bought at the height of the boom and with no rental income to meet mortgage repayments. In some cases these were bought with interest-only mortgages. In addition, capital allowances and other taxation reliefs are being removed, placing extra financial strain on many of these borrowers. In February 2011, BoSi announced it was prepared to do deals with buy-to-let mortgage holders that were in negative equity. At best, this will mean the bank crystallising significant losses on these loans. At worst, it will mean writing off the entire amount. In March 2011, the Central Bank produced a report detailing the amount of mortgage arrears in all of the banks and highlighted the fact that many mortgage holders had already negotiated revised payment terms and were now unable to meet these new terms. Many of those that bought at the top of the market with 100% mortgages are in a particularly bad way. With the ECB raising interest rates to fight inflationary pressures in the German and French economies, the situation is going to get a lot worse for the bank.

Though Bank of Scotland Ireland has now gone from the Irish market, it is its parent company that will have to deal with the fallout from such poor risk management. The late John Healy, a journalist with the *Irish Times* wrote a book in 1968 which chronicled the economic and social decline of rural life in the West of Ireland in a time of widespread poverty and emigration. Its title could equally be applied to risk management in the banks. The book was called: *No One Shouted Stop.*

Uncertainty

A distinction needs to be drawn between risk and uncertainty. Lunn (2008) suggests that risk is similar to playing roulette in a casino. With a roulette wheel, one knows how many red and black numbers there are. As a result, the level of risk can be calculated. However, when operating in global markets, there is a great deal of uncertainty. People do not know the odds. It is like playing poker without knowing how many aces are in the pack. Risk can be quantified, uncertainty cannot. So much of what is happening in global markets involves uncertainty. It is an important distinction that should be borne in mind by executives when making strategic decisions. When the Icelandic volcano Eyjafjallajokull erupted in April 2010, it sent a plume of volcanic ash high into the atmosphere. While the prevailing wind in Ireland comes from the southwest, for a number of weeks following the eruption, northerly airflows brought the ash clouds over Ireland, the UK and Northern Europe. As a result, airlines were forced to cancel flights, leaving passengers stranded. This caused major uncertainty in the industry and resulted in severe losses. The eruption of the volcano and the subsequent weather patterns were obviously outside the control of any country or organisation. Yet airlines were left to deal with the uncertainty. For Ireland, the uncertainty of the Icelandic volcano has been replaced by the uncertainty surrounding the banking industry, and the fear that the true cost of the financial crash has yet to be calculated. In addition to the banking collapse in Ireland, there is a great deal of uncertainty surrounding the Euro and its survival makes it a very difficult trading environment for Irish companies.

CONCLUSION

The corporate headquarters is the driving force that co-ordinates and drives the entire organisation. It creates the internal environment where all divisions can work together to achieve a level of synergy that ultimately enables the organisation to successfully implement its strategy. The issues dealt with in this chapter are general policy issues faced by organisations at the corporate level. The centre defines the personality of the organisation in terms of its culture and how it relates to the world around it through its policy on corporate social responsibility. One of the primary functions of a corporate headquarters is to provide a clear sense of direction for the entire organisation and this often has to be achieved against a background of conflicting stakeholder expectation. This means establishing a vision for the future direction of the organisation and also establishing goals and objectives that will stretch it in terms of what it can achieve. Ultimately, the corporate headquarters should add value to the company as a whole, which is greater than the sum of the divisions of that company if they were operating separately.

The next chapter will examine business-level strategy, either as a stand-alone competitive strategy or as part of the competitive strategy of a larger group. Chapters 9 and 10 will then examine a number of strategic directions that are open to the company to help it achieve its strategic objectives. Chapter 11 will examine the different methods by which companies can choose to pursue those directions. Chapter 12 will then consider the different tools that can assist in the decision-making process as the firm tries to choose the optimum solution given its particular circumstances.

Thereafter, the remaining chapters will consider the actions required to implement the strategies that a company uses, from gathering the right team together to the resources required to support them, the structure of the organisation and the control processes. This part will also include a chapter on change management. However, while change will be examined separately in order to understand the process better, it must be remembered that change is an on-going process that affects every organisation to some degree or other. For that reason, when executives are looking at making corporate decisions, flexibility is essential in that process.

SUMMARY

This chapter examined how the corporate headquarters defines the business in a number of ways:

- Scope – in terms of products and markets and whether it diversifies
- Leadership – how the centre provides leadership for the entire organisation
- Employees – recruiting the right employees is of vital importance
- Motivation – motivating the people in the organisation to achieve success
- Culture – instilling a high-performance culture
- Creativity – creating the environment where people will solve problems in creative ways
- Corporate governance – ensuring legal and ethical compliance
- Information systems – to achieve maximum efficiency and effectiveness

The structure of a company, as depicted graphically by an organisational chart, is effectively the skeleton that provides shape and form to that organisation. It depicts the various departments, the layers of management and the lines of responsibility in the company. Some of the basic structures are:

- **No formal structure** – start-up companies with just a couple of people working in them. Sooner or later, it will have to adopt some form of structure.
- **Functional** – where the organisation is divided up into different functional areas such as marketing, finance, production, etc. The organisation requires this form of functional expertise and this structure is likely to remain in place regardless of how the company grows.
- **Multi-divisional** – where the organisation is divided along geographical or product divisions. It allows the company to grow and there is flexibility in how more divisions are added. It facilitates the company concentrating its efforts in separate divisions.
- **Matrix** – a combination of, say, geographical divisions and product divisions that allows the company to adapt products for specific markets.

Every company will develop some variation of the various structural types to suit their own particular circumstances. There is no set formula for designing an organisation's structure. Goold and Campbell suggest nine 'tests' to facilitate the selection of an appropriate structure for an organisation. Over time, it is natural that the structure of organisations will evolve. On the other hand, it is important to have some continuity so that organisational members will understand the structure of the company and, in particular, the lines of responsibility.

With **centralised decision-making**, the corporate headquarters makes strategic and operational decisions that provide direction for the entire organisation. It is highly prescriptive and works on the basis that executives in the headquarters have greater knowledge and experience and thus can make more informed decisions.

At the other end of the spectrum is **decentralised decision-making**. Here the authority to make decisions is pushed down to the lowest level in the organisation that is capable of making such decisions. It means that unit managers are then responsible for what happens in that division, but takes into account that each market is different and these managers are best equipped to make decisions by considering all relevant factors. Individual companies will differ in how they relate to their units. Goold and Campbell suggest different styles that describe the relationship between the centre and the different divisions.

An important role of the corporate headquarters is in allocating the necessary resources to, and developing the potential of, each SBU. There are a number of factors to be considered in this regard, including finance, deciding which markets to compete in, and the product range on offer.

Financial decisions required at corporate headquarters level relate to the financing of the organisation including:

- Capital structure – how the corporation is financed between debt and equity
- Policy on dividends – a decision to be made by each individual company with regard to whether they will pay a dividend and, if so, how much?
- Incentive schemes to attract and retain top managers and employees
- Managing risk, recognising that the risk profile of every company will differ. Some will be risk-averse, some risk neutral, and others will be risk-takers.

All of these factors will impact on the other corporate decisions that are made.

DISCUSSION QUESTIONS

1. Differentiate between the various types of organisational structures and state the circumstances in which each type might be appropriate.
2. Distinguish between the different types of parental control that a corporate headquarters might use in controlling a subsidiary company.
3. Explore the various types of financial decisions that need to be made at corporate level.
4. Financial incentives have come in for a lot of criticism in recent times. Explore the role of such incentives in motivating managers.
5. Distinguish between risk and uncertainty.

Useful Websites

The following organisations have been referred to in this chapter:

- General Electric: www.ge.com/company
- IBM: www.ibm.com/us/en/sandbox/ver2
- Kerry Group: www.kerrygroup.com
- Royal Dutch Shell: www.shell.com
- Ryanair: www.ryanair.com/ie
- Virgin Group: www.virgin.com

REFERENCES

Accenture, 2010, http://www.accenture.com/us-en/Pages/service-banking-global-risk-management-study.aspx, Accessed 27 February 2011

Amabile, T. and Kramer, S., 2010, "What really motivates employees", *Harvard Business Review*, January/February 2010, Vol. 88, Issue 1, pp.43–44

Bartlett, C. and Ghoshal, S., 1990, "Matrix Management: Not a Structure, a Frame of Mind", *Harvard Business Review*, Vol. 68, Issue 4, pp.138–145

Bettis, R. and Prahalad, C., 1995, "The Dominant Logic: Retrospective and Extension", *Strategic Management Journal*, [January 1995], Vol. 16, Issue 1, pp.5–15

Brousseau, K. *et al.*, 2006, "The seasoned executive's decision-making style", *Harvard Business Review*, February 2006, Vol.84, Issue 2, pp.110–121

Carey, B., 2008, "Fund boss wants DCC broken up", *Sunday Times*, 29 June 2008

Chandler, A., 1962, *Strategy and Structure*, Cambridge, MA, MIT Press

Clancy, P. *et al.*, 2010, *Mapping the Golden Circle*, Dublin, TASC

Collins, J., 2001, *Good to Great*, London, Random House

Cooke, N., 2008, "Irish firms must look to foreign markets for growth", *Sunday Business Post*, 29 June 2008

Creaton, S. and O'Cleary, C., 2002, *Panic at the Bank*, Dublin, Gill & Macmillan

Dess, G. *et al.*, 2004, Strategic *Management, Boston*, McGraw-Hill

Dibb, S. *et al.*, 2006, *Marketing Concepts and Strategies*, Boston, Houghton Mifflin

Digby, D. and Vishwanath, V., 2006, "Localisation: The Revolution in Consumer Markets", *Harvard Business Review*, April 2006, Vol. 84, Issue 4, pp.82–92

Early, P.C. and Mosakowski, E., 2004, "Cultural Intelligence", *Harvard Business Review*, October 2004, Vol. 82, Issue 10, pp. 139–146

Fitzroy, P. and Hulbert, J., 2005, *Strategic Management: Creating Value in Turbulent Times*, Chichester, Wiley

Forfás, 2005, *Making Technological Knowledge Work*, Dublin, Technopolis/Forfás

Ghemawat, P., 2001, "Distance Still Matters", *Harvard Business Review*, September 2001, Vol. 79, Issue 8, pp.137–147

Ghemawat, P., 2003, "The Forgotten Strategy", *Harvard Business Review*, November 2003, Vol. 81, Issue 11, pp.76–84

Ghemawat, P., 2010, "Finding your strategy in the new landscape", *Harvard Business Review*, March 2010, Vol. 88, Issue 2, pp.54–60

Goold, M. and Campbell, A., 2002, "Do You Have a Well-designed Organisation?", *Harvard Business Review*, March 2002, Vol. 80, Issue 3, pp.117–224

Goold, M. and Campbell, A., 1987, *Strategies and Styles*, Oxford, Blackwell

Goold, M. and Campbell, A., 1998, "Desperately seeking Synergy", *Harvard Business Review*, September/October 1998, Vol. 76, Issue 2, pp.131–145

Goold, M. *et al.*, 1994, *Corporate-level Strategy: Creating Value in a Multibusiness Company*, Chichester, Wiley

Grant Thornton, 2010, *Corporate Governance Review 2010*, Dublin, Grant Thornton

Gunnigle, P., *et al.*, 2006, *Human Resource Management in Ireland*, 3rd Edition, Dublin, Gill & Macmillan

Hamm, J., 2006, "The Five Messages Leaders Must Manage", *Harvard Business Review*, May 2006, Vol. 84, Issue 5, pp.115–123

Harper, N. and Viguerie, P., 2002, "Are you too focused?", *The McKinsey Quarterly*, 2002, Special Edition: Risk and Resilience

Hayes, R. and Wheelwright, S., 1979, "The Dynamics of Process–Product Life Cycles", *Harvard Business Review*, March/April 1979, Vol. 57, Issue 2, pp.127–136

Huselid, M., 1995, "The impact of human resource management practices on turnover, productivity and corporate financial performance", *Academy of Management Journal*, Vol. 39, Issue 3, pp.635–672

Kanter, R.M., 1999, "From Spare Change to Real Change", *Harvard Business Review*, [May/June 1999], Vol. 77, Issue 3, pp.122–132

Kanter, R.M., 2003, "Thriving Locally in the Global Economy", *Harvard Business Review*, August 2003, Vol. 81, Issue 8, pp.119–127

Kaplan, R. and Norton, D., 2006, "How to implement a new strategy without disrupting your organisation", *Harvard Business Review*, March 2006, Vol. 84, Issue 3, pp.100–109

Kerry Group PLC, 2011, www.kerrygroup.com/page.asp?pid=82, (Accessed 27 February 2011)

Kotler, P. *et al.*, 2007, *Principles of Marketing*, 4th European Ed., Upper Saddle River, NJ, Prentice Hall Europe

Lane, B., 2008, *Jacked Up: The Inside Story of How Jack Welch Talked GE into Becoming the World's Greatest Company*, New York, McGraw-Hill

Levitt, T., 1983, "The Globalisation of Markets", *Harvard Business Review*, May/June 1983, Vol. 61, Issue 3, pp.92–102

Levitt, T., 2002, "Creativity is not enough", *Harvard Business Review*, Aug 2002, Vol. 80, Issue 8, pp.137–14

Liu, Y., 2007, "The value of human resource management for organisational performance", *Business Horizons*, November/December 2007, Vol 50, Issue 6, (2007) 50, pp.503–511

Lunn, P., 2008, "Economic Uncertainty Takes Revenge on Hubris of Traders", *Irish Times*, 24 September 2008, p.14

Mankins, M., 2006, "Stop Making Plans: Start Making Decisions", *Harvard Business Review*, Vol. 84, Issue 3, pp.76–84

Markides, C., 1997, "To Diversify or Not To Diversify", *Harvard Business Review*, November/December 1997, Vol. 75, Issue 6, pp.93–99

Nichols, J. and Roslow, S., 1986, "The S Curve: An Aid to Strategic Marketing", *Journal of Consumer Marketing*, Vol. 3, Issue 2, pp.53–64

O'Brien, J. and Marakas, G., 2008, *Management Information Systems*, 8th Edition, New York, McGraw-Hill

Ohmae, K., 1989, "Managing in a Borderless World", *Harvard Business Review*, May/June 1989, Vol. 67, Issue 3, pp.151–161

Ohmae, K., 1989, "The Global Logic of Strategic Alliances", *Harvard Business Review*, March/April 1989, Vol. 67, Issue 2, pp.143–152

Ohmae, K., 1982, *The Mind of the Strategist*, New York, McGraw-Hill

O'Leary, J., 2010, "I should have been more pushy in opposing risk-taking at bank", *Irish Times*, 24 July 2010, p.11

Peters, T. and Waterman, R., 1982, *In Search of Excellence*, New York, Warner Books

Schein, E., 2010, *Organisational Culture and Leadership*, 4th Ed., San Francisco, Jossey-Bass

Suarez, F. and Lanzolla, G., 2005, "The Half-Truth of First Mover Advantages", *Harvard Business Review*, April 2005, Vol. 83, Issue 4, pp.121–127

Tansey, P., 2008, "Innovate or Stagnate", *Irish Times*, 29 February 2008

Yip, G., 2003, *Total Global Strategy II*, London, *Financial Times*. Prentice Hall

Business-level Strategy

LEARNING OBJECTIVES

On completion of this chapter, you will be able to:

- Distinguish between business-level strategies and corporate-level strategies
- Differentiate between the various strategies that can be adopted at business unit level
- Analyse the extent to which each strategy will contribute to the competitive advantage of an organisation
- Critically examine the overall suitability of a particular business-level strategy for an organisation

"So much of what we call management consists of making it difficult for people to work."

Peter Drucker

INTRODUCTION

Throughout this text there are examples of organisations that are both large and small. The subject of this chapter is smaller, single business organisations where the business-level strategy is the same as the organisation's strategy. This also applies to much larger organisations that are divided into different strategic business units (SBUs). Each of these SBUs is operating in a different market, with its own set of customers, and different customer needs. The competitive environment will differ from one market to another and the strategy and business model being pursued must also be tailored for that market. The purpose of the strategy is to create value for the customer and generate profit for the company. If it can outperform rivals in so doing, it will achieve above-average profitability.

The concept of generic strategies was first developed by Michael Porter in his 1980 book: *Competitive Strategy: Techniques for Analysing Industries and Competitors*. He described **three internally consistent, generic strategies** that could be followed by any business:

- Cost leadership
- Differentiation
- Focus

The first two ('cost leadership' and 'differentiation') were aimed at a broad market segment, while 'focus' was aimed at a narrow market segment. By 'internally-consistent', Porter meant that the strategy should form the basis of everything the SBU does and requires total commitment. They were termed 'generic' as they could be applied to any business situation, and companies should choose one of those options.

In the 1980s, Porter's work was considered to be seminal but, like many theories, it has been since developed by others, reflecting the many changes that have taken place in industry in the intervening time. Johnson *et al.* (2008) refer to the strategy clock, which is adapted from the work of Bowman (1995). This is an eight-point clock representing different positions (generic strategies) in a market that reflect different customer requirements in terms of value for money. However, many writers, including Lynch (2008), Hill and Jones (2004), Thompson *et al.* (2008) and others, have taken Porter's original framework and developed it further. Despite their criticisms (some of which will be discussed here), it remains an important piece of work as part of a broader analysis in generating strategic options. According to Lynch (2008: 309) it "forces exploration of two important aspects of corporate strategy: the role of cost reduction and the use of differentiated products in relation to customers and competitors."

GENERIC STRATEGIES

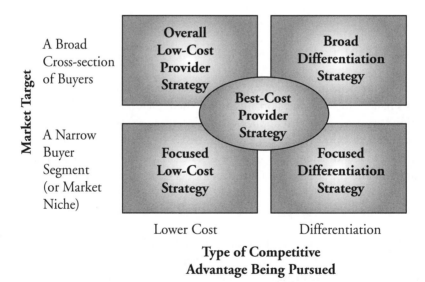

Source: Thompson *et al.* (2008: 134) *Crafting and Executing Strategy: The Quest for Competitive Advantage Theses and Cases*, 16th Edition, Boston, McGraw-Hill

Figure 8.1 *Five Generic Strategies*

According to Thompson *et al.* (2008: 134), there are five generic strategies. They are:

1. **Low-cost provider strategy.** This strategy involves attaining overall lower costs than rivals and appealing to a broad segment of consumers by charging a lower price.
2. **Broad differentiation strategy.** In this case, the product is differentiated from rivals by way of quality or service that appeals to customers, thus allowing the provider to charge a premium price.
3. **Best-cost provider strategy.** This strategy would have been considered unattainable by Porter, but involves a combination of good quality at a competitive price.
4. **Focused low-cost strategy.** This is based on low price and is aimed at a narrow market niche whose needs are not being met by the companies pursuing a broad-based cost leadership strategy.
5. **Focused differentiation strategy.** This strategy is also aimed at a niche market, but with differentiated needs.

Each of these strategies will require different distinctive competences to implement them successfully, and will now be discussed in detail.

Low-cost Provider Strategy

Chapter 6 examined in detail how an organisation can reduce its costs to become competitive. In every industry, there will be a segment that is price sensitive, either out of necessity, or because they regard the product or service to be worth only a certain price and no more. There are two different ways in which pursuing a low-cost strategy can work. First, charge a lower price than rival companies, and so attract customers. Any organisation can sell products or services at a low price. The acid test is whether it can do so and still make a profit. Secondly, once the company has attained low costs, it can also charge the standard industry price and make a much larger profit.

To achieve a low-cost provider strategy, the company must examine its cost base to see where costs can be reduced, or even eliminated in some cases. A low-cost provider strategy is attained when the organisation becomes *the* low cost provider in the industry. It involves a relentless pursuit of reducing costs to the bare minimum throughout the entire organisation. Once this has been attained, the company then has a competitive advantage. It should be noted that costs will vary with each industry, so any discussion about cost will be relative to rival companies in that industry.

Cost leadership requires a business model based on lowering the company's cost structure, and developing a distinctive competence that will separate the company from rivals. The value chain (see Chapter 6) is a useful strategic tool to examine the organisation to see where costs are generated and value is created. As such, it can be used to apply a generic strategy to the organisation. **Illustration 8.1** highlights many aspects of Dell's strategy to reduce costs. Each of the primary and secondary activities of the value chain can be examined to see where costs might be minimised. This can be achieved either by performing elements of the value chain better than rivals, or through by-passing some of the activities, e.g. Dell ship directly to the customer, thereby cutting out the retail distribution channel. There are numerous ways in which an organisation can reduce costs. The product or service is generally a standard, 'no-frills' product that will appeal to a large segment of the target market.

Generally, cost reduction requires attaining a large market share, as the profit margin per unit sold tends to be small. The large market share will, in turn, reap economies of scale (where unit costs decrease as production increases) and economies of scope (gained by expanding the scope of their activities and managerial skills). Cost reduction also requires exploitation of the experience curve and high capacity utilisation. It involves increasing stock turnover, reducing the cost of goods sold, skilled materials' management and flexible manufacturing/operations.

All of these methods are not proprietary: they can be copied by any rival company. Ryanair did not invent the low-cost strategy for the airline industry. The first airline to use a low-cost strategy was the Texan company, Southwest Airlines, which was established in 1971 by Herb Kelleher. It has been consistently profitable ever since, even after the events of 9/11 when the US airline industry was in turmoil. In the early 1990s, Ryanair's CEO visited Southwest Airlines to observe how they operated and then replicated their business model. There are other low-cost airlines operating in Europe, but none has been as profitable as Ryanair. What separates it is the determination of Ryanair to minimise costs throughout the entire organisation at every juncture.

Illustration 8.1: Low-cost Provider Strategy at Dell

The computer manufacturer Dell pursues a low-cost provider strategy by minimising costs across its entire business model. The strategy has evolved over the years, and the company is constantly seeking to cut costs from its system. Some of the principal ways in which this is achieved include:

- **Links with Suppliers** Dell works very closely with its suppliers and establishes long-term relationships with them. It limits the number of its suppliers and maintains relationships as long as suppliers keep at the cutting edge in terms of technology development.
- **Just-in-time** Dell has built up a perfect just-in-time relationship with its suppliers, many of whom are located close to Dell's manufacturing plants. The just-in-time arrangement ensures that a minimum amount of money is tied up in its supply chain, benefiting both the suppliers and Dell.
- **Operations** Dell operates with a minimum supply of parts on site, and as soon as these parts are used, just-in-time arrangements replace them. Working with their suppliers, Dell has consistently reduced the amount of stock it holds, and it is currently at roughly three days' supplies. Their operations are based on building computers to order. This allows them to customise the computer to meet the needs of the customer, while being able to capitalise on mass production efficiencies. Working to order also allows the company to track latest trends in terms of what customers want.
- **Research and Development** In addition to the feedback from customers' orders, the company also has a dedicated research and development unit employing a few thousand engineers dedicated to developing new products that leverage off existing production facilities and expertise.
- **Payment** Dell assembles its computers only when it has received payment from the customer. This up-front payment minimises the amount of working capital required in the business and also ensures that there are no bad debts.

- **Direct sales** While the company has recently modified its sales strategy, it is still primarily based on direct sales to customers. This allows Dell to remove the cost of distribution from their value chain. Their sales staff deal with all segments of the market, including home use, small businesses, large corporations, government departments, etc.
- **Customer service** The company provides online after sales service and uses contracts with local service providers to facilitate on-site business repairs. Their direct link to customers also allows the company to target existing customers for replacement models and computer peripherals such as printers.

Low-cost provider strategy requires a company to scrutinise each cost to see how it can be reduced or eliminated. It also requires creating a corporate culture that supports such attention to costs. It must be remembered that costs change constantly, and so the model must also change. For example, technology is constantly evolving, but it also creates opportunities to further reduce costs. However, in cutting costs, the organisation needs to have a good understanding of what the customers consider to be an integral part of the product/service and what is an optional extra. Customer sensitivity to price will also vary over time as living standards increase.

In recent years, Dunnes Stores, particularly their household department, has moved upmarket, reflecting the increased prosperity in the country. Other examples of cost leadership companies include Wal-mart, Lidl and Aldi in supermarkets, Bic in ballpoint pens and razors, Nucor in steel production, and Briggs & Stratton in small petrol engines.

Broad Differentiation Strategy

With a broad differentiation strategy, companies are trying to achieve a competitive advantage by selling a product or service that customers perceive as being different and are willing to pay a premium for that difference. By building up brand loyalty, they can create an advantage over rivals. Costs are the main concern with cost leadership. Costs remain important with differentiation, but they are not the primary concern. Differentiation can be achieved through a number of different approaches:

- Superior design and performance – Mercedes and BMW cars
- Superior service – Four Seasons hotels, FedEx logistics
- Innovation and technological leadership – 3M
- High quality durable products – Caterpillar earth-moving equipment
- Prestige design or brand image – Rolex watches, Fieldcrest towels and linen

The more attributes that a company can use to differentiate itself from rivals, the more difficult it will be for those rivals to imitate that product or service. All of these differentiating factors increase the cost. In including extra product features, the company must still be mindful of costs, as the selling price has to cover the total costs involved. There is, generally speaking, a ceiling to the price that customers are willing to pay for the product if the differentiation is based on product features, as customers will compare the various products. When the product conveys a prestige image, which conveys status, people are less price-sensitive and in many cases the product would lose some of its appeal if the price were to be dropped. Modern digital watches are probably as accurate as Rolex watches, but do not have the image that allows Rolex to charge a premium price.

The value chain can also be used to identify opportunities for differentiation. In terms of quality, it begins with the design of the product (R&D) and the sourcing of the components (high specifications). In operations, there has to be strict adherence to quality and attention to detail. The marketing of the product has to be in keeping with the image being portrayed and there needs to be a high level of customer service. The linkages between all of the elements of the value chain are also very important, because differentiated products are more expensive and companies following such a strategy have smaller market share. The premium price, however, allows the company to make significant profits on each item sold.

Illustration 8.2: Differentiation Strategy – Four Seasons Hotels and Resorts

Four Seasons Hotels and Resorts is a Canadian company that operates an international chain of luxury hotels, including one at Ballsbridge in Dublin. It was founded in 1960 and has grown continuously since then. Four Seasons is an example of a company operating a differentiation strategy. The group is dedicated to providing the highest standards of hospitality. It instils a culture of dedication and service among its employees. Four Seasons currently operates almost 90 hotels in 35 countries, with many more under development. It is considered a leader in the hospitality industry in terms of quality and service, and is the recipient of numerous prestigious awards.

Its founder, chairman and CEO, Isadore Sharp, has based his approach on four strategic decisions, which he has termed the 'Four Pillars'. First, they only operate medium-sized hotels of *exceptional quality*, and aspire to be the best. Secondly, Four Seasons distinguish themselves by the quality of their service – and build a competitive advantage based on that service. Thirdly, their values (their golden rule) are based on helping others, and there is also a code of ethics that forms the basis of their corporate culture. This is something that is universal and transcends national cultures. Finally, from a customer perspective, the brand is synonymous with quality that reflects the people working in the organisation. They recognise staff contribution and are quick to share the credit.

In terms of its strategies, how then does Four Seasons differentiate itself from its competitors?

Central to the concept of quality are the people working in the organisation. This begins at the recruitment and selection stage. Employees are hired for their attitude – people who have a natural affinity for customer service. Whether at recruitment stage or being selected for promotion, each employee is interviewed by four managers including the hotel's general manager. Training is also an essential element in the provision of a quality service. There are two distinct aspects to training. First is customer service: developing the emotional connection to people. Second is developing the technical skills that are required. Taken together, it ensures that the level of consistency and service exceeds customer expectations and builds on the reputation for quality. Refinement of the process is also important – examining procedures to ensure there is constant improvement on what they do. Staff that are professional and deliver a consistently high quality of work will inevitably derive great satisfaction from that work. The acid test is in staff turnover. Four Seasons have an exceptionally low turnover of staff – the lowest in the industry among the big brands. In the words of Isadore Sharp: "That which we do not own is our most valuable asset. They stay by choice because they are all highly qualified."

Delivering on customer service is essential. However, it must be remembered that Four Seasons is a business like any other. Four Seasons was a public company but it was taken private in 2007 by investors including CEO Isadore Sharp and Bill Gates. It was bought at 40 times' earnings, which demonstrated tremendous confidence in the potential of the brand. Indeed, the hotel group is a market leader with regard to financial returns – approximately 25–30% RevPar (revenue per available room) above other branded competition. Four Seasons charges a premium that customers are happy to pay in return for a blend of luxury combined with exceptional service levels. Four Seasons aims to be the best hotel in each market in which it operates. For the investors who own the hotel buildings (the company has a management contract to run the hotels on behalf of the owners), they too get an exceptional return as the brand generates a valuation premium on their investment.

Source: www.fourseasons.com and interview with Mr John Brennan,
former Regional Vice-President with Four Seasons Hotels and Resorts

(See also the Four Seasons Hotels and Resort case study at the back of this text.)

Best-cost Provider Strategy

Porter (1980: 41) suggests that companies need a clear understanding of their strategy, be it low-cost or differentiation, and should pursue that strategy rigorously. To do otherwise is to be "stuck in the middle" and involves "almost guaranteed low profitability". Many writers now see this as being inaccurate. It is possible to attain low cost *and* differentiation simultaneously.

Since the 1980s, when Porter developed his theory on the generic strategies, much has changed with regard to the notion of costs. The last chapter examined many ways in which costs can be reduced in an organisation through processes such as outsourcing, total quality management (TQM) and business process re-engineering (BPR) – see Chapter 13. Such processes deliver improved quality and reliability, particularly for Japanese companies, while at the same time reducing costs. Thus the combination gives customers more value for their money. It requires manufacturers to include features at a lower cost than rivals as well as quality and performance. It meets the needs of buyer segments that are looking for quality but are more price sensitive than those in the differentiated bracket.

When Toyota launched Lexus, they created it as a separate brand in order to be able to compete with prestige brands such as Mercedes, BMW and Jaguar. While Lexus is marketed as a separate brand, it is still able to benefit from the entire R&D, sourcing and production economies of scale available to Toyota. Lexus has won many awards for quality and reliability, and because of its lower manufacturing costs its cars are sold at a more competitive price than its prestige rivals.

Toyota has successfully pursued a best-cost provider strategy, but this is a difficult strategy for many organisations to achieve. The danger with pursuing a best-cost strategy is that a company may not achieve low enough costs while not having enough product features. Consequently, it appeals neither to price sensitive buyers or those willing to pay a premium for top quality. Nevertheless, it can be achieved, e.g. many international brands operating in the four-star hotel market are able to blend economies of scale that provide competitive prices, with a level of comfort bordering on five-star hotels.

Focused Low-cost Strategy

The discussion above on overall low-cost provider strategy and broad differentiation was centred on a broad market segment. The target segment with focus low cost and focus differentiation is directed at a niche market whose needs are not being met by the bigger players. The niche market can be segmented on the basis of geographical area, and special product or user requirements. It requires a clearly defined target market.

With focus low-cost strategy, the company needs to achieve lower costs than rivals for that particular market segment and, in so doing, can achieve a competitive advantage. From a cost perspective, the methods of achieving low cost are similar to those used in overall low-cost provider strategy for the broader market.

While there has been an enormous increase in the number of '4×4' sports utility vehicles in the last number years, the vast majority will be used only in an urban environment. Land Rover has been around for the last 60 years and caters for those who need a rugged 4×4 off-road vehicle. The Land Rover Defender is used by organisations and individuals that require such capability, but are not prepared to pay for the luxury found in many prestige SUVs.

Focused Differentiation Strategy

Focus differentiation strategy is at the other end of the scale, catering for a niche market that is willing to pay premium prices. By meeting the specific needs of this niche group, a company can attain a competitive advantage and above-average returns. Keeping with the example above, the Range Rover has excellent off-road capability for pulling horse boxes, while encompassing top of the range luxury. Porsche manufactures sports cars that have enormous engine power suited to German autobahns in a way that other sports cars could not match. Gore-Tex clothing is upmarket outdoor clothing that combines durability and quality for those out in extreme weather. Fisher-Price manufactures electronic equipment for young children. Tag Heuer aims its products at those requiring rugged waterproof watches.

Managerial Skills

Different core competences will be required for managing individual strategies. For an overall low-cost strategy, the main emphasis is on cost reduction and a company will require very tight control mechanisms to ensure that all costs are kept to a minimum. Staff training and control will be very prescriptive, and standardised manuals will direct staff in particular situations. For a broad differentiation strategy, costs still need to be managed, but the emphasis here is on the quality and service for which people are paying a premium price. It requires a core competence in customer service. It needs a totally different type of staff training – one that develops individual initiative and responsibility. As managers cannot be everywhere at the same time, there needs to be much greater latitude on the part of management with regard to the decisions made by staff in an effort to please the customer.

It is often a moot point as to whether a company is following an overall low-cost strategy or a focused low-cost strategy and similarly for broad differentiation/focused differentiation strategies. The theory of the broad versus narrow segments is often clearer than the reality. Are they distinguished by the size of the market or limited to geographical location or customer type? Apart from developing an appropriate marketing strategy, such distinction has probably little value. As with many aspects of strategy, the environment is constantly changing and organisations must be mindful of these changes. For differentiation strategies, the image created by marketing is central to generating a demand for the product or service. It has to create a sophisticated message that will appeal to wealthy customers. In some instances, it will be a global appeal such as in high-end fashion. In others, it will have to be tailored for a specific group and so cultural awareness will be important (Early and Mosakawski, 2004).

Information technology plays an important part in the management of generic strategies. For a cost leadership strategy, managers need to have accurate, real-time information about costs, so that measures can be taken to reduce them. O'Brien and Marakas (2008: 364) describe the attributes of information quality along three dimensions:

- Time – information should be up-to-date and available when needed and it should cover past, present and future performance.
- Content – it should be accurate, relevant, complete and concise and it should reveal performance by measuring activities, progress made or resources accumulated.
- Form – it should be clear and presented in a form that contains sufficient detail for the level of manager concerned.

Yield management will also play a very important role in industries such as the airline industry.

Linking with Corporate Level

For smaller companies with a single-business market, there will be an overlap between the generic strategy it is pursuing and corporate-level strategies. In essence, they will be woven into one overall strategic approach. For business units that are part of a much larger organisation covering many different markets and possibly different industries, there will be some degree of autonomy in the decisions that the SBU makes. There are many factors that will dictate the level of autonomy that applies, and this will vary greatly from one organisation to another. Regardless of the amount of decision-making latitude involved, the objectives set by the SBU must support the overall objectives of the corporation.

Having decided on a particular generic strategy, the organisation must then consider the possible strategies that will enable it to achieve its overall corporate objectives, and these will be considered in Chapter 9. There are a variety of factors that need to be considered and, while there are many strategic tools that will assist in the process, experience and judgement will also play an important role.

SUMMARY

Business-level strategies apply to smaller, single business organisations. In such cases, the business-level strategy is one and the same as the organisation's strategy. It also applies to much larger organisations that are divided into different strategic business units (SBUs). Each of these SBUs is operating in a different market, with its own set of customers, and different customer needs. The competitive environment will differ from one market to another and the strategy and business model being pursued must also be tailored for that market. The purpose of the strategy is to create value for the customer and generate profit for the company. If it can outperform rivals in so doing, it will achieve above-average profitability.

The concept of generic strategies was first developed by Michael Porter, who used the term 'generic' in that they are strategies that could be applied to all types of organisations. Thompson *et al.* (2008) and others, have taken Porter's original work and developed it further and now refer to the five generic strategies, which are:

Overall low-cost leadership This strategy involves attaining overall lower costs than rivals and appealing to a broad segment of consumers by charging a lower price. It appeals to price-sensitive buyers. To achieve cost leadership, managers must target costs throughout the organisation. The value chain will help identify where costs are being generated. The strategy requires tight managerial control.

Broad differentiation In this case, the product is differentiated from rivals by way of quality or service that appeals to customers, thus allowing the provider to charge a premium price. Costs remain important, but they are not the primary concern. Differentiation can be achieved in many different ways.

Best-cost provider strategy This strategy would have been considered unattainable by Porter, but involves a combination of good quality at a competitive price. Developments over the last 15 years or so have led to improved quality, while keeping costs low. A best-cost provider strategy is difficult to achieve and sustain as there is the possibility of failing to achieve low costs and high quality simultaneously.

Focus low-cost leadership This is based on low price and is aimed at a narrow niche market whose needs are not being met by the companies pursuing a broad-based cost leadership strategy. It requires having a clearly defined market niche.

Focus differentiation This strategy is also aimed at a niche market, but with differentiated needs.

Each of these strategies will require different distinctive competences to implement them successfully.

DISCUSSION QUESTIONS

1. Evaluate the importance of developing business-level strategies for an organisation.
2. Differentiate between the different generic strategies.
3. Critically analyse an overall low-cost leadership strategy and the managerial competences required to underpin the strategy.
4. Evaluate the best-cost provider strategy and state whether you think such a strategy is sustainable or is 'stuck in the middle'.

Activity

Taking the example of Dell in **Illustration 8.1**, use the value chain (see Chapter 6) to examine where Dell reduces its cost base.

REFERENCES

Dell, 2011, www.dell.com, accessed 7 March 2011

Dess, G. *et al.*, 2004, *Strategic Management*, Boston, McGraw-Hill

Early, P.C., and Mosakowski, E., 2004, "Cultural Intelligence", *Harvard Business Review*, October 2004, Vol. 82, Issue 10, pp.139–146

Four Seasons, 2011, www.fourseasons.com, accessed 7 March 2011

Johnson, G. *et al.*, 2008, *Exploring Corporate Strategy*, Harlow, Essex, Prentice Hall, Financial Times

Hill, W. and Jones, G., 2004, *Strategic Management: An Integrated Approach,* Boston, Houghton Mifflin

Lynch, R., 2008, *Strategic Management*, 5th Ed., Harlow, Essex, Prentice Hall, Financial Times

O'Brien, J. and Marakas, G., 2008, *Management Information Systems*, 8th Ed., New York, McGraw-Hill

Porter, M., 1980, *Competitive Strategy*, New York, The Free Press

Porter, M., 1985, *Competitive Advantage*, New York, The Free Press

Thompson, A. *et al.*, 2008, *Crafting and Executing Strategy: The Quest for Competitive Advantage*, New York, McGraw-Hill

Developing Strategy Options

"Success is on the far side of failure."

Tom Watson, Founder, IBM

INTRODUCTION

Chapter 9 examines the different strategy directions from which a company can choose. These include: consolidating what a company has already achieved and increasing market share, developing a range of products to keep abreast with new technology, developing new markets and going international. In making the decision to enter foreign markets, there are many factors that need to be taken into consideration. This chapter examines the choices available to enter new markets: exporting, licensing and franchising, strategic alliances and joint ventures, and also foreign direct investment. There are also different strategic options for operating internationally: global strategy, transnational strategy and multi-domestic strategy.

Chapter 10 will continue this theme of strategy development and examine the nature and types of diversification.

The strategies discussed in Chapters 9 and 10 are by no means mutually exclusive, and companies will develop along a number of these lines simultaneously. Chapter 11 deals with the different options open to an organisation to help achieve these strategies such as organic growth, mergers and acquisitions, and strategic alliances. Chapter 12 then looks at a number of different evaluation tools that executives can use to help choose the strategy best suited to the circumstances under which a particular firm is operating. These circumstances and the resources available will differ significantly from one organisation to another and, while the various strategic tools will assist in the selection process, the ultimate decision still requires managerial judgement.

CORPORATE STRATEGY DIRECTIONS

In 1965, the Russian-born writer H. Igor Ansoff published his famous work *Corporate Strategy* (it was subsequently republished in 1988 as *The New Corporate Strategy*). Having worked for the Rand Foundation and Lockheed Electronics Company, he subsequently taught at the Carnegie Institute of Technology. Along with his other books, his teaching on strategy and corporate planning was regarded as seminal. He argued that there are four broad strategic directions open to a company (known as 'Ansoff's Matrix' – see **Figure 9.1**).

1. **Market penetration** – consolidating the company's position in the market and developing a larger market share.
2. **Product development** – developing new products to meet market needs.
3. **Market development** – developing new markets (including international markets) as well as new market segments and new uses for products.
4. **Diversification** – related and unrelated diversification (see Chapter 12).

While these are listed as alternative directions, in reality, companies will pursue most, if not all, options possibly at the same time. These options will now be looked at in detail.

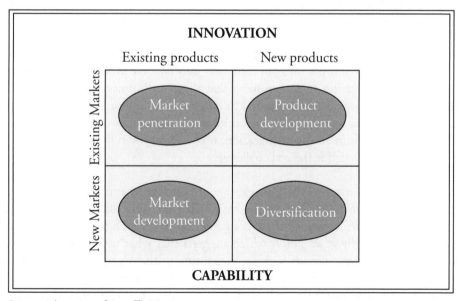

Source: Adaptation of Ansoff's Matrix

Figure 9.1 *Ansoff's Matrix*

CAPABILITY AND INNOVATION

Capability

The capability of the organisation was examined in Chapter 6. In pursuing the various strategic options outlined in this chapter, it is assumed that a company has the strategic capability to follow through on their chosen strategy. If such capability does not currently exist, the company will need to develop or acquire that capability. If, in the short-term, such a capability cannot be obtained, the company will have to settle for a more realistic option. However, care must be taken that the company is not always pursuing the safe option. Attaining 'stretch' goals requires that a company move out of its comfort zone to reach difficult targets.

The various options presented here: market penetration; product development; market development; and diversification, all require an innovative approach by the organisation to differentiate itself from competitors. It requires fresh thinking by managers to spot and develop new approaches and the determination to pursue them.

Innovation

There is a distinction between invention and innovation. According to Smith (2006:5) invention is the discovery of a new product. Innovation goes one step further in bringing that new product, process or service into use. The Economist Joseph Schumpeter defined innovation as "getting things done". It is an important distinction. An invention may be a piece of great ingenuity, but the primary focus here is on the commercial viability of new products in the marketplace.

As Ireland competes in the global knowledge economy, companies must realise that their most important assets are creative people who can turn ideas into valuable products and services that will satisfy their customers. Creating an environment that allows such innovation is a major challenge for the leadership of any organisation. Central to innovation in any organisation is the quality of its workforce. That process begins with the recruitment and selection of people who are creative and will fit in with the culture of the organisation. It continues when those people decide to stay. Keeping such people motivated is the real challenge.

There has been much controversy in recent years about bonus payments in banks. Such payments were justified by senior management on the basis that they were essential to motivating and holding on to talented staff. However, there is a good deal of research (Floriday and Goodnight, 2005; Catmul, 2008; Rigby *et al.* 2009) which suggests that what motivates creative people is primarily a range of intrinsic factors such as: the culture of the organisation where collegiality and trust bind people together and success is recognised; where experimentation can take place in a no-blame environment; people are allowed their own time for creativity rather than fixed to 9 to 5 days; where managers work to remove obstacles to creativity; and where non-performers are dealt with (including non-performing managers). The challenge for managers, therefore, is to keep creative people intellectually engaged. The culture of the organisation is clearly an essential element in facilitating innovation, along with open communication where ideas can be shared and discussed.

Staff motivation is important, but so is keeping the customer satisfied. Customer loyalty can have immense benefits for any organisation. Engaging with customers allows the organisation to understand precisely what their needs are. Working with customers and listening to their problems can also be a key source of innovation.

Innovation comes about in many ways. Smith (2006:86) suggests that innovation is not usually a particularly structured process, but comes about as a result of developing an "insight" that follows perhaps years of painstaking research. Such insight can manifest itself in various ways:

- Association – when people make an association between two apparently unconnected things
- Adaption – by adapting an existing product for a different use
- Analogy – where a principle in one situation is used for a completely different process
- Serendipity – when people discover something purely by chance

The danger for many companies in the middle of a recession is that they will cut back on investment in innovation. Chesborough and Garman (2008) suggest that "the companies that continue to invest in their innovative capabilities during tough economic times are those that fare best when growth returns". They suggest that not all of the investment need come from internal resources and instead companies can look at entering into partnerships with other organisations, while other projects can be spun off as separate ventures that will allow retention of some equity. Innovation can be hard to manage and also hard to measure, and the temptation is to cut back on investing, but it must be seen as of long-term benefit. The real challenge according to Rigby *et al.* (2009) is how to evaluate the merit of projects, and that too often decisions are made by overly-analytical leaders. They suggest that executives require complementary – creative and analytical – styles. Innovation should be seen as core to business, not a marginal activity.

In Chapter 4, we examined the importance of corporate social responsibility, and how it can bring benefits to the organisation as well as the wider community. It is also important that executives view sustainability not as a burden on the bottom line, but that being environmentally-friendly can lower costs and increase revenues. Nidumolu *et al.* (2009) believe that sustainability should be the "touchstone for all innovation". They see it as a five-stage process:

- Viewing compliance as opportunity – ensure that compliance with norms becomes an opportunity for innovation.
- Making value chains that are sustainable – increase efficiencies in the value chain.
- Designing sustainable products and services – make them eco-friendly.
- Developing new business models – try to find novel ways of delivering value to the customer and that will change the basis for competition.
- Challenging existing paradigms and creating next-practice platforms – critically examine today's accepted way of thinking and develop innovative solutions.

A culture of innovation is a critical aspect of any business operating in a competitive environment. Such a culture is pervasive throughout the organisation and not confined to those involved directly in research and development. It requires a constant search for better ways of doing things, and staying ahead of rival companies in all aspects of their operations.

MARKET PENETRATION

Market penetration discusses how a company will grow its share of its current market. In order to do this it may also require consolidation or even withdrawal from other parts of the market.

Market Penetration

Market penetration is a growth strategy dealing with the development of the company using existing products and in existing markets. In essence, it is about gaining customers from a company's competitors. It can also be achieved by convincing existing customers to buy more of your products or services. This can be done through increased advertising or direct selling. Market penetration is perhaps the option with the least amount of risk.

Most companies will try to develop greater market share, the main reason being that there is a strong correlation between high market share and profitability. This is primarily due to fixed costs, which can be spread over a greater number of units. Once market share has been built up, companies will want to protect their investment and ensure that competitors do not erode any advantage. Companies can defend their position in many different ways, such as increasing advertising, price cuts or building in customer loyalty e.g. with supermarket loyalty cards. In most instances, companies operating on an industry will each have only a relatively small slice of the market. Perhaps the best way to protect that market share is to gain an even greater share (and so increase profitability, which in turn can be reinvested). Each company has the advantage that it knows the market well and will spot opportunities when they arise. Though most Tesco stores are large outlets in out-of-town retail centres with ample parking, the company has also targeted underserved segments in urban centres with smaller outlets designed for convenience shopping for those who may not have cars, and thus access to the larger stores. In this way, Tesco is achieving even greater market penetration than they could just by building the larger stores.

In a static market, if one company gains market share, it will be at the expense of another, and so they can expect retaliation. Increased advertising or price reduction by one company is usually met with a similar tactic by competitors, resulting in smaller profits made in the market and a more competitive environment for consumers.

An easier method of gaining market share is to acquire other players in the industry, as this does not directly impact on the market share held by competitors, at least not in the short term. In the longer term, the consolidated company will have a greater combined market share and profitability. If the market is growing, it is easier for one particular company to gain market share, as other companies are also expanding but not at the same rate. For rival companies, they might be perfectly happy with increased sales, and not too concerned about their overall share of the market, which has fallen in relative terms.

Consolidation

While the ultimate objective of market penetration is to increase market share, it may not always be possible and companies may be forced to consolidate part of their current market share. Consolidation is a defensive measure (and should not be regarded as a primary objective in itself). It is important that what the organisation has, it holds. In a mature market where demand is static or falling, a company may want to close some spare capacity in order to reduce costs, and concentrate on other production facilities. Likewise, in mature markets many smaller or weaker firms will either go out of business or be taken over by larger competitors, leading to a consolidation of the industry. This can lead to problems with the Competition Authority or the EU Commission if it is seen that one particular company is becoming dominant in the marketplace. The result can be the blocking of a particular move or forcing the company to sell other related businesses to bring their overall holding back down to an acceptable level. Some industries are seen as being very sensitive in this regard, such as the media, where a dominant position can place a company or individual in a very powerful position. Consolidation takes place in service industries as well as manufacturing. Over the last 10 or 15 years, many accountancy firms have merged in an overall consolidation of the industry.

Withdrawal

On some occasions, in order to consolidate the main business, it may become necessary to withdraw from certain markets to concentrate on core markets or business units. **Illustration 7.2** examined how Bank of Scotland Ireland (BoSi), a subsidiary of Halifax Bank of Scotland, expanded very rapidly in the Republic of Ireland from 2000–2007. However, this expansion was not based on proper risk analysis, and when the financial crisis erupted, BoSi began losing enormous sums of money, as did its parent company, which was subsequently taken over by Lloyds Banking Group in January 2009. In order to stem the losses, Lloyds Banking Group took the decision to close down the retail and commercial sections of BoSi, and transferred the debts to a new company, Certus, whose function is to collect as much of the outstanding loans as possible. Having acquired Halifax Bank of Scotland, along with all its debt, Lloyds Banking Group now wishes to consolidate its core banking business, and withdrawing from the Irish market is central to that strategy.

Closer to home, AIB sold its 70% share in Bank Zachondi WBK in Poland for €3.1 billion in 2010. AIB also sold another subsidiary, Goodbody Stockbrokers to Fexco for €24 million (Simmons, 2011). Both of these sales were necessitated by the perilous state of AIB's finance, also as a result of disastrous lending decisions. The bank is now effectively in state ownership, and it needs to raise capital urgently to shore up its main banking business.

Along with consolidating the business, there can be a speculative reason behind divesting. In 2005 Jurys Doyle hotel group sold the 20 hotels in Jurys Inns group for €1.2 billion to Quinlan Private. They also sold three hotels in Ballsbridge, including their flagship hotel, the Berkeley Court Hotel, for a staggering €379 million to developer Sean Dunne. Finally, they sold the Burlington Hotel to another developer, Bernard McNamara, for €288 million. Of the €1.8 billion raised, the group's shareholders netted €400 million when all debts were cleared. The group also has 20 remaining hotels valued at three quarters of a billion Euro. This was probably the best property deal ever done in Ireland, as the timing was perfect. The hotels were sold at the height of the property boom. It would be hard to put a precise figure on it, but it is safe to say that, if the properties were being sold now, they would fetch perhaps 60% less.

In any economic downturn, cash is king. The man who cemented the deal for Jurys Doyle Hotels was John Gallagher. In an interview in the *Irish Times* he said he believed that "sensible people will wait for the froth to come off the market". He maintained that, as an asset class, hotels were valued incredibly high and when the market returns to normality, "there will be opportunities and they will grow the business" (Beesley, 2007). Apart from property prices plummeting, there is now great over-capacity in the hotel market, as a result of which average occupancy rates and RevPar (revenue per available room) have both fallen significantly. There have already been a number of hotels placed in receivership and NAMA, and more are likely to follow.

In Chapter 10, we will examine portfolio issues, whereby corporations manage their portfolios of different businesses. In some instances, it makes sense for companies to divest under-performing subsidiaries or ones that may be peripheral to their main business and concentrate on the parts that are central to what the company does – what Peters and Waterman (1982) refer to as 'stick to the knitting'.

PRODUCT DEVELOPMENT

Product development should be seen as an integral part of what a company does, rather than being viewed as an optional extra. By product development we mean developing brand new or modified products for existing markets. This text has already looked at how product life cycles have become shorter and shorter. Consequently, in a competitive environment, any firm that does not keep up-to-date with new product development will quickly lose market share and may go out of business as other companies innovate. Customer demand is not just for new products, but also for updated existing ones. Computers double their processing power every 18 months, and customers expect that all manufacturers are constantly improving their product. Otherwise a company would very quickly lose market share to competitors.

According to Tansey (2008), Ireland needs to increase its level of innovation significantly for two reasons. First, Irish goods and services are losing competitiveness on international markets as our costs are rising higher than in competitive countries. Secondly, Ireland's trade-weighted exchange rate has risen against a falling dollar and sterling. These two factors combined have meant that

Ireland's real exchange rate has appreciated by almost one-quarter since we joined the Single European Currency in 1999. To compensate for this, we have to innovate so that our products and services are in demand despite our loss of competitiveness. Innovation can take the form of a new product, a new production process, opening up a new market, funding a better supply source or developing new organisational techniques.

The former Intel Chief, Dr Craig Barrett, believes that education, technology and innovation are the key to opportunities for Ireland in the 21st Century. Speaking at an Education for Innovation conference at NUI Galway in November 2010, Dr Barrett called on the Goverment to increase funding for research and development (R&D) calling it "seed corn for new businesses". He believes that a 3% investment of GDP in research and development is "no longer a reasonable target". The Republic of Ireland is currently spending between 1.5 and 2% on R&D. This figure is skewed by the large multinationals located in Ireland who invest much more than indigenous Irish companies. According to McCall (2010), 73% of the money spent on R&D in Ireland is spent by foreign-owned companies operating here.

Dr Barrett believes that we "have now to compete with the rest of the world to get paid" and that we require a "sustained commitment" to R&D, connecting the private sector involved with universities and institutes of technology. He spoke about the success of Silicon Valley in the US and its relationship with Massachusetts Institute of Technology and Stanford University as examples of focused investment. Ireland's low investment in R&D is in contrast with countries such as Israel, which invests 5% of its GDP into research and development. Dr Barrett believes that Ireland should be doing likewise and, unless we pursue it with vigour, passion and resources, there will be no future for the country (Fallon, 2010).

While new product development may be regarded as essential, it does present certain problems in terms of cost and the management of products coming on stream. The process is very much linked with the environmental analysis carried out in Chapter 5 and the strategic analysis in Chapter 6, as companies have to be aware of opportunities in the market and their own capabilities in terms of being able to exploit such opportunities for profit.

There are a number of issues that need to be taken into consideration. These include:

- Definition of products
- Product line and product mix
- Research and development
- Product life cycle
- First mover advantage
- Brand management

Definition of Products

According to Kotler *et al.* (2007: 561) **a product** is "anything that is offered to a market for attention, acquisition, use or consumption and that might satisfy a want or need".

Products include more than just tangible goods. Broadly defined, products include physical objects, services, persons, places, organisations, ideas or mixes of these entities. In marketing terms there are three different levels to a product:

1. **Core product** This is the essential part of the product – the core benefits that consumers are really buying. The core product of a car is an independent means of transport.
2. **Actual product** This includes the brand name, the quality of the product, its features and other attributes that combine to deliver core product benefits, for example, a Renault Laguna or Volvo V70.
3. **Augmented product** Additional consumer services and benefits that come as part of the overall package of the core product and augmented product. When we buy a car, it will come with a warranty, after-sales support, there may be credit provision, etc. These will differ from one manufacturer to another.

In terms of new product development, it is often a moot point as to whether it is a 'new' product or a modification of an existing one. When a new car model comes out, it is generally a modification of an existing model (described in motoring terms as 'evolutionary'). In other cases, the product on offer simply did not exist before, as when MP3 players first appeared on the market. Sometimes the core product remains the same but the actual product is quite different. For example, as a core product, a flat screen television is still a television, but the quality of picture is far superior and the technology involved is quite different from the technology in older cathode-ray tube televisions.

A distinction needs to be drawn between a **product innovation**, which is a change made to an existing product, and a **process innovation,** which is a change made to the way that the product is manufactured or distributed.

Hayes and Wheelwright (1979) suggest that in the early stages of industry development, product innovation is very important as firms try to create technological advantage. Over time, this becomes less important and the emphasis switches to process innovation. Here the emphasis is on streamlining the operation and, in particular, reducing costs.

In the banking industry, when interest-only mortgages were first introduced, they represented a product innovation. Prior to that, mortgage holders were required to pay back interest *and* capital each month. It allowed people to borrow much more than they previously would have been able to do on the basis that, after a few years, their salary would have risen and they would then be able to switch to an annuity mortgage. Internet banking when it was brought in represented a change in the process by which banks interacted with their customers. It was a process change designed to reduce costs as Internet banking costs are a mere fraction of the cost of operating a high street branch.

Product Line and Product Mix

It is important to look at new product development in the context of the overall products sold by a company. In broad terms, products can be directed at industrial (business-to-business) markets or consumer markets. There are a number of marketing terms used to distinguish the different aspects of product offerings.

Definition According to Dibb *et al.* (2006: 302) a **product item** is a specific version of a product that can be designated as a distinct offering among a business's products, for example, a particular type of biscuit such as a cream cracker.

Definition A **product line** is a group of closely-related product items that are considered a unit because of marketing, technical or end-use considerations. This would include all the different types of biscuits manufactured by the company.

Definition A **product mix** is the total group of products that a company manufactures for its customers.

The **width** of a product mix is the number of different product lines that it offers, while the **depth** means the number of different products offered in each product line. Procter & Gamble are a large multinational consumer company whose product-mix width includes laundry detergents, toothpastes, soaps, deodorants, shampoos and tissues. If we take one of those product lines, say shampoos, the depth includes five different brands, among them Head and Shoulders, Pantene, Vidal Sassoon, Pert Plus and Ivory.

Making decisions about the type of products, product lines and product widths are very important choices for the company in terms of building up a market profile and the revenues that will follow from the sales. On the other hand, it also has to consider the costs involved, as well as the resources needed to manage those brands.

Research and Development

Product development requires considerable investment in research and development (R&D). This investment takes two forms. First is the investment required in the actual R&D facilities and, with larger multinationals operating in Ireland, this can amount to tens of millions of Euro in building and equipment costs. Secondly, there is the cost of the R&D activity itself.

In July 2008 EMC, the US data storage company, announced that it was spending €20 million in research and development activity in its Cork plant. This money will be spread over a five-year period and will involve the creation of 50 new engineering positions in the company. In February 2009, the US company Intel, announced that it was creating 134 jobs in R&D in its Shannon plant developing "the most advanced silicon technology on the planet". This represents a €50 million investment in the development of Intel's nanotechnology capability, and puts the company at the leading edge in terms of nanotechnology development (Deegan, 2009). In 2008, 43% of all new projects negotiated by IDA Ireland were R&D investments, valued at €420 million (Hunt, 2010: 54).

In general, any new R&D jobs created are for graduates, often requiring people with PhDs. This is obviously good for the economy as they are high-end jobs. In turn, it requires a high level of investment by the government in third-level facilities to produce the required number of suitably qualified graduates.

The cost of R&D will vary from one industry to another. In the pharmaceutical industry, it can take around €1 billion to bring a drug from concept stage to where it can be sold to the public in pharmacies. For other industries it may not be so expensive. Either way, it still requires specific funding that may not show an adequate return on investment and so there is an inevitable level of risk involved in the process. For decades, Eastman Kodak had a strong lead in traditional cameras, but did not invest heavily enough in digital photography. As a result, they lost out in the digital age to companies like Sony and Canon.

Illustration 9.1: Investment in Broadband

Ireland lags behind most of Europe in terms of broadband speed for both mobile and fixed line connections. With an increased emphasis on mobile telephony, mobile phone companies are investing huge sums of money to develop the network. It is estimated that broadband (3G) speeds could reach 84 megabits per second (Mbs) within a couple of years. In 2011, connection speeds of 2 Mbs to 4 Mbs are what most users could expect in reality.

Mobile telephony companies are currently upgrading the system to prepare for the rollout of the next generation, 4G long-term evolution (LTE), which could deliver speeds of up to 100 Mbs. Vodafone has spent €800 million on their network over the last 10 years. Such investment is necessary to develop the network and conduct trials that will eventually deliver those speeds. In turn, this has pushed fixed-line operators to increase their speeds in order to compete.

One of the limiting factors in developing faster speeds is the limitation of the broadbrand spectrum. High-speed data requires greater capacity networks. By 2011, half of new phone sales were for smartphones. To enable greater use of smartphones, the Commissioner for Communications Regulations (ComReg) will auction new spectrum bands to the operators. It is expected that this will raise €250 million for the Irish exchequer. For their part, the operators want the cost kept to a minimum and argue that it leaves less money for reinvesting in new product development, given the huge capital costs involved in developing networks (Wrecker, 2011).

It is somewhat ironic, however, that despite the investment by Vodafone in 3G connectivity, the strength of the 3G signal is quite poor in many areas. The lack of signal strength is such that Vodafone are advertising "Vodafone Sure Signal" – a device for ensuring a strong signal in the home or office, and which is for indoor use only, similar to a land line. The whole point of a mobile phone is its mobility. In other words, it will make and receive calls on the go. A system that fails to achieve that represents poor value for money for the customer and will require much greater investment by Vodafone.

The risk involved in new product development can be quite substantial as it is estimated that the majority of new products fail. It is difficult to measure precisely the level of new product failure, but according to Dibb *et al.* (2006: 307), it could be between 60% and 90% depending on the nature of the industry. However, companies must persist. Tom Watson, the founder of IBM once said: "Success is on the far side of failure." The reasons for this high level of failure are many. Perhaps the main one is the company's failure to match the product offering to customers' need. Other reasons include ineffective branding, technical or design problems, poor timing, over-estimation of market size, ineffective promotion, and distribution.

Failure to meet customers' needs raises a fundamental question for the company. What factors are driving the development of new products? There are different levels of new product failure. Some products can be outright failures where the company loses considerable money on a product that just never takes off with consumers. Other products may make a small profit, but fall well short of the financial and market share objectives that have been set for it. While the product may be making a profit, it must be remembered that there is an opportunity cost in terms of resources and management time for the company in continuing with production.

In some companies, researchers are given large amounts of money to pursue development in certain areas. Over a period of time, knowledge and expertise in the area is built up and eventually a new product is developed. This product is then launched onto the market. There are occasions where these products can be very successful, even though a prior need was not identified.

Post-it® notes are a simple example. These were developed by the US company 3M as a result of a fault in the production of a batch of glue for binding books. An internal memo was sent around describing the characteristics of the glue (particularly that it did not stick very well and could be peeled off without leaving any residue) and inviting suggestions as to what could be done with it. The result was a new product that has been a huge commercial success. In general, however, with such a high rate of failure in new product development being due to those products not meeting consumer needs, clearly a 'push' strategy is generally not the best approach.

Ohmae (1982) believes that customer-based strategies are at the heart of all strategy. He refers to the 'strategic triangle' consisting of the company, its customers and competition. Responding to customer needs is clearly an integral element of research and development. This means listening to customers, directly and indirectly. Sales personnel are coming into daily contact with customers and obtain feedback about the adequacy of current products and services and, in particular, what requirements are not currently being met. Feargal Quinn, former president of the supermarket chain Superquinn has always had a policy of spending as much time as possible on the shop floor, talking to customers to get their views. Companies can also receive information on customer requirements indirectly through market research. In relative terms, the costs involved in market research are little (when compared to the cost of product failure) and could mean the difference between success and failure. Having an understanding of customer needs is one thing; fulfilling those needs is another. Research should therefore be directed to those areas where there is a clearly identified need.

According to Tansey (2008), innovation is market-led, not science-based. The traditional view was that science caused innovation by increasing the flow of new knowledge. A 2005 report by Forfás entitled "Making Technological Knowledge Work" challenged this view. It believes that innovation can be stimulated in two ways. First, competition must be strengthened and the domestic market liberalised as this competitive pressure will force firms to innovate. Secondly, the absorptive capacity of enterprises must be improved so that they can utilise, in a creative manner, the existing stock of knowledge. This requires a more extensive investment in education as innovation requires better educated managers and workers.

The section dealing with organisational structures above included a discussion on project teams. Cross-functional project teams are an important part of new product development as it is imperative that the different functional areas of the company have an input right throughout the process, from the very beginning right through to when the product is launched. Such an approach will greatly increase the chances of the product being commercially successful. According to Dibb *et al.* (2006: 348), there are seven phases of new product development including:

- **Idea generation** – the process by which businesses seek product ideas that will help them achieve their objectives.
- **Screening ideas** – assessing which product ideas match organisational objectives and resources.
- **Concept testing** – seeking potential buyers' responses to a product idea.
- **Business analysis** – evaluating the idea to determine the likely commercial benefit to the company in terms of sales and contribution to profits.
- **Product development** – examining the feasibility of the company actually making the product.
- **Test marketing** – a limited introduction of the product in specific regions picked to represent the overall market. The purpose of test marketing is to confirm that there is an actual demand for the product and to ascertain whether any modifications need to be made before full-scale production.
- **Commercialisation** – making the final changes prior to production.

Very often companies are formed as a result of an entrepreneur coming up with an idea for a new product. The big challenge then for such people is to ensure that it is not just a once-off product and that other product ideas will follow. Trying to obtain funding to establish a company to develop products can be particularly difficult as banks are often reluctant to lend money to people who do not have a proven record in business. The gap is often filled by venture capitalists who will lend money to the entrepreneur. This is usually done by taking a stake in the new company with an exit mechanism in place to realise their investment.

The primary focus here is on existing organisations that need a constant stream of products to satisfy consumer demand. Different companies will have different policies for new product development. Some will have dedicated R&D departments whose remit will be to come up with a succession of products. In other cases, organisations may allow employees follow up on ideas that they have in their spare time and provide them with the facilities and funding they require.

This policy of allowing independent development to take place within the organisation is known as **intrapreneurship**. In situations where the product proves successful, the person behind the idea would generally share in the revenues that accrue to the company. It generally requires a champion for it to succeed. A champion is a senior executive in the organisation who personally backs the project in terms of mentoring and providing the resources required by the intrapreneur, as well as facilitating the process through the bureaucracy of the organisation. In some situations, if the product development is different to the existing range, the organisation may establish a new spin-off company to exploit the concept. This might be for various reasons, such as a requirement for different plant and equipment, or because it requires the support of a different culture to that of the parent organisation. Whatever forum is used for new product development, it requires a policy by the organisation that is actively promoting new ideas and encouraging independent thinking.

Product Life Cycle

Every product goes through a life cycle, consisting of four phases (see **Figure 9.2**). First is the **Introduction** when the product is introduced to the market. The company will be making a loss on the product at this point as all of the development costs will have been incurred, but sales are only beginning. The **Growth** stage comes next when sales begin to rise rapidly. It requires aggressive advertising to help promote sales. The pace of diffusion will vary greatly depending on the industry and product type as well as a wide range of consumer factors. Nichols and Roslow (1986) refer to the 'tipping point' when there is a rapid increase in sales. The next stage is **Maturity,** when the sales curve peaks and starts to decline. Competition is extremely strong at this stage. The final stage is **Decline** when sales fall rapidly. Promotion is generally kept to a minimum and the company has to make decisions on the withdrawal of the product from the market – either an immediate or a phased withdrawal.

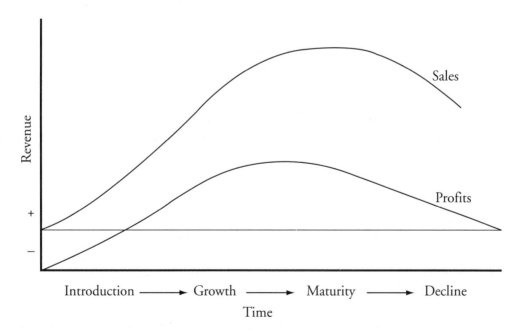

Figure 9.2 *Product Life Cycle*

In **Figure 9.2** it will be seen that the Sales line begins at zero on the Revenue line (there cannot be minus sales) and the Profit line begins below zero indicating start-up losses. Each stage of the product life cycle will require different strategies by the organisation. Identifying each stage of the product life cycle can be difficult, as it is quite subjective. A fall in sales may be just a temporary blip or the beginning of the decline of the product. Johnson *et al.* (2011: 303) suggest that the rate of diffusion (take-up of the product) depends on supply-side factors such as the level of improvement in the product, its compatibility with other factors, and its complexity. There are also demand-side factors, including consumer awareness and consumers' perception of the benefits arising from the product.

Promotion plays an essential part in product adoption by consumers. The nature of the promotion will differ greatly depending on the type of product, but the underlying principle of promotion is essential, regardless of product category. There is a five-stage product adoption process that includes awareness of the existence of the product, interest in it, evaluation, trial and adoption. In promoting the product, the company will first of all bring to the attention of the market that the product exists and in order to generate a need in consumers' minds for the product category. Once there is that need, advertising will try to create a favourable attitude towards the company's brand and then encourage consumers to make the actual purchase decision. If they are happy with the product, they will hopefully buy it again and again, thus building up brand loyalty.

For a product to be a commercial success, there has to be a large take-up in the target market. This can be a gradual process as not everybody will buy new products at the same rate. Dibb *et al.* (2006: 519) describe consumers according to five product adoption categories. The figures in brackets represent a typical breakdown of a market:

- Innovators (2.5%) – the first to adopt a new product.
- Early adopters (13.5%) – they chose new products carefully and are seen as 'the people to check with' by others.
- Early majority (34%) – they buy just before the average person.
- Late majority (34%) – somewhat sceptical about buying and do so out of social pressure.
- Laggards (16%) – these are suspicious of new products, and when they get around to eventually buying them, newer products are coming out.

First Mover Advantage

Sony and Walkman will forever be associated together. While many companies manufactured similar music devices, Sony was the first to the market with their product and the term Walkman is a registered trade mark of Sony Corporation. Being the first to the market has many benefits, known as **'first mover advantage'**. At this stage, there are probably no other suppliers, so the company is the only company meeting consumer demand, generating strong brand recognition and loyalty.

Brand loyalty can confer huge benefits in terms of repeat sales and in referral for new customers. The ultimate in brand recognition is when the brand name becomes a generic term in the industry, such as with Walkman, or Biro (made by the French company Bic) for ball point pens. In addition, the first mover may also have patent protection, slowing down the entry of rivals into the market. Sony invented the Walkman in 1979 and the market for the personal stereos grew rapidly, selling 40 million units in 10 years. While numerous rival companies manufactured similar stereo devices, 10 years later Sony still managed to hold on to 48% market share due to its strong brand reputation (Suarez and Lanzolla, 2005: 125). The Walkman brand continues in the MP3 market.

First maker advantage means the company can also gain considerable experience (the concept of the experience curve has already been discussed) and, when rivals do enter the market, the company will have a strong lead over them in this respect. They can use the experience to modify and improve the quality of the product, as well as build up greater knowledge of the nature of consumer demand for the product. An early lead in sales volume can allow the company to reap economies of scale, and allow them to use the financial gain to either improve quality or reduce price or both. This will further differentiate the first mover from later rivals.

However, as Suarez and Lanzolla (2005) point out, first-mover advantage is more than a myth, but also far less than a sure thing. For every success story, there is an equal number of examples of first movers who lost out to later followers. For many years, Xerox, a company with a strong brand name and resources, enjoyed first mover advantage in photocopying. In fact, their name had become a generic term and turned the brand name into a verb: to Xerox a page meant to photocopy it. However, they failed to hold on to the first mover benefits with latecomers like Canon taking away their market share.

Building a first-mover advantage depends on whether a company can build a durable or a short-lived advantage. With slow moving markets and technologies, a durable advantage is more likely. Industry dynamics are also crucial. Where the technologies involved are changing rapidly, first movers are unlikely to enjoy lasting benefits. Sometimes those coming afterwards have the advantage. They are able to evaluate what worked well for the pioneers and, just as importantly, what did not work. They can learn from other people's mistakes. They can also benefit from learning about the processes involved in the manufacturing process. Patents often give just limited protection and there are many countries around the world that do not respect patent rights.

While first mover advantage often confers great benefits on the company in question, it does not always follow that such benefits will accrue. The question then is does the company try to be a first mover, or follow up behind? And a much more important question is the level of new product development that the company engages in. The industry that the company is operating in will have some bearing on the issue, as some industries change faster than others. While the pace may vary, the development of new products has to be an integral part of every company's continuing existence.

Brand Management

Definition According to Kotler *et al.* (2009:245), a **brand** is "a name that is given to a particular product or service, or range of products or services".

In developing new products, it is very important that the company protects those products by branding them. Branding helps buyers by enabling them to identify and evaluate products, and it facilitates repeat purchases. The ultimate aim of a company is to try and engender brand loyalty among its customers, so that they will buy only from that company. Promotion, be it in the form of advertising, public relations, publicity and other marketing devices, plays a very important part in building up brand recognition and loyalty. Brand names can be legally protected by registering those brands through patent and trademark offices.

Companies can choose different options when branding their products. Some opt for what is termed family branding, where all of the company's products include the name of the company, for example, Campbell's Soups. With Campbell's, the labels are similar, differing only in describing the type of soup such as mushroom or tomato, but they all have the name Campbell's prominently displayed. This approach facilitates adding new brands to the line-up as consumers will instantly associate the new product with the company. Branding applies to companies as well as to products. The Virgin Group applies the brand name 'Virgin' to all its companies.

Other companies such as Procter & Gamble (see section on product mix above) use different brand names for each product, and there is no visible association with the company on the product label. It does not confer the advantage of existing brand recognition when launching a new brand. However, if the new product is a failure, it will not damage the existing brands.

Brands (and products) have to be actively managed. The company has to take an overview of all of its products and make decisions about the allocation of resources. There are a number of tools available to enable managers to manage the company's product and brands, such as the Boston Consulting Group Matrix (see Chapter 10) and others. These strategic tools will be looked at later on in the context of managing SBUs and companies.

MARKET DEVELOPMENT

From a business perspective, Ireland is a very small market and for many Irish companies development inevitably means looking overseas in order to grow the market for their goods or services. In a globalised world, this is increasingly becoming the norm. The main theme of this section will deal with developing international markets. In addition to developing international markets, Johnson *et al.* (2008: 261) identified two other forms of market development that are important and must also be examined. These are new segments and new uses.

New Segments

In any market, there will be only certain groups of people who are interested in a company's products. This is because the needs and wants of people will vary considerably and their purchasing habits will reflect that. Segmentation of the market is a central part of what companies do to identify the different groups and exploit market opportunities. It allows for better planning and a much more effective use of resources, and hence profitability. Those segments that the company is able to satisfy with its products and services are prioritised and targeted. The company will then develop a marketing mix that will suit the targeted segment(s). The marketing mix is the combination of: the product, how it is promoted, its price, how and where it is distributed and the people providing the service that goes with it.

Targeting can involve a concentration strategy where the company directs its efforts towards a single market segment by using a single marketing mix or a differentiated targeting strategy where it develops different marketing mixes for different segments. In both cases, the company needs to have the strategic capability to satisfy those needs. Once the company has decided which segments of the market to target, it must then position the product or service to create a clearly defined image in the minds of its chosen customers. This is particularly evident in the fashion industry, where companies are not just selling clothing; they are selling a whole lifestyle image.

A product will be developed for a specific market segment or segments and may satisfy those segments very well. As time passes, the company may identify other segments of the market to which they could also sell. Satellite navigation systems have now become very popular with motorists. The technology for these devices was initially developed for the US forces in the first Gulf War in 1991. Navigation is a very important military skill. To determine one's current position involves taking back-bearings from a few clearly identifiable points, and from the back-bearings doing a triangulation to determine one's location. Commanders and their troops must be able to navigate to seize the ground objectives that they have been entrusted with taking. Once they have their current position and know their target, they can then follow an axis of advance along that bearing. The problem with deserts is that very often there are no clearly defined reference points. One sand dune looks like the next, and these dunes are constantly shifting in strong winds. Global positioning system (GPS) technology was developed using satellites to determine one's position. Having been developed for military use, it was subsequently adapted for civilian use for hill walkers and boating enthusiasts, and then for motorists. It is essentially the same technology, but it is now being targeted at a much wider range of segments.

Another example is the drink Lucozade®. When Lucozade was first developed it was aimed at people convalescing in hospital. It is a glucose-based drink and glucose is the most basic form of energy used by the body. It does not require any breakdown by the body and because it is isotonic it can be absorbed straight through the stomach wall into the blood stream. The company repositioned the product and it is now seen as an energy replacement for people leading active, sporting lives (the opposite segment for which it was originally designed!). While the company added some extra flavours such as orange, the product is still a basic glucose drink. The brand was extremely successful and now sells to a much larger segment of the market, in addition to the original segment.

New Uses

New products are normally developed with a specific use in mind. Again, with the passage of time, new uses for products can appear that were not there when the product was first developed. There are some similarities between 'new uses' and new segments. Throughout the 1980s, silicon chip makers and consumer electronics companies put much effort into reducing the size of electrical appliances. This involved both improving existing technology but, more importantly, developing new technology. This technology was then taken and modified and used to create totally different products such as mobile phones and MP3 players. Such devices would not have been possible without the process of miniaturisation, but that was not the original intended purpose.

Stainless steel is another example. Stainless steel was first used to manufacture mass-produced cutlery, and for years was synonymous with Sheffield in England. It was later used for beer kegs. While wood is necessary for the maturation of spirits such as brandy, there is no need to mature beer. The manufacture of wooden barrels is a skilled trade for coopers, and so wooden beer kegs were expensive to produce and very brittle. Steel kegs are extremely robust and last for years. Stainless steel is also used in the automotive and the aeronautical industries. Such industries (and uses) were not envisaged when the product was first developed, but have greatly increased the size of the market for the product. Finally, researchers at General Electric adapted technology for aircraft engine fan blades into the blades used by wind turbines (of which GE is one of the world's leading manufacturers).

International Markets

In the middle of a severe downturn, many companies will retrench and focus on home markets. While this may be necessary, the company should be certain that growth opportunities do not exist elsewhere. In terms of market growth for Irish companies, by far the most important way of growing markets is to look at international markets for opportunities. International expansion is a form of diversification, and this will be developed in detail in Chapter 10. The strategic tools used in carrying out environmental analysis and understanding strategic capability are an important foundation for identifying possibilities for future expansion. Ultimately, international expansion should exploit environmental opportunities.

Chapter 5, in discussing the European Union, highlighted the opportunities available to Irish companies in terms of the sheer size of the market that is available without any restrictions such as tariffs or barriers, or import quotas. In the earlier years of EU membership, Ireland saw many of its indigenous industries close, as they could not compete with more competitive European companies. Over the last couple of decades, Irish companies gradually, but consistently, improved to a point where the quality of its products and the productivity of its workers could match the best. Clearly, exposure to the international arena of the European Union has been very beneficial to Ireland, apart from benefits such as the structural funds.

Now Irish companies are competing very successfully on international markets and, once the home market is saturated, this allows Irish firms to gain access to potentially much larger markets. Opportunities are not just restricted to the EU. In recent years, many Irish companies have established a strong presence in China, which has a population of 1.3 billion people. According to Ghemawat (2010), China accounted for 66% of global growth in GDP in 2009, and India for

11%, and emerging markets are likely to increase in importance quite substantially in the future. Apart from increasing the size of the market, operating in international markets can play a large part in reducing risk, as the company is no longer dependent on one particular market if there is a down-turn. It can also increase the life cycle of a product that may be reaching decline in the home market but could still be in the growth or maturity phase in a less developed country. As the development costs of the product will have been well recouped, it can offer great possibilities as a 'cash cow' (a product generating large profits — see Chapter 10). Cultural intelligence (Early and Mosakowaski, 2004) was discussed in Chapter 2 in the context of leadership. In developing foreign markets, cultural intelligence is vitally important in terms of forging relationships with potential buyers.

International Drivers

Yip (2003) refers to various factors that are driving internationalisation. While these will vary from one industry to another, they provide a useful insight into the nature of how international factors are impacting on Irish companies, and how they need to respond.

The Irish economy is a very open one (it exports and imports a very high percentage of its GDP), and even in terms of protecting market share of the home economy, Irish companies must be able to compete with the best international businesses. The section on 'Porter's Diamond' in Chapter 5 highlighted the importance of competition in developing the strategic capability of a firm. Irish companies have made enormous improvements in this respect in the last couple of decades. From that perspective, Irish companies can be confident that they can compete in the international arena. The World Trade Talks are also aimed at reducing restrictions on international trade and increasing greater interdependence between countries. Technical specifications are becoming increasingly standardised and this also facilitates greater trade.

Satellite television and the Internet have played an important role in opening up Western culture to other parts of the world, and the reverse is also true. This has contributed enormously to what can be termed a mass homogenisation of global demand for products, ranging from consumer goods to clothing to music. Electronic goods come with instruction booklets printed in perhaps 20 different languages, reflecting the fact that the same item is sold in Tokyo and in Dublin.

Driving down costs is an essential element of running any organisation. The value chain and system is increasingly becoming globalised as firms strive to find the lowest costs, wherever they may be in the world. International expansion can help an organisation to lower costs by selecting the optimum location for every part of their value chain. By selling to a global market (with its size implications), it provides enormous possibilities for achieving economies of scale in manufacturing. This is critical in the pharmaceutical industry where development costs are so high that it is essential for each company to achieve global sales. There are also economies of scale in marketing. Large international hotel chains such as the Marriott Group, which has a few thousand hotels around the globe, can reap huge economies in marketing, as well as other areas such as purchasing.

Competitive Advantage

One main objective in operating on an international basis is to develop a competitive advantage. Porter's Diamond looked at how some countries can be more competitive than others and some industries within those countries. These are important factors in deciding competitive advantage. Many Irish software companies have located in Silicon Valley to be at the cutting edge of developments in the industry. This allows companies access to technology and know-how that they otherwise may not have, and leverages the core competences that they have developed. As a result, once Irish companies can compete there, it means that they have developed a level of expertise and competences that can allow them to compete successfully anywhere in the world.

While most of the pharmaceutical companies in Ireland are foreign-owned multinationals, the development of clusters has resulted in a competitive advantage, and it is Ireland's most important industry in terms of the value of exports. As with the software industry, this in turn has led to the development of many related and supporting domestic industries. Horse breeding is very much an indigenous industry in which Ireland is regarded as a global leader. The industry is responsible for considerable employment and supports many other businesses indirectly.

The discussion on the value system can also be widened to look for international benefits in locating elements of the value chain that will yield greatest advantage. Many Irish companies are out-sourcing part of their value chain to lower cost economies, particularly to avail of cheaper labour. Improvements in information technology are greatly facilitating this process. Differences in labour costs, taxation, energy costs, productivity rates, inflation and the environment for doing business are all factors that will create large variations from one country to another. While labour costs are high in Ireland by international standards, other factors such as the low rate of corporation tax, and a highly-educated and productive workforce place this country in an advantageous position compared to developing foreign markets. As with the example of EMC (see the section on Product Development above), many foreign companies are locating R&D facilities in this country because of the above-mentioned factors. The presence of foreign multinationals operating here has had a highly beneficial impact on Irish companies, which in turn has brought them to a level where they can operate successfully in the international arena.

Selecting Markets

Notwithstanding the discussion on the drivers of globalisation, there remain many differences between various markets. Cultures and lifestyles still reflect national variations and, while they may have been eroded somewhat, they still exist. One major difference between markets is their purchasing power, so even if the desire for certain goods exists, the purchasing power may not match that desire. Markets have to be prioritised in terms of their attractiveness. Johnson *et al.* (2008: 307) differentiate between market characteristics and competitive characteristics.

Market characteristics The market characteristics (using the PESTEL framework) take into account the relative attractiveness of each particular market. From a political perspective, various countries will have very different business environments that may or may not be attractive for a company doing business there. This environment can also change significantly with a change in government. While the overall size of a market is important, economic factors will vary a great deal. As stated, there must be sufficient purchasing power available in a particular market, otherwise it will be of no benefit. (For example, though the people of a certain country may have a passion for horseracing, it does not follow that they can afford to buy Irish racehorses, and so there will be no market.) Economic indicators such as GNP/GDP, inflation rates, interest rates, and currency rates will give a good indication of the attractiveness of a country. Social factors, including favourable demographic segments, suitably qualified workers and cultural factors are important. Finally, the legal situation is important from the perspective of protecting and enforcing commercial contracts and intellectual property.

Ghemawat (2001) has stated that these factors are important, not just in terms of comparing one country with another to prioritise them, but also the compatibility in terms of culture and language between the country and the company that is considering operating there. If we examine this from the perspective of American companies such as Intel operating in Ireland, there is a very strong compatibility in language, culture, work ethic, education, etc.

Cultural variations can be important factors to consider from a number of perspectives. In dealing with people, either customers or employees, one must be conscious of major differences in things such as body language, how people greet one another, the use and meaning of different colours and the significance of numbers, as well as shapes and symbols. These are particularly relevant in the use of advertising. In addition to being aware of cultural variations, companies must make a conscious effort to bridge any cultural divide, while respecting the differences.

Competitive factors The factors affecting competition are also just as important for foreign markets as they are for the domestic market. Porter's Five Forces analysis can be used to determine the existence of competitive forces and their intensity. If the level of competition in a country is deemed to be very high in your industry, then that particular market would be an unattractive location for you to establish a presence in. Johnson *et al.* (2011: 280) suggest that one must examine the likelihood of retaliation from other competitors in that market, along with their power to fight back. This is usually related to their share of the market. The likelihood of retaliation and their power in the market can significantly modify the attractiveness of choosing a particular country to enter. This analysis can also be used to determine the benefits of expansion in an existing foreign market.

Emerging markets and the BRIC countries (Brazil, Russia, India and China) have a growing middle class population with high disposable income and offer enormous opportunities for expansion by Irish companies. Part of the remit of Enterprise Ireland is to help Irish companies expand abroad. They can provide significant assistance by way of country-specific market information as well as supporting companies in the process.

Risks

There are, however, certain risks that are part of international operations which need to be taken into consideration. Dess *et al.* (2004) suggest that there are four risks:

Political risk – forces such as conflict and military action, terrorism, social unrest, etc., make some countries across the globe unattractive as locations in which to become involved. There have been numerous kidnappings of western workers in Iraq, and companies would have to bear this in mind when considering locating there. Host countries may impose restrictions on the amount of trade that can take place or impose tariffs to protect home companies from competition. Other restrictions may require foreign companies to operate as part of a joint venture, or there may be stringent bureaucratic requirements.

Economic risk – when the political situation is unstable it also increases the economic risk to a company. Destruction of property, non-payment of debts or loss of revenue through piracy of intellectual property can result in significant financial loss.

Currency risks – currency fluctuations can pose serious risks to a company. In recent years, there has been a substantial devaluation in the US dollar vis-à-vis the Euro. This means that Irish goods are a lot more expensive in the US compared to American ones, and profits of Irish companies operating in the US that are being repatriated to Ireland have lost much of their value.

Management risk – the cultural variation (discussed above) adds to the complexity of managing an international workforce, and other factors such as distribution systems, customer preferences, etc., can all make the process of managing a company more difficult.

These risks will vary with the level of involvement in a particular foreign country. If the firm is just exporting, the risk will be relatively low and confined primarily to currency devaluation or non-payment for a consignment. The company can then make a decision to withdraw from operating in that country. At the other end of the scale, a wholly-owned facility will expose the company to considerable risk.

STRATEGIES FOR ENTERING FOREIGN MARKETS

In Chapter 7, we were introduced to organisational structure. It must be remembered that the structure of an organisation should support the strategy it is pursuing. The structure will therefore have to change, depending on the nature of its geographical operations, probably to some form of multi-divisional, transnational, or matrix structure. The structure will reflect the level of involvement in international markets. There are many choices available and each one requires a different level of organisational resources:

- Exporting
- Licensing and franchising

- Strategic alliances and joint venture
- Foreign direct investment (wholly-owned subsidiary)

Some of these methods are also used by companies operating solely in the home market. For that reason, they will be examined in greater detail in the next chapter. They will be addressed briefly here in the context of entering foreign markets.

Exporting

Exporting involves manufacturing goods in one country and selling them in another. Exporting is the most flexible form of international trade, involving the least amount of risk. Companies will normally begin the process of going international by exporting to a neighbouring country. For many years, Irish companies would have exported to the UK, particularly agricultural produce. This process would have been facilitated by a common language and geographical proximity.

In 2009, Irish companies supported by Enterprise Ireland had total exports of €12,903 million, a drop of €1,411 million from the previous year. The fall was as a result of the recession in Ireland as well as falling demand in target markets. The UK remains the biggest market for Enterprise Ireland client companies and to which the total figure of exports was €5,485 million. The rest of Western Europe accounted for €2,153 million and North America was worth €1,341 million in exports. The only region to show an increase in exports was the Asia/Pacific market, which was up 6%. In terms of indigenous Irish companies backed by Enterprise Ireland, the food sector remains by far the biggest industry in terms of exports with a total value of €7,020 million (Enterprise Ireland, 2010). Irish companies need to do much more to identify expansion opportunities in other markets, particularly in France, Belgium and The Netherlands, which from a logistical perspective are natural extensions of the UK market (Cooke, 2008). Enterprise Ireland offers advice and support for businesses considering exporting, as does the Irish Exporters Association.

According to the Irish Exporters Association, the total value of all goods and services exported from Ireland reached €161 billion in 2010 and, despite the recession, is expected to reach €172.6 billion in 2011, an increase of almost 8%. Such growth is dependent on the level of increase in world trade and, according to the OECD, it expects world trade to grow by 8.3% in 2011. The services industry is one of the most important in terms of overall growth and, despite the collapse of the domestic retail banking sector, the International Financial Services Centre (IFSC) in Dublin is a major contributor to the economy. In 2011, assets under management at the IFSC reached €2.5 trillion, an increase of 8% on the previous year (O'Halloran and Lynch, 2011).

In recent decades, the importance of the food and drink industry in Ireland has declined as other industries such as pharmaceuticals and computers have moved centre stage. Nevertheless, the food and drink industry remains an integral part of the Irish economy. In 2010, there was an 11% growth in the value of Irish food and drinks' exports. There is considerable confidence in the industry for further growth and, according to a Bord Bia survey, 70% of exporters rated their prospects for 2011 as either good or very good. In addition, 20% of food exporters increased full-time staff members in 2010 and another 61% maintained staff levels – both figures are at variance with the high number of redundancies announced by Irish companies in recent years. There were a number of factors behind the increase in food exports including reduced exchange rate pressures, improved relative competitiveness and also rising global prices for most agricultural commodities. European markets accounted for 34% of the industry's total exports of food and drink (MacConnell, 2011).

The Foreign Direct Investment (FDI) sector remains the most important element of Ireland's exports. Foreign-owned companies operating in Ireland account for over 70% of total exports and employ 240,000 people. US companies alone account for 600 companies and 100,000 jobs in our economy. Bilateral trade between the US and Ireland amounts to €27 billion. In total, some 55% of corporation tax paid in Ireland is paid by foreign companies. Ireland's low rate of corporation tax is under threat from Europe – Germany and France in particular. It is regarded by foreign companies operating in Ireland as very important in their decision as to where to make investments. Ireland is competing with countries such as Singapore and Switzerland where the effective rate is zero. We have a good record in attracting foreign manufacturing companies, although Craig Barrett, former Intel Chairman, believes that Ireland should be weaning itself off FDI and building its indigenous high-tech sector to drive the economy (McCall, 2010).

Exporting increases the market for a company's products, allowing them to reap economies of scale, without any major financial exposure. The Internet has greatly facilitated this process. As such, exporting is a relatively inexpensive way of entering the market, especially if a foreign wholesaler who has experience in distributing imports is used, although the exporter may choose to set up their own distribution network. Export agents bring together buyers and sellers from different countries, earning a commission for their work. Compared to other methods of entering foreign markets, it is very cheap. An export house and export merchants buy products from different companies and then sell them in other countries. Certain modifications may be needed for packaging and labelling in order to sell into other markets. Market research should be carried out to ascertain the level of demand and to see if there are any problems with regard to brand names, etc. Often, brand names do not have the same meaning in other languages and may have negative connotations. For that reason, sometimes companies make up brand names that have no inherent meaning as such, e.g. Kodak or Esso.

There are also some drawbacks in exporting. Manufacturing costs in the home country may be more expensive than the host country. This is often the case with Irish goods at present, as labour costs here have increased dramatically in recent years compared to other countries. In addition, the depreciation of the US Dollar and Sterling has made Irish exports more expensive in those countries. Fortunately, this does not apply in the Euro zone. Being an island nation, there are also higher transportation costs than, for example, French goods being sold in Germany. Because a company's exposure to the host country is limited, they do not benefit from any advantages that might accrue from being located there. In most cases, companies will begin to export after they have established a solid presence in the home market, but there are exceptions. Some companies might be very specialised in their nature and the home market might be too small. The Internet has also changed the nature of exporting and, for many companies, their goods can be sold right across the world just as in easily as in the home market.

Licensing and Franchising

There are occasions when a company may not have the resources or organisational capability to operate directly in another country and it may license a company in another state to manufacture the product and use its trademark in return for a royalty. It also has the advantage of minimising financial exposure as it does not involve committing resources. In some cases, it may be a government condition to operate in that market.

An example of a licensing arrangement operating in this country is Carlsberg beer. Guinness has been licensed by the Danish company to brew Carlsberg in Dublin and distribute it in Ireland. Beer is a heavy, bulk item to transport. In this case, it is cheaper for Carlsberg to accept a royalty fee from Guinness than export it from Denmark. One problem with licensing is in giving up a certain amount of control over the product and how it is distributed, and foregoing potential revenue and profit. Picking a suitable partner can be difficult.

Franchising is another form of contractual arrangement, whereby a supplier (franchisor) grants a dealer (franchisee) the right to sell products in exchange for some form of consideration. It is becoming a very popular form of international expansion. While licensing works well for manufacturing and proprietary technology, franchising is better suited for international expansion involving retail outlets or services. There are many examples in fast food such as McDonald's, Pizza Hut, Taco Bell and the Irish companies O'Brien's Sandwich Bars and Abrakebabra.

According to the Irish Franchise Association, there are around 300 franchise businesses in Ireland with a turnover of €2.1 billion and employing 25,000 people. Between 2006 and 2008, the sector grew by 64%.

Strategic Alliances and Joint Ventures

Joint ventures and strategic alliances involve sharing risk with a partner and have become increasingly popular as a way for companies to enter foreign markets. They differ in that strategic alliances comprise two companies working in co-operation with each other, while joint ventures involve setting up a new company that is jointly owned by the parent companies. By combining resources and expertise, companies can do better together than they could by operating on their own. In some cases, it is a requirement by the host government before granting permission to operate in that country. Together, they can develop new core competences that will allow them to compete.

Again, choosing partners that can work together is a vital part of the process. In the mid-1980s, Ballygowan went into partnership with Budweiser to distribute bottled water in the US, but the relationship came undone a few years later. Managing any alliance can be difficult, particularly when the other company is a foreign one.

Foreign Direct Investment

A company may decide to invest directly in a foreign market. This can be achieved by purchasing an existing company or establishing a greenfield site where it builds a manufacturing facility from scratch. It involves a good deal of risk, which, unlike a joint venture, is borne solely by the parent company. On the other hand, it allows full control of the facility and distribution network. Potentially, it also offers the highest level of return. Acquisition is quicker than developing a greenfield site, but it can create problems in regard to integrating separate corporate cultures. A greenfield site would allow the company to build a state-of-the-art facility, and this could give the company a competitive advantage.

In addition, and depending on the host country, there may be financial incentives available to attract such investment. (Companies like Intel received millions of Euro in grants from the IDA to attract them to Ireland.) Either option still involves a considerable financial outlay, so it is extremely important that the parent company has carried out sufficient research on the market beforehand.

STRATEGIES FOR OPERATING INTERNATIONALLY

Operating internationally raises issues as to whether the company should localise its products and services for each individual market, or whether they offer the same product around the world without any modification. There are three possible strategies, ranging from standardised products sold globally to products that are adapted for each individual market:

- Global strategy – standardised throughout the world
- Transnational strategy – a global strategy adapted for individual markets
- Multi-domestic strategy – a localised approach to each individual market.

These are part of a continuum rather than discrete strategies, and there is considerable overlap between them. The strategies highlight the different approaches required by companies depending on a whole variety of factors and conditions. This will be examined in greater detail below, having first looked at the three approaches.

Global Strategy

A global strategy involves treating the world as a single, large market. It is sometimes referred to as a 'think global, act global strategy'. It is based on the premise that demand for products throughout the world is similar and companies can achieve lower cost and reap large economies of scale by manufacturing standardised products (and quality) that can sell around the globe. While minor changes might sometimes be made, it is not appropriate if there is a requirement to make major changes to suit the local market.

It is a highly centralised strategy that is defined in the corporate headquarters and involves strong co-ordination between all units. It requires the same competitive approach and utilises the same capabilities across all markets. Global strategy is particularly relevant to industries that have large R&D costs such as the pharmaceutical and semiconductor industries. It is also relevant to the fashion industry. Gucci products are in demand around the globe and the same items are sold in Japan and the US. Likewise, it is the same demand for Rolex watches that entices buyers in Dublin and New Delhi. However, Ghemawat (2010) believes that in the last couple of years many changes have taken place in terms of the nature of global demand and that it makes sense to adopt a vision in which national differences remain pronounced. The primary challenge for organisations is how to manage those differences. It will require a fundamental shift in strategy to cater for regional varieties of offering in terms of taste, price sensitivity, and infrastructure for service and delivery.

Transnational Strategy

In reality, there are very few truly 'universal' products that can be sold unaltered around the world. Products such as commercial aircraft seem universal, but each airline will want different layout configurations and will have different specifications for on-board equipment. A transnational strategy takes the benefits of a global approach, but adapts it to the different markets in which it is operating. It is a 'think-global, act-local' approach. It is a trade-off between the scale efficiencies that can be gained from a global product and the benefits from increased sales due to local adaptation. In essence, it overcomes the limitations of global and multi-domestic strategies. Competition will differ in each country. It recognises the importance of being responsive to the needs of various markets, but only as a means of achieving greater global sales in the international arena. A certain amount of knowledge transfer can take place between various parts of the organisation around the world, but the peculiarities of the different markets can make this difficult to achieve in reality. The company will operate globally and establish its activities in the most beneficial locations for each. For example, manufacturing could be in a low-cost country, while R&D is located where there is a ready supply of suitable graduates.

A transnational strategy is much less centralised in terms of decision-making, which is pushed down as far as possible in the organisation. At the same time, it recognises that such decentralisation increases the complexity (and costs) of its operations. Not all aspects of decision-making are decentralised. Value chain activities can be divided up between those that are kept central, such as supply-chain activities and operations (as these will reap economies of scale), and other activities that can be devolved, such as marketing and customer service (these will help make the product more appealing to customers in each market).

Sometimes product modifications will be needed. Cars being sold in the UK and in Ireland require the steering column on the right-hand side, compared to the left in European and American markets. There is even a further difference in the right-handed version. In Ireland, the speedometer is in kilometres per hour, while in the UK it is in miles per hour. In most European countries washing machines are front-loaded, while in France they are traditionally top-loaded. These are relatively basic, but necessary modifications that are needed to succeed in each market. The clothing company Benetton has its operations configured to allow for maximum flexibility, while minimising costs, in catering for differing demands in each country.

Marketing will obviously differ in each market, taking into account language, culture, religious beliefs and social norms. Sometimes the advertising content needs to be adapted, as different markets will respond to different unique selling propositions (USPs).

A **Unique Selling Proposition** is the unique product benefit that the company promotes in a consistent manner in a target market.

In Belgium, a dishwasher is regarded as a labour-saving device to take care of the wash-up after dinner and, so, in advertising it there, its USP would reflect that. By contrast, in Switzerland, its USP is the hygienic nature of the machine leaving dishes and cutlery sterilised.

Multi-domestic Strategy

In some instances, there are considerable variations in tastes between different regions and, consequently, companies will need to respond with a range of products to reflect those needs. The company will tailor its competitive approach and product offerings to fit the specific conditions in each country in which it operates. It is a 'think-local, act-local' approach that produces goods locally for independent markets. There are many reasons for such localisation.

Demand for items and competition will differ in each market and businesses need to respond to that. As markets are in different stages of development, product life cycles can also vary. In developing, or less affluent markets, consumers often prefer purchasing smaller quantities rather than larger economy packs, which might be better value but cost considerably more. Sometimes, it might be a requirement of the host government, which may have strict specification requirements; or there may be tariffs or quotas to be circumvented by sourcing materials locally.

For clothing items, climatic conditions will vary considerably and this will be reflected in wide variations in demand. Generally, food items require considerable localisation as tastes differ according to ethnic background and culture. Other products such as car lubricants also require adaptation for local climate conditions, vehicle types and equipment applications. Castrol, for example, has an enormous number of different product variations to suit different local climatic conditions, variations in vehicle types and equipment uses. Services are different to tangible products and various economic, legal and social structures will mean that services will usually have to be tailored for each country in which they are being provided. This will diminish the ability to achieve global economies in service provision.

The company's regional managers will have considerable latitude in making decisions concerning what changes are required allowing for local tastes and preferences, as they are considered to know the market best. Co-ordination between the different parts of the company may be quite loose, given the varying conditions, and there is little opportunity for knowledge transfer as the competences required for each market can be different. A 'localisation' strategy will add considerable expense to the product, but is necessary if the company is to sell its products in that market. From that perspective, it is generally not suited to a low-cost strategy unless the company has the ability to customise products and still reap economies of scale. Finally, as consumer demand does become more globalised, the degree of customisation will change over time. In recent years, the Chinese market has become much more Western in its outlook, and demand is reflecting those changes.

Globalisation or Localisation

Various writers on strategy have their own views on the globalisation/localisation debate. An examination of the literature suggests that, in reality, while there are examples at either end of the continuum, the majority of international companies operate on the basis of having a global strategy that is adapted to a greater or lesser extent to the needs of the various locations in which they are operating.

Earlier in this chapter, we examined the international drivers that promote globalisation, common customer demand, competition, the need to minimise costs and moves by governments and international bodies (Yip, 2003). This move towards global demand is not a new phenomenon. Back in 1983, Levitt believed that a company could develop a sustainable competitive advantage by operating globally because of a similar demand worldwide and the efficient use of resources. Likewise, Ohmae (1989a) suggested that "most managers are near-sighted" and they should be looking at home and overseas markets as "equidistant". He suggests that, through the flow of information, people have become global citizens that demand universal products. However, while the product is universal, it often requires approaching each market differently and building a complete local infrastructure to create local demand. Profits too will differ from one market to another, and companies need to adjust their expectations. Ohmae (1989b) also suggests that the best way to achieve globalisation for most companies is to form strategic alliances. Fixed costs in many industries have grown so large that it is better to share the burden by collaborating with other companies and, through such collaboration, increase global sales.

Ghemawat (2003) believes that the world is not so homogenous. He believes that there are opportunities to be gained by exploiting differences and that there are "many forms of arbitrage that offer sustainable sources of competitive advantage". These include cultural, administrative, geographic and economic arbitrage.

Rigby and Vishwanath (2006) suggest that, in the past, consumer markets were dominated by companies that pursued strategies of standardisation. This is no longer the case and success for retailers and product manufacturers now rests on their ability to adapt for local preferences while maintaining economies of scale: "Combining sophisticated data analysis with innovative organisational structures, they're gaining the efficiencies of centralised management without losing the responsiveness of local authority." They believe that standardisation undermines innovation throughout the supply chain. Technological advances now provide both retailers and suppliers with considerable information about consumers' buying habits and preferences, and this facilitates the process of localising stores, products and services with precision.

It is important to get the balance right. Too much localisation can dilute the brand and lead to escalating costs. Too much standardisation can diminish market share and profitability. It is vital that managers understand the business in terms of the cost involved in localising and what impact it will have on sales. Store-by-store customisation is very expensive.

They suggest that one way around the problem is to use clustering techniques. Companies analyse data to identify communities or clusters that display similar buying habits, and products are then customised on the basis of clusters. This simplifies the process and the company still benefits from economies of scale, reducing costs considerably. The company collects as much data as possible on key elements of each store's business over a period of time. From this data, they then identify perhaps three to five different cluster types for customisation opportunities. VF, the apparel maker that owns brands such as Lee, Wrangler and North Face, combines "demographic and lifestyle data with daily store-level sales data, extensive consumer research and competitor analysis to develop localisation strategies". As a result, they have reported an improvement in sales by up to 50% while reducing store inventories and markdowns. Tesco gains an enormous volume of data from its loyalty cards, and using that knowledge has built five specialised food formats in the UK, clustered to meet local demand.

Rigby and Vishwanath (2006) believe that too much decentralisation can backfire as local managers lack the level of skill and data to make the right decisions on a constant basis. It also makes the process too complicated and costly. Most decisions need to be co-ordinated centrally by managers who have a good overview of the entire business and demand patterns. Central co-ordination is also essential in developing relationships between suppliers and retailers. Store managers play an important part in information gathering about local events and market conditions. By having most of the merchandising decisions made by headquarters, it frees up store managers to concentrate on running the daily operations and engaging with customers.

Finally, Rosabeth Moss Kanter (2003) looks at the effect that globalisation has on communities. She believes that companies can meet global standards and tap into local networks. It is a symbiotic relationship that develops the local communities in which global companies are based, and these communities provide the company with one or more of the intangible assets that make customers loyal: concepts (leading-edge ideas); competence (the ability to translate ideas into applications); and connections (alliances among businesses to leverage core capabilities). Her research looked at five American communities or regions that have become world-class centres for manufacturing, including Spartanburg-Grenville in South Carolina where BMW established its first-ever manufacturing facility outside Germany. These clusters develop over time, which in turn attracts more foreign direct investment. It also leads to greater assimilation of the global company into the local community. She believes that there are four factors critical for success:

- Visionary leaders in the community who have a very clear economic development strategy
- A hospitable business climate and work ethic
- Customised training and development of workers' skills
- Collaboration within the business community, and between business and government to improve quality and business performance.

This outside investment develops local communities, which has a positive spin-off effect on the local economy. Communities need to be able to attract these companies in the first instance, and then provide a forum which brings them all together to develop the common good. There are many similarities between her findings and the effect that foreign direct investment has had on Ireland in the last 20 or so years.

Despite the economic downturn in the Irish economy in 2008, the IDA is still attracting new industries to the country. In August 2008, an American medical devices company, Abiomed, announced that it was establishing a facility in Athlone to manufacture heart pump supports (there is a cluster of 50 international medical device companies operating in Ireland). Abiomed's chief operations officer stated that the mixture of a well-trained workforce (with an institute of technology located nearby), combined with a very favourable corporate tax regime, IDA grants for set-up costs and research and development, all combined to make Ireland a very attractive location. From the community perspective, multinational companies locating in towns and cities have utterly transformed those communities beyond all recognition.

CONCLUSION

Nothing stays the same in the business world for very long. Companies must be constantly reviewing their position and developing new strategies to achieve their organisational objectives. In times of a downturn in the economy, some companies will want to consolidate their business and are happy to tread water until the economy shows signs of improving. Others will constantly look for opportunities to increase their market share.

With improvements in technology, product life cycles are getting ever shorter. Organisations must be constantly monitoring the markets in which they operate to develop a good understanding of what their target market is looking for. If the company cannot develop new products and services to satisfy consumer demand, customers will move their business to rival companies. The dilemma for companies then is to understand and meet consumer demand with a range of products in a profitable manner. New product development in most cases is expensive and firms need to make decisions balancing the need for consumer-driven demand with keeping costs under control.

The Irish market is small and puts a limit on the amount of growth a company can achieve unless it looks to foreign markets. Indeed, in many industries, international drivers are putting competitive pressure on companies to operate on a global basis. Because of the nature of some companies' product and technology, they have no option but to start on an international footing. Indeed, Irish companies are succeeding very well in the international arena. There are a number of strategies that companies can use to compete in foreign markets, but one policy issue they have to decide is whether to adapt their products for each market or operate with a global product.

Many companies will operate in one particular industry and build up expertise that cements their reputation in that industry. Others will diversify into related or unrelated industries. Unrelated diversification requires very different corporate parenting skills by the centre, and the portfolio of companies has to be actively managed.

Chapter 11 will examine how these four broad development directions can be achieved by an organisation, either through organic growth, strategic alliances or mergers and acquisitions. Once again, companies will use a variety of these methods, depending on the particular circumstances, to achieve their objectives.

SUMMARY

H. Igor Ansoff argued that there are four broad strategic directions open to a company:

- **Market penetration** – consolidating the company's position in the market and developing a larger market share.
- **Product development** – developing new products to meet market needs.
- **Market development** – developing new markets (including international markets) as well as new market segments and new uses for products.
- **Diversification** – related and unrelated diversification (Chapter 10).

While these are listed as alternative directions, in reality companies will pursue most, if not all, options, possibly at the same time. They are driven by innovation and organisational capability.

Market penetration Most companies will try to build up a greater share of the current market with their current products. There is a strong correlation between high market share and profitability. In turn this profitability can be reinvested and so build up further market share. If the market is growing, it is easier for one particular company to gain market share, as other companies are also expanding, but not at the same rate. In a static market, for one company to gain market share it is at the expense of another, and so they can expect retaliation. An easier method of gaining market share is to acquire other players in the industry, as this does not directly impact on the market share held by competitors, at least not in the short term.

Once market share has been built up, companies will want to protect the investment that they have made. This is done by increasing advertising, price cuts or building customer loyalty. While consolidation is a defensive measure, it is important that, what the organisation has, it holds. In a mature market where demand is static or falling, a company may want to close some spare capacity in order to reduce costs, and concentrate on other production facilities. Likewise, many smaller or weaker firms will either go out of business or be taken over by larger competitors, leading to a consolidation of the industry. Consolidation may also include withdrawing from certain markets to concentrate on core areas. There can be a speculative reason behind divesting. In some instances, it makes sense for companies to divest underperforming subsidiaries or ones that may be peripheral to their main business and concentrate on the parts that are central to what the company does best: 'sticking to the knitting'.

Product development The development of new products should be seen as an integral part of what a company does. This involves developing brand new or modified products for existing markets. In a competitive environment, any firm that does not keep up-to-date with new product development will quickly lose market share and may go out of business as other companies innovate. Invention is the discovery of a new product. Innovation goes one step further in bringing that new product, process or service into use. The economist Joseph Schumpeter defined innovation as 'getting things done'. The primary focus is on the commercial viability of new products in the marketplace.

New product development presents certain problems in terms of cost and the management of products coming on stream. The process is very much linked with the environmental analysis as companies have to be aware of opportunities in the market and their own capabilities in terms of being able to exploit such opportunities for profit. There are a number of issues that need to be taken into consideration including: Definition of products; Product line and Product mix; Research and development; Product life cycle; First mover advantage; and Brand management.

Market development There are three forms of market development: new segments, new uses, and geographical spread. Segmentation of the market is a central part of what companies do to identify the different groups, and exploit market opportunities. Those segments that the company is able to satisfy with its products and services are then prioritised and targeted. New segments can be identified. Targeting can involve a concentration strategy where the company directs its efforts towards a single market segment while using a single marketing mix or a differentiated strategy where it develops different marketing mixes for different segments. It must then position the product or service to create a clearly defined image in the minds of its chosen customers. This is particularly evident in the fashion industry where companies are not just selling clothing: they are selling a whole lifestyle image.

New uses for the product can appear that may well have not been there when the product was first developed. The third, and by far the most important way of growing markets, is to look at international markets for opportunities. Ultimately, international expansion should exploit environmental opportunities. The European Union has created opportunities for Irish companies in terms of the size of the market that is available without any restrictions.

Going international There are various factors that are driving internationalisation. The Irish economy is a very open one, and even in terms of protecting their market share of the home economy, Irish companies must be able to compete with the best international companies. One main objective in operating on an international basis is to develop a competitive advantage. There are a number of different factors that must be taken into account in choosing which markets to enter. There are certain risks with international operations that need to be considered. Strategies available for entering foreign markets are: exporting; licensing and franchising; strategic alliances and joint ventures; and foreign direct investment. There are three possible strategies, ranging from standardised products sold throughout the world to products that are adapted for each individual market:

- Global strategy – standardised throughout the world
- Transnational strategy – a global strategy adapted for individual markets
- Multi-domestic strategy – a localised approach to each individual market

These are part of a continuum rather than discrete strategies, and there is considerable overlap between them.

DISCUSSION QUESTIONS

1. Differentiate between the various elements of a market penetration strategy.
2. Critically analyse the importance of research and development in supporting product development as a strategic option.
3. Discuss the factors that need to be taken into consideration in managing new product development.
4. Evaluate the importance of market development as a strategy for Irish companies.
5. Discuss the various factors that need to be taken into consideration when selecting foreign markets.
6. Explore the various options open to Irish companies when entering foreign markets.

REFERENCES

Bartlett, C. and Ghoshal, S., 1990, "Matrix Management: Not a Structure, a Frame of Mind", *Harvard Business Review,* July/August 1990, Vol. 68, Issue 4, pp.138–145

Beesley, A., 2007 (a), "Jurys Financier Opts Out of Irish Property", *Irish Times,* 20 July 2007, Finance, p.1

Beesley, A., 2007 (b), "Quinn Holds Forth on the Path to Success", *Irish Times,* 8 March 2007, Finance, p.1

Brennan, C., 2007. "Cleaning up", *Irish Times,* 20 July 2007, Finance, p.26

Chandler, A., 1962, *Strategy and Structure,* Cambridge, MA, MIT Press

Chesborough, H. and Garman, A., 2008, "How Open Innovation Can Help You Cope in Lean Times", *Harvard Business Review,* December 2009, Vol. 87, Issue 12, pp.68–76

Cooke, N., 2008, "Irish firms must look to foreign markets for growth", *Sunday Business Post,* 29 June 2008

Creaton, S. and O'Cleary, C., 2002, *Panic at the Bank,* Dublin, Gill & Macmillan

Deegan, G., "Intel to invest €50m in R&D jobs at Shannon", *Irish Times,* 28 February 2009, p.17

Dess, G. *et al.,* 2004, *Strategic Management,* Boston, McGraw-Hill

Dibb, S. *et al.,* 2006, *Marketing Concepts and Strategies,* Boston, Houghton Mifflin

Digby, D. and Vishwanath, V., 2006, "Localisation: The Revolution in Consumer Markets", *Harvard Business Review,* April 2006, Vol. 84, Issue 4, pp.82–92

Early, P.C. and Mosakowski, E., 2004, "Cultural Intelligence", *Harvard Business Review,* October 2004, Vol. 82, Issue 10, pp.139–146

Enterprise Ireland, 2010, *Chief Executive Officer's Report,* http://www.enterprise-ireland.com/annualreport2009/ceo_report_2.html, Accessed 28 March 2011

Fallon, J., 2010, "Outsmart and outthink them: ex Intel chief gives his vision", *Irish Times,* 17 November 2010, Business Today, p.19

Florida, R. and Goodnight, J., 2005, "Managing for Creativity", *Harvard Business Review,* July/August 2008, Vol. 83, Issue 7/8, pp.124–131

Forfás, 2005, *Making Technological Knowledge Work,* Dublin, Technopolis/Forfás

Ghemawat, P., 2001, "Distance still matters", *Harvard Business Review,* September 2001, Vol. 79, Issue 8, pp.137–147

Ghemawat, P., 2003, "The Forgotten Strategy", *Harvard Business Review,* November 2003, Vol. 81, Issue 11, pp.76–84

Ghemawat, P., 2010, "Finding your strategy in the new landscape", *Harvard Business Review,* March 2010, Vol. 88, Issue 2, pp.54–60

Goold, M. and Campbell, A., 1987, *Strategies and Styles,* Oxford, Blackwell

Goold, M. and Campbell, A., 2002, "Do you have a well-designed organisation?" *Harvard Business Review,* March 2002, Vol. 80, Issue 3, pp.117–224

Hayes, R. and Wheelwright, S., 1979, "The Dynamics of Process–Product Life Cycles", *Harvard Business Review,* March/April 1979, Vol. 57, Issue 2, pp.127–136

Hunt, C., 2010, *National Strategy for Higher Education,* Dublin, Strategy Group for Higher Education

Johnson, G. *et al.,* 2008, *Exploring Corporate Strategy. Text and Cases,* 8th Edition, Harlow, Essex, Prentice Hall, Financial Times

Johnson, G. *et al.,*2011, *Exploring Strategy: Text & Cases,* 9th Edition, Harlow, Pearson Education Ltd

Kanter, R.M., 1999, "From Spare Change to Real Change", *Harvard Business Review,* May/June 1999, Vol. 77, Issue 3, pp.122–132

Kanter, R.M., 2003, "Thriving Locally in the Global Economy", *Harvard Business Review,* August 2003, Vol. 81, Issue 8, pp.119–127

Kotler, P. *et al.,* 2007, *Principles of Marketing,* 4th European Edition, Upper Saddle River, NJ, Prentice Hall Europe

Levitt, T., 1983, "The Globalisation of Markets", *Harvard Business Review,* May/June 1983, Vol. 61, Issue 3, pp.92–102

Levitt, T., 1960, "Marketing Myopia", *Harvard Business Review Reprint,* July/August 2004, Vol. 82, Issue 7/8, pp.138–149

Lyons, T., 2008, "Irish IT Blow as Dell Boss Quits", *Sunday Times,* 11 August 2008, Business + Money, p.1

MacConnell, S., 2011, "Bord Bia says 70% of exporters are confident about outlook", *Irish Times,* 13 January 2011, p.18

McCall, B., 2010, "Are we ready to wean off FDI?", *The Irish Times,* 26 November 2010, Innovation, p.45

Mankins, M., 2006, "Stop Making Plans: Start Making Decisions", *Harvard Business Review,* January 2006, Vol. 84, Issue 1, pp.76–84

New, S., 2010, "The transparent supply chain", *Harvard Business Review,* October 2010, Vol. 88, Issue 10, pp.76–82

Nichols, J. and Roslow, S., 1986, "The S curve: an aid to strategic marketing", *Journal of consumer marketing,* 1986, Vol. 3, Issue 2, pp.53–64

Nidumolu, R. *et al.,* 2009, "Why sustainability is the key driver of innovation", *Harvard Business Review,* September 2009, Vol. 87, Issue 9, pp. 57–64

O'Brien, J. and Marakas, G., 2008, *Management Information Systems,* 8th Ed., New York, McGraw-Hill

O'Halloran, B. and Lynch, S., 2011, "Exports to exceed €1170bn, predicts trade body", *Irish Times,* 6 January 2011, p.16

Ohmae, K., 1989 (a), "Managing in a Borderless World", *Harvard Business Review,* May/June 1989, Vol. 89, Issue 3, pp.151–161

Ohmae, K., 1989 (b), "The global logic of strategic alliances", *Harvard Business Review,* March/April 1989, Vol. 67, Issue 2, p.143–152

Ohmae, K., 1982, *The Mind of the Strategist,* New York, McGraw Hill

Rigby, D. and Vishwanath, V., (2006) "Localisation: The Revolution in Consumer Markets", *Harvard Business Review,* April 2006, Vol. 84, Issue 4, pp.82–92

Rigby, D. *et al.,* 2009, "Innovation in Turbulent Times", *Harvard Business Review,* June 2009, Vol. 87, Issue 6, pp.79–86

Simmons, J., 2011, "Mergers & Acquisitions hit €10.3bn in 2010", *Irish Times,* 7 January 2011, Business This Week, p.5

Smith, D., 2006, *Exploring Innovation,* Maidenhead, McGraw-Hill

Suarez, F. and Lanzolla, G., 2005, "The Half-Truth of First Mover Advantages", *Harvard Business Review,* April 2005, Vol. 83, Issue 4, pp.121–127

Tansey, P., 2008, "Innovate or stagnate", *Irish Times,* 29 February 2008

Thompson, A. *et al.,* 2008, *Crafting and Executing Strategy: The Quest for Competitive Advantage,* New York, McGraw-Hill

Waldmeir, P., 2011, "Beijing presses motor groups to share technology", *Financial Times,* 19 February 2011, p.17

Wrecker, A., 2011, "Getting Ireland up to speed", *The Sunday Business Post,* 6 February 2011, p.M9

Yip, G., 2003, *Total Global Strategy II,* London, Financial Times/Prentice Hall

Diversification

"Sometimes it's better not to listen when people tell you that something can't be done. I didn't ask for permission or approval. I just went ahead and did it."

Michael Dell

INTRODUCTION

As organisations grow in size, they often develop in different ways compared to their original business. Chapter 9 dealt with companies expanding into other markets, but companies can also branch into different types of businesses or technologies, becoming diversified. According to Fitzroy and Hulbert (2005: 244), "the degree, nature, and direction of diversification are some of the most important corporate strategy decisions" that a company will have to make. Strategy-making becomes a much more complicated affair for diversified companies. It involves assessing a number of different business environments and developing strategies for each business and for the overall corporation.

Chapter 10 examines the impact diversification has on corporate parenting styles, including the reasons why a company might diversify. There are two main types of diversification: related and unrelated. However, the distinction between the two types can often be blurred. In turn, related diversification can be subdivided into two further divisions: horizontal or vertical. The impact of diversification on performance is also examined in this chapter. Each form of diversification requires different types of managerial skills and corporate parenting styles. The aim of any strategy is to add value to the organisation, and so the type of corporate parenting style must be aligned to the specific nature of diversification in the company.

The chapter also discusses various strategies by which diversification can take place: internal start-up, joint ventures, and acquisitions. As the diversified company grows in size, managing the portfolio is a vital component of the success of the business and different techniques of managing the portfolio are examined.

CHOOSING A DIVERSIFICATION STRATEGY

As companies grow, they will sometimes develop in different directions from their original business. Such development is known as diversification, and it can take many forms. In some instances there may be a strong common theme running through the different businesses – related diversification. On other occasions, the expansion may be into business areas that have no relationship with the original business.

Definition **Diversification** is a strategy whereby a company expands from being a single business operation into different businesses of varying relatedness.

The parenting style for each organisation will differ considerably as to how centralised or devolved the decision-making process is. This is generally related to the level of diversification in the company. It may involve detailed planning for each business unit by the corporate headquarters, or at a minimum giving approval for plans drafted by the SBU. Either way, the corporate parent must have a vision and a coherent plan for the entire organisation, towards which all elements of the company focus their attention.

According to Thompson *et al.* (2008: 267), the task of crafting a diversified company's overall strategy involves four distinct aspects:

1. Picking new industries to enter and deciding on the means of entry. Should the focus be a broad or narrow diversification, and should it be achieved by organic growth or acquisition?
2. Initiating actions to boost the combined performance of the businesses the firm has entered. It must strengthen the long-term competitive position of each company and the overall group.
3. Pursuing opportunities to create cross-business leverage – looking for ways to reduce costs and create efficiencies.
4. Establishing investment priorities and steering corporate resources into the most attractive business units.

Reasons for Diversifying

There are a number of reasons why a company might diversify. The acid test is ultimately whether diversifying increases shareholder wealth (other stakeholders' interests must also be taken into account). It can achieve such an increase in wealth in a number of ways, primarily through efficiency gains obtained from better utilisation of the company's resources in achieving economies of scope (where the company has underutilised resources or competences that can be deployed elsewhere in the company, such as management skills or financial resources). There can be opportunities to expand into related businesses that complement the current product line and technology.

Later in this chapter, we will examine portfolios and this can provide opportunities to cross-subsidise businesses that show potential. The company may also have an established brand name that can be applied to other businesses in a profitable manner, such as the Virgin Group. On occasion, a company may have exhausted all opportunities to further expand in its present business and, in order to achieve further growth, it will have to diversify into other areas. Likewise its current market may be in decline. Finally, by diversifying, a company is spreading risk across a number of industries. Most industries are cyclical to some degree, but not to the same extent and timing. By increasing the range of businesses, a company is lessening the impact that a downturn would have on its profitability.

According to Markides (1997: 94–9), there are six questions that a manager should ask when considering diversification:

1. What can the company do better than any of its competitors in its current markets? Managers must have a clear definition of their business and of what sets them apart from their competitors. This will increase the likelihood of success.
2. What strategic assets do we need in order to succeed in the new market? Success in one market does not ensure success in another unless the company has the strategic assets it requires.
3. Can we catch up to or leapfrog competitors at their own game? If we lack some strategic assets, can they be bought or developed?
4. Will diversification break up strategic assets that need to be kept together? By breaking up strategic assets, will this diminish their overall effectiveness?
5. Will we be simply a player in the new market or will we emerge a winner? Can our competitors imitate our strategic assets and outperform us?
6. What can our company learn by diversifying, and are we sufficiently organised to learn from it? Diversification is potentially a learning experience that can improve overall organisational efficiency.

TYPES OF DIVERSIFICATION

Diversification can be divided into two broad classifications:

- **Related diversification**: where there are common links between the value chains of each company. There are two subdivisions:
  - o Vertical integration, either forward or backward integration
  - o Horizontal integration

- **Unrelated diversification**: where the company moves into a business where there is no common link in their value chains.

Related Diversification

Related diversification is seeking to develop a strategic fit between the value chains of similar companies. This strategic fit can be in areas such as marketing or using a common brand name, sharing R&D resources, transferring valuable skills or know-how between companies and building up common capabilities.

Vertical integration Vertical integration describes the company moving either backwards or forwards along the value system. The inbound logistics of a company describes the movement of goods from a supplier to a manufacturer. **Backward vertical integration** is where the manufacturer moves back along the value system and takes control of a company that supplies it with raw materials, components or machinery. This might be done in a situation where the supplier has strong bargaining power and is demanding high prices. By moving back along the supply chain, the manufacturer is now achieving control over its inputs, particularly quality. A brewing company might take over farms supplying it with grain in order to ensure that its grain is of an appropriate quality and standard.

Outbound logistics is where a company interfaces with its distribution network in the value system. **Forward vertical integration** is where a company moves forward along the value system and takes over distribution systems or retail outlets. In the UK, many breweries own public houses (known as tied houses) which promote the beer of their parent companies. In 2006, BMW took over control of the importation of BMW cars into Ireland and now distributes them directly to dealers around the country.

Horizontal integration Horizontal integration involves moving into activities that are either competitive products or complementary products. Examples of companies/products competing with one another include some of the international hotel companies that own different chains offering different facilities and levels of comfort. While different star ratings are aimed at different segments, there is a large overlap between those segments and they are effectively competing for customers in the same industry. We previously examined the product mix of the fast-moving consumer goods company Procter & Gamble. The company manufactures a number of different washing powders, including Bold, Dreft, Tide and these are individually branded products that also compete with one another.

An example of related diversification into **complementary products** is Eircom Phonewatch. Eircom, the former semi-state organisation, is a telephone operator involved in voice telephony. While home security alarm systems is a different industry, its effectiveness as a deterrent is largely dependent on telephone contact between the security company and the Gardaí to notify them that there has been a break-in at the house. The alarm system is connected to the phone system and there is a technological similarity in monitoring the alarm through the phone network. It is a complementary product that builds in switching costs and reinforces the relationship between the company and the customer.

Synergy Related diversification (and to a lesser extent, unrelated diversification) should produce synergy. Synergy is achieved when the total is greater than the sum of the parts. In terms of diversification, the capability of the combined organisation should be greater than the capabilities of all the individual companies. However, research carried out by Goold and Campbell (1998: 131) suggests that "synergy initiatives often fall short of management's expectations". Rather than assuming that synergies will exist, managers need to adopt a more sceptical view. When synergy is not realised it is usually due to the corporate executives. They suggest there are four common pitfalls that make synergy seem more attractive than it is:

- **Synergy bias** – overestimating the benefits and underestimating the cost involved.
- **Parenting bias** – a belief that synergy will be obtained only by forcing the business units to co-operate.
- **Skills bias** – the assumption that the competencies and know-how required are available in the organisation.
- **Upside bias** – when executives concentrate on the potential benefits and overlook the negative aspects.

The company needs to be clear about the objectives and benefits of the potential synergy that they have identified. They also need to be clear about how and when they should intervene in terms of extracting the benefits, and should take into account the skills of the managers involved. When synergy can be achieved, it can create additional value with existing resources, but it is often difficult to realise in practice.

It should be stated, in examining related and unrelated diversification, that the two types are not dichotomous, but are part of a continuum. At first glance, it may appear that there is no relationship between particular businesses, but on closer examination, a connection can often be found. With Procter & Gamble, for example, the product mix includes laundry detergents, toothpastes, soaps, deodorants, shampoos and tissues. They also manufacture snack items such as Pringle's crisps. The raw materials and manufacturing process for cleaning agents are very different to those for snacks, and it would appear there is little synergy involved. However, they are both classified as fast-moving consumer items and both are sold in supermarkets. There is little or no difference from a marketing perspective in terms of brand management, advertising and logistics. Therefore, it can be argued that it is related rather than unrelated diversification.

With a large, diversified company, there can be some parts of the group that conform to related diversifications. There can also be other parts that are clearly unrelated companies and there is no synergy with the remainder of the company. In reality, most conglomerates are probably a mixture of related and unrelated diversification, and they also vary considerably in size. The make-up of individual companies can range from one core business accounting for most of the revenues, with a small number of other diversified companies. Other companies might be narrowly diversified with around three or four businesses that may or may not be related. Finally, there can be larger companies that are diversified into a number of unrelated areas, but within each of these areas there can be clusters of related companies. A good example of the latter type is the Quinn Group, which will be discussed in detail below.

Unrelated Diversification

Unrelated diversification occurs when a company expands its portfolio into businesses where there is little or no relationship between the various companies. It is often referred to as a **conglomerate,** and many holding companies fall into this category. Conglomerates became very popular in the US and Britain in the 1980s as many large companies expanded across industries and geographical markets. The following decade subsequently saw many de-mergers (for reasons which we will examine) where the conglomerates were split up into separate companies, which allowed for a more clearly defined core business and market focus – what Peters and Waterman (1982) referred to when they coined the phrase "stick to the knitting".

The main rationale behind unrelated diversification is that the company headquarters can make better capital allocation to the various units than financial markets could if the businesses were separate companies. With a spread of businesses and, industries, there should be a more even flow of cash compared to a single business where it can be quite cyclical.

Economic cycles are effectively beyond a chief executive's control, but what they do have control over is the scope of the business. Apart from cash flow, diversification also spreads business risk across a number of different businesses and, using its corporate parenting skills, the conglomerate can invest in industries that are showing attractive returns rather than restricting growth to related industries.

While industries appear different, there can be opportunities to exploit what Bettis and Prahalad (1995: 5–14) referred to as "**the dominant logic**". The research in their original paper in 1986, and then revised in 1995, drew attention to managerial rather than economic forces in environmental-driven organisational change and the problems they face. Information technology has led to "information-rich but interpretation-poor systems" (p.6) that lack appropriate actionable knowledge. They define the dominant logic "as the way in which managers in a firm conceptualise the business and make critical resource allocation decisions" (p.7). It acts as an information filter that focuses organisational attention only on data deemed relevant by the dominant logic, which in turn is incorporated into the strategy of the organisation. This can direct organisations in certain directions, or also prevent them from taking certain action. They cite IBM in the early 1990s as an example, whose dominant logic revolved for years around the centrality of the mainframe business (rather than personal computers) and which became embedded in their strategy. In such cases, the dominant logic prevents new learning and must be changed.

Performance

There has been much research into the correlation between diversification and performance. Focused companies are subject to the cyclical effects of industry and declining industries. To generate further growth, they have to diversify. In general (and there are many exceptions), limited related diversification produces better results than either single business companies or highly diversified companies. This is often depicted graphically as an inverted 'U' with the vertical axis representing performance and the horizontal axis representing the level of diversification. This suggests that profitability increases with diversity, but only to the point known as the 'limit of complexity'.

Harper and Viguerie (2002: 30) found that "moderately diversified companies share a common approach to managing scope – an approach applied at the right time in the life cycle of a business, generates superior returns through higher growth that is both realised and anticipated by capital markets". They refer to the balance between focus and diversification as a "strategic sweet spot", but finding that balance can be difficult as it varies widely from company to company and from point to point in the stages of a business's life cycle. It is not a steady state and needs to be managed. Their research, carried out on 412 S&P 500 companies, found that, on average, moderately diversified companies notched up 13% per year in annual excess returns compared to highly diversified companies.

Managing conglomerates is extremely challenging, given the wide variety of industries and business environments. Increasing the variation of companies adds to the complexity involved. The greater the spread, the more difficult it is for corporate managers to have an understanding of the individual businesses and to keep abreast of the changes taking place. As a result, they are not in a position to properly evaluate proposals from individual companies. For that reason, the form of parenting style known as 'financial control' is most suited where the role is that of a portfolio manager. The corporate headquarters would set financial objectives for the companies and allow the company to develop its own strategies to achieve the required results.

There are many arguments that suggest that investors allocate capital across different businesses more effectively than a conglomerate can do. Markets often discount the valuation of conglomerates as they perceive that the full financial benefits do not materialise due to a number of shortcomings associated with broad diversification, such as the cross-subsidisation of unprofitable businesses.

One example of this was in June 2008, when Nigel Hart, the Chief Executive of Reachcapital, an American fund manager, called on the board of the Irish holding company DCC to begin the process of breaking up the company. The investor believed the share price was considerably less than the group's intrinsic value, possibly by as much as 50%. Hart believed that the valuation gap was due to "the conglomerated nature of the group's structure and distraction caused by the ongoing insider trading dealing litigation with Fyffes". The company has five main divisions: healthcare, energy, food and beverages, energy, and IT distribution. He stated that he had "never understood the synergies that exist from a conglomerate of businesses as disparate as DCC". Despite the high returns, Hart added that the stock market will never record a fair valuation of the company in its current form (Carey, 2008).

There are occasions when diversification across a broad spectrum can produce superior results such as when it takes over a company that has undervalued assets or is in financial distress. In 2008, the value of many Irish companies, and in particular banks, dropped very significantly. In such situations companies are always vulnerable to a takeover bid.

Adding Value – Diversification

Examining the performance of diversified companies again raises the issue of corporate parents and whether they add or destroy value. As public companies can be taken over if they are under-performing, corporate parents must demonstrate that they are able to contribute to the value of the company. Goold *et al.* (1994) suggest that a corporate parent can add value by: providing a clear vision and strategic intent for the organisation; developing strategic capabilities and synergies; providing financial support and expertise; monitoring business performance; and making necessary interventions. Corporate parents can also destroy value: in that they add to the cost as they do not generate revenue in a direct way; they slow down decision-making and add to the "bureaucratic fog"; and internal cross-subsidisation can cover poor performance in parts of the organisation.

The more related the various companies are to each other, the easier it can be for the corporate parent to intervene in a meaningful way in businesses that they understand – what Goold *et al.* refer to as 'parental development'. In a hotel chain, executives at head office will have worked in the group in different positions and locations, giving them a wealth of experience that they can apply to an individual hotel that is not performing to its potential. In addition to providing expertise, a strong brand and the ability to provide finance can assist the individual units. For a highly diversified company, this form of parenting would do great damage and instead require, what Porter (1987) termed, a 'portfolio manager'.

There are many examples of major conglomerates that are very successful. General Electric is one of the biggest and most successful companies in the world. GE is involved in a vast range of different industries such as aviation, consumer electronics, oil and gas, energy, finance, media (NBC), and healthcare. During his time as chief executive, Jack Welch bought and sold 1,900 companies, earning him the sobriquet 'Neutron Jack' after the variation of the atomic bomb that was developed by the US and was designed to destroy people but leave buildings intact (Lane, 2008).

Berkshire Hathaway, another very successful conglomerate, is run by one of the richest men in the world, Warren Buffet. Each year, at the company AGM, analysts as well as shareholders wait with bated breath to listen to 'the sage of Omaha', to hear his views on a wide range of economic issues. Buffet, who is in his seventies, is a self-confessed technophobe. No one should use that as an excuse for ageism. During the 1990s when billions of dollars were being invested in dot-com companies, he stayed clear of them stating that he did not understand them and therefore would not invest (they were outside his 'dominant logic'). His judgement proved correct when the dot-com bubble burst and proved that many of these companies lacked a sound business model. While the personal wealth of many other big names has decreased, Buffet's has increased each year. He also wants to give his wealth away while he is living, rather than set up a trust that would disperse it after his death. He claims that attempting to control the spending of his money after his death would give a new meaning to the term 'thinking outside of the box'!

Illustration 10.1: Diversification Strategy – The Quinn Group

An Irish company, the Quinn Group, became a successful conglomerate. It is a private company located in Derrylin, County Fermanagh and was established by Seán Quinn and his family. It began in 1973, when he inherited his father's farm. The farm was not big enough to provide a decent lifestyle, but Quinn saw the potential of the quarry located on the farm, and so with a £100 loan from the bank, he began a quarrying business. The company has expanded at a phenomenal pace over the years and now employs 6,500 people in a broad range of industries located across Europe.

There are a number of main divisions in the company, and examining them will give the reader a good indication of the nature of the businesses engaged in unrelated diversification. The divisions are:

Financial Services This covers three areas. *Quinn Insurance*, founded in 1996, offers a full suite of general insurance products covering motor, home, liability and property insurance. The company also offers *private health insurance* in competition with the Vhi. In 2007, the company bought British-owned Bupa Ireland in Fermoy, in a high-profile takeover. In 2000, it established *Quinn Life*, which offers pensions and savings under the Freeway brand, and customers can invest in equity and bond funds in the European and US stock market. It also has a stake in a stockbroking business, owning a 25% share in NCB stockbrokers.

Radiators Quinn Radiators is one of Europe's leading producers of domestic and specification radiators with production facilities in Ireland, the UK and Belgium. Quinn spent €84 million taking over Barlo (an Irish-listed radiator manufacturer) when Tony Mullins tried to privatise it in a management buy-out in 2004.

Quinn Cement Established in 1989, Quinn Cement has been taking on the Irish giant, CRH. In one of his rare interviews, Seán Quinn spoke about being confronted with "strong, systematic and sophisticated industry opposition" to setting up a cement factory. Quinn Cement uses the raw material from Quinn's original quarry, and another in Williamstown in County Galway, to manufacture 1.7 million tonnes of cement annually and concrete products such as pre-stressed concrete, roof tiles, lightweight thermal blocks, insulation products and tarmac.

Quinn Hotels The Quinn Group owns the Slieve Russell Hotel in Cavan and Buswell's Hotel in Dublin. It also owns the Holiday Inn in Nottingham and the Crown Plaza in Cambridge, as well as the Belfrey near Birmingham, famous for hosting the Ryder Cup on four occasions. On the continent, Quinn hotels include the Ibis hotel in Karlin in the Czech Republic, Hilton hotels in Prague and Sofia, and the Sheraton in Krakow, Poland. This division also includes pubs.

Property This division of the Quinn Group operates office blocks, retail shopping centres and warehouses in Eastern Europe and Russia.

Plastics Quinn Plastics offers a range of industrial and domestic products that are used mainly in the construction sector, and it now includes a chemical company in Leuna, near Leipzig in Germany.

Glass This division operates from Derrylin, and in Cheshire, England, and manufactures glass containers for the food and beverage industries.

Quinn Power The manufacturing base of the group uses a considerable amount of electricity and so they entered the green energy market by constructing a 5 megawatt wind farm in 1995. In 2004, the company added a 13.5 megawatt wind farm at Ballyconnell in County Cavan, with further expansion planned.

Source: www.quinn-group.com

As discussed above, very often, large diversified companies have a number of unrelated divisions, but, within these divisions, there can be clusters of related companies.

The Quinn Group is an example of such a conglomerate in that there are perhaps some synergies between different parts of the group. For example, stone from the quarry is used in the manufacture of cement. In turn, cement is a primary product in much of the building materials that the company manufactures for use in the construction sector in Ireland, both north and south. Insulation products are also used in the construction industry. With energy costs rising, this is becoming a very profitable business. Most of the hotels were already in existence and so would not have benefited from the use of the company's building materials in construction. Apart from that, the majority of them are abroad, so the materials would not be used in the construction process as they are heavy, bulky items that are expensive to transport.

Therefore, the hotels division of the Quinn Group can be seen as a very separate division. From a managerial perspective, running hotels is very different from manufacturing building products. The financial services division is different again. There is a relationship between car, home, and health insurance, and this can be seen as a cluster within the financial services division. There is a synergy between the insurance and the building divisions. One of the reasons that prompted Quinn into the insurance field was the enormous cost of insuring his own fleet of trucks used in the delivery of building materials around the country. That fleet is now insured in-house, thus reducing costs significantly. However, managing this division is again very dissimilar to managing the remainder of the businesses in the group.

Competences

Clearly, there is no obvious synergy across the Quinn Group. However, when analysing conglomerates, there are certain competences that are required by all constituent businesses, and by corporate headquarters in managing them together as a portfolio. These apply also to single businesses, but given the complexity involved in managing conglomerates, they are particularly important here.

The first competence needed is **financial**. Financing structures, cash flows, profits, control measures, etc., will differ from one industry to another, but the basic underlying skills are common to all. In dealing with individual business managers, it is vital that head office executives have the ability to understand the financial implications of decisions that are being made and the financial information that is coming to them. Quinn has stated that the company avoids investments with "modest rates of return". In 2006, group sales were €1.3 billion, with profits of €425 million. The company has delivered an average annual profit growth of 30% over the last 30 years.

The second competence required is **leadership**. In a diversified company, it is very difficult to forge a common vision that unites all the elements under one banner. The Virgin Group achieves it under a common brand that signifies an innovative approach to established businesses. General Electric achieves it to some extent by requiring each business to be number one or number two in the industry in which they operate.

The Quinn Group is also building up a strong brand image that unites the various divisions. There has to be strong leadership from the centre that motivates and inspires each company to achieve good results. Part of such leadership is the ability to spot talented people. Each company is only as good as its management team and staff, and so picking the right people and keeping them motivated is a vital ingredient. Seán Quinn has stated that in the future the Quinn Group will 'leverage a lot of the profits towards management and staff'. Quinn's management style is designed to help people realise their own potential and, if the company does not have the people to do a particular job, they recruit them. Likewise, if someone wants to leave, they do not ask them to stay (Beesley, 2007).

The future of the Quinn Group, however, is quite uncertain at the time of drafting this edition. Lyons and Carey (2011) present a very detailed analysis of the financial dealings involving Seán Quinn and the Quinn Group. Over a number of years, Seán Quinn and his family borrowed €2.3 billion from Anglo Irish Bank and €1.3 billion from other banks to fund investments that are now worth a fraction of what they cost. In addition, Mr Quinn built up contracts for difference (CFDs) in Anglo Irish Bank shares, which at one point were valued at 28% of the market value of the bank. A CFD differs from ordinary share trading in that the person does not take ownership of the shares (and consequently does not appear on a share register), but bets on their price movement. The investor is required to put down only a percentage of the value (perhaps 10%), known as a 'margin'. As the share price of Anglo was dropping, Mr Quinn continued to build up his holding. When it became known that his position was so high, he came under pressure to convert the CFDs to ordinary shares and also reduce his holding quite substantially. Quinn transferred money from Quinn Insurance to fund the share purchase, bringing Quinn Insurance below permitted solvency levels. The manner in which Mr Quinn's holding in Anglo Irish Bank was reduced is the subject of current inquiries. It is reasonably certain that the eventual outcome will have serious consequences for the Group as it is currently structured.

STRATEGIES FOR ACHIEVING DIVERSIFICATION

There are different methods for achieving diversification in a company, including:

- internal start-up (organic growth),
- joint ventures, and
- acquisitions.

These will be discussed briefly here in the context of diversification. As they are also general strategies for all types of companies, they will be dealt with in greater detail in Chapter 11.

Internal Start-up

An internal start-up is where a company builds up a new subsidiary company (different from the parent company) from the beginning. It involves the parent company investing considerable time and resources to build up all aspects of the new company internally and externally in forming relationships with suppliers and distributors. An internal start-up takes a considerable period of time compared to making an acquisition, so time cannot be a critical factor as it would be in a highly competitive and fast-moving industry. The response from competitors will also be related to time. The parent company must already have all the necessary skills and competences to compete in an area different from its own or else be able to hire people with those skills. Many of the companies examined above in the Quinn Group example were internal start-ups, for example, cement manufacture. Other companies in the group were added by acquisition.

Joint Venture

A joint venture involves forming a new company that is jointly owned by two or more companies. In some countries, the host government makes a joint venture with a local company a requirement for foreign companies wishing to operate there. This method of achieving diversification is particularly useful where a company does not have all the necessary skills to operate in a new venture. This is often the situation in technology-related areas where the boundaries of current industries are constantly changing and merging with other industries. Sometimes these ventures can be extremely expensive and so it also spreads the risk involved. There are a number of pitfalls in joint ventures, which will be dealt with in the main discussion on the topic in Chapter 11.

Acquisition

Making acquisitions of existing companies is probably the most common form for achieving diversification. It is quick, and in taking over an existing company the new parent is acquiring all of the assets, resources, personnel and know-how as part of the deal. It also means that the company has an immediate relationship with suppliers and distributors, who no doubt will want to continue doing business with the company.

The above strategies can be used singly or in combination. Decisions have to be made with regard to the scope of the diversified company. It may decide to broaden the base of the company through further acquisitions in new areas or complement the existing line-up. If some companies are not performing, it may decide to divest those areas and concentrate its efforts on those parts that are performing. It might also look at keeping the existing range of businesses, but perhaps pursue international diversification. The environment is constantly changing and diversification requires constant management of the portfolio.

MANAGING THE PORTFOLIO

In a conglomerate, not all constituent companies are going to have the same characteristics and perform at the same level. Therefore, the corporate headquarters needs to maintain a watching brief on the entire organisation and take corrective measures in individual companies whenever necessary. This will also involve adding or subtracting companies from the portfolio to keep an overall balance. As a result of the recession, many companies may find that some parts of their portfolio subtract rather than add economic value. Ghemawat (2010) believes that companies will have to be more ruthless about terminating long-standing loss makers – and pursuing new opportunities. Some of this can be achieved by creating more stringent investment criteria and adopting more realistic assumptions about future growth. There will still be opportunities for growth, but, in order to pursue these opportunities, other avenues may have to be closed off.

There are a number of different techniques to assist managers in the process. The original model was developed by the Boston Consulting Group (BCG), who developed a growth/share matrix. It was initialy designed to manage a portfolio of products, but it can equally be applied to manage a range of businesses in a company's overall portfolio.

Boston Consulting Group Matrix

The Boston Consulting Group (BCG) Matrix plots each business on a two-dimensional basis, showing market growth rate and the market share held by each company, resulting in a four-quadrant matrix – see **Figure 10.1** below.

Market share is important as there is a strong correlation between high relative market share and profitability. Growth rate is important for the future success of a company. In putting resources into a company, it is obviously better to invest them in one that is located in a growing, rather than a contracting, industry. It will, however, require a good deal of investment to ensure growth. The purpose of the matrix is to get an overview of the entire portfolio so that managers can see where resources are needed and where they emanate from. Individual businesses within the company are allocated to the different quadrants according to their characteristics.

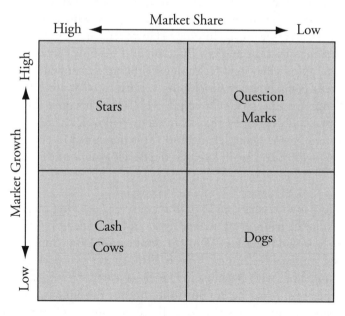

Figure 10.1 *The Boston Consulting Group (BCG) Matrix*

The resulting quadrants are labelled stars, cash cows, question marks (also called a problem child), and dogs.

Stars A 'star' is a business that has high market share and high market growth. This is a good position to be in as it has high market share at present (which makes the company more likely to be profitable) and it is also in an industry that is growing, thus showing future potential growth for the company either in just maintaining its existing market share percentage or even growing its market share. However, that is by no means guaranteed. Rival companies will also try to increase their market share, so the future position is by no means secure and it will require substantial investment to maintain a favourable position. High market share should mean good profitability, and these profits can be reinvested, but it will probably require additional investment from the cash cows quadrant.

Cash Cows A 'cash cow' is a business that has high market share, but one that is located in a mature market that is no longer growing. High market share means that it is in a dominant position and is yielding worthwhile profits. As the market is mature, it can be taken that all development costs such as R&D have been well recouped and it is now generating good profits. These profits are not required for reinvestment in the business and so they can be diverted to help support 'stars' and question marks. One drawback to this transfer of funds from cash cows is that it can have a de-motivating effect on the management of cash cow companies as they see their hard work going to other companies that may not put in the same effort.

Question Marks (or Problem Child) A 'question mark' has low market share in a growing industry. The low market share needs to be built up to a star position, where it will be much more profitable. To achieve this, it will require substantial investment in marketing, particularly in advertising, and in developing technology. However, such investment is certainly not guaranteed. While some question marks will go on and become successful, others will fall by the wayside. For example, when new technology is being developed in an industry, it often happens that different companies are developing variations of the technology simultaneously. The industry will opt for one particular type, which will become the 'industry standard', and the company that has developed that technology will quickly move into a star position. For the others, it often means being left behind. This happened in the development of video recorders in the early 1980s, and again lately in the development of the latest generation DVD technology.

Dogs 'Dogs' have low market share and are in a static or declining market. This is the worst possible position to be in from every perspective, and the business will at best be breaking even, but most likely is making a loss. Thus, it drains cash from the other companies in the portfolio. With the market declining, there is little or no prospect of a turnaround. The accepted wisdom in dealing with business in the 'dogs' category is to sell them or close them down, provided other businesses in the portfolio are not dependent on them. However, the most rational decision is not always taken, as there are often political considerations to be taken into account. For example, the chief executive could have been associated with that company in the past, might have a strong emotional attachment to it, and it could be that no one in the company wants to state the obvious! There are occasions when such a company may be held on to for strategic regions; for example, it might have a valuable distribution network in a particular market that could be used for new products about to come on stream in another company within the group.

The BCG matrix can be a useful tool for managers to gain a good overview of the entire portfolio of companies, not just singly but in how they relate to one another in the group in terms of the transfer of resources. It is not just financial resources that can be transferred. Earlier in this chapter attention was focused on how corporate parents may intervene in a particular company to help turn it around. Such intervention may require moving managers with particular skills from one company to another. It is standard procedure in large multinational companies for executives to be moved around from one company and location to another. While this is done to give executives personal experience for future promotion within the company, it is also done for very practical reasons, such as bringing their expertise to parts of the company that need it.

There are some limitations with the Boston Consulting Group Matrix as a tool. First, it examines only two variables: market share and market growth rate. While these are very important, there are also other important criteria that should be considered. These will be discussed below when considering the GE matrix. Secondly, high market share and high market growth are often very subjective terms. In some industries, it is possible to calculate these criteria reasonably accurately. In the motor industry, for example, because all new cars have to be registered and taxed, it is possible to get accurate figures on the total amount of new cars sold which can be compared with previous years to determine growth in the market. It will also show the relative market share of each car manufacturer. However, the car industry is something of an exception in that regard, and such accurate figures will often be unavailable for most industries. As a result, it requires a lot of speculation, which may not present an accurate figure. As Mark Twain once quipped: "Get your facts first, then you can distort them as you please."

Thirdly, the BCG Matrix perhaps implies that the resources needed by one company must come from others in the group. In many situations, financial resources may well be raised by the company itself through bank loans or share issues. This can have the benefit of focusing the attention of management in that company to the issues facing it, rather than automatically assuming that if resources are needed they will be provided by the corporate head office. If a company believes that a certain decision could secure its future or, on the other hand, mean its demise, it will think very carefully before making that decision. The other side to transferring resources from one company to another is, as mentioned above, that it can have a de-motivating effect on the management in the company that is providing the resources. They may resent having to give over those resources having worked hard to build them up in the first instance.

Directional Policy Matrix

McKinsey, another consultancy company, in conjunction with General Electric, developed the directional policy matrix, also known as the attractiveness matrix. The directional policy matrix looks at different companies in the portfolio and places them according to:

1. The attractiveness of the market in which the company is operating.

2. The competitive position of the company compared to others in the market.

The attractiveness of the industry can be termed as high, medium or low and it is an overview of that industry taking many different criteria into account. In this case the resulting matrix is a nine-box grid, thus giving a much more accurate picture of the position of the company/SBU.

Once again, much of the information that is fed into the criteria can be quite subjective. However, the object of the exercise is to gain a good, overall understanding of the position of each company in the matrix. This text has already discussed the importance of ongoing environmental analysis. Executives should have a reasonably accurate picture of the information required, and it will assist them in making the decisions that are needed to develop the portfolio. This information can be discussed and debated by executives until there is some form of consensus with regard to the issues facing the company (from Chapter 1, it will be recalled that, in general, organisations are moving towards a more pluralist approach to strategy-making rather than a top-down approach by the CEO).

The following are some of the criteria that should be included in the analysis.

Table 10.1: *Market Attractiveness*

Factor	Impact
Market growth rate	As discussed above in the BCG matrix.
Market size	A big market will have greater potential than a small market.
Competitive structure and profitability	Looking at Porter's Five Forces to determine the competitive structure of the industry and to see how profitable it is.
PESTEL	Using the PESTEL framework to gain an overall understanding of the factors affecting the industry. For example, the economic factors will also determine profitability, but this can be moderated by other factors such as political forces or sociological forces, etc. As with the PESTEL analysis, the most relevant factors should be included.
Cyclicality	Many industries are cyclical in nature. In terms of entering a particular industry, the optimum time is just as it is about to emerge from a downturn. For divestment, the time to get out is when it is still on top of the cycle and is attractive to buyers.

Table 10.2: *Relative Strength of the Company*

Factor	Impact
Market share	As per BCG matrix above.
Financial resources	A major benefit of a portfolio is having financial resources that can be transferred from one company to another in the group.
Research and development	In discussing new product development, it was stated that new product development is the lifeline of any company, and with product life cycles getting ever shorter, it is imperative that companies have a constant stream of new products in production.
Managerial strength	Parenting skills are very much dependent on the calibre of the management team in the corporate HQ.
Marketing	Marketing ties in with R&D to ensure that the products being developed will have market appeal. It is also vital that when they are developed they will be marketed effectively, and the public has a positive image of the company.

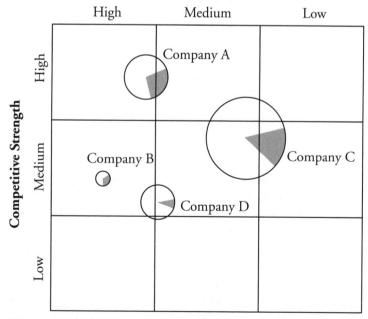

The size of the circle indicates overall market size.
The size of the wedge within a circle indicates size of market share held by the company.

Figure 10.2 *Industry Attractiveness – Competitive Strength Matrix*

The level of detail here is considerably greater than the Boston Consulting Group Matrix and consequently should provide a much more comprehensive picture to executives. The information from the above criteria can then be plotted on a nine-box Industry Attractiveness – Competitive Strength Matrix.

Each company or SBU is shown graphically on the matrix as a circle. The size of the circle should represent the size of the market that the SBU is operating in, and it should also show the market share of the SBU within that market. The matrix also gives guidance to managers with regard to each business. The company should invest in strong, attractive industries (top left). At the opposite end of the scale, those that are not in attractive industries and are weak should be divested (bottom right). For those companies in the middle, the decision is not so clear-cut.

This is illustrated in Figure 10.3 below – the GE/McKinsey Portfolio Planning Matrix.

Industry Attractiveness

	High	Medium	Low
High	STRONG INVESTMENT	INVEST	SELECTIVE INVESTMENT
Medium	INVEST	SELECTIVE INVESTMENT	HARVEST/ DIVEST
Low	SELECTIVE INVESTMENT	HARVEST/ DIVEST	DIVEST

(Vertical axis label: **Competitive Strength**)

Figure 10.3 *The GE/McKinsey Portfolio Planning Matrix*

Corporate Parenting

We saw in Chapter 7 that the main function of the corporate headquarters is to add value to the organisation as a whole. According to Grant (2010: 433) one major drawback with both the Boston Consulting matrix and the GE/McKinsey matrix is that they regard each of the business units in the matrix as being a separate entity, while one of the most basic arguments in favour of a multi-business organisation is the existence of synergy between all the various companies. There is an implicit assumption in the above models that there is a balance between each of the companies in the portfolio. However, there may not be any synergy present, and the inclusion of any one company in a portfolio does not automatically represent added value. To overcome these weaknesses, Campbell *et al.* (1995) proposed a parenting framework to examine where companies create value in the portfolio of businesses they own. The focus is thus on the competences of the parent and the value created from the relationship between the corporate parent and its businesses. Where there is a good fit between the parent and the business, value will be created. If none exists, then value will be destroyed.

The parenting framework assessment process has two parts. It begins with identifying the Key Success Factors (KSFs – see Chapter 5) of each business in the portfolio. Every business has activities that are critical to its performance and the creation of competitive advantage, and these will vary in different industries. (A corporate parent that does not understand the KSFs in a business is likely to destroy value.) Identifying KSFs will also enable the headquarters to compare how similar the KSFs are among the various businesses and where there is a parenting opportunity.

In the second part of the parenting framework process, the parent examines where performance can be improved – where it can add value to the business. This might be in a wide variety of areas such as reducing costs or creating economies of scale in marketing, better management, providing a clearer business definition, common capabilities, access to finance or perhaps the business may need to undergo a major restructuring.

A business may be performing well or poorly without the parent having any real influence on that performance. Therefore, it can be difficult for companies to judge exactly the level of value added by the parent. Campbell *et al.* recommend that the performance of the business in the portfolio is compared with the industry average return on investment using the Profit Impact of Marketing Strategies (PIMS) methodology. PIMS is a database containing detailed information about various aspects of performance submitted confidentially by participating companies. These results are combined and companies can then compare their results, thus indicating whether their performance is on par, above or below the average for that industry.

The examination of the compatibility of KSFs and where the parent can add value can then be brought together in a matrix (see **Figure 10.4**).

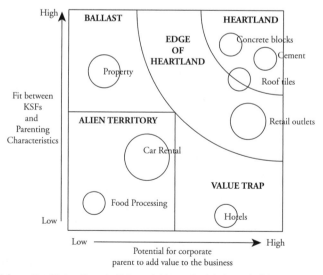

Source: Adapted from Goold A., Campbell A. and Alexander M. (1995), "Corporate Strategy: The Quest for Parenting Advantage", *Harvard Business Review*, March/April 1995, Vol. 73 Issue 2, pp. 120–132.

Figure 10.4 *Parenting Matrix: (the Ashridge Portfolio Display) A Diversified Buildings Material Group*

Each business in the portfolio can be plotted on the matrix and its position can then direct corporate strategy for those businesses. Campbell *et al.* categorise them as follows:

Heartland businesses – these are the core of the company's strategy, as the parent understands the Key Success Factors very well and there are ample opportunities to add value. In **Figure 10.4**, the concrete block and cement businesses are central to the company.

Edge of heartland – judgement is difficult here as some businesses will fit and others may not match very well. In the example in **Figure 10.4**, the retail outlets can benefit in many ways from the corporate parent but there is some gap between the KSFs of the parent and the retail business. This can take up a lot of management time in the beginning as the corporate parent tries to understand it better. If they succeed, the retail outlets business may move into the heartland.

Ballast – here the potential for further value is low, but the business sits well in terms of the KSF fit with the parent. The important thing is there is also little opportunity to destroy value as the parent is familiar with, in this case, the property business. Ballast businesses are usually a good source of cash flow and steady earnings, but slow growth can be a drag on the company and may drift into alien territory or be taken over.

Alien Territory – here, there is little potential for adding value and a poor match between the KSF of the business and parenting characteristics, as depicted by the food processing and car rental business in the example in **Figure 10.4**. These companies may well be quite profitable, but in all probability, the parent will be destroying value by having them in the portfolio, and in most cases would be better off divesting them.

Value Trap – here, there are opportunities to add value, but there is little fit between the KSF of running a hotel (such as service and yield management) and building materials businesses. The opportunity to create value often blinds senior managers to the risks involved. Value is usually destroyed and the business usually ends up worth a good deal less.

Portfolio frameworks such as the Boston Consulting Matrix and the GE/McKinsey Matrix look at companies primarily as stand-alone entities rather than addressing the more fundamental question of whether the businesses are better off as a result of the influence of the corporate parent. The Parenting Matrix addresses this important issue. Parenting skills are usually developed from deeply held values making change difficult. In most cases, therefore, it is easier to change the company mix in the portfolio to suit the corporate parent rather than trying to get the corporate headquarters to develop new parenting skills. As a result, the corporate parent can then develop strategy that is more likely to create value across its portfolio because it is using parenting fit as the criteria rather than an excess of cash on its balance sheet prompting the company to make acquisitions.

CONCLUSION

For many conglomerates, the path to diversification was probably due more to emergent strategy than any particular design. Such diversification poses many challenges for managers as they try to maximise the value from the overall group. In many cases, value may well be increased by divesting some of the companies. Perhaps one of the biggest challenges for senior executives is developing enough expertise in all of the different industries represented by the group's constituent companies. Providing such depth of knowledge is a very difficult process and, in reality, those at the top are highly reliant on the CEOs of the various companies in the group. Consequently, it requires a more hands-off approach to corporate parenting and, again, this highlights the importance of selecting the right people that will fit in with the organisation. Larger companies such as General Electric also go to great lengths to develop its managers so that they can assume such responsibility.

SUMMARY

As companies grow in size, they often develop in different ways from their original business, branching into different types of businesses or technologies and becoming diversified. The task of crafting a diversified company's overall strategy involves four distinct aspects:

- Picking new industries to enter and deciding on the means of entry. Should the focus be a broad or narrow diversification and should it be achieved by organic growth or acquisition?
- Initiating actions to boost the combined performance of the businesses the firm has entered. It must strengthen the long-term competitive position of each company and the overall group.
- Pursuing opportunities to create cross-business leverage – looking for ways to reduce costs and create efficiencies.
- Establishing investment priorities and steering corporate resources into the most attractive business units.

There are a number of reasons why a company might diversify. The acid test is ultimately whether diversifying increases shareholder wealth. Diversification can be divided into two broad classifications:

- **Related diversification**, where there are common links between the value chains of each company. There are two subdivisions:
  o Vertical integration, either forward or backward integration
  o Horizontal integration

- **Unrelated diversification**, where the company moves into a business where there is no common link in their value chains.

There are different methods for achieving diversification in a company, including internal start-up (organic growth), joint ventures and acquisitions. In a conglomerate, not all constituent companies will have the same characteristics and perform at the same level. Therefore, the corporate headquarters needs to maintain a watching brief on the entire organisation and take corrective measures in individual companies whenever necessary.

The Boston Consulting Group Matrix and the Directional Policy Matrix can be useful tools for managers to gain a good overview of the entire portfolio of companies, not just singly but in how they relate to one another in the group in terms of the transfer of resources. The Parenting Matrix examines whether the corporate parent can add value to businesses in its portfolio and whether there is an understanding of the KSFs of that business. Those businesses that fall into the 'Heartland' category will benefit from the parenting skills, and consequently add value to the corporate parent.

DISCUSSION QUESTIONS

1. Critically analyse the reasons why a company might choose a strategy of diversification.
2. Differentiate between the various forms of diversification.
3. Select a diversified company and identify its various constituent businesses. Identify any common theme that links the various elements together.
4. With reference to question 1 above, in your opinion does the corporate parent add or destroy value?
5. Discuss how an organisation might analyse the contribution of various businesses in its portfolio.

REFERENCES

Bettis, R. and Prahalad, C., 1995, "The Dominant Logic: Retrospective and Extension", *Strategic Management Journal*, Vol. 16, Issue 1, 1995, pp.5–15

Carey, B., 2008, "Fund Boss Wants DCC Broken Up", *Sunday Times*, 29 June 2008

Campbell, A. *et al.*, 1995, "Corporate Strategy: The Quest for Parenting Advantage", *Harvard Business Review*, March/April 1995, Vol. 73, Issue 2, pp.120–132

Early, P. C. and Mosakowski, E., 2004, "Cultural Intelligence", *Harvard Business Review*, October 2004, Vol. 82, Issue 10, pp.139–146

Fitzroy, P. and Hulbert, J., 2005, *Strategic Management: Creating Value in Turbulent Times*, Chichester, Wiley

Ghemawat, P., 2010, "Finding your strategy in the new landscape", *Harvard Business Review*, March 2010, Vol. 88, Issue 2, pp.54–60

Goold, M. and Campbell, A., 1998, "Desperately Seeking Synergy", *Harvard Business Review*, Sept/Oct 1998, Vol. 76, Issue 2, pp.131–145

Goold, M. *et al.*, 1994, *Corporate Level Strategy: Creating Value in a Multi-business Company*, Chichester, Wiley

Grant, R., 2010, *Contempory Strategic Analysis: Text and Cases*, 7th Edition, Chichester, John Wiley & Sons Ltd

Harper, N. and Viguerie, P., 2002, "Are You Too Focused?", *The McKinsey Quarterly*, 2002 Special Edition: Risk and Resilience

Johnson, G. *et al.*, 2008, *Exploring Corporate Strategy, Text and Cases*, 8th Edition, Harlow, Essex, Prentice Hall, Financial Times

Lane, B., 2008, *Jacked Up: The Inside Story of How Jack Welch talked GE into Becoming the World's Greatest Company*, New York, McGraw-Hill

Lyons, T. and Carey, B., 2011, *The Fitzpatrick Tapes*, Dublin, Penguin Ireland

Markides, C., 1997, "To Diversify or Not to Diversify", *Harvard Business Review*, November/December 1997, Vol. 75, Issue 6, pp.93–99

O'Brien, J. and Marakas, G., 2008, *Management Information Systems*, 8th Edition, New York, McGraw-Hill

Peters, T. and Waterman, R., 1982, *In Search of Excellence*, New York, Warner Books

Thompson, A. *et al.*, 2008, *Crafting and Executing Strategy: The Quest for Competitive Advantage*, New York, McGraw-Hill

www.quinn-group.com, Accessed 6 August 2008

Alternative Methods of Developing Strategy Options

"Interdependence is and ought to be as much the ideal of men as self-sufficiency."

Gandhi

INTRODUCTION

The previous two chapters looked at Ansoff's Matrix to explore the four possible development directions a company can take. There are a number of methods by which these strategies can be achieved:

- Internal development (also known as organic growth) is concerned with how a company grows incrementally year after year, using its own resources such as retained earnings along with borrowings. It is a very important method of achieving growth for the vast majority of companies.
- Strategic alliances involve teaming up with other companies and pooling resources in a mutually-beneficial way. They can take many different forms and vary in duration from short-term arrangements to ones lasting many years.
- Mergers and acquisitions are where one company takes control over another. As the Irish economy grows, so too do the number of M&As each year.
- Particular industry conditions will mean the tailoring of specific strategies to accommodate those conditions.

Each one will be examined in detail and it will be seen that these methods are quite different from one another in a number of respects. Once again, the methods shown here are by no means mutually exclusive and it would be quite common for a company to pursue a number of these methods simultaneously.

Strategy is largely dependent on the context surrounding the organisation. The final part of this chapter deals with various industry conditions and examines which method is more appropriate for any given situation.

INTERNAL DEVELOPMENT

Internal development, or organic growth as it is sometimes called, is common to every type of organisation and is generally the main method of development. It involves the company growing using its own resources and capabilities. Internal development can be used as a means to achieve all of the directions discussed in the last two chapters: growing market share, developing new products, market development, or diversification. Normally, the investment in organic growth can be either for offensive (taking the initiative) or defensive (reacting to moves by competitors) reasons.

The funding required for internal development may come from a number of sources. For most established companies funding would come from retained earnings – profits built up over a few years, along with bank borrowings. In recent times, bank borrowings are getting more difficult to obtain due to the current credit squeeze. The availability of credit tends to go in cycles and is also dependent on the rates of interest prevailing at the time. For most of this decade, interest rates in Ireland were at a historical low, making borrowing very cheap. Once companies can earn a greater return on their development, it makes sense in most cases to borrow.

If large amounts of funding are needed, the company may raise fresh equity, probably in the form of a rights issue. (Issues about the nature of funding have been discussed in Chapter 7.) Suffice to say, retained earnings will form an important element of the funding as companies will want to reinvest this money to create greater profitability in the future. The amount of funding raised in the various forms would depend on the nature and scope of the growth involved, depending on whether it is incremental or adding a major amount of new capacity. Especially in the case of incremental development, it has the advantage of spreading the cost over a greater period of time, thus easing pressure on cash flow in any one particular year. While borrowing has positive tax implications (interest payments can be offset against tax), it does place a level of financial risk on the company, and this is minimised when the development takes place over a number of years.

Organic growth avoids one major issue that occurs with the various forms of alliances and with mergers and acquisitions, and that is cultural compatibility. (The implications of this are presented in greater detail below.) Any new staff being recruited as a result of the development will, as part of their induction and training, be slotted into existing structures and work patterns and will be absorbed into the culture of the organisation. As a consequence, growth does not have a disruptive effect in terms of the internal politics of the company (the impact of company politics on organisational strategy was examined in Chapter 1).

In order to enter new markets, a business may initially use an indigenous company to distribute its exports or maybe form a joint venture. This is often the practice as the business may have very limited knowledge and experience in operating in such a market. In further developing that market, it may decide to do so by internal development and establish its own greenfield site. This would then give an organisation far greater control in that it is not dependent on any other company and can therefore develop at its own pace. In turn, this will build up the company's own internal capability and knowledge, which will assist it in further development either in that market or in others.

There are situations where there is no other choice open to a company if it is to grow. In the case of brand new technology, it may well be that one company is far more advanced than any of its rivals, and there are no suitable firms to acquire or with which to form a joint venture in terms of advancing the development. As a result, there is no option but to continue the development internally. On other occasions, a suitable acquisition opportunity may just not present itself.

Internal development is quite common, for example, in the hotel industry where companies add extra facilities (such as building a spa) and capacity on an incremental basis. In Chapter 9, we looked at how the Jurys Doyle Group sold the 20 Jurys Inns to the private investor group, Quinlan Private. Since then, the new owners have added another three hotels to the group and have another six in the pipeline (Curran, 2008).

Illustration 11.1 gives an example of an Irish company that has grown since it was established in 1997 using a mixture of organic growth and acquisition. It also illustrates how a company chooses to outsource some aspects of its operations in order to concentrate on core areas.

Illustration 11.1: Insomnia Coffee Company

Insomnia Coffee Company (Redcoral Catering Ltd) was founded in 1997 by four Irish entrepreneurs who identified an opportunity in the rapidly growing market for premium coffee. They opened their first outlet in Galway and this was quickly followed by six outlets in the Dublin area. Insomnia is now the largest premium coffee and sandwich retail chain in Ireland.

What led to this successful growth? The company initially started off selling freshly-roasted premium coffee in retail outlets. In 2002, the company acquired the Bendini & Shaw sandwich chain to provide sandwich and food products alongside its range of coffee. The range includes 29 different varieties of homemade sandwiches and a selection of 11 different breads. To ensure top quality, the sandwiches are freshly made throughout the day. There is also a wide variety of freshly baked bagels, pastries and desserts. These are outsourced to selected suppliers who can meet high standards of quality, and this allows Insomnia to concentrate on their core area of expertise. They also offer a range of soups and gourmet Italian panini. In 2005, Insomnia signed a deal with Fairtrade Ireland, which represents the biggest Fairtrade deal and 20% of all Fairtrade coffee business in Ireland.

Insomnia's stores are designed to offer a relaxing atmosphere to enjoy the coffee experience. Service is an essential element of any company. In order to maximise sales, Insomnia delivers its products to offices around Dublin catering for early breakfast, or after-hours meetings.

In October 2005, Insomnia acquired the Perk chain of coffee shops. The company now has 52 outlets in total including partnership arrangements with Spar, Meadows & Byrne and Gardenworks. In addition, it has 65 'bean to cup' self-service facilities in Spar shops. In 2007, the Penninn Group purchased a 51% stake in the privately-owned company. Penninn is a major Icelandic-based diversified group with interests in retail, coffee roasting and distribution, office supplies and book stores. The original shareholders still retain a 49% shareholding and are actively involved in managing and growing the business.

Source: www.insomnia.ie and interview with CEO Mr Bobby Kerr

STRATEGIC ALLIANCES

Strategic alliances have grown enormously in popularity over the last 20 years or so. Not only are more and more companies recognising the benefits of entering alliances; some larger companies can be involved in dozens of different alliances simultaneously. Strategic alliances can be contractual, involving ownership, or looser collaborative arrangements between companies.

Definition A **strategic alliance** is when two or more separate companies agree to collaborate on a strategic basis and share resources, risk and control for their mutual benefit.

Globalisation has changed the nature of competition and, according to Ohmae (1989), "in a complex, uncertain world filled with dangerous opponents, it is best not to go it alone". In a globally competitive industry, it can be particularly useful for launching a product around the world simultaneously rather than using a 'cascade' effect moving from one market to another.

As with internal development (above) strategic alliances can be used by companies in achieving the four different development directions discussed in the last chapter. Briefly, these are:

- consolidation – loose, non-contractual agreements to protect market share
- product development – defraying the huge cost and risk involved in research and development and speeding up the development process
- market development – entering new markets internationally using joint sales and distributions systems
- diversification – developing the skills and resources needed to diversify from the main line of business

337

There are many benefits from alliances. Generally speaking, they are a much quicker form of development than internal development. In technology markets in particular, speed is of the essence in developing new products and this can be achieved by collaboration. Alliances are also used to improve various value chain activities and can reduce costs in production and marketing as well as research and development. These costs savings make the members of the alliance more competitive. As mentioned, when discussing entering international markets, alliances can sometimes be a requirement by host governments in foreign markets, either by way of joint ventures or other forms. In other cases, it may not be an actual requirement, but it can help the company in navigating its way through the cultural peculiarities of a foreign market or through the layers of bureaucratic red tape, or both. The need to adapt products for particular markets was also examined and, where a company lacks experience of a certain market, alliance with foreign companies can assist in the process of adaptation.

As with all the other options being examined, strategic alliances should be seen as a means to an end – to achieve a specific and important goal for the organisation. An alliance can either be an offensive move to take advantage of an opportunity, or defensive to ward off a threat.

Types of Alliances

There are a wide variety of types of alliances from which to choose. Alliances can vary from long-term agreements to temporary arrangements. Generally speaking, they tend to be long-term when the companies involved are collaborating on either supply or distribution contracts. Alliances based on the development of technology tend to be shorter as the companies realise the benefits in terms of new products coming on stream and then they move on. The different types of alliance include:

- Consortia
- Joint ventures
- Licensing
- Franchising
- Outsourcing
- Networking

Consortia

Contractual alliances involve consortia and joint ventures. A consortium is a group that consists of two or more companies that have come together for a particular purpose, such as developing a large venture. A Public Private Partnership (PPP) is a type of consortium between the state and a private company to develop, for example, hospitals and schools as well as major infrastructural projects. In many cases, because the cost of the project is so immense, a number of banks would be part of the consortium, as the financial risk would be too great for any one bank to bear on its own. The total cost of completing the Dublin Port Tunnel was approximately €700 million (which was almost twice the original estimate) and development costs such as this are best spread over a number of different groups.

The redevelopment of the Docklands area in Dublin has seen some magnificent new buildings being constructed. The cost of some of these developments has been enormous – in some cases too expensive for any one developer – and one of the most expensive sites ever bought in Ireland was the old Glass Bottle site in Ringsend, Dublin. It was purchased in 2006 for €413 million by a consortium consisting of builder Bernard McNamara, financier Derek Quinlan, the Dublin Docklands Development Authority and Davy private clients. This has proved to be a controversial purchase with the site now worth a fraction of the price that was originally paid. Another consortium that hit the headlines in 2010 relates to the Gulf of Mexico oil disaster. While BP took the brunt of the criticism for the disaster, the Deepwater Horizon rig was in fact owned by a consortium comprising BP (65%), Anadarko (25%) and the Japanese group Mitsui (10%). There are many other companies actually involved in the extraction of the oil. The Deepwater Horizon rig was built by Hyundai and was supplied by the world's largest offshore drilling contractor, Transocean. In turn, the US company Halliburton had responsibility for cementing the rig in place. The blowout preventer was manufactured by Cameron International, a specialist engineering company. BP is hoping to share the cost of the damage with its consortium partners, but this is being disputed by the other members.

(See also the case study, "BP and Deepwater Horizon" at the back of this book.)

For expensive projects such as this, consortia are a common method of development, as it spreads the risk between a number of individuals and institutions.

Joint Ventures

 A joint venture is when two companies come together and create an alliance in the form of a third company that is jointly owned and managed by the two parents, who remain separate entities.

Both companies will contribute dedicated assets and resources to the joint venture, in order to spread the risk involved. Firms wishing to enter some markets such as China will often be required by the government there to form a joint venture with a Chinese company. China is rapidly making the transition to a market economy and joint ventures are seen by the government as a means for domestic companies to develop the resources and skills required to compete in global markets. The Chinese car market is a rapidly growing and competitive market. Foreign car manufacturers are obliged to form joint ventures with Chinese manufacturers. There were 13.8 million passenger cars sold in China in 2010. Chinese car manufacturers have about 30% of the domestic market and are keen to grow that market share, particularly in the small car market, which is the fastest growing and most competitive segment. Foreign car manufacturers are under pressure from the Beijing government to transfer more technology to their Chinese partners to boost "indigenous innovation". This arrangement has been in place for the last 25 years, and the Chinese are frustrated at the slow level of technology transfer.

Volkswagen has partnered with two local manufacturers: FAW Volkswagen and SAIC Volkswagen and is currently in talks about a joint brand. Another group, SGMW, a joint venture between General Motors, SAIC and Wuling manufactures mini-commercial vehicles and recently produced its first own-brand car, the Baojun 630. Nissan, and its joint-venture partner Dongfeng Motors, hope to launch a car in 2012. Honda and Guangzuhou Automobile also hope to launch a car in 2012. Foreign manufacturers are dissatisfied with this arrangement, but have little choice if they wish to operate in China. For GM, its rationale is that, through joint ventures, it can get access to a market of about six million cars that otherwise it would not be able to operate in. By jointly producing small cars with Chinese partners, foreign manufacturers are creating further opportunities that would not otherwise be available to them. This is seen as being particularly important as the small car market is where the big growth is expected to be for the foreseeable future. While existing joint ventures are based on a 50:50 basis, the Chinese government is insisting that any new-energy vehicle joint ventures (such as electric cars) will be majority controlled by Chinese companies (Waldmeir, 2011).

Some Irish semi-state companies have entered into joint ventures abroad. One such company that has engaged in many joint ventures in foreign countries is ESB International (a subsidiary of the Electricity Supply Board), which provides consultancy services overseas in building and managing power plants. Since its establishment in 1973, ESB International has been involved in over 150 countries. Another company involved in joint ventures abroad is Aer Rianta International, a subsidiary of the Dublin Airport Authority. It has developed airports and duty-free facilities in cities around the globe. Joint ventures can create great opportunities for many companies who are trying to access foreign markets. However, according to Walsh (2010), not every company is willing to take on board the restrictions imposed by joint venture agreements. Louis Vuitton, part of LVMH (Moët Hennessy Louis Vuitton) is the world's biggest luxury leather goods brand and the company has recently expanded and opened stores in Lebanon, Poland and the Dominican Republic. Their major expansion in the last few years has been to China. Overall, the Asian market now accounts for 25% of the group's revenues, beating Europe (19%) and America (23%). The company has plans to expand further in China. There are 1.3 billion people there who, according to Yves Carcelle, CEO of Louis Vuitton, "want to treat themselves, and it will continue. In China, there is a genuine sense of aspiration." He believes that people can migrate from the country, work hard and achieve prosperity.

However, Mr Carcelle sees India as being different, where there is little change in many people's lives. Louis Vuitton has only four stores in India. Carcelle cites poor infrastructure, protectionist policies and slow decision-making as the reasons for not expanding more in India. He is particularly scathing on the ban on foreign companies having full ownership of any company in India. Mr Carcelle believes "it's an unfair and stupid policy because it slows down investment. I'm not risking opening 20 stores if I have to share the capital with somebody I don't know."

Louis Vuitton exercises very tight control over its brand, and the company directly controls each of their 460 stores worldwide and does not operate using joint ventures, licences, or franchises. In 2009, though sales in the luxury goods market worldwide were down 20% because of the recession, Louis Vuitton managed to break-even. It achieved double-digit growth for 2010.

While Louis Vuitton has chosen not to use joint ventures as a means of greater expansion into foreign markets, it must be remembered that the size and success of the company has given it many options that would not be available to other smaller companies.

One of the main issues to be decided in forming a joint venture is the management of the assets being dedicated to the joint venture, and how the assets of the joint venture relate to, and can be separated from, the parent companies. While the joint venture might spread risk on one hand, this form of alliance also brings risks in terms of the management of the assets and whether one side might take them for their own exclusive use.

Licensing

In Chapter 9 it was stated that there are occasions when a company may not have the resources or organisational capability to operate directly in another country, and it may license a company in another state to manufacture the product and use its trademark in return for an initial fee and an annual royalty based on production. It also has the advantage of minimising financial exposure as it does not involve committing resources and, as such, is an alternative to foreign direct investment. As discussed above in the section on joint ventures, it may be a government condition to operate in that market. In other cases it may just suit a company to issue a licence to another company in order to reduce the production or distribution cost, as in the Carlsberg example. The capital cost of building a brewery is quite substantial, and by licensing its product, Carlsberg avoids this huge capital cost and large transportation costs in what would be a relatively small market for its product. Another licensed product that consumers in Ireland would be familiar with is the French yoghurt, Yoplait.

Licensing can also be particularly useful in a situation where the political climate in a country is somewhat unstable. It is then seen as an attractive alternative to foreign direct investment as it minimises the financial exposure involved. Licensing is normally more common with technological products. Airlines now have the ability to allow passengers to use mobile phones on board aircraft. The technology underpinning this was developed by Altrobridge, a Tralee-based company founded by entrepreneur Mike Fitzgerald. The technology, which creates a base station and then uses satellites to create links, has been licensed to airlines, shipping companies and emergency services. The company is now targeting remote villages in developing countries in conjunction with large mobile phone operators. Licensing allows Altrobridge (a company of 130 employees) to expand at a much greater pace than would otherwise be possible.

Franchising

Definition

Franchising is a form of licensing whereby the franchisor grants the franchisee the right to use certain intellectual property rights such as brand names, copyrights, patents, etc., in return for various fees.

Franchising is another alternative to direct investment and one that is growing worldwide at a phenomenal pace, particularly in various service industries. Brand recognition is an inherent part of franchising. The examples listed in **Table 11.1** below are all well-known brand names. In a survey carried out for the Irish Franchise Association by Franchise Direct in 2006, there are now more than 270 different franchises in operation in Ireland, employing 25,000 people, accounting for a turnover of €2.1 billion.

By comparison, in the US, there are over 3,000 different franchise operations, and many of the franchises operating here in Ireland originate in the US, including McDonald's. Indeed, only 14% of franchise systems in Ireland originated here. Indigenous franchise businesses include Supermacs, O'Brien's Irish Sandwich Bars and Golden Discs. McDonald's is the largest franchise system in Ireland with 68 outlets. Of these, 48 outlets are franchised to 30 operators; the remaining ones are operated directly by McDonald's Ireland. This part-owning, part-franchising arrangement is quite common among companies that have franchised their business. The following table gives a sample of the various franchise businesses operating in Ireland, and the types of industries in which they operate.

Table 11.1: *A Selection of Franchise Businesses Operating in Ireland*

Abrakebabra	Avis	Topaz
Burger King	Budget Rent-a-Car	Chemdry
Domino's Pizza	Snap Printing	Carraig Donn
Four Star Pizza	Mace	Hilton Hotel
McDonald's Restaurants	Fairplay	Ramada
Supermac's	Centra/Supervalue	Holiday Inn
Pizza Hut	Spar	Radisson
O'Brien's Irish Sandwich Bars	The Body Shop	Senator Windows
Sign Express	Golden Discs	Tilesavers
The Tanning Shop	Weight Watchers	Value Tile
		Source: www.aib.ie/business

Franchising is an ideal way for someone with limited commercial experience to start a business, as they are buying into a tried and tested business model, with training and backup support, and a marketing network. This expertise and backup reduces the time required to set up a successful business. There would also be a performance clause to ensure that the conditions and standards must be met, particularly, for example, in food safety, hygiene and storage arrangements.

While franchising is a very good idea for someone setting up in business, there are also some downsides. The franchise agreement is quite prescriptive in how the business is operated, and any deviation from the required model would terminate the franchise. Thus, it offers little scope for initiative by the franchisee (the person taking out the franchise). If there is any damage done to the franchise brand in general, it will obviously impact directly on the franchisor (the company that is franchising its business) as well as on each franchisee of that brand. Unlike a normal business, the franchisee does not have the freedom to sell the franchise without the prior agreement of the franchisor, and goodwill would not be part of the sale price as it remains with the franchise owner. It is important that care is taken in selecting franchise operators as there must be compatibility between the two parties to ensure a smooth operation, as it is, after all, a binding legal agreement.

The fees involved vary considerably depending on the franchise but would normally include an initial franchise fee. According to the Irish Franchise Association, these fees vary from €2,500 to €125,000, with an average fee around €25,000. The franchisee would also be expected to have sufficient working capital to operate the business on a day-to-day basis. There will also be other investment requirements to fit out the premises to the standard required by the franchisor as part of the business concept, and to fund equipment and vehicles. This could amount to perhaps €500,000 for bigger operations, but for most businesses the average would be about €150,000. In addition, a percentage of the turnover would be paid as a royalty fee (typically 6.5%) and a marketing fee (typically 2.5%). Normally the franchisee would also be obliged to buy all their supplies and materials from the franchisor (an additional form of income for the franchisor). Because of the split of income between the franchisor and franchisee, the franchise arrangement can only operate in an industry with reasonable margins. Generally speaking, the franchisee would have exclusive rights to a certain geographic area, so that two franchise operations are not competing for the same customer base.

According to McGarry (2007), there are certain preconditions necessary before considering franchising a business. It must have:

- A profitable track record to allow for profits for both the company and investors.
- Name protection, so that the company has exclusive rights to that trademark.
- A clear identity that separates the business from competitors.
- Transferable operations – one that can be transferred from one location to another while delivering consistency of product or service to the customer.
- Management depth to provide potential franchisees with training, and all of the operating manuals and other material that they need.

From a strategic perspective, franchising is an ideal way to rapidly expand a business while incurring little risk in the process. It is each individual franchisee that is putting up their own capital to invest in the business, while the franchisor gets the fees. The total amount raised by the fees may not be the equivalent of the profits from owning businesses outright, but they still amount to considerable profit once the business concept is sound, with good consumer appeal. In 1987 Starbucks was a modest nine-store operation in the Northwest of the United States. In the intervening time, Howard Schultz, its founder and chairman, has transformed the company into a multinational enterprise which now has 15,000 stores around the world. This enormous expansion could not have been achieved by organic growth alone, leaving aside the inherent risk involved in such rapid growth. It is easy to see how franchising is becoming such a popular strategy for expanding businesses.

Outsourcing

Outsourcing is a form of alliance that is becoming more and more popular with a wide variety of firms. This is when a company makes a decision not to perform some value chain activities itself and subcontracts them to another business specialising in that activity. Many companies are gaining a better understanding of their strategic capabilities and, just as importantly, any value chain activities in which they do not excel. Traditional economic theory would suggest that it is better to spend time and effort concentrating on those parts of the operation where one has a comparative advantage. The remaining activities can be farmed out to a company that can perform them better or cheaper than they can be in-house (see **Illustration 11.1** — Insomnia Coffee Company above).

The company providing the service can also be expected to keep up-to-date with all aspects of that service and any new developments. This reduces the risk to the main company regarding any changes in technology that may take place within the outsourced activity area. The other side to the decision to outsource is that it then allows the company doing the outsourcing to concentrate on the core areas that are critical to its success. In cases of expansion into new markets or product areas, it also gives the company the flexibility to acquire access to the skills that they need but may not have already. The one critical factor is picking the right activities to be outsourced.

In choosing those activities, it is best to pick ones that are non-crucial to the firm in achieving competitive advantage. A common example of an activity suitable for outsourcing is office cleaning. Offices need to be cleaned in the evening when most staff have left. By outsourcing this activity a company is not employing cleaning staff that are underutilised for long periods of time. Instead, cleaning companies will have a team that can get through the offices in a very short time and then move on to the next office block.

Companies can outsource many other activities. Various administrative functions such as payroll activities are outsourced. A company that passes on all legal matters to a particular firm of solicitors is effectively outsourcing. We have already seen in Chapter 6 how Nike outsources its manufacturing process to companies mainly situated in the Far East. At first glance, the manufacture of their product line might seem like a critical activity and one that should not be outsourced. However, the actual manufacture of clothing apparel is an activity that could be carried out by many manufacturers. What is critical to Nike is the design of their clothing and the lifestyle image that they are creating, and it is that image that people are buying into.

In developing relationships with suppliers, a firm is building up a strong, dedicated arrangement with those suppliers to ensure delivery of goods at the right quality and the right time. This is a central part of the process in controlling cost and quality of the brand. It is also a departure from a more adversarial arrangement based purely on the cheapest price. 'Just-in-time' requires a very close relationship where much information is exchanged between the two companies and it is in effect an alliance between the manufacturing company and the supplier for the delivery of its inputs. As with most other types of alliances, it is critical to pick a suitable partner.

Networking

The final type of alliance is networking. This is very much a non-contractual arrangement that is extremely loose, but nevertheless is beneficial to all concerned. Each company maintains full control over its activities. There are many different types of networking arrangement. Most industries have representative bodies acting on behalf of all members in areas of common interest. Take licensed premises, for example: each pub is in competition with all other rival pubs for business. Like other industries, there are also areas of common concern on which publicans would like to see action taken, such as the level of excise and VAT. In these cases, their representative bodies provide a forum for each industry to voice its concerns.

Code sharing agreements between airlines is another type of networking. Code sharing agreements are where airlines feed business into rival airlines that are members of the network, but are not competing on the same route. They will sell tickets that can be used by passengers using the other airlines and would recognise each other's frequent flyer miles, etc. The One World Alliance is an example. This consists of 10 members: American Airways, British Airways, Cathay Pacific, Finnair, Iberia, Japanese Airlines, LAN Argentina, Qantas, Malév (Hungary) and Royal Jordanian. Until recently, Aer Lingus was also a member, but since it is now concentrating mainly on budget routes, it has withdrawn from the arrangement. The code sharing agreement works on the basis that a business person going on a work trip to a number of destinations might book a ticket through, e.g. British Airways to fly from London to Singapore, then go to a meeting in Tokyo with JAL and then on to Melbourne with Qantas – all on the one ticket.

Managing Alliances

There is a wide variety of possible alliances and each one has its own requirements in terms of how it might be managed. Some large organisations may have a number of alliances operating simultaneously and so the process needs to be managed similar to a portfolio. At the outset, senior management needs to be very clear about what it hopes to achieve in terms of strategic and financial objectives from an alliance and, indeed, as to whether an alliance is the best way to achieve those objectives. According to Dyer *et al.* (2004: 109), "alliances typically create very little wealth for shareholders". Thompson *et al.* (2008: 167) quotes research carried out in 1999 by the global consulting company Accenture in saying that "61% of alliances were either outright failures or 'limping along'." Oscar Wilde's observations on marriage would appear to have some similarities:

> "Men marry because they are bored. Women marry because they are curious. Both are disappointed."

All parties to the arrangement must have a shared understanding of what it will bring to them. It will take a considerable amount of management time to make it work and to achieve the synergies involved. The previous chapter looked at how synergies can be greatly over-estimated in diversified companies. This can also apply to managing alliances. It will be easier to achieve synergies when management has definite objectives in mind, before crafting the alliance to achieve them. Both sides will need to be clear about the rules for decision-making in terms of the scope of decisions, as well as what level in the organisation they are made and the process by which those decisions are made. It is also important that the mechanism allows for decisions to be made in a timely fashion.

Cross-business teams will have to work closely together on all aspects of the relationship. As people get to know one another, it is easier to iron out potential problems. Different corporate and national cultures complicate the process and this will have to be worked on to ensure that both parties are culturally sensitive to the other. Choosing partners is not just about the sharing of technology but also the compatibility of people. Kanter (1994) believes that top executives spend more time screening potential partners in financial terms than in managing the partnership in human terms. "They worry more about controlling the relationship than about nurturing it." It is therefore important to choose potential partners with great care. Alliances are about organisations working together and that implies trust.

It takes time to build up trust and, according to Ohmae (1989), one problem many organisations have is a fixation on control of equity, which "equates 51% with 100% and 49% with 0%". The trust has to be maintained for the duration of the alliance. For a successful alliance to happen, both parties must be able to see things from the perspective of the other side and to continue to live up to their commitments.

In Chapter 3, we discussed the Balanced Scorecard. Kaplan and Norton (2010) also recommend the use of the Balanced Scorecard for managing strategic alliances as a means of increasing the chances of success. They argue that an alliance usually gets defined by service level agreements that focus on what each side will contribute to the arrangement rather than what they hope to gain. By developing a Balanced Scorecard specifically for the alliance, it shifts the emphasis from operational performance metrics to a strategic focus that cuts across organisational boundaries.

Circumstances can very often change an alliance. There has to be flexibility built into the arrangement so that it can evolve as the environment takes on a different shape. Technology is constantly developing and nothing stays proprietary for very long. Similarly, market conditions change and companies must be in a position to respond. Some alliances may be intended as short-term arrangements. This is often the case where the arrangement is based on technology, with quickly changing conditions. Other alliances, for example between suppliers and manufacturers, have long-term potential, provided that the relationship can evolve in a way that remains satisfactory to all sides.

MERGERS AND ACQUISITIONS

Mergers and acquisitions happen when two organisations come together, but differ in terms of ownership and management.

Definition　A **merger** is where the companies involved, normally similar in size, agree to come together to form a new company, generally changing the name in the process.

Unlike alliance, merger is a reasonably permanent arrangement, although there are circumstances when the companies subsequently demerge.

Definition An **acquisition** is where one company takes over or acquires another one.

Generally, acquisition involves a large company acquiring a smaller company and absorbing it into its own operations. The acquired company may continue to trade under its own name or it may be changed to that of its new owner.

Occasionally, there can be a 'reverse takeover' such as Alpyra's reverse takeover of Cardpoint Plc in 2007 to create Payzone, a consumer payment and cash distribution group. A reverse takeover is the purchase of a publically traded company by an unlisted one.

Worldwide, there are tens of thousands of mergers and acquisitions each year. It is not just manufacturing companies that engage in mergers and acquisitions. In July 2008, for example, after six months of negotiations, accountancy firm Farrell Grant Sparks merged with Dublin accountancy firm Moore Stephens Caplin Meehan. The merged group is named FGS.

Currently, however, a lot of uncertainty hangs over M&A activity in Ireland due to the recession. According to Simmons (2011), the market picked up in 2010 from the previous year and there were 197 deals worth some €10.3 billion involving Irish companies. The previous year, 2009, saw 134 deals totalling just €3.4 billion. Some of the bigger transactions in 2010 included the acquisition of Impress Holdings by Ardagh Glass for €1.7 billion and the ESB's acquisition of Northern Ireland's electricity network from Veridian for €1.4 billion. While the year started off slowly, the value of M&As picked up as the year went on.

One feature of the deals conducted in 2010 was the number of foreign acquisitions by Irish companies (see below). According to the NCB Corporate Finance M&A Tracker Survey, CRH plc took the lead with 28 transactions, while Kerry Group made four acquisitions in total. The most active sectors during 2010 were information technology and telecoms; building; construction and property; and industrial. The food and food services industry was also busy, accounting for 24 deals, as were the health and pharmaceutical sectors.

One reason for the pickup in M&A activity in 2010 was the mopping up of distressed businesses and assets, such as Énergie Group's acquisition of Jackie Skelly Fitness Clubs. This is a trend that is likely to continue for the foreseeable future. One major constraint at present is the difficulty in getting sufficient funding, although for larger companies, with a proven track record, it should not be an insurmountable problem.

A sample of recent acquisition deals showing a variety of industries, nationalities and prices includes:

- United Drug (Ireland) purchased InforMed Direct PLC (UK) for €13.8 million
- Premira (UK) acquired a majority shareholding in Creganna-Tactx Medical (Ireland) for €158 million

- Singapore Technologies Telemedia (Singapore) acquired Eircom (Ireland) for €47.6 million
- Aryzta AG (Ire/Swiss) bought Fresh Start Bakeries (USA) for €791 million
- Kerry Group plc (Ireland) bought Newmarket Co-operative (Ireland) for €33 million
- Fexco Holdings Ltd (Ireland) acquired Goodbody Holdings Ltd (Ireland) for €24 million
- Smurfit Kappa Group (Ireland) bought Mondi plc (UK) for €51 million
- CRH plc (Ireland) acquired an additional 50% stake in Bauking (Germany) for €126 million
- Kingspan plc (Ireland) bought CRH Insulation Europe (Ireland) for €120 million
- Greenstar Environmental Ltd (Ireland) acquired Veolia Environmental Services (Ireland) for €50 million
- Investricity (Ireland) bought French Power Station (France) for €14 million
- Biffa Waste Management (UK) bought Greenstar UK (Ireland) for €162 million
- W&R Barnett (Northern Ireland) bought a 50% stake in R&H Hall (Origin Enterprises plc) (Ireland) for €52 million
- Eason & Son (Ireland) acquired Hughes & Hughes (Ireland) (seven Irish airport stores) for an undisclosed sum
- Deloitte Ireland (Ireland) acquired Curach Consulting (Ireland) for €7 million

Source: NCB Corporate Finance 2011

Benefits of Mergers and Acquisitions

There are many benefits to mergers and acquisitions (M&As). The premier one is the timeframe involved. Like alliances, M&As allow a company to expand much more quickly than would be possible solely with internal development. With an ongoing target acquisition process to identify suitable candidates for possible acquisition, negotiations may be conducted, due diligence carried out and the whole deal completed in a matter of months. Depending on the size of the merger or acquisition, this could substantially increase the size of the organisation. Kerry Group's new Chief Executive, Stan McCarthy, has stated his intention to double the company's sales to €10 billion over the next few years, mainly through acquisitions.

M&A can also be used as a means of acquiring skills or expertise that a company does not currently own but needs for future development. This is particularly important when industry conditions are changing rapidly. Then speed is of the essence, and internal development may not be a viable option, while an alliance may not provide the desired level of control.

In the previous chapter, it was seen that the share price of a company can sometimes fall significantly for a number of reasons. If there is no immediate prospect of it rising again, its shareholders may wish to sell the company in order to realise their investment. This could present an immediate opportunity for a company to acquire another at a considerable discount, integrate it into its own operations or, in some cases, strip its assets. Likewise, the privatisation of former semi-state companies provides opportunities for acquisition. Having changed hands on a number of occasions, the Australian finance group Babcock & Brown paid €2.4 billion in 2006 for the former state telecommunications company Eircom.

An acquisition can be a good way for a company to enter a static market. Generally, competitors will not see it as a direct threat as it does not increase the capacity of that market and thus cause retaliation by incumbent players. It is also a way in which a fragmented market can be consolidated.

The concept of synergy was discussed in detail in Chapter 10. Acquiring or merging companies can be a way of realising cost efficiencies in a number of areas such as advertising, sales, distribution and transport, research and development, managerial and administrative processes. In 1997, two of Ireland's leading publicly-quoted dairy companies merged to form Glanbia: Waterford Foods Plc and Avonmore Foods Plc. These two companies, in the same industry, were located in close geographical proximity to each other, so the merger allowed considerable efficiencies to be gained.

One big danger with M&As is that executives will pursue them to increase their own power base rather than for the benefit of the organisation. For that reason, board approval should only be given when there are demonstrable benefits to be obtained from the process.

Variety of Mergers and Acquisitions

A common mistake managers make is to consider all mergers and acquisitions to be the same. Bower (2001) conducted a considerable amount of research on M&A deals, and identified the following five categories:

The overcapacity M&A These account for 37% of all deals. The strategic objectives of the acquiring company are to eliminate excess capacity, gain market share and create a more efficient company. It requires the merged company to decide quickly what needs to be rationalised. This will present a number of problems, particularly in the battle for control by managers, as will the merging of different cultures.

The geographic roll-up M&A This may appear similar to the above category but it differs substantially as it generally occurs earlier in the industry's life cycle. It involves the company expanding geographically into desired locations. The acquired companies remain local and maintain their relationship with their customers. In areas of overlap, duplicate facilities can be closed. In both cases, it is creating scale and scope efficiencies. Irish banks expanded in this manner.

Product or market extension M&A This is the next biggest category at 36%, and it is done to extend a company's product line or international reach. It is different from geographic roll-up as it involves bigger companies and moving into different countries, not just adjacent towns and cities. It is more difficult to execute as there will be greater cultural differences and, because it is further from home, difficulty in assessing the deal. Likewise, expanding into new product lines that are different from existing ones can cause difficulties. The company must know what it is buying. It will also require a lot of consideration to develop the acquisition to its full potential. The bigger the acquiring company is compared to its target, the easier the integration process will be.

The M&A as R&D In this case, the acquisition is a substitution for in-house R&D, and allows the company to build market position quickly. Many biotech and IT companies expand in this manner (research shows that it is particularly suitable for IT). The company needs a robust evaluation process in order to ensure that it is acquiring the specific technology that it requires. It does not allow for a slow assimilation of the new company. It is imperative that the company holds on to its human talent in order to reap the entrepreneurial and technological benefits.

The industry convergence M&A In this case, a company anticipates that a new industry is emerging and tries to establish a position by culling resources from existing industries whose boundaries are eroding. The acquirer should rationalise the non-essential elements and install its own accounting and control processes. Thereafter, it requires giving the subsidiary a considerable amount of freedom, and choosing links carefully and diplomatically. Integration should be driven by specific opportunities to create value, not by a perceived need to create a symmetrical organisation.

Process

In Chapter 1, we saw that there is often less emphasis now on the role of detailed format planning in developing corporate strategy. However, any form of alliance or acquisition requires a considerable degree of planning. There are various frameworks to guide the acquisition process. In most instances, there are six main elements that are generic to acquisition programmes:

- Strategic review
- Identifying a suitable company to acquire
- Carrying out due diligence
- Making the acquisition
- Integrating the acquired company
- Review of acquisition

Strategic Review In Part One of this text, we looked at the process of how a company sets strategic and financial goals that it hopes to achieve. Strategy represents the process by which these goals are attained. In that regard, acquisitions like alliances should be seen as a means to an end. They must add value to the company. Thus, there must be a good reason for any proposed acquisition that fits in with the organisation's well-defined strategy. Developing an acquisition strategy requires a full understanding of the business environment and strategic review of the organisation. Uhlaner and West (2008) believe: "One of the most often overlooked, though seemingly obvious, elements of an effective M&A programme is ensuring that every deal supports the corporate strategy". As with strategic alliances, senior managers need to be very clear as to what their strategic and financial objectives are in relation to acquisitions and what they hope to achieve, e.g. a 7% increase in market share. It was stated earlier that Kerry Group plans to expand its sales to €10 billion over the next few years. In this case, they have a clear strategy of expansion using acquisitions as a vehicle.

Part of the strategic review should be the development of a synergy plan. If the acquisition is to add value, then clear synergy objectives need to be identified. In the previous chapter, it was noted that Goold and Campbell (1998) had stated that synergy is often overestimated. The possible synergies that are identified as part of the strategic review should be confirmed during the due diligence process.

Once a decision is made with regard to acquisitions, management then needs to establish criteria to identify the types of opportunities that they could realise. Different deals will involve different approaches and execution, and will have to be tailored for the specific circumstances that currently exist. The company will also need to develop an acquisitions team representing various business functions and SBUs that will search for suitable targets. It is important to get the number and combination of this team correct. Given the huge cost of the acquisition, the process has to be right. This team will need clear guidance as to their function, and will often be assisted by consultancy firms specialising in mergers and acquisitions. Deals will need to have approval in principle from the board of directors.

Identifying a suitable company to acquire In addition to identifying particular companies that may be suitable in terms of strategic and financial objectives, the company must be realistic about what it can achieve in terms of price and the skills required in making a deal. Therefore, they will need specific parameters to guide their search, and a priority for the various factors. It may well be an organisation with which they have a strategic alliance already in place already. The team may examine a few dozen companies. It will draw up a list of possible candidates and this will have to be examined and reduced to a shortlist of those companies that are most likely to fulfil the company's objectives and achieve both a strategic and cultural fit. This will obviously require considerable resources, which must be put in place if the process is to succeed. Eventually, the team will come up with a preference. Procedures for opening discussions and conducting negotiations will also have to be formulated. This will have to include price limits. Initial plans should be made for how the new company will be integrated if the deal is completed.

Carrying out due diligence When the company has identified a specific target that fits the appropriate criteria, it will carry out a process of due diligence on that firm. Due diligence is an essential part of purchasing any company in order to ensure that it will form a proper strategic fit in line with the objectives and to ascertain a reasonable price for the acquisition. It needs to identify the synergies to be realised and how the deal will generate value. It involves doing a review of all aspects of the company's operations in all its functional areas, including product range, sales and marketing, research and development, human resources, and finances (in particular its liabilities). The importance of doing proper due diligence is borne out by the following example.

In 1983, AIB, which had a stake in the Insurance Corporation of Ireland (ICI), bought the remaining shares for £40 million and, according to Carswell (2006), carried out just 'superficial' due diligence. It used auditors Ernst Whinney to value the company. ICI had become a large organisation, covering a wide variety of risk in Ireland and the UK. However, it was poor at evaluating the risk it was underwriting. By 1984, ICI was building up huge losses, particularly in London, and did not have the cash reserves to cover those losses. By the end of the year, the losses were out of control and AIB had to plough another £40 million into the company. The problem was compounded by the fact that insurance is a 'long tail' business, meaning that it is often years after an event that the insurance cover is paid out.

By March 1985, given the enormous scale of the losses in ICI to date, along with unknown future liabilities, AIB informed the Government that it would not underwrite its subsidiary any longer. The scale of the problem was such that it would have brought down AIB, Ireland's largest bank, along with the entire Irish banking industry. The potential impact was so great that the Fine Gael-led Coalition Government was effectively forced to buy ICI from the bank (which wrote off its £86 million investment) for a nominal £1. In so doing, the State also took responsibility for its massive debt. By October 1985, it was estimated that debts would amount to £164 million. The Central Bank set up a rescue package and a new administration company, Icarom, was established to look after the winding up of ICI to meet its ongoing liabilities. In the early 1990s, AIB had agreed to contribute to the cost of the administration and, by 2004, had contributed €134 million with another €80 million due. Ernst Whinney was sued by AIB over the due diligence it had carried out on ICI. In 1993, Ernst Whinney settled out of court, without admission of liability for £39 million (Carswell, 2006). Clearly, it was an expensive exercise for all concerned. It is a sad irony that a quarter of a century later AIB had to be bailed out once again by the citizens of the State. Both of these incidents highlight the critical importance of proper governance structures.

Making the acquisition Once the company is satisfied that the target company represents good value and will help the company achieve its objectives, it can proceed with the deal and finalise arrangements with the company being acquired. All items included in the sale will have to be clearly stated. The company also needs to determine how the deal will be structured and financed. The acquisition will need the approval of the board of directors and other relevant stakeholders. Legal agreements will have to be drawn up by solicitors for both parties, and arrangements made for the closing of the deal.

Integrating the acquired company The acquiring company must act quickly to integrate the new acquisition as seamlessly as possible. It needs to draw up long-term, medium-term and short-term objectives. A priority of work also needs to be established, with an emphasis on the tasks that need to be tackled immediately. Integration involves a considerable amount of change, especially for the acquired company, and this process needs to be managed carefully.

According to Ashkenas and Francis (2000), the integration of an acquired company is a delicate and complicated process. The problem for most organisations is that the team that makes the acquisition then hands over to a management team, which will eventually run the merged organisations, but often, no-one is responsible for the integration process itself. They recommend appointing an integration manager, or what Uhlaner and West (2008) call a 'deal owner' – a senior, experienced, manager who will oversee the process from the very beginning to when integration has been completed. Functional heads would deal with the issues pertaining to their area of responsibility but report to the deal owner who would coach all those involved along the way.

Merging the two cultures is not an easy process. The two companies will have different objectives and priorities. Their corporate values will also be different, as will the way they approach work. Both management and staff in the new company will naturally be fearful. Their tenure needs to be clarified as soon as possible and expectations made clear. Bower (2001) has stressed the importance of holding on to talented personnel. The company will have to make a determined effort to hold on to key people by putting appropriate measures in place.

As with all aspects of management, good communication is vital, so there is a need to develop a communications plan for both organisations to ensure that all people have the information that they need and when they need it. In particular, each employee must understand what the priorities are and how it impacts on their work. Choosing the most appropriate medium for communicating is also important. In some situations, an all-staff email might suffice; on other occasions it will require face-to-face meetings.

The integration process will involve a merging of the two corporate frameworks as well as each of the functional areas. The type of decisions required will include the desired locations for areas such as production facilities, R&D and the various staff functions. There will have to be a review of all contracts for supplies, distribution, advertising, training, etc. One of the most important areas for consideration is a review of operations to identify opportunities for synergies and then ensure that those synergies are created. While each of the functional areas will develop their own objectives, these must be developed in a co-ordinated fashion using frameworks such as the balanced score-card. This can be used both as a planning and a control device to check progress.

Another consideration that must be taken into account is what technology will be used by the company after the acquisition. It may well be that the acquired company has better technology or systems in place than the parent company. A decision should be made to adopt the best technology/systems regardless of their origin. This needs to be done as quickly and seamlessly as possible.

Finally, it must be remembered that with larger organisations there may be a number of acquisitions being integrated at the same time. This obviously complicates matters quite considerably. According to Uhlaner and West (2008), in 2007, IBM's software group was integrating 18 acquisitions simultaneously, involving over 100 full-time experts in a variety of functions and locations in addition to the specialised teams mobilised for each deal.

Review of Acquisition

The importance of constantly monitoring the environment is stressed throughout this book. Circumstances change and, as a result, so too must the organisation. This ongoing review should also take into account the strategic capability of the organisation, as that too will evolve. The nature of an acquisition means that the organisation will change and, depending on the size of the acquisition, that change can be substantial. In some cases, an acquisition will be a rare occurrence that may happen only once in the lifetime of the organisation. For other companies, such as Kerry Group, acquisitions are a very regular occurrence and there may be a number of them carried out in any one year. In all instances, a review of the process should be carried out to ensure that it is realising the value and benefits that were expected. This review should be done at a strategic level to see whether an acquisition was the most appropriate way to achieve the strategic and financial objectives of the company and also to review whether the target acquisition process identified the most suitable target. At an operational level, the integration process itself also needs to be reviewed to see can any improvements be made to the company's performance. It can be compared against any previous acquisitions completed by the company and it can also be benchmarked against similar acquisitions carried out in the industry by other companies. Any issues arising from the review need to be tackled without delay by senior management.

The concept of the learning organisation has already been discussed in this text. With regard to the learning organisation, the review process is not just about examining the performance of a particular acquisition: it should also be a learning experience to see what lessons can be put to use for the future direction of the organisation and whether acquisitions will form part of that. There will be lessons drawn from every deal, and it is important that these are shared throughout the company so that organisational learning takes place.

M&A Approval

When companies merge or are acquired, it can create a dominant position for that company in the market place. Such dominance is open to potential abuse, and for that reason both the European Union and national governments encourage as much competition as possible. If a merger or acquisition is likely to create such dominance, it must receive approval from the Competition Authority before it can proceed (the UK equivalent is the Competition Commission). The Competition Authority reviews on average between 75 and 100 mergers and acquisitions each year. The Authority, under its chairman, Bill Prasifka, is currently reviewing its procedures and has invited a large number of companies and law firms to make submissions on how these procedures can be improved.

The Competition Authority has a two-phase process for vetting M&As. The majority of referrals are cleared after an initial Phase One investigation, but it has the power to carry out a full investigation if one is deemed necessary. In many cases, it may impose conditions on any approval given. For larger or international deals, approval may be sought from the European Commission before the deal can proceed. In 2007, Ryanair acquired a substantial minority stake (29%) in rival company Aer Lingus. Under company law, any holding above 29.9% requires that the company makes a bid for the entire company that it holds shares in. In the Aer Lingus case, there was considerable opposition to the Ryanair move among other shareholders, which includes the Government holding of 25%. Apart from this opposition to Ryanair taking control of Aer Lingus, the European Commission would have to give its approval (which is probably unlikely) as it would put Ryanair in a dominant position on cross-channel routes.

While the majority of M&As that are referred to the Competition Authority receive approval, occasionally some deals do not get the go-ahead. In August 2008, Kerry Group's proposed €165 million acquisition of Reox's Breo Foods was blocked by the Competition Authority, who held that it would 'substantially lessen' competition in consumer markets for cooked meats and processed cheese. The deal would have seen Kerry Group add Dairygold, Galtee, Shaws, Mitchelstown cheese and Sno yogurt to their line-up. Kerry Group already owns well-known brands such as Denny, Dawn, Ballyfree, Charleville, Cheesestrings and Low Low. The failed acquisition netted Reox €20 million in a non-refundable deposit, which was agreed when the company entered into discussions about the takeover. When a deal such as this is turned down by the Authority, there is potential redress for the companies concerned in the High Court (Curren and Daly, 2008). Lawyers for Kerry Group appealed the decision of the Competition Authority to the High Court. In March 2009, the High Court overruled the Ruling by the Competition Authority and it allowed the acquisition to proceed.

A major corporate deal that received approval in 2008 was a merger between the Irish company IAWS (which owns the Cuisine de France brand, among others) and a Swiss company, Heistand. The merged company is now known as Aryzta, a €2.5 billion operation with 8,000 employees and a presence in Europe, North America, Asia and Australia. IAWS previously held a 32% stake in Hiestand and IAWS existing shareholders now hold 83% of the new company Aryzta. The Chief Executive of IAWS, Owen Killian, is the chief executive of the merged companies, with its headquarters in Switzerland. Talks on the merger began in February 2008 and were successfully concluded in June. A British investment group, Lion Capital, owns 8% of Aryzta (Clerkin, 2008).

Alliance or Acquisition

Alliances and acquisitions are alternative strategies. There are certain similarities between alliances and acquisitions, but both often fail to deliver the promised results. According to Dyer *et al.* (2004), acquiring companies experience a wealth loss of 10% over five years after a merger. In contrast, after an acquisition is announced, the target company's share price rises by 30%, implying they are taking home most of the value. It is estimated that up to 55% of alliances break down prematurely. One of the main problems, suggested by Dyer *et al.,* is that executives do not treat alliances and acquisitions as alternative mechanisms, and do not compare them before picking one. "Consequently, they take over firms that they should have collaborated with and ally with those that they should have bought." They both differ in many ways.

Acquisitions are competitive and, being based on market price, they are risky. On the other hand, alliances involve two companies that are cooperating, which is less risky.

As outlined above, few companies appoint an integration manager or deal owner who can steer the process through from the very beginning through to the end. With no one taking overall charge, the deal will most likely fail. To help in deciding whether an alliance or an acquisition is more appropriate, Dyer *et al.* (2004: 110) developed a framework which considers three sets of factors: resources and synergies; the market place; and their competences at collaborating.

Resources and synergies The company must first decide on the type of synergies that potentially can be achieved:

- Modular synergies where resources are managed independently and later pooled for profits, such as an airline and a hotel chain working together to generate business for each other. In this case a non-equity alliance is best.
- Sequential synergies where one company completes its task and submits it to the other partner, as in biotech companies producing drugs for larger pharmaceutical companies who will then market them. These require equity-based alliances.
- Reciprocal synergies where companies work closely together and share knowledge. Here companies are better off combining all assets in a merger or acquisition.

Synergies are achieved by combining resources, so the company must distinguish between hard resources such as manufacturing facilities and soft (human) resources. With hard resources, acquisitions are a better option as they are easy to value and the synergistic effect is achieved by combining the resources and eliminating any excess capacity. Mergers and acquisitions are the best and quickest method of doing this, like, for example, the Hewlett-Packard merger with Compaq.

On the other hand, if the synergies are dependent on talented people working together, acquisitions should be avoided and equity alliances used instead. Research shows that, when a company is acquired, many of its most talented people leave within a three-year period. An equity stake allows for better control and alignment of interests, without causing dissatisfaction among the staff.

Market place companies need to consider market uncertainty and competition. If there is market risk involved in the process, the companies are better off collaborating using an equity, or non-equity alliance, as this limits their exposure. If, later on, the level of certainty increases, they can then consider a merger or acquisition. Making an acquisition is based, among other things, on the market price of the target company. In a competitive environment, there may be rival companies also interested in the same target and this can push the price up to a level that may not be justified.

Competences at collaborating According to Dyer *et al.* the third consideration is the experience the company has in managing acquisitions or alliances. Previous experience tends to drive companies in a certain direction. If, in the past, the company negotiated a successful alliance, there is a strong likelihood that all future arrangements will be alliances, rather than considering whether an acquisition would be more appropriate. The opposite also holds true. It is important that the company develops skills in both areas so that it has the competence to deliver on an acquisition or an alliance, whichever is the more appropriate in the circumstances.

This again highlights the necessity to have one senior executive in charge of the entire process, with different expert teams reporting to them. Cisco is a company with significant experience in growing through alliances and M&As. The company has a senior vice president in charge of corporate development. There are two vice presidents representing alliances and M&As advising on how best to achieve their objectives. When the decision is made, the appropriate vice president takes over the day-to-day running of the process from beginning to end.

INDUSTRY CONDITIONS: TAILORING APPROPRIATE STRATEGIES

The last couple of chapters looked at the different directions in which a firm could develop and the various methods by which it could achieve its strategic objectives. These are all possibilities for a company but depend on so many other factors. Ultimately, it depends on the strategic and financial objectives that have been set. The company must also consider the particular industry conditions that prevail, as well as their own capabilities. The firm must then adjust its strategies accordingly.

Porter (1980) drew attention to the concept that the structures of industries change, often in fundamental ways, as they evolve through the phases of introduction, growth, maturity and decline. This has "critical importance for the formulation of strategy", and it impacts on buyer behaviour, products and product changes, marketing, manufacturing, R&D and overall strategy. These strategies were further developed by Thompson *et al.* (2008).

Emerging Industries

In emerging industries, companies are trying to discover the nature of that industry as there are no set rules in place and each company is trying its own approaches. Examples of emerging industries include e-book publishing, nanoelectronics and electric car engines. Different companies will often be coming up with their own version of the technology, hoping that their particular technology will eventually become industry standard. Companies are aiming to perfect technology, and there will be a steep learning curve. The price will normally be very high and the products are bought only by 'innovators' or some of the 'early adopters'. In general, companies will try to get the technology right and may well form alliances or acquire other companies to get the expertise that they lack. In order to recoup high R&D costs, the company will try to expand the market as quickly as possible, both at home and abroad (again possibly through alliances). There will be a high level of advertising, initially to create product awareness, but this will later change to creating brand awareness. As sales increase, the price will begin to drop which, in turn, will generate more sales. One of the biggest hurdles for young companies in emerging industries will be raising sufficient finance to fund the establishment of their operations until such time as they reach breakeven point. Other challenges include positioning themselves to take advantage of rapid growth when it does happen as well as managing the level of competition that will inevitably follow as the industry grows.

Growth

When the market starts growing, the company will try to achieve a greater level of growth than the industry average. To entice more customers, it is important to reduce price (through cost reduction). The company will also have to build up additional markets and distribution channels. As it receives feedback from sales, it will continue to improve upon the product and increase on the range of models available so as to appeal to wider segments. In order to take advantage of a growing industry, companies may have to look at expanding out of the markets that they are currently operating in. This is particularly relevant for Irish companies, as the home market will invariably be too small. The methods by which this can be achieved have already been discussed in this chapter.

Maturity

When the market reaches maturity, sales will slow considerably as the last of the 'late majority' and 'laggards' buy the product. Other than that, it is dependent on repeat purchases from those who bought earlier on. Competition will be very strong as rival companies (including foreign ones) are well established and customers are much more discerning. The emphasis will then switch to service and cost, and profits will begin to fall considerably. The company needs to respond by cutting out marginal products from their range and concentrating on those that produce the greatest profit margin. Costs will have to be reduced considerably by examining every aspect of the value chain to see where efficiencies can be made without compromising quality. Economies may be achieved by acquiring rival companies that are struggling. There may be opportunities for increasing sales in less developed markets that are in a different stage of the industry life cycle. Cigarette smoking is declining significantly in Western countries, but is very much on the increase in countries such as China – with a population of 1.3 billion. Foreign expansion could be achieved by foreign direct investment or through alliances or joint ventures. There will usually be a considerable amount of consolidation in the industry, as smaller or less efficient companies are taken over by their larger rivals. Whatever action is being taken, it is important to respond quickly and to have a clear strategy. The maturity phase may well be extended as new technologies emerge that effectively prolong the life of the industry. LCD technology has replaced cathode ray tube televisions, and, while modern TV sets are much slimmer and of better quality, the TV industry continues to provide entertainment, while embracing new technology, thus prolonging the maturity phase of the industry. It is similar for the motor car: though manufacturers are switching to engines based on green technology, the car industry adapts and continues.

Decline

Declining industries see sales drop off considerably. This can be for a variety of reasons: changing customer tastes and lifestyles, demographics, or improved substitute technology (personal computers replacing typewriters). Costs will have to be driven down further, but there may be segments of the market that still remain profitable. The pace of the decline can be slow (where good profits can still be made) or fast, and consequently the company has to make a decision as to what way it will exit the industry. In a slow-exit strategy a company may curtail any new investment and harvest as much cash as they can. In a fast-exit strategy, it sells out as quickly as possible and concentrates resources in other industries.

In picking appropriate strategies, the situation is further complicated by additional factors such as whether the industry is turbulent and changing rapidly or if it is concentrated or fragmented. The position of the company in the industry will also have a bearing on the matter, depending on whether it is the industry leader, a close second or a small player. Companies that are in a weak position need to make a fundamental decision about remaining in the market and trying to improve their situation or making a decision to quit.

Thompson *et al.* (2008) point out that some strategic options are more suited to certain industry conditions and environments than others, while the company must also take into account its own particular circumstances to create a tight strategy–situation fit. They suggest that the company pose four questions to point it in the right direction:

1. What competitive edge can it realistically achieve?
2. Which strategy best suits the company, given all of the different issues that it faces?
3. What offensive actions can be taken to capitalise on rivals' weaknesses?
4. Does it need to take any defensive action to protect its position?

Having assessed the general situation, the company must be clear in what it is trying to achieve in terms of strategy. It is important that it achieves its potential, but at the same time it should design a strategy that does not push its capabilities too far. Ideally, it should stick to what it knows best and has experience in, as this will lessen the risk involved. However, it may be that a familiar strategy is causing problems, so executives must also be prepared to develop in a radically different direction if necessary.

CONCLUSION

There are many strategic options open to companies to achieve growth. Internal growth will play an important role for every company, and for many it may well be the only way that it achieves growth – particularly smaller and family-run businesses. Strategic alliances are growing in importance as many companies realise that it is neither desirable nor possible to develop all the competences required to operate in particular markets. For bigger companies, many may choose mergers and acquisition as a means of expanding quickly or acquiring skills and resources that they do not currently have. While M&As can achieve rapid growth, they also need to be managed very carefully, as they do not always achieve the benefits that are expected.

Perhaps the key requirement is for managers to have a clear vision of what exactly it is they want to achieve for the company and then to analyse each of the options available to see which method can best deliver on their strategic objectives. As with all strategies, they must be tailored for the specific conditions within which the company is operating.

SUMMARY

There is an extensive range of choices available for a company in deciding how it is going to achieve further growth. This chapter looked at the three main methods of strategic development: internal growth, strategic alliances and mergers and acquisitions. Each has different characteristics and will achieve different objectives for the organisation.

Internal development is the main method of development for most organisations. It involves the company growing using its own resources and capabilities. Internal development can be used as a means to achieve all of the directions discussed in Chapter 10. The funding required for internal development usually comes from a number of sources, including retained earnings, borrowings and, perhaps, fresh equity. This form of growth is spread over a number of years and so causes little internal disruption in cultural terms. There are situations where internal development might be the only viable option open to a company, particularly if there are no suitable targets for acquisition.

Strategic alliances can be contractual, involving ownership, or looser collaborative arrangements between companies. A strategic alliance can be defined as 'a formal agreement between two or more separate companies in which there is a strategically relevant collaboration of some sort, joint contribution of resources, shared risk, shared control and mutual dependencies'. Much of the demand for strategic alliance has been brought about by globalisation and the changed nature of competition. Alliances are also used to achieve all four development directions. They are a much quicker form of development than internal development, which can be especially important in the technology industry. They are also used extensively to improve value chain activities.

There is a wide variety of types of alliances from which to choose. Alliances can vary from long-term agreements to temporary arrangements, including:

- **Consortia** – a consortium is a group that consists of two or more companies that have come together for a particular purpose, such as developing a large venture.
- **Joint ventures** – a joint venture is when two companies come together and form an alliance in the form of a third company that is jointly owed and managed by the two parents who remain separate entities.
- **Licensing** – licensing involves allowing another company to manufacture the product and use its trademark in return for an initial fee and an annual royalty based on production.
- **Franchising** – franchising is a form of licensing whereby the franchisor grants the franchisee the right to use certain intellectual property rights such as brand names, copyrights, patents, etc., in return for various fees.
- **Outsourcing** – outsourcing is when a company makes a decision not to perform some value chain activities in-house and subcontracts them to another company that specialises in that activity.
- **Networking** – there are many different types of networking arrangements where firms maintain full control over their activities and benefit one another.

Alliances involve substantial trust and need to be nurtured on an ongoing basis.

Mergers and acquisitions occur where two organisations come together in terms of ownership. A **merger** is where the companies involved, normally similar in size, agree to come together to form a new company, generally changing the name in the process. An **acquisition** is where one company takes over or acquires another one. There are many benefits to mergers and acquisitions (M&As). The premier one is the speed at which the process can be completed. It can also be used as a means of acquiring skills or expertise that a business does not currently own but needs for future development. An acquisition can be a good way for a company to enter a market that is static as the reaction by competitors tends not to be strong.

Achieving **synergy** is perhaps the most important reason for M&A, though experience shows that it is much more difficult to achieve in reality than on paper. There is a wide variety of mergers and acquisitions, and managers need to be clear as to their objectives before embarking on the acquisition trail. M&As require a significant amount of planning in order to be successful. The process involves a number of stages:

- Strategic review
- Identifying a suitable company to acquire
- Carrying out due diligence
- Making the acquisition
- Integrating the acquired company
- Review of acquisition

Before a company can proceed with a merger or acquisition, it may, depending on its size, require regulatory approval. Alliances and M&As are quite different vehicles for development and, once again, managers need to be clear in what they are trying to achieve before choosing one over the other.

The final part of this chapter dealt with different industry conditions. These include the various stages of the industry life cycle as well as the nature of the industry itself.

It is necessary to match the various strategies to the circumstances that exist in an industry at a particular time.

DISCUSSION QUESTIONS

1. Critically analyse the advantages and disadvantages of organic growth as a method of development.
2. Ohmae (1989) stated: "In a complex, uncertain world filled with dangerous opponents, it is best not to go it alone." Twenty years later, strategic alliances are just as important. Discuss.
3. Differentiate between the various forms of strategic alliances.
4. Explore the role that franchising has played in the development of business in Ireland.
5. Critically analyse the importance of acquisitions in the strategy of multinational companies.

REFERENCES

Aiello, R. and Watkins, D., 2000, "The fine art of friendly acquisitions", *Harvard Business Review*, November/December 2000, Vol. 78, Issue 6, pp.100–107

Ashkenas, R. and Francis, S., 2000, "Integration Managers, Special Leaders for Our Times", *Harvard Business Review*, November/December 2000, Vol. 78, Issue 6, pp.100–107

Bower, J., 2001, "Not all M&As are Alike – and That Matters", *Harvard Business Review*, March 2001, Vol. 79, Issue 3, pp.92–101

Carey, D., 2000, "Making Mergers Succeed", *Harvard Business Review*, May/June 2000, Vol. 79, Issue 3, pp.92–101

Carswell, S., 2006, *Something Rotten: Irish Banking Scandals*, Dublin, Gill & Macmillan

Clerkin, D., 2008, "IAWS Hold the Whip in Hiestand Merger", *Sunday Business Post*, 15 June 2008, Money and Markets, p.3

Coffey, A., 2008, "Irish boys score with Sunderland", *Sunday Times*, 17 August 2008, Business and Money, p.18

Curran, R., 2008, "Property slump gives Quinlan plenty to ponder", *Sunday Business Post*, 10 August 2008, Money & Markets, p.2

Curran, R. and Daly, G., 2008, "Kerry Group loses $20m on collapse of deal", *Sunday Business Post*, 31 August 2008, Money & Markets, p.1

Devine, J., 2008, "Mergers and acquisitions surge 32%, mainly in first half of year", *Irish Times*, 5 January 2008

Dyer, J. *et al.*, 2004, "When to Ally and When to Acquire, *Harvard Business Review*, July/August 2004, Vol. 82, Issue 7/8, pp.108–115

Early, P. C. and Mosakowski, E., 2004, "Cultural Intelligence", Harvard Business Review, October 2004, Vol. 82, Issue 10, pp.139–146

Ion Equity, 2008, "Mergers and Acquisitions 2007", *Irish Times*, 5 January 2008

Johnson, G. *et al.*, 2008, *Exploring Corporate Strategy*, Harlow, Essex, Prentice Hall, Financial Times

Kanter, R. M., 1994, "Collaborate advantage: The art of alliances", *Harvard Business Review*, July/August 1994, Vol. 72, Issue 4, pp.96–108

Kaplan, R. *et al.*, 2010, "Managing Alliances with the Balanced Scorecard", *Harvard Business Review*, January/February 2010, Vol. 88, Issue 1, pp.114–120

Lyons, T., 2008, "Dublin Port in Mekong Move", *Sunday Times*, 17 August 2008, Business and Money, p.1

McGarry, S., 2007, *Franchise Guide: A Short Guide to Franchising*, FranchiseDirect.com, http://www.wceb.ie/download/1/franchise_guide.pdf, Accessed 19 July 2011

O'Brien, J. and Marakas, G., 2008, *Management Information Systems*, 8th Ed., New York, McGraw-Hill

Simmons, J., 2011, "Mergers & Acquisitions hit €10.3bn in 2010", *Irish Times*, 7 January 2011, Business This Week, p.5

Walsh, K., 2010, "The world's not big enough for Louis Vuitton", *The Sunday Times*, 21 November 2010, Business, p.10

CHAPTER 12

Decision-making

LEARNING OBJECTIVES

On completion of this chapter, you will be able to:

- Examine the factors involved in the decision-making process
- Evaluate the rational model for decision-making
- Differentiate between individual and group decisions
- Critically assess the various factors that should be considered when making strategic decisions

"Time for you and time for me, and time yet for a hundred indecisions."

T. S. Eliot

INTRODUCTION

The previous chapters have examined the many possibilities for an organisation in terms of directions, methods and industry conditions. Such options offer an enormous choice, but it is essential that a company tailors its strategy to suit its own particular circumstances. This inevitably entails making a decision about its future. This chapter examines the process involved in making those decisions. It begins with examining the decision-making process itself: how do people and organisations make decisions?

The second section of the chapter goes on to explore the factors that managers need to consider in making specific choices. This section looks at ensuring that the strategies fit with the company's strategic position, which was explored earlier in Chapters 6 and 7, and ensuring that all possibilities are in line with established strategic and financial objectives. Financial objectives are reasonably straightforward, in that financial analysis will indicate whether each option is giving an acceptable return on investment. A number of tools that evaluate financial returns will be examined. Strategic returns are more subjective and therefore somewhat more difficult to analyse, but must also be considered as they are equally important.

Stakeholders will have differing expectations of an organisation and these also need to be considered. The purpose of this chapter is to show what executives will need to do in order to make decisions that can capitalise on any opportunities that may arise, or to protect a company from possible threats. Either way, informed, decisive action is a vital part of success.

DECISION-MAKING PROCESS

In Chapter 1, the strategic process was described as the long-term action of an organisation and also as usually involving significant spending. Strategic decisions are rather complex, and executives must consider many different factors. They involve both analysis and judgement. The implications of strategic decisions on the organisation can be quite profound. For that reason, they must be right.

Definition   **Decision-making** can be defined as "the selection of a course of action from among alternatives" (Weilrich and Koontz, 1993: 199).

Before examining various techniques for analysing strategies, it is first of all necessary to look at the conditions under which decisions are made including uncertainty, risk, the amount of information available and the reaction of various stakeholders.

There is inevitably going to be a level of uncertainty involved in strategic decisions, and the greater the timespan involved, the greater will be this level of uncertainty. In studying the macro-environment of an organisation, it may be seen that there are many factors outside its control, such as the cost of oil. A hurricane in the Gulf of Mexico, or the threat of conflict in the Middle East can send the price soaring. As we have seen, this impacts on all businesses, and sometimes in a major way. For a haulage company planning expansion, the cost of oil is therefore extremely uncertain, and will have serious implications for the company if the price rises significantly. While there are some decisions made where the outcome is reasonably certain, in reality, there is some level of uncertainty in most strategic decisions.

Executives also have to look at the amount of risk involved in the process. Chapter 7 examined how companies treat risk at corporate level. The tolerance for risk must be factored into decision-making. There could be a course of action that potentially is promising great returns, but as we have already seen, there is a strong correlation between risk and return. For that reason, it may be decided that the level of risk involved is too great as it could endanger the entire future of the organisation should things go wrong. Even within the same organisation, different executives will have alternative approaches to risk.

When we examine the rational model for decision-making, we will see that a presumption is made that the relevant information is available to the executives. Strategic decisions are, for the most part, non-programmed decisions. At operational level, most decisions are programmed decisions, where the manager has made similar decisions before and, if necessary, refers to operations manuals for guidance. Strategic decisions, on the other hand, are generally once-off, with no precedents for guidance. As a result, it is very difficult to ensure that all the relevant information for a decision has been gathered.

Various stakeholders can be expected to have different expectations from an organisation. As a result, there can be considerable opposition to a certain strategy from interested groups. Strategic decisions will often be modified to include the views of powerful stakeholders such as unions, or the government. All of these factors will modify the final decision, regardless of how objective the decision-makers perceive themselves to be.

THE RATIONAL MODEL

The rational model for decision-making originated with the Greek philosopher Plato. It assumes that people use a rational, sequential process in making decisions. This involves a number of stages, including diagnosing the problem, identifying all solutions, evaluating each one, making the optimum choice, implementing it and, finally, evaluating the decision.

Diagnosing the Problem

Executives have first to be aware that a problem exists (and this also implies that they are willing to take action to resolve that problem). A problem can be said to exist when the actual situation differs from the desired situation. It is important to diagnose the exact cause and nature of the problem rather than just the symptoms. High staff turnover can be a major problem for companies, but this may just be a symptom of a greater underlying problem with the quality of management. There will be considerable data from which executives can identify the problem, such as historical analysis and benchmarking. However, listening to staff and to customers can often highlight the existence of a problem, once the company has mechanisms in place for this information to filter through. It should be stated that a company that is intent on being a market leader should not have to wait for problems to arise, but should take initiatives to prevent them.

Identifying Different Solutions

The next stage of the process is to identify as many solutions as possible. It can often happen that the best solutions are not the most obvious, so for that reason, by generating as many potential solutions as possible, the correct one can be more readily identified. They will be evaluated in the next step. It will be seen later that groups can often generate a greater number of possible solutions. Techniques like De Bono's 'Six Thinking Hats' can be useful for generating alternatives that may not otherwise come to mind. While most interpretations of the rational model suggest that many possible solutions are generated, it must be remembered that this can complicate the process and can also delay it considerably. The danger is that the search for an exhaustive list of solutions can lead to 'paralysis by analysis'. Time is often not on the side of a company, and so the executive does not want to be always one consultant's report short of a decision.

Evaluating the Alternatives

Once the various alternatives have been identified (bearing in mind that there may be some possible solutions that have not been included), the next stage is to evaluate them in order to come up with the solution that offers the greatest value to the company. This is sometimes referred to as 'maximising the expected utility of an outcome'. The problem with this is that it can be quite a subjective process, as many of the values are not numerical. Consequently, the alternatives have to be weighed up in a holistic manner in terms of the ultimate benefits. The use of cost-benefit analysis should be part of the process. (This will be developed later in the chapter.) As a result, the final decision will probably be a mixture of objective analysis and the executive's own gut feeling. Thus, experience can play an important role in making the correct decision.

Making a Decision

Rarely will an organisation have the luxury of a long period of time with which to reflect on all aspects of a problem. More often than not, there will be just a narrow window of opportunity to make a decision and implement it. Thus, an important function of management is the decision-making capacity. The executive needs to be decisive. There are circumstances where executives may rightly feel that there is genuinely not enough information to make a decision. In that case, they will have to revert to stage one to ensure that they have correctly identified the problem, or stage two in order to generate further options. While all this is time-consuming, it may be the best course of action. On the other hand, if they have the information, the decision should quickly follow.

Implementing the Decision

Once the executives have made their decision, and they are happy that it is the correct one, it must now be implemented. It is not a simple process of issuing an edict. Buelens *et al.* (2006: 445) suggest that there are three managerial tendencies that reduce the effectiveness of implementing solutions. These are:

- The tendency not to ensure that everyone understands what needs to be done. Ideally, the decision-making process should be inclusive, but, one way or the other, the decision must be communicated clearly to all concerned so that there is no ambiguity about what is required.
- The tendency not to ensure the acceptance or motivation for what needs to be done. Once again, an inclusive approach to decision-making will allow for greater acceptance of that decision, as people's views have been included. This will increase ownership and overall acceptance.
- The tendency not to provide appropriate resources for what needs to be done. There are two aspects to this. First, the manager must provide adequate staffing and financial and physical resources to complete the job, as well as a realistic time frame. Secondly, there need to be proper structures in place to ensure cross-functional/departmental co-ordination.

These points will be addressed in Part Four of this text which deals with the implementation of strategy. Successfully implementing the chosen strategy is an integral part of the overall process of guiding an organisation towards its chosen objectives.

Evaluating the Outcome

Feedback is an essential element of any process. In decision-making, the aim of feedback is to assess the effectiveness of the choices that were made, ensuring that an organisation is on target to achieve its objectives. Circumstances are constantly changing and, for that reason, adjustments will often have to be made to get back on course. This evaluation process should include re-evaluating the diagnosis of the problem in the first instance. If the original summation of the problem was incorrect, then a different solution will, in all probability, have to be found. The process of monitoring the decision should continue until the objectives are finally achieved.

Limitations of the Rational Model

The rational model for decision-making, as described above, is a logical process that should be used in examining potential strategies. It makes the assumption that, when executives are making decisions, they are trying to find the optimum solution. It also makes the assumption that those executives have full knowledge of the issues facing them and all of the relevant information to make the decision, as well as understanding the consequences of each alternative. The model also implies that the executives concerned have the intelligence to weigh up all of the factors and choose the optimum solution. However, as in many instances, the theory and the practical reality are often different for a number of reasons. In Chapter 2, we saw that there is a strong link between politics and business, as political decisions ultimately create the environment within which business operates. Such decisions often take into account various political factors, many of which can over-ride better judgement. Barry (2010) catalogues a series of disastrous policy decisions that were taken by the Irish Government during the boom period in the 2000s that ultimately had a devastating impact on the economy. Simon (1979) suggests that, as such, the rational model is effectively aspirational as it largely ignores the human element in decision-making.

Decision-makers are limited by what March and Simon (1958) termed **'bounded rationality'**. Bounded rationality implies that the executive, when making decisions, is 'bounded' or limited by a number of different constraints. These include the environment within which executives are working and this is often outside their control. Individuals also have limited mental and emotional capacity. It will be very difficult to solve the problem, for example, if the problem is not clearly identified by the executives in the first instance. It may be that the problem is too complex for them to understand fully. Fatigue can also impair sound judgement. According to the road safety authority, one in five driver-deaths in Ireland is due to driver fatigue (RSA, 2011). Dr Charles Czeisler, Professor of Sleep Medicine at Harvard Medical School, believes that, due to the pressures of business and travel, many executives are not able to perform properly because of sleep deprivation and develop the same level of cognitive impairment equivalent to the legal level defining drunkenness (Czeisler, 2006: 54).

McShane and Von Glinow (2009) suggest that difficulties with problem identification include the fact that people sometimes block out bad news as a defence mechanism, and also people develop mental models to help them cope with the outside world, but these also produce assumptions that can limit people's ability to think clearly. These assumptions can produce biases which will affect their judgement. The reaction of different stakeholders will often impact on corporate decisions, as we saw in Chapter 1. A certain course of action could well prove to be unacceptable to particular stakeholders, be they investors, unions or the government. As a result, anticipation of their reaction is likely to have a modifying effect on the various outcomes that are being considered.

As a result of problems such as these, executives find it difficult to process all of the information, making it difficult to come up with an optimum solution. Instead of continuing the search for the best solution, people tend to 'satisfice'. **'Satificing'** is choosing a solution that meets the minimum, rather than the optimal solution: one that can be described as sufficient.

Time Requirement in Decision-making

Time to make decisions is another major constraint on people. One of the biggest economic decisions ever taken by an Irish Government was taken in an incredibly short time-frame. The €440 billion blanket guarantee for Irish banks given by the Government in the early hours of 30 September 2008 has been the subject of a lot of debate. The chairmen and chief executives of Ireland's two biggest banks, AIB and Bank of Ireland, had approached the Government on the previous evening. They believed that the collapse of Anglo Irish Bank and Irish Nationwide was imminent and that this would have a domino effect on the entire Irish banking system; they needed state support to ensure the future of AIB and Bank of Ireland. The decision to provide liquidity for the banks had to be taken before the markets opened at 7am on 30 September (at that stage the banks insisted it was just a liquidity issue rather than the major recapitalisation that would subsequently be required). Though that decision solved the immediate problem, the wider banking crisis will remain for a long time to come (Cooper, 2009).

Time given to decision-making also has broader implications for corporate governance. Clancy *et al.* (2010), in discussing the number of cross-directorships in top Irish companies, point to the danger that, because of the workload involved in each directorship, not enough time is given by these directors to the problems actually facing the companies in question. They showed that some directors were sitting on the boards of five PLCs or semi-state companies at the same time, in addition to which they were directors of up to 10 other companies. Some of these were in full-time positions as CEOs while also serving in multiple directorships. The capacity of individuals to undertake multiple directorships depends on the competence and experience of the individuals concerned, as well as the complexity and diversity of each company. The degree of change being undertaken by companies will also impact on the amount of time required by directors and managers to make decisions. According to Clancy *et al.* (2010:20): "Some of them may have been over-extended, and thus unable to fulfil all of their roles as directors effectively, which is in itself a serious issue for good corporate governance."

The Walker Review (2009:14-15) in the UK also recommended that non-executive directors of boards need to give much greater time commitment than has been the case before. They suggest that directors of banks should commit between 30 to 36 days per year. A chairman is recommended to commit a minimum of two-thirds of his or her time.

Escalation of Commitment

When a decision has been made, there is often a tendency to stay with that decision, no matter what. The final stage in the rational model outlined above is the necessity to review decisions to see how successful they are. In some instances, it will appear that it was a wrong decision.

Definition The term **escalation of commitment** refers to the tendency to stay with a particular course of action even though it now appears to be a poor decision.

Ross and Straw (1993) suggest that there are four reasons underlying escalation of commitment varying from: the ego of people involved in the decision-making process; internal politics and poor communication; the nature of the project itself and a natural tendency to stick with it and see it brought to a conclusion; and, finally, factors outside the organisation that may put pressure on them to continue.

An example of the concept of escalation of commitment on a grand scale was the American involvement in the Vietnam War. It began with the involvement of the US Army as advisers to the ARVN – the Army of the Republic of Vietnam (South Vietnam), and this led to the gradual introduction of US combat troops. In response to calls for additional troops by General Westmoreland, the US Commander in Vietnam, the Johnson Administration committed ever-increasing numbers to the war during the 1960s. There were a number of indications throughout the decade that should have alerted the Administration to withdraw the US troops. There was extremely strong Viet Cong resistance, particularly in the Tet Offensive in 1968, resulting in heavy American casualties, and diminishing international and domestic support for the war (Maclear, 1981). Ricks (2006) draws similar conclusions about America's involvement in Iraq following the US-led invasion in March 2003:

> "It now seems more likely that history's judgement will be that the US invasion of Iraq in the spring of 2003 was based on perhaps the worst war plan in American history. It was a campaign plan for a few battles, not a plan to prevail and secure victory. Its incompleteness helped create conditions for the difficult occupation that followed. The invasion is of interest now mainly for its role in creating those problems."
>
> Ricks (2006: 115)

The battle to take Iraq lasted just a couple of weeks. However, there was no coherent plan to govern the country after Saddam Hussein's regime fell. In the aftermath of the invasion, more and more American troops were required to maintain order in Iraq. Once again, military commanders requested a 'troop surge' to guarantee stability in the country. Six years later, the US still has a significant presence with over 100,000 troops in the country. It took a change in the administration in the US to announce a withdrawal from Iraq, with President Obama pledging to withdraw all combat troops by August 2010 and all remaining troops will have left the country by the end of 2011 (Staunton, 2009).

369

Illustration 1.1 (Chapter 1), dealing with the development of the PPARS Information Technology system for the Health Service Executive, also represents a commercial example of escalation of commitment. There were a number of reviews undertaken during the development of the system and, despite the fact that the project was not delivering on its promise, more and more resources were committed to its development, with costs spiralling out of control.

Escalation of commitment can clearly have disastrous consequences for an organisation. The development of the PPARS system by a private organisation would clearly have destroyed the company financially. In making decisions in an organisation, it is important that people are aware of the characteristics of escalation of commitment. It is important also that there is a supportive 'no blame' culture in the organisation that facilitates withdrawing from a project despite previous financial and emotional commitment to it. Such a culture can help reduce the potential negative impact. In addition, it can be useful to have other senior executives, not involved in the original decision, to review progress to determine if it is matching the original expectations.

GROUP DECISIONS

Many decisions will be taken by groups such as committees or work teams. According to Kreitner (1998: 234), there are a number of advantages and disadvantages to groups making decisions. The advantages include:

- 'Two heads are better than one.' Groups will generally speaking have a greater amount of knowledge and experience than an individual, and the group will be able to process more information than an individual.
- Groups will often have greater understanding of the issues under discussion and of the possible courses of action.
- Each member will have a different perspective on the issue.
- This greater comprehension should, in turn, lead to greater ownership and make the implementation process easier.
- Decisions can provide training for younger and less experienced team members.

It is said that a camel is a horse designed by a committee. It does not always follow that group decisions are better. Some of the disadvantages include:

- Groups can often be dominated by a few strong personalities.
- The contribution of individual members may be limited by social pressures to conform to group norms.
- Internal politics (see Chapter 1) can take precedence over the objectives of the group.
- Decision-making by groups can lead to what is described as 'groupthink' (see below) where the desire for unanimity overrides sound judgement.

Groupthink

The latter point is significant and requires further examination. The term **'groupthink'** was coined by Janis (1982) and he describes it thus:

Groupthink is "a mode of thinking that people engage in when they are deeply involved in a cohesive in-group, when members' strivings for unanimity override their motivation to realistically appraise alternative courses of action."

Groupthink impacts on the effectiveness of decision-making in a considerable way and can lead to ignoring reality, resulting in serious errors of judgement.

Illustration 12.1: Groupthink – Our Lady of Lourdes Hospital, Drogheda

One very disturbing Irish example of groupthink is the case of Dr Michael Neary and others in Our Lady of Lourdes Hospital in Drogheda. During the 25 years covered by the report into the case, 188 peripartum hysterectomies were carried out at the hospital, of which 129 were carried out by Dr Michael Neary (Harding Clark, 2006: 30–1). The number of operations was significantly out of line with international best practice (approximately 20 times greater than rates in large tertiary-care hospitals). Despite these alarming statistics, no one queried the practice. It finally took a whistle-blower (a midwife that had been trained outside of the State) to alert the attention of outside medical authorities (see also Chapter 4). Dr Neary was investigated and he was eventually struck off the Medical Register in 2003. The Lourdes Hospital Inquiry Report investigated practices in the maternity unit at the hospital (not just Dr Neary) from 1974 to 1998, and the report itself was published in January 2006.

The chairperson and sole member of the Inquiry was Judge Maureen Harding Clark SC. In summary, her report is damning in a number of areas including management, communication, and documentation keeping. With so many people involved and so many disciplines, how could this have happened? Judge Harding Clark noted that: "Few complained or questioned. Not the patients, their partners nor their families…; not the junior doctors nor the post membership registrars; not the anaesthetists who received the patients, administered the anaesthesia, wrote up the operation notes and spoke to each patient in the recovery room and were always present at the operations; not the surgical nurses, who were frequently midwives…; not the midwives who cared for the patients after their operations…; not the pathologists and technicians who received the wombs…; not the Medical Missionaries of Mary who owned the hospital and employed the obstetricians…" (Harding Clark, 2006: 32–3)

The Judge noted that there was a strong sense of loyalty by staff members to their hospital and they felt a sense of privilege in training and working there. There was little turnover in staff and there was significant job insecurity that "may have influenced a climate of silence" (Harding Clark, 2006: 38). The inquiry found "an extraordinary cocoon of confidence and self-assurance around itself. It simply did not occur to anyone within the body of management in the hospital that practices within the maternity unit were different from the accepted norm" (Harding Clark, 2006: 41). She went on to note the absence of a "healthy questioning environment" (Harding Clark, 2006: 42).

Judge Harding Clark also noted: "This is not a simple story of an evil man or a bad doctor, nor is it a story of wholesale suppression of the facts. The facts were there for all to see..." (Harding Clark, 2006: 34). There are a number of complex reasons for what happened in the Lourdes Hospital. Included in these reasons, however, was an appalling example of how a group of people, for whatever reason, can think in an unquestioning way about a practice (or strategy) that flies in the face of reason.

Source: Harding Clark (2006)

Clancy *et al.* (2010:2) refer to the danger of groupthink when boards of directors are drawn from a small group of people and there are many cross-directorships and also where there is a lack of diversity due to gender imbalance: "Similarities in world view and experience, risk persistent 'groupthink' which may diminish willingness to challenge decisions and may lead to a failure to understand and protect either the shareholders or the wider public interest." The Report of the Commission of Investigation into the Banking Sector in Ireland (the Nyberg Report) is equally critical of the level of groupthink within Irish financial institutions (Nyberg, 2011).

Notwithstanding the example of groupthink in **Illustration 12.1**, it is important to look at group decisions in a balanced manner. There are both advantages and disadvantages in group decision-making, and whether it improves the quality of decision-making in an organisation depends to a great extent on the particular context. In general, additional people should be included in the process if the information they possess would increase the quality of the decision being made. Chapter 1 examined the political nature of organisations and the development of strategy. There are times when acceptance of a decision by a particular group is vitally important, and so inclusion of those people in the process facilitates acceptance of the final decision.

One interesting point to note is that hierarchical organisations that do not involve employees in the decision-making process still have group decisions made by their boards of directors.

Buelens *et al.* (2006: 455) suggest that, in general, decisions made by groups are superior to decisions made by individuals. They further state that participative management and employee empowerment are highly touted as a means of improving organisational productivity. There are some important considerations here. First, groups tend to be less efficient than individual decision-makers. Time constraints would be a key factor in this regard. Secondly, groups are more confident about their decisions, but this does not guarantee quality. Thirdly, group size has an impact and there is a negative correlation between size and quality. Fourthly, group decision-making is better when the members know a great deal about the subject matter and group leaders can effectively evaluate individual contributions. Lastly, composition of the group is important – decisions are better when members possess lots of unique rather than common information. According to Parker (1990), in making decisions groups generally try to reach a consensus. There are different techniques that can be used to facilitate group decision-making, including brainstorming, the nominal group technique, and the Delphi technique.

Brainstorming The concept of brainstorming was developed by Osborn (1979) to increase creativity in the advertising industry, and is a technique used to facilitate the generation of many different ideas and solutions. The emphasis is on the generation of the ideas rather than evaluating them, and the process involves a lot of interaction by the group.

Nominal group technique In contrast, the nominal group technique separates the brainstorming from the evaluation. It gets people to work individually on the problem. Afterwards, their ideas are recorded on a flip chart, and then the group discusses each one. People are free to criticise and defend these ideas. Finally, the group members vote anonymously on their choice, using a weighted voting system and a decision is made.

The Delphi Technique The Delphi technique was developed by Dalkey *et al.* (1972) and is an iterative, group process involving experts who generate ideas anonymously from individuals who are physically separate from one another. Members are asked to fill in questionnaires and return them to the co-ordinator. This allows ideas to be generated without interference from groupthink. The findings are summarised and returned to the members for further evaluation. The process continues until there is a clear consensus on the way forward.

DECISION-MAKING STYLES

As discussed in Chapter 2, leadership at every level involves decision-making and is an essential element in the running of organisations. This chapter has examined the rational model of decision-making and some of its limitations, as well as comparing individual and group decisions. Inevitably, various individuals will have different decision-making styles. According to Brousseau *et al.* (2006), it is essential that the style of decision-making evolves as people move to higher levels in the organisation.

Brousseau *et al.* carried out extensive research on the decision-making styles of over 180,000 executives across the globe. They found that decision-making styles differ in two fundamental ways: how people use available information (whether they tend to maximise the amount of information available to them before making a decision, or do they "satisfice"); and also how they create options (single focus on one option or multi-focused – generating lists of options and pursuing multiple courses). Using these two dimensions of information, use and focus, they categorised four styles of decision-making:

- **Decisive** – value action, speed and efficiency. The decision is made and they move on to the next decision.
- **Flexible** – focuses on speed and also on adaptability. This kind of decision-maker will use enough information to make a decision and will change course if necessary.
- **Hierarchic** – they do not rush to judgement, but analyse a great deal of information and expect others to contribute. Their decisions should stand the test of time.

- **Integrative** – not necessarily looking for a single best solution. They frame every situation broadly, taking multiple elements that overlap into account. Decisions are broadly defined and consist of multiple courses of action. When working with others, they require extensive input, even when it conflicts with their own view. Decision-making for them is not an event, but a process.

Managers need to be able to adapt to all four styles of decision-making depending on circumstances e.g. an entrepreneur may not have the time for lengthy analysis, while periods of uncertainty may require a multi-focus approach. The main part of the Brousseau research focuses on how decision-making styles evolve as managers progress. In general, as managers rise in the organisation, there is a steady progression towards openness, diversity of opinion and participative decision-making. This reflects the move away from the type of direct, immediate action required from lower-level managers to more analytical, creative and exploratory decision-making. As the career of the manager progresses, there comes a point where all four styles of decision-making converge. Some managers can continue to adapt while others remain at this point. For those managers who cannot make the transition in style, it usually means the levelling off of their progression within the company. Successful managers can adapt and develop new styles. **Figure 12.1** illustrates the changes in leadership styles for successful managers (in their research, Brousseau *et al.* picked high financial compensation as an inexact measure for success).

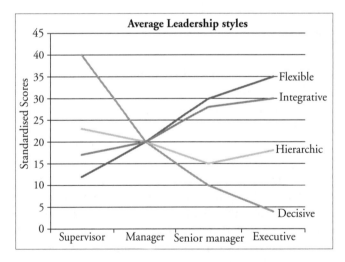

Source: Adapted from Brousseau *et al.* (2006) "The Seasoned Executive's Decision-making Style", *Harvard Business Review*, Vol. 84 Issue 2, p.116

Figure 12.1 *Average Decision-making Styles for Highest Compensated 20% of Managers*

While the illustration in **Figure 12.1** was based on US executives, the results for European and Asian managers were reasonably similar. Latin American executives, on the other hand, showed a similar convergence at manager level, which did not subsequently fan out at more senior levels.

The chart reflects different people at different levels, not the same people over the course of their careers.

This research has implications for organisations and how potential leaders are groomed for higher positions – how their competences are developed.

DECISION SUPPORT SYSTEMS

Information technology can greatly assist the decision-maker in making sense of the vast amount of information. Decision support systems (DSSs) are computer-based information systems designed to provide managers with interactive information support to enable them make better decisions. Decision support systems rely on model bases (software components used in computational and analytical routines) and databases. DSSs are designed to provide managers at every level with the type of information required to make decisions ranging from operational management, which requires regular, detailed reports for structured decisions, to strategic management where decisions are unstructured, infrequent and forward-looking. DSSs designed for this latter function are often referred to as Enterprise Information Systems and are geared specifically to the needs of senior executives.

People at different levels and in different managerial positions will vary in their requirements for report formats and information when making decisions. There are a number of reporting alternatives available from management information systems, including periodic schedule reports, exception reports, demand reports and push reporting (where reports are 'pushed' to appropriate individuals throughout a network station). According to O'Brien and Marakas (2008: 367), DSSs use a variety of different techniques such as analytical models, specialised databases, a decision-maker's own insights and judgements and an interactive, computer-based modelling process to support strategic decisions. They can enable managers to use a number of analytical modelling techniques ranging from 'what-if' analysis to optimisation analysis. In addition, data mining can analyse vast amounts of data and search for patterns, trends and correlations. This can provide very valuable information to managers on which to base decisions (see Chapter 13, **Illustration 13.1 – Data Mining in Tesco**).

The problem for many decision-makers is not the lack of information, but often that there is too much of it. Many organisations are now capitalising on increased information richness and analytics to gain a competitive advantage in the market place. Analytics involves applying statistical models to mine large data sets. It enables the user to make data meaningful and support decision-making. According to Balboni *et al.* (2010), top-performing companies are three-times more likely to be sophisticated users of analytics. The emphasis now is on emerging approaches that convert information into scenarios and simulations that make insights easier to understand and act on. Just as a fuel gauge is an essential indicator in a car, it is important that vital information is readily available to decision-makers. Data visualisation and 'dashboard' reporting mean that the output of data analytics are accessible in real time so that decisions are based on accurate and the most up-to-date information available.

STRATEGY EVALUATION

The process of evaluating different options is an important part of the process of developing and implementing strategy. It is likely that the development process may have thrown up many possibilities, and there is a need for a framework to consider each one and pick the one most appropriate to the organisation's position. Collins (2001:69) believes executives should display two disciplines of thought in evaluating strategy. First, they must infuse the entire process with the brutal facts of reality; and secondly, there must be a "simple, yet deeply insightful, frame of reference for all decisions". Executives must have a clear vision of what the organisation is trying to achieve.

Lynch (2008: 371) distinguishes between content and process in strategy selection. So far, this chapter has looked at the decision-making process in general, both at individual and group level. The content refers to what strategy is selected and what proposals it contains. The purpose of looking at decision-making is to ensure the organisation will be able to choose the best course of action from the various options available and, in so doing, meet its strategic objectives.

Each organisation will have its own methods of assessing strategy. The framework outlined here is adapted from Lynch (2008: 374–79) and will give some structure to the process. It should not necessarily be considered as a sequential process; rather these are the factors that need to be taken into consideration when examining the different options. Thus, if it appears at the beginning of the evaluation process that the strategy under consideration is too risky or would be unacceptable to key stakeholders, then it is likely that it will not be considered any further. On the other hand, an option may appear to be suitable under the present circumstances, but may not be consistant with the mission. While the mission gives consistency to the organisation, it could be that the time has come for the mission to be reappraised.

Consistency

The process of evaluating a strategy begins with examining its 'consistency' with the organisation's vision, mission and goals and objectives. Chapter 3 looked at setting a vision for the organisation. Part of that process involved the purpose for which an organisation exists. There needs to be a clear understanding by executives of what that purpose is and the objectives that have been set. The strategy that they choose should be consistent with those objectives, regardless of whether it is in the commercial sector or the not-for-profit sector. There should be an overall consistency from the vision through to the strategies that an organisation is following. If this consistency is lacking, the question must be asked as to why the proposal is being considered. Values are an integral part of the vision and they guide decision-making. Such values can range enormously from highly ethical ones to ones that may be without any element of integrity. Decisions being taken by people in an organisation should, therefore, be consistent with the values of that organisation, which should also reflect a sound ethical foundation.

Suitability

Suitability refers to how the various options relate to the business environment within which the organisation is operating and its strategic capability. Chapter 5 examined the business environment in great detail from the macro and the industry perspectives. Chapter 6 then examined the organisation's strategic capability to understand what the organisation is capable of achieving at the present time. The strategies under consideration need to be in line with the information coming out of this environmental analysis and examination of the organisation's strategic capability. For example, when the economy is stagnant or in recession, the strategies that an organisation should be concentrating on would probably be based more on consolidation than expansion. The following table is a broad outline of the major factors that would need to be taken into consideration.

Table 12.1: *Determining the Suitability of Strategic Options*

STRATEGIC TOOLS	USE IN DETERMINING STRATEGIC OPTIONS
External	
Global environment, Porter's Diamond, PESTEL analysis and Scenarios	While most of the information here will normally be outside the control of an organisation, it can have a major impact on the future profitability. While they cannot be controlled, they have to be taken into account when assessing opportunities and threats.
Industry economic features, Five Forces Analysis, Industry driving forces, Strategic groups, Market segmentation, and Critical success factors	These are more applicable for a single company operating in a particular industry, or a diversified company considering moving into that industry. As above, consideration of these analytical tools should give a good indication of the suitability of the various options under consideration.
Internal	
Resources, Competences, Capabilities, Cost Competitiveness, Value Chain and Value System Analysis	These factors look at the internal strengths and weaknesses of a company. It must be remembered that, while there may be some great opportunities in principle, it depends on the resources and competences of an organisation to capitalise on those opportunities.

Source: Adapted from Johnson *et al.* (2011: 364)

The internal and external analysis will have thrown up the main issues facing an organisation and its ability to respond. The purpose of using such strategic tools as listed above is to help develop a proper understanding of all of the factors that need to be taken into account when developing strategy. Any of the strategic options under review should be in line with the environment and the capability of a company to exploit any opportunities. Judgement will play an important part in the process as there are many factors that need to be considered. It is also likely that there may be many different possibilities facing a company. In the vast majority of cases, resources will be limited, so decisions will have to be made with regard to the relative suitability of each one. One useful way to consider which ones should be exploited is to rank them against appropriate criteria. Those with the highest marking are ranked number one and so on down the line. The purpose of looking at the suitability of the options is to get an overall understanding of them. There are also other factors that need to be considered before a final decision is made.

While Lynch (2008: 375) refers to 'validity', there is an overlap between suitability and validity. In considering the suitability of different strategies, much will depend on the assumptions underlying the future facing the organisation, the industry and indeed the macro-environmental factors. It is important that the executives consider the validity of the assumptions that they have made. In other words, are the assumptions grounded in accurate information rather than what the executives would like to happen? Once again, this is something that will require sound judgement and experience.

Feasibility

There are a number of different factors that need to be considered under the heading of feasibility. First we must look at resources. A firm has to have sufficient resources, particularly the necessary human resources, to pursue the strategy in question. A resource deployment analysis can assist in the process of identifying the resources required and where they may be obtained. In larger companies, it will often be the case that the resources are present somewhere in the organisation but will need to be located and redeployed. Such moves have to be planned, particularly if it means moving managers with specific skills and experience. This process must also be supported by the culture of the organisation, where such redeployment is considered a normal part of working in that corporation. Not every company would have the necessary flexibility to be able to respond quickly.

Specific strategies will require specific resources, which may not be present within an organisation. Implementing an IT programme, for example, would require people with specialised skills. In examining the Quinn Group in Chapter 10, it was seen that their company policy was: 'if we don't have the people, we just hire them'. If it is the case that personnel with specific skills are required, but are not available within the organisation, then a recruitment process will have to be put in place in sufficient time to allow new members to be employed in the company when they are required. It is not just a case of specialised skills that may be needed, but also the managerial competences necessary to support particular strategies, and at the appropriate level. In Chapter 8, we saw that the different generic strategies require very diverse managerial competences. This will all have to form part of the overall consideration.

If the strategy under consideration is a merger or an acquisition, then it will most probably be the case that there will be excess personnel, in which case it will require an integration plan that will most likely entail redundancies. Once again, this is a process that needs to be planned very carefully to ensure that the company ends up with the right people remaining. Redundancy payments will form part of the financial consideration, as well as HR planning. This process can be complicated when it is a cross-border situation where different laws apply. Communication is an integral part of all moves concerning the people working in an organisation. Lack of communication, or poor communication, may cause many problems down the line that can easily be avoided.

Supporting a strategic move will also require adequate financial resources. This will probably be a mixture of an initial capital allocation and ongoing working capital requirements. The timing of cash flows in and out of an organisation can be critical to the feasibility of a strategy. The ability of an organisation to raise the necessary finance is critical.

In Chapter 7, we saw that finance for strategies can come from a number of different sources, and probably a mixture of sources. For strategic business units within a larger organisation, it may be the corporate headquarters that supplies the necessary funding. Strategic options will not be considered in isolation but in the context of other, previous strategies, and moves that are likely to come in the near future. Committing finance to a strategic project will tie it up for a period of time. Strategies implemented a couple of years ago may well be yielding positive cash flow that could support the strategy now under consideration.

External to a company, there are also factors that may curtail the feasibility of a strategic option. Some takeovers may require regulatory approval because of their size, and such approval may not be forthcoming. Such moves must also be made with regard to relationships within the value system, particularly suppliers and distributors.

Business Risk

Every strategic move is going to entail some level of risk. This is considered to be a normal part of business.

 Business risk can be defined as the risk of loss or failure due to pursuing a particular strategy.

We have already seen that different organisations will have different tolerances to risk, and this will have to be taken into consideration when making a decision. A company will have to carry out a risk assessment to ascertain the exact level of risk involved. This assessment should also include examining ways in which the risk can be reduced or removed. When examining corporate social responsibility, it was seen that certain moves could damage the image of a company, and that such damage could have serious financial consequences. Inevitably, financial risk will be a central part of this process.

In the previous section, it was seen that strategies will require considerable financial investment. The ability of a firm to raise the necessary cash is central to the whole process. Putting money into a project inevitably produces risk, particularly when the nature of the financial package is taken into account. Debt finance can be offset against taxation, but it must be repaid regardless of the success of the project. This could place a considerable financial burden on a company. In 2008, with the downturn in the construction sector, many larger developers were faced with considerable pressure from lenders to repay loans, despite being unable to sell their apartments and office blocks.

Cash flow analysis is an essential part of this process. An operation can be profitable overall, but at times illiquid, and such illiquidity could bring about the demise of the company. Break-even analysis is another important criterion to consider. Break-even analysis examines the volume of sales required at a particular price to break even on the original investment, and before it starts making profit. Various financial ratio analyses should also be undertaken to examine all aspects of a project.

Sensitivity analysis should be applied to a project to examine the consequences if things do not go according to plan. It is often referred to as 'what if' analysis and it explores the impact that different factors would have on the strategy if they deviate from planned assumptions. For example, the project may necessitate borrowing a considerable amount of money. For a number of years, the European Central Bank's rates have been at a historical low at 1%. In recent times they have begun to rise. This obviously has a considerable knock-on effect on the financial viability of the strategy, and needs to be factored in when making the decision. Other factors that may not go according to plan are projected sales, economic growth, and currency movements. (The Euro has appreciated considerably in recent years against the dollar and sterling, making exports much more expensive. This might be partially offset against cheaper raw materials if they are sourced in the UK or the US.) It is important to take a realistic view of all of these factors when considering a particular course of action as they could have a material effect on the financial viability of the plan.

Return

For any commercially-focused organisation, return on investment will be an essential part of its *raison d'être*. It is not just the shareholders that will be looking for a satisfactory return, but the future viability of the company and its ability to employ staff rests on its capacity to pursue profitable strategies. For that reason, the process of evaluation must consider the expected returns for each of the options under consideration. There is a very strong correlation between the level of risk and return. There is an old adage: 'if it looks too good to be true, it usually is'.

There are a number of different financial analyses that can assist managers in their appraisal. In general, they can compare the capital investment involved with the expected return. It is worth bearing in mind that, while the different appraisal techniques might appear objective, they rely on projections that might be subjective and are based on predictions about the future. Such predictions will be coated in uncertainty as there will be many circumstances outside the control of a firm. These calculations are based on factors that can be measured in financial terms. Not all factors can be reduced to monetary value. This will be developed further in discussing cost-benefit analysis.

Before examining specific techniques, there are a few general considerations to be taken into account:

- For the most part, the financial outlay will be quite substantial, so care must be taken to make the correct decision.

- Along with the size of the investment, it must also be remembered that these decisions are generally long-term and this will have implications with regard to tying up finance for the duration of the project.
- The decision to invest will have to be taken against the background of all other financial decisions as there is an inter-relationship in terms of cash flow and total borrowings.
- There is an opportunity cost in making an investment. The money allocated cannot be used for other purposes for the lifespan of the investment. There may be other opportunities available that have not been considered.

These different techniques act as a guide to decision-making. They assist in the process, but it still requires managerial judgement. Each technique needs different types of information and they lead to different conclusions. Thus, it is useful to employ a number of different techniques, including:

- Payback method
- Accounting rate of return
- Discounted cash flow methods (net present value)

Payback Method It was stated above that when money is invested in a project there is an opportunity cost involved, and this also involves risk that the investment may not be recouped. From a risk perspective, it is preferable that the amount of time involved is kept to a minimum, as the longer the finance is tied up in the project, the greater the risk involved. The payback method is based on the amount of time it will take for the cumulative cash flows to equal the initial investment. From that point on, the project will be making a positive contribution. The payback period is arbitrary: the nature of the industry and the particular circumstances of the company will dictate what an acceptable payback period would be. The following is an example.

A factory is considering investing €10 million in a large extension. Using the projected net cash inflows each year, it wants to know how long the payback period will be.

Table 12.2: *Payback Period*

Year	Net annual cash inflow	Net *cumulative* cash inflow (€)
1	500,000	500,000
2	900,000	1,400,000
3	2,600,000	4,000,000
4	3,500,000	7,500,000
5	1,500,000	9,000,000
6	3,500,000	12,500,000
7	3,500,000	16,000,000

It can be seen that the time is somewhere between five years (which is €1 million short of the original investment) and six years (which is showing a cash inflow of €3.5 million). It can be estimated as:

$$\frac{1,000,000}{3,500,000} = 0.29 \text{ years}$$

Hence, the total payback period is 5.29 years.

The payback method is easy to use and it shows the amount of time the money will be tied up for, thus introducing some caution into the decision. Two major drawbacks of the method is that, first, it does not take into consideration the total net cumulative cash inflow, and, secondly, it ignores the timing of cash flows. In the above example, there could be very high cash flows in years 8, 9 and 10 by which time there could be a theoretical return of €50 million (which would be an extremely satisfactory return on investment).

Accounting rate of return The accounting rate of return looks at the overall profitability of an investment. There are different definitions of the return and different definitions of the investment. However, the following is an example. The profitability is related to the amount of money invested in the project and the amount of time for which it is required. Depending on the cost of capital, the company will set a required rate of return. If the cost of capital in XYZ Ltd is 5% per annum, the company will accept the project under consideration if it yields a return of 5% or greater. Using the example from the payback method above:

Total cash inflow from the project:	€16,000,000
Deduct the initial capital investment:	€10,000,000
Profit:	€ 6,000,000

The investment earns €6 million over the seven-year life span, yielding €857,143 per annum. The initial investment was €10 million. The amount invested at the end is zero as the initial cost has been recouped, plus yielding a profit. Therefore, the rate of return is:

$$\frac{\text{Average annual profit (cash inflows less depreciation)}}{\text{Initial investment}}$$

$$\frac{€857,143}{€10,000,000} \times 100 = 8.57\%$$

As a return of 8.57% is greater than the cost of capital at 5%, this project can be accepted.

One advantage of the accounting rate of return method is that it takes the overall profitability of the project into account. However, one major weakness is that it does not take the pattern of cash flows into account.

Discounted cash flow methods There are two methods of using discounted cash flow to evaluate capital investments:

- Net present value method
- Internal rate of return method (IRR)

Usually, the methods yield the same result, though there are advantages and disadvantages to each appraisal method. The main advantage of the IRR method is that the information it provides is more easily understood by managers (especially non-financial managers). The main disadvantage is that it ignores the size of the investment. The net present value takes into account the total size of the investment and is superior for ranking mutually exclusive projects. For these reasons it will be the method demonstrated here.

Net Present Value Method The one big advantage of the net present value method compared to the other methods used is that it takes the time value of money into account. Thus, projects that yield a good cash flow early on are preferable to others where the cash inflows come later in the project. This brings us to the concept that money has a time value. There is a cost involved in having money tied up for a particular time period – the cost of capital. The longer this period will be, the greater the cost, and therefore the return the project gives us will be less valuable as time progresses.

The timing of cash inflow is important, assuming the money is going to be reinvested in further projects. While a particular project may produce a satisfactory profit over its lifetime, the company may have to wait a long time for cash inflows. If significant cash inflows are received earlier in the project, this allows the company to reinvest that money in further projects and, consequently, is of far greater value to the company.

If we use a cost of capital of 10%, then a Euro in one year's time is the equivalent of just 90.9 cent today, while a Euro in two years' time would only be worth 82.6 cent today, and so on. This can be calculated using tables or using the formula:

Year one:

$$\frac{€1 \times 100}{110} = \frac{1}{1.10} = 90.9c$$

Year two:

$$\frac{1}{1.10^2} = \frac{1}{1.21} = 82.6c$$

This can be extended to cover the number of years that the project will last. The following is an example using *annual* (rather than cumulative figures, which were used above in the payback method), with the same initial investment of €10 million:

Table 12.3: *Net Present Value Method*

Year	Cash Inflow €	Discount Rate 10% (from tables or the formula)	Present Value of Cash Inflows
1	500,000	.909	454,500
2	900,000	.826	743,400
3	2,600,000	.751	1,952,600
4	3,500,000	.683	2,390,500
5	1,500,000	.621	931,500
6	3,500,000	.564	1,974,000
7	3,500,000	.513	1,795,000
Total	16,000,000		10,241,500

Present value of inflows = **€10,241,500**

The present value of the €16 million cash inflow is reduced to just €10.24m using the discounted cash flow method. The net present value is equal to the present value of the cash inflows (€10.24m) less the present value of the cash outflow (€10m). In this case, the original investment was €10 million, so the project is just about breaking even over the seven-year period, using a cost of capital of 10% and the projected income outlined above. In the above example, the initial investment of €10 million was made at the beginning of the project. It will often be the case that the investment will be spread over a few years in the life of a project, in which case it is the net figure (the expenditure in that year less the net cash inflow, is then discounted by the appropriate figure). It must also be remembered that, in addition to the capital investment, there may also be a requirement for working capital, which should be taken into consideration.

These examples demonstrated different ways of evaluating various strategic projects from a financial perspective. The project was examined looking at its merits in isolation.

Mutually Exclusive Projects

It will often be the case that one project will have to be compared with another because of capital rationing or where they are mutually exclusive. Capital rationing is when there is a restraint on the amount of capital available. In 2008, the international credit squeeze made it very difficult for businesses to borrow money. Mutually exclusive projects are where the acceptance of one project means that a company cannot accept another project. In this instance, a decision will have to be made as to which one is the most suitable. One other factor that needs to be considered when investing in a strategic project is that circumstances may change substantially and the project may have to be abandoned. Having invested what is perhaps a considerable sum, it may be difficult to do this. However, if it is no longer viable, it is better to treat it as a sunk cost and not waste further investment that could be used more productively elsewhere.

Cost–Benefit Analysis

The financial return from a project is obviously a very important consideration. It is not, however, the only issue that should be taken into account. A company should also take a strategic overview of its entire portfolio and look at the project against that background. For example, entering a new market using direct investment might be extremely costly for a SBU. However, once established, its distribution network may be of considerable benefit to other SBUs in the organisation. As a result, all of the costs and benefits, both tangible and intangible, should be taken into consideration when examining a strategic option. Cost–benefit analysis attempts to put a monetary value on all the costs and benefits of a project, whether they are tangible or not.

This applies to commercial bodies as well as to the public sector. Indeed, in the public sector, many facilities would never be built if a purely financial perspective were taken. Many of these facilities and services play an important part in society. Many small post offices, for example, do not make a profit, but it is considered that they play a very important social role in rural communities. Flights from many regional airports to and from Dublin are subsidised under a public service contract administered by the European Union, as they also are deemed to provide an important service in linking the regions. Without the subsidy, the cost of the flights would be regarded as prohibitive. The process of assigning a monetary value on intangible benefits is obviously difficult, but it does ensure that managers take a more holistic approach to decision-making rather than focusing purely on costs and revenues.

Stakeholder Reaction

In Chapter 5, we examined the role of the different stakeholders in an organisation. It was seen that they will have very different views on the strategies chosen. It follows then that these views must be taken into consideration when developing strategies. The use of stakeholder mapping is a useful tool that can be used to anticipate support and opposition to a strategy. Once again, the importance of communication must be stressed, as often opposition can result from a lack of understanding. Communicating openly and clearly with all concerned may well alleviate any fears particular stakeholders may have. It should also be stressed that just because there will be opposition does not mean that a certain course of action should not be pursued, particularly if it is the correct course of action. However, being aware of the issues in advance can allow appropriate action to be taken.

Some of the obvious measures that will likely cause strong reaction are those involving major changes to the organisation – particularly those that will require redundancies, such as mergers and acquisitions, outsourcing or closing down some production facilities. If an organisation takes a more inclusive approach then it should be able to reduce or even eliminate any negative repercussions.

STRATEGIC PLAN

An organisation may now be in a position to finalise its strategic plan. Having a written plan will assist senior managers in terms of clarity of thought, and it will also play an important part in the communication of that plan to all staff members in the relevant parts of the organisation. There is no specific template *per se*, but the following framework is adapted from Thompson *et al.* (2008: 264) and should provide guidance to those developing the strategic plan.

Table 12.4: *Strategic Plan*

No.	Content	Comments
1	**Strategic vision, mission and ethical stance**	This sets clear guidelines for the organisation and where it should be deploying its resources, and how the organisation should be conducting its affairs.
2	**Strategic goals**	These should be divided into different categories based on the Balanced Scorecard, and should include long-, medium- and short-term goals.
3	**Strategic objectives**	Stemming from the goals in stage 2 above will be the specific objectives that need to be set. Being specific, they are easier to measure. These should also be divided into long-, medium- and short-term objectives.
4	**Overall business model**	This should articulate the overall business model for the entire organisation and the specific strategic business units. It should cover what type of generic strategies will be used, as well as laying out the different directions and methods by which the organisation will achieve its goals.
5	**Functional strategies**	These are the various functional strategies to support the corporate and business strategies. Separate plans are made out for each functional division in the organisation: Operations, Marketing, Human Resources, Finance, Research and Development etc. As well as being specific departmental plans, they obviously need to be co-ordinated if they are to support the overall corporate plan.
6	**Monitoring**	It was seen from **Figure 1.2** (Chapter 1) that feedback is an integral part of this process. As the plan is being implemented, it must be carefully monitored to ensure that it is working as it was originally intended. In most cases, changes will have to be made in light of the feedback being received.

CONCLUSION

Strategic decisions have long-term implications for the organisation and generally involve considerable sums of money. Thus managers must get them right. In the real world, this does not always happen, for a variety of reasons. Decisions must be taken by those running the organisation and, once people are involved, it is inevitable that the quality of decision-making will vary greatly from one situation to another and from one company to another. If people follow a logical framework, such as that proposed in this chapter, the probability of making a correct decision will be greatly enhanced. Ultimately, however, strategic decisions are usually quite subjective in nature, and it is hard to argue definitively whether a particular decision was the 'optimum' course of action. Perhaps the biggest factor in deciding whether the decision is a correct one or not, is the professionalism with which that decision is implemented. The implementation of strategy is the subject of Part Four.

SUMMARY

The nature of strategic decisions is such that they generally involve a considerable amount of money and have significant long-term implications for an organisation. For that reason, it is important that executives choose the correct course of action. Having generated a number of possible strategies that an organisation might pursue, it is necessary to have a framework to examine all of those options and select the optimum one.

The chapter began by looking at the decision-making process itself. Decision-making was defined as 'the selection of a course of action from among alternatives'. In most cases, there will be a degree of uncertainty about the outcome, and this inevitably makes the process more difficult. There is also a degree of risk involved in the process and this also has to be taken into account. Every organisation will have its own tolerance to risk, as will each individual executive.

The rational model assumes that people use a rational, sequential process in making decisions. This involves diagnosing the problem, identifying all solutions, evaluating each one, making the optimum choice, implementing it and finally evaluating the decision. It makes the assumption that all information is available and that people will process it in a rational manner. The model also implies that the executives concerned have the intelligence to weigh up all of the factors and choose the optimum solution. However, as in many instances, the theory and the practical reality are often different.

Decision-makers are often limited by what is termed '**bounded rationality**' which implies that the executive, when making decisions, is limited by a number of constraints including the capacity of the executive, and the environment. Instead of continuing the search for the best solution, people tend to '**satisfice**'. The reaction of different stakeholders will often impact on corporate decisions and this is likely to have a modifying effect on the various outcomes. The time available to make decisions is another important factor.

Escalation of commitment is where more and more resources are allotted to a project, despite evidence that it is no longer viable. **'Groupthink'** is where people involved in decision-making see the problem from one perspective only, and that perspective may be severely flawed. In general, group decisions are better than decisions made by individuals. The advantages include greater knowledge and comprehension of the issues and a number of different perspectives. By involving people in the decision-making process, there tends to be better acceptance of it. Decision-making styles evolve as a person moves up the corporate ladder or progress through the organisation.

Decision support systems are playing a very important role in helping executives make decisions based on accurate and up-to-date information. Analytics involves using statistical models to mimic large data sets.

Strategy evaluation applies the decision-making process to the various strategies under consideration in order to pick the most suitable one. The strategies must be consistent with the mission and the objectives of the company. They must also be suitable – examined against the background of the environment the company is operating within and the organisation's own capability. The strategy must also be feasible – there must be the appropriate resources in place to support it, particularly human resources and finance.

There is a strong link between business risk and return. The greater the potential return, the greater the risk involved. In most instances, the financial return will be of great importance, so it must be properly evaluated. There are a number of financial tools to assist the manager to examine each option. It must be remembered that these are only as accurate as the projections used. This chapter looked at three common investment appraisal systems. First, **the payback method** which looked at how long it will be before the initial investment has been paid back. This is important as the money tied up in a project cannot be used in another project until it is freed up. The second method was the **accounting rate of return**. In this case, we examined the overall profitability of an investment and the length of the project. It takes into consideration the entire cash flow for the life of the project. If the return is greater than the cost of capital, the project can be accepted.

The third method examined was **net present value**. This method recognises that money has a time value. A given amount of money available to a company now is worth more than that same amount in a few years' time. The net present value discounts future earnings into today's value and the cumulative amount can then be compared to the initial investment. If it is greater than the initial outlay, it can be accepted.

Cost–benefit analysis involves putting a monetary value on the intangible aspects of a project so that it can be viewed in a more holistic way. Finally, the views of all the relevant **stakeholders** must be taken into consideration before a final decision is made.

The chapter ended by looking at a template for a strategic plan. Having a written plan is important in that it helps crystallise all the issues facing an organisation and how that organisation can best position itself to meet those challenges.

DISCUSSION QUESTIONS

1. Critically analyse the rational model as a tool for decision-making.
2. Differentiate between group decisions and decisions made by individual executives, and state under which circumstances one approach might be more suitable than the other.
3. Evaluate the various stages involved in choosing a particular strategy.
4. Identify a major strategic decision taken by a large company, and critically analyse its effectiveness with regard to the stages referred to in question 3 above.
5. Differentiate between the various forms of financial appraisal that may be used in deciding an appropriate return on investment.
6. Discuss the importance of having a strategic plan for an organisation.

REFERENCES

Balboni, F. *et al.*, 2010, "Analytics: The New Path to Value", *MIT Sloan Management Review*, Fall 2010

Barry, F., 2010, "Politics and Economics Policy Making in Ireland", in Hogan,J. *et al.* (Eds.), *Irish Business & Society*, pp.28–43, Dublin, Gill & Macmillan

Buelens*et al.*, 2006, *Organisational Behaviour*, Maidenhead, McGraw-Hill

Brousseau, K. *et al.*, 2006, "The seasoned executive's decision-making style", *Harvard Business Review*, February 2006, Vol.84, Issue 2, pp.110–121

Clancy, P. *et al.*, 2010, *Mapping the Golden Circle*, Dublin, TASC

Collins, J., 2001, *Good to Great*, London, Random House Business Books

Cooper, M., 2009, *Who really runs Ireland?*, Dublin, Penguin Ireland

Czeisler, C., 2006, "Sleep Deficit: The Performance Killer", *Harvard Business Review*, October 2006, Vol. 84, Issue 10, pp.53–59

Dalkey, N.C. *et al.*, 1972, *Studies in the Quality of Life: Delphi and Decision-making*, Lexington, Lexington Books

De Bono, E., 1985, *Six Thinking Hats*, London, Penguin

Huber, J.P., 1980, *Managerial Decision-making*, Glenview, Scott, Foresman

Janis, I., 1982, *Groupthink*, 2nd Ed., Boston, Houghton Mifflin

Johnson, G. *et al.*, 2008, *Exploring Strategy*, 9th Ed., Harlow, Essex, Prentice Hall, Financial Times

Judge Harding Clark SC., M., 2006, *The Lourdes Hospital Inquiry: An Inquiry into Peripartum Hysterectomy at Our Lady of Lourdes Hospital, Drogheda*, Dublin, Stationery Office

Knights, D. and Willmott, H., 2007, *Introducing Organisational Behaviour and Management*, London, Thomson Learning

Kreitner, R., 1998, *Management*, 7th Ed., Boston, Houghton Mifflin

Lynch, R., 2008, *Strategic Management*, 5th Ed., Harlow, Essex, Prentice Hall, Financial Times

March, J. and Simon, H., 1958, *Organisation*, New York, John Wiley & Son

Martin, J., 2005, *Organisational Behaviour*, 3rd Ed., London, Thomson Learning

Maclear, M., 1981, *The Ten Thousand Day War*, London, Thames Mandarin

McNamara, R., 1995, *The Tragedy and Lessons of the Vietnam War*, New York, TimesBooks

McShane, S. and Von Glinow, M., 2009, *Organisational Behaviour*, 2nd Ed., New York, McGraw-Hill

Nyberg, P., 2011, "Misjudging Risk: Causes of the Systemic Banking Crisis in Ireland", *Report of the Commission of Investigation into the Banking Sector in Ireland*, Dublin, Government Publications Office

O'Brien, J. and Marakas, G., 2008, *Management Information Systems*, 8th Ed., New York, McGraw-Hill

Osborn, A.F., 1979, *Applied Imagination: Principles and Procedures of Creative Thinking*, 3rd Ed., New York, Scribners

Parker, G.M., 1990, *Team Players and Teamwork: The New Competitive Business Strategy*, San Francisco, Jossey-Bass

Ricks, T., 2006, *Fiasco, The American Military Adventure in Iraq*, London, Penguin Group

Ross, J. and Straw, B., 1993, "Organisational Escalation and Exit: Lessons from the Shoreham Nuclear Power Plant", *Academy of Management Journal*, August 1993, Vol. 36, Issue 4, pp.701–732

RSA, 2011, http://www.rsa.ie/RSA/Road-Safety/Campaigns/Current-road-safety-campaigns/Drunk-With-Tiredness/Campaign-2/, Accessed 24 April 2011

Simon, A.H., 1979, "Rational Decision-making In Business Organisations", *American Economics Review*, September 1979

Staunton, D., 2009, "US Combat Troops to Leave Iraq Next Year", *Irish Times*, 28 February 2009, p.11

Walker, D., 2009, *A Review of Corporate Governance in UK Banks and Other Financial Institutions*, London, The Walker Review Secretariat

Weilrich, H. and Koontz, H., 1993, *Management*, New York, McGraw-Hill

PART FOUR

Implementation

Introduction to Strategy Implementation

The final part of the strategy process in any organisation is its implementation. It is arguably the most important part of the process. Up to this point, the organisation's strategic plan is merely a blueprint for action. The plan on its own will not achieve anything. The manner in which

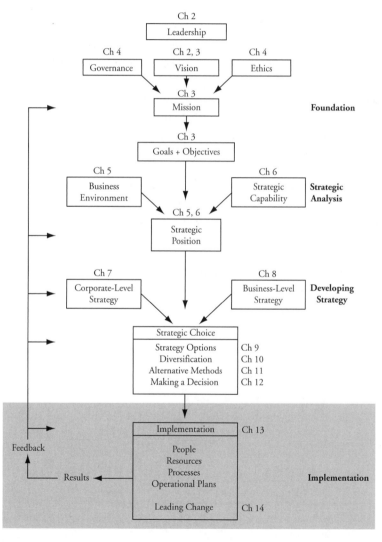

Figure 1.2 *The Strategic Planning Model*

it is implemented will have a direct result on the success or failure of the company, particularly in a competitive environment. Great consideration must therefore be given to how the strategic goals and objectives will be achieved. The Prussian General Von Moltke said that no plan survives contact with the enemy. Circumstances are constantly changing and the implementation process requires much flexibility as the organisation responds to new circumstances.

Part Four consists of two chapters. Chapter 13 deals with the implementation of strategy. Throughout this text the importance of the role that people play in the strategy plan has been highlighted. Nowhere is this more evident than in the implementation process. Regardless of how automated processes are, those employed in the organisation from the CEO down are central to the successful delivery of the plan. The implementation process will also require significant resources to support strategy. These include having sufficient finance (which can be difficult in the current climate), both from the point of view of the capital cost and also the day-to-day running costs, until such time as the project is generating positive cash flow. Operational efficiency is central to a profitable organisation and great care must be paid to how this process is designed. Various methods of ensuring quality are discussed here. Information systems will provide managers with the data required to make whatever adjustments are required to keep the process running smoothly. The final part of the chapter then deals with the variety of control mechanisms that can be employed to ensure targets are being met.

Chapter 14 examines organisational change. Change can be regarded as a certainty. Sometimes it is small incremental changes in the environment – often barely noticeable in the short term. On other occasions, it is like a train crash, and companies struggle to survive as they try to make sense of unfolding situations. This presents many challenges to managers as they must first understand the nature of the change and then bring the organisation to a safer place. As John Kotter argues, change must be led. While people are an organisation's greatest asset, we are also creatures of habit. People invariably fear change and find it difficult. One of the greatest tests of leaderships is dispelling that fear and bringing people to face the challenges head on.

Strategy Implementation

"We are what we repeatedly do. Excellence, then, is not an act, but a habit."

Aristotle

INTRODUCTION

Part Three of this text examined the types of strategic options that are potentially available to an organisation. It examined the possible strategies at business and corporate level, as well as the various different methods with which those strategies could be achieved. The final chapter in that Part, Chapter 12, provided a decision-making process to enable managers to make a decision on the best way forward for their organisations.

The strategy implementation process – Part Four – is the final process required for an organisation to achieve its strategic and financial goals. There are two related chapters in this Part: this chapter dealing with the actual implementation, and Chapter 14, which deals with the change process that inevitably happens when strategy is being implemented. The implementation of strategy is concerned with the delivery of results and creating the environment where things happen. It requires a different set of managerial skills from the development of strategy. The development of strategy demands market-driven skills to analyse the environment and the organisation's ability to respond. Strategy implementation, on the other hand, depends on working with and motivating people, and building up competitive capability. It is operations-oriented.

Each section of this chapter deals with a different aspect of the implementation process. The first section concerns the people in the organisation as, without the right people, nothing can be achieved. It also deals with the leadership required to initiate the process and see it through to a successful conclusion. Leadership and management go hand-in-hand in this process, so it is vital that the organisation assembles the right management team and has the right employees.

Chapter 6 looked at analysing strategic capability to gain an understanding of the strengths and weaknesses of an organisation. This is referred to as strategic fit: creating a fit between the capability of the organisation and the opportunities that match that capability. In reality, it does not always fit that neatly, and organisations often have to 'stretch' themselves in terms of the strategies being developed. In light of this, the company will have to reappraise its resources and competences to ensure that they are sufficient to support the chosen strategy or, if not, take immediate steps to rectify the situation. In particular, IT systems need to support the business model and ensure that the company can use technology to develop a competitive advantage.

Following on from this, the executives will have to fine-tune the structure so that it supports the strategies being pursued, and this process involves looking at factors such as the internal control processes, how the organisation relates internally and externally, where decisions are made within the organisation, and many more related issues. Policies and procedure will also have to be examined to enable the organisation to improve constantly and achieve best practice.

This chapter also examines strategies that will be required in the different functional areas such as marketing, R&D and, in particular, finance. It has been stated before that strategies by their nature require considerable finance, and appropriate measures must be put in place to support the strategy. All of these elements of strategy implementation are separate but need to be woven together in one co-ordinated plan, and this comes back to the managerial skills required.

STRATEGIC CAPABILITY

The starting point of implementing strategy is having a clear understanding of the goals and objectives that need to be achieved. Each set of circumstances will require different resources, which will need to be carefully controlled for cost reasons. The use of these resources will need to be carefully planned, along with appropriate budgets. Kaplan and Norton (2008) suggest that the use of the Balanced Scorecard will greatly assist in providing clarity to the process of implementation, along with providing relevant dashboards to alert managers to any deviation from the plan.

In examining the resources needed to implement a chosen strategy, it should be recalled that resources must be coupled with core competences if the organisation is to develop strategic capability and gain a competitive advantage in the marketplace. For most organisations, building core competences is a slow and incremental process. In a competitive marketplace, it is these competences that will separate the company from others in the mind of the consumer. In each of the resource areas detailed below, it must therefore be remembered that it is ultimately strategic capability that will give an organisation that edge. The distinction between possessing resources and combining those resources with core competences to create strategic capability will become apparent in the first section below which concerns people.

The organisation must have the capability to support the strategy it is endeavouring to implement. Chapter 6 examined various ways in which an organisation can evaluate its strategic capability. The emphasis there was primarily on what is known as 'strategic fit' – fitting the strategy to the resources and competences of the organisation. There are often occasions when the company has to push itself out of its comfort zone and stretch its capability to reach strategic goals. The organisation must assess the situation and understand the difference between where it needs to be and where it is currently. This is known as '**gap-analysis**', and it highlights what the organisation must do to reach its targets. If there is a shortfall in terms of resources and competences, these can be made good in a variety of ways. It may be done by purchasing the resources and developing the skills in-house, or it can be achieved by acquiring companies that have those resources and skills or by forming strategic alliances. Once the deficit is understood, it can be rectified.

PEOPLE

The first part of the implementation process concerns the people working in the organisation, as without the energy and determination of those who make up the company, nothing will happen. This applies to the top executives, middle management and all of the employees, as well as other relevant stakeholders, such as unions. 'Human Resources' (HR) is a standard term to describe the 'people' function in the organisation, and consequently it is used in this text.

However, from a strategic perspective, the term HR can be somewhat misleading in that people are a resource totally different to all of the other resources available to the firm, for two reasons. First, people can provide an organisation with a competitive capability different to all other resources. Secondly, the organisation does not own this resource. If people are not stimulated in their work and are not properly treated by the organisation, one of two things will happen: they will leave for a rival company and bring their skills with them; or else they will sit back and do enough so as to not get fired, but not enough to deliver a competitive edge to the company. It therefore requires a different paradigm than just looking on employees as another resource. In many cases, particularly in the knowledge economy, they are *the* resource.

For a company to be successful, everyone has to be working in unison to deliver on the vision. Collins (2001: 41–2) argues that:

> "The executives who ignited the transformation from good to great did not figure out where to drive the bus and then get people to take it there. No, they *first* got the right people on the bus (and in the right seats) and the wrong people off the bus and then figured out where to drive it."

Collins further adds: "If you begin with 'who' rather than 'what', you can more easily adapt to a changing world". Collins has modified the adage that 'people are your most important asset'. He argues that "People are *not* your most important asset. The *right* people are" Collins (2001: 13).

Leadership

Leadership forms an essential element in every aspect of running an organisation, from creating a vision and culture to laying down a proper ethical base on which staff at every level will make decisions. Making decisions, and seeing them through, are not the same thing. As the environment for most industries is changing at an ever-increasing rate, it becomes imperative that, when decisions are made in the best interests of the organisation, they are implemented quickly and decisively. Any discussion on managing the implementation process inevitably implies leadership to motivate all concerned to ensure the process is carried out efficiently and effectively.

There is an important distinction between efficiency and effectiveness. One can be carrying out a task with great efficiency, e.g. carrying buckets from the well to fill a large tank of water. Or one could put the effort into connecting a pipe to the tank and have a constant flow of water thereafter – effectiveness. Leaders are able to see the big picture and decide where the effort goes to ensure the effective use of scarce resources. According to Collins (2001: 86-7), it often involves operating under the 'Stockdale Paradox' (so called after an American admiral who was held as a POW by the North Vietnamese during the Vietnam War – or the 'American War' as it is termed in Vietnam – and who survived years of torture during his time in captivity). The Stockdale Paradox involves retaining faith that you will prevail in the end while confronting the most brutal facts of your current position. He added:

> "The good to great leaders were able to strip away so much noise and clutter and just focus on the few things that would have the greatest impact."

It requires clear thinking and the energy to make things happen quickly and effectively, as well as the ability to follow through. In the present economic climate where most organisations are facing extreme difficulties, it is vital that they can maintain optimism that they will succeed in the end, while at the same time being realistic as to the severe nature of this current crisis.

Management Team

Alongside visionary leaders, a strong management team forms an essential element of strategy execution. The two go hand-in-hand. Different managers will each bring their own set of skills and experience to the organisation, and it must be remembered that different strategies will require different managerial skills.

For a management consultancy organisation, the emphasis is on creating a learning organisation where knowledge is created and shared. For a low-cost airline, it is about reducing or eliminating costs at every juncture. With a lost-cost strategy, the emphasis is more on Taylor's 'scientific management' where there is one best way to do the job. It requires staff to follow these rules rather than act on their own initiative. In getting the 'right people on the bus', the organisation must pick managers with the right skills set. The company must also get 'the wrong people off the bus' as managers who do not have the appropriate skill or motivation will form a serious impediment to implementing the strategy. Creating the right team applies to management and to employees and how they both work together.

Depending on the size and scope of the strategic decision being implemented, the existing managerial team may or may not be sufficient to carry out the task. If not, the company will have to recruit additional managers with the appropriate skills. Alternatively, they can make an acquisition of a company with those capabilities or form some type of strategic alliance.

A corporate policy of promoting from within can have a positive motivational effect as people can see a career path within the company provided that they perform. There may, however, be occasions when the necessary managerial skills are not available in-house. An example could be a turnaround situation, where it may be that the existing managerial team did not take the necessary action to avoid the current situation. If the search to find suitable managers has been exhausted internally, the company will have to look elsewhere to appoint a suitable CEO and managerial team. While promoting from within often benefits an organisation, in recent times there has been much criticism of some internal appointments at senior executive level within the banking industry. In this instance the criticism centres on the fact that these appointees were in senior management positions when the banks ran aground. In situations such as these, there is often a requirement to recruit new executives from outside the organisation, or even the industry, who would bring fresh thinking with them and be unencumbered by the organisation's culture.

More and more, companies are beginning to realise the importance of developing appropriate managerial skills. A core competence of General Electric, for example, is its ability to pick and develop outstanding managers with a wide range of problem-solving and leadership skills. These skills are honed at their corporate development centre at Crotonville, and promotion and incentives are closely tied to successful completion of these courses.

The importance of good management is obvious when we examine examples of bad management. It often happens that, when things go wrong, management blame employees. There is an old military saying: 'there is no such thing as bad soldiers, only bad officers'. The fault often lies closer to home. Paul Tansey in an article in the *Irish Times* (2007) was deeply critical of falling productivity in the public sector in Ireland, and, in particular, the quality of its management:

"It would be deeply unfair to attribute these results to any lack of effort or dedication on the part of frontline public service staff…the central problem is a problem of management. It exists on two levels. First management and administration are wholly different functions. Management is active, administration is passive. This clear perceptual difference does not seem to have percolated through public services hierarchies. As a result, we have public services that are over-administered and under-managed. Secondly, it is simply a conceit to believe that inside every able administrator, there is a good manager struggling to get out.

"Management is a professional skill acquired only with time, effort and experience and usually backed by professional qualifications. It is simply not apparent, and indeed experience would speak otherwise, that whatever their undoubted administrative skills, the key management cadres within the public service are sufficiently qualified as professional managers."

The above comment is a generalisation: there are some extremely effective managers in the public service. There is also, however, much evidence to back up Tansey's view. There are many examples of poor management practices in the HSE. In many instances, the service provided could only be described as appalling, and if a commercial body were to deal with customers in a similar manner it would quickly fail. In his report published in September 2008, the Comptroller and Auditor General (C&AG) was highly critical of the financial management of many Irish public sector bodies, with millions of Euros being spent on poorly appraised projects (de Bréadún, 2008). There have been a number of inquiries into spending at the State Training Agency, FÁS.

The poor management is not confined to the public sector. If the discussion is broadened out somewhat from Paul Tansey's distinction between management and administration, there are many instances of private sector companies going out of business due to poor management. It is incorrect to assume that just because companies are in the private sector they always go bust if poor management decisions are made. In many cases, the company may not go out of business, but shareholder value is still impacted considerably. It is argued that many mergers and acquisitions do not create value for the company, and in many cases cause considerable losses. The DCC insider trading deal cost DCC €50 million in compensation to the various companies that had bought the shares from them, and in legal fees. In the cases of the various banking scandals, the evidence of unethical and illegal behaviour lies firmly with management.

Every organisation, whether in the public or private sector, has an absolute requirement for effective (and not just efficient) management if they are to deliver on their purpose. In terms of strategy formulation and implementation, it should not be taken for granted that the presence of a management team is enough. It must be 'the right people on the bus'. However, an important qualification with regard to the discussion in this text about managers achieving results is that it is predicated on the basis that those results are achieved in an ethical and legal fashion. Unfortunately, this is not always the case.

Managers at every level play a central role in the implementation of strategy. While there is a general trend towards flatter organisations, it must be remembered that middle managers are particularly important in that they need to translate the overall corporate strategy into meaningful goals and objectives for each section (and individual) within their area of responsibility. Problems that are being encountered at local level, and that cannot be solved at that level, will need to be referred back up along the line. The implementation of strategy will often require several iterations and fine-tuning before it is right.

Employees

While good managers are essential, without good employees they cannot deliver on the strategy. In most organisations, the divide between managers and employees is blurring considerably in that progressive companies place much greater emphasis on teamwork. In many cases, in the knowledge economy, employees are often as well-educated as managers, and will be the source of many of the ideas that underpin strategy development and implementation.

In terms of delivering on strategy, it is important not just to have the right people, but that they are in positions that suit their skills and aptitudes. Every person will have their own strengths and weaknesses and it is important that, in picking a team, each member can play in the position for which they are best suited. Rugby has been described as a game that caters for the gazelle and the elephant. The gazelle does not play in a second row position!

We saw in Chapter 1 how the American Bank, Wells Fargo, focused on "injecting an endless stream of talent" into the veins of the company. Many organisations, particularly the large multinationals, have a policy of recruiting the best and the brightest from college and from MBA programmes on the basis that the quality of their product is directly related to the quality of their employees. Considerable resources are spent on ensuring that the organisation gets the people that it wants, picking people with ability, the appropriate skills sets, initiative and drive, and, just as importantly, people who will fit in with the corporate culture.

On the Four Seasons' recruitment Website is a video clip of the CEO Isadore Sharp talking about the hotel chain. In the video, he talks among other things about the culture of customer service in the company. For potential employees, the video provides an important insight into the standards required by those who work in the group. Setting out clear expectations is an important element of attracting only those who will fit neatly into the existing culture and work with the values of the organisation. It must also be remembered that the policy of promotions from within stands for the entire organisation from front-line managers to senior executives. Today's young employees are tomorrow's senior managers.

Retention of employees goes hand-in-hand with the recruitment and selection process. As talented people within the organisation further develop their skills and knowledge, holding on to them becomes vital, as there are very large direct and indirect costs associated with staff turnover. Retention is achieved through a mixture of intrinsic and extrinsic rewards. This includes an integrated package of good remuneration, bonuses and perhaps share options, as well as providing challenging and rewarding jobs in a healthy corporate culture. Training is seen as an important and integral part of the process of attaining corporate goals. This includes initial training to facilitate the induction of the employee into the organisation and their particular job, and ongoing training to keep their skills up-to-date. Depending on the size of the organisation and the resources at its disposal, the training can be done either in-house or by outside consultants.

As noted earlier, many large companies have their own training centres that are, in effect, third-level institutions. Such centres obviously require significant financial resources that could normally only be justified for large companies. In other cases, organisations have specialised training centres as the skills required by the organisation could not be provided elsewhere. A good example of this is the Military College in the Curragh in County Kildare. While the college works in close conjunction with some universities for more general aspects of management, and other areas of study, most of its training and development requirements are esoteric to the military and can only be provided in-house.

The majority of smaller companies hire training consultants to run specific courses to meet their training needs. While such training and development is necessary, it can be disruptive in that the employees are away from their jobs for the duration of the course.

Many companies are turning to e-learning solutions where employees can do online training in their own time or in quieter periods at work. Companies such as PulseLearning (see **Illustration 1.3**) specialise in developing online courses tailored to meet the needs of individual companies. There are many obvious financial and time benefits to online training. On the other hand, the importance of networking and the opportunity to get to know work colleagues on traditional training and development courses should not be underestimated. Perhaps a blending of both methods is the answer. What is important is that there is a strategic focus to training and development that balances the short-term imperative of being trained for the immediate job requirements with the long-term development of the employee and the long-term goals of the organisation.

The ultimate purpose of training and development is to ensure that employees have the appropriate skills to underpin the strategic progress of the company. Once employees have these skills, the organisation can then develop a competitive advantage. Certain skills can be considered essential for employees to attain and are often linked to rewards and promotion. This applies to all levels in the organisation. In the Army, for example, promotion to the next level will only be considered when the person has successfully completed the appropriate course for that rank, in addition to all other requirements.

The Human Resources Function

The HR function also plays an important strategic role in planning the long-term human resource requirements of a company. It monitors sociological and demographic trends (see PESTEL analysis in Chapter 5), along with the organisation's future plans and conducts a gap analysis in terms of its requirement for people.

For example, when companies like Intel in Leixlip, County Kildare, consider a major expansion of their facility, the company has to plan well in advance to ensure that it has the right number of managers and employees, with the appropriate skills. It also has to ensure that they are available at the time they are needed. This process entails identifying leadership development requirements as well as the immediate technical and operational skills needed, and making the appropriate arrangements to ensure the gap is bridged. This process is carried out against the backdrop of the corporate culture to see what cultural changes, if any, need to be effected to ensure the company can properly position itself in the future.

On the other hand, companies such as Aer Lingus have needed to downsize in order to become competitive, and the process of redundancies is one that has to be carefully planned in terms of identifying the types of jobs that will go, and negotiating with the stakeholders concerned. All of these are strategic HR initiatives that have to be planned and executed in the medium to long term.

The HR strategy also has to be distilled down into the day-to-day operational issues. In recent years, there has been a raft of legislation dealing with various aspects of employment. The specialised nature of such legislation, and the importance and relevance of the HR function, has increased significantly. In most organisations, the HR function is primarily an advisory one, with the direct responsibility for employees resting with their line manager. There should be close liaison between the human resources manager and the various line managers to ensure that all aspects of employee rights are being upheld. Failure to do so could be costly for the organisation. The HR function maintains employee records and will normally co-ordinate training and development with the line managers.

OTHER RESOURCES

The people that make up an organisation are not just an essential resource: they can also become a competitive capability. However, there are also numerous other resources required by organisations in order to succeed. In most instances considerable finance will be required, and this has to be sourced and planned. Operational facilities will also be required and there are many possibilities here as to whether they are conducted in-house or outsourced. Information technology underpins almost all strategy and this has to be tailored to suit the unique circumstances of each company. Research and development is not forgotten about at this implementation stage, but is an ongoing process, not just in terms of constantly improving and modifying existing products and services, but also coming up with the next generation of products. Marketing resources will also be required to facilitate the sale of the product or service to the widest possible market. All of these will need to be considered in greater detail.

Finance

The finance required to support a strategy has to be carefully planned. There are two main aspects here, the capital cost required to finance the project and the current costs. There are two considerations that managers must plan for with regard to the financing of a project. First is the total amount of finance required for supporting a strategy, and second is the timing of cash payments.

Many of these aspects, such as funding strategies, have already been discussed in Chapter 7, which considered corporate-level strategy, and also Chapter 12, which examined the different financial appraisal systems as part of the decision-making process. In addition, Chapter 6 examined the principle of cost competitiveness in an organisation. That cost perspective now needs to be examined in relation to each specific strategy to ensure that it is lower than rival companies offering a similar product or service or, if it is higher, customers must be happy to pay a premium because they perceive the product or service to be of better quality. Costs are relative to what is being produced. The process, therefore, involves examining all of the cost drivers (those factors that create cost, both direct costs involved in production and overheads), and these must be compared to the value being created by the product and service. The latter is a function of the volume produced, multiplied by the sales price.

The cost of capital must also be taken into consideration and this applies to equity, bank and other borrowings, and retained earnings. Considerable amounts may well have been invested in capital costs involved in creating the necessary facilities (for large multinationals, this could amount to hundreds of millions of Euro). There will also have to be adequate working capital pumped in to ensure that day-to-day costs can be met and the organisation does not become illiquid.

Once the total costs and the total revenues are known, profitability can then be calculated. Corporate finance can be complicated. However, in any business, in any industry, profitability boils down to a very simple equation:

- If a company is selling its products or services at a price greater than what it is costing, it is making a profit.
- If a company is selling its products or services at a price lower than what it is costing, it is making a loss.

The above equation may seem simplistic in a book about corporate strategy, yet it is amazing how often it seems to be forgotten. It is fundamental to the continued existence of any business. Budgets form an integral part of the process of managing finance. Budgets are both a planning tool in setting out what the expenditures and revenues are likely to be, and they are also a control device to compare actual with planned expenditure. There are situations where a particular strategy may be deliberately loss-making in the short term. This may be done for strategic reasons, such as wanting to gain a foothold in a particular market that would have good long-term potential. However, it is vital that managers monitor the situation and keep it under tight control so that the strategy does not haemorrhage funding. When things do go wrong, managers also need to be decisive when corrective action is required.

Marketing

Marketing is an essential element of an implementation plan. Every organisation must have customers for its products and services. The company needs to make as many people as possible aware of the range of products and services on offer before they will make a purchase decision. As with other activities, it will involve considerable resources and these resources must be used as effectively as possible. A marketing plan will assist in this process.

 A **marketing plan** is a document that sets out how an organisation will market its products and services.

A marketing plan has many functions:

- It helps in ensuring that the organisation is customer-focused and aware of the requirements of the market place.
- It is a guide for the organisation for implementing marketing strategies and assisting management in controlling and monitoring those strategies.
- It ensures efficient use of resources and specifies how those resources will be used.
- It assigns responsibilities and timeframes to individuals for specific tasks.

Each Strategic Business Unit (SBU) has its own specific market separate to the other SBUs. Consequently, there should be a separate marketing plan for each major strategy being pursued by the company. There will be an overall marketing plan that co-ordinates the activities of the entire organisation.

Dibb *et al.* (2008: 722) suggest that marketing plans will generally conform to a similar outline, which includes: an executive summary of the plan; a statement of the goals and objectives to be achieved; the general background to the market; a general analysis of the market and an examination of realistic marketing opportunities; an examination of competitor activity; an outline of marketing strategy including target market priorities, differential advantage, as well as brand and product positioning; a statement of expected sales patterns; the detail of marketing mixes (price, product, place, promotion and people) required to implement the marketing plan; control mechanisms to monitor progress; financial requirements to implement the marketing plan and budgets; and finally any operational considerations that arise from the marketing plan.

Information Technology Systems

Information technology plays a vital role in supporting strategy and giving the company a competitive advantage in the market place. The term 'knowledge economy' has been used a number of times in this text to describe the evolution of the Irish economy away from basic manufacturing to more upmarket products and services. As companies develop, the importance of information technology grows substantially. Information technology has the ability to change the nature of the business in a strategic and operational manner. Information technology is primarily a strategic asset. In the context of this chapter, it impacts on the implementation of strategy in organisations in many ways benefiting the company itself and the customer.

The flow of information and strategic capability go hand-in-hand. Organisations need accurate and timely information about customers' needs in order to develop products and services that meet those needs. Managers also need IT systems to provide them with information from all parts of the company, particularly financial information in order to make sound decisions about the future. Financial statements can be compiled with much greater accuracy and in a fraction of the time compared to previously. This has also impacted on the structure of organisations and, as a general rule, organisations have become much flatter, cutting out layers of middle management and associated costs. Accurate and timely flows of information also has important implications in terms of leading change in an organisation, and this will be examined in the next chapter.

IT can transform how the company interacts with other businesses as part of the value system. In particular, it changes the nature of competition in the industry and how the level of competition is judged (using Porter's Five Forces analysis). Some businesses have transformed from traditional-type companies into 'virtual' businesses. As technology improves and companies become more comfortable with technology, it is moving to centre stage in the structure of many business organisations.

Business models have changed considerably as a result of developments in IT systems.

Definition	**A business model** describes the processes by which an organisation interacts with suppliers and customers to deliver its products or services.

The value chain explains how business models have changed. When discussing the supply chain, the importance of linkages was stressed, both internally in the organisation and with the wider value system. Information technology plays a vital part in such linkages. In the supply side, just-in-time manufacturing is dependent on integrated IT systems between the supplier of components and manufacturers. Dell, for example, holds on average only two days' supplies in order to minimise costs. As the components are used to assemble computers, suppliers are notified electronically and additional components are shipped to replace stocks. It also impacts on how customers interact with companies. Some organisations, such as airlines, have moved exclusively to online purchasing and others, such as banks, are attempting to move to online transactions as much as possible. These are all primarily strategic issues for IT systems, but they also have an enormous operational benefit with regard to the rollout of the strategy being followed.

While e-commerce benefits the customer in many ways, the main incentive for companies is that it reduces costs very significantly. When Ryanair first moved away from using travel agents, bookings were done by using call centres. This necessitated having people to take the calls, and in many cases perhaps deal with passengers who were indecisive about their arrangements, thus prolonging the transaction and increasing the costs. When an individual is browsing on an airline's Website, the time spent on the site is not costing the airline as it is only the customer's time that is being taken up. When the customer makes a decision, the transaction is conducted immediately. In addition, information technology is a vital part of yield management whereby airlines attempt to maximise the revenue from each flight. IT systems allow this to happen in real time, and the prices are adjusted according to the demand.

Another very important function for many industries is data mining. **Data mining** allows companies to extract from their IT systems information about customer demand, as well as trends and connections in that demand. Tesco is a prime example of a company that has exploited information technology to enormous effect.

Illustration 13.1: Data Mining at Tesco

An article in the *Financial Times* by Elizabeth Rigby illustrates the extent of the strategic capability contained in the Tesco Clubcard. In 1994, Tesco hired Dunnhumby, a firm that specialises in consumer data, to assist it with the development of 'Clubcard', its customer loyalty card. After an initial trial in a limited number of stores, Dunnhumby made a presentation to the Tesco board on the value the Clubcard could add to the company. At the end of the presentation, its chairman Lord MacLaurin responded:

"What scares me about this is that you know more about my customers after three months than I know after 30 years."

Tesco now owns 84% of Dunnhumby and Tesco's business accounts for 30% of Dunnhumby's turnover.

With scanning machines at each checkout, every supermarket knows what items are sold and at what time. For the majority of companies, this resource provides them with just a basic competence. Tesco has turned this basic competence into a core competence. The application form for the Clubcard contains personal information about the applicant. The Clubcard matches information on purchases with an individual person and builds up a very detailed profile. What separates Tesco from other supermarkets that have similar loyalty cards is the ability to process the information that the card provides. In the UK, two-thirds of British households shop in Tesco and £1 in every £7 spent in all shops is spent in Tesco. With such a large customer base and the ability to analyse individuals' shopping habits, it generates five billion pieces of data from the weekly shop in a 40-terabyte database (it probably has more frequently updated personal information about named individuals in the UK than any other organisation!). It also allows the company to target individuals with special offers that have been very successful in attracting customers into the stores.

This raw data is turned into useful information that allows the company to segment its customers into different categories and sub-categories and, in so doing, gives Tesco a competitive advantage across almost every aspect of its business. It has also informed strategic decision-making by the company to branch into other areas such as mobile phones and insurance. With every purchase made, more information is added to the person's purchasing profile. This information is added to other data received from various sources such as the statistics office and it builds up socio-economic profiles of customers and areas. This allows the company to spot trends in shopping habits. Not only is this information of enormous value to Tesco in deciding what to stock in each individual store, and indeed where to locate stores, but the information is sold on to over 200 consumer-goods companies, including giants like Unilever and Procter & Gamble, to assist them in product development that is tailored to suit customer demand.

(Rigby, 2006)

There are certain limitations and risks that must be taken into account with regard to IT systems. Ethical issues must be considered in relation to the use of information technology, especially in the use and distribution of confidential customer information. As well as ethical concerns, this is also covered by legislation and the company could be subject to fines for the misuse of information. The organisation should prepare a detailed policy statement for all departments in relation to the use of information and monitor its adherence. It is important for executives to have a realistic expectation regarding what information technology can do for the company. No matter how sophisticated the system is, it is not a substitute for sound managerial judgement. In most instances, competitors will also be using similar technology and so competitive advantage is gained not so much by the technology itself, but by how it is used. In other words, the use of technology has gone from being a core competence to a basic, threshold one.

Costs involved in IT systems have come down considerably, making its use more universal. However, because of competitive pressures, IT systems must be regarded as an essential resource, rather than believing the cost to be prohibitive. In addition, IT has raised the expectations of customers, because through different company Websites they are able to gain information about all the competitors in a particular market and compare one with the others.

There are many ways in which IT has changed and enhanced products that benefit the customer. As mentioned above, it provides quite an amount of pre-purchase information for the customer allowing them to make a better and more informed choice. As a result of making better and more informed choices, there should be greater customer satisfaction. It also enables customers to tailor products to their own specific needs. This is done by Dell, for example, in that their computers are built to the customer's exact specification. It also allows significant savings that are passed on to the customer. When things go wrong, IT systems can assist in problem-solving. Car maintenance, for example, has become much more sophisticated; garages use computers to identify problems and they also make certain activities such as fixing engine timing much more accurate. Computers are also used in the NCT to determine if vehicles are roadworthy.

By correctly identifying a problem, it can be fixed in a shorter period of time and at less cost. Finally, IT can improve customer service by sharing information between different parts of an organisation. There are many examples in the hotel industry where departments can share information on customers' requirements and this information can also be shared by hotel groups. Similarly in hospitals, departments can access information on a patient, thus improving the speed and accuracy of the treatment when collaboration between departments is required.

Operations

The operations element of strategy implementation will obviously differ significantly from one organisation to another, depending on the nature of the business. There are a number of general factors that must be considered. The importance of R&D was discussed in Chapter 9. There is an ever-increasing pressure on companies to constantly innovate by improving existing products and developing new ones. Such innovation is dependent on the people in the organisation having imaginative ideas and a system that fosters those ideas and brings them to fruition. This involves having a good understanding of customers and their requirements. In recent years, Ireland has been selected as the location for R&D facilities for many different reasons, not least being the ready availability of suitably qualified graduates. However, in Chapter 5 it was seen that our ability as a country to produce graduates in sufficient quantity should not be taken for granted.

Operations systems must support strategy. Innovation refers not only to new products but also new systems. Being able to increase efficiency in operations will increase profitability. Decisions must be made about conducting operations in-house or outsourcing to third parties, e.g. Nike and Benetton. If the company is to carry out operations in-house then a decision must be made as to whether the facilities are developed internally by the organisation or whether it acquires another company that has those facilities. Developing them in-house provides the opportunity to create state-of-the-art facilities that could have a very significant impact on efficiency, but is likely to take a number of years. Acquisition can provide the necessary facilities in a short period. The decision to opt for one or the other is dependent to a large extent on the industry and the nature of the technological changes taking place. The reader should refer back to Chapter 11 for a fuller discussion of the relevant issues. Considerable financial resources will be required and these will have to be provided either at corporate level or by the division concerned.

BUILDING COMPETITIVE CAPABILITIES

The development of competitive capabilities is an integral element of the entire strategy development and implementation process. Organisations have no choice but to develop the competitive capabilities required to operate in their industry. Chapter 6 examined the process by which strategic capability is identified as part of the development of strategy. In the implementation phase, the company needs to ensure the correct capabilities are in place and these must also be modified as conditions change in the marketplace. Building such capabilities takes a considerable amount of managerial time and effort. It requires identifying best practice, imitating it and eventually improving on it. This involves a number of stages. Companies must work on their basic skills and continuously develop them. Over a period of time, and as the organisational experience grows, these activities can be performed more efficiently ensuring acceptable quality at a competitive price. Further improvement should convert this activity into a core competence giving the company a strong competitive advantage.

The Japanese sum up this incremental improvement in one word: *Kaizen*.

 Kaizen is a philosophy that suggests that every aspect of our lives should be constantly improved.

In management terms, *Kaizen* underpins total quality control. Its key elements include quality, effort, involvement of all employees, willingness to change and good communication. The practical application of this concept is indeed difficult, but, in order to achieve excellence, it must be done. This once again raises the issue as to whether these capabilities are developed in-house or whether they are outsourced to key employers.

The competitive capability of an organisation consists of the resources and the competences that it possesses and the knowledge that has been built up, often over a period of time. Porter (1985) stressed the importance of linkages between elements of the value chain and the wider value system. These linkages therefore are not only internal, but also involve working closely with suppliers and, in particular, customers in order to improve not just the products but all the process flows as well. Such linkages also make it very difficult for other companies to imitate these competences. Identifying these competences in a competitor is one thing; being able to replicate them is entirely different. The *Kaizen* approach is a holistic approach based on constant improvement over a sustained period of time. It involves examining all aspects of the organisation to identify areas that can be improved. In particular, it involves improving activities from the level of a basic competence to a core competence. This requires concentrating more effort and talent than rivals into strengthening that competence. This point highlights the importance of having talented people in the organisation. The business environment is constantly evolving and so too should the organisation in response to changing market demands. The process of *Kaizen* should therefore be viewed as a continuous process, rather than an end destination.

PROCEDURES FOR GOOD STRATEGY EXECUTION

The strategy implementation process must be supported by appropriate policies and procedures. While the organisation will have policies and procedures in place, these will have to be updated and adjusted for the strategies that are being implemented. Thompson *et al.* (2008: 391) state that prescribing new policies and operating procedures will facilitate the process of execution in three ways:

- It provides top-down guidance on how the organisation does certain things. From that perspective, it helps align the actions and behaviour of company personnel with the strategy, and channels the energy of the organisation towards achieving their goals. It also provides parameters for employees on the types of decisions that they make.

- In larger organisations, it will help provide a certain consistency between the different geographical and product divisions of the company in terms of how the strategy is implemented and how the organisation interacts with its customers.

- It helps create an appropriate work climate that will enable the strategy to be implemented, and such a work climate will also facilitate change.

In a competitive environment, managers must constantly identify opportunities for adopting best practices in all aspects of strategy implementation. Such practices are essential in reducing costs and improving quality. When the company has identified best practice for the relevant activities, it must then adopt and implement such practices. An important part of this process will be the development of metrics by which improvements can be measured. Best practice is something that is constantly evolving, so the organisation must keep up-to-date with the best performers around the world. Such excellence is only achieved over a period of time and with much effort. Indeed, identifying best practice can often be difficult: while it is easy to identify companies that are successful, it is another matter identifying what internal processes make them so successful. When this is identified, it then has to be translated into the specific circumstances surrounding the company wishing to adopt the practice. There are a number of different tools that managers can use to help achieve excellence. These include Business Process Re-engineering, Six Sigma and Total Quality Management.

Business Process Re-Engineering

Business process re-engineering (BPR) was made popular in the early 1990s by James Champy and Michael Hammer in their book *Re-engineering the Corporation* (1993). BPR is based on the premise that, in order to stay competitive, organisations have to redesign themselves using a clean sheet of paper if they are to survive. The purpose of business process re-engineering is to examine the processes rather than the products and see what efficiencies can be gained by aligning those processes across functional and divisional units in an organisation.

Supply chain management, for example, involves purchasing the materials, storing them, manufacturing/assembly, storing finished goods and distributing them. This involves several different departments and personnel, as well as countless procedures. It was believed that most of the time wasted on any particular process is wasted in moving from one department to another, particularly the flow of information. By reorganising these processes on the basis of work teams, enormous productivity gains can be made and it can cut costs significantly. By the mid-1990s, it was estimated that four out of five Fortune 500 companies were using some form of business process re-engineering, and not just in manufacturing but in services and the public sector.

Micklethwait and Wooldridge (1996) believe that business process re-engineering is not without its critics. It is inextricably linked with 'downsizing' – getting rid of large numbers of employees and middle managers. It has been likened to Taylorism in that it treats employees like automatons rather than intelligent people, and this has a devastating impact on employee morale and a negative impact on innovation. Hammer and Champy (1993) consider that it is not the concept that is at fault but the manner in which it is applied. It may well be that in many cases companies involved in cost-cutting and large scale lay-offs have termed it business process re-engineering without any realignment of their processes – just merely making people redundant.

Total Quality Management

It is ironic that while total quality management (TQM) is very much associated with the Japanese, it was two Americans, William Denning and Joseph Duran, who were the pioneers behind the concept. Denning developed a set of 14 points which he believed were essential for attaining quality in a company. He believed that faults in manufacturing lay with the systems used rather than the people involved in the process. Juran believed that management could largely control quality defects. The two men worked with Japanese companies and their teaching gained widespread acceptance. This move towards quality led to the development of total quality management, which is essentially a customer-focused management philosophy aimed at achieving total quality at all levels of the organisation by all employees from the CEO down. It requires each and every employee to take responsibility for quality in their own work and for rectifying mistakes if they occur.

According to Stevenson (1989), TQM involves five stages: understanding what the customer is looking for; designing the product/service in a manner that exceeds the customers' needs; designing a production process that ensures everything is done correctly the first time; monitoring performance; and then working with suppliers and distributors to extend the process. It also emphasises continuous improvement – *Kaizen* – in every aspect of what the organisation does, including administrative functions as well as production and services. The process of TQM is an integral part of, and must be supported by, the corporate culture of the organisation. As a managerial tool, TQM has developed widespread appeal across the world.

Six Sigma Quality Control

Six Sigma quality control was originally designed by Motorola in the mid-1980s and has become an integral part of training in many top class companies such as Motorola, BMW, Nokia, Xerox,

General Electric and many more Fortune 500 companies. In the section on training above, it was stated that General Electric sends employees on various training programmes; this includes sending all new employees on a basic programme in Six Sigma. This is followed up with more advanced courses that are graded similarly to martial arts labels such as green belt, brown belt or black belt and these qualifications are regarded as a prerequisite for promotion.

Six Sigma is a statistics-based system with the objective of having no more than 3.4 defects per million opportunities (DPMO) in the entire business process. It is the equivalent of 99.9997% efficiency. It was originally designed for manufacturing but it was later applied to other business processes and can also be used in non-profit organisations. In Six Sigma a defect is regarded as anything that would lead to customer dissatisfaction. It was inspired by previous studies on quality control methodologies such as TQM. Sigma (represented by the Greek letter: σ) is used to represent the standard deviation of a statistical population. Six Sigma operates on the premise that continuous efforts to achieve top quality in business processes are vital for success. It considers that all business processes can be measured, analysed, improved and controlled, but this can only be achieved with commitment from the entire organisation, particularly top management.

Six Sigma Quality Control is aimed at improving various processes within an organisation. For new processes, the process involves five stages: Define, Measure, Analyse, Design and Verify (DMADV). However, in most instances, existing processes are probably already in place and so a different Six Sigma process – DMAIC – is used. The five stages of DMAIC include:

- **Define** – team members must define what constitutes a defect from the customers' perspective.
- **Measure** – develop a process flow chart to enable the team to collect data on the defects, such as how and why they occur, and how often.
- **Analyse** – the data must be analysed to understand the process and where it is failing.
- **Improve** – develop and document best practice for the process.
- **Control** – the best practice must be used by all employees with regard to this process.

Six Sigma Quality Control is a very effective programme for improving performance in companies where there is a wide variation in how different organisations perform a particular process. In can be used in manufacturing procedures or in the services end, where those products are being sold, e.g. in direct sales there could be a big difference between the top sales performers and poor sellers. If the techniques of the poor sellers are bad, then no amount of extra incentives will improve performance. But if the performance of the top sellers is studied using rigorous statistical techniques, it will show how they plan and spend their day, and the techniques they use for closing sales. The information obtained could be used in many ways, from improving the performance of the poor sellers, to being more selective in recruitment.

As with all such efforts to improve efficiency, it must have top managerial support and become embedded in the culture of the company. Many companies have championed the process ensuring that it has become a central part of how their company operates. While there are similarities between business process re-engineering, TQM and Six Sigma, the main difference between them is in the time frame for improvements. Processes like TQM and Six Sigma emphasise continuous improvements in quality and cost reduction over a long period of time, while business process re-engineering can achieve enormous gains in a very short period, although sustaining such improvement can be difficult. The different processes are not mutually exclusive and a dual approach may well achieve sustained long-term results. It is important to remember that improvements in quality can create excess capacity. This excess capacity must, in turn, lead to a greater level of sales, otherwise the excess capacity must be redirected to other uses. Reforms currently taking place in the public sector are aimed at increasing productivity and removing excess capacity. In some cases, people may be redeployed to other departments and organisations. In other cases, people are being offered voluntary redundancy packages such as in the Health Service Executive (HSE).

Operational efficiency is important, but it is not a substitute for strategy. Porter (1996) suggests that, while operational efficiency is needed, organisations must also keep a strategic focus. He believes that managers must respond quickly to competitive and market changes, but many fail to distinguish between operational effectiveness and strategy. They are both necessary but work in different ways. A company can only outperform if it can establish a difference that it can preserve, such as greater value. Cost advantages arise from performing activities more efficiently than competitors. Threats to strategy are often seen to emanate from outside the company because of changes in technology or competitors. Managers often start imitating everything about their competitors and chasing technology for its own sake. The pursuit of operational effectiveness is seductive because it is concrete, but it lacks a vision of the whole and the perspective to recognise trade-offs. The desire to grow has the most pervasive effect on strategy, particularly in targeting customers in other segments. But this blurs a company's strategic position. Companies should grow by concentrating on deepening a strategic position rather than broadening and compromising it. It should look for extensions of the strategy that lever the existing activity system. Globalisation can open up markets for a focused strategy.

According to Porter (1996), organisations depend on leadership – "a clear intellectual framework to guide strategy". It is far broader than making operational improvements, defining and communicating the company's unique position, making trade-offs and forging fits among activities. The leader must decide what industry changes and customers' needs the company will respond to. This may mean saying no to certain courses of action in some instances. Porter suggests that improving operational efficiency is necessary but it is not strategy. "Both are essential, but the agendas are different." While operational efficiency requires constant change and flexibility for best practice, strategy demands a unique position, clear trade-offs, discipline and continuity.

Illustration 13.2 is a good example of how an Irish company, Shannon Aerospace, has responded to global pressures by introducing lean techniques, and in the process, has radically transformed how the company operates. It demonstrates a strategic approach from corporate level to operational level with regard to issues facing the company. The illustration highlights the importance of senior managers realising that good ideas can come from anywhere in the organisation and that one of the most important functions of managers in an organisation is creating a forum and a climate whereby such ideas can filter through and be translated into a strategy that will work (see Chapter 1). It is also a good example of leading change (see Chapter 14).

Illustration 13.2: Shannon Aerospace – Lean Transformation

Shannon Aerospace Limited (SAL) is a company that specialises in the maintenance, repair and overhaul of commercial jet airframes. Operating in a global industry, it is based in Shannon, County Clare. The company is a wholly owned subsidiary of Lufthansa Technik AG. Like many big companies, it has responded to challenges in the past that significantly changed its business environment, including the Gulf wars, 9/11, low-cost airlines changing the rules of the industry (and reducing maintenance business volume), deregulation and the collapse of former shareholder companies, GPA and Swissair. Perhaps one of the biggest challenges was the Celtic Tiger impact on costs and staff turnover. The company had to respond radically by growing business volume and transforming how they operated. Lean tool techniques were seen as essential in helping to reduce maintenance turn-around time (TAT), which in turn would reduce costs.

The company began the process by communicating the necessity for the programme with staff members. To bridge the gap between their lean strategy and actual implementation, Value Stream Mapping (VSM) was used. The company mapped its end-to-end business processes with the specific goals of reducing aircraft turn-around time by 35% and cost of production by 30%. The company brought together a team of 28 people from all levels and areas of the company as well as the technical director of EasyJet to represent customers. The team received training in Lean principles, VSM and paradigm-shift training. The team applied their training by reviewing all practices within the organisation from the perspective of the customer. It was a very open approach to the problem and all company employees witnessed the executives spend a full week on the shop floor, questioning their own processes in terms of the value that each activity was adding. The process identified bottlenecks and inefficiencies, and the team learned to brainstorm for ideas to overcome these problems. From this, the team agreed an 'Ideal State Map' for the value stream analysis and developed realistic goals to enable the company to grow and transform the business.

The implementation plan involved a number of projects with several Process Preparation and Planning events, some 'just do it' tasks and many *Kaizen* events called Rapid Improvement Events (RIEs). Using the implementation plan, the team then brought in all relevant employees and briefed them on the plan. Employees were given training in areas that impacted on their team's participation in the process. This process was not a one-off event but became part of the development of a continuous improvement culture that persists in the organisation.

The implementation plan required new processes to be created, old processes to be made more efficient, safer or more reliable, and a relentless drive to identify and eliminate waste. It involved full engagement with staff members. Rapid improvement events involved the 'process owner' developing a plan that specified the purpose of the event, the specific deliverables, the benefits to be derived and the metrics that will be used to verify results. The critical path of the project would be identified. Team members would then be selected, which also included people from outside the company to bring a fresh perspective. The process is tied in with a number of lean companies from around the world with which SAL collaborates and shares information. The team is open to input from any source.

When an event is being planned, the team forms on a part-time basis three weeks prior to the event to start the planning process and define the scope and understand what success will look like. The team gets intensive training in the various tools, such as value stream mapping, etc., to plan their schedule effectively, with all the various manuals and other requirements available online. One of the biggest benefits of the RIE teams was the breaking down of barriers between different sections and the streamlining of the organisation. One innovation was the creation of a 'hub' on the hangar floor acting as a single point of contact between hundreds of various technicians as well as support teams.

Changes such as these have made enormous improvements, such as the time taken to strip and paint an aircraft, which has been reduced from 13 shifts (12-hour shifts) to nine shifts, taking two days off each ground time and opening up new revenue slots for sale. Likewise, technicians contributed significantly to the success achieved in improving cash flow by reducing invoicing time from 78 days to 7 days. The company has benchmarked a number of different lean processes and adapted them to their own particular needs, such as their '6S' workplace organisation. Here, the workplace is laid out so that it is easy to operate following an agreed new process, from which it is difficult to deviate. As improvements are made, both management and colleagues are briefed on those improvements, and the changes are then converted into new operating procedures.

There were many lessons learned by SAL along the way. Initially, a lot of the change taking place was opposed. In response, the company realised that it was essential to create ownership of the process by all those involved and to include them in the problem-solving process. Some managers initially did not fully appreciate this, or carry out their role as 'facilitator of change and improvement'. As time went on, the quality of internal communications improved as this was seen to be an integral part of its overall success. Managers also underestimated how long the transformation would actually take. Some areas of excellence emerged, while other areas were initially left behind. This proved divisive, but created a positive demand and interest in these areas for improvement. However, SAL learned from their mistakes and the company now has a culture of continuous improvement. SAL employees are rated by their customers as being among the best in the world. This is a source of genuine pride in the company, and, more importantly, it generates a lot of business in a globally-competitive industry.

Source: Mr Tom Caffrey, Head of Safety, Quality, Training and Continuous Improvement, Shannon Aerospace Limited

PROJECT MANAGEMENT

Depending on the nature of the strategy, project management techniques are often used to implement major strategic initiatives. The Project Management Institute defines a project as a "temporary endeavour undertaken to create a unique product, service, or result" (Schwalbe, 2010: 4). Projects can be large or small; they differ from normal operations in that projects end when their objectives have been reached or the project terminated. While every project is unique, they all share three common constraints:

- **Scope** – defining what will be covered by the project and how it will be verified.
- **Time** – what is the time frame for completion?
- **Cost** – what will be the total cost and how can it be contained?

There is a natural tendency for these constraints to impact on the success of the project; people will want the scope to be expanded, and this will have an impact on time and inevitably on cost. As with all strategy implementation, the project manager plays a crucial role in ensuring its success and satisfying all stakeholders. According to Schwalbe (2010: 10), there are nine knowledge areas in project management. Four **core functions** include: scope management; time management; cost management; and quality management. In turn these are supported by four **facilitating functions**: human resource management; communications management; risk management; and procurement

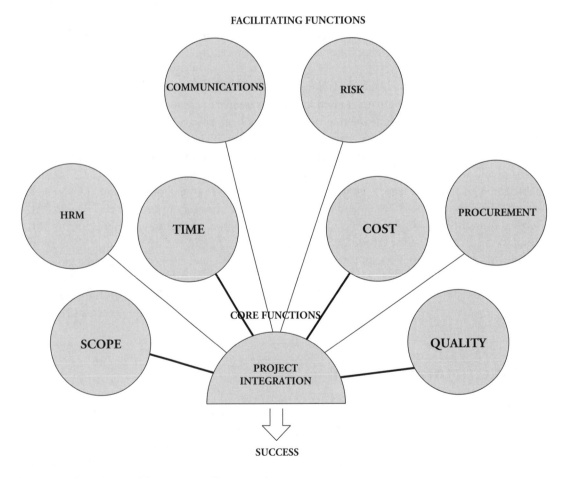

Figure 13.1 *Project Management Framework*

management. The four core functions and the four facilitating functions are all co-ordinated under **Project Integration Management**. Each of these functions is supported by various tools and techniques. While projects form a discrete body of work, they operate within a much broader context of operational strategy and, in some instances, such as strategic alliances, within the context of a number of organisations. The role of the project manager, therefore, is not just to co-ordinate all aspects of the project, but also to satisfy multiple stakeholders across organisations, bearing in mind each organisation will have its own culture and internal politics.

Project Life Cycle

A project was described above as a 'temporary endeavour' which implies that each project undergoes a number of stages. The first phase is the **concept**, where the business case for the project is discussed and the ideas teased out, along with an outline of the work involved and preliminary costs. If the initial idea seems worth pursuing, the second stage is development. The **development stage** involves expanding on the initial work to formalise the scope of the project, the time frame and accurate costs. Stage three is its **implementation**, where the work is actually carried out. Most of the cost will be incurred during implementation. The fourth and final stage is the **close-out** when all the work is finally completed. The first two stages: concept and development are known as **Project Feasibility**. The last two stages: implementation and close-out are known as **Project Acquisition**.

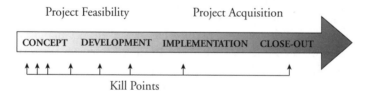

Figure 13. 2 *Project Life Cycle*

Not all projects go through all four stages. There should be a constant review as circumstances change and new information comes to light that might render the project no longer viable. As a result, a decision might be taken at any stage to terminate the project; such a decision is called a **kill point**.

Processes

There are a number of processes involved in project management, all of which are interlinked. The processes define the type of work managers do at each of the various stages of the project life cycle. In effect, these processes are superimposed on the four stages of the project life cycle outlined above. The processes involved in project management include:

- **Initiating** – initiating occurs primarily in defining the project itself and, to a lesser extent, at each stage of the project. Essentially, it gets the project team operating together for that particular phase.
- **Planning** – developing a plan that will ensure successful completion of each stage of the project taking into account the scope, time and cost.
- **Executing** – co-ordinating all of the resources (and people) to deliver on the project.

- **Monitoring and controlling** – every project needs systems in place to ensure it is running according to plan.
- **Closing** – bringing the project to a close and formal acceptance by stakeholders.

The balance between the various processes will vary considerably depending on the particular stage of the project life cycle. For example, the planning process will be very prominent during Project Feasibility, though each stage of Project Acquisition will also need to be planned. Planning is therefore a continuous process throughout the project. Likewise, control will be required from start to finish, although it will be most prominent during the implementation phase.

Project Integration Management

As with all elements of strategy implementation, there must be clear strategic objectives to be achieved, and these objectives must be understood by all. Thus, the project must be an integral part of the company's strategic plan. It may be that there are a number of projects running simultaneously in the organisation, or that a number of projects have been identified, but need to be prioritised due to limited funding. For those projects that are going ahead, **Project Integration Management** is where all elements of the project – people, finance and other resources – are co-ordinated and brought together as required. In this regard, the project manager is like the conductor of an orchestra: he will utilise the five processes discussed above in order to deliver the project – getting it started, planning the various stages, co-ordinating all the people and resources, ensuring everything is going according to plan. One of the project manager's most important roles is to get agreement on the Project Charter. The **Project Charter** is the formal document that authorises the project and commits the necessary resources to it. This involves working with all the stakeholders to get agreement on what exactly the project will entail. If different stakeholders have differing expectations about the outcome, the project will be on a collision course from the very beginning. The charter also sets out the time frame for the project: when it begins and ends, and key milestones. It also includes a budget for the project.

Project Scope Management

The **project scope** refers to the parameters of the project – defining exactly what it is going to achieve, and just as important, what will *not* be included. The project scope helps formulate the project charter at this stage and the work involved is examined in much greater detail in the form of a **Work Breakdown Structure (WBS)**. A Work Breakdown Structure examines the project in its entirety and breaks it down into specific modules that will be carried out by different people and perhaps at different times. The WBS is an important document because it forms the basis for the resources required, costs and the schedule of work. The use of Gantt charts assists in the process of 'decomposition' – subdividing the project into smaller elements, which in turn allows the project manager to estimate the time involved in each stage and thus schedule the entire project. While stakeholders will want to tie down the scope, it is important to build in flexibility as circumstances will change, in which case, agreement will have to be reached as to who has the authority to make changes to the scope, bearing in mind it will have implications for cost and time.

Project Time Management

Using the activities listed in the WBS, it will be possible to develop a schedule of work for the project. In turn, it will allow the project manager to estimate the resources required at each stage. This schedule will also include the sequencing of activities and the relationship between those activities. This is a very important process as some activities can be carried out at the same time, while other activities can only be carried out when another activity is completed. Using **network diagrams** (a schematic display of the relationship between the different elements of a project) and critical path analysis (see below) the shortest time for the completion of the project can then be estimated. There are different types of network diagrams, but the most common one is a precedence diagramming method (PDM) network. Software such as Microsoft Project can construct these networks and show the various forms of dependencies.

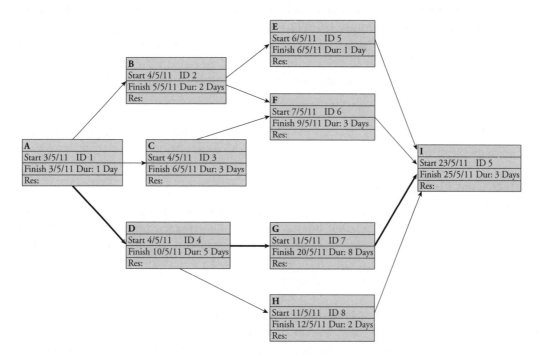

Figure 13.3 *Precedence Diagramming Method (PDM) Network Diagram*

In the diagram in **Figure 13.3** above, each particular activity is listed in a box and labelled with an ID number. The box shows: the start date and finish date of the activity; its duration (based on a five-day working week); and also lists the resources required. The diagram also displays the dependency between the different activities. The project starts with Activity A and goes simultaneously to Activities B, C, and D. In the case of Activity F, it cannot start until both Activity B and Activity C is finished (therefore its start date is the 7 of May).

The dependencies between the activities will show up the critical path. **Critical Path Analysis** is a network diagramming technique which is used to predict the total length of time a project will take. The critical path shows the series of activities that determine the **earliest** time that the project can be completed. It is the **longest** path (in terms of time) through the activities of the project, and has the least amount of slack time (the amount of time an activity can be held up without delaying the entire project). Understanding the critical path is important in preventing delays and in determining where resources are needed most urgently. In **Figure 13.3** above, the critical path is highlighted (A to D to G to I) and in this example is 17days long (1 + 5 + 8 + 3 days). There is slack time at various parts of the project, e.g. Activity H could be delayed by up to six days without adding to the overall length of the project. Knowing where there is slack time might present an opportunity to divert resources to the critical path and so speed up the project.

Estimating the amount of time required for each activity is largely a matter of prior experience. In some cases, there may be a lot of uncertainty about these time estimates, in which case the **Programme Evaluation and Review Technique (PERT)** may be used. PERT is a weighted average for the estimated time for each activity, which takes risk into account. It is based on the following formula:

$$\text{PERT weighted average} = \frac{\text{optimistic time} + 4 \times \text{most likely time} + \text{pessimistic time}}{6}$$

As with all aspects of controlling strategy, the project manager needs to monitor progress and take corrective action when required.

Project Cost Management

The PPARS system that was discussed in Chapter 1 is a perfect example of a project that not only went far beyond the original timeframe, but the final cost was perhaps 15 times the original budget. In major projects, there can be enormous costs involved. Approval for such projects is based on a certain monetary cost. The project must, therefore, be managed in such a way to ensure that costs are contained within the approved budgets, while delivering on the objectives.

By constructing a detailed work breakdown structure listing all of the activities involved in the entire project, and examining the resources that will be required for these activities, it will be possible to come up with an accurate costing for the project. This will then determine the overall budget required. Importantly, the finance needed is unlikely to be required all at once, but will be staged over the lifetime of the project.

Project Quality Management

There are many definitions of 'quality', and, in many ways, it is a subjective term that means different things in different situations. When a project is commissioned there is, however, an expectation that it will be 'fit for purpose'. In other words, it will satisfy the needs of the end user. Those needs will have been clearly defined in the project charter, and the entire project then needs to be planned based on those expectations. Quality, therefore, has to be planned and built in to the project from the start, rather than an extra attached at the end. The project manager must then ensure that those quality requirements are being met as the project progresses, as rectifying mistakes later can be very expensive. There are a variety of quality assurance techniques that can be used to assist the process.

Project Human Resource Management

Throughout this text, the importance of having the right people on board has been constantly stressed. Managing projects is no exception, and, within projects, managing people is probably one of the most challenging tasks. In keeping costs under control, the project manager will have to make the most effective use of all team members. That requires planning the exact requirement for human resources in terms of numbers and skill sets, and the reporting relationship within the team. This will have to be formalised in a human resource plan. Team members will then have to be selected and their roles allocated. The requirement for people will vary considerably from one phase to the next, and so team members will be assigned and removed from the project as required. There may be many talented individuals on board, but they will be required to operate as a team, and creating such a team will require investment in time and effort. Motivating members to work hard and resolving personal conflict, should it arise, are all part of the challenges the project manager must face. A **responsibility assignment matrix** can be used to assign responsibility for specific tasks to different individuals. **Resource levelling** is a form of network analysis that may be used to ensure an even demand for personnel, and avoid staff shortages at critical times.

Project Communications Management

The project charter (see above) identifies all the stakeholders involved in a project. Each of these stakeholders will have different requirements in terms of the frequency and detail of progress reports. Ensuring effective communications can alleviate many problems. A communications management plan should be developed to provide people involved with the information they require, at the time they require it and in the form they require. For some it might be an oral briefing once a month, while others may require a detailed written report each morning. The project manager must understand the communication needs of different stakeholders and establish appropriate communication channels.

Project Risk Management

The importance of analysing risk was discussed in Chapter 7. Every project is going to entail some risk and the level of risk involved needs to be calculated and accepted. There are a whole variety of types of risk, not just financial. These include damage to the company's brand or image, technology risk, process risk and the risk of not having the right people on board. **A risk management plan** sets out the procedures for analysing and dealing with risk throughout the project. As with all risks, the probability of the risk occurring and the potential impact on the organisation should be assessed. Once risks are identified, contingency plans can then be drawn up to deal with those risks, and reserves built in to minimise the impact if they should happen.

Project Procurement Management

Managing resources to contain the cost of the project is an important element of the project manager's job. Many of the resources required to complete the project may have to be sourced from outside the organisation. The most appropriate suppliers will have to be identified and contracts drawn up to ensure a just-in-time delivery of those components. They will then have to be issued to the different individuals as and when they are required, and their use will have to be accounted for. A **procurement management plan** will detail all the arrangements for procurement, including the planning of the resources that are needed, their ordering in a timely manner, authorisation for use and all the documentation required. There are various forms of E-procurement software packages that can assist in this process.

Successful Implementation

The successful implementation of any project requires leadership and a broad range of managerial and other skills (particularly soft skills) on the part of the project manager, including strong communication skills and the ability to build trust, team-building and conflict-resolution skills, critical thinking and the ability to set priorities. It also requires a detailed knowledge of all of the issues involved in the particular circumstances in which the project is being undertaken. The history of major infrastructural projects in this country paints a poor picture, with many projects, such as the Dublin Port Tunnel, delivered late and in some cases costing almost twice the original estimate.

Projects also need the support of all stakeholders. In the case of the Corrib Gas Project, it was originally planned that gas would come ashore in Co. Mayo in 2003. While other aspects of the project might have been meticulously planned, a narrow view of stakeholders was taken. Both Enterprise, the original exploration company and Shell, who acquired the gas field in 2001, seemed to brush aside the environmental concerns of a wide number of groups as well as the health and safety concerns of residents in Erris in Co. Mayo. The approach by Enterprise and Shell has set the project timeframe back by 10 years, and added tens of millions of Euro to the cost.

Notwithstanding these costly failures, project management techniques are an extremely effective way of implementing strategy. As with all aspects of strategy implementation, what matters is the efficiency with which the strategy is implemented.

INCENTIVES AND STRATEGY EXECUTION

In strategy execution, employees must be enthusiastic and committed to achieving the targets that have been set. To achieve good performance over a sustained period, the company must provide appropriate monetary and non-monetary incentives. In most cases it will be a combination of the two. Monetary incentives include pay increases, performance bonuses, profit-sharing and contributions to pension funds. Non-financial incentives include making the company an attractive place to work. This entails, in addition to suitable financial rewards, challenging job assignments, providing recognition for work well done, promoting from within and generally creating an atmosphere where their suggestions are valued and, where appropriate, adopted. In many larger organisations, greater emphasis is being placed on the physical surroundings of the business, and many include leisure and recreation facilities for staff members and their families. It requires a flexible approach by managers as people are motivated by different things and in different ways. The management of rewards, therefore, requires good people skills. It must also be transparent and be seen to be fair by all concerned.

The attainment of organisational results will inevitably bring a certain element of pressure with it. The pressure on employees must, however, be appropriate as undue pressure on achieving results will culminate in a demoralised workforce and work-related illnesses such as stress. Targets must be realistic and within the capability of staff to achieve them, and appropriate training and other resources must be put in place.

When targets are difficult, but achievable, and employees see that attaining these targets is linked directly to generous rewards and recognition, it can have a powerful motivating effect that will generate commitment. These targets must be set for every level of the organisation. Within each area, they must be linked to both team and individual performance.

In a competitive environment, the emphasis needs to be on achieving results rather than just performing particular tasks. For senior executives, this is usually tied in to overall sales growth, share performance, return on investment, etc. For others in the company it is usually linked more closely with their area of responsibility. In hotels, a service charge is paid to all staff as only some members of staff have direct contact with customers, while others such as kitchen staff, do not. The greater the level of sales in the hotel in terms of bed-nights, meals, bar sales, etc., the greater the financial reward will be. As a consequence, even those staff members who do not have direct contact with customers still have an incentive to maintain high standards.

There are a couple of important caveats in linking rewards with the attainment of results. First is the ethical foundation underpinning the achievement of those results. If there is a culture of achieving results at *any cost*, it may lead to managers and employees using unethical methods to attain targets. A study of the near-collapse of the banking industry around the world illustrates this point very clearly. There is an important ethical aspect to this. Incentives are linked to achieving objectives such as reaching specific sales targets. The Financial Services Ombudsman has had to deal with many complaints of mis-selling of financial products to bank customers, e.g. selling products with a 10-year maturation date to people in their eighties. Such products are clearly unsuitable for such customers, but the sale attracts commission for the seller, as well as helping achieve sales targets for their managers – a clear conflict of interest. In many instances, either systems were not in place in the banks to detect such inappropriate behaviour or else such systems were ignored in order satisfy performance targets.

Secondly, there have to be measures in place to ensure that the underlying trend is one of sustained growth, rather than just focusing on the short-term (in the case of public limited companies on six months' results, or three months in the case of the US). In such cases, cutting back on costs in the short-term can increase sales, but have detrimental long-term effects in areas such as staff training or research and development.

STRUCTURAL DESIGNS

Chapter 7 introduced different structural designs for the corporation. It was introduced there to give the reader an understanding of what larger organisations look like from a structural perspective. However, structure must follow strategy and senior managers must make whatever changes are necessary to the structure of the organisation to ensure that it supports the chosen strategy. Flexibility is key, and, for that reason, there will be much emphasis on cross-functional and cross-divisional teams. The use of strategy maps was discussed in Chapter 3 (Kaplan and Norton (2008)). Strategy maps are very useful in overcoming structural difficulties in organisations and assisting executives in achieving strategic objectives. In other cases, it may be necessary to change the basic structure of the organisation.

In recent years, Kerry Group plc has re-aligned its organisational structure to better support its strategy. It is important that companies ensure that the organisational structure is best suited for the type of strategy that is being pursued, and in particular, provides the appropriate level of control for the type of organisation. Depending on the type of industry in which they operate, some organisations will require tight control and procedures, and the type of structure chosen will assist in this process. Creative organisations, such as marketing companies, will need a much more flexible approach. Foreign expansion will often precipitate structural change. The domestic market for many Irish companies is very small, and they will look to foreign markets as a means of further growth. Such a move will often necessitate change in the type of structure in place. It will be recalled from Chapter 6 that each company will develop a structure for their own needs, and there is no prescriptive formula. Goold and Campbell (2002) proposed nine 'tests' to facilitate the selection of an appropriate structure for the organisation.

In Chapter 14 we will examine organisational change, and changing the organisational structure will often be a part of this change. In reality, such restructuring will only take place occasionally as it also causes a considerable amount of disruption and uncertainty within the organisation. It is also dependent on the nature of change taking place and, in particular, the speed by which it is taking place.

CONTROL PROCESSES

While every organisation will have an organisational structure in place, of equal importance is how all of the parts of the organisation are linked together. Each organisation will have to develop appropriate control processes that will provide managers with the means of implementing strategy and ensuring that the results are in line with expectations. A structure on its own will not achieve this. Just as the structure must be appropriate for the type of organisation, so too must the control processes as they can either help or hinder the implementation of strategy. There are many different types of control processes, both direct and indirect. Just as strategy is developed in many ways (see Chapter 1), likewise, an organisation will most probably employ a mixture of these control processes.

Direct Controls

Direct control processes include:

- Strategic planning process
- Performance targeting.

Strategic planning process This process is used to a greater or lesser extent by most organisations. It involves the setting of goals and objectives and detailing how these will be achieved. This is best illustrated by the use of budgets, which are a planning and a control device. It lays out the planned expenditure for the organisation as a whole (the master budget) and for each division and section within that organisation. For example, in the marketing plan described above, a budget for the proposed marketing activities is an integral part of that plan. Within the budget, each item of expenditure will be listed.

The benefit of planning will depend on the nature of the industry within which the company is operating. In stable conditions, planning can be very effective, as any assumptions about the future are likely to remain valid for the duration of the plan. Most organisations involve a 'bottom-up' process in developing the plan rather than a prescriptive top-down approach. Each organisation will have different arrangements concerning the relationship between the corporate headquarters and each of the different divisions.

In addition to budgets, other forms of planning systems that control process include measures to standardise work practices, which include product and service features. Standard operating procedures (SOPs) ensure that each unit performs the service to a uniform standard across the organisation. Franchise operations use such standard operating procedures to ensure a uniform quality in each outlet that provides the customer with a standard of service that, if properly applied, will consistently meet or exceed their expectations. Such SOPs are internal to the organisation. External control measures include quality standards like ISO 9000 systems. These are externally-validated quality programmes that certify a high level of product reliability and service delivery.

All of these processes require tight managerial control. In smaller organisations, or family-run companies, this involves hands-on supervision by the owner/manager of the processes to ensure a high standard. In larger organisations, particularly those pursuing a cost-leadership strategy, it will involve each individual manager exercising stringent control within their area of responsibility.

This is particularly so with regard to financial control. Fraud is an ever-present danger in any organisation and appropriate measures must be put in place to ensure that it does not happen. In June 2008, Scottish Mineral Water, a subsidiary of Greencore Group, was found to be at the centre of a €21 million financial fraud. The fraud, which was uncovered by a new audit committee, was spread over a three-year period. The fraud hit Greencore's share price badly and caused considerable damage to the confidence of the Group's internal control systems (Curran, 2008).

Performance targeting Setting targets and attaining them is a vital element of strategy. One of the big problems with many control measures, particularly financial control measures, is that they are lagging indicators. They reflect past performance which is not necessarily a good indicator of future performance. Leading indicators of the company's future strategic position indicate whether the company will be in a stronger or weaker position in the market place. For example, by setting ambitious targets for the coming year, and achieving those targets, in all likelihood the end of year financial results will be strong. On the other hand, if the company sits on its laurels, it is unlikely that the results will be anything more than mediocre. The targets that are set for the organisation must reflect a balance between financial and strategic goals. Chapter 3 examined the use of the Balanced Scorecard, which combines both qualitative and quantitative measures that reflect different aspects of the company. The four measures included are:

- Financial perspective
- Customer perspective
- Internal perspective
- Innovation and learning perspective

The objectives should be based on the key success factors relevant to the market that the company is operating in. All four elements of the scorecard are linked together and what impacts on one will impact on the others, thus providing a forward-looking and holistic perspective on the performance of the organisation. Control is then exercised by ensuring that each element of the organisation is achieving the goals that have been set for it. Where these goals have not been met, appropriate action to rectify any problems needs to be taken. In taking such action, it is important that management has a clear understanding of the true nature of the problem and are not just tackling the symptoms (see the rational decision-making model in Chapter 12).

Indirect Controls

In addition to the direct controls, there are also indirect controls. Indirect control can be exercised by:

- The culture of the organisation, or
- Internal markets

Organisational culture The culture of the organisation was discussed in detail in Chapter 2. It was seen that the culture has an all-pervasive effect and so will impact on the effectiveness and control of the organisation. As organisations move up the value chain, the calibre of the employees changes correspondingly. While tight control might be appropriate for a cost-leadership situation, it is inappropriate for a company in the knowledge economy that depends on bright, innovative employees. In such a situation, formal control would stifle creativity. While some form of control is of course appropriate, the emphasis here must be more on the internal motivation and self-control of the individuals concerned. For aid agencies operating in the developing world, the volunteer staff will, by necessity, have considerable latitude in how they do their work. The enormous impact they have in destitute parts of the world is driven by a common culture and work ethic, rather than by any traditional controls.

The culture can standardise control as it dictates 'the way things are done around here'. The pressure from colleagues can exert a powerful influence on the performance of others. The impact of peer pressure on workers' performance was first noted by Elton Mayo in the famous Hawthorne experiments carried out in the 1920s and 1930s at the Western Electric Company. In the Bank Wiring Observation Room Experiments conducted in 1931–32, colleagues developed what they regarded as an acceptable rate of output. Those that produced more were known as 'rate busters' and those who produced below that rate were known as 'chisellers'. Pressure was put on both groups to conform to the group average (Tiernan *et al.*, 2006).

The workers in the Hawthorne experiments were doing relatively basic jobs in a very different work environment. In modern, high-performance companies such as Motorola and Microsoft, the culture is internalised and supports creativity and a strong work ethic. This ethic is pervasive within the organisation and exerts strong pressure on individuals to conform to the high standards expected by the company. In such situations, the culture exerts much more effective control than any traditional methods.

High-performance culture attracts a certain type of individual that will conform and fit in. It also dictates the type of person that is selected by the organisation in recruitment drives. Training courses and socialisation reinforce this culture, not just in the initial training but throughout the person's career. People who do not fit in with the culture will, generally speaking, leave after a short period of time.

Internal Markets When examining the value chain, it was seen that an organisation consists of primary and secondary activities. It is a useful tool for examining the organisation from the perspective of costs and value creation. This was then extended out to the value system. In both the value chain and the wider value system, linkages between the different activities was said to be a vital element. Each of these elements is involved in providing services to one another. In many organisations, there is a 'contracting out' of the goods and services that each unit needs from other units. In addition, these different units are often treated as profit centres.

For example, many foreign companies operating in Ireland use transfer pricing within the company to avail of the lower rate of corporation tax. This raises a few issues. First, there has to be a price agreed by the corporate headquarters for the internal transfer of goods or the provision of services to another unit. Secondly, there has to be an agreement about the quality of service that one unit provides for another. If the price is too high, or the quality of service is poor, then it will reflect on the receiving profit centre. Therefore, if that profit centre were to obtain the necessary supplies or services from outside the organisation, they could do so at a more favourable rate or service level. By agreeing prices and service quality, it overcomes this dilemma, and effectively imposes a level of control on each of the units of the organisation. Mobil, the multinational oil company, implements the Balanced Scorecard for its different business units and applies it to all of its shared service units. These units sell their services to the main business units and get agreement from them on price and service levels provided (Kaplan and Norton, 2001: 46).

Johnson *et al.* (2008: 543) highlight certain limitations to internal markets. First, they can increase bargaining between different units of the organisation, taking management attention away from critical issues. Secondly, in drafting regulations to cover such transfers, it adds to the bureaucracy of the organisation. Finally, it can lead to dysfunctional competition between the units, thus destroying a collaborative culture in the organisation.

In addition to the control processes mentioned above, the way the organisation, and all of the units within the organisation, relate to one another is central to the success of the company. These were discussed in dealing with corporate strategy in Chapter 7. However, in the context of implementing strategy, these will have to be revisited to ensure the smooth functioning of the organisation.

CONCLUSION

It is worth recalling the quote from Alice in Wonderland when Alice asked the Cheshire Cat in which direction she should go, and the Cat advised her:

"That depends a good deal on where you want to get to."

Just as it is vital for organisations to have a clear picture of where they want to go, it is equally important that they have the energy and determination to see the plan through. Up to this point, it is exactly that – just a plan. To deliver on the strategic goals and objectives that were developed, the organisation must implement the strategies that were designed to reach those targets. Everybody must have a clear understanding of the plan in so far as it impacts on their particular work and how that work fits in with the team around them.

In many cases, it is not so much the nature of the plan that ensures success in the marketplace, but the professionalism in seeing it implemented. This point is well illustrated by Ryanair. There is no rocket science in what the company does to deliver such consistently high profits. There are many other airline companies that pursue a low-fares strategy. What separates Ryanair from the rest is the absolute determination in examining every aspect of its operations and cutting costs at every opportunity. It is in the implementation of its strategy that it is different.

In a competitive world, successful implementation plays a central role in how companies perform, and central to the implementation process are the people within the organisation. Throughout the company, there has to be a determination by all concerned to achieve excellence in what they do. With a flexible and creative approach, all obstacles can be overcome. The best form of control for implementing strategy is a high-performance culture that creates a desire in each member to do their best. The following quotation from Darwin Smith (Collins, 2001:20) sums it up:

"I never stop trying to become qualified for the job."

SUMMARY

Implementation is the final stage of the four-stage process of strategy formulation and implementation. Up to this point, it is simply just a plan, and will have no impact one way or another on the organisation until it is put into effect. Resources must be coupled with core competences if an organisation is to develop **strategic capability** and support its strategies.

There are many different aspects to the implementation process. The organisation must have all of the necessary resources and a well-motivated team. It requires very different **managerial skills** than the previous stages. The resources must be coupled with the appropriate competences to have the capability to deliver on the strategy. The implementation phase is a make-things-happen process that requires **leadership** and strong management. Each of the different sections of the organisation will have to interpret the strategic plan and develop their own functional and divisional plans to secure those objectives. While each of these relates primarily to its own area, they must all be co-ordinated to achieve synergy. The plan will rarely go as expected, and an important part of the skill-set needed for implementation is the ability to lead change in the organisation. These skills include being able to recognise the forces that are driving change in the macro economy and in the industry within which the company is operating. These forces have to be analysed in terms of their impact on the organisation and how the organisation will respond.

The most important resource identified was **the people** in the organisation as, without them, nothing will happen. There are three different elements to this. The first is leadership – providing the right direction for the entire organisation. It creates the vision and the culture and lays down the ethical parameters for all other decisions that are made. It also plays an important part in motivating staff to implement the chosen strategy effectively.

Secondly, a strong management team is essential. Different managers will each bring their own set of skills and experience to the organisation, and it must be remembered that different strategies will require different managerial skills. In getting the 'right people on the bus', the organisation must pick managers with the right skills set. The company must also get 'the wrong people off the bus', as managers who do not have the appropriate skills or motivation will form a serious impediment to implementing the strategy. Creating the right team applies to management and to employees and how they both work together.

Thirdly, great care must be taken in picking employees with an appropriate mix of skill and enthusiasm that will fit in with the prevailing culture. It is important not just to have the right people, but to ensure they are 'sitting in the right seats'. Every person will have their own strengths and weaknesses and it is important that in picking a team each member can play in the position for which they are best suited. Their skills must be constantly updated, particularly by companies operating in the knowledge economy. The company must also get the right blend of training and development. The human resource function in an organisation provides the expertise required by line managers in dealing with people-related issues.

In most instances considerable **finance** will be required to support strategy execution, and this has to be sourced and planned to cover both capital and operating costs. The cost of capital must also be taken into consideration and this applies to equity, bank and other borrowings, and retained earnings. Companies must be aware of their costs and the revenues arising from a particular strategy. **Budgets** are both a planning tool in setting out what the expenditures and revenues are likely to be, and a control device to compare actual with planned expenditure.

The company will need to create a **marketing plan** to support the strategy. This is a blueprint governing all of a business's activities, including the implementation and control of those activities. Each SBU has its own specific market separate to the others. Consequently, there should be a separate marketing plan for each major strategy being pursued by the company. There will be an overall marketing plan that co-ordinates the activities of the entire organisation.

Information technology plays an essential element in supporting strategy and providing linkages between all the various elements of the company. Information technology has the ability to change the nature of the business in a strategic as well as operational manner, benefiting the company and the customer. Managers need IT systems to provide them with information from all parts of the company, particularly financial information in order to make sound decisions about the future. **Data mining** allows companies to extract from their IT systems information about customer demand, as well as trends and connections in that demand. IT has also changed the structure of most companies, and how the company interacts with other businesses as part of the value system. **Business models** map out how companies interact with their customers. There are certain limitations and risks that must be taken into account with regard to IT systems and ethical issues must be considered.

The **operations** element of strategy implementation will differ significantly from one organisation to another but it must support the strategy. Innovation, both in systems and products is vital, and the strategic capability of the organisation must be constantly upgraded. This is a slow and incremental process. Decisions must be made concerning the location of operations and whether they are conducted in-house or outsourced.

The strategy implementation process must be supported by appropriate **policies and procedures**. They provide top-down guidance on how the organisation does certain things and help align the actions and behaviour of company personnel with the strategy. It provides a consistency between the different geographical and product divisions of the company. Best practice for all activities must be a central part of strategy execution. There are a number of different tools that managers can use to help achieve excellence. These include **Business Process Re-engineering, Six Sigma** and **Total Quality Management**.

Project management techniques are often used as a means of implementing strategy. It is based on four core functions which involve managing: scope, time, cost and quality. In turn, these are supported by managing: HR, communications, risk and procurement. The project manager integrates all of these functions to deliver the project on time and within budget.

In strategy execution, employees must be enthusiastic and committed to achieving the targets that have been set. To achieve good performance over a sustained period, the company must provide appropriate monetary and non-monetary incentives. Targets must be realistic and within the capability of staff to achieve them, and appropriate training and other resources must be put in place. Targets must be set for every level of the organisation.

There are many different types of control processes that are both direct and indirect. **Direct control processes** include strategic planning and performance targeting. A strategic planning process is a formal planning process that makes extensive use of budgets. It involves the setting of goals and objectives and detailing how these will be achieved, and entails tight managerial control. Performance targeting is a more holistic and forward-looking control process that balances four separate perspectives – financial, customer, internal and innovation. All four elements are interlinked.

Indirect control can be exercised by the culture of the organisation and internal markets. The culture can have an important impact on the performance of an organisation, particularly where staff are well trained and motivated. Internal markets provide measurable standards for the exchange of goods and services. In addition to the control processes, the way the parts of the organisation relate to one another is central to success.

DISCUSSION QUESTIONS

1. Critically evaluate the role that people play in the implementation of strategy.
2. With reference to question 1 above, to what extent does leadership play an important part in the implementation process?
3. Distinguish between the various functional strategies and their importance in the overall strategy.
4. Discuss the role of information technology systems in implementing strategy.
5. Critically evaluate the part that Total Quality Management plays in ensuring sound strategy execution.
6. Discuss the role of culture in supporting the implementation of strategy.

REFERENCES

Buelens, M. *et al.*, 2006, *Organisational Behaviour*, Maidenhead, McGraw-Hill

Collins, J., 2001, *Good to Great*, London, Random House Business Books

Curran, R., 2008, "Scottish Water Fraud has Hurt Greencore", *Sunday Business Post*, 29 June 2008

de Bréadún, D., 2008, "Still a Culture of Non-compliance and Non-payment of Tax", *Irish Times*, 23 September 2008, p.9

Dibb, S. *et al.*, 2006, *Marketing Concepts and Strategies*, Boston, Houghton Mifflin

Ghemawat, P., 2010, "Finding your strategy in the new landscape", *Harvard Business Review*, March 2010, Vol. 88, Issue 2, pp.54–60

Goold, M. and Campbell, A., 2002, "Do you have a Well-Designed Organisation?", *Harvard Business Review*, March 2002, Vol. 80, Issue 3, pp.117–224

Hammer, M. and Champy, J., 1993, *Reengineering the Corporation*, New York, Harper Business

Johnson. G. *et al.*, 2011, *Exploring Strategy: Text and Cases*, 9th Ed., Harlow, Pearson Education Ltd

Johnson, G. *et al.*, 2008, *Exploring Corporate Strategy*, Harlow, Essex, Prentice Hall, Financial Times

Kaplan, R. and Norton, D., 2008, "Mastering the management system", *Harvard Business Review*, January 2008, Vol. 86, Issue 1, pp.62–77

Kaplan, R. and Norton, D., 2001, *The Strategy-Focused Organisation*, Boston, Harvard Business School Press

Kaplan, R. and Norton, D., 1993, "Putting the Balanced Scorecard to Work", *Harvard Business Review*, Sept/Oct 1993, Vol. 71, Issue 5, pp.134–147

Kaplan, R. and Norton, D., 2005, "The Balanced Scorecard: Measures that Drive Performance", *Harvard Business Review*, Jul/Aug 2005, Vol. 87, Issue 7/8, pp.172–180

Kaplan, R. and Norton, D., 2001, *The Strategy Focused Organisation: How Balanced Scorecard Companies Thrive in the New Business Environment*, Boston, Harvard Business School Press

Micklethwait, J. and Wooldridge, A., 1996, *The Witch Doctors*, London, Heinemann

O'Brien, J. and Marakas, G., 2008, *Management Information Systems*, 8th Ed., New York, McGraw-Hill

Porter, M., 1985, *Competitive Advantage*, New York, The Free Press

Porter, M., 1996, "What is Strategy?", *Harvard Business Review*, Nov/Dec 1996, Vol. 74, Issue 6, pp.61–78

Rigby, E., 2006, "Eyes in the Till", *Financial Times Magazine*, 11/12 November 2006, pp.16–22

Schwalbe, K., 2010, *Managing Information Technology Projects*, Augsburg, Cengage Learning

Stevenson, W., 1989, *Production/Operations Management*, Illinois, Irwin

Tansey, P., 2007, "Public Sector Reform Would Aid Productivity", *Irish Times*, 23 November 2007, p.34

Tiernan, S. *et al.*, 2006, *Modern Management: Theory and Practice for Irish Students*, Dublin, Gill & Macmillan

Welch, J., 2001, *Jack: What I've Learned Leading a Great Company and Great People*, London, Headline

Leading Organisational Change

"Change is not made without inconvenience, even from worse to better."

Samuel Johnson

INTRODUCTION

The implementation of strategy involves translating the strategic plan into meaningful goals and objectives throughout the organisation. It is an iterative process which will involve much adjustment before it is successfully completed. One of the biggest challenges in implementing the strategy is that everything does not stay still while the strategy is being rolled out (which could take many months, even years). The world around us is constantly changing. Most of the time, the business environment is probably changing at a reasonably slow, incremental rate. On occasion, it can happen quite quickly, such as the meltdown in global financial markets in August and September 2008, when some of the biggest names in the financial world went out of business or were taken over.

Such change provides a great challenge for managers. In some cases, it may mean that strategic plans, which were so long in the making, now have to be abandoned (see Chapter 1). In other cases, it will involve substantial changes to the plan. In the previous chapter, it was seen that people play a central role in the implementation process. It is axiomatic that in implementing organisational change, the people that make up the organisation will be fearful and resistant to that change taking place. Such fear is not restricted to the lower levels of the organisation, but can exist right up to the top. In implementing change, it is therefore necessary to overcome that fear.

This chapter will examine organisational change from a number of different perspectives. First, it will examine the internal and external factors that are forcing change and the importance of the organisation being able to respond accordingly. Second, it will explore the different types of change and how these can be recognised. Each type will present its own difficulties in how the organisation deals with it. Some change may just have a small impact on the organisation as it is incremental. Other forms of change can radically alter the way the company operates, and all of these will impact on its culture. A number of different models of change will also be examined. In leading change the senior managers must be aware of the type of change and be able to respond, taking into account the particular circumstances facing the organisation. There is no universal prescription and each set of circumstances will impact on the approach taken by the company in dealing with change. Just as there are many factors driving change, there can also be a number of people using different styles involved in implementing the change process. Approaches to each situation may also differ, depending on timing.

In many respects, this chapter is a summation of the entire process in that it involves feedback into the strategic plan, while making any appropriate adjustments that may be required. In other cases, leading change involves using an entirely different paradigm than was used before as the circumstances are radically altered, and the old order no longer applies.

Illustration 14.1: Ernest Shackleton – Leading Change

The expedition led by Irishman Ernest Shackleton to cross the Antarctic in 1914, is an incredible account of leadership as the expedition changed from its original vision of being the first to cross the Antarctic continent (in 1911, Norwegian explorer Roald Amundsen beat Scott in the race to the South Pole), to one of survival under horrendous conditions. Shackleton's ship, the *Endurance* became trapped in the ice and was eventually crushed. Shackleton led his men over the ice floes, dragging three lifeboats, until they got to the open seas and eventually reaching Elephant Island. However, this was away from the main shipping routes and so there would be little hope of rescue. Shackleton believed that their best chance of survival would be to reach the whaling station at South Georgia Island – some 800 nautical miles away. Leaving most of the crew on the shelter of Elephant Island, Shackleton picked five men and together they made the incredible journey in an open lifeboat in probably the world's roughest ocean to South Georgia Island. He then had to set about rescuing the remaining men on Elephant Island.

While the nature of this expedition is without parallel in the business world, it demonstrates extraordinary leadership and human insight. It also demonstrates that, with the right leadership, people are capable of achieving incredible results. In the present economic downturn, many companies are faced with making hard decisions that will hopefully ensure their survival. The story of Shackleton is one of inspiring leadership that brought men through unimaginable hardship over an incredibly long period of time. The crew of the *Endurance* displayed all the normal characteristics of a group of individuals, and no doubt fear was a common emotion. When their original vision was no longer viable, Shackleton created a new vision – returning safely to England.

His immediate mission changed to one of survival and he achieved this through character, resolution and personal courage, that held his crew together and got them to buy-in to that vision. He achieved it not by authoritarian rule but by creating an environment that brought out the best in each individual. It illustrates what Kotter (2002) suggests, that change must be led not managed. Lao Tsu defined a great leader as one "who the people say: 'we did it ourselves'". In Shackleton's case, his men would disagree. They would all say it was the "Boss" who brought them home.

(See also the case study about Shackleton in the section at the back of this book.)

FORCES OF CHANGE

There are many factors driving change in the business environment. These forces are largely external but there are also some internal forces that must be considered. The external forces include rapidly changing technology, market changes, and changes in demographics and society. Some of these forces impact on organisations over a long period of time. In other cases, their effect is much more short term. Every organisation must accept change as a given and managers have to develop the necessary skills to understand the forces of change that are operating in their industry, and how they react to such changes.

Technology

Throughout this text, the importance of innovation in products and processes has been stressed. Some companies such as 3M are synonymous with innovation. When technology changes, it will diffuse down and impact on all companies in that industry. In turn, each one will be forced to develop new products or risk losing valuable market share or eventually going out of business. The pace of technological change is happening at an ever-increasing rate, and companies can no longer rely on long periods of unrivalled dominance after introducing new products, no matter how innovative they may be. For that reason, 3M has as a corporate goal that 40% of its profits must come from products that are less than three years old. This is done to ensure the company does not become complacent in an ever-changing world.

In manufacturing, technology has impacted on the type of products on offer and how those products are made. In terms of products, technology can cause small modifications or fundamental changes. In some instances, changes to products that have been around for a long period of time are evolutionary, such as a car company bringing out a new model. In other cases, it can represent a major shift in the nature of the product and how it is produced, such as the move from traditional film-based photography to digital photography. Technology has also altered the way products are made. Car manufacturing used to be a very labour-intensive industry (Henry Ford pioneered assembly-line production using Fredrick Taylor's principles of 'scientific management'), now car manufacture is largely undertaken by robotic tools and computerised systems, including computer-aided design (CAD) and computer-aided manufacturing (CAM). In addition, it was seen in the last chapter that the integration of the different parts of the value chain are heavily dependent on computerised systems, particularly for just-in-time production.

It was also seen that managers are dependent on information and communications technology to provide them with accurate and up-to-date information on which to base decisions. Management information systems and financial information systems are essential tools in both manufacturing and service industries. The use of technology has radically changed the manner in which organisations interact with their customers and the nature of business models. Kenny's bookshop was a traditional store in Galway city for generations. Like many businesses, they established an internet site to sell books, aimed particularly at the Irish-American market. In 2007, the company decided to close their traditional city-centre shop and concentrate exclusively on internet sales, similar to Amazon. com. The move has been hugely successful in a business environment that is changing rapidly. This text has many examples of other industries – from airlines to banks – that have used technology to change they way they operate. In most instances, change involves reducing the cost of doing business. The use of technology can greatly increase productivity, and hence it can have a positive impact on costs.

Market Changes

Globalisation has radically altered markets and how they operate. Ireland has witnessed many company closures as costs here are uncompetitive in many industries compared to Far Eastern countries. Global competition has radically altered markets that existed for decades, if not centuries. Countries like Japan moved from manufacturing cheap products of relatively poor quality, to high quality products that now dominate many industries from cars to electrical consumer goods. While many Irish businesses have not been able to compete on cost grounds in industries such as footwear and clothing, other industries have been transformed and are competing very successfully on the world stage. Such global pressures have also brought about many mergers and acquisitions as companies need to acquire scale and skill-sets in order to survive. Even those companies that remain small and are competing here at home have also changed radically as a result of globalisation. For every large multinational company such as those in the computing or pharmaceutical industries that are operating in Ireland, there are hundreds of small, indigenous companies that are supplying them with vital services. The quality of the output of these small companies has to be equal to the standard of the larger multinationals with which they do business.

Governments often intervene in the markets. This is particularly the case in providing an environment in which there is free competition. It has long been recognised that restricted markets are bad for the consumer. In times past, many companies in this country were effective monopolies, and gave a very poor service or at a very high cost. Industries such as telecoms and airlines have changed radically as a result of open markets. As the nature of markets change, customers' demands also change and so managers need to be aware of the nature of these changes and respond accordingly. As with all aspects of strategy, this necessitates keeping in close touch with your customers – and listening to them. The challenge is then to respond to those needs. Such response might vary from new products to entirely new business models. In recent times, there have been many failures in governance in Ireland which has had a dramatic impact on the economy and individual firms. Over the next few years, we are likely to see changes not just in terms of rules and regulations, but also closer scrutiny of the ethical approach taken by companies. This will result in significant changes in how companies are run.

Demographics and Sociological Changes

For decades Irish people emigrated to Great Britain or the United States as there was no work for them at home. The sociological impact of such emigration is outside the scope of this book. Suffice to say it had a devastating impact on Irish society. In the 1990s, many Irish people began to return, especially those who might have left just a few short years before, having received valuable experience in high-tech industries abroad. For those who spent longer abroad and only came home in recent years, they returned to see changes in Irish society that they could never have imagined.

The population of Ireland is now higher than at any time since the 1870s (CSO, 2007). Growing affluence and increasing numbers have led to the rise of many new industries and services that simply did not exist before, such as crèches. The nature of the workforce in Ireland has also been radically altered, and some 10% of the working population are now foreign nationals. They have brought with them a variety of new skills and knowledge, but it has also meant challenges for businesses in how they are integrated into the workforce. The current downturn in the economy will bring with it further changes. The impact of the downturn is such that we are now witnessing a return to the level of emigration last experienced in the 1980s.

While the main focus of the factors outlined above are primarily external, many of them also impact on the organisation from within. This is particularly so with changes in societal factors. While human resource legislation will dictate issues such as the entitlements of employees in areas like health and safety or maternity leave, the expectations of employees have also changed dramatically and work practices that may have been considered acceptable in the past are no longer so. In the knowledge economy, people expect interesting and stimulating jobs and a management style that supports, rather than just controls, their efforts. Legislation cannot dictate employee satisfaction, but if management cannot respond to the legitimate demands of a changing workforce, they cannot hope to remain competitive.

TYPES OF CHANGE

There are many different types of change impacting on organisations. To deal with changing circumstances, it is necessary to understand the nature or type of change facing the organisation. This section will examine three models for analysing the types of change taking place in organisations:

- Balogun and Hope Hailey's matrix
- Generic typology of change
- Theory 'E' and Theory 'O'

Balogun and Hope Hailey

Some theorists, such as Balogun and Hope Hailey (1999: 21), categorise the nature of the change taking place, and the extent of its cultural impact on the organisation, in terms of a matrix. The problem in using such matrices is the difficulty in correctly identifying the nature of the change and placing it categorically in one box as opposed to another. It is often difficult for a manager to make this call during the process of change, whatever about identifying it in retrospect. However, understanding the type of change, and its likely impact on the organisation, particularly on its culture, is a crucial part of the process of responding effectively. Balogun and Hope Hailey define change along two dimensions. First, the **Impact of Change** varies from *adjustment*, which can be a substantial change but does not impact on the organisation's beliefs and values, to *transformation* – where there is a fundamental change in the organisation. The second dimension is the **Speed of the Change** – how quickly it is implemented. This varies from *gradual* to *immediate*.

There are four positions resulting from these two dimensions:

- **Adaptation** – this occurs gradually and does not impact on the organisation's culture in any significant way. For example, aid agencies are adapting to new demands in a gradual way, but it is important that they maintain their fundamental culture.
- **Evolution** – transformational change implemented in a gradual way, probably using several different phases. Oil companies are adapting quite significantly to environmental concerns, and are diversifying into alternative fuels, though this is happening slowly.
- **Reconstruction** – where the organisation responds quickly to major changes, but it does not impact on the culture in any significant way. For example, though many exporting organisations have had to respond very quickly to the recession by cutting costs, there has been no immediate demand for a more fundamental change.
- **Revolution** – this change is immediate and has a profound impact on the organisation and its culture. At the time of writing, the severe state of public finances in Ireland means that the public sector will be required to change in a very fundamental way.

These four positions are represented in **Figure 14.1** below.

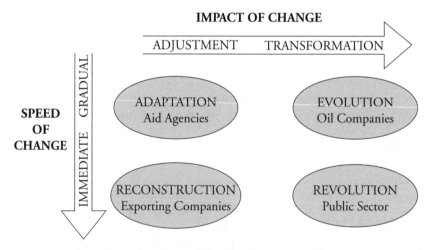

Source: Adapted from: Balogun, J. and Hope Hailey, U. (1999: 21),
Exploring Strategic Change. Harlow, Prentice Hall

Figure 14.1 *Types of Change*

Generic Typology of Change

In simple terms, a generic typology of change effectively describes parts of a continuum between minor, adaptive changes that happen very slowly, through the mid-way point of innovative change and on to radically innovative change that significantly alters the nature of the company (Nutt, 1986). As change moves along the continuum from adaptive to radically innovative change, it will impact more and more on the degree of complexity, cost and uncertainty associated with that change. The potential for resistance to change will also move from low (for adaptive change), to high (for radically innovative change).

Theory 'E' and Theory 'O'

A third model, by Beer and Nohria (2000), examines how change is implemented in organisations. Theory E and Theory O are based on the context of change and use a range of assumptions. Theory E is based on the economic value of the change programme to the organisation and is a top-down approach. It is based on formal structures and systems being changed, and generally involves downsizing and financial incentives. It is a planned approach to change and often involves outside consultants. Theory E is more suited when change needs to be focused in one direction. Business process re-engineering would fit this description.

Theory O on the other hand focuses on organisational capability and development of culture through learning (both individual and organisational). This form of change is not planned and it is much more emergent. It is generally a slower process and involves considerable experimentation. It is more suited to situations that call for more sensitivity at local level as well as autonomy in how the process is handled.

Theory E and Theory O are different in their approach in terms of the goals being pursued, the leadership style, the focus of change, the actual process involved, the rewards system used to provide incentives, and the use of consultants in the process. Each one has its own advantages and disadvantages. Beer and Nohria suggest that the two theories should not be seen as dichotomous, but can be blended together to suit circumstances.

CHALLENGES FOR UNDERSTANDING CHANGE

There are many challenges to understanding change. These challenges are complex and cannot be examined in isolation, as they are all interconnected. The factors affecting change examined at the beginning of this chapter act on an organisation in different ways. This happens at international, national and industry level. Against this background it has been suggested that it is vital for an organisation to carry out environmental analysis on a continuous basis, and not as a once-off event before developing a new strategy. There are a number of issues that should be considered:

- Leadership
- Context
- Culture

Leadership

In the previous section, we have already examined the forces driving change. These forces are placing constant pressure on the organisation. The need for change must be recognised by those leading the organisation, and they must create a sense of realisation among staff members of the need to adapt to new circumstances. Fitzroy and Hulbert (2005: 297) suggest that the ability to lead the firm into new ways must become a core competence of the firm. Change must also be effected within an ethical framework.

The CEO must take a central role in both the design and implementation of the change process within the organisation, by either taking a lead part in directing the change programme or indirectly through facilitating the process. However, common to both will be the need for a clear vision as to the direction in which the organisation is going. There will be many factors driving change, but managers must ensure that the response to them is more strategic rather than operational. The vision, it must be remembered, is the long-term direction of the organisation and is underpinned by leadership, values and purpose. It is what guides the company through difficult times. From the vision, the mission evolves and then the goals and objectives. A company must keep a clear focus on what it is trying to achieve. As with all aspects of strategy, the CEO must lead by example, and personify the type of change being advocated.

While the vision remains constant, it may well be that the goals and objectives that were previously established are no longer relevant, particularly in the short term. Thus, new goals and objectives will therefore have to be set and communicated throughout the organisation. Leadership is particularly important in situations of post-acquisition integration, as there will inevitably be a large change programme in place. One of the big challenges in leading change is keeping that vision alive and giving people within the organisation a clear sense of direction – and hope.

Pettigrew and Whipp (1999) examined change in a variety of organisations in the UK on a longitudinal basis to see what constituted effective change in terms of organisational performance. They found that high performers led the change process. The managers in the companies that were examined conducted rigorous environmental analysis, linked strategic change and operational change, managed people in the organisation in terms of assets and liabilities (this is similar to the findings of Collins (2001)), and, finally, there was a coherence in the overall change process.

Miles (2010) suggests that change initiatives can often run into gridlock, as different change projects are often launched with little or no strategic alignment. Senior executives need to select no more than three or four initiatives, each with just a couple of carefully selected areas of focus that are tied to clear outcome metrics. Fitzroy and Hulbert (2005: 308) believe that a limited number of themes also make it easier to communicate the change process throughout the organisation. A Balanced Scorecard and, in particular, a strategy map (Kaplan and Norton, 2008), could be used for this purpose as it develops just a few specific themes, and then applies appropriate measures, targets, initiatives to achieve those targets, and necessary budgets to support those themes. This will allow the company to achieve more by concentrating resources where they are most needed.

In Chapter 3, the use of the Balance Scorecard was discussed in detail. **Figure 3.3** picks three themes that were superimposed on the Scorecard: operational excellence, customer service and customer relationship management (CRM). The third theme, CRM, was further developed in **Figure 3.4** and is reproduced here in **Figure 14.2**. It demonstrates how a particular theme that is driving change is supported by specific measures, targets, initiatives to achieve those targets, and the necessary budgeting allocation.

(Theme 3): Customer Relationship Management					
	Strategy Map (Figure 3.3)	**Measure**	**Target**	**Initiative**	**Budget**
Financial perspective	Increase revenue and ROCE ↑	Revenue mix Revenue growth	New: + 10% Existing: + 25%		
Customer perspective	Add and retain high value customers ↑	New customers Increase in repeat visits Longer stay	15% increase in new customers 10% increase in repeat visits (calendar year) 1 night extra per guest per visit	Marketing campaign Discount for extra night	€ __
Internal Processes Perspective	Create a comprehensive customer database to include detailed information about likes and dislikes ↑	Targeted marketing Improve process for customer feedback Develop integrated database	Complete database of all customers c/w personal preferences, interests, etc.	Data mining Social media E-mail/write to targeted customers	€ __ € __
Innovation and Learning Perspective	Develop a capable and efficient Workforce Develop customer-focused competences	Staff training Staff development	Certification awards Top rating for Customer feedback Staff Incentive scheme	Internal training External Training Secondment/ Posting to other hotels and resorts Profit sharing	€ __ € __ € __ € __

Figure 14.2 *Customer Relationship Management*

Context

Every organisation is different and the nature of change in the environment will impact on each company in various ways. Consequently, the response of the company will also differ. The nature of the change taking place must be examined in its context. Balogun and Hope Hailey (1999: 14) provide a framework for examining this context under eight headings. Each of these factors needs to be considered before formulating a response. The contextual features are:

- **Time** – as mentioned above, the business environment in Ireland has changed substantially over 20 years. In most cases, industries have been able to deal with this in a gradual response. On other occasions, such as the current financial crisis, the response of many organisations in both the public and private sectors has to be immediate.
- **Scope** – how much change is required in terms of the breadth of change across the entire organisation or one particular part? This would also include changing the culture of the company.
- **Preservation** – the company must decide what it needs to preserve in its culture and traditions and what must change.
- **Diversity** – how diverse is the organisation in terms of geographical location and business types?
- **Capability** – is the organisation under its present management capable of making the required changes?
- **Capacity** – does the organisation have the resources needed?
- **Readiness** – how ready is the workforce for change?
- **Power** – does the CEO have sufficient power to execute the change process?

The context will vary considerably, depending on a wide range of factors, from the type of organisation under consideration to the particular environmental circumstances. Understanding the nature of the above factors and their relevance to the circumstances within which the company is operating is of central importance in deciding how to deal with the situation. Each situation will be different and, therefore, there is no specific formula to guide the process. It is a matter of judgement and interpretation.

In addition to the contextual features listed above, Buelens *et al.*(2006: 641) suggest that change in an organisation should also be studied on a longitudinal basis. This should examine previous instances of change, such as mergers and acquisitions, or other events where change would have taken place, as this will give some indication as to how future change might be handled.

Culture

The different aspects of the context discussed above must be considered in managing change. In addition, they must be understood, along with the culture of the organisation, which forms a backdrop to the change process. Johnson *et al.* (2011: 176) recommend the use of a 'cultural web' to analyse the nature of an organisation's culture. Evaluating the culture of an organisation will give managers or those attempting to effect change a better understanding of the type of change needed and how successful it is likely to be. The cultural web examines the organisation under a number of different headings including symbols, power structures, operational structures, control systems, rituals, routines and stories. No one of these will give an accurate picture, but taken together they will provide a good appreciation of the type of prevailing culture.

It will be recalled from Chapter 2 that the culture of an organisation has a profound impact on its strategy, and that changing a culture is a slow and difficult process. Nonetheless, there are times when cultural change is an imperative. Miles (2010) outlines a number of cultural challenges that may derail transformation processes. A cautious management culture may hold the organisation back when change is badly needed. All senior executives need to confront reality and agree on ground rules for tackling the problems they face. There may be other managers who are aware of the issues, but who do not want to come on board, or who are incapable of performing within the parameters of the change programme. Miles recommends that these executives are quickly confronted so that they do not undermine the transformation. Dealing with these individuals can send a powerful message to others in the organisation. It is equally important to confront disengaged employees. While employee training and development can play an important role in facilitating change, this must be preceded with a "rapid, high-engagement, all-employee cascade" where the importance of the change is defined with clear objectives, and a clear line of responsibility is established throughout the entire organisation. Then, when managers and employees are engaged, staff will be better motivated to adapt and take on board the necessary changes, and training will be more effective.

Throughout the change process, people play a central role. There are many different facets to change but yet most corporate turnaround situations focus on cutting costs – the bottom line. Hassan (2006) believes that cost cutting is not always the answer and that change should be led from the top line. This involves creating a motivated and respected sales force that will increase revenues from sales and develop the right kind of customer relationships. In turn, Hassan believes that focusing on people will have a quicker positive response for the company.

RESISTANCE TO CHANGE

In the discussion above, it was stated that there will be differing levels of resistance to change. An important element of the process of conducting change is to understand and manage this resistance.

> "To be worst, The lowest and most dejected thing of fortune, stands still in esperance, lives not in fear: The lamentable change is from the best; the worst returns to laughter."
>
> *King Lear.* Act 4, Sc.1

Why People are Resistant to Change

People are creatures of habit. Habit gives people a sense of security and confidence, and enables them to cope with life. Anything that will change everyday habits is going to be difficult for employees and managers as they attempt to get to grips with new circumstances. The organisational structure with which they are familiar gives them a sense of security that enables them to deal with the complexities of their job. This security can also lead to inertia when change is needed to cope with different market challenges. In most cases, people take comfort in the familiar, and there is a fear of the unknown. There are many reasons for resistance to change:

- Will their job still exist or will it be replaced by machinery? This has happened in many industries as more and more automation is introduced. Even if their jobs are secure, it could mean a drop in income as work practices change. The Irish Government is currently seeking 25,000 redundancies from the public sector in an effort to reduce costs. Remaining staff will be expected to increase productivity substantially in addition to significant pay cuts and pension levies.
- Will they still be working with the same group of people? As people get older, they find it more difficult to get to know new groups of people and there may be personality clashes. The Hawthorne experiments demonstrated the moderating effect of peer pressure, and while some individuals may be happy to go along with change, pressure from colleagues may prevent them from giving their support. Changing group structures will impact on the cultural dynamics at play in that group. When new members join, there can be a strong distrust of them.
- If new technology is being introduced, will employees be able to develop the necessary expertise to use it? Many employees will have a fear of failure that they will not be able to make the transition. Many work practices are changing with a move towards multi-skilling.
- What is their perception of the change taking place and the reason for that change? There is often a mistrust of management's intentions and the rationale for making the changes. This is often accompanied by either a lack of communication or poor communication, and the grapevine takes over. The absence of accurate information will fuel the fear of staff members. It is imperative that managers take appropriate measures to keep people properly informed.
- Is the change affecting the entire organisation or just one part, and how will it affect how the different parts of the organisation link together? Understanding new systems will take time and effort. There may also be a fear that the necessary resources will not be provided to make the transition.
- When change is introduced, it is inevitably going to affect the power balances between different groups. This often impacts on the availability or call on resources by certain groups. These power structures may well prove a formidable force to implementing change.

There are many reasons for fear and these usually occur in various combinations. Managers must understand these reasons and the strength of these reasons before overcoming such resistance. Forcefield analysis is one method for understanding the forces operating in an organisation that support change and those resisting it.

Forcefield Analysis

In every situation, there will be factors pushing change and factors operating against it. The factors that impact in a positive way on change are obviously of great importance to managers. In all cases, they must be recognised, and in some cases they may need to be strengthened. Likewise, managers need to be aware of the factors operating against change. Forewarned is forearmed, and managers can take appropriate measures to ensure that any resistance to change is either removed or at least lessened. **Forcefield analysis** is somewhat similar to stakeholder mapping which was discussed in Chapter 2. The main difference between stakeholder mapping and forcefield analysis is that stakeholder mapping is looking at strategy in the context of people and the amount of power and interest they have in a particular strategy. Forcefield analysis involves listing all of the factors, and not just people, that must be considered. It provides a list of these factors, but does not necessarily rank them or measure their impact.

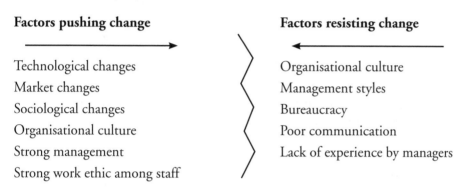

Figure 14.3 *Forcefield Analysis*

Managers will have to form a judgement on each of the items listed above. Any one item could be a significant factor either supporting change or operating against it, such as culture. It is particularly important that managers understand each of these factors, as overcoming resistance is essential in the programme for change.

Manifestations of Resistance

Managers must be cognisant of the way resistance will manifest itself. Resistance to change can vary quite significantly, depending on each situation . . . the people involved, the organisation and industry and many other factors. A necessary part of the process of dealing with resistance is being able to judge its strength. Judson (1991: 48) suggests resistance can be measured on a continuum going from Acceptance, Indifference, Passive Resistance, to Active Resistance. Each one of these divisions has several degrees, e.g. enthusiasm at the top of acceptance, to deliberate sabotage at the extreme of active resistance. The response by managers will obviously differ quite significantly, depending on the level of resistance encountered. Employees showing different forms of acceptance such as co-operation or even passive resignation will make the change process easily. On the other hand, those showing active resistance such as doing as little as possible or deliberately working against the process will make the task extremely difficult. There are a number of strategies for overcoming resistance to change, and these will be looked at below in the context of implementing a strategic change model.

It is important to note that, while many people will be resistant to change, there are others who are quietly embracing change. Change is usually seen as a top-down process, but Pascale and Sternin (2005) remind us there are often people in organisations that are good at finding a way around problems and constantly looking at better ways of doing things. Managers must recognise that these employees can make a major contribution to the change process and their ideas should be infused into the corporate consciousness, and leveraged throughout the organisation.

MODELS OF PLANNED ORGANISATIONAL CHANGE

There is a difference between planned, anticipatory change and the type of change that forces an organisation to react immediately. The latter form of change can impact negatively on a company as it is taken by surprise, and the response may not be appropriate. By using the analytical techniques outlined in Part 2 of this book, managers should be in a position to spot the forces of change before they strike. By analysing the situation and planning a response that fits the circumstances, the company is in a much stronger position in a competitively-advantageous way.

Lewin's Change Model

Much of the seminal work in change management was carried out by social psychologist Kurt Lewin who saw change as a three-stage process. The three stages proposed by Lewin (1951) are unfreezing, changing and refreezing. He suggested that change involves altering current attitudes and behaviours and requires motivation to change if it is to succeed. What makes change particularly difficult to implement is that people are at the heart of it. Irrespective of whatever changes are made to structures and other factors, people have to change. Even when people recognise the need for change and perhaps welcome it, it is still a difficult process to overcome fear and natural resistance.

- **Unfreezing** – Managers need to create the motivation and urgency in staff to change their old behaviours and attitudes and embrace new ones. There are different ways in which this can be achieved. A crisis facing an organisation can focus attention of all concerned to the need for change. In other situations, it may be that staff members are unaware of the need for change, but by presenting them with data showing much lower productivity or competitiveness compared to key rivals, they recognise the need for change.
- **Changing** – Having recognised the need for change, managers then need to move the organisation to the point where change begins to take place. This may consist of installing new technology or systems, changing behaviour and helping employees embrace all aspects of the change programme. Benchmarking is often used to set standards for the change programme and outside consultants are often used to assist the process. It must be remembered that, during this transition, normal business must be transacted. No organisation has the luxury of being able to close down for the duration of the process and then start up again. Kanter (1987) suggests using a transition manager to assist the process and to keep all stakeholders informed.

- **Refreezing** – Once all the necessary change has taken place, the final phase is refreezing. This is a critical part of the process and involves reinforcing the new behaviour so that it now becomes the accepted norm. Otherwise there is the danger that staff will revert to their old ways. Leisure centres make considerable money out of people who join in January full of good intentions at the start of the New Year, but fail to maintain those intentions. Coaching, training and development can help reinforce the new behaviour, as can various positive incentives.

Lewin's model is criticised for not considering the range of factors that impact on the process from outside the organisation. However, like all seminal models, it forms the basis of other and more recent models of organisational change that take into consideration the relevant outside factors, as well as what the company actually needs to do in order to implement the change programme successfully.

STRATEGIC CHANGE MODEL: AN INTEGRATED APPROACH

While Lewin's model provides a basic framework for change, the process clearly is much more complex and requires an integrated, strategic approach. The outline of this chapter provides the first part of the essential framework. The remainder of the framework requires making choices about the steps needed to be taken to address the situation and how they will be implemented. This can be summed up under the headings:

Phase One – Identifying the need for change

- Identification of the forces of change impacting on the organisation
- Identification of the type of change
- Challenges for understanding change and the levels of resistance

Phase Two – Choosing the appropriate change strategy

- Making the necessary changes to the organisation's strategy
- Choosing the appropriate time to introduce change
- Resources

Phase Three – Implementing the change programme

- Choosing the appropriate managerial style
- Managing different situations
- Symbolic processes
- Change agents

Phase Four – Monitoring results

- Monitoring the results of the change programme and making necessary adjustments.

Phase One – Identifying the Need for Change

Identification of the Forces of Change Impacting on the Organisation In any industry, there are many drivers of change. These are primarily external forces, which like King Canute and the tide, we have no control over. The fact that we might have little control does not mean that these forces will not have a significant impact on our business. This chapter has already examined how technology has radically changed many industries and how companies interact with their customers. Combined with changes in global markets and demographic changes, the nature of the business environment is constantly changing. Sometimes these changes are easily identified, on other occasions they fall into the category of 'unknown unknowns'. Chapter 5 dealt with the subject of monitoring the external environment. Such monitoring is not a one-off event. It is imperative that managers are constantly examining the environment within which they operate and identify both the trends, as well as the events, that are taking place.

Type of Change The type of change that is taking place will vary considerably from one situation to another. In some instances, it can be so incremental that it is almost imperceptible. This type of change is often very difficult to identify. Some companies are continuously making minor incremental adjustments to their strategy keeping them in line with these changes. For many companies, they continue to operate as normal, and, over a period of time, their strategy begins to drift from the demands of the market, and this will require a more definite change programme to realign their strategy. Occasionally, as a result of significant changes in the environment, a very fundamental change in the company's strategy and culture will be required, resulting in a turnaround strategy being implemented.

Understanding Change One of the greatest challenges for senior managers is to make sense of the business environment and the significance of the changes that are taking place for their individual company. Such understanding is important because it will underpin the decisions that they make. In leading the process of change, managers must keep a firm focus on the vision of the organisation and its mission. In responding to change, the strategies chosen must be consistent with the values and purpose of the company. Another major challenge for managers leading change is trying to understand the likely level of resistance from various stakeholders and where it will manifest itself. It is important to note that some of the root causes of resistance are lack of trust in management and poor communication. People must be led through the change process and, therefore, clear, open communication is a central component of any change programme and building trust. There must be a shared perception of the need to change.

Phase Two – Choosing the Appropriate Strategy

Before any particular strategy is chosen, it is necessary to decide on what the organisation is trying to achieve. While the overall vision will remain, most likely the organisation will have to develop new goals and objectives that reflect the current situation. Those leading the change should have a clear understanding of what the organisation will look like at the end of the programme. The process of generating strategic options and selecting the most appropriate strategy has already been described in detail in this text. It was stated that strategies must be tailored to meet the needs of each organisation. Strategies are the means to an end. In a change situation, circumstances will dictate that the original strategies are no longer appropriate and need to be altered. To what extent they need to be altered is dependent on the context within which the change is happening. Earlier in this chapter, we identified the various contextual features: time, scope, preservation, diversity, capability, capacity, readiness and power. The new strategy will have to be tailored to fit those particular circumstances. Lynch (2009: 580) stresses the need for a "balanced approach that is both focused and efficient internally, while adapting successfully to external changes".

Changed circumstances may also require a new paradigm: a new way of looking at the world and how things have changed. For that reason, the type of change taking place will also be central to the new strategy as major cultural changes will be required. Though cultural changes are likely to meet with strong resistance, resistance will not be the same for each option being considered. Some options may be regarded as totally unacceptable by key stakeholders. This does not mean that such strategies cannot be considered. It simply means that managers will have to weight up the consequences of either choosing or not choosing that strategy. If opposition is likely, it just places greater onus on managers to lead the change process and to bring dissenters on side.

Timing The timing of introducing a change programme is an important element in the overall process of change. It was stated above that the organisation must be ready for change. If there is an obvious and major threat to the organisation's existence, or the danger of a hostile takeover, managers can use this moment to galvanise the workforce into change. Similarly, if there is a change of ownership of the organisation or a new CEO, there will often be an expectation by staff that a 'new brush will sweep clean', and that significant changes will be made. Therefore, there is a certain window of opportunity in which management can act.

Some companies will be proactive and be constantly initiating gradual change. For others, the need has to be quite obvious before they will initiate change, in which case more effort will be required. According to Fitzroy and Hulbert (2005), initiating a change programme is a delicate balancing act. If major change is initiated too early, greater employee resistance is likely. If it is done too late, the survival of the company may be at stake.

Resources Most change programmes require significant resources to implement. For example, payroll costs often have to be reduced and this will involve redundancies. Though this will effect savings in the long-run in terms of salaries and other payroll costs, there is an up-front cost in redundancy payments. This was the situation in the HSE in 2010 when the Minister for Health and Children stated that the Government wished to reduce staff numbers by 5,000. Change will often involve other costs, such as staff training, new buildings, new machinery, etc. These will have to be planned for and included in the budget.

Phase Three – Implementing the Change Programme

Choosing the Appropriate Managerial Style Every change situation is going to be different and, consequently, the response must be tailored to the exact circumstances. There were four types of change identified earlier according to the speed of change and the impact of that change on the organisation: adaptation, evolution, reconstruction and revolution (Balogun and Hope Hailey (1999):

Adaptive change poses the least challenge as it allows managers plenty of time and the impact on the organisation is small.

Evolutionary change will have a transforming impact on the organisation, but is achieved in a gradual fashion. Leaders should create a clear vision of what the organisation will look like, and work to bring people on board. They must also empower people at every level in the organisation to work towards that vision. It allows experimentation – within clear guidelines.

Reconstruction is required when there is an immediate threat to the existence of the organisation, and costs will have to be cut drastically and/or revenues increased significantly. Generally, management will first of all try to stabilise the company and then initiate change. Quick wins are important so that staff can see that the changes are having the desired effect. Clear priorities will have to be decided on what needs to be done. New markets may well have to be found if there are problems with current markets. One of the main difficulties with a turnaround situation is the possible weakness of management. By allowing such a serious situation to happen in the first instance, they may not be the right people to lead the firm out of it. There were many criticisms of senior bank appointments following the collapse of the industry in Ireland. Management changes may have to be made as fresh thinking is required:

> "The significant problems we face cannot be solved at the same level of thinking we were at when we created them."
>
> Albert Einstein

Clear strategic thinking is required to analyse the factors facing an organisation and how to refocus on its target market. There will have to be solid support from key stakeholder groups and resistance will have to be minimised.

Finally, **Revolutionary change** involves not just great haste, but a major cultural change as well. Many of the problems outlined in the reconstruction scenario above may also be present here, particularly the fact that the situation was allowed to develop in the first place, but is compounded by the need to change the culture of the organisation as well. The perilous state of Ireland's finances as a result of the recession, and the subsequent need for the EU/IMF bailout has put enormous pressure on the Government to reduce the cost of running the country. However, getting the required efficiencies will also require major cultural changes in how certain parts of the public sector operates.

Managing different change situations One major factor that will obviously differ in each situation is the likely level of resistance. Consequently, in rolling out the change strategy, management must tailor their approach to minimise this. Different writers have proposed various methods of overcoming resistance, but there is no universal method as each situation will be different and different methods may be required at various stages of the process. Thus, those leading the change will need a broad repertoire of change strategies as well as flexibility in their application. The types of leadership styles that may be used in bringing about change are summarised in **Figure 14.4**:

		Style	Description
High		**Coercion**	Using power to force change through in the organisation. May be imperative in a crisis situation, but unlikely to get much support.
		Direction	There is a clear focus on what needs to be done. Change is still forced by senior management, but there may be some concessions in regard to the approach.
Degree of Control		**Participation**	There is some move towards involving staff in putting forward ideas, but managers are still retaining overall control of the direction that the change is taking. It is likely to build some element of support.
		Collaboration	Widespread involvement of employees throughout the organisation about the direction and methods of change. It is a lot slower, and there is little control over the eventual outcome, but there is likely to be widespread acceptance by staff members. Quite time-consuming.
Low		**Education**	Here the objective is to meet with small groups of people and convince them of the need to change, and gain their commitment. Staff members will then have the authority to effect change. Very time-consuming.

Source: Adapted from Balogun, J. and Hope Hailey, V. (1999) *Exploring Strategic Change*, Harlow, Pearson Education Ltd

Figure 14.4 *Styles of Leadership Change*

The styles outlined above will be more or less effective depending on the particular circumstances such as the amount of time available and the willingness and capability of staff members for change. They are also dependent on the particular leadership style of the CEO. Different styles will also have more relevance at different stages of the change process.

There are a number of factors that need to be taken into account when deciding what approach might be used. In the initial stage, clear direction might be needed to impress upon staff members that change is required. It might then switch to a more collaborative style. Time is a critical issue. If the organisation is facing a crisis situation, there will not be time to engage in a long consultative process and clear intervention is needed. The types of organisation will also have a bearing on the leadership style. Highly-trained professional staff will most probably want to be central to the process and will react strongly to change being forced upon them without consultation.

It must also be remembered that, when an organisation is facing a change situation, management will be dealing with a variety of stakeholders and each group will require a different approach. For that reason, the styles outlined above are not mutually exclusive and it may be that a combination of styles is used.

According to Buelens *et al.* (2006: 646), there are four factors that should be borne in mind when attempting to overcome resistance to change:

1. An organisation must be ready for change. The emotional evaluation of change is of more importance than the cognitive evaluation. Kotter (1996) makes the distinction that change must be led rather than managed.
2. Change is less successful when management fail to keep employees properly informed about the process.
3. People do not always resist change consciously. Managers should use a systems method of change which maps out the process and how it will impact on the organisation.
4. Employees' perceptions affect their resistance. They are less likely to oppose change if they perceive that the benefits outweigh the personal costs.

Symbolic processes Symbolism can play a significant part in changing an organisation, particularly where the culture of the organisation is also changing. Symbols can transmit important messages about the organisation and how it perceives the world around it. They are part of the normal routines and processes of the organisation and so any changes made can help refocus the beliefs and expectations of members of the organisation. Company logos and uniforms are obvious examples that are clear for all to see. Changes in staff dress codes will not in itself change work practices. In isolation, this would be purely a cosmetic exercise. However, as part of a wider programme, such details will help signify the greater change that is taking place and can send an important subliminal message to staff members. Where improved teamwork is required, a move to open-plan offices can help facilitate direct communication. One very powerful symbolic message that can be sent to employees is where certain staff members that are openly opposed to the change programme are transferred to other appointments. Other staff members then see that the change is going to happen, one way or the other.

Routines Day-to-day routines will also have to be changed to reflect the new circumstances. Best-practice routines should be an integral part of the change process. This should be a bottom-up as well as a top-down process, as those involved in the various departments will have constructive ideas as to how these processes can be made more efficient. There are many changes to staff routines that can be made, starting with the recruitment and selection process, and also in requiring staff members to undergo certain training programmes such as cultural awareness. Changes in the criteria used for promotion can also clearly communicate the model of behaviour that the organisation requires from staff.

Internal politics Different people in the organisation are going to react to change in different ways. Some will be supportive and others implacably opposed. Block (1987) suggests that in implementing change, those affected in the organisation should be assessed along two dimensions: the level of agreement with the change; and the level of trust that they have in management. Trust is a long-term investment and will be difficult to import if it has not been present all along. If trust is present, it will make the process of winning over those who might be against the proposals a lot easier. Most programmes are unlikely to win everyone over and much effort could be wasted in trying. The important thing is to get key players behind the process, what Kotter (2007) describes as a "powerful guiding coalition".

Any change programme is likely to disrupt the political power structures in the organisation. Management should use this opportunity to assess the situation and strengthen the official structures. This will reduce any negative influence in the rollout of strategy and may prevent similar situations arising in the future. The use of resources can assist senior managers in re-aligning power. By diverting necessary resources to a particular group, it will greatly strengthen their position, and likewise, removing resources can weaken their power base. Thompson and Martin (2005) point out that there will often be casualties and some people may leave the organisation because they are unhappy with the changes.

Change Agents Much of the discussion so far about implementing change is centred on the chief executive. The chief executive must play a central role in the process as he/she is ultimately responsible for the success of the organisation. They need to provide the vision and the necessary clarity about how the organisation is going to achieve its goals. However, they may not be directly involved in the day-to-day implementation of the change. It must be remembered that the organisation must continue with the normal daily routines in meeting customers' needs as the change process takes place. For that reason, CEOs may well appoint senior executives as change agents, while they continue to run the company as normal. A change agent is either an individual or a group responsible for implementing change.

It must also be remembered that everyone in the organisation plays an important part. This is particularly true of middle managers, who play a dual role in the process. On one hand, they are responsible for implementing the change in their own departments according to the wishes of senior management. They also play an important role in feeding information to senior managers about the situation at the interface between the organisation and its customers. Ultimately, the success of any change programme lies with the willingness of the staff to embrace change. If they resolutely refuse to support the change, the chances of success are greatly diminished.

Managerial Imperatives

The change process is designed to realign the organisation in response to different circumstances. The future of the company could well depend on the success of the process. Yet, according to Kotter (2007), organisational change often fails because of management's short-comings in eight areas. Management must:

1. Establish a sense of urgency with regard to the crisis, and the need to change in response.
2. Form a powerful guiding coalition that will take responsibility for the implementation of change.
3. Create a vision that will guide the process.
4. Communicate the vision to all employees and other stakeholders.
5. Empower others to act on the vision by removing institutional structures, and encourage them to take risks.
6. Plan for and create short-term wins. This demonstrates that the plan is working and encourages others to continue with the progress.
7. Consolidate improvements and continue with the change process. Hire, promote and develop staff that will support the vision.
8. Institutionalise the new approaches in the organisation's culture. Demonstrate the connection between the new behaviours and the success of the programme.

Kotter recommends that companies should follow the above steps in sequence. However, change doesn't always follow such a logical process and therefore cannot always be managed in that way. It does not, for example, describe the process of incremental change that takes place over a prolonged period with small, iterative changes. It does, however, provide managers with a solid framework on which to base their change programme when a more management-led approach is required. In addition to the above factors, Johnson *et al.* (2011: 489) suggest that change programmes can fail for a number of other reasons: inability to move quickly in response; loss of focus by senior managers; staff members not being convinced of the credibility of the programme; lack of trust; as well as a variety of forms of resistance from passive to active.

Implementing change is a long and difficult process. It should not be underestimated.

Phase Four – Monitoring Results

Planning the change programme is necessary to achieve the desired results. In a change situation, it is likely that the environment will be turbulent and, as a result, management will need to be flexible in implementing change. This applies not only to achieving the goals and objectives that were set, but it also requires managers to constantly assess whether they have analysed the situation correctly and whether those goals are realistic. It is also unlikely that the change programme will follow a logical sequence. Therefore, results must be constantly monitored throughout the entire change process.

Assuming that the correct course of action has been taken, then managers must be consistent in implementing the programme and ensure compliance so that targets are met. Perhaps the most significant challenge is preventing slippage and a return to the old ways. The process must be embedded in the new culture.

CONCLUSION

Nothing remains the same for very long. Every organisation will, over a period of time, adapt to changing circumstances, or else it will go out of business. Change is all around us and, as managers, we must learn to accept and deal with it.

The whole process of strategic management, as outlined in this text, is set against a background of changing circumstances. Managers must be aware of these changes and constantly assess their environment to examine what changes must be made. It was stated in the definition of corporate strategy that it was the long-term direction of a company. Therefore, there can be a time lag between the formulation of a strategic plan, and its rollout. During that time, events can impact on the validity of the plan which may cause it to be abandoned or altered significantly. That is ultimately a judgement call by management. Either way, adjustments to the original plan will have to be made.

Implementing change requires a broad range of skills by management, and, most of all, it requires the ability to work with people and help them overcome their fears. By overcoming such fears, managers will remove many of the obstacles that might otherwise impede the successful implementation of the change strategy.

SUMMARY

One of the biggest challenges in implementing the strategy is that everything does not stay still while the strategy is being rolled out. Leading change is therefore an integral part of running any organisation. This chapter examined organisational change from a number of different perspectives.

There are many external and internal factors that drive change. The external forces include rapidly changing technology, particularly information and communication technology; globalisation and the effect of market changes; and changes in demographics and society, both internationally and at home. Some of these forces impact on organisations over a long period of time. In other cases, their effect is much more short term. There are many different types of change impacting on organisations. In order to be able to deal with changing circumstances, it is necessary to understand the nature or type of change facing a company.

Three different models for analysing the types of change were examined:

- Balogun and Hailey's matrix which looks at the type of change and its impact on the culture of an organisation.
- Generic typology of change which measures change along a continuum, from adaptive change to innovative change to radically innovative change. The level of complexity, risk and potential resistance increases as it moves along the scale to radically innovative change.
- Theory E is based on the economic value of the change programme to the organisation and is a top-down approach. It is based on formal structures and systems being changed, and generally involves downsizing. Theory O focuses on organisational capability and development of culture through learning. This form of change is not planned and it is much more emergent.

There are many challenges to understanding change which are complex and interconnected. These include the organisation's vision, creating a link between change and the outcomes, the context surrounding the change, including the time frame, scope, preserving aspects of the organisation, the diversity of the organisation, its capacity and readiness for change, and the power of the change agents. The culture also needs to be understood.

An important element of the process of conducting change is to understand and manage the resistance to change. People are creatures of habit and are fearful of change. Many of these are legitimate fears based on their perception of the security of their tenure and their ability to cope with change. It will also impact on the social aspect of their jobs. Managers must understand these reasons and the strength of those reasons before overcoming such resistance. **Forcefield analysis** is one method for understanding the forces operating in an organisation that support change and those resisting it. **Resistance** to change can vary quite significantly, depending on each particular situation, the people involved, the organisation and industry and many other factors. Resistance can be measured on a continuum going from Acceptance, Indifference, Passive Resistance, to Active Resistance. The response by managers will obviously differ quite significantly, depending on the level of resistance encountered.

Lewin saw change as a three-stage process: unfreezing – creating the motivation to change; changing the process; and refreezing – embedding the changes in the culture of the organisation. The model is regarded as simple, and it is criticised for not considering the range of factors that impact on the process from outside the organisation.

A strategic change model has the following elements:

Phase One – Identifying the need for strategy change. This includes identification of the forces of change impacting on the organisation, the type of change, challenges for understanding it and estimating the level of resistance.

Phase Two – Choosing the appropriate strategy. This involves making the necessary changes to the organisation's strategy.

Phase Three – Implementing the change programme: choosing the appropriate time, managerial style, how to manage the different change situations, the symbolic processes and the use of change agents.

Phase Four – Monitoring Results and making necessary adjustments.

Every change situation is different, so the response must be tailored to the exact circumstances. If the change is **adaptive**, the organisation has the time to assess the situation and experiment with different approaches. **Radically innovative** change presents very difficult challenges for managers. Time is of the essence in responding to a crisis situation. It will require clear strategic thinking to analyse the factors facing the organisation and how to refocus on its target market. One major factor that will obviously differ in each situation is the likely level of resistance. There are different strategies for dealing with resistance including education, collaboration, intervention, direction and coercion. Symbolism can play a significant part in changing an organisation, particularly where the culture of the organisation is also changing. The day-to-day routines will also have to be changed to reflect the new circumstances. There are often a number of people – change agents – involved in the process, each with their own role to play.

The change process is designed to realign the organisation in response to changing circumstances. The future of the company could well depend on the success of the process. Kotter proposed eight steps that managers should take to ensure success.

However, while it provides a framework, change doesn't always follow such a logical process.

DISCUSSION QUESTIONS

1. Differentiate between leading change and managing change in organisations.
2. Taking an industry of your choice, critically analyse the various forces of change impacting upon it.
3. Explore the various challenges that managers face in attempting to understand the nature of change impacting upon their organisation.
4. Discuss the various reasons why employees in an organisation might be resistant to change.
5. Critically analyse the various elements required in a strategic change model.
6. Explore the different methods that managers might use in overcoming resistance to change.

REFERENCES

Balogun, J. and Hope Hailey, V., 1999, *Exploring Strategic Change*, Harlow, Essex, Prentice Hall, Financial Times

Beer, M. and Nohria, N., 2000, *Breaking the Code of Change*, Boston, Harvard Business School Press

Block, P., 1987, *The Empowered Manager*, San Francisco, Jossey-Bass

Buelens, M. *et al.*, 2006, *Organisational Behaviour*, Maidenhead, McGraw-Hill

Darwin, J. *et al.*, 2002, *Developing Strategies for Change*, Harlow, Essex, Prentice Hall, Financial Times

Drucker, P., 1995, *Managing in a Time of Great Change*, Oxford, Butterworth Heinmann

Fitzroy, P. and Hulbert, J., 2005, *Strategic Management: Creating Value in Turbulent Time*, Chichester, John Wiley & Sons Ltd

Ghemawat, P., 2010," Finding your strategy in the new landscape", *Harvard Business Review*, March 2010, Vol. 88, Issue 2, pp.54–60

Hassan, F., 2006, "Leading Change from the Top Line", *Harvard Business Review*, July/August 2006, Vol.84, Issue 7/8, pp.90–97

Johnson, G. *et al.*, 2011, *Exploring Strategy*, 9th Ed., Harlow, Essex, Prentice Hall, Financial Times

Judson, A., 1991, *Changing Behaviour in Organisations: Minimising Resistance to Change*, Cambridge, MA, Basil Blackwell

Kanter, R., 1987, "Managing Traumatic Change: Avoiding the 'Unlucky 13' ", *Management Review*, May 1987, pp.23–24

Kotter, J., 2007, "Leading Change: Why Transformation Efforts Fail", *Harvard Business Review*, January 2007, Vol. 85, Issue 1, pp.96–103

Kotter, J., 2002, *The Heart of Change*, Boston, Harvard Business School Press

Lewin, K., 1951, *Field Theory in Social Science*, New York, Harper & Row

Lynch, R., 2009, *Strategic Management*, 5th Ed., Harlow, Prentice Hall

Miles, R., 2010, "Accelerating Corporate Transformations (Don't Lose Your Nerve)", *Harvard Business Review*, January/February 2010, Vol. 88, Issue 1, pp.68–75

Nutt, P., 1986, "Tactics of Implementation", *Academy of Management Journal*, June 1986, pp.230–261

O'Brien, J. and Marakas, G., 2008, *Management Information Systems*, 8th Edition, New York, McGraw-Hill

Pascale, R. and Sternin, J., 2005, "Your Company's Secret Change Agents", *Harvard Business Review*, May 2005, Vol.85, Issue 5, pp.73–81

Pettigrew, A. and Whipp, R., 1999, *Managing Change for Competitive Success*, Oxford, Blackwell Publishing

Thompson, J. and Martin, F., 2005, *Strategic Management: Awareness and Change*, London, Thomson Learning

Wind, J. and Main, J., 1999, *Driving Change*, London, Kogan Page

Introduction: Case Study Analysis

Case studies are an important element in learning about corporate strategy. They illustrate the kind of problems that organisations actually face, and the strategic decisions that they make in the quest for survival and competitive advantage in the market place. The purpose of studying cases is to allow you to put yourself in the position of senior management and analyse all the factors that impact on the organisation in question, and then consider or, in a class setting, debate the issues in order to come up with an appropriate response.

There is, of course, a marked difference between debating the issues raised in a case study and being in the position of a CEO having to make a decision in pressurised circumstances, where full information may not always be available. While a poor answer in a case study might merit lower marks, poor decisions taken by managers can have enormous personal consequences for them, as well as shareholders who can lose life savings with plummeting share prices and staff members who may lose their jobs. This has become very clear in recent times where so much wealth has been destroyed by reckless decisions.

While case studies will not reproduce the same pressures of real-life situations, they can nevertheless provide you, as a student of corporate strategy, with the opportunity to develop your diagnostic and analytical skills. In analysing the case material and developing solutions, you can apply the range of strategic tools contained in this text. It is by applying these tools, and examining how they have been used, that you can develop the managerial skills required to hold executive positions. You can also develop decision-making skills in developing your answer to specific questions about the cases within a limited timeframe, determining and then justifying an appropriate course of action or approach taken.

The case studies included with this textbook (both with the print edition and as an online resource) involve a wide variety of companies and organisations, both large and small, and from a variety of industries. In many situations, the problems or issues discussed might be on-going. When analysing a case, you should focus on the information provided in the case itself rather than trying to find the latest news on the company on the Internet, etc.

Also, it is important to note that there is rarely a definitive answer to the problems presented in case studies. The decisions made by organisations can be examined in retrospect to see if they improved the situation or not. For some cases, the answer will be clear; for others the answer may be open to debate. Strategy is not a precise science. What is important is that in the process of examining cases, you can develop critical thinking skills and learning to articulate those views in writing and/or class debate. In reviewing your answer, you should seek to understand where your answer is strong and where it is weak. Gradually, your analytical skills will improve with each case studied. Eventually, you should be able to identify the issues in the case without being prompted by case questions provided by your lecturer.

As with other aspects of study, you will benefit most when you fully participate in the process. This is not a 'spectator sport'. It will require a number of iterations before you will fully understand the issues presented in the case. Each case is different, but a general approach can be applied to all. You may find the following approach useful:

- Briefly review the case to get a broad understanding of the problems facing the company. At this stage, do not concern yourself with the finer details.
- Now read the case in detail, reviewing any tables, graphs or financial information included. What are these telling you? Many students find using a yellow highlighter useful to draw their attention to important detail. For maximum effect, use the highlighter sparingly.
- Re-read the case, analysing the strategic issues facing the organisation, making notes of the main points. In developing answers, you should be looking for information to be able to answer the following questions: who, what, where, when, why and how.
  Who are the main players?
  What are the problems facing the organisation, and what is their significance to the company?
  Where are they happening?
  When did these events happen – *what* was the time sequence?
  Why are they happening? Is it the result of previous action – or inaction?
  Finally, *how* is it happening?

There are a wide variety of strategic tools used throughout this text. Choose the appropriate tools and apply them to understand fully the implications of the situation for the company. Analyse the information in the tables, particularly the financial information. Use the financial ratios in **Chapter 6** to analyse the figures and interpret their meaning. If it is a group case study, debate the issues among the group. Be able to justify your position, but also be open to other opinions. Throughout this process, you should be developing a clearer understanding of the problems and their solutions.

When you receive the questions relating to the case from your lecturer, you can begin preparing the answers based on the analysis that you have conducted. If the case is an in-class exam, care should be taken to answer all of the questions within the allotted time, paying particular attention to the breakdown of marks for the different questions. Be able to support your answers with reference to the information contained in the case. Be objective in your analysis. Avoid using terms such as "In my opinion". Instead, use statements such as: "the evidence in Figure 4 demonstrates…".

Develop recommendations for the company involved in the case. These recommendations should be based on your analysis of the information presented in the case and should be designed to improve the company's situation. These recommendations should be prioritised in terms of importance for the company and the time-frame involved. They should also be realistic in regard to the resources available to the company.

Finally, while case study analysis can be time-consuming, the return for you in terms of your understanding of strategy is immense.

Case Study – Subject Matrix

The Subject Matrix provided on the following page illustrates the content of each of the various case studies. The column on the left lists the cases, and the row along the top shows the various strategic themes from the text.

One asterix under a particular theme indicates that the case contains minor discussion on that point, and two asterixes indicates that the case covers that theme in considerable detail.

The subject matrix will assist in choosing cases that demonstrate specific aspects of strategy.

Eight of these case studies, those marked in bold, are included here with the printed edition:
- BP and Deepwater Horizon
- HSBC – Changes at the Top
- Four Seasons Hotels and Resorts
- Eason & Son Ltd – A New Chapter
- Bonuses at the Bank
- Ryanair
- ESB International
- Ernest Shackleton – Leading Change

Other full case studies are published as an online resource and can be available through your lecturer (or Chartered Accountants Ireland). These include:
- Marks & Spencer
- Altobridge
- Houlihan's Butcher Shop
- Clarion Hotels
- Kerry Group
- Newbridge Silverware

Case Study – Subject Matrix

Case Study	Strategy Formulation	Leadership	Culture	Vision	Business Environment	Capability	Corporate Level Strategy	Business Level Strategy	Product/ Market Development	Strategy Methods	Implementation	Leading Change
BP	*	**	**		*		*			*	*	**
HSBC	*	**	**				**					
Four Seasons	*	**	**	**	*	**	*	**	**	**	**	**
Marks & Spencer	**	**	**	*	*	*			*			**
Altobridge	*	**	**		*				**	*		*
Eason & Son Ltd					**	*	*		**	*		*
Houlihan's Butcher's					**	*		*	*	*		
Clarion Hotels	*	*	*		**	*	**		**	*	**	*
Bank Bonuses	**	**	**		*		**				*	
Ryanair	**	**	**	*	*	**	*	**	**	*	**	
ESB International	*	*	*		*	**	*		**	**	*	
Kerry Group	*	*	*	*	*	**	**	*	**	**	**	
Newbridge Silverware			**		*	*	*		**			*
Ernest Shackleton	**	**	**	**		*					**	**

Legend:
** = Detailed discussion
* = Minor discussion
Bold title = Case included with print edition

BP and Deepwater Horizon

Gerry Gallagher[1]

This case illustrates a number of issues arising from the Gulf of Mexico oil disaster in 2010 including how corporate culture impacts on strategy and how corporate culture impacts on strategic alliances. The case also examines the importance of corporate social responsibility and the enormous cost for large multinationals when things go wrong.

Tony Hayward (53) has always enjoyed sailing. It is a perfect way to spend time with his wife and children, and to get away from the pressures of work. While life as CEO of BP was rewarding, it brought its own pressures; sailing was the perfect antidote.

Hayward joined BP nearly 30 years ago, after graduating with a 'First' in geology from Birmingham University and then earning a PhD from the University of Edinburgh. Working for BP brought him all around the globe and he rose to the very top of Britain's largest corporation, BP.

In June 2010, when Tony Hayward was participating in the 'Round the Island' yacht race at the Isle of Wight, his PR advisors must have been looking at each other in disbelief. Public reaction in the US was incredulous. There was possibly 60,000 barrels of oil flowing into the Gulf of Mexico following an explosion on BP's Deepwater Horizon rig on 20 April in which 11 crew members were killed. The leakage from the rig was the equivalent of the 1989 Exxon Valdez spill every four days. And the CEO was off sailing! While the focus of the anger was directed at Tony Hayward, BP was suffering irreparable damage. How did it come to this?

Company History

In 1901, the English entrepreneur, William Knox D'Arcy got exclusive rights to search for oil in Southwest Persia. In June 1908, he finally struck oil and the Anglo-Persian Oil Company was born. To secure supply of oil for its strategic military interests, the British Government became a major stakeholder in the company. In 1917, the Anglo-Persian Oil Company bought a small oil company called British Petroleum, and the company began using 'BP' as its trademark. It grew continuously and emerged into a truly global organisation, with oil fields across the globe.

BP did not have a retail network in the US, so it bought a 25% stake in the American company Sohio. In October 1987, as part of Margaret Thatcher's policy of privatisation, the government's remaining shareholding was sold off at 330p a share. In 1988, production at their North Sea rig

---

[1] This case is intended for class discussion rather than to illustrate effective or ineffective management of a situation.

became the first field in Western Europe to produce 2 billion barrels of oil. In 1989, BP acquired full ownership of Sohio, and this became the cornerstone of a new division of the company: BP America.

In 1997, Lord Browne of Madingley, CEO of BP at that time, became the first CEO of an energy company to warn against the danger of global warming. He maintained that no single organisation could fix the problem but that his company would do its part. In 1998, BP set itself a target to cut its carbon emissions to 10% below its 1990 levels by 2010. Later that year, BP and Amoco merged, thus combining their worldwide operations into a single organisation, BP Amoco. In 2000, BP created a new global brand – a sunburst of green, yellow and white. In the early part of this century, BP began experimenting with alternative sources of energy such as solar power and, in 2005, created a new global business dedicated to low-carbon power: BP Alternative Energy.[2]

Lord Browne had conducted a series of takeovers such as Amoco, that turned BP into one of the industry's giants. Critics say this growth was at the expense of proper operational standards, as evidenced by the 2005 Texas City oil refinery explosion. Despite making the takeovers, Lord Browne failed to integrate the new companies properly with the parent company, nor did he tackle the growing bureaucracy within BP. After the Texas City disaster, Hayward, then a senior executive in BP, was highly critical of the senior management at the company for "a leadership style that is too directive and doesn't listen sufficiently well". His willingness to speak out and get involved in the issues facing workers earned him widespread respect at lower levels within the company.

When Hayward took over at the helm of the company in 2007, he was appalled by the lack of technical and safety rigour and set about modelling standards on Exxon Mobil (the 'Exxon Way'), regarded as the industry leader in safety procedures. He streamlined the management structure of the company and brought the focus back on to its core business – oil:

> "BP makes its money by someone, somewhere, every day putting on boots, overalls, a hard hat and glasses, and going out and turning on valves. And we'd sort of lost track of that".[3]

According to internal safety audits, Hayward had implemented changes in safety procedures across 80% of the company when the Gulf of Mexico accident happened. However, early indications from the congressional investigation into the disaster did not look good for the company and reflect poorly on some of the decisions that it made.

While implementing these safety changes, Hayward was also delivering good results for shareholders. Just a few weeks before the accident, Hayward had delivered record profits of $5.6 billion in the first quarter. BP also had low gearing, with a debt to capital ratio of less than 30%.

---

2 www.bp.com/extendedsectiongenericarticle.do?categoryId=10&contentId=7036819 (accessed 4 November 2010).

3 *The Economist*, 8 May 2010, p.64.

When the Gulf of Mexico explosion happened, Hayward acted quickly in coming to grips with the clean-up operation; he even moved to Houm, Louisiana, where he set up headquarters to oversee the operation. On behalf of BP, he took responsibility for the accident, but he also pointed out that a sub-contractor, Transocean, operated the rig.

The Drilling

As a result of rising oil prices, oil companies are moving to deep, offshore fields that were previously considered too expensive to exploit the oil reserves they contain. The move by BP to the Macondo field in the Gulf of Mexico was part of that process. BP has a number of wells in the Macondo field, including the Deepwater Horizon rig. According to the US Department of Energy, technically-recoverable wells in the Gulf of Mexico are equal to approximately 41 billion barrels, about 25% of which are in deep waters. The depth of water poses many technical challenges for oil companies. The Minerals Management Service (MMS), which comes under the control of the US Department of the Interior, oversees off-shore drilling. It issues permits for drilling and it is also tasked with regulating the industry. (In this case, officials from the MMS approved the blowout preventer that ultimately failed.[4])

The Deepwater Horizon rig, with its crew of 126, was located 64km off the coast of Louisiana. The well itself is some 4,000 metres beneath the seabed, in water that is 1,500 metres deep. BP leads the consortium that owns the Gulf of Mexico well. BP's share is 65%, Anadarko owns 25% and the Japanese group Mitsui owns the remaining 10%. There are many other companies involved in the extraction of the oil. The Deepwater Horizon rig was built by Hyundai and was supplied by the world's largest offshore drilling contractor, Transocean. In turn, the US company Halliburton had responsibility for cementing the rig in place. The blowout preventer was manufactured by Cameron International, a specialist engineering company. BP is hoping to share the cost of the damage with its consortium partners, but this is being disputed by the other members. Initially, Hayward attempted to blame Transocean: "It was operated by another company. It was their people, their systems, their processes."[5]

Drilling for oil poses many technical problems. The oil comes up from reservoirs under the ground or seabed at immense pressure, and the drilling pipes need to be held in place with concrete strong enough to withstand that pressure. When the well was being drilled, BP was advised by its subcontractor Halliburton, that 21 mechanical centralisers would be required (centralisers keep the central pipe steady and prevent the cement casing from cracking, allowing gas to escape). To save time and money, BP opted to use only six. Some engineers claim that only four or five were ever used. There was clear concern within BP regarding the quality of the work done on the well and in particular the centralisers. One BP engineer, Brett Cocales, sent an email to colleagues: "Who cares? It's done, end of story, will probably be fine and we'll get a good cement job".[6]

---

[4] *The Economist*, 15 June 2010, p.50.
[5] Marlow, L. (2010), *Irish Times*, 19 June 2010, Weekend Review, p.5.
[6] Caesar, E (2010), "Deepwater Horizon: The Big Picture" *The Sunday Times*, 12 September 2010, Magazine. p.31.

On 20 April 2010, the crew on the rig was sealing the well before moving off to another position. The drilling hole was being filled with seawater, and capped with concrete seals. Drilling mud should have been used instead of seawater. Drilling mud is a complex and viscous substance that helps equalise the pressure in the well. On the day of the explosion, BP managers misread data relating to pressure on the well and gave orders for oil rig workers to replace heavy drilling mud in the well with sea water. One of these concrete seals is thought to have failed, allowing gas to escape which was then sucked up to diesel engines on the rig and caused at least two fatal explosions, killing 11 of the crew.

The Deepwater Horizon rig had a blowout preventer in place on the seabed, the purpose of which was to seal off the well in an emergency with a number of hydraulic systems. There were two systems in place that should have activated the blowout preventer when the pressure built up, but neither of them worked. The preventer had not undergone a full inspection since the rig was completed in 2000. In evidence given to the congressional investigation into the disaster, 26 of its components were rated as being in 'poor' or 'bad' condition. The US government official whose job it was to inspect the blow-out preventer admitted that he had never done so.

Once in position in the Macondo field, the rig was costing BP nearly $1 million per day and, when the incident happened, the project was 43 days behind schedule. BP hired Transocean to dig the hole, and BP is one of its most important customers. Transocean knew that they would have to accelerate the programme to keep their client happy. On the rig, BP's employees were the senior decision-makers and they 'called the shots'. In turn, they answered to their bosses in Houston, who set the strategy.

Many of the Transocean employees felt under pressure to deliver on the project, but were unhappy with some of the procedures. One of the senior Transocean employees on the rig, Jason Anderson, said to his father shortly before the explosion: "They are doing things that I really don't like. They are pushing us to do things that are not safe." He was one of the 11 people who lost their lives. One of Transocean's engineers stated that several of the rig's computers were continually "on the blink" and the alarm system, which might have allowed the 11 men who died time to escape, was permanently set to bypass. Some 115 survivors managed to make it to the rescue boats and they were picked up by a ship that was servicing the rig. They were forbidden to use satellite phone on board. When they finally got to Port Fourchon, Louisiana, around 28 hours after they were picked up, they were asked to sign disclaimers drafted by Transocean lawyers before they disembarked, including those who were badly injured. The disclaimers read:

> "I was not a witness to the incident requiring the evacuation [of the Deepwater Horizon] and have no first-hand or personal knowledge regarding the incident… I was not injured as a result of the incident or the evacuation."[7]

---

[7] Caesar, E (2010), "Deepwater Horizon: The Big Picture" *The Sunday Times*, 12 September 2010, Magazine. p.28.

Previous Disasters

There have been numerous other major accidents in the oil exploration industry. The biggest oil spill in history took place in 1979 in the Gulf of Mexico when there was a blowout on a Mexican rig, Ixtoc-1, releasing 3.3 million barrels of oil into the Gulf between June 1979 and March 1980.

On 6 July 1988, there was an explosion on the Piper Alpha platform in the North Sea, which killed 167 people. Piper Alpha was owned by a US company, Occidental Petroleum.[8] The official inquiry was scathing about the company's safety standards and the disaster ushered in a new era of regulation for the British oil industry.

In 1989, the Exxon Valdez oil tanker ran aground 15km from the Alaskan coastline spilling 250,000 barrels of heavy viscous crude into the sea. It had an immediate and devastating impact on the environment. Exxon Mobil suffered great harm to its reputation as it tried to fight off claims arising from the spill. Total costs to the company were about $4 billion in legal fees and for the clean-up operation. In 2008, the US Supreme Court allowed punitive damages to be slashed from $2.5 billion to $507.5 million (a judgement that BP will no doubt have welcomed as it will have set a legal precedence that their lawyers can use).

In 2004, some 4,800 barrels of oil leaked from a BP pipeline in North Slope, Alaska, and in 2007, BP was accused of fixing the propane gas market in 2004 and the company paid more than $300 million in settlement. The Chemical Safety Board is an independent federal agency that investigated BP's previous disaster at the company's Texas City refinery in 2005 when an explosion killed 15 workers and injured 75 others. That inquiry found that budget cuts and poor safety practices were factors in the explosion.

The US investigation following the Deepwater Horizon disaster was tasked with examining the company's safety culture as well as the regulations that govern the industry. BP received 97% of all health and safety citations that were issued to oil companies in the US between June 2007 and February 2010. While Mr Hayward put much effort into changing the corporate culture, many commentators think that these citations reflect the culture of the company where promotion was traditionally dependent on the ability to cut costs rather than technical competence.

Containment Measures

In the period after the explosion, there were various estimates about the amount of oil flowing from the ruptured pipe. At its peak, it was thought to be about 60,000 barrels per day ('bpd'). By early June, BP was managing to capture 16,000 bpd of this. By mid-June, the company was capturing another 10,000 bpd by 'flaring', or burning off the excess oil. However, in turn, this was creating a different environmental problem by generating plumes of acrid smoke.

---

[8] Allright, T. (2010), *Irish Times*, 2 July 2010, p.15.

There were numerous attempts to fix the problem. BP started drilling a relief well after the accident, and began a second relief operation some time later in case the first one failed. In the meantime, BP tried several times to get the blowout preventer to close, but these attempts were unsuccessful. By June, it was estimated by the National Incident Command Flow Technical Group that the rate of flow had dropped to about 25,000 bpd. BP managed to stem the flow of oil on August 4, with a procedure known as 'static kill'. Four days later, the company announced that no more oil was flowing into the Gulf. During the clean-up, BP employed over 1,000 boats out at sea using booms, skimmers and dispersants in an attempt to block the oil coming ashore. BP also had 500 claim adjusters processing tens of thousands of claims received by the company for financial loss as a result of the spill.

Environmental Impact

According to the US Government's Fish and Wildlife Service, the oil spill had a devastating impact on birds – coast gulls, terns and cormorants, and a whole range of mammals. The oil came ashore and caused damage to Louisiana's fragile wetlands that is expected to last for years. With most oil spills, dispersants can be used for a brief period when the oil first makes its way to the surface. After approximately two days, some of the lighter elements of the oil will evaporate (up to 40% of the total). While dispersants help break up the oil on top, under the surface, the oil is mixed with the water causing problems for fish life. Furthermore, measures such as the use of dispersants and boats with booms attached to gather up the oil on the surface are dependent on the prevailing weather being favourable. BP was spending approximately $6 million per day on the clean-up operation. [9]

Accidents such as these are also likely to strengthen the case of environmentalists who are pressing for further restrictions on oil companies. Environmental groups in the US are attempting to turn America away from its dependency on oil towards cleaner, more environmentally-friendly energy sources. The fallout could ultimately spell the end of off-shore drilling. While that is probably unlikely, what does seem certain is that there will be much greater restrictions placed on oil companies, with safety-related costs set to rise substantially.

As the weeks passed into months, reaction from the US Federal Government was intensifying and the pressure on the company continued to grow. Much of the American public believed that President Obama was not doing enough to stop the flow of oil. In turn, the President was directing public anger back on to "British Petroleum" (the company changed its name from British Petroleum in the 1990s). In one poll, more than 80% of Americans disapproved of BP. Across the country, BP service stations were being boycotted, and many investors dumped BP shares. The company announced that it was setting up a $20 billion escrow fund (a fund administered by an independent third party) to cover damages from the disaster.

Meanwhile, Hayward became the focus of anti-BP sentiment. While he was taking a very hands-on approach to dealing with the problem, some of his press conferences did not run smoothly. At one

---

[9] *The Economist*, 8 May 2010, p.66.

point, in talking to reporters about the impact the crisis was having on him personally, he stated: "I would like my life back". Discussing the amount of oil flowing into the sea, he stated: "The Gulf of Mexico is a very big ocean. The amount of oil and dispersant we are putting into it is tiny in relation to the total volume of water." He told Sky News: "I think the environmental impact of this disaster is likely to be very, very modest." As described above, in June, Hayward competed in the Isle of Wight Round the Island yacht race, a move that enraged Americans. At another point, the company chairman, Carl Henric Svanberg, referred to the people living and working on the Gulf coast as "the small people".

Congressional Hearings

On 16 June 2010, Hayward appeared before a US Congressional committee meeting. These meetings can be bruising affairs, often aimed at the gallery as much as getting to the bottom of the matter. Referring to earlier comments made by BP, the chairman of the subcommittee for Oversight and Investigations said: "We are not small people, but we wish to get our lives back. For people on the Gulf Coast, it will take a while. The 11 dead workers will never get their lives back. I'm sure you will get your life back Mr Hayward, with a golden parachute." Mr Stupak added: "BP blew it. You cut corners to save money and time." Henry Waxman, chairman of the House energy and commerce committee accused Mr Hayward of "Not taking responsibility. You are kicking the can down the road and acting as if you had nothing to do with this company." The brother of one of the 11 people killed on the rig told the committee: "Mr Hayward, I want my brother's life back".

In answering the questions put to him on what had happened, Hayward relied on four stock answers provided by his army of PR advisors: "Since I have been the CEO of this company I have focused on safe, reliable operations"; "I think it is too early to reach a conclusion"; "I wasn't part of the decision-making process on this well"; "I just can't recall".[10] The committee found several instances where BP managers had cut costs. Early indications have shown that the use of only a few centralisers cementing the pipe in place was a major factor in causing the explosion. The nature of the questioning by the committee was similar to the queen in *Alice in Wonderland* – find him guilty and then hold the trial.

Market reactions

At the beginning of June 2010, ratings agencies downgraded BP, which had serious implications for BP in terms of the cost of its borrowing. The company's share price fell 45% to 375p between April and June, valuing the company at £67 billion. BP hired advisors to help prevent a takeover, with Exxon Mobil and Chevron seen as the most likely bidders, although any bid is unlikely until the final cost of the disaster is eventually known. The company's board has ring-fenced €20 billion to cover the cost of the clean-up.[11] The markets would normally expect a substantial dividend from BP – representing 12% of all the dividends from London-listed companies. Senator Charles

---

[10] Marlow, L. (2010), *Irish Times*, 19 June 2010, Weekend Review, p.5.
[11] *The Economist*, 19 June 2010, p.57.

Schumer told Mr Hayward that it would be "unfathomable for BP to pay a dividend before the full cost of the disaster was known". The company bowed to pressure and cancelled its dividend for the remainder of 2010.

Costs

There are three main elements to the total cost to BP as a result of the disaster. The first relates to the plugging of the well and cleaning up the pollution that the leak caused. The US "Oil Pollution Act"(1990) firmly places responsibility for this on the offending company. Estimates vary from $12 billion up to $16 billion. Depending on how responsibility is fixed between the members of the consortium, BP would be liable for two-thirds of these figures.

Secondly, the company faces fines under the US "Clean Waters Act" (1972), ranging from $1,100 to $4,300 per barrel of oil spilled, depending on the level of negligence attributed to the company. This could add a further $17 billion to the bill.

Finally there are the compensation claims and other economic costs, such as taxes foregone. While the Oil Pollution Act caps at $75 million the total costs that oil companies are liable for in the event of major environmental damage, BP has stated that it will waive this cap and honour all legitimate claims. Estimates here vary from $5 billion to $10 billion.

The disaster has had a devastating impact on the company's share price. One of the main reasons for this is the level of uncertainty in relation to compensation that will be paid. BP has waived the cap on the amount that might be paid, and this has frightened investors. While the company is asset-rich, such payments will have a big impact on cash flow. The company was due to spend $20 billion on capital programmes in 2010, which will not go ahead. The company was also due to pay $10 billion in dividend payments to shareholders, but took the decision to freeze such payments for 2010.

Following the incident, BP had approximately $5 billion available in cash and bank lines. However, there is around $17 billion in maturing debt due in 2011. As a result of the down-grading by the debt agencies, the cost of borrowing for BP has soared, and may make the availability of funds hard to get causing severe liquidity problems. Its credit-default-swap spread rose to six percentage points over government rates. The cost of the clean-up and compensation will be spread over a few years. The whole affair has left BP in a very vulnerable position, although it is unlikely to go bankrupt. The company is also vulnerable to being taken over by either some of the big US companies such as Exxon Mobil or European oil companies including Royal Dutch Shell or Total.

Drilling Moratorium

There is likely to be a whole new set of strict regulations brought in to cover drilling in the future and this will impact on the bottom line of oil companies such as BP. Shortly after the explosions on 20 April, the Obama administration imposed a six-month moratorium on deep-water drilling in the Gulf of Mexico. In mid-June, however, a federal court sided with the oil companies in overturning the moratorium believing that the ban was unreasonable and that it was "arbitrary and capricious" to argue that just because one well failed, that others were likely to fail also. The government appealed the decision, and re-imposed the ban. In the meantime, BP has appointed Bob Dudley to head up the damage-limitation campaign. Mr Dudley was a former head of its joint venture in Russia. When Mr Hayward announced his resignation on 27 July, BP confirmed Mr Dudley as his successor. On 12 October, the Obama Administration lifted the moratorium on deep-water drilling, six weeks before the bitterly contested suspension was due to expire. The Interior Secretary, Ken Salazar, said the Administration had drawn up a stringent list of new safety requirements to which all oil companies must adhere. Many organisations reacted with anger to the announcement believing that scientists had not fully assessed the ecological damage caused by the disaster. According to Greenpeace: "It is irresponsible to say the least, reckless at worst."[12]

The challenges facing Mr Dudley and the board of directors are very significant, not just in terms of their own safety culture, which will need to be tackled as a matter of urgency for BP. Size is also an issue for the company. BP produces 4 million barrels of oil per day, which is about 5% of global demand. Since 1995, it has spent about $95 billion in finding new resources, yet it now produces 16,000 barrels per day less than it did then. Its reputation has been severely damaged as a result of the Gulf disaster. Morgan Stanley recommends that BP needs a four-point plan: prune non-core assets; greatly increase spending on exploration; slash future dividends; and examine large-scale mergers. BP has also started selling many assets in its "shrink to grow approach". One option would be break up BP, divesting its loss-making petrol station and refinery division and concentrate on an independent exploration business, which investors tend to rate higher than integrated rivals. The oil exploration industry is a slow growth one, with a surplus of players. When Exxon merged with Mobil, it pruned $8 billion of annual costs and is now the biggest oil company in the world.[13]

Presidential Commission

The report issued in 2011 by the presidential commission that investigated the Gulf of Mexico disaster was scathing in its findings. It attributed the disaster in the Gulf of Mexico to a failure of management by BP, Halliburton and Transocean. It said most of the mistakes and oversights that happened at the well can be traced back to a single overarching failure of management. Better management by all three companies would almost certainly have prevented the blowout. Decisions made by all three companies saved those companies both time and money. While the report was scathing, shares in BP rose 2% to 509p – the highest value since the spill, although it fell back again to 496p. The reason for the investor confidence was that the report did not accuse BP of gross negligence, which will result in savings of tens of billions of dollars to the company. A finding of gross negligence by BP would also have made it much more difficult to recoup money from its partners. So far, both partners (Halliburton and Transocean) have refused to pay. It is considered unlikely that the US Department of Justice will override the recommendation of the Commission regarding gross negligence.

---

[12] Phillis, C. (2010), *Irish Times*, 13 October 2010, p.29.
[13] Forston, D. (2010), *The Sunday Times*, 12 September 2010, p.9.

Another piece of good news for BP was when Ken Feinberg, the lawyer appointed to oversee the escrow fund that BP set up to compensate people affected by the spill, stated that he expected to need only half of the €20 billion fund that was established. Now that the share price has recovered from a low of 299p in June 2010, it looks less likely that Exxon Mobil or Royal Dutch Shell would pursue a takeover bid. However, with fines and compensation to be paid, the company is not out of the woods yet. BP is conducting its own strategic review. Changes that Mr Dudley has already made include splitting the exploration arm into three units, all of which report directly to him. Bonus payments are now linked to safety targets. The company will be smaller in the future. Whether these changes will be enough to regain the confidence of the US government to be able to operate in the United States remains to be seen. Structural changes are relatively easy. Overseeing changes to a culture that allowed such a disaster to happen will be an entirely different and greater challenge.

HSBC – Changes at the Top

Gerry Gallagher[1]

This case illustrates issues of the transition of leaders running a major international plc and the importance of leadership in defining the values of a company, and its strategy. It also examines corporate-level decision-making, as well as aspects of corporate governance.

Company History

The Hong Kong and Shanghai Banking Corporation Limited was established in 1865 to finance the growing trade between Europe, India and China. It was the inspiration of a Scot, Thomas Sutherland, who was working for the Peninsular and Oriental Steam Navigation Company and realised that there was a considerable demand for banking facilities in Hong Kong and on the China coast. The new bank quickly became established throughout the region. In 1959, it purchased the Mercantile Bank and the British Bank of the Middle East, and began a period of expansion in Europe and the United States. In 1991, it created a new holding company, HSBC Holdings plc. In 1992, it acquired full ownership of the Midland Bank and HSBC moved its headquarters to London.

HSBC Group was established in 1999 as a uniform, international brand name for discrete legal entities, each of which is wholly or partly owned by HSBC Holdings plc. HSBC uses the phrase "the world's local bank" to distinguish itself from its competitors, and is now one of the largest global banking and financial services organisations.[2] HSBC group operates in six regions: Europe; Hong Kong; the rest of Asia Pacific; the Middle East and Africa; North America; and South America. It employs 307,000 people and has a market capitalisation of $180 billion. It has a network of 7,500 offices in 87 countries. Its products and services are delivered through two customer groups: personal financial services and commercial banking; and through two global businesses: global banking and markets, and global private banking. Combined, HSBC's five largest customers do not account for 1% of the bank's income.[3]

Corporate Values

HSBC is recognised for having a strong culture supported by core values which guide the bank in its dealings with its staff, customers and the wider community. The bank considers its culture to be central to its success over the years. These can be summarised as follows:

- Openness to different ideas and cultures
- Connected with our customers, community and each other
- Dependable and doing the right thing

---

[1] This case is intended as a basis for class discussion and not as an illustration of good or bad practice.
[2] www.hsbc.com/1/2/about/history/history (accessed 27 April 2011).
[3] www.hsbc.com/1/2/about/group-structure (accessed 27 April 2011).

Connecting its values with its business strategy, the group uses the following business principles in its dealings:

- Outstanding customer service
- Effective and efficient operations
- Strong capital and liquidity
- Prudent lending policy
- Strict expense discipline

Changes at the Top

Such values and business principles require strong leadership to ensure that they are not just platitudes that look good on the group corporate website. In September 2010, HSBC – by now Britain's biggest bank – was pushed into an early announcement of its new leadership team, as a result of the publication of a newspaper article on the subject. The board named Douglas Flint, its finance director, as the new chairman to replace Stephen Green who had resigned to take up the post of Trade Secretary in the UK Government. Flint gave up his non-executive role at BP (chairman of the audit committee) in 2011 to focus on the full-time role of HSBC chairman. He was heavily involved with BP during the disaster in the Gulf of Mexico in 2010. The existing CEO, Michael Geoghegan, who had 37 years' service with the bank, was passed over for the chairmanship and subsequently resigned, creating another vacancy at CEO level.

HSBC then confirmed that Stuart Gulliver, the head of the investment banking division, would take over as the bank's new CEO. Gulliver has been 30 years with HSBC and started in Hong Kong in January 2011 on a salary of £1.25 million along with a relocation package. His total package as CEO is less than he received in his earlier appointment (he received a bonus of £9 million for 2009). Gulliver was then replaced as finance director by Iain Mackay. Michael Geoghegan, who took over as CEO in 2006, stayed on in an advisory role until March 2011. He received €1.42 million on his departure along with a bonus for 2010 and a £200,000 consultancy fee, which he intended to donate to charity.[4]

After an emergency board meeting and accelerated approval by the Financial Services Authority, Stuart Gulliver was confirmed as the new CEO of HSBC. Described as a 'visionary', he seems to command universal praise. He keeps a very low profile, despite being one of the world's highest paid investment bankers (his remuneration package in 2010 was almost £10 million). This is in keeping with HSBC's relatively low-profile investment banking operations. When he took over in 2006 as head of investment banking, Gulliver transformed the business into something that aligned with the group's broader focus on emerging markets. "Over the three years of the financial crisis, when other parts of HSBC – notably its US subprime lending operation

---

[4] Goff, S. and Jenkins P. (2010), *Financial Times,* 25 September 2010, p. 1.

'Household' – were dragging down results, Mr. Gulliver's division generated €20 billion of pre-tax profit". (HSBC made more money from this division alone in the first half of 2010 than Barclays and Standard Charter put together.) He hired very few big name bankers and expanded the banks expertise slowly and steadily.

Stuart Gulliver grew up in Plymouth, went to a state school and then went to the University of Oxford where he obtained a degree in jurisprudence. Many praise his prescience in anticipating many of the recent events in banking, such as the danger of sub-prime lending in the US, the debacle at Northern Rock, and constantly reducing HSBC's exposure to rival Wall Street investment banks almost to zero, before the Bear Stearns collapse in March 2008. Mike Powell, a former colleague at HSBC, described him as very decisive and he is "a natural leader because he communicates so well". He has strong diplomatic skills. Others, however, criticise his elevation because of his perceived inexperience outside of investment banking, particularly in HSBCs retail and corporate sectors. One of his immediate challenges was to strengthen the leadership of the investment bank now that he has been promoted to CEO.

Many wait to see what sort of "double act" Stuart Gulliver will play with Douglas Flint, the new chairman. Like Gulliver, Flint also understood the problems in US banking at an early stage. When the crisis first began to emerge in late 2007 and early 2008, Gulliver moved his office from the management floor at HSBC's Canary Wharf building down to the dealing room to ensure he fully understood the risks to which HSBC was exposed. His typical working day began at 7am and finished at 11 pm.[5]

> "In some ways the management shake-up, which will see Douglas Flint make the fairly unusual move from Finance Director to chairman, will bring a new balance to the relationship between chairman and chief executive. Mr Flint is regarded as a highly capable and mild-mannered banker with a keen eye for detail and a deep understanding of the mechanics of banking and the intricacies of regulation".[6]

Others believe, however, that unlike his predecessor, Stephen Green, Flint does not have the ambassadorial flair needed to successfully engage with politicians and regulators.

Gulliver has spent most of his career in Asia and is regarded as having very good people skills. Flint trained as an accountant before joining HSBC in the mid-1990s and is regarded as a safe pair of hands who, along with Gulliver, will represent stability in terms of strategy. Both men perceive Asia as a priority for potential market growth, particularly Shanghai and Mumbai.

---

[5] Jenkins, P. and Sender, H. (2010), *Financial Times,* 25 September 2010, p.13.
[6] Goff, S. and Jenkins, P. (2010), "HSBC puts safe pair of hands at top". *Financial Times,* 25 September 2010. p. 15

There will be many challenges facing Gulliver from a strategy perspective. What remains to be seen is whether he will continue over the next few years to pursue the acquisition strategy led by Mr Geoghegan (HSBC recently bought Nedbank of South Africa). Gulliver recently hit out against the move to split up British banks into smaller entities saying that this could shift the focus of financial markets away from London to Hong Kong. Over the next few years, he will also have to try to rebuild HSBC's presence in the US.

Many observers of the banking industry had expected Stephen Green to be replaced by John Thornton in a relatively straightforward succession process. Thornton, an American, was a former Goldman Sachs executive who became a non-executive director of HSBC a few years ago. He was seen as someone who had considerable experience as a banker and who knew the Asian markets well. More importantly, he had many contacts in China and could open doors for HSBC's expansion there. The ability to open doors is essential. Others, however, considered his management style to be at odds with the culture at HSBC, where the focus is on building consensus.

Strategic Direction

During the latter part of his time as CEO, Michael Geoghegan had the freedom to direct strategy at HSBC in whatever direction he saw fit. Had Thornton been appointed as Chairman, it may have locked HSBC into a US-focused strategy at the expense of other growth areas which may provide a better balance. In the end, the board selected two HSBC executives (i.e. Flint and Gulliver) that were likely to maintain a British focus.

Figure 1 below shows the breakdown of HSBC's pre-tax profit by geographical region:

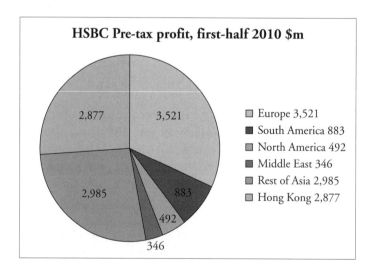

Figure 1 – *HSBC Pre-tax profits by Geographical Area*

Stephen Green had originally planned to step down as chairman of HSBC in 2011–2012. The search for a new chairman began in a timely manner in March 2010, and was led by the senior independent director, Sir Robert Simon. Initially, the two most likely candidates were the chief executive, Michael Geoghegan, and non-executive director John Thornton. These plans were upset, however, when Green announced that he would be retiring early from the post to become David Cameron's Trade Minister.

The announcement of the new chairman and chief executive followed a hastily convened conference call press briefing to confirm the disclosure of the appointments the previous day by the *Financial Times*. Stephen Green stated that the decision by the board was completely unanimous and was a "superb way forward". According to Sir Robert Simon, the nominations committee had made the decision on the chairman 10 days previously and had broken the news to Michael Geoghegan over dinner. The board had expected that Geoghegan would accept being passed over, but instead he chose to resign, prompting a quick decision by the board and the subsequent press call. (There were rumours that Geoghegan had threatened to resign if he were passed over for the role of chairman – a rumour denied by the board of the bank.) At the conference call, the Board sought to minimise the damage caused to the bank's reputation (HSBC had always been noted for its internal cohesion). In addition, the simultaneous replacement of chairman, chief executive and finance chief, despite getting regulatory approval, would inevitably cause a certain amount of anxiety in the markets.

HSBC has a long tradition of promoting people to the top positions from within the bank. The bank takes pride in its prudent succession planning. In fact, in May 2009, Stephen Green had stated that succession plans were being developed for key executives. It seems strange then that, when Green announced his early retirement in September 2010, the bank was not able to make an immediate announcement on his replacement.

HSBC, the world's largest bank in terms of market capitalisation, used to have a clear division of responsibilities: the chairman set the strategy and the chief executive implemented it. That changed in 2009 when the Chief Executive, Michael Geoghegan, moved from London to Hong Kong taking responsibility for strategy with him. The Chairman, Stephen Green, then took a much less active role. For the first 127 years of its existence, HSBC did not have a chief executive, but when HSBC took over the UK's Midland Bank in 1992, it then had to conform to British corporate governance rules. In 2006, Green became the third chief executive to move to the position of chairman.[7]

2010 Annual Results

The new senior management team at HSBC was in place just three months when the 2010 results were published.[8] Pre-tax profit more than doubled to $19 billion, with every region and every

[7] The Lex Column, *Financial Times*, 25 September 2010, p.26.
[8] www.hsbc.com/1/PA_1_1_S5/content/assets/investor_relations/hsbc2010ara0.pdf (accessed 27 April 2011).

customer group being profitable. Total operating income was $80 billion, up 2%. There was continued capital generation with core tier 1 ratio increased to 10.5% (up from 9.4%). This was largely due to profit retention during the year. Deposits were up 7% to $1.2 trillion and customer lending was up 8% to $958 billion. Earnings per share were $0.73, up 115%. Loan impairment charges to total operating income dropped to 16.9% from 31.7% in 2009, reflecting improving world economic conditions. The cost-efficiency ratio rose to 55.2%, up from 52% in 2009. The cost efficiency measures total operating expenses divided by net operating income before loan impairment and other credit risk provisions.

Challenges facing the Industry and the Bank

The global banking industry faces many major regulatory issues. While a new top management team is in place at HSBC, all those involved have worked with the bank for many years and have considerable experience from which to draw. The primary objective for CEO Stuart Gulliver is to deliver sustainable long-term value for shareholders, while recognising the importance of all other stakeholders. The corporate reputation of HSBC is the overriding imperative. A key challenge for the chairman is engaging in the regulatory reform debates that will shape the future of the industry, while also providing stewardship to the board in leading the organisation. One of the biggest regulatory changes made in the aftermath of the world-wide financial crisis was the revision of the common equity tier 1 ratio to 7%, in line with Basel III recommendations,[9] which is designed to protect taxpayers and governments from future banking collapses. This is a threshold that has been comfortably met by HSBC. Certain aspects of the Basel III rules seem open to interpretation by national regulators, but many of the changes will be implemented gradually up to 2019. This will ultimately impact on shareholder return. HSBC is targeting a return on average shareholders' equity of 12–15% in the future.

A major debate that is currently running concerns the designation of "Systemically Important Financial Institutions" (SIFIs). Consideration is being given to higher capital requirements as well as more intense supervision. HSBC believes that systemic importance should not be considered by size alone. Another major issue is the proposal by the UK Government to raise a bank levy of £2.5 billion, and this will have implications for HSBC, which though registered in the UK, operates globally.

Perhaps one of the biggest challenges facing banks worldwide is to reflect on the events that led to the 2008 financial crash, the biggest since the Great Depression of the 1930s, and its far-reaching consequences. Every country needs a functioning banking system to facilitate the provision and protection of capital as wells as the basic banking facilities that society needs to operate effectively. The banking system has to achieve this at a cost that is proportionate to the value it is creating. What happened in Ireland, as well as many other parts of the world, is that bankers, regulators, legislators and others lost sight of that basic fact. People will play a central role in future value creation, and for

---

[9] A new global regulatory standard which prescribes the level of capital and liquidity that banks need to hold. It was developed in response to the global financial crisis in 2008.

HSBC and other banks, that means recruiting, training and retaining the right people to develop financial products and manage the inherent risk. Compensation packages will have to be designed to attract suitable talent that are aligned to best practice and long-term shareholder interests. Values will play a central role in shaping these organisations.

HSBC is headquartered in London, the world's premier financial centre. The bank must therefore conform to UK banking regulations, and this has implications for many aspects of their operations, including the imposition of a banking levy. CEO Stewart Gulliver's principal office will be in Hong Kong, a financial hub of growing importance to HSBC. Recent events in the Middle East may have implications for expansion in the Arab regions. Increases in world oil prices will have an impact on economic growth and, coupled with large debt overhangs in some countries, many Western markets may under perform in the short term.

All banking involves risk to varying degrees, which needs to be measured, evaluated and managed. HSBC classify risks as 'top' or 'emerging'. A 'top risk' is a current visible risk that could have a material effect on its financial performance or reputation. An 'emerging risk' is one that could have a material effect on its long-term strategy. These risks can be viewed under four broad categories:

- Business operations
- Governance and internal controls
- Macro-economic and geopolitical risk
- Macro-prudential and regulatory risk to their business model

HSBC's progress is monitored against its strategic objectives using both financial and non-financial KPIs. Its strategic objectives are:

1. Deliver consistent earnings and superior risk-adjusted returns (risk-adjusted revenue growth; basic earnings per ordinary share; and dividends per share growth).
2. Enhance efficiency using economies of scale (cost efficiency).
3. Motivate staff to deliver strategy (employee engagement).
4. Maintain capital strength and strong liquidity (return on average total shareholders' equity; tier 1 capital; and advances to core funding ratio).
5. Reach new customers and expand services to existing customers using the HSBC brand and global network (brand perception; and customer retention).

Delivering on these objectives for 2011 and beyond will be quite a challenge for HSBC in the face of difficult economic circumstances and regulatory changes. Will the new management team be up to the challenge?

Four Seasons Hotels and Resorts

Gerry Gallagher[1]

This case illustrates the role of leadership in forming corporate culture and values, and in running a major international hotel company. It highlights the importance of people in a service industry and how value is created by developing people to their full potential. It also illustrates product and market development.

"So much of long-term success is based on intangibles. Beliefs and ideas. Invisible concepts."

Isadore Sharp

Background

At 79, Isadore Sharp, the founder of Four Seasons Hotels and Resorts ('Four Seasons') is still active as CEO. Known throughout the company and the industry as 'Issy', he regards retirement as a product of age and that he has the privilege of being able to decide when he wants to go. A number of years ago he mentioned to his wife that he hoped he would know when he should step down. Rosalie, his wife of 55 years, said: "For sure you're going to know." When he asked her how she was so certain, she replied: "Because I am going to tell you."[2]

The son of Polish immigrants, Sharp was born in Toronto Canada in 1931. He qualified as an architect in 1952 from Ryerson Polytechnical Institute in Toronto and followed his father, Max, into the family construction business. In his youth, he was a keen sportsman, which influenced his thinking on the importance of teamwork. In sport, one has to learn to lose as well as win, and it is from losing that one learns to try harder. Winning is the result of team effort rather than any talented individual. The role of the coach is getting the best out of people.

At first, Max Sharp & Son built houses, later expanding to begin constructing apartment buildings. Sharp's first introduction to the hotel business was when he built a hotel in the mid-1950s for a friend, Jack Gould. Seeing the hotel do well, he began thinking of building his own and approached some friends for financial backing. After some persuading, Cecil Forsyth, Murray Koffler and his brother-in-law, Edmund Creed, put up funding, and along with a $125,000 loan from the Bank of Nova Scotia, he set about building the hotel on Jarvis street, Toronto.[3] He consulted widely with

---

[1] This case is intended as a basis for class discussion and not as an illustration of good or bad practice.
[2] Walker, V. (2007:40) "Isadore Sharp Four Seasons' CEO", *Portfolio*, Issue 24 October/November 2007.
[3] Sharp, I. (2009) *Four Seasons: The Story of a Business Philosophy.* New York, Penguin Group.

professionals on the design, interior décor and other aspects of the hotel finish, and in so doing began many partnerships that would last for decades. He also negotiated with suppliers and many others to hold off on payment until the hotel was built, which they did.

Sharp's hotel was originally going to be called 'The Thunderbird', but that name was already registered. His brother-in-law, Eddie, was just back from Germany where he had stayed at a fine hotel called *VierJahrzeiten*, which translated as 'Four Seasons'. That was the limit of their market research on the name, and it stuck. Opened in 1961, and built around a central courtyard and pool, providing it with an oasis of calm in the middle of the city, the hotel was a different concept. Sharp hired an experienced hotelier, Ian Munro, to manage the new hotel, and the two became friends as well as colleagues. Together, they generated many ideas to attract customers to the hotel, and to ensure they came back. The Four Seasons was across the road from the headquarters of the Canadian Broadcasting Corporation, which provided considerable business.

The Golden Rule

Originally, there was no grand vision for the company. Coming from a building background, Sharp, did not know anything about the hotel business. However, from the start he always approached it from the perspective of the customer and how the hotel could add value to their experience. For example, Four Seasons was the first hotel company to make shampoo available in the guests' bathrooms. He recalls that growing up in a house with three sisters, there was always shampoo in the bathroom, and he just expected it to be there.[4]

In many ways, Four Seasons has defined the concept of the luxury hotel in terms of service excellence and top-class facilities and operations. It has focused on the affluent, frequent traveller and built a worldwide reputation and brand. Sharp considers brand names to be only as good as what they represent and the confidence that people have in them. Central to its definition of luxury are the people who work in Four Seasons and its unique culture. The guiding philosophy that rules how the company treats all its stakeholders, including its employees, is the "Golden Rule" – treat others as you would like them to treat you. This particular value is the cornerstone of its corporate culture.

The first hotel was a success and another hotel followed, also in Toronto. Sharp saw a 16-acre site for sale near a park and though he convinced his original backers to go again, none of them had any spare cash. They would have to leverage the entire amount. He went back to the Bank of Nova Scotia and, much to his surprise, the bank agreed to lend him the $600,000 he needed. Once again, suppliers and workers agreed to hold off on payment until the hotel was complete. Sharp asked Ian Munro to find another manager for the first hotel and to come over and manage the new hotel himself. The hotel – the Inn on the Park – also had a new fitness institute for guests (the first in the industry) and a cabaret club.

---

[4] Sharp, I. (2009).

London

Sharp's third hotel venture was in London, where he linked up with the McAlpine Group, a large construction company and owner of the Dorchester Hotel. Primarily dealing with Sir Gerald Glover, who became a life-long friend, the negotiations took a number of years. McAlpines wanted a large, mid-range hotel, as they believed London was more than adequately serviced by long-established luxury hotels such as The Savoy, Claridges, The Dorchester, The Grosvenor and The Ritz. However, Sharp believed that international travel was on the increase and kept holding out for a luxury hotel. He finally got approval and work commenced. Once again, he picked the best furnishing, even personally testing numerous beds for comfort, before choosing a German-made bed. (Four Seasons was the first hotel group to make the quality of their beds such an important feature.) The London Inn on the Park opened in January 1970. Ian Munro was now overseeing three hotels. The new hotel quickly established itself and in its first year was awarded European Hotel of the Year.

Toronto Revisited

Around the same time, Sharp became involved in a bid to build a massive, 1,600-room hotel in Toronto. The project was way out of the league of his original backers. Instead, he approached the conglomerate ITT, which was in the process of taking over Sheraton Hotels. Sharp convinced them that he could build a flagship hotel for them, and invested $3.5 million for a 49% partnership with ITT to develop the hotel. Sheraton, now controlled by ITT, kept making changes to the new hotel in Toronto that did not meet with Sharp's approval, and which he believed were not in keeping with five-star standards. He decided to exercise his right to sell his share in the ITT partnership at the then market price, making an $18 million profit on his $3.5 million investment. This meant that he was able to clear his debts on his other hotels; it also taught him many lessons about dealing with large corporations.

Soon after pulling out of the ITT partnership, which had netted him a handsome profit, another deal Sharp got involved in cost him a lot of money. He had bought and prepared land on the waterfront in Vancouver, Canada, for building 1,000 apartments. He was approached by the city council and was asked to move the development a few hundred feet away from a nearby park. When he refused, they expropriated the land and he ended up with nothing. Had the development gone ahead, he would have made an enormous profit and, by his own admission, may not have built any more hotels. Along with some other deals that potentially could have ruined the company, Sharp decided to limit their financial liability in any future deals.[5]

Vision

From that point on, Sharp began developing a vision of specialising in medium-sized hotels (200–400 bedrooms) of exceptional quality and with the aim of being the best. Years after the London hotel opened, he asked Sir Gerald Glover why he trusted him with such a large project as the London Inn on the Park knowing that he did not have the financial wherewithal if things

---

[5] Sharp, I. (2009).

went wrong. Sir Gerald's response surprised but inspired Sharp: "My dear boy, over time you make a judgement about people. You develop a belief and a trust."[6]

Expansion

Four Seasons now manages 84 hotels in 35 countries worldwide. Three-quarters of their hotels are built by developers and then managed by Four Seasons. The company plans to double the number of hotels in its portfolio over the next 10 years. It was not all plain sailing getting to this point, and some deals did not work out, such as the Sheraton partnership in Toronto. As the company grew, some hotels were developed as greenfield sites and in other cases the company acquired established hotels and renovated them to Four Seasons standards. When Canada appeared to have no more potential for expansion for the company, Four Seasons looked to the United States, where the level of competition was a great deal stronger. The company landed some big deals, taking over the Clift in San Francisco and the Ritz-Carlton in Chicago. The Four Seasons in Washington was the first hotel they acquired in the US to bear the Four Seasons name. Perhaps their biggest coup was in 1981, when they secured the Pierre in New York, described by *The New Yorker* when it opened in 1930 as "a millionaire's Elysium". The Pierre proved a difficult assignment; numerous owners with different agendas had to be satisfied, as well as a unionised staff, many of whom participated in a city-wide hotel strike in 1985 when managers took over many roles themselves and staff from other Four Seasons hotels were drafted in to keep the hotel open. Four Seasons relinquished the management contract in 2007, when they opened a hotel under the Four Seasons name in New York.

In the early 1980s, the company experienced a lot of demand from other hotel owners to take on the management of their hotels on a contract basis. Finding enough staff of the right calibre for rapid expansion was going to be a problem, and Four Seasons declined most of the offers. It proved to be a fortuitous decision as recession hit world markets and demand for hotels dropped. The company was already highly-geared and under pressure from the banks. However, while most major hotel chains made drastic cuts at this time, Four Seasons did the opposite: they continued to invest in upgrading facilities. To get the extra funding from the banks, Sharp had to use all his Four Seasons' shares as collateral. The hotel industry is cyclical and, once the recession passed, the company grew at varying levels over the years as they expanded into other countries.

The 1990s saw further expansion. The Four Seasons Maui opened in Hawaii in 1990; this was the first resort the company built, providing a wide range of sporting and leisure amenities for their guests. A new hotel in Tokyo soon followed. Doing business in Japan proved to be a challenge initially as the company found the business culture very different. A hotel in the Caribbean proved challenging from a different perspective as a hurricane destroyed the West Indian island of Nevis soon after the hotel had opened. Opportunities in Europe were harder to find as so many of the main cities had well-established luxury hotels. Soon after the collapse of the Berlin Wall in 1989, Four Seasons built a hotel in Berlin, but the city did not grow according to their expectations and the hotel was sold at a loss some years later.

---

[6] Sharp, I. (2009).

The company's biggest deal to date was when it bought the troubled Regent hotel chain in August 1992, giving Four Seasons control of 15 hotels in choice Asian locations. In one move, the size of the group greatly increased. It was also a tremendous coup for the company as they acquired control from the Regent's bankers at a knock-down price. Unfortunately, the acquisition happened at the time of the slump following the first Gulf War, and the group's earnings dropped substantially. Four Seasons tried to enter the Indian market on a number of occasions and protracted and costly negotiations proved fruitless as different investors pulled out at the last minute. However, in 2008 the Four Seasons Mumbai opened. The company also ran into difficulty in Caracas, Venezuela, in the mid-1990s when they partnered with a developer in the city to build a luxury hotel. Having put much time and effort into the deal, the hotel opened in January 2001. Soon after, relations with the developer turned sour and Four Seasons lost $10 million. The case is being pursued in the courts in the US, but the company is not hopeful of a successful outcome.

Competition

There are numerous luxury hotels in every country. (In Ireland alone, there are 35 Five Star hotels – a considerably high number for the size of the country.) Michael Porter's work examines how businesses can create a competitive advantage over their rivals. What makes the Four Seasons different from its competitors and what makes people want to pay a premium for this product? A necessary part of creating a difference is preserving the elements that separate a business from its rivals and ensuring that competitors do not imitate the very aspects of that business that made it different in the first place. Worldwide competition for Four Seasons comes from other luxury chains like Ritz-Carlton, Marriott, Westin, and Sheraton. In each major city there will also be single stand-alone hotels that have achieved superior reputations, such as the Savoy in London.

The 'Four Pillars'

Four Seasons differentiates itself based on what the company terms the "Four Pillars", which were developed at different stages over its history.[7] Isadore Sharp describes the four pillars thus:

- **Quality:** "We will only operate medium-sized hotels of exceptional quality with an objective to be the best." (1972)
- **Service:** "True luxury will be defined not by architecture or décor, but by service. So we must make the quality of our service our distinguishing feature and a competitive advantage." (1976)
- **Culture:** "We will create a work ethic based on the Golden Rule to give our people a frame-work to pursue a superior service culture." (1980)
- **Brand:** "We will grow as a management company and build a brand synonymous with quality." (1986)

Four Seasons has recently added another strand, or fifth pillar:

"To become our industry's undisputed leader, known globally as number one."

---

[7] Higley, J. (2007:26), "The Man Behind the Brand", *Luxury Hotelier*, September 2007.

Over the years, Sharp spent much time travelling around the group, talking to managers and staff in the different hotels, preaching the Four Seasons 'gospel' and getting everyone to understand the importance of service and trust. However, not all of the managers were buying into this new culture, and changing their management style from command and control to one based on mutual respect, where the emphasis was on leadership and developing the full potential of each individual staff member was not an easy task. In some cases, it had to be made clear that those managers would not have a future in the company if they could not adapt their approach. This was personally a difficult process for Issy, but one he was absolutely convinced had to be done. As new managers replaced the ones who left, they were hired first and foremost for their compatibility with the Four Seasons' corporate culture, excellent communication skills, and strong leadership and coaching skills.

The Product

'Luxury' is a relative concept and it can be easily imitated. While sumptuous facilities at Four Seasons hotels must be taken for granted, other aspects of the five pillars can help separate the company from its competitors. Brands represent a sense of promise to the guest in terms of what to expect. It is then up to the hotel to exceed that promise, and in so doing, generate loyalty and repeat custom. In that regard, Four Seasons differentiates itself from its competition. At one point, a prominent guest stopped coming to one of the Toronto Four Seasons hotels. Staff made enquiries and found that he was dissatisfied with the quality of the pillows. When management further investigated the matter, it was found that some other hotels had better quality pillows, and the pillows in all the Four Seasons hotels worldwide were duly changed. The former guest was invited back, and he has remained a loyal customer ever since.

Each Four Seasons hotel is designed and furnished to reflect its locality, and this is intended to give it a sense of place. Sharp personally approves the plans before any development starts. Many aspects of five-star luxury that today are taken for granted by travellers were first developed by Four Seasons, such as big bedrooms, sound-proofing from external noise, large bespoke beds, luxurious bathrooms with telephones, 24-hour room service, overnight laundry, non-smoking floors, twice-daily housekeeping service, and valet parking. While all of these factors could now be considered to be standard industry practice, the Four Seasons maintains its differential in the quality of its service. Employees are encouraged to note and remember guests' likes and dislikes. The company was the first to computerise a reservations system which would record guests' individual preferences. This would allow each hotel in the group to tailor its services accordingly.

Service is the product of people, systems and culture. These factors are built up over a period of time. In a globalised world, while comfort levels are constantly increasing, the one factor people value most of all is time. In that regard, good service can make the guests' time more productive and enjoyable. Service in the Four Seasons is therefore built around the guest's individual requirements and not restricted to set times for activities. Service standards are developed for all aspects of guest interaction. These are not prescriptive, but act as a general guide that allows the individual staff member to tailor the service to the needs of the customer, and is based on the 'Golden Rule'. In turn, it places a large degree of trust on the employee: on their character and their competence to do the job impeccably.

Mission Statement

Four Seasons created a corporate mission statement that would guide the actions of everyone in the organisation. It is designed to underpin their goals and beliefs, and how they interact with their guests.[8] This mission statement is shown below:

Four Seasons' Mission Statement

Who we are

We have chosen to specialise within the hospitality industry by offering only experiences of exceptional quality. Our objective is to be recognised as the company that manages the finest hotels, resorts and residence clubs wherever we locate.

We create properties of enduring value using superior design and finishes, and support them with a deeply instilled ethic of personal service. Doing so allows Four Seasons to satisfy the needs and tastes of our discriminating customers, and to maintain our position as the world's premier luxury hospitality company.

What we believe

Our greatest asset, and the key to our success, is our people.

We believe that each of us needs a sense of dignity, pride and satisfaction in what we do. Because satisfying our guests depends on the united efforts of many, and we are most effective when we work together co-operatively, respecting each other's contribution and importance.

How we succeed

We succeed when every decision is based on a clear understanding of and belief in what we do, and we couple this conviction with sound financial planning. We expect to achieve a fair and reasonable profit to ensure the prosperity of the company and to offer long-term benefits to our hotel owners, our customers and our employees.

How we behave

We demonstrate our beliefs most meaningfully in the way we treat each other and by the example we set for one another. In all our interactions with our guests, customers, business associates and colleagues, we seek to deal with others as we would have them deal with us.

---

8 See www.fourseasons.com/about_us/service_culture/ (accessed 28 April 2011).

Achieving the Mission

While increasing staff numbers can improve the quality of service that a hotel delivers, it will also push up costs. However, competing on service has allowed Four Seasons to achieve and maintain Rev PAR (revenue per available room) leadership.[9] It is not just about staff numbers but more about the quality of those people delivering that service. While the nature of the Four Seasons product has evolved, one constant that has remained, and is central to repeat business, is the quality of its employees. Well-trained staff are invaluable in generating repeat custom and in making guests less price sensitive.

Four Seasons has, over the years, developed a deep understanding of what their guests expect and a culture that facilitates meeting, and exceeding those expectations. The company is also constantly innovating. A major trend in recent years in the luxury market is for families to travel together, rather than just parents/individuals on their own. In response, Four Seasons has developed a broad range of services designed to meet the needs of families, which include programmes especially tailored for children and teenagers. It is all part of generating guest loyalty and repeat custom.

Hotel Divisions

Depending on their location, Four Seasons hotels are normally operated on the following lines, all of which are designed to provide a seamless service to the guest:

Operational hotel divisions
- Rooms
- Food and beverage
- Spa and fitness facilities
- Four Seasons Residences

Administrative hotel divisions
- Sales and marketing
- Engineering
- Administrative and general

Four Seasons' head office is in Toronto and is the base for a number of senior management positions including HR and Administration, Marketing, Finance, Worldwide Development, Business Administration and General Counsel. In 2011, Irishman Jim Fitzgibbon retired as President of worldwide hotel operations. In addition to the above positions, there are numerous vice presidents with responsibility for various functional roles and different geographical locations. Each hotel has a general manager responsible for all that happens in that hotel. By 2010, Four Seasons was

---

[9] Talbott, B. (2006) "The Power of Personal Service: Why it Matters. What Makes it Possible. How it Creates Competitive Advantage", *CHR Industry Perspectives*, No. 1, September 2006 (Cornell University).

running 39 hotels in North America and Canada, 22 in Asia/Pacific, and 12 in Middle East/Africa. In Europe, there are Four Seasons hotels in Budapest, Dublin, Florence, Geneva, Istanbul (2), Lisbon, London (2), Hampshire (England), Milan, Paris, Prague and Provence.

People

The company's overall philosophy for treating its staff is that, in a service environment, staff members cannot properly look after guests if they themselves are dissatisfied.

Four Seasons believes in treating every employee with dignity and respect. It aims to be fair and just in all its dealings, including selection, transfers, promotions, scheduling, training assignments, discipline and benefits. It has consistently ranked high in *Fortune* magazine's 100 Best Companies to Work For, and in other similar ranking systems around the world. Individual employees are recognised for their contribution.

In every country that Four Seasons operates, it has been able to find the exceptional employees which makes the company what it is. Team members develop camaraderie that makes co-operation the norm. People play a central role in service delivery. One of the main differentiators between service industries (such as hotels) and manufacturing is that, in service industries, production and consumption are largely simultaneous. Unlike quality control in manufacturing, service cannot be pre-checked for quality. Thus, the delivery of service in a hotel can make or break its reputation. The quality of its outcome is therefore solely dependent on its frontline employees, such as porters, receptionists and restaurant staff, and in most instances, these are not highly paid jobs. Managers cannot be everywhere at the same time, so trust plays a large part in daily operations. It is estimated that in a 200-room hotel, there can be as many as 5,000 interactions between guests and staff each day.[10] This provides a lot of opportunities to excel or to fall short of expectations. Four Seasons aims to have no mistakes in interacting with its guests; however, human nature being what it is, this will not always be achieved. While guests can therefore be disappointed, such situations can also provide new service opportunities and what guests usually remember is not the original problem, but how it was handled. Employees are encouraged to think for themselves and empowered to make decisions to solve the problem immediately.

The role of managers therefore is not so much tight supervision in the form of Taylor's "Scientific Management", but to act as mentors and develop their staff. Good communication is vital as all employees must always know precisely what is expected from them. They are given much latitude, but they also have challenging goals to meet. Managers must be up front with employees and let them know how they are getting on. Managers must also be visible – and accessible – and are expected to lead by example. Managers must realise that they operate in a glasshouse where everything they do is observed, and commented upon by staff. They are therefore expected to live up to company values.[11]

---

[10] Talbott, B. (2006).

[11] Sharp, I. (2010) Conference on Entrepreneurship at the Graduate school of Business, Stanford University. Available at www.videosurf.com/video/2010-conference-on-entrepreneurship-keynote-speaker-1237262530 (accessed 6 May 2010).

Many companies focus on remuneration as a means of attracting and retaining employees. While pay is important, Four Seasons also believes that other factors are even more important. Research among *Fortune* 100 companies[12] indicates that the three main things employees consider most important in choosing employers are:

- To work for leaders who inspire the best in individuals
- A physical environment that makes work more enjoyable
- A sense of purpose – a feeling that one is working for more than just a pay cheque, but that they are helping to build a company in which they can take pride.

It is this common sense of purpose that helps build teamwork and shared values that inspires commitment to the company's success. While the "Golden Rule" which mandates everyone to treat others as they would want to be treated is not a unique philosophy, in Four Seasons it is strictly enforced, as nothing will destroy management credibility faster than espousing the importance of its employees, while clearly demonstrating otherwise in its daily operations. The company treats staff complaints as seriously as it deals with guest complaints. Whenever hotel renovations are taking place, staff facilities are also upgraded. There is no class distinction – all employees from the general manger down eat together and there is no reserved parking for managers. Employees are nurtured to develop their full potential. There is a clear career path developed for them and all promotions are internal.

Training plays an essential part in ensuring that Four Seasons personnel deliver a high level of service on a consistent basis. It is regarded as an investment by which the company develops competences and builds confidence in staff members. Particular emphasis is then placed on the application of new learning in the workplace, thus creating a "learning organisation", designed to assist managers to get the best from their employees. Training managers, or "learning managers" as they are termed, are available to assess training needs and advise on appropriate solutions. Such solutions may not always involve additional training. The problem could be caused by poor morale, equipment or systems.

Overall, the company's approach to training is a dynamic one, allowing true development to take place.[13] People are seen as an asset, and not as a cost. Training is thus made easier by the quality of the employees that the company hires. In training its staff, the company places great emphasis on anticipating guests' needs rather than just learning to respond to requests. Training programmes are tailored to each individual and are provided at each stage of a person's career to help them develop their full potential. Such training is designed also to align the skills of the individual with the goals of the company, and throughout, there is a strong emphasis on teamwork, and particularly, the Golden Rule.

---

[12] Sharpe, I. (2010) (see above, n.11).

[13] http://jobs.fourseasons.com/workingatfourseasons/learninganddevelopment/Pages/LearningandDevelopment.aspx.

In recruiting staff, most hotels will usually look for experience. Four Seasons looks primarily for attitude. Sharp believes that anyone can be trained to be a waiter, but attitude is ingrained. Potential employees must be interested in people and be comfortable working in a service role. Sharp believes that these are qualities that people are brought up with. It is this common value system that binds people together irrespective of ethnicity, and therefore helps create a corporate culture that transcends borders. The company aims to have 90% of the staff in any hotel coming from the local area. Irrespective of the position for which they are applying, each employee is interviewed normally around four or five times, the last one by the general manager.

When Four Seasons opened in New York, it had 15,000 applicants for 400 places. Such a rigorous recruitment and selection procedure is inevitably very time-consuming and costly, but the company believes that it is not expensive in the long run as they do not have to deal with employees who are clearly unsuited to their jobs. Staff turnover at Four Seasons is less than half the industry average. Their highly-valued managers are constantly being head-hunted by recruitment companies, but by and large, they prefer to stay. Working for Four Seasons provides many intangible rewards in addition to the normal benefits that attract talented personnel. For all Four Seasons personnel, these benefits include free meals, medical care, pension arrangements and complimentary holidays at Four Seasons hotels. Staff members are also free to apply for transfer to other Four Seasons hotels around the world. Whenever a staff member leaves the company, HR conducts an exit interview and the information obtained is discussed by managers with a view to lessons learned.

Implementation

Many companies have espoused values that are never actually seen in practice or implemented. Four Seasons ensures that its values are enacted on a daily basis with its guests. It begins with the morning meeting, which includes the hotel manager, all departmental heads, and the guest relationship manager (departmental head level). The guest relationship manager goes through the guest list for the hotel, and everyone who will be arriving and checking out that day. The purpose is to identify the guests and their individual needs.

In a service industry that is so dependent on people, it is inevitable that things will go wrong from time to time. The daily meetings also include the "glitch report" – a review of anything that went wrong in the previous 24 hours, and what was done to rectify the matter. It ensures that all departments know that a particular individual was dissatisfied with an aspect of service, and all other staff members can make an extra effort to ensure nothing else goes wrong with that customer. The policy is that, if something is not up to standard, it must be rectified straight away, beginning with a sincere apology, and then whatever additional steps are required to ensure that the guest is satisfied. The third part of the meeting is a review of the coming day – the events that might be happening and the relevant times, as well as a staff review and any other matters that the hotel staff may need to know about. Good service can only come through teamwork, and that requires co-ordination.

Ownership

Though Four Seasons went public in 1985, launching on the New York stock exchange, it went private again in 2006 in a deal worth $3.4 billion.[14] Normally, the rationale for companies floating on the stock exchange is to raise equity for further development. There are also significant downsides, not least of all is the relentless demand for profits every quarter. Four Seasons needed an equity injection, but the primary reason was to secure its future free from such demands that would place short-term profitability above long-term success. It was funding, without the pressure. The investors: Cascade Investment, controlled by Microsoft's Bill Gates, and Kingdom Hotels, controlled by Saudi Prince Al-Waleed bin Talal, were viewed by Sharp as long-term investors who considered the hotel industry worldwide to be a major growth industry. Sharp still retains a 5% interest and remains as CEO.

In any company, succession is an important issue, but while Four Seasons is very much associated with Sharp, there is an extensive senior management team in place that has on average 17 years' experience of the company and how it operates. Since Ian Munro died in 1976, the company has hired many other experienced hoteliers including Michael Lambert, John Sharpe, John Richards and Barbara Talbott. These managers have been promoted internally, and have undergone training and development programmes that prepared them for their next managerial role.

The Four Seasons culture is so ingrained in the company that it will remain long after Isadore Sharp retires. Going private has effectively secured the future for the 84 hotels it currently manages, and those about to come on stream.

The Four Seasons hotel in Dublin was owned by an 18-strong syndicate known as the Nollaig Partnership, which was put together by financier Derek Quinlan. The hotel has 183 rooms and 14 suites, as well as a number of private, serviced apartments on the top floor. Prices for rooms range from a few hundred euro per night up to €2,000 for a presidential suite. The hotel cost around €90 million to build and was opened in 2001. Anglo Irish Bank part-financed the deal and is owed €50 million, of which it has recourse to only €5 million from the syndicate.[15] The hotel lost €2 million in 2009, although it has since improved its position. The hotel was sold in June 2011 to British property investors for €15 million – a fraction of what it cost to build. This reflects the downturn in the hotel sector in Ireland as well as the onerous terms of the lease signed by the Four Seasons and the owners of the land on which the hotel was built, the Royal Dublin Society. The lease comes with an annual rent of €700,000 and the contract stipulates that a five-star hotel must operate there.

Corporate Social Responsibility

The Sharp family suffered personal tragedy in 1978 when their son Chris died of cancer, aged 17. Two years later, it was brought to Issy's attention that a young man, Terry Fox, who had lost

---

[14] Higley, J. (2007:26) "The Man Behind the Brand", *Luxury Hotelier*, September 2007.
[15] Lyons, T. (2011) "Brothers Eye Four Seasons Deal", *The Sunday Times*, 1 May 2011. Business, p.1.

a leg to cancer, and had an artificial leg fitted, was running across Canada to raise money for cancer research. Inspired by his tenacity, Issy told Terry that Four Seasons would help raise $10 million for the fund. Terry was making great progress, but having covered 3,339 miles, the cancer had spread to his lungs forcing him to retire. By that stage they had raised $24 million. Terry died the following June, but before he died, Issy pledged that he would organise an annual Terry Fox memorial run. By 2008, some $500 million has been raised by volunteers worldwide for the fund.[16] Four Seasons is also involved in many other fundraising events as well as instigating many initiatives for protecting the natural environment in locations where it operates hotels.

The Future

Four Seasons currently has 50 new hotels at various stages of development around the globe, and it is planned to have up to 150 new hotels over the next eight to 10 years. Europe, in particular, is providing the company with some of its best opportunities.

Sharp says he was often asked: what was the ideal size of the hotel group? How many more hotels could he add and still maintain the focus on customer service? These were questions to which he did not know the answer for many years. The figure kept constantly changing. The criterion he set for limiting growth was when the next hotel he built was not an improvement on previous hotels; it would then be time to stop. As time went by, he realised it was not about size, but focusing on a plan that helped each hotel become the best they could be. Now that the company has grown, it can provide considerable support at corporate level to each individual hotel, and so help build the reputation of the brand. In terms of goals, the focus for Four Seasons is on the three Ps: people, product, and profit. Given the size of the investment by Bill Gates and Prince Al-Waleed, it would appear that the prioritising people and product-before-profit is still providing adequate return on investment.

---

[16] Sharp, I. (2009).

Eason & Son Ltd – A New Chapter

Sheila O'Mahony[1]

This case study provides an overview of Eason & Son Ltd, Ireland's largest retailer of books, newspapers, stationery and cards. Despite its iconic stature, the business has faced many difficulties that have challenged the viability of its business model. These difficulties arose due to significant developments in the book retailing industry, including changing economic, competitive and technological factors. This case explores these changing market conditions and illustrates the challenges faced by the Eason company in responding to these changes.

Introduction

The book retailing industry in Ireland has undergone significant changes in recent years. The US bookstore Borders pulled out of Ireland in August 2009; this was followed by the collapse of Irish book chain Hughes & Hughes in February 2010 (six Hughes & Hughes stores have since reopened under different ownership and seven of its airport stores were taken over by Eason & Son Ltd); and the closure of Dublin's two branches of Waterstone's in February 2011.

These developments have certainly sent a shiver up the spine of the Irish book-selling trade and, indeed, the Irish publishing sector in general. This shake-up of the book retailing market has not been unique to Ireland, with many booksellers and bookstores around the world either downsizing or going out of business. Factors such as increasing competition from supermarkets and online retailers, the growing market for e-books, along with the economic downturn, have all contributed to the decline of more traditional book-selling businesses.

Ireland's largest and best-known bookseller, Eason, has not gone unscathed by the adverse market conditions. The company suffered losses of €10.09 million and a decline of 16.4% in total turnover in the financial year ended January 2010.[2] A reassessment of Eason's position in the marketplace and an examination of the strategic options available to the company are duly required. Providing an overview of Eason's current business model, this case study focuses primarily on Eason's Irish retail book business and the market conditions in which it operates.

---

[1] Sheila O'Mahony is a Lecturer in Marketing at the Institute of Technology, Tralee. This case study is intended to be used as the basis for class discussion rather than to illustrate either effective or ineffective handling of a management situation. The case was compiled from published sources.

[2] www.cro.ie (accessed 22 April 2011).

About the Company

Eason & Son Ltd was originally founded in 1819 as Johnston & Company, a newspaper advertising agency based on Eden Quay, Dublin. The firm was subsequently taken over by W.H. Smith, who appointed Charles Eason, a British printer who had been running one of Smith's UK bookstalls, as its manager in 1856. Charles Eason's arrival to run Smith's Irish operation coincided with the rapid growth of the bookselling and newspaper industry in Ireland due to the expansion of the railway network, the emergence of national daily newspapers and a growing literacy rate.[3]

Eason eventually bought the Irish business from W.H. Smith in 1886 and together with his son John, they formed the present private company, Eason & Son Ltd. Under its new ownership, the company expanded rapidly, with the addition of wholesale book and stationery departments, an advertising section and a circulating library. The company was also closely involved in the literary revival that occurred in Ireland in the 19th Century. With the growth in literacy, printed information became more important and Eason's railway bookstalls became increasingly popular. By 1900, the company controlled most of the bookstall and newspaper trade in Ireland.[4]

The business continued to expand throughout the 20th Century and today Eason is Ireland's largest book retailer with 60 stores in both the Republic of Ireland and Northern Ireland employing over 1,000 people.[5] Eason also operates a newspaper magazine distribution arm and two companies in South Africa, which sell mobile phone card 'top-ups' and prepaid electricity. Details of Eason's current business divisions are outlined in **Figure 1** below.

Eason's Retail Business

Eason's retail outlets are located in prime positions throughout the island of Ireland, including high street locations, shopping centres and train and bus stations. In 2010, Eason secured its presence in Dublin Airport (Terminal 1) and Cork Airport with the acquisition of seven airport stores from the insolvent Hughes & Hughes book retailer. These airport stores operate under a five-year licence from the Dublin Airport Authority (DAA).

Eason has a total of 60 stores throughout the island of Ireland, more than a quarter of which are franchises. Eason's franchising strategy enables the business to grow its market share while avoiding the logistical problems and financial outlay involved in opening new stores. It opened its first franchise store in Monaghan in 2004 and now has a total of 16 franchise arrangements spread across the country from Donegal to Dungarvan.[6]

---

[3] Brennan, C. (2004), "Brought to Book", *Business & Finance*, 8 April 2004.

[4] *Ibid.*

[5] www.irishpublishingnews.com/2011/03/30/eason-reveals-more-details-of-its-new-strategic-plan (accessed 21 April 2011).

[6] www.eason.ie/stores (accessed 20 April 2011).

Principal Group Companies and Joint Ventures	Principal Activity
Incorporated in the Republic of Ireland	
Eason & Son (NI) Ltd.	News agents, booksellers and stationers.
EM News Distribution (Irl) Ltd.	Newspaper and magazine distribution.
Eason Advertising Service Ltd.	Advertising agency (disposed of in 2010).
Incorporated in Northern Ireland	
Eason Library Supplies Ltd.	Property holding.
Eason Electronic International Ltd.	Investment company.
EM News Distribution (NI) Ltd.	Newspaper and magazine distribution.
Incorporated in South Africa	
Eason Electronic (Pty) Ltd.	Distributor of mobile phone pre-paid credits.
Eason Electricity (Pty) Ltd.	Distributor of electricity pre-paid credits.

Source: www.cro.ie (2011)

Figure 1 – *Eason's Business Divisions 2010*

Eason stores stock an extensive range of books, newspapers, magazines, greeting cards and stationery. Some shops also stock music, DVDs, toys, arts and craft supplies, computer accessories and confectionery. In-store cafes are also available at selected Eason's high street stores.

Eason's Internet Presence

Eason's online store was set up in 1998 to enable customers to purchase books and Eason gift cards through its website at http://www.eason.ie. This website sells both books available in its retail shops as well as over 4.5 million additional titles not normally carried in all its shops.[7] Eason started selling electronic books (e-books) on its website in March 2010 and now offers a limited range of new releases, classics and Irish books at prices somewhat higher than their physical world counterparts. The store also sells Sony Readers (electronic reading devices) to enable customers to read the e-books at their convenience, anytime, anywhere.[8]

Eason maintains a social media presence on both the Twitter and Facebook social networking websites. Eason has over 1,700 followers on Twitter (@easons)[9] and its Facebook page has developed a significant online book club community with almost 7,000 members.[10] This is used primarily to

---

[7] www.eason.ie/about (accessed 20 April 2011).

[8] www.irishpublishingnews.com/2010/03/23/eason-launches-a-new-ebook-store (accessed 21/04/2011).

[9] http//:twitter.com/#!/easons (accessed 28 April 2011).

[10] http//:facebook.com/EasonBookClub (accessed 25 April 2011).

communicate directly with customers, enable customers to interact with each other and to highlight book-related events. Eason is satisfied with the popularity of its Facebook page and regards it as useful for brand-building rather than as a sales outlet.[11]

Factors Affecting the Retail Book Industry

Traditional, high street book retailers are encountering many challenges at present. Due to the global nature of businesses today, similar challenges face all book retailers regardless of where they are located in the world. These challenges include the worldwide economic downturn, increased competition from supermarkets and online retailers and the rapidly growing market for e-books.

Ireland's recession commenced in 2008 when economic activity began to decline in response to rising interest rates and the bursting of the property bubble. The pace of decline accelerated markedly in 2009 as the global economy suffered the deepest economic slump since the 1930s. During this time, many businesses folded altogether, unemployment soared and pay rates declined. The retail sector suffered from a major decline in consumer spending and the book trade has not been immune from this. While books, magazines, etc., remain relatively inexpensive products to buy, they are regarded by most consumers as non-essential purchases, with the resultant decline in sales. Sales of books, newspapers and stationery in Ireland fell by 9.3% in 2010.[12] Figures from Nielsen, which relate only to book sales, show that Irish book sales fell by about 10% in 2010 to €135 million.[13]

Traditional 'bricks and mortar' booksellers such as Eason continue to face stiff competition from supermarkets and pure online retailers such as Amazon. Supermarkets such as Tesco and Dunnes Stores offer their customers best sellers at discounted prices and the convenience of purchasing newspapers, magazines, stationery and greeting cards alongside the necessities. They also offer consumers the convenience of doing all their shopping under one roof rather than visiting a store at a prime location, where access, traffic and parking might be a problem.

Online book retailers and resellers such as Amazon, The Book Depository and eBay are continuing to make inroads into the sales of books sold at traditional retailers through their sales of new and secondhand books. These 'click-only' retailers enjoy the benefits of lower operating costs as well as the ability to offer their customers access to an unprecedented range of titles, 24-hour shopping and home delivery, all at hugely discounted prices. Irish consumers are increasingly spending more time and money online availing of the discounts offered by these online retailers. Research into the Irish consumer's online shopping habits has found that over 30% of their online purchases are on books/magazines/newspapers/e-learning material.[14] 23% of Irish book readers are now buying their books online, with only 46% still buying books through bookshop chains like Eason.[15]

---

[11] O'Mahony, C. (2010), "Eason goes face to face with readers", *Sunday Business Post*, 21 March 2010.

[12] www.cso.ie/releasespublications/documents/services/2010/rsi_nov2010.pdf (accessed 24 April 2011).

[13] Hancock, C. (2011), "One more thing", *Irish Times*. 4 February 2011.

[14] www.cso.ie/releasespublications/documents/information_tech/2008/ictireland2008.pdf (accessed 24 April 2011).

[15] www.amarach.com/blog/2010/04/a-world-of-books.html (accessed 23 April 2011).

The growth in the availability of electronic books (e-books) is increasingly affecting the sales of printed books available through high street bookstores. E-books can be read from a laptop, PC, PDA, Smart phone (such as an iPhone or Blackberry) or from a specialised electronic reading device such as Amazon's 'Kindle' or the Sony 'Reader'. The ability to buy and start reading a new book instantly from wherever the consumer happens to be is an advantage that conventional book retailers cannot offer without embracing the digital format.

The demand for e-books has grown particularly in the wake of Smart phones, e-reading devices and tablet computers. In 2009, Amazon's sales of e-books outstripped its sales of physical books.[16] Industry sources predict that e-book sales will make up between 10% and 40% of all book sales within five years' time.[17] 30% of Irish adults have already read e-books on some form of electronic device (mostly PCs/laptops) and 48% of them plan to read e-books at some time in the future as depicted in **Figure 2** below.[18] Irish data on actual sales of e-books is not yet available. However, sales of e-books in the US market increased by 116% to total $69.9 million in 2010.[19] Competition in this emerging market

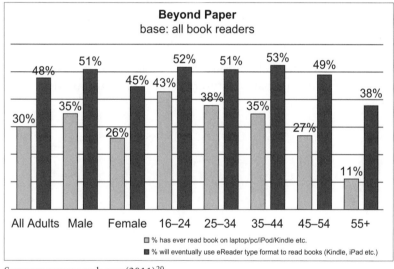

Source: www.amarach.com(2011)[20]

Figure 2 – *Irish Usage of e-Books*

---

[16] www.guardian.co.uk/books/2010/jul/20/amazon-ebook-digital-sales-hardbacks-us (accessed 23 April 2011).

[17] Foley, C. (2010), "E-book sales are expected to make up as much as two-fifths of the publishing market within five years, so can Irish publishers afford to be left on the shelf?", *Sunday Times,* 2 May 2010.

[18] www.amarach.com/blog/2010/04/a-world-of-books.html (accessed 23 April 2011).

[19] www.irishpublishingnews.com/2011/03/22/briefly-noted-e-book-sales-exploded-by-116-this-january-totaling-69-9-million-in-the-u-s (accessed 21 April 2011).

[20] www.amarach.com/blog/2010/04/a-world-of-books.html (accessed 23 April 2011).

is fierce with major Internet players such as Amazon, Apple and Google having introduced their own technologies and continuing to stake out their positions. Many conventional book retailers have also entered this evolving market space by selling e-books through their own websites and one US bookstore, Barnes & Noble, has even developed its own e-reading device, the 'Nook'.

Time for Change at Eason

The rapid economic, competitive and market-based changes taking place in the retail book industry present many challenges for Eason. The company has already suffered losses of €10.09 million in the year ending 31 January 2010, and company turnover for all its businesses (including joint ventures and discontinued operations) fell from €375.4 million to €313.7 million or 16.4% in 2009.[21] Retail revenue in particular fell by 5% across the company's operations in the Republic of Ireland.[22] In light of these difficulties, Conor Whelan, Eason's Managing Director, has set about overhauling the company. As a starting point, he commissioned research amongst consumers, employees and other stakeholders to gain an insight into the inherent problems at Eason. He and his team also visited 'best in class' retailers in the UK and US as a benchmarking and learning exercise. Two of the biggest problems identified by the research were the company's "archaic and clunky IT" and its "retailing weaknesses, such as cluttered, dated stores, poor brand positioning and lack of innovation".[23] Armed with these insights, Whelan now needs to examine the strategic options available to the company and implement new business and marketing strategies that will turn the company around and safeguard the future of this iconic Irish retailer.

---

[21] www.cro.ie (accessed 22 April 2011).

[22] Percival, G. (2010), "Eason halves losses to €10m as retail revenues fall 5% in Republic", *The Examiner*, 21 August 2010.

[23] Coffey, A (2011), "Eason must turn over a new leaf", *The Sunday Times*, 3 April 2011, p.6.

Bonuses at the Bank

Gerry Gallagher[1]

This case examines organisational leadership and culture. It looks at the concept of bonus payments as a motivational tool for achieving organisational goals. It also examines the ethical nature of such payments as well as the implications for other stakeholders.

Few events caused such a public outcry in 2010 as AIB's announcement that it was going to pay bonuses to some of its staff. When the news broke, the bank pulled back on its promise to pay the bonuses, but not before there was more reputational damage done. For those staff members concerned, they were not happy that public opinion had blocked their payments. One of them initiated High Court proceedings to force AIB to pay what he saw was his legal entitlement. The case was listed for hearing in late 2010.

High Court Case

As a result of a High Court ruling in November 2010, AIB was directed to pay a bonus of €161,000 (along with 8% interest) to John Foy, an employee in its Capital Markets division (which comprises Global Treasury, Investment Banking and Corporate Banking). As a result of that decision, the bank was of the opinion that it also had to pay backdated bonuses to approximately 90 employees who had also initiated court action. The High Court ruling affected employees in the Capital Markets Division of AIB and relates to their performance in 2008. The case was taken by one trader who sued the bank for non-payment of a €161,000 bonus and who claimed in court that the non-payment would cause "unjustified hardship" to himself and his family. The bank said it would honour contractual payments for 2008 but that it had no plans to pay any bonuses for 2009. Staff in other parts of AIB were also claiming they should be paid bonuses.[2]

The Minister for Finance at the time, Mr Brian Lenihan, stated that the bank was obliged to pay the bonus to John Foy because of the decision of the High Court. However, the Court's judgment was not after deliberation of both sides of the argument, as AIB did not defend the test case brought against it by Mr Foy. In turn, this judgment triggered the payment of bonus payments to some 2,400 other staff members across AIB. The High Court did not decide that the bank was legally obliged to make the payments *per se*. Rather, it was a foregone conclusion because the bank did not enter a defence. As a result, the Court had no option but to allow the claim. A spokesperson for the bank stated that the bank was not in a position to enter a bonafide defence as it had been advised that the payments were legal obligations, and it could only enter a defence to the claim by swearing

---

[1] This case is intended for class discussion and not as an illustration of good or bad practice.

[2] Lynch, S. (2010), "AIB to pay up to €10m in backdated employee bonuses", *Irish Times*, 10 November 2010, p.18.

an affidavit that it had a bona fide defence and that the bank was not going through the motions of entering a defence simply to delay or frustrate the legal process. The bank also stated that the payments were for 2008 only, and that no bonus payments were being made for 2009 or for 2010.

In December 2010, Larry Broderick, General Secretary of the Irish Bank Officials Association, made a statement that bank executives should consider deferring bonus payments until a time when the bank sare in a better financial position. Mr Broderick stated that bonuses had generated a "bad culture" in banking and should not be part of future pay structures:

> "The excessive pursuit of narrowly-focused targets by AIB and other institutions in order to maximise shareholder-value in the short-term, while inevitably undermining the long-term stability of the bank, lies at the heart of the current financial crisis which has done so much damage to the Irish economy."[3]

He added that most AIB workers did not receive bonuses and that frontline members of his association had experienced abuse from members of the public over the conduct of the bank.[4] One banker who regularly received bonuses took a different view. He complained of long hours working in trading rooms: "Let the people who are currently trying to slit your throats make up the profit and tax shortfall. I am currently supporting about 10 people on the dole through my taxes."[5]

The payments by AIB were bonuses for "exceptional effort" during 2008, which was the year the bank in effect became insolvent due to its reckless lending practices. The Executive Chairman of the bank, Mr David Hodgkinson, said the payments "reflected AIB's past and was not the way we intend to conduct ourselves in the future". A number of charities called on those receiving bonuses to donate their bonuses to them as corporate donations had fallen off considerably due to the recession. As a result of the High Court ruling, AIB was to pay €40 million of public money in bonuses to 2,400 staff members, but the organisation did a U-turn in regard to the bonus payments.

The bank traditionally regarded the payment of the bonuses as a normal part of banking practice designed to motivate staff to work harder. This would have been normal practice across the financial services industry for many years. In many cases, staff remuneration was based on a basic salary and an additional bonus, payable when certain agreed targets were met. It was seen as aligning the setting of strategic goals with the successful implementation of those goals. It was regarded as a 'win-win' situation: the bank increased its profits and the individuals that contributed to the greater profits were rewarded for the extra effort involved. That would have been the traditional procedure. On this occasion, however, while the Capital Markets division of the bank may have been profitable overall, these bonus payments were announced when senior managers in AIB knew that the bank itself would require a rescue package from the State. On December 21, 2008, the Minister for Finance, Mr Lenihan announced that AIB would need an initial public recapitalisation amounting to €3,500,000,000. This money was paid to the bank less than two months later on 11 February 2009.

---

[3] Carrol, S. (2010), "Banks should defer bonuses – union", *Irish Times*, 11 December 2010.

[4] "Lenihan 'powerless' to stop AIB paying out bonuses", *Irish Independent*, 13 December 2010.

[5] Bielenberg, K. (2010), "Of course I deserve a bonus. My taxes pay for 10 people on the dole", *Irish Independent*, 18 December 2010.

AIB would subsequently require many more billions of Euros from the State, with the State eventually owning 99.5% of the bank's share capital.

Writing in the *Irish Times* in December 2010, Fintan O'Toole stated that the procedure for the payment of annual bonuses in AIB was that the amount of the bonus that each individual would get for the previous year would be announced at the end of March and staff would receive the bonus by the end of April, along with their salary. If this procedure had been adhered to in 2009, the Government would have been in a position to block any such payments before they were announced. However, it appears there was a change in policy at AIB, and staff members who were eligible for a bonus were called individually to a special meeting with senior managers on 29 January 2009 and were informed that their bonus for the previous year was being brought forward and would instead be paid on 25 February. Staff would normally get a letter detailing the payments that they were to receive. However, on this occasion, they did not receive such a letter, but were told that the meeting constituted a verbal contract that was legally binding and to treat the matter as confidential.

In addition to the bringing forward of the payments, what also surprised staff was the size of the payments they were to receive – they were much bigger than they had received in previous years:

> "Not only were the bonuses brought forward ... they were also unexpectedly large. According to my source: 'It was the general view of staff that this was the largest bonus that had been paid in any year by the bank, much to the surprise of employees. However, it was also the [well-informed] belief that this would be the last bonus paid for some time, hence the overcompensation'."[6]

The payments to staff were also unusual in a number of ways. For most of the staff concerned, their contracts did not specify any bonus payments. Instead, they were regarded by staff as custom and practice and, over the years, became an expectation. The payments were announced after the Government had stated that AIB would require public money to remain in operation, but before the transfer of the funding was completed. On this occasion, the payments were also much larger than in previous years as if to compensate staff as payments would certainly cease for a number of years.[7]

News of the 29 January 2009 meeting concerning the bonus payments to staff leaked out to the *Irish Times*, and following a report in the paper by John Collins, AIB announced that the payments were being deferred. The bank also stated that the decision to pay the bonuses in February was as a result of a change in policy regarding bonuses that was taken in 2007.

Blocking of Payment

Initially, the Government took no action to stop the payment by AIB to its staff. Nor did it instruct AIB to mount a legal challenge to the case being taken by John Foy. Junior Minister Barry Andrews stated: "To be honest, it seems this money will be paid out." Finance Minister, Brian Lenihan said after the High Court judgment that the decision was made by the courts. The AIB bonuses triggered a wave of public anger that finally provoked the Government into action. On 13 December 2010, Mr Lenihan wrote to the executive chairman of AIB and informed him that the Government would

---

[6] O'Toole, F. (2010), "Inflated bonuses rushed through as bailout loomed", *Irish Times*, 14 December 2010, p.12.
[7] *Ibid.*

withhold any further state aid to the bank if it proceeded with paying staff bonuses, irrespective of when those payments were earned. The letter reads as follows in **Figure 1**[8]:

Dear Mr Hodgkinson,

As I have already indicated, I am extremely unhappy at the prospect of substantial sums being paid in bonuses to AIB staff. I am aware that those claiming the bonuses did so under the terms of their employment contracts. However, it is obvious that the situation of the bank has changed drastically since the period in which the bonuses were supposedly earned and indeed that the foundations of the bank's problems were laid down in that and earlier periods. Furthermore, the bonuses are referable to a period in which the State had to provide financial support to enable the bank to meet its financial and regulatory obligations. The financial difficulties of the bank were clearly a supervening event which was not contemplated at the time of any agreement in relation to bonus payments.

You will be fully aware of the extent to which state support, in a variety of forms, has already been provided, and of the fact that without such support AIB could not have survived until now. I am sure you are also conscious, as I am, of the urgent need for further support, on an enormous scale. Without such support, these bonuses clearly could not be paid. Furthermore the bank could not have continued to operate without this financial support and the employees claiming the bonuses would almost certainly have had their employment contracts terminated.

Keeping systematically important banks functioning is not something that is done in a vacuum, and State support since the crisis began has been provided subject to various conditions. Those conditions were designed not only to achieve important economic and financial outcomes but to demonstrate to the Irish public, who must ultimately fund the support being provided, that their interests are being taken into account by the Government and the banks. Without a measure of public acceptance, no Government could provide support for the banks on the scale needed. Accordingly, I wish to inform you that the provision of further State funding to AIB will be conditional, inter alia, on the non-payment of bonuses no matter when they may have been earned. As AIB could not be in a position to pay without State support, past, present and to come, I believe that this condition is reasonable and proportionate. Nothing in this letter is intended to prevent the bank meeting its obligations on foot of a Court Order already obtained.

Yours sincerely,
Brian Lenihan TD
Minister for Finance

Figure 1 – *Government Directive to AIB on Bonus Payments*

---

[8] O'Halloran, B. (2010), "Payments could not be tolerated in light of €13.5 bn bill for taxpayer", *Irish Times*, 14 December 2010, p.7.

On receipt of the letter, the Board of AIB held an emergency meeting and made a decision not to pay the bonus payments to the 2,400 staff members. Subsequent to the meeting, on 13 December 2010, AIB issued the following statement

The Board of Allied Irish Banks, plc. met this evening to consider a letter received from the Minister for Finance in relation to the payment of bonuses to certain employees. Previously the board had received strong legal advice that it was obliged to pay these bonuses. However, the letter from the Minister conveys a decision by him to legislate which overtakes this obligation. In his letter, the Minister stated that the provision of further State funding to AIB will be conditional on the non-payment of any bonuses awarded, no matter when they may have been earned. The letter to the board stated that without the State support which had been provided in a variety of forms, AIB could not have survived until now.

The bank very much appreciates the support it has received to date from the State and the Irish taxpayers and acknowledges that it will continue to rely on this support for some time to come. Accordingly, the board has decided not to pay the bonuses. The executive chairman of AIB, David Hodgkinson said: "The board of AIB very much welcomes the actions of the Minister and is relieved to be in a position not to pay these bonuses. We are determined to position the bank to play a full role in the recovery and development of the Irish economy. In doing so we are committed to treating our customers, staff, the taxpayer and the public in a fair and transparent manner."[9]

Figure 2 – *Response of the AIB Board*

The following day, 14 December, the Minister made amendments to the Credit Institutions (Stabilisation) Bill 2010, which gave legislative effect to the memorandum of understanding with the European Union and the International Monetary Fund. The President of Ireland, Mary McAleese, called a meeting of the Council of State to see if the Bill might be unconstitutional. Following a meeting of the Council, the President subsequently signed the Bill into law.

Minister Lenihan also stated that AIB was correct in not entering a defence in relation to the case taken by John Foy stating that a sworn defence was required and AIB was not in a position to swear a defence as the employees had entitlements to bonuses under their contracts. In the Dáil, opposition members stated that the Minister was only reacting to public outrage on the matter. Labour TD, Pat Rabbitte, said it was a U-turn by the Government and the board of AIB:

"This is another case of where the Government and the board of a State-funded bank have had to be shamed into reversing a decision that was patently unjustifiable. What this episode has shown is that the Government is not exercising the degree of supervision of the banks

---

[9] O'Halloran, B. (2010), "Payments could not be tolerated in light of €13.5 bn bill for taxpayer", *Irish Times*, 14 December 2010, p.7.

that the present crisis requires and that there is still little or no change in the governance culture in the banks."[10]

Subsequently, the executive chairman of AIB, David Hodgkinson, issued a statement to staff saying:

"The issues we are facing mean that the bank currently relies on Government and taxpayer support and I am working to ensure that, in future, our pay and benefits policy is more reflective of our organisation's responsibilities, performance and of the economic climate."

Subsequent to Mr Hodgkinson's letter, 16 senior executives in the Capital Markets division filed new High Court cases against the bank, which were separate to the cases initiated by other traders. The group, using a different firm of solicitors, includes Michael Foley, who is head of corporate operations in the division along with other senior managers. They have initiated a case for specific performance of their contracts. This brings the total number of High Court cases relating to the bonus payments and which remain outstanding to 115, in addition to many Circuit Court cases.[11] In all, the bank was due to pay €58.7 million in bonuses, with some senior executives receiving up to €780,000.[12] Those taking Circuit Court cases have a limit of €38,000 on their claims. The payments were working out at an average of €110,000 each for 90 staff members and another group of 1,950 staff sharing an average of €15,000 each. Despite the change in ownership of the bank, many of these staff members would traditionally have received a large part of their annual remuneration in the form of bonuses. As with workers in every sector, they would have taken on financial commitments commensurate with their income. New pay structures for bankers is part of the reform demanded by Basel III,[13] with the emphasis shifting from bonuses to salary.

Many believe that despite the Minister's letter to AIB, staff members still have a legal entitlement to their bonuses. In the future, however, under section 51 of the Credit Institutions (Stabilisation) Act 2010 (enacted on 21 December 2010), it will be unlawful for a bank to make bonus payments in breach of a ministerially-imposed condition.[14] From 2011 onwards, it will be quite clear-cut: there will be no further bonuses payments. Whether it can apply retrospectively will be a matter for the courts to decide. AIB paid almost €1 million to retain some 30 staff members working in their Capital Markets division in London and New York. Their contracts of employment were drawing to a close and the bank paid an average of just over €30,000 to each employee in an effort to stop them leaving. AIB insisted that the payments were not a bonus and were made to prevent damage being done to business if they had left. It claimed that there is a high rate of turnover in the London and New York labour markets.

---

[10] McGee, H. (2010), "AIB in U-turn over bonuses as Lenihan warns bank over funds", The *Irish Times*, December 14, 2010 p.1.

[11] Paul, M. (2010) "AIB staff step up legal action", *Sunday Times*, 9 December 2010.

[12] O'Halloran, B. (2010), "New group plans to claim for AIB bonuses", *Irish Times*, 17 Friday December 2010, Business this Week, p.1.

[13] A new global regulatory standard which prescribes the level of capital and liquidity that banks need to hold. It was developed in response to the global financial crisis in 2008.

[14] Barrett, G. (2010), "Burning the bonus takers", *Sunday Business Post*, 19 December 2010.

Of course, AIB is not alone in terms of paying bonuses to staff during the current crisis. Prior to December 2010, Bank of Ireland has managed to 'fly under the radar' and avoid impinging on the public consciousness. Bank of Ireland also received considerable state aid, but when approached by various newspapers, it refused to answer any questions in regard to bonus payments. The Minister for Finance sought a report from the Court (board) of the Bank of Ireland about any bonus payments that might have been made.

It emerged that Bank of Ireland had made payments of €66 million in bonuses from September 2008 to December 2009, including a €500,000 bonus paid to an executive in the bank's fund management department. The CEO of Bank of Ireland, Mr Boucher, had previously told the Minister for Finance that no bonus payments had been made, and the Minister used this information in response to a Dáil reply, thus causing the Minister to inadvertently mislead the house.[15] Some 1,200 Bank of Ireland staff members signed a letter to the Chairman of the bank, Pat Molloy expressing their anger over the payments stating: "it is outrageous that these bonuses have been paid" and added that they had been asked to make considerable sacrifices from pay freezes to changes in their pension entitlements. The bank subsequently apologised to the Minister for supplying inaccurate information. In 2010, Mr Boucher was asked to forego a pension top-up of €1.5 million. Mr Lenihan had approved the pension payment which would have allowed Mr Boucher to retire at 55 as was the normal practice at Bank of Ireland. As a result of the controversy, Mr Boucher announced that he would not now be retiring at 55 and would work until the age of 60, and as a result, the pension top-up was not needed.[16]

Perhaps the payment that received most condemnation was the €3 million payment to former AIB managing director, Colm Doherty. Mr Doherty was forced to resign as a condition of AIB's recapitalisation by the state in September 2010. The €3 million payment was made up of salary payments from January to November of €432,000, a termination payment of €707,000 in lieu of a year's notice, and a payment of circa €2 million contribution to his pension fund.[17] This payment is against a loss in 2010 by AIB of €12 billion.

The Lex column in *The Financial Times* has an interesting slant on bankers' pay and risk:

> "For all its ills, economies that leave markets to follow Gordon Gekko's greed-is-good mantra generally support a higher standard of living than those with hard-left ideologies. Chasing the bucks weeds out inefficient operators and sometimes society is best served by liquidating a dysfunctional company. What lawmakers subsequently forgot is that fear is also good. Markets work best when greedy investors worry that taking one risk too many may cause bankruptcy. This is not good if they believe they will be bailed out from losing bets. Every banker must be just 'one trade away from humility'."[18]

Where is humility when it is needed most?

---

[15] Carswell, S. (2010), "Lenihan rightly angry at BOI 'catalogue of errors'", *Irish Times*, 3 March 2011, p.2.
[16] Keena, C. (2010), "Lenihan approved a €1.5 m deal for Boucher pension". *Irish Times*, 24 April 2010. p.1.
[17] Carswell, S. (2011), "AIB managing director received €3m in 2010". The *Irish Times*, 19 April 2011, p.1.
[18] *Financial Times*, Lex Column, 26 September 2010, p.26.

Ryanair

Catherine Moylan and Gerry Gallagher[1]

This case illustrates how leadership has driven developments in Ryanair and how the company has developed a core competence in how it exercises very tight controls over its operational cost base, revenue generation and the implementation of its strategy. The case also examines a number of corporate-level issues, from funding to how the company interacts with different stakeholders and also how it maximises publicity at little or no cost to the organisation.

In the early 1980s, with high unemployment at home, there were many Irish people working in the UK. Most of them travelled home only occasionally, and then it was mostly by ferry on routes such as Dun Laoghaire–Holyhead. Aer Lingus and British Airways offered scheduled flights to Ireland, but the cost for most people was prohibitive. At that time, there were international rules governing air travel which gave national flag carriers (such as Aer Lingus) considerable control over landing rights at airports. As a result of such restrictions, competition was severely curtailed. The European Union recognised that a lack of competition was damaging to the consumer and the European Commission deregulated the industry in Europe in the mid-1980s. On 28 November 1985, Tony Ryan, a former Aer Lingus employee and chairman of Guinness Peat Aviation (GPA), established Ryanair. It flew initially from Waterford to London Gatwick and then from Dublin to Luton charging £99 – half the rate charged by Aer Lingus at the time.[2]

The first CEO of Ryanair was Eugene O'Neill; two of Tony Ryan's sons, Cathal and Declan, were also involved. It was a brave new venture and it immediately met with strong opposition from Aer Lingus, which quickly matched Ryanair's lower fares, believing that the new airline would not be able to sustain that level of pricing. Though Ryanair was set up as a low-cost, no frills airline, in the early days it did not have the same approach to cost reduction that it has now. Over the next couple of years, the airline expanded its routes, taking in other cities in Ireland and the UK. However, it was losing a considerable amount of money and, in 1988, Eugene O'Neill and Ryanair parted ways.[3] He was replaced initially by Declan Ryan and later by P.J. McGoldrick. With accumulated debts of £20 million, Tony Ryan's personal assistant, Michael O'Leary advised his boss to close the airline and cut his losses. Ryan refused and put a case to the Minister for Transport, Seamus Brennan, to be given exclusive rights to fly into Stansted airport. The Minister agreed and in

---

[1] IT Tralee. This case is intended as a basis for class discussion and not as an illustration of good or bad managerial practice.

[2] Creaton, S. (2004) *Ryanair: How a Small Irish Airline Conquered Europe.* Aurum, 2004.

[3] *Ibid.*

September 1989 Aer Lingus was restricted to flying to Gatwick and Heathrow, while Ryanair would fly to Luton and Stansted.

At this stage, O'Leary was controlling the finances at the airline, and he began cutting costs. The Gulf crisis in 1991 hit the airline industry badly and passenger numbers worldwide were down. Tony Ryan called an old contact Herb Kelleher, founder of Southwest Airlines in Texas, and asked if they could study Southwest's operations. O'Leary was duly dispatched to learn from America's most successful low-cost operator.[4] Today, what separates Ryanair from all the other European low-cost operators is its ability to successfully and consistently cut costs down to the bare minimum.

By 2010, Ryanair had a fleet of 232 Boeing 737-800 aircraft carrying 66.5 million passengers, up 14% from the previous year. It operated 940 routes across Europe and its average load factor was 82%. The company generated €318 million in profits.[5] How did the small airline that was once just an annoying blip on the radar of Aer Lingus come to dwarf the former national carrier and redefine air travel? The answer lies with Ryanair's CEO Michael O'Leary and the strategies he developed over the last 20 or so years that have changed the way the industry operates.

	2006	2007	2008	2009	2010
Scheduled number of passengers (million)	34.8	42.5	50.9	58.6	66.5
Number of aircraft operated	103	133	163	181	232
Average number of employees	3063	3991	5262	6369	7032

Figure 1 – *Ryanair Holdings Plc: Passengers, Aircraft and Employees*

Operating Costs

Achieving a fast turnaround is central to keeping operating costs low. This is particularly important on the Dublin–London route, where Ryanair can achieve a 25-minute turnaround at Stansted compared to 60 minutes for Aer Lingus at Heathrow. From the very beginning, Ryanair flew only point to point – any connecting flight by Ryanair would be treated as a totally separate journey. This had implications for passengers in terms of check in and baggage transfer. Flying on specific routes to and from the base airport also facilitates crew rosters and ensures that crew will be back in their home station at the end of their shift.

Ryanair fly to secondary airports, where landing charges are much lower than the main airports. The drawback for passengers is that some of these airports are a considerable distance from the intended destination. The flight from Dublin to Frankfurt Hahn, for example, will leave the passenger over 120 kilometres from the city, a bit like branding Knock Airport as 'Dublin West'.

---

[4] *Ibid.*

[5] www.ryanair.com/ie/about (accessed 24 April 2011).

While Ryanair has been able to negotiate good deals from some of these airports, this has not always been a smooth process. In 2004, the European Commission ruled that Ryanair had received illegal state subsidies from Charleroi airport in Belgium. The airline seems to be in constant battle with airport authorities over landing charges, not least of all with the Dublin Airport Authority (DAA). Michael O'Leary has consistently criticised the DAA over what he terms excessive charges to pay for the building of Terminal 2 – which he describes as a "white elephant" project. O'Leary believes that Ryanair could have built and operated the new terminal for a fraction of the cost incurred by the state.

Unlike most other airlines, Ryanair has a *common fleet*, i.e. all of its aircraft are Boeing 737-800s. Having a common fleet has many advantages in terms of flight deck and cabin crew training (crew have to be 'rated' separately for different models of aircraft). Given that fuel costs represent the single biggest operating expense as a percentage of operating costs, these newer jets are significantly more fuel efficient, and less noisy than their older counterparts. Newer aircraft also save considerable money on maintenance compared to older models.

In the aftermath of the 11 September 2001 terrorist attacks, Ryanair reduced their prices to boost demand. The response was a significant increase in demand, so much so that Ryanair needed more jets. They bargained hard with Boeing, and given that worldwide demand for flights, and therefore aircraft, had fallen significantly, O'Leary got a reputed 50% price reduction on 100 new 737-800s, with options on another 50 aircraft. It was a brilliant deal, for even if Ryanair did not need the extra 50 aircraft, they would be able to sell the options to other airlines when the industry picked up (the airline industry is notoriously cyclical). Speaking about the deal, Michael O'Leary stated that being a farmer's son gave him a huge advantage:

> "I grew up in Mullingar and farmers know that the time to buy is when everybody else is selling and the time to sell is when everybody else is buying. It was quite simple. We had money. Boeing and Airbus couldn't give away planes. So we went and bought up about two years' worth of production."[6]

The latest version of the Boeing 737-800 has a bigger capacity, carrying 189 passengers, but without the need for extra cabin crew.

There are no 'free meals' on Ryanair flights, which as well as being a saving on food costs, also allows cabin crew the time to sell drinks, sandwiches, scratch cards and other items that generate money for the airline. They also work on a commission basis for in flight sales which helps boost their take-home pay. Cabin crew ensure the plane is clean by the time the aircraft has landed. Leather seats facilitate quick cleaning, and ready for the next flight. The company made a decision in the early 1990s not to carry cargo as the revenue generated would easily be offset by delays in unloading and thus missing take-off slots. Ryanair was the first airline to take on the travel agents' industry, first by reducing their 12% commission and then as the Internet came into common

---

[6] Creaton, S. (2004: 212).

usage, eliminating the commission altogether and getting passengers to book online. This also facilitates yield management, thus maximising revenue from each flight. Now all bookings are made on their website www.ryanair.com.

In recent years, the airline has introduced hefty fees for checked-in luggage. The company would like to see all passengers carry their own luggage on board as this saves on baggage handlers, check-in staff and fuel, as the fewer people bringing extra luggage means a lighter load and less fuel burn. Many choose to bring just hand luggage and save the €30 fee for one checked-in bag (less than 15kg). Other optional fees include priority boarding, €8; SMS confirmation, €1; and travel insurance, which will vary in price. Not all Ryanair charges, however, can be avoided such as the web check-in, €12 (it seems strange that the company that drove online check in should charge passengers for the process); delay/cancel levy, €4; and credit card booking fee, €12. If passengers turn up without their printed ticket, the company will charge them €30 for printing another boarding card. Combined fees quickly add a considerable amount to what first appears to be a reasonable fare and firmly switches the emphasis from 'low fares' to low cost.

Ryanair generates considerable revenue from its ancillary services. In 2009, ancillary revenues amounted to €598 million. These services include advertising on its website, selling hotel accommodation and car rental, livery advertising on jets, as well as the in flight sales, priority bookings, etc.

		2006	2007	2008	2009	2010
Operating Revenue	$m	1,692.5	2,236.9	2,713.8	2,942.0	2,988.1
Net profit	$m	306.7	435.6	390.7	(169.2)	305.3
Adjusted Net Profit	$m	301.5	401.4	480.9	104.9	318.8
Adjusted EPS	cent	19.66	25.99	31.81	7.10	21.59
Closing Share Price	cent	783.00	583.00	280.00	289.50	368.00

Figure 2 – *Extracts from Ryanair Holdings Plc. Financial Statements (prepared in accordance with IFRS)*

Publicity

Michael O'Leary has come up with some other ideas to generate extra revenue which are probably aimed more at generating publicity rather than serious proposals, including two controversial ones: a €1 charge for passengers using the toilet on board, and a so-called "fat tax" for overweight passengers. Like many of his antics, these proposals have generated much publicity for the airline, which seems to operate on the Irish writer Brendan Behan's maxim that "the only bad publicity is an obituary". The company does not use an advertising agency. Instead, staff members come up with advertising ideas that form the basis of newspaper advertising, much of which can be controversial, and sometimes leads to litigation.

An example of the latter was in early 2008 when Ryanair used a photograph of President Nicolas Sarkozy of France and Carla Bruni before their wedding. The photo had a bubble with Ms Bruni saying "With Ryanair, all my family can come to the wedding". The couple sued Ryanair, with Ms Bruni seeking €500,000 damages – based on her normal appearance fee. President Sarkozy sought a more modest €1 in damages, which the court awarded, while Ms Bruni received €60,000, plus legal fees.[7] Publicity surrounding the advertisement and subsequent court case received constant front-page coverage in newspapers right across Europe at a fraction of the cost of placing regular advertisements.

In Ireland, Government Ministers are often the butt of Ryanair advertisements, with former minister Mary O'Rourke and former Taoiseach Bertie Ahern frequently lampooned in full-page advertisements in the daily newspapers. On occasions, Michael O'Leary appears in Dublin Airport in various costumes ranging from Santa Claus to the Pope in order to launch a particular promotion. When interviewed, his turn of phrase is usually quite colourful, particularly when people or organisations are criticising Ryanair's customer service. He tends to get particularly exercised when discussing the DAA or the EU Commission. While many may find some of these incidents amusing, the airline frequently goes beyond what most find acceptable.

In 1988, the then CEO of Ryanair, P.J. McGoldrick, saw an opportunity for publicity as the airline was about to carry its one-millionth passenger. Jane O'Keeffe, a 22 year-old secretary from Dublin, was identified as the lucky passenger and, in a blaze of publicity, offered free flights for life along with a friend. By 1997, the arrangement was turning sour and Ms O'Keeffe was finding it very difficult to arrange flights and subsequently sued the airline for breach of contract. Ryanair claimed there was no contract, but in June 2002, Mr Justice Peter Kelly in the High Court believed otherwise, and found Ms O'Keeffe's version of events to be very clear. He awarded the plaintiff €67,500 plus costs in lieu of lost past and future flights.[8] In January 2004, a court in London awarded a disabled passenger, Mr Bob Ross, £1,336 in compensation after the airline had charged him £18 for the use of a wheelchair to transport him from the terminal building to the aircraft. While the airline accepted the judgement, it responded with a 50p per ticket "wheelchair levy".[9] In 2010, in a dispute over landing charges in Dublin Airport, Ryanair managers gave evidence in the High Court in Dublin which did not find favour with the judge. Mr Justice Peter Kelly stated that "the truth and Ryanair are uncomfortable bedfellows"[10]. Legal cases take up a lot of management time in Ryanair, and must amount to a considerable cost to the airline, although this cost is not broken down in their annual accounts.

Industrial Relations

While Ryanair has modelled itself very successfully on Southwest Airlines, one major difference between the two airlines is that Ryanair does not recognise trade unions. In December 1998, baggage handlers in Dublin airport sought union recognition, and when this was not forthcoming, they began a series of strikes the following month. The dispute did not cause much disruption

---

7 "Ryanair's wings clipped as Sarkozy, Bruni win damages" *Irish Times,* 6 February 2008, p.1.

8 www.rte.ie/news/2002/0619/ryanair.html

9 Colby, R. (2004), "Compensation: Low points of the no frills carriers", *The Guardian,* 21 February 2004, p.10

10 www.irishexaminer.com/business/kfcwkgbmhql/rss2/ (accessed 25 April 2011).

as senior managers, along with a number of "volunteers" from the airline, loaded and unloaded baggage. After a number of weeks, the dispute fizzled out. Michael O'Leary told the workers that he would close the airline rather than negotiate with a trade union. There have been a number of attempts over the years by Ryanair pilots to be represented by groups such as the Irish Airline Pilots Association and similar bodies across Europe. There have been claims by the pilots, who have accused the airline of intimidation relating to what the pilots believed was the unilateral imposition of terms and conditions.

Corporate-level Strategy

Ryanair became a Plc in 1997, floating on the Dublin and London stock exchanges and later on the NASDAQ exchange in New York. The shares were 20-times oversubscribed. Ryanair employees received free shares, which at the end of the first day's trading were worth a combined €100 million. That year it carried 3.7 million passengers and the UK Civil Aviation Authority said it had the best record for punctuality on the Dublin–London route.[11]

Most of Ryanair's expansion over the years has been by organic growth. In 2003, Ryanair purchased Buzz, the Dutch low-cost airline from KLM. Buzz, with a staff of 570 people, was losing €1 million a week and Ryanair moved quickly saying they would make one-quarter of its pilots and 80% of its cabin crew redundant, and discontinue the brand. The real attraction for Ryanair was the valuable slots that Buzz held at Stansted, which would give it considerable latitude for further growth. Ryanair set up a subsidiary company called Buzz Stansted Limited in order to get around legislation protecting employees in redundancy situations. The unions representing the workers put pressure on the parent company KLM and a new deal was struck, which saw Ryanair acquire Buzz for €20.1 million, along with 130 staff members out of the original compliment of 530 staff in the Dutch airline. KLM would retain the other 400 staff. Ryanair also assumed responsibility for outstanding leases and other costs, bringing the total payment to €46.7 million.[12]

Shortly after Aer Lingus was privatised in 2007, Ryanair purchased a 25% stake in the rival airline. It was a move that caught the markets by surprise and Michael O'Leary had to follow up the purchase with a series of meetings with senior investors in Ryanair to explain the rationale behind the move. The stake in Aer Lingus was increased later to 29.8%. Anything above 29.9% would trigger a bid for the entire company. There would inevitably be strong opposition from the unions representing Aer Lingus workers who held 12.6% of the company's shares through an employee share-ownership trust (ESOT). Aer Lingus pilots controversially used their pension fund to buy Aer Lingus shares in a bid to stop the takeover. When the company was privatised, the Government held onto a 25.4% holding. Combined, there was enough voting power to block the takeover. While "hostile takeovers" often succeed, what made this move unusual is the likely response of the European Commission. Had the takeover succeeded, it would have placed Ryanair in a very dominant position on the Dublin–London route, one of the busiest air routes in the world. It was

[11] www.ryanair.com/ie/about (accessed 24 April 2011).
[12] Creaton, S. (2004).

no surprise that the Commission ruled against the move. In January 2009, Ryanair made a revised offer for Aer Lingus with revised terms, but that too was rejected.

An airline has two options when it comes to obtaining aircraft: either to lease them (from a leasing company such as GE Capital Aviation Services), or purchase them outright, which Ryanair has done. To grow the airline, therefore, requires large sums of money which can be obtained from borrowings and retained profits. Over the years, Ryanair has not distributed any of its profits as dividends to shareholders. Instead, it has used the money to fund further expansion believing that, in the long-run, shareholders would get better return on their investment from capital growth alone. In 2009, Ryanair had been negotiating with Boeing over the purchase of new aircraft. As part of their negotiating strategy, Ryanair stated that, if they did not get a satisfactory price for the aircraft, they would cancel negotiations and distribute the retained profits as dividends. Perhaps Boeing thought Ryanair was bluffing but Ryanair withdrew from the negotiations and instead paid a dividend to its shareholders for the first time. Ryanair paid a dividend of 33.57 cent per share on 1 October 2010.[13]

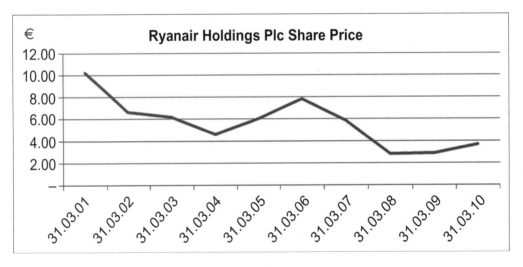

Figure 3 – *Ryanair Holdings Plc Share Price*

Fuel costs have always been the largest cost factor for the airline, and they fluctuate considerably on world markets. Airlines the world over are subject to these variations, as oil prices are beyond the control of countries let alone individual companies. A common practice to overcome these peaks and troughs in oil prices is to hedge the cost – enter into a contract that will fix the price for a certain period, normally 12 months. If the cost of oil rises in the meantime, the airline will profit from the hedging, but if the price drops on world markets, it will lose out. It is a gamble, but it brings a level

---

13 Clark, P. (2010), "Ryanair to pay first dividend since flotation", www.ft.com, 1 June 2010 www.ft.com/cms/s/0/aa79c924-6d4f-11df-bde2-00144feabdc0,s01=1.html#axzz1MhHYaAJf (accessed 16 May 2011).

of certainty for the airline that allows them to accurately assess their costs for budgeting. In 2008, the airline had not hedged fuel costs, when oil reached $147 a barrel on international markets which resulted in a huge increase in fuel costs (they subsequently hedged the following year). Rising fuel costs, along with a major depreciation of the value of its Aer Lingus investment on its balance sheet, saw the airline making a loss of €169 million in their financial year ending 31 March 2009. This was the first time the company lost money since the early years.

	(Prepared in accordance with IFRS)				
	2006	**2007**	**2008**	**2009**	**2010**
	€m	**€m**	**€m**	**€m**	**€m**
Non-current assets	2,581	3,337	3,940	3,845	4,500
Fixed Assets – Aircraft Net book value	2,520	2,858	3,553	3,602	4,275
Current Assets	2,054	2,354	2,387	2,543	3,063
Current Liabilities	846	1,118	1,557	1,379	1,550
Long term debt	1,524	1,683	1,900	2,196	2,691
Shareholders' funds-equity	1,992	2,540	2,502	2,425	2,849
Total liabilities & shareholders' equity	4,634	5,691	6,328	6,388	7,563

Figure 4 – *Ryanair Holdings Plc. Consolidated Balance Sheet*

The airline is named after its founder Tony Ryan, but for a variety of reasons it is associated throughout Europe with its CEO Michael O'Leary. Mr O'Leary has announced his intention to leave Ryanair within the next couple of years and has stated that he will make a clean break rather than remain on the board or take over as chairman from David Bonderman. It remains to be seen whether deputy CEO, Michael Cawley, will take the helm or will the new CEO be appointed from outside. The big question is when that change happens, will the airline continue its exponential growth and profitability or will it lose altitude?

ESBI – Internationalisation in Action

Chris O'Riordan and Dr Felicity Kelliher[1]

Lighting up...

ESB International (ESBI)'s beginnings can be traced back to the 1970s, when the Arab–Israeli war in 1973 created a major oil crisis and 'growth came to a halt over a period of years' (Moore[2], 2007). For ESB (the Electricity Supply Board of Ireland),[3] this meant that hard decisions were required – the engineering resource was a significant cost but, with expansion curtailed, had little benefit to add in its existing form. One option was to scale it back and, realistically, lose it forever. ESB chose, instead, to find alternative uses for this resource, due primarily to the division's insightful and dedicated leadership at the time:

> "We were very fortunate at the time that we had very strong and visionary leadership in the ESB ... They were all very strong guys who had come through the rural electrification period and who weren't daunted by anything."(Moore, 2007)[4]

In the beginning, international growth was slow and measured and began in the Middle East in Saudi Arabia and Bahrain. The flip side of the oil crisis was that money was plentiful in these oil-rich states, but infrastructure was underdeveloped. In 1981, ESBI was a successful bidder for a sizeable contract in the city of Jubail in Saudi Arabia – a brand new industrial city in the desert, built from scratch and to be powered by gas that was otherwise being flared[5]:

> "This was the single biggest project ever undertaken on the planet at that time, to build a city of 370,000 people from scratch. ... We won a [big] contract, against international competition, to design the transmission and distribution system for the city ... The job went very well, it was very challenging, [with] huge publicity and the management and board of ESB sat up and noticed."
>
> (Moore, 2007).

---

[1] Both of the School of Business, Waterford Institute of Technology. The authors wish to acknowledge their appreciation to Mr Don Moore, former Managing Director of ESBI, and the staff of ESBI, for their time, help, guidance and support in the production of this case. This case is an abridged version of O'Riordan, C. and Kelliher F. (2008) "ESB International – A Bright Future", in Cunningham, J.A. and Harrington D.G. (Eds.), *Irish Management 2.0: New Managerial Priorities in a Changing Economy*. Dublin, Blackhall Publishing, pp. 117–139. Global Market statistical updates are with the approval of Data Monitor.

[2] Mr Don Moore is the former Managing Director of ESBI.

[3] The Electricity Supply Board is Ireland's main (and State majority-owned) electricity utility provider.

[4] Moore, D. (2007), Interview with Mr Don Moore, former Managing Director, ESB International, conducted on 17 April, 2007.

[5] Flared gas is a by-product of oil refining.

A decision now needed to be taken by ESB: would they continue to pursue such business in an active and co-ordinated way, or allow ESBI to continue as a small niche in the bigger company? The management of ESB decided to take the requisite risk and moved the Design and Construction Organisation in ESB into the new division.

ESBI – a New Division…

ESBI was set up as a separate division in ESB in 1989 and, in 2000, became a separate wholly-owned subsidiary of the group. This was a novel move, or as Don describes it, "a huge step" – staff with effectively lifetime contracts in the nation's largest semi-state organisation were being asked to move – physically, culturally and conceptually – into a new, more commercially-based entity in new offices. This was handled through seconding the relevant staff from ESB into the new firm, whereby they retained their terms and conditions of employment. However, all new staff hired directly by the new entity would be on ESBI terms and conditions. The new firm was different to ESB – the benchmark was to be the competition, not just internally devised targets.

Since its establishment, ESBI has completed numerous projects worldwide, and today ESBI's services and expertise are demanded the world over by multinational and state-owned utilities. To date, ESBI has completed projects in over 115 countries, and are recognised as one of the world's most successful utility engineering, contracting and consultancy organisations (see the ESBI Website). ESBI's technical expertise is derived from resources in engineering design, planning, construction, investment, commissioning and operation for all types of power plant and electrical networks. The company employs approximately 1,200 people who work in partnership with clients, within four main divisions in the organisation (**Figure 1**).

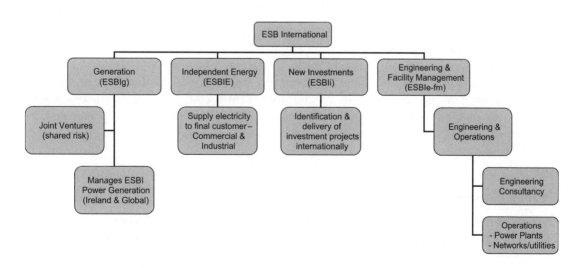

Figure 1 – *ESB International Corporate Chart 2007*

ESBIg This division manages ESBI's power generation assets, both in Ireland and worldwide. The division holds a portfolio of assets including CCGTs, windfarms, combined heat and power (CHP) units and renewable generation assets. Some of these assets are held in joint venture (JV) businesses, where ESBIg has a partial holding, thus sharing the risk with other parties, and in these cases the JVs are led by a general manager and operated by teams from the facility management division. A number of the generation assets held are situated abroad, including the first internationally-owned independent power plant in the Spanish market.

ESBIE This division is a competitive supply business, established in January 2000 "to supply electricity to the liberalised electricity markets and build long-term relationships with customers" (ESBI website). The division does this by tailoring its offering to the customers' needs with a focus on the industrial/commercial market, differentiating it from the competition. Customers include Intel, British Telecom and Tesco Ireland. ESBIE also provides 'value adding' services to customers in the form of green electricity supply, energy monitoring and management services, and electronic billing.

ESBIi This division "is responsible for the identification, development and bringing to commercial operation of power-related projects in the deregulated markets both at home and overseas" (ESBI website). Spain and the UK have proven to be the most successful markets for the division to date, with two 800MW and one 400MW plants at varying stages of completion. ESBIi is also responsible for the group's renewable energy business. According to the 2007 White Paper on Energy, the Government wants one-third of Ireland's electricity to be supplied from renewable sources by 2020.

ESBIe-fm This is the main engineering and operations wing of ESB International. The engineering division is the centre of engineering services for ESB, and also provides consulting services to foreign governments and private businesses. Consultancy services provided by ESBI Engineering are wide and varied, and include power plant engineering, automation and telecommunications, restructuring/privatisation, strategic consultancy, civil and structural engineering, environmental and climate services, and architectural/building services. In total, the division carried out operations in 25 countries during 2005. The facility management business provides full operation and maintenance services to ESBI power plants and to international clients.

Gaining Momentum...

Over the years, the company has won contracts all over the globe for a variety of jobs and assignments. The focus has been on consultancy/technical projects and taking on the role of transmissions operator as these contracts are profitable, numerous and quick paying. **Figure 2** below highlights key successes over the years:

Year	Location	Value €m	Contract Description
1994	Corby, UK		ESBI took a small fractional share as part of the terms as the operating and maintenance contractor.
1996	Pakistan	€57m	ESBI took a 7% share to operate & maintain a power plant for 13 years.
1997	Malaysia	€80m	Operate the power supply to an industrial park for 9 years.
2001	Nigeria		Provide consultancy services to the National Electric Power Authority.
2002	Georgia	€12m	Manage the electricity services of the former Russian state of Georgia.
2004	Kosovo	€8.8m	Oversee the operation of Kosovo's electricity service and provide training to workers (extended in 2005).
2005	Manjung, Malaysia	€9m	Operate, manage and maintain a 2,100 MW coal fired plant – ultimate owner is the national electric company.
2005	Vietnam	€4.5m	Consultancy contract relating to a 600 MW coal fired plant, including technical project design, preparation of specifications, tender evaluation and contract negotiation.
2005	Indonesia	€5m	Advisory services relating to the construction of a 1,200 MW coal fired plant.
2006	South Africa		A five-year contract with the state electricity supplier for consultancy services in the construction of new power plants.
2005	Amorebieta (Basque Region)	€500m	Completed CCGT gas toiling plant: ownership: 50% ESBI / 50% Osaka Gas Group. This plant represents the largest ever inward investment in the region and will be managed and maintained by ESBI for an initial 20-year period.
2005	Northern Ireland	€300m	Completed 400 MW CCGT plant in Coolkeeragh.
2006	Galway	€72m	Completed 60MW windfarm project at Derrybrien.
2007	Southampton England	€563m	The construction of a new combined cycle gas turbine plant is a joint (50/50) project between ESBI and Scottish and Southern Energy plc (SSE).

Figure 2 – *ESBI Contract Highlights 1994–2007*

Not all contracts worked out in ESBI's favour. As the size, risk and complexity of projects grew, so too did the dynamics relating to contract negotiation and acceptance (see **Figure 3**).

Year	Contract	Value €m	Reason for failure
2001	Bid for purchase of a network of energy distributors – Poland	€950m (annually)	The Irish Government vetoed the deal because of the scale of the spending involved (€1.7 billion) & the perceived risk involved.
2002	Awarded Setrans project – US contract to manage a regional transmission organisation, accounting for 10% of the market	€750m	Deal fell through (2003) primarily due to the US Energy Bill – electricity companies were no longer obliged to join regional transmission systems, forcing a suspension of the contract.

Figure 3 – *ESBI Disappointments 1994–2007*

As for the Setrans Project, Don Moore is notably philosophical:

> "We got paid for our time and effort … There was no loss, at the end of the day … You always learn something, even from failure – the next time an opportunity presents itself, you'll be better."

Considering ESBI's 'minnow' size in international terms, alliance and joint venture activity has also been a valuable tool in the creation of sustainable competitive advantage for the organisation over the years: "One of the things we do, because of our size, is to team up with others to win the job" (Moore, 2007). These partnerships work well, as ESBI can bring technical expertise and partners provide other key elements. For example, in the Southampton project (in 2007 – **Figure 2**), SSE will supply the plant with fuel and will purchase the electricity generated, while 80% of the investment was secured as debt finance from a consortium of five banks, with the two equity partners putting in the balance evenly.

Mutual respect between ESBI and individual stakeholders is evident in ESBI's interaction with customers, alliance partners and financiers: "Most Irish people working abroad make a very favourable impression in the most difficult of circumstances" (Moore, 2007). This reputation facilitates country, partner and financier/World Bank business relations and in ESBI's experience, partners "want us to lead" in these arrangements. This amounts to a "key competency of Irish companies … that's why Irish companies are doing so well out of globalisation" (Moore, 2007).

The Future Looks Bright?

ESBI has built up a significant international business over the years, and has completed medium and large-scale projects in 115 countries over that time. The company has built a reputation for advanced market knowledge, technical expertise and a professional approach, and pride themselves on a reputation for getting the job done. As Don Moore remarks:

> "In all of my 25 years in ESBI, I can't remember a single instance where we failed to deliver a project. We might have had difficulties, but we always delivered. If we had to spend, we spent. It's a business of long-term relationships; it's all about repeat business."

The future for ESBI looks to be promising and lucrative. This is an organisation "always on the lookout for something new" (Moore, 2007), and in recent years, the company has been more aggressive in targeting high profile and more long-term projects than in the 1990s. The company now has the capacity to invest in power plants and wait the requisite time to recoup its investment. In addition, ESBI has used the partnership model to great success with Osaka Gases and SSE and hopes to continue to create such mutually beneficial alliances. However, competition in the global market is intensifying (**Appendix 1**), and the ownership situation surrounding the ESB and its divisions is likely to resurface in the coming years also.

REFERENCES

Datamonitor (2010a) – Global Electricity: Industry Profile, August

Datamonitor (2010b) – Electricity in Europe: Industry Profile, August

Datamonitor (2010c) – Electricity in the United Kingdom: Industry Profile, August

DETE – Department of Enterprise, Trade and Employment (2005) *Irish Electricity Market: Principal Challenges* (Discussion Paper)

Eirgrid (2010) *Transmission Forecast Statement*, 2010–2016

ESB International website – www.esbi.ie

Moore, D. (2007), Interview with Mr Don Moore, former Managing Director, ESB International, conducted on 17 April, 2007

APPENDIX – THE GLOBAL ELECTRICITY MARKET

According to Datamonitor, the global electricity market in 2009 generated total revenues of over $1,601 billion, an increase of 2.1% on the previous year:

Global Electricity Market	2005–2009	2009 (bn)	2009–2014	2014 (bn)
CAGR (Datamonitor, 2010a)	8.3%		11.0%	
Revenue		$1601		$2,693
Market consumption rates (kilowatt hrs)		15,303		19,909
European Electricity Market				
CAGR (Datamonitor, 2010b)			6.2%	
UK CAGR (Datamonitor, 2010c)	15%		5.1%	

Figure 4 – *Global Market Consumption Rates & Compound Annual Growth Rate (CAGR)*

The compound annual growth rate (CAGR) over the period 2005–2009 was 8.3%, and forecasts for the market over the period 2009–2014 show the CAGR rising to 11%, resulting in predicted 2014 revenues of $2,693 billion (Figure 4). As market consumption rates are expected to hit 19,909 billion kWh in 2014, this would suggest that prices will rise faster than output, possibly because of the increased cost of fuel sources as oil, gas and fossil fuel resources approach total depletion.

In Europe (which accounts for 29% of the global market), the story is similar, though with considerably lower growth rates (**Figure 4**). The European market consists of four significant players[6] with over 40% share between them, while the remaining companies are smaller and more fragmented. Notably, while 100 per cent of the EU market was supposed to be fully liberalised by 2007, this is still in progress.

The Irish electricity market grew at an average annual rate of 5% during the 1990s (DETE, 2005), which is significantly above that of the EU25. This is on the back of a sustained period of growth as Ireland's economy expanded at a rapid rate – average real growth in GDP was 7% per annum between 1991 and 2001. While growth has slowed significantly in recent years due to the recession, the infrastructure is playing catch-up – although current ESB capacity is able to accommodate peak national demand, there is an awareness that, with forecast power demand predicted to increase by approximately 2% per annum between 2010 and 2016 (Eirgrid, 2010), further investment from existing suppliers and incoming players is certainly needed.

---

[6] These four companies are FGC UES (Russia), E.ON (Germany), EDF (France) and RWE (Germany). The latter three also dominate the UK market.

Ernest Shackleton – Leading Change

Gerry Gallagher

This case is an incredible example of human resilience and survival under extraordinary conditions and how the leadership of Ernest Shackleton brought his men through changing circumstances that could never have been originally envisaged. It demonstrates that, while aspects of change may be managed, primarily change must be led.

The race to the South Pole had ended when the Norwegian explorer Roald Amundsen reached it in 1911. In 1913, Sir Ernest Shackleton, a polar veteran who had accompanied Scott on earlier expeditions, came up with an ambitious plan: to be the first person to walk 3,000km across the Antarctic continent from the Weddell Sea to the Ross Sea. He planned the trip meticulously and chose the expedition members. Shackleton understood the necessity of selecting the main trans-Antarctic team (as opposed to support teams) from the outset, and also the resources required – especially the use of skis and dogs. To the crew he was always 'The Boss', though his authority derived from his well-developed leadership skills, and his understanding of human nature rather than any hierarchy. In short, his approach to the expedition showed that there was a clear, consistent line running from his vision through to his goals.

Though he failed in his bid to cross the continent, and the expedition turned to a two year-quest for survival, Shackleton succeeded in the greater task of leading his men to safety in unimaginable conditions earning him the reputation of "the greatest leader that ever came on God's earth, bar none". Sixty years after the expedition, Lionel Greenstreet, the first officer of the *Endurance,* was asked how they survived when so many other expeditions had perished. The 82-year-old answered in one word: "Shackleton".[1]

Early Life

Ernest Shackleton was born on 15 February 1874 in Kilkea, County Kildare. His parents were Quakers and this seemed to influence many of his values later in life and gave him a strong moral compass. The family later moved to Dublin and then to London, where he attended Dulwich College. He did not like student life and decided to join the Merchant Marine with whom he completed a four-year apprenticeship, later taking exams to secure promotion. Proving to be very popular with his fellow crew members, he served on a number of ships and learned much from their captains about what constituted good and bad leadership. He was an avid reader on a broad range of topics and began developing an interest in exploration. In 1901, Robert Falcon Scott, a

---

[1] Morrell, M. and Capparell, S. (2001), *Shackleton's* Way. London, Nicholas Brealey Publishing

Royal Navy captain, led an Antarctic expedition and Shackleton was selected as a junior officer on the *Discovery*. He threw himself into his work and was chosen by Scott to be part of the three-man team to make the 2,500km round-trip to the South Pole. Some 700km from the Pole, the men developed scurvy and were forced to turn back. Shackleton suffered the most and then was wrongly blamed by Scott for having to abort the mission. Though the two men never really reconciled their differences, Shackleton managed to put the episode behind him, even offering to help Scott to organise his famous but ill-fated expedition of 1910.

On his return from the first expedition, Shackleton worked at a variety of jobs, including journalism, and in April 1904 he married his long-time sweetheart Emily Dorman, who was six years his senior.

The Nimrod

In 1907, Shackleton launched his own expedition on board the *Nimrod*, with the aim of reaching the South Pole. He had learned a great deal from the mistakes that Scott had made about food and clothing, and in particular, leadership. He quickly earned the respect of his men who called him 'the Boss', a name that stuck. In fact, the contrast in leadership styles between Scott and Shackleton could not have been more pronounced. Scott had been brought up in the tradition of the Royal Navy. He was controlling, strict and believed in tough discipline, putting the mission above everything else. In contrast, Shackleton, though physically tough, was kind and considerate. He had a strong, clear focus on his goal, but was never foolish or obstinate. He always put his men's safety before personal glory. There would be other opportunities: "better a live donkey than a dead lion".[2] In many ways, Shackleton was way ahead of his time in leadership style in terms of giving his men individual responsibility and independence to achieve their goals. In everything he did, he led by example. He drew out the best in his men, and they responded with absolute loyalty.

In November 1908, Shackleton, with Dr Eric Marshall, Lt Jameson Boyd Adams and Frank Wild, set out for the South Pole. By 9 January 1909, however, they were forced to turn back or face certain starvation. They reached 88 degrees, 23 minutes south – just 155km from the Pole. Shackleton had beaten Scott's previous record by 570km. On the way back, they were desperately short of food. One of the men, Frank Wild was feeling particularly weak. Shackleton gave Wild his limited rations so that he could continue. They made it back safely to the ship. This was a gesture that Wild never forgot. Wild wrote: "I do not suppose that anyone else in the world can thoroughly realise how much generosity and sympathy was shown by this. I DO and GOD I shall never forget it."[3] On their return to England, Shackleton was knighted and he received many exploration awards from governments around the world.

---

[2] *Ibid,* see above, n.1.
[3] Alexander, C. (1999), *The Endurance: Shackleton's Legendary Antarctic Expedition*. New York, Alfred Knopf.

The Race to the South Pole

At this time, though there were many countries planning polar expeditions, the two main contenders were Captain Scott and the Norwegian Roald Amundsen. In 1910, Scott initiated another expedition. The *Terra Nova* set sail for the Antarctic via New Zealand, the intention being to reach the South Pole from the Ross Sea. A group of Norwegians was also making for the South Pole across the Ross Sea and, using skis and dogs, they made much quicker progress. The epic race was won by Amundsen when he reached the South Pole on 14 December 1911. Scott's group (which included Irishman Tom Crean, though Crean was not included in the final dash), reached the pole on 17 January 1912, only to find a Norwegian flag planted in the snow. On the way back to his ship, Scott, along with Wilson, Oates, Bowers and Taff Evans perished.[4]

The Vision

Shackleton was clearly bitten by the exploration bug. The race for the South Pole was over, but in 1913, he came up with a new vision: to be the first to lead an expedition 3,000km across the continent from the Weddell Sea to the Ross Sea. He wrote to *The Times* to announce the "Imperial Trans-Antarctic Expedition", and in January 1914 set up an office to plan for the men, the supplies, the scientific team (necessary to get official backing) and the considerable financial support that would be required.

The success of the expedition would depend on the personnel chosen. Shackleton began by picking the key players – his second in command and the ship's captain (these expeditions consisted of two main groups – the ship that would transport them and the shore party that would participate in the discovery). Frank Wild, a veteran of previous Antarctic trips, was a natural choice as Shackleton's second in command, and he had all the qualities needed. Captain Frank Worsley, who had excellent navigational skills, was chosen to command the main ship the *Endurance*, named after Shackleton's family motto: *Fortitudine Vincimus* (by endurance we conquer). Shackleton did not fit any conventional mould and he sought similar qualities in the men he would lead to the windiest, coldest place on earth, where the lowest temperature ever recorded was minus 89.6° C. Despite the danger involved, there was no shortage of applicants (over 5,000 in all), including three young women who wrote:

> "We 'three sporty girls' have decided to write and beg of you, to take us with you on your expedition to the South Pole. We are three strong, healthy girls and also gay and bright, and willing to undergo any hardships that you yourselves undergo. If our feminine garb is inconvenient, we should just love to don masculine attire. We have been reading all books and articles that have been written on dangerous expeditions by brave men to the polar region and we do not see why men should have all the glory, and women none, especially when there are women just as brave and capable as there are men."[5]

---

4 Smith, M. (2000), *An Unsung Hero*. Cork, The Collins Press.
5 Heacox, K. (1999), *Shackleton: The Antarctic Challenge*. Washington DC, National Geographic.

While the three women may have been ahead of their time, this was one challenge that Shackleton did not take on. The intrepid Antarctic explorer from Kerry, Tom Crean, was made second officer. All personnel were chosen first and foremost for their temperament; then their proven ability. While each in his own right was talented, Shackleton also wanted positive, optimistic people who would work together as a team. The group included biologists, geologists, physicists and other scientific personnel that would be required to attract funding from organisations such as the Royal Geographical Society. Each man was given detailed instructions as to their entitlements and what would be expected from them in return. It was an extraordinary collection of individuals, taking in a wide variety of trades and professions, and, in a highly class-conscious society, a broad spectrum of social backgrounds. On this trip there would be no passengers and each individual, regardless of any professional or social standing, would be required to put their hand to all tasks.

Shackleton's exploits had caught the public imagination and he was able to raise the huge sum of £50,000 (the equivalent of £10 million today) needed to finance the trip. He sent an individualised fund-raising prospectus for the voyage to numerous wealthy people. Various industrialists, including Dudley Docker and Janet Stancomb-Wills made contributions, and Sir James Caird alone donated £24,000. (The ship's three life boats, which would later play such an important role, were named after these benefactors.[6]) Shackleton also pre-sold the rights to all photographs and books that would arise from the trip.

The original plan was that the *Endurance* would drop off the main shore party at the Weddell Sea side of the Antarctic and then sail around to the opposite side, to Cape Evans in the Ross Sea, where a second shore party would be dropped off. Their role was to lay food depots at intervals along the second part of the route that would sustain Shackleton and his group as they made their way towards their pick-up point at the Ross Sea. However, at an early stage he changed this plan and organised a second ship, the *Aurora*, which would go directly to Cape Evans.[7]

Shackleton paid great attention to the selection of the equipment required for the journey. Experience had taught him that poor equipment can cost a great deal of time and destroy morale. He had also learned first-hand the limitations of poor clothing. He chose the best materials available (made then by Burberry), and used the latest scientific information on nutrition and food packaging, ensuring that they would have a balanced diet sufficient to match the demanding needs of the rough climate.

The Journey

The *Endurance* left England on 4 August 1914, and sailed for the Antarctic via South America and South Georgia Island. Shackleton was now 40 years old. He had a wealth of experience behind him and he understood what men were capable of achieving. He also understood their limitations. Some of the crew, however, did not shape up well on the voyage south, and when they reached Buenos Aires, Shackleton decided to send four of them back to England. He demanded total commitment.

---

[6] Smith, M (2000), *An Unsung Hero*. Cork, The Collins Press
[7] Heacox, K. (1999), *Shackleton The Antarctic Challenge*. Washington DC, National Geographic

The *Endurance* left Buenos Aires for South Georgia on 27 October. At this stage, Shackleton had established a strict schedule that ensured everyone participated in the ship's daily routine, regardless of rank. Such routine, balanced by periods of recreation, lessened the social division among the crew members and helped forge deep friendships. In all tasks, 'the Boss' led by example. Before he made any changes, he carefully weighed up the situation, rather than making change for change sake. Any breach of discipline was dealt with immediately and fairly. It was then forgotten about. They arrived at the whaling station at Grytviken in South Georgia at the beginning of November 1914, and remained there for a month as they were informed by the whalers that the pack ice in the Weddell Sea was the worst in living memory for that time of year. They waited for a while for it to clear and finally left for Antarctica on 5 December.[8]

The Weddell Sea

As the expedition approached the Weddell Sea, they made very slow progress, encountering a considerable amount of pack ice. They eventually sighted land on 12 January 1915. Days later, they were caught in a storm which surrounded the *Endurance* with ice, trapping the ship and its crew of 28. Though they were only one day's sailing from their landing base, they would have to wait for the ice to break up before continuing. A number of attempts were made to force a channel through the ice, but without success. The precarious nature of the pack ice rendered it impossible to attempt to trek across it to their original landing point. For the time being, Shackleton's vision was put on hold. The crew settled in until conditions improved. However, the summer months of the southern hemisphere passed and the ice did not free them. On a few occasions, breaks in the ice floe appeared further out and Shackleton had the men out trying to break up the ice in front of the ship to create a channel, but their efforts still proved fruitless. All the time, the dogs that would pull the sledges had to be exercised each day and trained to work together in harness.

On 24 February 1915, with the Antarctic summer drawing to a close, and no let-up in sight, Shackleton designated the ship a winter station. According to the surgeon, Alexander Macklin, Shackleton never showed any outward sign disappointment or frustration. He told them that it would be necessary to winter in the pack ice and he explained the dangers and possibilities, but never lost his optimism.[9] During this time, the ice, and with it the *Endurance,* was drifting further north from their landing point. The ship's radio operator tried unsuccessfully to make contact with the Falkland Islands. The war in Europe was raging, and no one even knew they were stranded. Winter clothing, intended for the shore party, was issued to all. Adjustments were made to the interior of the ship to make it better suited for winter conditions and the crew moved to the interior where it would be warmer. Shackleton however remained in his cabin in the aft, where anyone could come to him in private with their concerns. He spent a considerable amount of time talking individually to each crew member, getting to know all about their background and aspirations.

---

[8] Morrell, M. and Capparell, S. (2001), *Shackleton's Way*. London, Nicholas Brealey Publishing.

[9] Alexander, C. (1999), *The Endurance: Shackleton's Legendary Antarctic Expedition*. New York, Alfred Knopf.

This was balanced by ensuring they stayed together as a group. He had extraordinary skill in communication and earned their trust and respect. He also put enormous effort into keeping up their morale. If any crew member was sick, Shackleton personally nursed him back to health. He rarely slept more than a couple of hours a night. He ensured they all kept fit, and regularly practiced emergency drills should the situation worsen. For relaxation, they would read, played games of charades, listen to the gramophone or have sing-songs with Hussey playing the banjo. All were expected to participate, regardless of any talent. Individual birthdays were always celebrated. The months passed, and the ship, stuck in the pack ice, drifted northwest. Despite living in such confined quarters for such a long period, the men's diaries show no sign of anguish.

The Sinking

The ice around *Endurance* became more solid, putting pressure on the sides of the ship. Eventually, on 27 October 1915, the *Endurance* began taking in water and Shackleton gave the order to abandon ship, and move onto the ice. They salvaged essential supplies along with three small life boats, and camped on the ice. Shackleton was the last to leave. The *Endurance* had drifted 1,950 km from its original point of entrapment, and was 1,600km from the nearest human settlement. Though now listing badly, it was still held up by the ice. Over the next few weeks, the crew made a number of foraging trips to the ship to retrieve more equipment, but it was no longer home. *Endurance* finally sank on 21 November 1915. Shackleton's vision of the Imperial trans-Antarctic expedition was at an end. No one outside the expedition knew where they were, or even that they were in trouble. They were on their own. His mission now became one of survival for his crew and getting them home safely. The remainder of the crew also had their dreams of glory shattered and viewed the situation as desperate. Shackleton wrote: "The task was likely to be long and strenuous, and an ordered mind and a clear programme were essential if we were to come through without loss of life."[10] He had, however, considered this eventuality many times during their entrapment and thought about different contingencies.

Situation: Desperate

Shackleton called his team together and explained the situation in matter-of-fact, realistic terms. He offered a number of options, putting forward his preferred option, and asking for their support. He spoke from the heart. To Shackleton, "optimism is true moral courage". His plan was that that they would march across the ice, hopefully making five miles per day, pulling the lifeboats, until they got to open water. His proposal seemed logical and no one argued. Macklin wrote:

> "As always with him, what had happened had happened. It was in the past and he looked to the future … without emotion, melodrama, or excitement he said the ship and stores have gone – so now we'll go home."[11]

---

[10] Morrell, M. and Capparell, S. (2001), *Shackleton's Way*. London, Nicholas Brealey Publishing.

[11] Alexander, C. (1999), *The Endurance: Shackleton's Legendary Antarctic Expedition*. New York, Alfred Knopf.

From the beginning, Shackleton took control, leading by example. He realised that they would only be able to take the absolute necessities with them. He ordered the crew to jettison anything that was not essential. He made a point of being the first to throw away personal items, casting his gold cigarette case and watch into the snow. He made some exceptions – he allowed Hussey to keep his banjo - "vital mental medicine", the surgeon was allowed to keep his medical instruments for obvious reasons and Frank Hurley was allowed to salvage some of his photographic plates which survive to this day (in the possession of the Royal Geographical Society), and give an incredible visual record of the events. Trapped on an ice-floe, "Ocean Camp" was established. Between them, they had five tents and Shackleton assigned each man to a particular tent, mindful of the personalities involved, and he appointed a team leader for each of those groups. He assigned the most difficult to his own tent, including the photographer Hurley, who was a potential rival for group leader. They had only 18 reindeer-fur sleeping bags among the 28 men; the remainder being poorer quality woollen bags. To ensure that morale would not be affected, Shackleton drew lots for the better quality bags. Now that they were off the ship, rank, including his own, did not confer any privilege. Those that did not get the good sleeping bags didn't seem to mind. They knew the way the Boss handled it was fair. Likewise he ensured that the small food portions were evenly distributed.

Over the next few days, they made very poor progress, and the Boss changed the plans and called a halt to the march. The Boss held frequent emergency drills to pack up camp if the ice split, and every man was assigned a specific duty. Hopefully they would drift near to Paulet Island where he knew there were emergency supplies left by a previous Swedish expedition. The weeks passed and fresh supplies began to diminish. Their diet was supplemented with fresh seal which would provide vitamin C, vital to prevent scurvy. From his own first-hand experience with Scott, the Boss saw that it was imperative that everyone should take it. Knowing there would be resistance to its strong flavour, the Boss pronounced that it would be available only for the officers. After a while, a delegation came to Shackleton demanding that the rest of the men have their fair share. After brief consideration, he agreed to their request!

Even in blizzards, the Boss went to each tent every day to talk to the men and inquire as to their welfare. It was an opportunity to listen to their concerns. It was also an opportunity to plant ideas the Boss had about what needed to be done, and give people time to come to terms with the proposition. One example was when he believed the time had come to put the dogs down because they were a drain on scarce food resources. This prolonged period of idleness was difficult for all. Shackleton decided to make another attempt to march across the ice to Paulet Island in order to give the men a sense of control over their destiny. After many days of very hard work and very little progress, he once again called a halt to the effort. Dragging the boats was just too much work and outweighed any mental benefit. He decided to set up a new camp – "Camp Patience" – and let the 2-metre thick ice drift until they reached the open sea. At Worsley's insistence, Shackleton agreed to send a team back to retrieve one of the lifeboats, the *Stancomb Wills,* which had been left behind at "Camp Ocean".

Trouble Brewing

Morale was beginning to sag as any hope of survival diminished, and one member of the group, the carpenter McNeish, was became mutinous. He was refusing to do certain work when ordered by

Captain Worsley, saying that his contract had terminated with the sinking of the ship. Shackleton pulled McNeish aside and made clear to him he would have to obey orders. Later that evening, he called together the crew and read from the ship's Articles. Shackleton had originally added extra rules to the normal articles to include: "To perform any duty on board, in the boats, or on the shore as directed."[12] He told the men that they were still under the command of the ship's officers until they reached safe port but that, unlike the situation under normal ships' articles, they would also be paid during this time. It was enough to diffuse the situation. McNeish backed down, and Shackleton's action held the group together at a vital time. Their only hope of salvation was by operating together as a cohesive unit. Shackleton later denied the Polar Medal to McNeish over the incident.

The ice on which they were camped was drifting away from the uninhabited Paulet Island. Elephant Island was now the nearest landfall, but it was uninhabited. As they drifted north away from the Antarctic, the pack ice was slowly breaking up, and eventually on 9 April 1916, they were able to launch the three lifeboats: the *Dudly Docker*, *Stancomb Wills* and the *James Caird*. Again, the Boss picked the crew for each boat, putting the best men in the worst boat, knowing their seafaring skills would handle it. So far, there had been no casualties, though the months of idleness had left them extremely unfit. During the day, they rowed, and at night, tied up alongside the ice floes. There were a few isolated whaling stations some distance away where they could get help. Shackleton tried to head to these, but they were at the mercy of the strong currents. He had to change the plan on a few occasions. Days later, they hit the open sea and made a run for Elephant Island. Whenever he felt morale sagging, the Boss ordered extra rations to be distributed. After 170 days adrift, and seven days in open boats, they finally found a landing spot between the 600 metre high cliffs on the island. It was 497 days since they last set foot on solid land. Many in the group were at the point of mental and physical exhaustion.

Elephant Island

The uninhabited, and inhospitable Elephant Island was 1,000km from the tip of South America and some distance away from any known shipping routes. While the island provided plenty of fresh water from glaciers as well as seal and penguin meat, it could only ever be a staging post. Shackleton quickly set up a routine, and designated different tasks to the men. There were many different views among the group as to what they should do. He decided that the best hope for rescue was to take six men in the biggest and most stable boat – the *James Caird* – and try to reach civilisation and return with a rescue ship for the remaining men. There were three options open to them. The two nearest options were South America (1,000km) and the Falkland Islands (885km), but both would have entailed crossing Drake Passage, probably the most treacherous piece of ocean on the planet. Shackleton believed that the best option was to make for the whaling station on South Georgia Island, some 1,300km away but with prevailing winds to help them.

---

[12] Lansing, A. (1959), *Endurance: Shackleton's Incredible Voyage*. New York, Caroll & Graf.

The next major decision he had to make was who should be included in the crew, and who would remain behind. Shackleton would lead the attempt, and asked his second in command, Frank Wild, to stay on the island and maintain discipline and morale among the 22 men remaining behind. Shackleton had implicit trust in Wild that he would hold the group together in his absence. He called for volunteers for the trip, but he knew precisely who he was going to bring. The other five men that travelled with Shackleton included Captain Frank Worsley, who was captain of the *Endurance* and was chosen for his navigational skills – an essential requirement on the trip; Irishman Tom Crean for his mental and physical strength, all-round ability and good humour; another Irishman, Timothy McCarthy, a strong and experienced seaman; and "Chips" McNeish who had already caused trouble – Shackleton wanted to keep a close eye on him and not leave him behind where he could destroy morale; and finally Jack Vincent, another man who needed to be watched. To his credit, McNeish proved very resourceful and did a splendid job preparing the *James Caird* for the journey, taking pieces from the other two boats to build up the sides and create a canvas deck cover which would prove vital in keeping out the Antarctic swell. They packed the boat with supplies and ballast and on April 24, 1916 (Easter Monday – the same day that Patrick Pearse led the 1916 Rebellion in Dublin) they set out on the 1,300km journey for South Georgia. For the crew of the *James Caird* and those remaining on Elephant Island, their troubles were far from over.

Journey to South Georgia

The *James Caird* experienced some dreadful conditions on the journey, and the crew was continuously pumping water out of the boat. Their clothes were totally unsuited to the conditions and the men were constantly wet in freezing temperatures. The crew split into two groups, taking four-hour shifts. Those on watch would man the tiller, keep lookout and bail the boat. The others would try and snatch some sleep in wet sleeping bags lying on top of the supplies. Crean was designated cook, and preparing hot food under those conditions was an almost impossible, yet essential, task. He also played an invaluable role in keeping up morale with his appalling singing and his infectious good humour.

Worsley was incredibly skilled at navigation. Determining their position required using a sextant to calculate the angle of the sun on the horizon. With appalling weather conditions, most of the time no opportunities presented themselves. In total, they had only four sightings of the sun during their entire voyage to South Georgia. When those opportunities arose, It took two men to hold Worsley steady as he stood up in the mountainous swell to use the sextant, while Shackleton quickly recorded the readings and did the calculations. A tiny margin of error would mean that they would miss South Georgia and perish. The southern winter was approaching and conditions were deteriorating rapidly. The waves were running 20 metres high. Thick ice was forming on the canvas shelter and this had to be constantly chipped away or the weight of it would topple the boat. To make matters worse, salt water had now contaminated their fresh-water supply. It was imperative that they reach South Georgia soon. Again, Shackleton kept a close eye on each member's health, and ability to cope. When morale was sagging, he would call for hot food for all, so as not to single out any man in difficulty.

As dawn broke on May 8, small birds were seen flying overhead. They knew land was near. At midday they spotted the island. It was an incredible feat of navigation and seamanship. They wanted to land on the north eastern side of the island near the harbours, but 90km winds were blowing them to the South side, and were also preventing them from landing. Finally on May 10, with the sail broken, the men rowed the remaining few miles to shore. They had spent 17 days at sea, were exhausted and were out of fresh water. It was 522 days since they last set foot on South Georgia. They had completed the most extraordinary sea journey ever taken, but their problems were still far from over.

They struggled to get the boat safely out of the water and off-load the food. They cooked a meal and slept for 12 hours. The Boss surveyed the situation. During the last night at sea, the boat's rudder had been lost, thus preventing them from going by sea around to the whaling station at Stromness on the other side of the island. In addition, strong winds would most likely blow them away from land. The alternative was to cross the island to the other side, a distance of 48km as the crow flies, but over alpine-like peaks – the Allardyce mountains. McNeish and Vincent were physically unable to make the journey and Shackleton asked McCarthy to look after them, while Crean, Worsley and Shackleton would attempt to cross the mountains and get help. Once again, the weather had deteriorated and it was the evening of May 19 before the three could set out. McNeish demonstrated great ingenuity by taking brass screws out of the *James Caird* and fixed them to the soles of their boots to give them traction on the ice.

Crossing the Allardyce Mountains

They made many attempts to cross the mountains, and had to retrace their steps on numerous occasions and try a different route as their way was blocked by sheer cliffs. Nevertheless, they made good progress, but as the second night descended, so too did fog. They were at an altitude of 1,500m, and without tents or sleeping bags they needed to get down to a lower altitude quickly. They made an improvised toboggan out of a length of rope, and linked to one another, slid down a 900m slope in a couple of minutes. Exhausted and dehydrated, they continued on their trek. The Boss knew the lives of all the other men depended on his keeping the show on the road. Later they stopped for a rest; Crean and Worsley quickly fell asleep. Shackleton too was dozing off but realised that without protection, sleeping would be fatal in the freezing temperatures. He woke the other two after a few minutes and told them they had been asleep for a couple of hours and it was time to move on. His thinking saved their lives. As dawn broke, they heard the steam whistle at Stromness. Thirty hours after they had set off, they knew they were almost there. But the terrain was still extremely difficult, and dangerous. By early afternoon, they were on a ridge above Stromness, and made their way down, at one stage having to climb down an icy waterfall. It was thirty-six hours of a continuous trek across inhospitable mountains. Their clothes were tattered, their faces black and their hair long and matted when they arrived at the station. The station manager looked at them and asked "who the hell are you?" and the Boss addressed the startled men inside: "My name is Shackleton". The men were bathed and fed and given fresh clothes. A rescue party set out immediately by sea to collect NcNeish, Vincent and McCarthy from the west coast of the island.

Rounding up the Crew

Shackleton then organised a steamer, the *Southern Sky* to rescue the remaining 22 men from Elephant Island, but the ship ran into heavy ice and was unsuited for the task. Shackleton then headed for the Falkland Islands to get another ship. With the First World War still raging, it proved impossible, but he then appealed to the Uruguayan government who sent a steamer, the *Instituto do Pesca No 1*, to Port Stanley in the Falkland Islands where it picked up Shackleton, Worsley and Crean (the other three had already returned to Britain). The second attempt also failed to get through the ice to Elephant Island and they sailed to Punta Areanas in Chile where they chartered a schooner, *Emma*. That attempt also failed, and once again they returned to Port Stanley. Shackleton appealed to the Chilean government for help and they dispatched a steel-hulled steamer, the *Yelco*. This time they succeeded, and on 30 August 1916, Shackleton led the rescue party ashore – 128 days after they had originally set out for South Georgia Island. His first words to the astonished men were: "Are you all well?" All 22 men on Elephant Island were still alive, although some were in bad condition after their ordeal. Shackleton had chosen well in picking Wild to look after the men. In turn, Wild based his leadership style on Shackleton. With all the men on board the Yelco, the ship returned to Punta Arenas in Chile on September 20, 1916. From there, the crew made their way to Buenos Aires and back to Britain. Shackleton then set about rescuing the remaining men from the *Aurora,* who had been stranded on the Ross Sea side of the Antarctic. He finally arrived back in Britain in May 1917.

Shackleton hadn't succeeded in the difficult task of crossing the Antarctic. He did succeed, however, in leading the most amazing turnaround situation ever imagined. The 28 men of the *Endurance* arrived safely home to their families. To paraphrase the words of the BBC journalist Brian Hanrahan during the Falklands War in 1982 – he counted them all out, and he counted them home again.

Bibliography

Accenture, 2010, http://www.accenture.com/us-en/Pages/service-banking-global-risk-management-study.aspx, Accessed 27 February 2011

Adair, J., 1983, *Effective Leadership*, Aldershot, Gower

Aiello, R. and Watkins, D., 2000, "The Fine Art of Friendly Acquisitions", *Harvard Business Review*, November/December 2000, Vol. 78, Issue 6, pp.100–107

Alexandre, C., 1998, *The Endurance: Shackleton's Legendary Antarctic Voyage*, New York, Alfred A. Knopf

Amabile, T. and Kramer, S., 2010, "What really motivates employees?", *Harvard Business Review*, January/February 2010, Vol. 88, Issue 1, pp.43–44

Ambrose, S., 2003, *Eisenhower: Soldier and President*, London, Pocket Books

Argyris, C. and Schon, D., 1978, *Organisational Learning: A Theory of Action Perspective*, Wokingham, Addison-Wesley

Aristotle, Translated by Thomson, J., 1976, *Ethics*, Harmondsworth, Penguin

Ashkenas, R. and Francis, S., 2000, "Integration Managers, Special Leaders for Our Times", *Harvard Business Review*, November/December 2000, Vol. 78, Issue 6, pp.108–116

Balboni, F. *et al.*, 2010, "Analytics: The New Path to Value", *IBM Institute for Business Value and MIT Sloan Management Review*, Fall 2010

Balogun, J. and Hope Hailey, V., 1999, *Exploring Strategic Change*, Harlow, Essex, Prentice Hall, Financial Times

Barney, J., 2002, *Gaining and Sustaining Competitive Advantage*, 2nd Ed., Upper Saddle River, NJ, Prentice Hall

Barney, J.B., 1986, "Organisational Culture: Can it be a source of sustained competitive advantage?", *Academy of Management Review*, 1986, Vol. 11, No. 3

Barrington, K., 2010, "Truth-seekers are left to whistle down the wind for real protection", *The Sunday Business Post*, 23 May 2010, p.5

Barry, F., 2010, "Politics and Economic Policy Making in Ireland" in J. Hogan *et al.* (Eds), *Irish Business & Society*, pp.28–43, Dublin, Gill & Macmillan

Bartlett, C. and Ghoshal, S., 1990, "Matrix Management: Not a Structure, a Frame of Mind", *Harvard Business Review*, July/August 1990, Vol. 68, Issue 4, pp.138–145

Bass, B., 1990, "From Transactional to Transformational Leadership: Learning to Share the Vision", *Organizational Dynamics*, Winter 1990, p.22

BBC, 2011, "Cut in corporation tax 'could cost NI £280m', PwC says", http://www.bbc.co.uk/news/uk-northern-ireland-12128999, Accessed 23 February 2011

BBC, 1998, http://news.bbc.co.uk/2/hi/europe/221508.stm, Accessed 23 July 2010

Beasley, A., 2010, "McCreevy quits over 'privileged' position", *The Irish Times*, 9 October 2010, p.17

Beer, M. and Nohria, N., 2000, *Breaking the Code of Change*, Boston, Harvard Business School Press

Benis, W. and Nanus, B., 1985, *Leaders: The Strategies for Taking Charge*, New York, Harper & Row

Berton, E., 2010, "Dress to impress, UBS tells staff", *The Wall Street Journal*, 14 December 2010, http://online.wsj.com/article/SB10001424052748704694004576019783931381042.html?mod=djemTMB_t, Accessed 21 February 2011

Bettis, R. and Prahalad, C., 1995, "The Dominant Logic: Retrospective and Extension", *Strategic Management Journal*, Vol. 16, Issue 1 (1995) pp.5–15

Bloom, M., 1999, "The Performance Effects of Pay Dispersion on Individuals and Organisations", *Academy of Management Journal*, February 1999, pp.25–40

Bohan, H., 2009, "A new kind of leadership now required", *Irish Times*, 6 October 2009, p.14

Bower, J., 2001, "Not All M&As Are Alike – and That Matters", *Harvard Business Review*, March 2001, Vol. 79, Issue 3, pp.92–101

Bower, J. and Gilbert, C., 2007, "How everyday decisions create or destroy your company's strategy", *Harvard Business Review*, February 2007, Vol. 85, Issue 2, pp.72–79

Breen, J., 2008, *Interview with the Author*, September 2008

Brousseau, K. *et al.*, 2006, "The seasoned executive's decision-making style", *Harvard Business Review*, February 2006, Vol. 84, Issue 2, pp.110–121

Brown, A., 1994, "Transformational Leadership in Tackling Technical Change", *Journal of General Management*, Vol. 19, Issue 4, pp.1–10

Bruntland, G.H., 1987, http://www.thegoalfocusedway.com/?p=112, Accessed 12 March 2011

Buelens, M. *et al.*, 2006, *Organisational Behaviour*, Maidenhead, McGraw-Hill

Campbell, A. *et al.*, 1995, "Corporate Strategy: The Quest for Parenting Advantage", *Harvard Business Review*, March/April 1995, Vol. 73, Issue 2, pp.120–132

Carey, B., 2008, "Fund boss wants DCC broken up", *Sunday Times*, 29 June 2008

Carey, D., 2000, "Making mergers succeed", *Harvard Business Review*, May/June 2000, Vol. 79, Issue 3, pp.145–154

Carroll, L., 1989, *Alice's Adventures in Wonderland*, London, Hutchinson

Carswell, S., 2006, *Something Rotten: Irish Banking Scandals*, Dublin, Gill & Macmillan

Carswell, S., 2009, "Bankers must create Climate of Responsibility says Archbishop", *Irish Times*, 29 January 2009, p.21

CER, 2011, http://www.cer.ie/en/about-us-overview.aspx, Accessed 22 March 2011

Chandler, A., 1962, *Strategy and Structure*, Cambridge, MA, MIT Press

Chesborough, H. and Garman, A., 2008, "How Open Innovation Can Help You Cope in Lean Times", *Harvard Business Review*, December 2009, Vol. 87, Issue 12, pp.68–76

Clancy, P. and Murphy, G., 2006, *Outsourcing Government: Public Bodies and Accountability*, Dublin, TASC

Clancy, P. *et al.*, 2010, *Mapping the Golden Circle*, Dublin, TASC

Clerkin, D., 2008, "IAWS hold the whip in Hiestand Merger", *Sunday Business Post*, 15 June 2008, Money and Markets, p.3

Coffey, A., 2008, "Irish boys score with Sunderland", *Sunday Times*, 17 August 2008, Business and Money, p.18

Coffey, A., 2010, "Managing Cash Flow", *The Sunday Times*, 7 October 2010, Business Section, p.5

Collins, J. and Porras, J., 1996, "Building your company's vision", *Harvard Business Review*, September/October 1996, Vol. 74, Issue 5, pp.65–77

Collins, J., 2001, *Good to Great*, London, Random House Business Books

Collins, L., 2007, *Irish Family Feuds*, Dublin, Mentor Books

Committee on Standards in Public Life, 2010, *Review and Annual Report 2008-2009*, London, Committee on Standards in Public Life

Coogan, T.P., 2003, *Ireland in the Twentieth Century*, London Hutchinson

Cooke, N., 2008, "Irish firms must look to foreign markets for growth", *Sunday Business Post*, 29 June 2008

Cooke, N., 2011, "Plane Talker", *The Sunday Business Post*, 30 January 2011, p.17

Coonan, C., 2010, "Chinese developing taste for Irish Tayto", *The Irish Times*, 28 December 2010

Cooper, M., 2009, *Who really runs Ireland?*, Dublin, Penguin Ireland

Covey, S., 1994, *The Seven Habits of Highly Effective People,* London, Simon & Schuster

Covey, S., 2004, *The 8th Habit: From Effectiveness to Greatness*, London, Simon & Schuster

Creaton, S., 2004, *Ryanair*, London Aurum

Creaton, S. and O'Cleary, C., 2002, *Panic at the Bank*, Dublin, Gill & Macmillan

Csikszentmihalyi, M., 1990, *The Psychology of Optimal Experience*, New York, Harper Collins

CSO, 2010, http://www.cso.ie/Quicktables/GetQuickTables.aspx?FileName=TRDA1.asp&TableName=Overseas Visits to and from Ireland&StatisticalProduct=DB_TM, Accessed 30 January 2011

Cúl Green, 2011, "A cleaner, greener Croke Park", http://www.culgreen.ie/en/About_en.aspx, Accessed 12 March 2011

Curran, R., 2008, "Property slump gives Quinlan plenty to ponder", Dublin, *Sunday Business Post*, 10 August 2008, Money & Markets, p.2

Curran, R., 2008, "Scottish Water Fraud has hurt Greencore", Dublin, *Sunday Business Post*, 29 June 2008

Curran, R., 2011, "How BoSi paid a heavy price for its Irish property gambles", *Sunday Business Post*, 20 February 2011, p.N8

Curren, R. and Daly, G., 2008, "Kerry Group loses €20m on collapse of deal", *Sunday Business Post*, 31 August 2008, Money & Markets, p.1

Czeisler, C., 2006, "Sleep Deficit: The Performance Killer", *Harvard Business Review*, October 2006, Vol. 84, Issue 10, pp.53–59

Dalkey, N.C. *et al.*, 1972, *Studies in the Quality of Life: Delphi and Decision-making*, Lexington, Lexington Books

Dallek, R., 2003, *John F. Kennedy: An Unfinished Life 1917–1963,* London, Penguin Group

Darwin, J. *et al.*, 2002, *Developing Strategies for Change*, Harlow, Essex, Prentice Hall, Financial Times

De Bono, E., 1985, *Six Thinking Hats*, London, Penguin

De Bréadún, D., 2008, "Still a Culture of Non-compliance and Non-payment of Tax", *Irish Times*, 23 September 2008, p.9

Dess, G. *et al.*, 2004, *Strategic Management*, Boston, McGraw-Hill

Devine, J., 2008, "Mergers and Acquisitions Surge 32%, Mainly in First Half of Year", *The Irish Times*, 5 January 2008

Dibb, S. *et al.*, 2006, *Marketing Concepts and Strategies*, Houghton Mifflin

Digby, D. and Vishwanath, V., 2006, "Localisation: The Revolution in Consumer Markets", Boston, *Harvard Business Review*, April 2006, Vol. 84, Issue 4, pp.82–92

Donaldson, T. and Dunfee, T., 1994, "Towards a Unified Conception of Business Ethics: Integrative Social Contracts Theory", *Academy of Management Review*, Vol. 19, Issue 2, April 1994, pp.252–84

Donovan, D., 2011, "Loss of fiscal sovereignty inevitable if euro is to survive", *The Irish Times*, 13 January 2011, p.16

Dose, J.J., 1997, "Work Values: An Integrative Framework and Illustrative Application to Organisational Socialisation", *Journal of Occupational and Organisational Psychology*, September 1997, pp.219–40

Drucker, P., 1954, *The Practice of Management*, New York, Harper & Row

Dublin Docklands Development Authority, 2008, *6th Annual Social Regeneration Conference*, Dublin, DDDA

Dyer, J. *et al*, 2004, "When to Ally and When to Acquire", *Harvard Business Review*, July/August 2004, Vol. 82, Issue 7/8, pp.108–115

Early, P.C., and Mosakowski, E., 2004, "Cultural Intelligence", *Harvard Business Review*, October 2004, Vol. 82, Issue 10, pp.139–146

Enterprise Ireland, 2010, *Chief Executive Officer's Report*, http://www.enterprise-ireland.com/annualreport2009/ceo_report_2.html (accessed 28 March 2011)

ESB, 2011, http://www.esb.ie/main/sustainability/strategy-to-2020.jsp, Accessed 26 January 2011

ESRI, 2010, *Quarterly Economic Commentary Winter 2010*, Dublin, ESRI

Europa, 2011, http://europa.eu/index_en.htm, Accessed 22 March 2011

Fáilte Ireland, 2007, "Tourism and the Environment", *Fáilte Irelands Action Plan 2007–2009*, Dublin Fáilte Ireland

Fallon, J., 2010, "Outsmart and outthink them: ex Intel chief gives his vision", *The Irish Times*, 17 November 2010, Business Today, p.19

Feldman, D., 1981, "The Multiple Socialisation of Organisation Members", *Academy of Management Review*, April 1981, pp.309–18

Finlay, P., 2000, *Strategic Management*, Harlow, Essex, Prentice Hall Financial Times

Fitzroy, P. and Hulbert, J., 2005, *Strategic Management: Creating value in Turbulent Times*, London, Wiley

Flemming, L., 2010, "Whistleblowing and White Collar Crime, Why Ireland needs Legislative Change", *Accountancy Ireland*, December 2010, Vol. 42, Issue 6

Florida, R. and Goodnight, J., 2005, "Managing for Creativity", *Harvard Business Review*, July/August 2008, Vol. 83, Issue 7/8, pp.124–131

Forfás, 2005, *Making Technological Knowledge Work*, Dublin, Technopolis/Forfás

Forfás, 2009, *Forfás Annual Report 2009*, http://www.forfas.ie/media/forfas100602-Annual_Report_2009_English.pdf, Accessed 21 March 2011

Forston, D., 2008, "Five Lehman Chiefs Scoop $100m—Days Before Collapse", *Sunday Times*, 12 October 2008, Business This Week, p.3

Franklin, D. *et al.*, 2008, "Just Good Business" Special Report, London, *The Economist*, 19 January 2008

Freeman, R.E., 1985, *Strategic Management: A Stakeholder Approach*, Boston Ballinger

French, J. and Raven, B., 1959, "The Basis of Social Power" in *Studies in Social Power*, Ed. Cartwright, D., Michigan, University of Michigan Press

Gerstner, L., 2002, *Who Says Elephants Can't Dance*, London, Harper Collins

Ghemawat, P., 2001, "Distance Still Matters", *Harvard Business Review*, September 2001, Vol. 79, Issue 8, pp.137–147

Ghemawat, P., 2003, "The Forgotten Strategy", *Harvard Business Review*, November 2003, Vol. 81, Issue 11, pp.76–84

Ghemawat, P., 2010, "Finding your strategy in the new landscape", *Harvard Business Review*, March 2010, Vol. 88, Issue 2, pp.54–60

Giuliani, R., 2002, *Leadership*, London, Time Warner

Goleman, D., 1995, *Emotional Intelligence*, London, Bloomsbury

Goleman, D. *et al.*, 2002, *The New Leaders*, London, Little, Brown

Goold, M. and Campbell, A., 2002, "Do You Have a Well-designed Organisation?", *Harvard Business Review*, March 2002, Vol. 80, Issue 3, pp.117–224

Goold, M. and Campbell, A., 1987, *Strategies and Styles*, Oxford, Blackwell

Goold, M. and Campbell, A., 1998, "Desperately Seeking Synergy", *Harvard Business Review*, September/October 98, Vol. 76, Issue 2, pp.131–45

Goold, M. *et al.*, 1994, *Corporate Level Strategy: Creating Value in theMultibusiness Company*, Chichester, Wiley

Grant, R., 2010, *Contemporary Strategic Analysis: Text and Cases*, 7th Ed., Chichester, John Wiley & Sons Ltd

Grant Thornton, 2010, *Corporate Governance Review 2010*, Dublin, Grant Thornton

Greenpeace, 2007, http://www.greenpeace.org/international/en/about/history/the-brent-spar/, Accessed 23 July 2010

Griffeth, R. and Horn, P., 2001, *Retaining Valued Employees*, Thousand Oaks, CA, Sage Publications

Griffin, R., 2005, *Management*, Boston, Houghton Mifflin

Guerrera, F., 2009, "Welsh Condemns Share Price Focus", *The Financial Times*, 12 March 2009

Gunnigle, P. *et al.*, 2006, *Human Resource Management in Ireland*, 3rd Ed., Dublin, Gill & Macmillan

Handcock, C., 2008, "Kerry to Appeal Competition Authority Ruling On Breo", *Irish Times*, 30 September 2008, p.23

Hamel, G. and Prahalad, C., 2005, "Strategic Intent", *Harvard Business Review*, July/August 2005, Vol. 83, Issue 7/8, pp.148–161

Hamm, J., 2006, "The Five Messages Leaders Must Manage", *Harvard Business Review*, May 2006, Vol. 84, Issue 5, pp.115–123

Hammer, M. and Champy, J., 1993, *Reengineering the Corporation*, New York, Harper Business

Handcock, C., 2010, "Elderfield says level of mortgage arrears likely to get worse but should not destabilise banks", *The Irish Times*, 9 November 2010, p.18

Harding Clark, S.C., M., 2006, *The Lourdes Hospital Inquiry: An Inquiry into Peripartum Hysterectomy at our Lady of Lourdes Hospital, Drogheda*, Dublin, Stationery office

Handy, C., 1999, *Understanding Organisations*, London, Penguin

Harper, N. and Viguerie, P., 2002, "Are You Too Focused?", *The McKinsey Quarterly*, 2002 Special Edition: Risk and Resilience

Harrison, R., 1972, "Understanding your Organisation's Character", *Harvard Business Review*, May/June 1972, Vol. 50, Issue 3, pp.119–128

Hartman, L., 2002, *Perspective in Business Ethics*, New York, McGraw-Hill

Hassan, F., 2006, "Leading Change from the Top Line", *Harvard Business Review*, July/August, 2006, Vol. 84, Issue 7/8, pp.90–97

Hayes, R. and Wheelwright, S., 1979, "The Dynamics of Process-Product Life Cycles", *Harvard Business Review*, March/April 1979, Vol. 57, Issue 2

Heacox, K., 1999, *Shackleton: The Antarctic Challenge*, Washington, National Geographic

Hesselbein, F. and Cohen, P. (Eds.), 1999, *Leader to Leader: Enduring Insights on Leadership*, New York, Jossey-Bass

Hesselbein, F. and Shinseki, E. (Eds), 2004, *Be-Know-Do: Leadership the Army Way*, San Francisco, Jossey-Bass

Higgs, D., 2003, *Review of the role and effectiveness of non-executive directors*, London, The Stationery Office

Hill, C. and Jones, G., 2004, *Strategic Management: An Integrated Approach*, Boston, Houghton Mifflin

Hill, C. and Jones, G., 2009, *Theory of Strategic Management with Cases*, New York, South-Western Cengage Learning

Hines, P., 1993, "Integrated Material Management: The Value Chain Redefined", *The International Journal of Logistics Management*, Vol. 4, Issue 1, pp.13–21

Honohan, P., 2010, *The Irish Banking Crisis: Regulatory and Financial Stability Policy 2003–2008*, Dublin, Central Bank of Ireland

House, R., 1971, "A Path-goal Theory of Leader Effectiveness", *Administrative Science Quarterly*, 16 September 1971, Vol. 16, Issue 3, pp.321–338

Huber, G.P., 1980, *Managerial Decision-making*, Glenview, Scott Foresman & Co.

Huff, A. *et al.*, 2009, *Strategic Management: Logic and Action*, Hoboken, NJ, Wiley

Humphries, J., 2004, "Women hold 5 per cent of seats on Irish Boards", *The Irish Times*, 23 January 2004

Hunt, C., 2010, *National Strategy for Higher Education*, Dublin, Strategy Group for Higher Education

Hurley, F., 2001, *South With Endurance: Shackleton's Antarctic Expedition 1914–1917. The Photographs of Frank Hurley*, London, Bloomsbury

Huselid, M., 1995, "The impact of human resource management practices on turnover, productivity and corporate financial performance", *Academy of Management Journal*, Vol. 39, Issue 3, pp.635–672

Interbrand, 2010, *Best Global Brands 2010*, http://www.interbrand.com/en/best-global-brands/best-global-brands-2008/best-global-brands-2010.aspx, Accessed 12 March 2010

Irish Management Institute, 2010, *Closing the Gap*, Dublin, IMI

Ion Equity, 2008, *Mergers and Acquisitions 2007*, Dublin, *The Irish Times*, 5 January 2008

ISE, 2010, *Irish Stock Exchange Adopts New Rules in relation to Corporate Governance*, Dublin, Irish Stock Exchange

Janis, I., 1982, *Groupthink*, 2nd Ed., Boston, Houghton Mifflin

Johnson, G. *et al.*, 2008, *Exploring Corporate Strategy*, 8th Ed., Harlow, Essex, Prentice Hall, Financial Times

Johnson, G. *et al.*, 2011, *Exploring Strategy: Text and Cases*, 9th Ed., Harlow, Essex, Prentice Hall. Financial Times

Judson, A., 1991, *Changing Behaviour in Organisations: Minimising Resistance to Change*, Cambridge, MA, Basil Blackwell

Kanter, R.M., 1987, "Managing Traumatic Change: Avoiding the 'Unlucky 13'", *Management Review*, May 1987, pp.23–24

Kanter, R.M., 1989, *When Giants Learn to Dance*, London, Simon & Schuster

Kanter, R.M., 1994, "Collaborate Advantage: The Art of Alliances", *Harvard Business Review*, July/August 1994, Vol. 72, Issue 4, pp.96–108

Kanter, R.M., 1999, "From Spare Change to Real Change", *Harvard Business Review*, May/June 1999, Vol. 77, Issue 3, pp.122–132

Kanter, R.M., 2003, "Thriving Locally in the Global Economy", *Harvard Business Review*, August 2003, Vol. 81, Issue 8, pp.119–127

Kanter, R.M., 2004, "The Middle Manager as Innovator", *Harvard Business Review*, July/August 2004, Vol. 82, Issue 7/8, pp.156–161

Kanter, R.M., 2008, "Transforming Giants", *Harvard Business Review*, January 2008, Vol. 86, Issue 1, pp.43–52

Kaplan, R. and Norton, D., 1993, "Putting the Balanced Scorecard to Work", *Harvard Business Review*, September/October 1993, Vol. 71, Issue 5, pp.134–147

Kaplan, R. and Norton, D., 2001, *The Strategy Focused Organisation: How Balanced Scorecard Companies Thrive in the New Business Environment*, Boston, Harvard Business School Press

Kaplan, R. and Norton, D., 2005, "The Balanced Scorecard: Measures that Drive Performance", *Harvard Business Review*, July/August 2005, Vol. 87, Issue 7/8, pp.172–180

Kaplan, R. and Norton, D., 2006, "How to Implement a Strategy Without Disrupting your Organisation", *Harvard Business Review*, March 2005, Vol. 84, Issue 3, pp.100–109

Kaplan, R. and Norton, D., 2008, "Mastering the Management System", *Harvard Business Review*, January 2008, Vol. 86, Issue 1, pp.62–77

Kaplan, R. *et al.*, 2010, "Managing Alliances with the Balanced Scorecard", *Harvard Business Review*, January/February 2010, Vol. 88, Issue 1, pp.114–120

Katzenbach, J. and Smith, D., 1993, *The Wisdom of Teams: Creating the High-Performance Organisation*, New York, Harper Business

Keena, C., 2008, "DCC to Pay €41m in Fyffes Case Settlement", *Irish Times*, 15 April 2008

Keena, C., 2011, "Corporation Tax: Unravelling the Myths", *The Irish Times*, 11 February 2011, Finance, p.5

Kenny, I., 1987, *In Good Company: Conversations with Irish Leaders*, Dublin, Gill & Macmillan

Kenny, I., 1991, *Out On Their Own: Conversations with Irish Entrepreneurs*, Dublin, Gill & Macmillan

Kenny, I., 2005, *Achievers, Visionary Irish Leaders who Achieved their Dream*, Cork, Oak Tree Press

Kerry Group PLC, 2011, www.kerrygroup.com/page.asp?pid=82 (accessed 27 February 2011)

Ket de Vries, M., 2001, *The Leadership Mystique*, London, Financial Times, Prentice Hall

Kiberd, D., 2007, "There's no Stopping the Service Sector", *The Sunday Times*, 28 October 2007, Business, p.4.

Kim, C. and Maubourgne, R., 2002, Charting your company's future, *Harvard Business Review*, Vol. 80, Issue 6, pp.76–82

Kimes, S. (2003), "A Strategic Approach to Yield Management", in Ingold, A. *et al.* (Eds.) *Yield Management: Strategies for the Service Industry*, London, Continuum

Knights, D. and Willmott, H., 2007, *Introducing Organisational Behaviour and Management*, London, Thomson Learning

Kotler, P. *et al.*, 2007, *Principles of Marketing*, 4th European Ed., Upper Saddle River, NJ, Prentice Hall Europe

Kotter, J., 1996, *Leading Change*, Boston, Harvard Business School Press

Kotter, J., 2007, "Leading Change: Why Transformation Efforts Fail", *Harvard Business Review*, January 2007, Vol. 85, Issue 1, pp.96–103

Kotter J. and Cohen D., 2002, *The Heart of Change*, Boston, Harvard Business School Press

Kouzes, J. and Posner, B., 1995, *The Leadership Challenge*, San Francisco, Jossey-Bass

Kreitner, R., 1998, *Management*, 7th Ed., Boston, Houghton Mifflin

Lane, B., 2008, *Jacked Up: The Inside Story of how Jack Welch Talked GE into Becoming the World's Greatest Company*, New York, McGraw-Hill

Lansing, A., 1959, *Endurance: Shackleton's Incredible Voyage*, New York, Carroll and Graf

Largo Foods, 2011, www.largofoods.ie/about_us/corporate_history.asp (accessed 21 March 2011)

Lavery, B. and O'Brien, T., 2005, "Insurers' trails lead to Dublin", *The New York Times*, http://query.nytimes.com/gst/fullpage.html?res=9805EED9103FF932A35757C0A9639C8B63, Accessed 30 January 2011

Leahy, P., 2009, *Showtime: The Inside Story of Fianna Fáil in Power*, Dublin, Penguin Ireland

Lencioni, P., 2002, "Make Your Values Mean Something", *Harvard Business Review*, July 2002, Vol. 80, Issue 7, p.113–117

Levitt, T., 1960, "Marketing Myopia", *Harvard Business Review Reprint*, July/August 2004, Vol. 82, Issue 7/8, pp.138–149

Levitt, T., 2002, "Creativity is not enough", *Harvard Business Review*, August 2002, Vol. 80, Issue 8, pp.137–14

Levitt, T., 1983, "The Globalisation of Markets", *Harvard Business Review*, May/June1983, Vol. 61, Issue 3

Lewin, K., 1951, *Field Theory in Social Science*, New York, Harper & Row

Likert, R., 1961, *New Patterns of Management*, New York, McGraw-Hill

Liu, Y., 2007, "The Value of Human Resource Management for Organisational Performance", *Business Horizons*, November/December 2007, Vol. 50, Issue 6, pp.503–511

Locke, E. and Latham, G., 1990, *A Theory of Goal Setting and Task Performance*, Upper Saddle River, NJ, Prentice Hall

Lonergan, J., 2006, *Address to Social Care Conference*, Institute of Technology, Tralee

Lunn, P., 2008, "Economic Uncertainty Takes Revenge on Hubris of Traders", *Irish Times*, 24 September 2008, p.14

Lynch, R., 2003, *Corporate Strategy*, 3rd Ed., Harlow, Essex, Prentice Hall. Financial Times

Lynch, R. 2008, *Strategic Management*, 5th Ed., Harlow, Essex, Prentice Hall, Financial Times

Lynch, S., 2010, "AIB to Pay up to €10m in Backdated Employee Bonuses", *The Irish Times*, 10 November 2010, p.18

Lynch, S., 2010, "Irish Management Skills Weak", *The Irish Times*, 21 December 2010, p.17

Lyons, T., 2008, "Dublin Port in Mekong Move", London, *Sunday Times*, 17 August 2008, Business and Money, p.1

Lyons, T., 2008, "Irish IT blow as Dell boss quits", London, *Sunday Times*, 11 August 2008, Business and Money, p.1

Lyons, T. and Carey, B., 2011, *The Fitzpatrick Tapes: The Rise and Fall of One Man, One Bank and One Country*, Dublin, Penguin Ireland

Macaro, A. and Baggini, J., 2010, "The Shrink and the Sage", *Financial Times Magazine*, 27 November 2010, p.51

MacConnell, S., 2011, "Bord Bia Says 70% of Exporters are Confident About Outlook", *Irish Times*, 13 January 2011, p.18

Maclear, M., 1981, *The Ten Thousand Day War*, London, Thames Mandarin

Magee, B., 1998, *The Story of Philosophy*, London, Dorling Kindersley

Mankins, M., 2006, "Stop Making Plans; Start Making Decisions", *Harvard Business Review*, January 2006, Vol. 84, Issue 3, pp.76–84

Mankins, M. and Steele, R., 2005, "Turning Great Strategy into Great Performance", *Harvard Business Review*, July/August 2005, Vol. 83, Issue 7/8, pp.64–72

March, J. and Simon, H., 1958, *Organisation*, New York, John Wiley & Son

Margolis, J. and Stoltz, P., 2010, "How to Bounce Back from Adversity", *Harvard Business Review*, January/February 2010, Vol. 88, Issue 1, pp.86–92

Markides, C., 1997, "To diversify or not to diversify", *Harvard Business Review*, November/December 1997, Vol. 75, Issue 6, pp.93–99

Martin, J., 2005, *Organisational Behaviour and Management*, 3rd Ed., London, Thomson Learning Ltd

Martin, J. and Schmidt, C., 2010, "How to Keep Your Top Talent", *Harvard Business Review*, May 2010, Vol. 88, Issue 5, pp.51–61

Martin, R., 2010, "The Age of Customer Capitalism", *Harvard Business Review*, January 2010, Vol. 88, Issue 1, pp.58–65

McCall, B., 2010, "Are We Ready to Wean Off FDI?", *Irish Times*, 26 November 2010, Innovation, p.45

McCaughran, S., 2008, "Investors Looking for Blue Gold", *Sunday Business Post*, 20 July 2008

McClelland, D., 1961, *The Achieving Society*, New York, Free Press

McElhaney, K.A., 2008, *Just Good Business: The Strategic Guide to Aligning Corporate Responsibility and Brand*, Williston, Barrett-Koehler

McGarry, S., 2007, "Franchise Guide: A Short Guide to Franchising", Dublin, Franchise Direct.com, www.wceb.ie/download/1/franchise_guide.pdf (accessed 22 June 2011)

McGreevy, R., 2008, "Hibernian Insurance to Outsource Jobs", Dublin, *Irish Times*, 3 July 2008

McKay, S., 2009, "The Kindness of Strangers", *Irish Times*, 14 March 2009, Magazine, p.17

McKinsey & Co., 2009, *Management Matters in Northern Ireland and Republic of Ireland*, Dublin, Forfás

McNamara, R., 1995, *The Tragedy and Lessons of the Vietnam War*, New York, Times Books

McShane, S. and Von Glinow, M., 2009, *Organisational Behaviour*, 2nd Ed., New York, McGraw-Hill

Micklethwait, J. and Wooldridge, A., 1996, *The Witch Doctors*, London, Heinemann

Miles, R., 2010, "Accelerating Corporate Transformations (Don't Lose Your Nerve)", *Harvard Business Review*, January/February 2010, Vol. 88, Issue 1, pp.68–75

Miles, R. and Snow, C., 1978, *Organisational Strategy, Structure and Process*, New York, McGraw-Hill

Mintzberg, H., 1979, *The Structuring of Organisations: A Synthesis of Research*, New Jersey, Prentice Hall

Mintzberg, H., 1994, "The Rise and Fall of Strategic Planning", *Harvard Business Review*, January/February 1994, Vol. 72, Issue 1, pp.101–114

Mintzberg, H. and Waters, J., 1985, "Of Strategies: Deliberate and Emergent", *Management Journal*, Vol. 6, Issue 3, pp.257–272

Moore, G., 2005, "Strategy and Your Stronger Hand", *Harvard Business Review*, December 2005, Vol. 83, Issue 2, pp.62–72

Morley, M. and Heraty, N. (Eds), 2000, *Strategic Management in Ireland*, Dublin, Gill & Macmillan

Mourkogiannis, N., 2006, *Purpose – The Starting Point of Great Companies*, New York Palgrave Macmillan

Murphy, D. and Devlin, M., 2009, *Banksters: How a powerful elite squandered Ireland's wealth*, Dublin, Hachette Books Ireland

Murphy, Y. *et al.*, 2009, *Report into the Catholic Archdiocese of Dublin*, Dublin, The Stationery Office

Neilson, G. *et al.*, 2008, "The Secrets to Successful Strategy Execution", *Harvard Business Review*, June 2008, Vol. 86, Issue 6, pp.60–70

New, S., 2010, "The Transparent Supply Chain", *Harvard Business Review*, October 2010, Vol. 88, Issue 10, pp.76–82

Nichols, J. and Roslow, S., "The S Curve: An Aid to Strategic Marketing", *Journal of Consumer Marketing*, 1986, Vol. 3, Issue 2, pp.53–64

Nidumolu, R. *et al.*, 2009, "Why Sustainability is the Key Driver of Innovation", *Harvard Business Review*, September 2009, Vol. 87, Issue 9, pp.57–64

Nonaka, I. and Takeuchi, H., 1995, *The Knowledge Creating Company*, Oxford, Oxford University Press

Nugent, F., 2003, *Seek the Frozen Lands: Irish Explorers 1940–1922*, Cork, The Collins Press

Nutt, P., 1986, "Tactics of Implementation", *Academy of Management Journal*, June 1986, pp.230–261

Nyberg, P., 2011, "Misjudging Risk: Causes of the systemic banking crisis in Ireland", *Report of the Commission of Investigation into the Banking Sector in Ireland*, Dublin, Government Publications Office

O'Brien, J. and Marakas, G., 2008, *Management Information Systems*, 8th Ed., New York, McGraw-Hill

O'Cleary, C., 2007, *The Billionaire Who Wasn't*, New York, Public Affairs

O'Donovan, H., 2009, "CRAIC – A Model Suitable for Irish Coaching Psychology", *The Coaching Psychologist*, Vol. 5, Issue 2, December 2009

OECD, 2009, *Corporate Governance and the Financial Crisis: Key Findings and Messages*, OECD, http://docs.google.com/viewer?a=v&q=cache:ZaMONnyAq7EJ:www.oecd.org/dataoecd/3/10/43056196.pdf+oecd+corporate+governance+and+the+financial+crisis&hl=en&gl=ie&pid=bl&srcid=ADGEESgGKyXtMlC1TWuVFGm1I6IvAzmGpo0xtzE50tf-3wtURuUuB8r7uUQT7bno816D_r6yIjOXvfzSEqUEottHhAPr054o7D1V5LBoI2R8WD MjDXSsl9yJb7D-APpANpMNfNMpMiSs&sig=AHIEtbQOp4BQvgUaxAya5bbhFWdmZP 9i7g (accessed 14 November 2010)

O'Halloran, B., 2008, "BordnaMóna to Invest €1.4bn over Five Years", Dublin, *Irish Times*, 22 July 2008

O'Halloran, B. and Lynch, S., 2011, "Exports to exceed €170bn, predicts trade body", *Irish Times*, 6 January 2011, p.16

Ohmae, K., 1982, *The Mind of the Strategist*, New York, McGraw-Hill

Ohmae, K., 1989, "The Global Logic of Strategic Alliances", *Harvard Business Review*, March/April 1989, Vol. 67, Issue 2, pp.143–152

Ohmae, K., 1989, "Managing in a Borderless World", *Harvard Business Review*, May/June 1989, Vol. 67, Issue 3, pp.151–161

O'Leary, J., 2010, "I should have been more pushy in opposing risk-taking at bank", *Irish Times*, 24 July 2010, p.11

O'Leary, K., 2010, "Partnership in Enterprise Level in Ireland", in Hogan, J. *et al.* (Eds), *Irish Business and Society*, Dublin, Gill & Macmillan

Osborn, A.F., 1979, *Applied Imagination: Principles and Procedures of Creative Thinking*, 3rd Ed., New York, Scribners

O'Toole, F., 2009, *Ship of Fools: How Stupidity and Corruption Sank the Celtic Tiger*, London, Faber and Faber Ltd

O'Toole, F., 2010, "Balancing profit and loss, ups and downs, right and wrong", *The Irish Times*, 6 March 2010, Weekend, p.7

Parker, G.M., 1990, *Team Players and Teamwork: the New Competitive Business Strategy*, San Francisco, Jossey-Bass

Pascale, R., 1984, "Perspectives on Strategy: the Real Story behind Honda's Success", *California Management Review*, Vol. 26, Issue 3 (Spring 1984), pp.47–72

Pascale, R. and Sternin, J., 2005, "Your Company's Secret Change Agents", *Harvard Business Review*, May 2005, Vol. 83, Issue 5, pp.73–81

Paul, M., 2008, "Ireland Misses Out on New Google jobs", *Sunday Times*, 21 December 2008, Business and Money, p.1

Pedigree, 2011, *Adopt a dog*, http://www.ie.pedigree.com/adopt-a-dog, Accessed 12 March 2011

Peters, T.J. and Waterman, R.H., 1982, *In Search of Excellence: Lessons from America's Best-run Companies*, New York, Harper Collins

Pettigrew, A. and Whipp, R., 1999, *Managing Change for Competitive Success*, Oxford, Blackwell Publishing

Plato, Translated by Lee, D., 1974, *The Republic,* Harmondsworth, Penguin

Pocock, T., 1987, *Horatio Nelson*, London, Brockhampton Press

Porter, M., 1980, *Competitive Strategy: Techniques of Analysing Industries and Competitors*, New York, The Free Press

Porter, M., 1985, *Competitive Advantage*, New York, The Free Press

Porter, M., 1996, "What is Strategy?", *Harvard Business Review*, November/December 1996, Vol. 74, Issue 6, pp.61–78

Porter, M. and Kramer, M., 2006, "Strategy and Society", Boston, *Harvard Business Review*, December 2006, Vol. 84, Issue 12, pp.79–92

Prahalad, C.K., 2010, "The Responsible Manager", *Harvard Business Review*, January/February 2010, Vol. 88, Issue 1, p.36

Prahalad, C.K. and Hamel, G., 1990, "The Core Competence of the Organisation", *Harvard Business Review*, May/June 1990, Vol. 68, No. 3, pp.79–91

Press, G., 1990, "Assessing Competitors' Business Philosophies", *Long Range Planning*, October 1990, Vol. 23, Issue 5, pp.71–75

Quinn, J., 1980, *Strategies for Change*, Homewood, Ill, Irwin

Reddan, F., 2008, "Steady Flow of Deals Continues", *The Irish Times*, 13 June 2008

Regling, C. and Watson, M., 2010, *A Preliminary Report on the Sources of Ireland's Banking Crisis*, Dublin, Government Publications Office

Reich, R., 2008, *Supercapitalism: The Battle for Democracy in an Age of Big Business*, Cambridge, Icon

Ricks, T., 2006, *Fiasco: The American Military Involvement in Iraq*, London, Penguin

Rigby, D. and Vishwanath, V., 2006, "Localisation: The Revolution in Consumer Markets", *Harvard Business Review*, April 2006, Vol. 84, Issue 4, pp.82–92

Rigby, D. *et al.*, 2009, "Innovation in Turbulent Times", *Harvard Business Review*, June 2009, Vol. 87, Issue 6, pp.79–86

Rigby, E., 2006, "Eyes in the Till", London, *Financial Times Magazine*, 11/12 November 2006, pp.16–22

Roche, B. and Coyle, D., 2007, "IDA Confident Despite Loss of Amgen Plant", *Irish Times*, 4 October 2007, p.1

Rokeach, M., 1973, *The Nature of Human Values*, New York, The Free Press

Rokeach, M., 1979, *Understanding Human Values*, New York, The Free Press

Ross, J. and Straw, B., 1993, "Organisational Escalation and Exit: Lessons from the Shoreham Nuclear Power Plant", *Academy of Management Journal*, August 1993, pp.701–32

Ross, M. *et al*, 1999, "Basic Individual Values and the meaning of Work", *Applied Psychology: An International Review*, January 1999, pp.49–71

Ross, S., 2009, *The Bankers: How the Banks Brought Ireland to its Knees*, Dublin, Penguin Ireland

Ross, S. and Webb, N., 2010, *Wasters*, Dublin, Penguin Ireland

RSA, 2011, http://www.rsa.ie/RSA/Road-Safety/Campaigns/Current-road-safety-campaigns/Drunk-With-Tiredness/Campaign-2/, Accessed 24 April 2011

Rust, T. *et al.*, 2010, "Rethinking Marketing", *Harvard Business Review*, January/February 2010, Vol. 88, Issue 1, pp.94–101

Ryan, S.*et al.*, 2009, *The Commission to Inquire into Child Abuse*, Dublin, Government Publications Office

Schein, E., 1997, *Organisational Culture and Leadership*, San Francisco, Jossey-Bass

Schein, E., 2010, *Organisational Culture and Leadership*, 4th Ed., San Francisco, Jossey-Bass

Schwalbe, K., 2010, *Managing Information Technology Projects*, Augsburg, Cengage Learning

Schwartz, S. and Sagie, G., 2000, "Value Consensus and Importance: A Cross-National Study", *Journal of Cross-Cultural Psychology*, July 2000, p.468

Selden, L. and Colvin, G., 2003, "M&A needn't be a loser's game", *Harvard Business Review*, June 2003, Vol. 81, Issue 3, pp.70–79

Senge, P., 1990, *The Fifth Discipline: The Art and Practice of the Learning Organisation*, London, Doubleday

Simmons, J., 2011, "Mergers & Acquisitions hit €10.3bn in 2010", *The Irish Times*, 7 January 2011, Business This Week, p.5

Simon, A.H., 1979, "Rational Decision-making in Business Organisations", *American Economics Review*, September 1979

Smircich, L., 1983, "Concepts of Culture and Organisational Analysis", *Administrative Science Quarterly*, September 1983, Vol. 28, Issue 3, pp.339–58

Smith, D., 2006, *Exploring Innovation*, Maidenhead, McGraw-Hill

Smith, M., 2000, *An Unsung Hero*, Cork, Collins Press

Staunton, D., 2009, "US Combat Troops to Leave Iraq Next Year", *The Irish Times*, 28 February 2009, p.11

Stevenson, W., 1989, *Production/Operations Management*, Illinois, Irwin

Stewart, J. and Rigg, C., 2011, *Learning and Talent Development*, London, CIPD

Stewart, T.A., 1999, "The Conquest for Welch's Throne Begins: Who will Run GE?", *Fortune*, 11 January 1999, p.27

Stogdill, R. and Coons, A., 1957, *Leader Behaviour: Its Description and Measurement*, Columbus, Ohio, Ohio State University Press, Bureau of Business Research

Stogdill, R.M., 1948, "Personal Factors Associated With Leadership: A Survey of the Literature", *Journal of Psychology*, 1948, pp.35–71

Suarez, F. and Lanzolla, G., 2005, "The Half-Truth of First Mover Advantages", Boston, *Harvard Business Review*

Tansey, P., 2007, "Public Sector Reform Would Aid Productivity", *Irish Times*, 23 November 2007, p.34

Tansey, P., 2008, "Innovate or Stagnate", Dublin, *Irish Times*, 29 February 2008

Taylor, C., 2010, "The Four Year Challenge", *The Sunday Business Post*, 10 October 2010, p.10

The Economist, 2011, "Irish Mist", *The Economist*, 19 February 2011, p.14

Thomas, M., 2008, *Belching out the Devil*, London, Ebury Press

Thomas, T. *et al.*, 2004, "Strategic Leadership in Ethical Behaviour", *Academy of Management Review*, Vol. 18, Issue 2, May 2004, p.58

Thompson, A. *et al.*, 2008, *Crafting and Executing Strategy: The Quest for Competitive Advantage*, New York, McGraw-Hill

Thompson, J. and Martin, F., 2005, *Strategic Management: Awareness and Change*, 5th Ed., London, Thomson Learning

Tian, X., 2007, *Managing International Business in China*, Cambridge, Cambridge University Press

Tiernan, S. *et al.*, 2006, *Modern Management: Theory and Practice for Irish Students*, 3rd Ed., Dublin, Gill & Macmillan

Trompenaars, F. and Hampton-Turner, C., 1998, *Riding the Waves of Culture: Understanding Cultural Diversity in Global Business*, 2ndEd., New York, McGraw-Hill

Uhlaner, R. and West, A., 2008, "Running a Winning M&A Shop", *McKinsey Quarterly*, Spring 2008

Vroom, V., 1964, *Work and Motivation*, New York, John Wiley & Sons

Wagner, S. and Dittmar, L., 2006, "The Unexpected Benefits of Sarbanes-Oxley", *Harvard Business Review*, April 2006, Vol. 84, Issue 4, pp.133–140

Waldmeir, P., 2011, "Beijing Presses Motor Groups to Share Technology", *Financial Times*,19 February 2011, p.17

Walker, D., 2009, *A Review of Corporate Governance in UK Banks and Other Financial Institutions*, London, The Walker Review Secretariat

Walker Review, 2009, *A Review of Corporate Governance in UK Banks and Other Financial Industry Entities*, London, The Walker Review Secretariat

Wall, M., 2006, "Inefficiency and High Labour Costs Blamed for Expensive Electricity", *Irish Times,* 2 October 2006, p.5, Computers in Business section

Walsh, K., 2010, "The world's not big enough for Louis Vuitton", *The Sunday Times*, 21 November 2010, Business, p.10

Weckler, A., 2008, "The evolution of invention", Dublin, *Sunday Business Post*

Weilrich, H. and Koontz, H., 1993, *Management*, New York, McGraw-Hill

Welch, J., 2001, *Jack: What I've Learned Leading a Great Company and Great People*, London, Headline

Whole Foods Market, 2011, http://www.wholefoodsmarket.com/values/, Accessed 11 February 2011

Wind, J. and Main, J., 1999, *Driving Change*, London, Kogan Page

Woodall, P., 2003, "House of Cards", *The Economist*, 31 May 2003, pp.3–16

Wrecker, A., 2008 "The Evolution of Invention", *Sunday Business Post*, 20 July 2008

Wrecker, A., 2011, "Getting Ireland up to speed", *The Sunday Business Post*, 6 February 2011, p.M9

Yip, G., 2003, *Total Global Strategy II*, London, Financial Times, Prentice Hall

Glossary

Acquisition – One company purchases a controlling interest in another company.

Architecture – The network of relationships both within the organisation and between the organisation and other groups.

Authority – Where an individual has legitimate power within the organisation to give work-related orders.

Autonomy – The extent to which employees have freedom to take the initiative with regard to their work.

Backward integration – The development of activities into areas concerned with the supply of inputs into the organisation.

Balanced Scorecard – Performance measurement that combines qualitative and quantitative measures in a balanced manner across the organisation.

Barriers to entry – Factors that prevent an organisation entering a market.

Benchmarking – The comparison of performance between an organisation and other organisations, regardless of which industry they might be in.

Boston Consulting Group Matrix – A matrix used to place business units according to the level of market share and market growth.

Bounded rationality – The mental limitations of managers which makes them choose a course of action that may not be the optimum course.

Brands – A name, term, design, symbol or any other feature that differentiates one seller's products or services from another.

Break-even – The point where total costs equal total revenue.

Break-even analysis – A method of examining the relationship between costs, revenue and the volume produced.

Budget – A statement of plans and expected outcomes for various activities within the organisation. It is normally expressed in financial terms.

Bureaucracy – A form of management or organisational structure which is hierarchical and based on detailed rules and procedures.

Business Ethics – The ethical conduct of people within organisations and the impact it has on decisions they make at corporate and individual level.

Business-level strategies – Strategies that relate to a single business unit.

Business model – How an organisation produces products and services and interacts with customers.

Business process re-engineering – Carrying out a substantial and radical redesign of business processes within an organisation in order to improve efficiency.

Cash Cows – Products or companies that have high market share in a low growth industry, and generate substantial profits.

Change agent – A person or group of people tasked with leading change within an organisation.

Cognitive dissonance – Where an individual has conflicting attitudes with regard to a decision that they made.

Competences – The skills and abilities by which resources are used in an organisation. They can be basic or core competences.

Competitive advantage – The significant advantages that one company possesses over its competitors.

Competitive strategy – The basis by which an organisation competes in a competitive environment.

Computer-aided design (CAD) – The use of computer technology in designing products.

Computer-aided manufacturing (CAM) – The use of computer technology in manufacturing products.

Computer-integrated manufacturing – The use of CAD and CAM to sequence the production process efficiently.

Consistency – Where the strategy being pursued by an organisation is consistent with its goals and objectives.

Consolidation – When an organisation concentrates its efforts on maintaining its current market share.

Context – The circumstances in which a company is operating and how it impacts on its strategy.

Contingency theory – Applying a management style to suit the particular circumstances.

Control – A management function which compares actual performance with planned performance. If there is a deviance, corrective action should be taken.

Core competences – The distinctive set of skills that an organisation possess that bring significant benefit to the customer.

Core values – The values and principles considered fundamental to an organisation.

Corporate governance – The control mechanism by which senior executives are held accountable to stakeholders for the legal and ethical operations of a company.

Corporate-level strategies – Strategies pursued by the headquarters of an organisation that impact on all divisions of the company.

Corporate social responsibility – A strategy that is integrated with (1) core business objectives and (2) core competences to create financial and social/environmental returns and is embedded in corporate culture and day-to-day business operations.

Corporate strategy – Charting the future direction of a company by developing long-term goals which reflect stakeholders' interests and achieves competitive advantage.

Cost Benefit analysis – The examination of a strategy that takes in broader criteria in addition to the main financial benefits.

Cost leadership – A competitive generic strategy which aims to minimise costs.

Cultural web – Shows the behavioural, physical and symbolic manifestations of a culture within an organisation.

Culture – See organisational culture.

Data mining – The interrogation of information systems for trends and insights into customers' buying habits or preferences.

Delegation – The process by which a manager assigns responsibilities to a member of staff.

Devolution – The extent to which the corporate headquarters empowers business units to make strategic decisions.

Differentiation – A competitive generic strategy aimed at developing goods and services that are viewed as being of superior quality.

Direct supervision – The direct control of work in an organisation.

Discounted cash flow – The sum of projected future cash flows from a strategy, converted into present day values. It takes account of the time value of money.

Diversification – A strategy whereby a company expands from being a single business operation into different businesses of varying relatedness.

Divestment – When a company sells a business or division.

Division – A separate and self-contained part of a company, usually with responsibility for profits.

Dogs – Business units in low-growth markets with low market share.

Driving forces – Those changes taking place that are altering the fundamental nature and competition of that industry.

E-commerce – The conduct of business transaction through electronic media.

Economies of scale – When the unit cost of production decreases as the volume increases.

Economies of scope – The cost savings derived from the internal sharing of competences.

Effectiveness – The degree to which a company achieves its objectives.

Efficiency – Using the minimum amount of resources to achieve results.

Emergent strategy – A strategy that develops through the everyday routines of an organisation that become part of the long-term direction.

Empowerment – The devolution of power and decision-making to members lower down in the organisation.

Entrepreneurship – The process of starting a new business venture, and undertaking risk.

Environment – All of the factors that impact on an organisation, both internal and external.

Environmental complexity – The number of environmental factors impacting on an organisation and the difficulty in understanding them.

Environmental scanning – The process of collecting information about the forces in the business environment.

Existence-related-growth (ERG) – A theory by Alderfer which examines the level of motivation in an employee.

Expectancy theory – A model of motivation (Vroom) which considers the level of effort required to do work and the subsequent level of performance.

First mover advantage – The competitive benefits that accrue by being first into the market with a product or service.

Five Forces Analysis – A framework for understanding the competitive forces at play in an industry.

Flexibility – The ability to change organisational direction when required.

Focus – A generic competitive strategy aimed at a niche market.

Forcefield analysis – Identifies the factors forcing and blocking change in an organisation.

Foreign direct investment – Investment of manufacturing or other facilities by a foreign company in another country.

Foreign Trade – The exporting and importing of goods and services, to and from foreign countries.

Franchise – A form of licensing whereby the franchisor grants the franchisee the right to use certain intellectual property rights such as brand names, copyrights, patents, etc., in return for various fees.

Functional departmentalisation – The division of a company along functional lines, e.g. marketing.

Gearing ratio – The ratio of debt to equity in a company.

Generic strategies – Originally developed by Michael Porter, they are general strategies that can be used by companies to compete in a particular market. They consist of cost leadership, differentiation, niche markets and best cost provider strategies.

Group think – A form of thinking that people engage in when making decisions that is so pervasive it clouds clear thinking.

Human resource management – The management of employees of the organisation. It is a strategic approach that recognises people as the company's most important asset.

Hybrid strategy – A competitive strategy that combines high quality with good value.

Implementation – The final part of strategy generation, whereby the plan is put into effect, and results are monitored.

Industrial relations – The rules, practices and conventions governing the relationship between employees and their managers. It often includes collective employee representation and bargaining.

Innovation – The application of new knowledge and approaches to developing products or services that have application in the market place. It is different from invention, which is the creation of an entirely new product.

Intangible resource – Non-physical assets including brand name, goodwill, reputation and knowledge.

Intellectual capital – The future earnings of a company that are derived from the calibre of people working in the organisation.

Intended strategy – The desired strategy that an organisation had planned to achieve.

Intrapreneurship – The development of new enterprise within an organisation, along with the necessary support.

Joint venture – When two companies come together and create an alliance in the form of a third company that is jointly owned and managed by the two parents who remain separate entities.

Just-in-time – Management processes which ensure that stock is delivered just as it is needed for production, thus keeping stock costs at a minimum.

Kaizen – The Japanese concept of continuous improvement in an organisation.

Key success factors – The resources and competences required by an organisation to be successful in a competitive industry.

Key value and cost drivers – The factors that most influence the generation of profits as well as the costs associated with them.

Leadership – The ability to inspire and motivate others to work willingly towards achieving organisational goals.

Learning organisation – An organisation that has a culture that supports knowledge generation, continuing learning and the development of staff skills.

Leasing – A type of debt where an organisation hires a particular asset for a defined period, often with an option of purchase at the end of the lease.

Leverage – The exploitation of assets by a company.

Life cycle – The evolution of a product or industry from its introduction to its eventual decline.

Logical incrementalism – The development of strategy by experimentation and learning from partial commitment rather than through global formulations of total strategies.

Logistics – The management of the sourcing of materials right through to the delivery of goods to customers.

Market development – The development of new markets by creating new segments for products, new uses for existing products or geographical spread.

Market positioning – The selection of a strategy that allows a company to compete at a particular level in the market place.

Market segment – Dividing the market into distinct groups based on different variables such as age, gender etc.

Matrix structure – A form of multi-divisional structure which combines two overlapping structures e.g. product line and geographical area.

Merger – Where two companies, generally of roughly equal size, decide to join operations and form a new company.

Mission – A mission guides the members of an organisation in making decisions that will achieve strategic goals and objectives.

Mission statement – A mission statement is the articulation of a company's mission to employees. It describes the company's current business – 'who we are; what we do and why we are here'.

Multidivisional structure – An organisational structure that divides the company into different divisions based on product lines or geographical areas.

Multinational company (MNC) – A company that operates in many countries around the world.

Net cash flow – The sum of pre-tax profits arising from a strategy.

Niche market – A small market segment with its own distinctive characteristics.

Objectives – Statements of specific outcomes that the organisation intends to achieve.

Oligopoly – A market that is dominated by a small number of companies.

Operational strategies – Strategies concerned with how the organisation will convert corporate and business-level strategies into day-to-day routines in the various parts of the company.

Opportunity costs – The cost of not taking a particular course of action in terms of benefits foregone.

Organic development – Development of the organisation through its own capabilities.

Organisational culture – The basic assumptions and beliefs that are shared by members of an organisation.

Organisational knowledge – The knowledge, values, understanding and experience that have been built up throughout an organisation over a period of time.

Organisational politics – The power relationships within an organisation.

Outsourcing – Contracting out certain parts of the organisation's value chain to companies who specialise in that work.

Paradigm – The manner in which an organisation views the world around it.

Parenting – How a corporate headquarters guides and assists divisions within the group.

Payback period – The time it takes a company to recover the cost of a strategy.

Performance targets – Targets that the organisation sets based on output. It is based on quality, products etc.

PESTEL framework – A framework for examining the environment from six related perspectives including political, economic, sociological, technological, environmental and legal.

Porter's Diamond – A framework for examining the competitiveness of industry clusters within a country. It has four inter-related factors.

Portfolio – A collection of businesses owned by a company.

Primary activities – The parts of a value chain directly concerned with the production of goods or services.

Product development – The development of new products in an organisation.

Product life cycle – The cycle that a product undergoes from introduction, growth, maturing and eventual decline.

Product mix – The variety of different products that a company has on offer.

Production management – The management of the process of transforming materials into finished products.

Quality – The test of whether a product is fit for its intended purpose.

Realised strategy – The strategy that an organisation is actually following.

Related diversification – Corporate development into different areas but within the same value chain.

Resource allocation – The allocation of resources to support strategy.

Retained profits – Previous profits that have been retained by a company.

Risk – Concerns the probability and consequences of a strategy failing.

Scenarios – An outline of alternative future developments and their impact on an organisation.

Short-term debt – A short-term loan that is normally repayable within one year.

Stakeholder mapping – It plots different stakeholders' likely position regarding a proposed strategy according to their interest and power.

Stakeholders – People, both groups and individuals, who have a direct or indirect interest in the organisation and its goals, including shareholders, directors, managers, employees, trade unions, government and the wider community.

Star – A business unit which has a high market share in a growing market.

Strategic alliance – When two or more separate companies agree to collaborate on a strategic basis and share resources, risk and control for their mutual benefit.

Strategic business unit – A part of an organisation for which there is a distinct external market for its goods and services.

Strategic capability – The combination of resources and competences needed to support strategy and succeed.

Strategic choices – Analysing the various strategic options that are open to an organisation.

Strategic drift – When the strategies of an organisation diverge from the demands of the market.

Strategic fit – The matching of a company's strategy and its resources.

Strategic gap – An opportunity to exploit a gap in a market segment that is not being served by competitors.

Strategic group map – A graphical depiction of the positioning of various companies competing within an industry.

Strategic intent – Envisions a desired leadership position and establishes the criteria the organisation will use to chart its progress.

Strategic planning – The systematic planning required to develop and implement strategy.

Strategy – The direction and scope of an organisation over the long term, which achieves advantage in a changing environment though its configuration of resources and competences with the aim of fulfilling stakeholder expectations.

Suppliers – People or organisations who supply the company with the necessary materials and components for production or support activities.

Supply chain management – The development of partnerships with suppliers and distributors to facilitate the movement of goods or services.

Support activities – The parts of a value chain directly concerned with supporting the primary activities in the production of goods or services.

Sustainable development – Development that meets the needs of the present without compromising the ability of future generations to meet their needs.

SWOT analysis – An analysis of the internal strengths and weaknesses and the external opportunities and threats of an organisation.

Synergy – The benefits gained by the creation of a whole that is greater than the sum of the parts.

Tangible resources – The physical resources of the organisation such as plant and machinery.

Technology transfer – An agreement which involves the transfer of technology or use of technology between organisations.

Tipping point – A tipping point is reached when the demand for a product or service takes off exponentially.

Total costs – The combination of fixed and variable costs.

Total quality management – A systematic approach to improving quality in the production of goods and services.

Turnaround strategy – A strategy aimed at turning a company around in a crisis situation and bringing it back to viability.

Uncertainty – Factors that impact on the organisation, but are difficult to quantify.

Unrelated diversification – Diversification into products or services that have no connection with the current value chain.

Value chain – Developed by Michael Porter to examine the elements of a company where costs and value are created.

Values – Standards or criteria for choosing goals or guiding actions.

Value system – The expansion of the value chain to include all of the suppliers and distributors involved in delivering a product to the end customers.

Venture capital – Capital provided by individuals and organisations to support the creation of new enterprise.

Vision – The desired end-state of an organisation, which consists of its values and purpose, underpinned by leadership and expressed in motivating terms to inspire its members.

Vision statement – Articulation of the long-term vision of the organisation – what it aspires to be.

Whistle-blowers – People who report unethical or illegal behaviour being conducted in organisations to outside bodies.

Yield management – The application of information systems and pricing strategies to maximise revenue from resources of a relatively fixed, but perishable capacity, by anticipating and directing consumer behaviour.

Index

3M 84, 164, 267, 285, 435

abandoned strategies 23
Abiomed 305
accounting rate of return 382–3, 388
acquisitions 14, 61, 322, 332, 346–56,
    360–61, 476, 484, 511–12
Action-Centred Leadership model 46
activity-based costing 210
activity maps 213–14
actual products 282
Adair, John 34, 45–6
Adams, J.S. 47
Adams, Jameson Boyd 522
adaptive change 438, 450, 457
adaptive cultures 60
Aer Lingus 22, 59, 114, 215, 345, 354, 402,
    506–7, 511–12, 513
Aer Rianta International 340
AIB 101, 110, 120–21, 126, 172–3, 197,
    253, 254, 279, 350–51, 368, 499–505
Alpyra 347
Altobridge 341
Amabile, T. 238, 239
Amazon 210, 496, 498
American Airlines 217
Amgen 23
Amundsen, Roald 40, 521, 523
Anadarko 339, 465
Andrews, Barry 501
An Post 18
Anglo Irish Bank 121, 157, 255, 321, 368, 491
Ansbacher affair 120
Ansoff, H. Igor 275, 306, 334
Ansoff's Matrix 275, 306, 334

Antarctic expeditions 39–40, 434–5, 521–31
Apollo space programme 86
Apple 498
Aquinas, Thomas 118
Ardagh Glass 347
Aristotle 116, 142–3
artefacts 54, 67
Arthur Andersen 83
Aryzta 355
Ashkenas, R. 352
Atlantic Philanthropies 136
attractiveness matrix *see* directional policy
    matrix
audit committees 111
augmented products 282

Babcock & Brown 348
backward vertical integration 314
Baggini, J. 172
Bailey, Mick 121
Bailey, Tom 121
bailouts 156–7, 450, 502–4
balanced scorecard 86, 91–7, 98, 103, 346,
    396, 426, 427, 440–41
Balboni, F. 375
Ballygowan 299
Balogun, J. 437–8, 442
Balogun and Hope Hailey's matrix 437–8, 456
Bank of Ireland 197, 368, 505
Bank of Nova Scotia 480, 481
Bank of Scotland Ireland 255–6, 279
banks 4, 29–30, 43–4, 51–2, 100–101,
    110–12, 120–21, 126, 156–7, 172–3, 197,
    254, 255–6, 276, 279, 351–2, 368, 372,
    423, 473–9, 499–505

bargaining power 178–80
Barney, J.B. 65
Barrett, Craig 281, 298
Barry, F. 367
Bartlett, C. 244, 245
Basel III regulations 478, 504
basic assumptions 54, 55, 67
basic competences 198–9, 225
Bass, B. 41
Beer, M. 439
behavioural theories (leadership) 38–40, 66
beliefs 54–5, 67
benchmarking 214–17, 446
Benetton 197, 301, 408
Bennis, Warren 34, 79
Bentham, Jeremy 117
Berkshire Hathaway 318
best-cost provider strategy 269–70, 272
Bettis, R. 316
Bhopal 130
Bic 289
bin Talal, Al-Waleed 491, 492
Blake, R. 39, 66
Block, P. 453
Bloom, M. 100
BMW 267, 304, 314, 411
board of directors 108–14, 142
Bohan, Harry 52
Bonaparte, Napoleon 42, 50
bonus payments 100, 113, 252, 276, 474, 499–505
Bord na Móna 190
Boston Consulting Group Matrix 290, 323–5, 328, 330, 332
bounded rationality 367, 387
Bower, J. 21, 349, 352
Bowman, Cliff 264
BP 339, 463–72, 474
brainstorming 373
brand equity 137
brand loyalty 138, 176, 267, 288–9
brand management 289–90, 307, 484
Branson, Richard 42, 235

break-even analysis 380
Breen, Jim 20, 76–7
Brennan, Seamus 506–7
British Nuclear Fuels 134
broad differentiation strategy 267–9, 272
broadband 169–70, 284
Broderick, Larry 500
Brousseau, K. 50, 373–4
Brown, A. 50
Bruni, Carla 509–10
budget deficits 156–7
budgets 404, 425, 429
Budweiser 299
Buelens, M. 36, 46, 47, 61, 79, 98–9, 366, 372, 442, 452
Buffet, Warren 12, 318
business environment see environmental analysis
business ethics 115–22, 126, 142–3
business-level strategy 9, 13, 24, 263–73
business models 405–6, 430
business process reengineering 269, 410–11, 430
business risk see risk assessment; risk management
Buzz 511

Cadbury report 109, 112
Cameron International 339, 465
Campbell, A. 246, 248, 258–9, 314–15, 328–30, 350, 424
Campbell's Soups 290
Canon 85, 198, 289
capital investment 177
capital structure 250, 259
carbon footprints 135
Carcelle, Yves 340
Carey, B. 321
Carlsberg 299, 341
Carroll, Liam 255
Carswell, S. 351–2
cash flow analysis 380
cash flow management 201
Castleknock College, Dublin 89

Castrol 302
Caterpillar 267
Cawley, Michael 513
centralised decision-making 248, 258
chain of governance 108, 142
Champy, James 410, 411
Chandler, A. 240
change 4, 49–50, 394, 433–57, 474–6
change agents 453
change drivers 435–7, 448
change management 450–55, 456–7
change models 446–55
change types 437–9, 448
charismatic leadership 41–2, 67
Chesbrough, H. 277
Chevron 469
China 157–8, 292, 302, 339–40
Churchill, Winston 79
Cisco 356
Clancy, P. 109–10, 254, 368, 372
close-out stage (projects) 417
clustering techniques 303–4
clusters 162, 163, 304
coaching 47–8, 50
Coca Cola 137, 212
Code of Practice for the Governance of State
    Bodies 125–6
code sharing 345
codes of ethics 119–20, 143
coercive power 33
Collins, Jim 6, 20–21, 42–4, 76, 78, 80,
    83–4, 101, 119, 237, 376, 397–8
Collins, L. 21
Commission for Energy Regulation 174–5
communications management (projects)
    416, 421
company directors see board of directors
company law 112–13, 125–6
Company Law Reform Group 125
competences 198–9, 225, 320–21
Competition Authority 354–5
competitive analysis 219–22, 226
competitive capabilities 409–10

competitive environment 4, 174–86, 293,
    295, 484
competitiveness 2, 52, 159–64, 206–7, 294
compliance approach (ethics) 126
concept stage (projects) 427
conglomerates 174, 315–16, 317–20
consistency assessment 376, 388
consolidation 279, 337
consortia 338–9, 360
control processes 424–8, 431
control styles 247–9, 259
core competences 138, 198–9, 225,
    271, 396
core ideology 76
core products 282
corporate culture see organisational culture
corporate governance 30, 107–15, 142, 235,
    258, 478
Corporate Governance Code 112–13
corporate headquarters 234–40
corporate-level strategy 9, 13, 24, 233–57
corporate parenting 328–30
corporate social responsibility 30, 127–41,
    143–4, 171, 212, 463–72, 491–2
corporate strategy see strategy
corporation tax 166–7, 427
Corrib gas project 131, 132–3, 422
cost-benefit analysis 385, 388
cost competitiveness 206–7, 226
cost drivers 206–7, 226, 403
cost leadership strategy 13, 263–4, 265–7,
    272–3
cost management (projects) 416, 420
cost of capital 200, 403
cost reduction 216–17
countercultures 61
Covey, S. 87
CRAIC framework 50
Crean, Tom 39, 523, 524, 529, 530
creativity 239–40, 258
CRH plc 347
critical path analysis 419–20
critical success factors 186–9, 192, 329–30

Croke Park 140–41
Csikszentmihalyi, M. 99
Cúl Green 140–41
cultural differences 65–6, 68, 295, 296
cultural intelligence 38, 293
cultural strength 58–60, 64–5, 68
cultural web 23, 64, 68, 200, 442–3
Curran, R. 255
currency risk 296
current ratio 216
customer relationship management 96, 441
customer service see service

Dalkey, N.C. 373
damage control approach (ethics) 126
D'Arcy, Gay 190
data mining 375, 406–7, 430
data visualisation 375
DCC plc 121, 317, 400
de Bréadún, D. 121
debt 200, 250
decentralised decision-making 248, 258–9
decision implementation 366
decision-making 50–51, 248–52, 258–9,
    363–88
Decision Support Systems 204, 375, 388
decisive decision-making style 373
decline stage (life cycles) 181, 287, 358
Deepwater Horizon 339, 463–72
Dell, Michael 87, 241
Dell Computers 87, 202, 203, 208, 217,
    241, 265, 266–7, 406, 408
Delphi technique 373
Denning, William 411
deontological ethical systems 117–18, 143
Dess, G. 296
detachment, fallacy of 16
development stage (projects) 417
Diageo 80–81
Dibb, S. 88, 201, 283, 284–5, 286,
    288, 405
differentiation strategy 13, 263–4, 267–70,
    272–3, 482–3, 484–5

direct controls 424–6, 430
directional policy matrix 326–8, 330, 332
directors see board of directors
DIRT inquiry 121
discounted cash flow analysis 201, 383–4
distribution channels 177, 217
distributive justice 117
Dittmar, L. 112
diversification 13, 234–5, 275, 306,
    311–31, 337
dividend policies 251, 259, 469–70
Doherty, Colin 505
dominant logic 316
Donaldson, T. 118, 143
Dongfeng Motors 340
Donovan, D. 156
Dose, J.J. 79, 102
Dove 139
Dream Ireland 170
dress codes 55–6
Drucker, Peter 45, 99, 201
Dublin Docklands Development Authority
    17–18, 130, 339
Dudley, Bob 471, 472
due diligence 351–2
Duffy, Mark 255
Dunfee, T. 118, 143
Dunne, Sean 280
Dunnes Stores 129, 267
Duran, Joseph 411
Dyer, J. 345, 355, 356
Dyson, James 204

e-books 497–8
e-commerce 236, 406, 495–6
Early, P.C. 38
earnings per share 216
Eason & Son Ltd 493–8
Eastman Kodak 85, 182, 284
eBay 496
economic risk 296
economic influences 167–8
economic structure 173–5, 192

economies of scale 176, 206
education 136, 161
efficiency *see* operational efficiency
Einstein, Albert 204, 450
Eircom 314, 348
ESB 18–19, 140, 347
ESB International 340, 514–19
electronic data interchange 210
EMC 283
emergent strategy development 19–23, 25
emigration 52, 168, 437
emotional intelligence 36–8
employees *see* human resources
Énergie Group 347
Enron 82–3, 119
Enterprise Information Systems 375
Enterprise Ireland 89, 295, 297
enterprise resource planning systems 236
environmental analysis: macro environment
    153–73; micro environment 173–91;
    overview 12–13, 149, 151–2
environmental issues 134–5, 140–41, 144,
    171, 468–9, 470–71
environmental scanning 151–2
envisioned future 76, 84
Ernst and Whinney 351–2
equity 200, 250, 491
equity theory (motivation) 47
escalation of commitment 369–70, 388
ethical culture approach (ethics) 126
ethical relativism 119, 143
ethical systems 117–19, 143
ethics *see* business ethics
European Central Bank 155, 167, 352, 380
European Union 153–7, 166–7, 169, 183,
    191, 292, 354
evolutionary change, 438, 450
expansion 483–4, 511–13
executive directors 109
expectancy model (motivation) 41, 47
expenses as percentage of sales 215
experience curve 207
expert power 33–4

explicit knowledge 205
exporting 297–9
Exxon Mobil 464, 467, 469, 470, 471, 472

Farrell Grant Sparks 347
FÁS 33, 400
FBD Insurance 89
feasibility assessment 378–9, 388
FedEx 267
Feeney, Chuck 136
Feldman, D. 63
Felt, Mark 122–3
Fielder's Contingency Model 40
finance 200, 250, 429
financial capabilities 200–201
financial control style 248
financial crisis 4, 29–30, 51–2, 156–7, 168,
    172–3, 197, 200, 368, 450, 475, 478,
    499–505
financial decision-making 250–52, 259
financial ratios 215–16
Financial Regulator 110, 111, 126
financial resources 197, 225, 403–4, 429
Fingleton, Michael 100
firm infrastructure 209
first mover advantage 288–9
Fitzgerald, Mike 341
Fitzgerald, Niall 111–12
Fitzpatrick, Sean 121
Fitzroy, P. 250, 311, 440, 449
Five Forces analysis 129, 175–80, 192, 295
Flavin, Jim 121
flexible decision-making style 373
flexible structures 246–7
Flint, Douglas 474, 475
Flood report 121
focus strategy 13, 263–4, 270, 273
focused differentiation strategy 270, 273
focused low-cost strategy 270, 273
forcefield analysis 444–5, 456
Ford, Henry 87
foreign direct investment 164, 166,
    298, 300

foreign markets *see* international markets
formulisation, fallacy of 16
forward vertical integration 314
Four Seasons Hotels 80, 184, 267, 268–9, 401, 480–92
Fox, Terry 491–2
Foy, John 499, 501, 503
franchising 299, 341–3, 360
Francis, S. 352
Franklin, D. 129
fraud 253, 425
French, J. 33
Friedman, Milton 127
functional strategies 10, 24
functional structures 241–2, 258

Gaelic Athletic Association 140
Gallagher, John 280
gap analysis 397
Garman, A. 277
Garratt, R. 48
Gates, Bill 491, 492
GE/McKinsey Matrix *see* directional policy matrix
gearing 216, 250
gender balance 109, 372
General Electric 17, 36, 49, 86–7, 109, 137, 235, 292, 318, 320, 326, 399, 412
General Motors 242, 339–40
generic strategies 263–73
generic typology of change 439, 456
Geoghegan, Michael 474, 476, 477
Gerstner, Louis 77
Ghemawat, P. 212, 292–3, 295, 301, 303, 323
Ghoshal, S. 244, 245
Gilbert, C. 21
Glanbia 349
global environment 153–9
global strategy 300–301, 307
globalisation 4, 5, 127, 182–3, 303–5, 337, 436
Glover, Sir Gerald 482–3
goals 30, 75, 89–101, 103, 440

Golan Heights 135
Goldman Sachs 129
Goleman, D. 36–7
Google 137, 161, 241, 498
Goold, M. 246, 248, 258–9, 314–15, 318, 350, 424
Gore-Tex 270
government intervention 436
Grant, R. 328
Green, Stephen 474, 475, 476, 477
Greencore Group 425
Greenpeace 134, 471
Greenstreet, Lionel 521
gross profit percentage 215
group decisions 370–73, 388
groupthink 371–3, 388
growth stage (life cycles) 180, 287, 357
Guangzuhou Automobile 340
Gucci 301Guinness 299
Gulf of Mexico 339, 463–72
Gulliver, Stuart 474–6, 478, 479

Halifax 279
Halliburton 339, 465, 471
Hamel, G. 84–5, 198
Hamilton, James 125
Hamm, J. 45
Hammer, Michael 410, 411
Hampden-Turner, C. 53
Handy, Charles 53, 56–7, 68
Handy's Four Types (organisational culture) 56–7, 68
Harding Clark, Maureen 125, 371–2
Harper, N. 317
Hart, Nigel 317
Hassan, F. 443
Hayes, R. 282
Hayward, Tony 463, 464–5, 468–70, 471
headquarters *see* corporate headquarters
health 135–6
Health Service Executive 6, 89, 370, 400, 413, 449
Heistand 355

Herlihy, John 161
Hewlett, Bill 90
Hewlett Packard 83, 90, 164, 356
Hibernian Insurance 216
hierarchic decision-making style 373
Hierarchy of Needs 47
Higgs report 109, 113
high-performance cultures 59–60, 239, 258, 427
high-performance organisations 48–9
Hill, C. 264
Hines, P. 210
Hodgkinson, David 500, 502–4
Hofstede, G. 65
Honda 198, 340
Hope Hailey, V. 437–8, 442
horizontal integration 314
House, R. 41
House's Path–Goal Theory 41
HSBC 473–9
Huff, A. 3
Hulbert, J. 250, 311, 440, 449
human resources 161, 196–7, 225, 237–8, 249, 253, 258, 397–403, 427, 478–9, 488–90
human resources function 402–3
human resources management 199–200, 209, 210, 237–8, 416, 421
human rights 137, 212
Hunt report 161–2
Huselid, M. 237
Hyundai 339, 465

IAWS 355
IBM 77, 82, 137, 245, 316, 353
implementation stage (projects) 417
implicit knowledge 205–6
imposed strategies 18–19
Impress Holdings 347
inbound logistics 208
incentives 100–101, 422–3, 430, 489; see also bonus payments; management incentive schemes

India 292–3
indirect controls 426–8, 431
individual development 47–8
Industrial Development Agency 305
industrial relations 510–11; see also human resources
industry conditions 173–5, 356–9
industry driving forces 181–3, 192
industry life cycle 180–81, 357–9
informal structures 241, 258
Information Systems 204–5, 235–7, 258, 436
information technology 5–6, 169–70, 182, 197, 204–5, 206, 210, 218, 225, 271, 405–8, 430; see also technology
infrastructure 161, 166
innovation 161–4, 169–70, 276–8, 435
Insomnia Coffee Company 336–7
Institute of Directors in Ireland 113
Insurance Corporation of Ireland 351–2
intangible resources 197, 225
Integrated Materials Management 210
integration (acquisitions) 352–3
integrative decision-making style 374
integrative social contracts theory 118–19, 143
Intel 89, 283, 402
intended strategy development 15–19, 24–5
interest rates 167, 256
internal development 14, 335–7, 359
internal markets 427–8
internal politics 453
internal rate of return 249, 383
internal start-ups 321–2, 332
international drivers 293
International Financial Services Centre 17, 168, 297
international markets 292–305, 307
intrapreneurship 286–7
introduction stage (life cycles) 180, 287, 357
investment information 114–15, 142

Iraq 369
Irish Nationwide Building Society 100, 157, 368
Irish Stock Exchange 113

J.J. Kavanagh & Sons 89
Jackie Skelly Fitness Clubs 347
Janis, I. 371
Japan 84–5, 157, 198, 210, 436
Johnson, G. 6–7, 9, 21, 22–3, 61, 64, 68, 164, 199, 200, 206, 264, 288, 290, 294, 295, 427, 442, 454
Johnson & Johnson 81–2, 202, 237
joint ventures 299, 322, 332, 339–41, 360
Jones, G. 264
Judson, A. 445
Jurys Doyle hotel group 280, 336
just-in-time management 206, 208, 215, 217, 266, 344, 406

kaizen 198, 409, 411, 414
Kant, Immanuel 117, 119, 143
Kanter, Rosabeth Moss 82, 209, 211, 304, 346, 446
Kaplan, Robert 7, 91–5, 247, 346, 396
Keena, C. 167
Kelleher, Herb 507
Kennedy, David 255
Kennedy, John F. 42, 86, 87
Kenny's bookshop 436
Kerry Group 7, 49, 237, 243–4, 249, 347, 348, 350, 354–5, 424
Kets de Vries, Manfred 42, 45
key success factors 186–9, 192, 329–30
Killian, Owen 355
Kim, C. 187–8
Kimes, S. 218
King, Martin Luther 87
KLM 511
knowledge economy 196, 205, 225, 405
knowledge management 205–6, 225
knowledge management systems 206
Kotler, P. 88, 281, 289

Kotter, John 34, 36, 49–50, 76, 394, 435, 452, 453, 454
Kouzes, J. 36
Kramer, M. 138–40
Kramer, S. 238
Kreitner, R. 370

Land Rover 270
Lanzolla, G. 289
Largo Foods 158
Latham, G. 100
Lay, Kenneth 83
leadership 12, 15, 30, 32–52, 66, 78–9, 102, 199–200, 237, 258, 320–21, 398, 429, 434–5, 440–41, 450–51, 474–6, 506–13, 521–31
leadership failures 51–2
leadership functions 44–52, 67
leadership prototype 36
leadership theories 35–44
lean production 203
lean techniques 414–15
learning organisations 48, 67, 354, 489
Leeson, Nick 124
legal influences 171
legitimate power 33–4
Lencioni, P. 119
Lenihan, Brian 499, 500, 501–3, 505
'Level 5' leadership 42–4, 66
Levitt, T. 240, 303
Lewin, Kurt 446–7
Lewin's change model 446–7
licensing 299, 341, 360
Liu, Y. 238
Lloyds Banking Group 279
localisation 303–5
Locke, E. 100
logical incrementalism 19–21
logistics *see* inbound logistics; outbound logistics
Lonergan, John 86
long-term goals 85–7
long-term strategies 4–5
Louis Vuitton 340–41

Lourdes Hospital Inquiry 125, 371–2
low-cost provider strategy 265–7, 273
Lunn, P. 256
Lynch, R. 9, 197, 264, 376, 378, 449
Lyons, T. 321

McAleese, Mary 503
McAlpine Group 482
Macaro, A. 173
McCall, B. 281
McCarthy, Stan 348
McCarthy, Timothy 529, 530
McClelland, D. 99
McDonald's 205, 342
McElhaney, Kellie, A. 127, 138, 141
McErlean, Eugene 126
McGarry, S. 343
McGoldrick, P.J. 506, 510
Mackay, Iain 474
Macklin, Alexander 525, 526
McKenna, Peter 141
McNamara, Bernard 255, 256, 280, 339
McNeish, Harry 528, 529, 530
macro environment 13, 152, 153–73, 191
McShane, S. 60–61, 64–5, 367
management 34, 66, 398–400, 429, 488
Management by Objectives 99
management consultants 18
management incentive schemes 251–2, 259
management philosophies 60, 68
management risk 296
managerial grid 39, 66
Mandela, Nelson 42
Mankins, M. 97–8
Mann, Richard 36
Mansfield, Jim 255
Marakas, G. 206, 235, 246–7, 271, 375
March, J. 367
Margolis, J. 50
market changes 436
market characteristics 295
market development 13, 275, 290–305, 306,
    307, 337

market penetration 13, 275, 278–80, 306
market segmentation 183–4, 192, 290–91
marketing 201–3, 208, 210, 301–2,
    404–5, 430
marketing concepts 201
marketing plans 404–5, 430
Markides, C. 313
Marks and Spencer 129, 130
Marshall, Eric 522
Martin, Diarmuid 121
Martin, F. 453
Martin, J. 48, 61, 237
Martin, R. 202
Maslow, A. 47
materials management 210
matrix structures 244–6, 258
Mattel 137, 212
maturity stage (life cycles) 180–81, 287,
    357–8
Mauborgne, R. 187–8
Mayo, Elton 61, 62, 426–7
mentoring 48
Mercedes 267
mergers 14, 61, 322, 346–56, 360–61, 471
Merke, Sharp and Dohme 130
Michigan leadership study 39, 66
Micklethwait, J. 411
micro environment 13, 152, 173–91, 192
Microsoft 137, 164, 427
Miles, R. 57, 68, 440, 443
Miles and Snow typology (organisational
    culture) 57, 68
Mill, John Stuart 117
Mintzberg, H. 15, 16, 34
mission 12, 30, 75, 88–9, 101, 103, 440,
    486–7
mission statements 88–9, 103, 486
Mitsui 339, 465
Mobil 427
Molloy, Pat 505
Molloy, Rody 33
Moore, Don 514, 518
Moore Stephens Caplin Meehan 347

moral philosophy 116–19, 142–3
Morris Tribunal 125
Mosakowski, E. 38
motivation 37, 47, 67, 99–101, 238–9, 258, 276–7, 422–3
Motorola 411, 427
Mourkogiannis, N. 84, 101
Mouton, J. 39, 66
multi-divisional structures 242–4, 258
multi-domestic strategy 302, 307
multiple directorships 109–10
Munro, Ian 481, 482, 491
Murphy report 35, 52
mutually exclusive projects 384–5

Nanus, B. 34
natural resources 161
Neary, Michael 125, 371–2
Nelson, Horatio 42
Nestlé 141
net present value 249, 383–4, 388
net profit percentage 215
network diagrams 419–20
networking 345, 360
New, S. 212
new entrants, threat of 176–7, 180
Nichols, J. 287
Nidumolu, R. 277
Nike 87, 129, 203, 208, 344, 408
Nissan 340
Nixon, Richard 122–3
Nohira, N. 439
Nokia 137, 249, 411
Nollaig Partnership 491
nominal group technique 373
Nonaka, I. 205
non-executive directors 109
North American Free Trade Agreement 157
Norton, David 7, 91–5, 247, 346, 396
Nyberg report 372

objectives 30, 75, 89–101, 103, 440, 479
O'Brien, J. 206, 235, 246–7, 271, 375

O'Donovan, H. 50
Office of the Director of Corporate Enforcement 112
Ohio leadership study 38, 66
Ohmae, K. 285, 303, 337, 346
oil prices 158–9, 167, 171, 172, 253, 364, 512
O'Keeffe, Jane 510
O'Leary, Jim 110, 172–3, 254
O'Leary, Michael 114, 189, 506–13
O'Neill, Eugene 506
operating costs 507–9
operational efficiency 394, 408–15
operational strategies 9–10, 24
operations 203–4, 208, 266, 408–9, 430
opportunities 13, 189–91, 223
opportunity costs 200–201
organic growth 321–2, 332, 335–7
Organisation for Petroleum Exporting Countries 158–9
organisational capabilities see strategic capabilities
organisational change see change
organisational culture 22–3, 30, 53–66, 67–8, 200, 239, 258, 276–8, 426–7, 442–3, 467, 471, 472, 473–4, 481, 484–5
organisational development 48
organisational knowledge 205, 226
organisational leadership see leadership
organisational learning 172, 206, 489
organisational politics 21–2
organisational structure 107–8, 142, 240–47, 258, 423–4
Osborn, A.F. 373
Our Lady of Lourdes Hospital see Lourdes Hospital Inquiry
outbound logistics 208
outsourcing 197, 203–4, 211–12, 344, 360, 408
Oxfam 89

Packard, David 83
Palmisano, Sam 82

parenting bias 315
Parenting Matrix 329–30
Parker, G.M. 372–3
partnership agreements 168
Pascale, R. 20, 446
payback method 201, 381–2, 388
Pedigree 137
Pepsi Cola 211
performance: and diversification 316–17; and organisational culture 64–5; and strategy 97–8
performance evaluation 46
performance metrics 94, 215–16
performance targeting 425–6
person culture 57
personalised power 32–3
PESTEL analysis 164–71, 191, 295
Peters, T.J. 58, 64, 68, 280, 316
Peters and Waterman Excellence Model 58, 64, 68
Pettigrew, A. 440
Pfizer 154
physical resources 197, 225
Pierse Contracting 201
planning see strategic planning
Plato 116, 142, 364
political influences 166–7
political risk 296
Porsche 270
Porras, J. 76, 78, 80, 83–4, 101, 119
Porter, Michael 13, 129, 138–40, 159–64, 175–80, 207–10, 212, 263–4, 269, 295, 318, 357, 409, 413, 484
Porter's Diamond 138, 159–64, 191, 293, 294
portfolio management 322–30
positioning 184
Posner, B. 36
power 32–4, 35
power culture 56
PPARS computer system 6, 370, 420
Prahalad, C.K. 45, 50, 84–5, 198, 316
Prasifka, Bill 354

prediction, fallacy of 16
precedence diagramming method 419
Press, G. 60
price/earnings ratio 216
primary activities 207–8
process design 206–7
process innovation 282
Procter & Gamble 202, 283, 289, 315
procurement 208, 416, 421–2
product design 206–7, 209, 210, 268
product development 13, 275, 280–90, 306–7, 337, 435
product differentiation 176, 179, 267–9, 482–3, 484–5
product innovation 282
product life cycle 169, 287–8, 307
product line 283, 307
product mix 283, 307
Profit Impact of Marketing Strategies method 329–30
profit margin 209
profitability 210, 404
Programme Evaluation and Review Technique 420
project acquisition 417, 418
project charters 418
project feasibility 417, 418
project integration management 417, 418
project life cycle 417
project management 415–22, 430
property crash 255–6
Public Interest Disclosure Act 125
Public Private Partnerships 338
publicity 509–10; see also marketing
PulseLearning 20, 76–7, 402
Purdy, Stuart 216
purpose 83–4, 102

quality 210, 409–15, 416, 420, 484
quick ratio 216
Quinlan, Derek 255, 339, 491
Quinlan Private 280, 336
Quinn, Feargal 285

Quinn, J. 20
Quinn, Seán 318, 320, 321
Quinn Group 315, 318–21, 322, 378

Rabitte, Pat 503–4
rational model (decision-making) 365–70, 387
ratios see financial ratios
Raven, B. 33
Rawls, John 117
reconstruction 438, 450
referent power 33–4
Regling, C. 51
regulation 51, 121–2, 163, 174–5, 478
Reich, Robert 127
related diversification 314–15, 331
research and development 162, 164, 169, 204, 209, 210, 266, 283–7, 307, 408; see also innovation; product development
resilience 50
resistance (to change) 443–6, 450, 456
resource allocation 3, 21, 249, 259
resource audits 196–7
resources 196–7, 225, 396, 403–9, 428–9, 449
responsibility assignment matrix 421
retained earnings 200
return evaluation 380–84, 388
return on capital employed 201, 215
return on shareholders' funds 215
reverse takeovers 347
revolutionary change 438, 450, 457
reward power 33
rewards see incentives
Rigby, D. 277, 303–4
Rigg, C. 47
risk assessment 254, 364, 379–80, 388
risk management 252–7, 259, 416, 421, 475, 479
risks, international markets 296
rivalry 177–8, 180
Roddick, Anita 42

Rokeach, M. 79
role culture 56–7
Rolex 267, 268, 301
Roslow, S. 287
Ross, J. 369
Ross, S. 33, 80
routines 452–3
Royal Dutch Shell 132–3, 134, 244, 470, 472
Rusnak, John 126, 253
Rust, T. 202–3
Ryan, Cathal 506
Ryan, Declan 506
Ryan, Jean 135
Ryan, Tony 506, 507, 513
Ryan report 52
Ryanair 21–2, 65, 87, 113–15, 154, 178, 189, 213–14, 217, 251, 266, 354, 406, 506–13

Sagie, G. 79
SAIC 339–40
sales and marketing see marketing
Sarbanes-Oxley Act 112
Sarkozy, Nicolas 509–10
satisficing 368, 387
scenarios 172–3
Schein, Edgar 53–4, 62–3
Schmidt, C. 48, 237
Schultz, Howard 343
Schumpeter, Joseph 276
Schwalbe, K. 416
Schwartz, S. 79
scope: organisations 234–5, 258; projects 416, 418
scope creep 6
Scott, Robert Falcon 39–40, 521–2
segmentation 183–4, 192, 290–91
Sellafield 134
Senge, P. 48
sensitivity analysis 380
service 208, 484–5
service industries 8, 168

SGMW 339–40

Shackleton, Ernest 40, 434–5, 521–31

Shakespeare, William 21, 22, 37–8, 48, 49, 122, 123, 253, 443

Shannon Aerospace 414–15

share options 251

Sharp, Isadore 80, 268–9, 401, 480–85, 490, 491–2

Shaw, George Bernard 83

Simon, A.H. 367

Simon, H. 367

Simon, Sir Robert 477

Simmons, J. 347

single market 154–5

situational theories (leadership) 40–41, 67

Six Sigma quality control 411–15, 430

skills bias 315

Smircich, L. 61

Smith, D. 47, 276, 277

Snow, C. 57, 68

socialisation 63, 68

socialised power 32

sociological influences 168–9, 437

Socrates 116, 142

Sony Corporation 84, 182, 288–9

Southwest Airlines 507

stakeholder mapping 21, 131–4

stakeholders 5, 128–31, 385, 388

standard operating procedures 205, 425

Starbucks 86, 343

Steele, R. 97–8

Sternin, J. 446

Stevenson, W. 411

Stewart, J. 47

stock turnover 216

Stockdale Paradox 398

Stogdill, R.M. 36

Stoltz, P. 50

strategic alliances 14, 157–8, 299, 337–46, 355–6, 359–60

strategic analysis 12–13, 24, 149–50; *see also* environmental analysis; strategic capabilities; SWOT analysis

strategic business units 9, 263–4, 271–2, 404

strategic capabilities 13, 149, 195–224, 276, 396–7, 428

strategic change model 447–55

strategic control style 248

strategic drift 6–7, 61

strategic fit 314, 396–7

strategic group mapping 184–6, 192

strategic inflection points 249

strategic intent 84–7, 102–3

strategic planning control style 248

strategic planning model 11, 29, 150, 232, 393

strategic planning process 425

strategic plans 16, 386, 388

strategic reviews 350–51

strategic themes 94

strategy 1–14

strategy canvasses 187–9

strategy clock 264

strategy development: alternative methods 334–59; business-level strategy 263–73; corporate-level strategy 233–57; diversification 311–31; overview 13–25, 231–2; strategy options 274–305, 311–31

strategy evaluation 376–85, 388

strategy foundations 12, 24, 29–30

strategy implementation 14, 24, 393–4, 395–431, 490

strategy maps 94–7, 213–14, 424, 440

strategy options 274–305, 311–31

strategy workshops 16–18, 172

Straw, B. 369

strengths 13, 222

strong cultures 58–9

structure *see* organisational structure

Suarez, F. 289

subcultures 60–61, 68, 239

substitute products, threat of 178

succession planning 49

suitability assessment 377–8, 388

Superquinn 285

suppliers 162, 179–80, 217, 266
supply chain transparency 212–13
supply costs 206
support activities 207, 208–9
supporting industries 162
sustainability 4, 30, 128, 277
switching costs 177, 179
SWOT analysis 13, 149–50, 222–4, 226
symbolic processes 452
synergies 314–15, 349, 350, 353,
    355–6, 360
synergy bias 315

Tag Heuer 270
tailor-made strategies 3
Takeuchi, H. 205
Tansey, Paul 280, 285, 399–400
targeting 184, 291
targets 423, 425–6, 430
task culture 57
tax avoidance 120–21
Tayto Crisps 158
team building 45–6, 67, 489
technology 5–6, 169–70, 182, 197, 212–13,
    435–6; see also information technology
teleological ethical systems 117, 143
Tesco 198, 278, 406–7
Theory E 439, 456
Theory O 439, 456
Thomas, T. 113, 212
Thompson, A. 9, 58–60, 68, 76, 85, 118,
    126, 219, 264, 265, 312, 345, 357, 358,
    386, 410
Thompson, J. 453
Thornton, John 476, 477
threats 13, 176–7, 178, 189–91, 223–4
time management (projects) 416, 419–20
Total 470
total quality management 210, 269, 411, 430
Toyota 135, 203, 208, 215, 269–70
trading blocks 157–8, 191
training 401–2, 489
trait theories (leadership) 35–8, 66

transactional leadership 41
transformational leadership 41
transnational strategy 301–2, 307
Transocean 465, 466, 471
'Transport 21' 161, 166
Traynor, Des 120
Trompenaars, F. 53

Uhlaner, R. 350, 352, 353
uncertainty 256–7, 364
unconcerned approach (ethics) 126
unemployment 52, 168
unethical behaviour 120–22
unhealthy cultures 59
Unilever 139
Union Carbide 130
unique selling propositions 301–2
unrelated diversification 315–16, 331–2
upside bias 315
utilitarianism 117

value addition 317–20, 481
value chain 138, 140–41, 207–14, 226,
    406, 427
Value Stream Mapping 414
value system 211–12, 226, 427
values 45, 54–5, 79–83, 102, 119, 239,
    473–4, 479, 488–90
Veridian 347
vertical integration 314
VF 304
Vietnam War 369
Viguerie, P. 317
Virgin Group 235, 290, 313, 320
virtual companies 246–7
virtue ethics 118
Vishwanath, V. 303–4
vision 12, 30, 41, 45, 75–87, 101–2, 440,
    482–3
Vodafone 284
Volkswagen 339
Volvo 199
Von Glinow, M.A. 60–61, 64–5, 367

Vincent, Jack 529, 530
Vroom, V. 41, 47
Visions

W.H. Smith 494
Wagner, S. 112
Walker report 110, 115, 368
Walsh, K. 340
water conservation 135
Watergate scandal 122–3
Waterman, R.H. 58, 64, 68, 280, 316
Watson, M. 51
Watson, Tom 285
weak cultures 59
weaknesses 13, 222–3
Webb, N. 33
weighted average cost of capital 200
Welch, Jack 17, 36, 49, 86–7, 109, 318
Wells Fargo 20–21, 401
West, A. 350, 352, 353
Wheelwright, S. 282

Whelan, Conor 498
Whipp, R. 440
whistle-blowers' charters 124–6
whistle-blowing 122–6, 143
Whole Foods Market 62
Wild, Frank 522
withdrawal 279–80
Wooldridge, A. 411
Work Breakdown Structures 418
workshops 16–18, 172
World Business Council for Sustainable
    Development 128
World Trade Organisation 159, 183
Worsley, Frank 523, 528, 529, 530
Wuling 339–40

Xerox 85, 289, 411

yield management 204, 206–7, 217–19, 509
Yip, G. 293
Yukl, G. 32